Java for Engineers and Scientists

D1408303

Stephen J. Chapman

BAE SYSTEMS Australia

Java for Engineers and Scientists

Stephen J. Chapman
BAE SYSTEMS Australia

An Alan R. Apt Book

Prentice Hall
Upper Saddle River, NJ 07458

Library of Congress Cataloging-in-Publication Data

Chapman, Stephen J.
    Java for engineers and scientists / Stephen J. Chapman
        p.   cm.
    ISBN 0-13-919523-8
    1. Java (Computer program language) I. Title.
QA76.73.J38C477   1999
005.7'2--dc21

                                                    99-17733
                                                       CIP

Editor-in-chief: **MARCIA HORTON**
Publisher: **ALAN APT**
Director of production and manufacturing: **DAVID W. RICCARDI**
Exeecutive Managing Editor: **VINCE O'BRIEN**
Managing editor: **EILEEN CLARK**
Editorial supervision/Page composition: **SCOTT DISANNO**
Cover director: **HEATHER SCOTT**
Creative director: **AMY ROSEN**
Marketing manager: **DANNY HOYT**
Manufacturing buyer: **PAT BROWN**

© 2000 by Prentice-Hall, Inc.
Upper Saddle River, New Jersey 07458

10 9 8 7 6 5 4 3 2

ISBN 0-13-919523-8

Prentice-Hall International (UK) Limited, *London*
Prentice-Hall of Australia Pty. Limited, *Sydney*
Prentice-Hall Canada, Inc., *Toronto*
Prentice-Hall Hispanoamericana, S.A., *Mexico*
Prentice-Hall of India Private Limited, *New Delhi*
Prentice-Hall of Japan, Inc., *Tokyo*
Prentice-Hall (Singapore) Pte., Ltd., *Singapore*
Editora Prentice-Hall do Brazil, Ltda., *Rio de Janeiro*

This book is dedicated to my son Avi, on the occasion of his leaving home for University.
May he enjoy a long and happy career in Computer Engineering.

Preface

The basic purpose of this book is to simultaneously teach the Java programming language, structured programming techniques, and good programming practice to an audience of science and engineering students.

Java is a relatively new programming language, but it is taking the world by storm. The language has enormous appeal for many reasons. One major reason is that it is largely *platform independent*, meaning that an application written for one computer is very likely to run unchanged on another computer. Thus, a single application can be written to execute across all of a company's computers, whether they are PC's, Macs, or Unix workstations. A second major advantage is that Java has a C-like syntax, but drops many of the more obscure and messier features of C. Having a C-like syntax means that it is already partially familiar to millions of people. This fact aids its acceptance. An example of Java's improvement over C is its treatment of character strings. In Java, strings are treated as objects and are manipulated by a set of standard methods. In C, strings are manipulated with pointers, which is a much more error-prone process.

A third major advantage of Java is that it is object oriented, which should make code written in Java more re-usable between applications. With a little forethought, classes and methods written for one application are usable in another application without change, because the way that the data and methods are encapsulated in the objects prevents undesirable interactions among them.

A fourth major advantage of Java is that it is possible to write *device-independent* graphics applications. Languages such as C and Fortran do not provide device-independent graphics, because the programmer must concern himself / herself with the specific details of the hardware being used to display the graphics. The language definitions do not include standard APIs for working with graphics at a higher level. By contrast, Java's AWT and Swing Graphics classes provide a higher-level abstraction that is the same across any Java implementation, making device-independent graphics practical.

A final advantage of Java is that it is free. Sun provides a free Java Development Kit for download from its World Wide Web site (http://java.sun.com). This kit includes free Java compilers, development tools, and class libraries. Other vendors such as IBM offer free trial editions of their Java Integrated Development Environments, which include excellent debuggers. This is the right price for many budgets. The Unix operating system and C language reached their current strong positions because AT&T made Unix available essentially free to universities in the 1970's and 1980's, where generations of students were trained to use them, and went on to spread their use widely throughout the working world. Java is poised for a similar but more rapid spread.

Java also makes it easy to create applets that can be exchanged and executed freely across the Web. This adds enormous appeal in today's interconnected world.

The principal disadvantage of Java is that it is a new language, and there is no large library of reusable classes available to solve scientific and engineering problems. These libraries will appear over the next few years as more and more universities adopt Java. A secondary disadvantage of Java is that the Java I/O system is very complex and confusing. This book avoids that problem by providing convenience classes for reading and writing data to files, hiding the complexities of Java I/O from the student until Chapter 14.

THE BOOK

The idea for this book was conceived as a result of my experience writing and maintaining large programs in both the defense and geophysical fields. During my time in the industry, it became obvious that the strategies and techniques required to write large, *maintainable* programs were quite different from what new engineers were learning in their programming classes at school. The incredible cost of maintaining and modifying large programs once they are placed into service absolutely demands that they be written to be easily understood and modified by people other than their original programmers. The Java programming language is especially suitable for this purpose, because its platform independence allows a program to be easily transported from computer to computer as a company's needs grow, and its straightforward syntax (compared to C) and strict object orientation encourage a cleaner programming style. My goal for this book is to teach simultaneously both the fundamentals of the Java language and a programming style that results in good, maintainable programs.

It is quite difficult to teach undergraduates the importance of taking extra effort during the early stages of the program design process in order to make their programs more maintainable. Class programming assignments must by their very nature be simple enough for one person to complete in a short period of time, and they do not have to be maintained for years. Because the projects are simple, a student can often "wing it" and still produce working code. A student can take a course, perform all of the programming assignments, pass all of the tests, and still not learn the habits that are really needed when working on large projects in the industry.

From the very beginning, this book teaches Java in a style suitable for use on large projects. It emphasizes the importance of going through a detailed design process before any code is written, using a top-down design technique to break the program up into logical portions (classes and methods) that can be implemented separately.[1] The book demonstrates object re-usability by building later examples on the classes and methods created in earlier examples. Finally, it emphasizes the importance of exhaustively testing the finished program with many different input data sets before it is released for use.

The book attempts to make learning an interactive experience by providing all sources for all examples at the book's Web site, and encouraging the student to download, execute, and modify them, since some end-of-chapter exercises are built on the examples. The Web site also contains the book's library of packages to solve technical problems (array manipulations, plotting, statistics, complex numbers, FFTs, etc.).

This book also caters to the structure of the introductory programming course taken by most engineers. In many cases, this course is a module within an "Introduction to Engineering Problem Solving" course, and the time available for learning the language is quite limited. Such courses usually teach simple procedural programming in some computer language such as Fortran, C, Basic, or Pascal, with advanced materials occurring in a separate course. Chapters 2 through 6 of this book provide a sound introduction to procedural programming, and can be used as the basis for such an introduc-

---

[1] While this book emphasizes the importance of breaking down problems into classes and methods, it does not introduce any of the formal object-oriented design methodologies. That is a topic for a separate text.

tory course. The students learn the structural programming techniques inherent in a language such as Pascal, but in a language that has more practical day-to-day use. In addition, novice programmers can begin creating plots in Chapter 5, something that is not possible in standard Fortran, C, Basic, or Pascal.

TOPICS COVERED IN THIS BOOK

A quick glance at other Java books shows that most of them are 1000+ pages long, and that most of that space is taken up in providing examples of how to use the thousands of classes in the Java API. This book takes a different approach to teaching Java, concentrating on only the small subset of the Java API necessary to perform technical calculations and to display the results. This choice leaves more time to concentrate on programming techniques and solving technical problems, while still leaving the book about half the length of many competitors.

The book introduces Java *applications* (as opposed to Browser-based *applets*) in Chapter 1, and uses applications to illustrate all of the basic principles introduced in the book. Applications are better suited to teaching basic principles, because they can be very simple, and they don't obscure the point that example is trying to illustrate. The book builds from the basics of the programming language (Chapters 2 through 4) to arrays (Chapter 5), methods (Chapter 6), classes (Chapter 7), and object-oriented programming features in a series of logical steps. Graphics and GUIs are introduced in Chapters 11 through 13 as the culmination of the book, along with a brief discussion of applets in Chapter 13.

Since this is fundamentally a *technical* programming book, it emphasizes technical calculations and the graphical display of technical data. It provides classes to create plots of data, perform array manipulations, format output data, solve simultaneous equations, calculate statistics, use complex numbers, and perform signal-processing functions such as FFTs, convolutions, etc. Such basic infrastructure is readily available for older languages such as Fortran and C, but it is not yet widely available for Java. These classes may be reused by students to solve their own technical problems in a device-independent manner.

FEATURES OF THIS BOOK

Many features of this book are designed to emphasize the proper way to write reliable Java programs. These features should serve a student well as he or she is first learning Java, and should also be useful to the practitioner on the job. They include:

Emphasis on Problem Solving

The book starts from the beginning developing and executing practical examples useful for solving problems in an engineering environment. It emphasizes solving problems in the language, and only introduces the bare minimum of Java classes required to make a program execute. The earlier chapters hide the complexity of Java I/O by using simple convenience classes to read and write files. The book starts with standalone Java programs to solve a particular problem, rather than applets designed to run within a Web browser. Arrays, strings, and graphics, and details of class libraries are introduced in a gradual fashion in later chapters.

Emphasis on Interactive Learning

All examples in the book are available for download from the book's Web site. Students are encouraged to execute each example as it is encountered on their own computers. In addition, end-of-chapter exercises require the students to modify and enhance the on-line code. The packages that accompany this book provide basic tools to manipulate complex data and arrays and to perform signal-processing functions such as FFTs. Students are encouraged to re-use these components in their own programs.

Emphasis on Strong Typing and Data Dictionaries

Every variable and reference in Java classes and methods must be explicitly typed, so strong typing is an inherent feature of the language. In conjunction with the explicit declaration of every variable and reference in each method, the book emphasizes the importance of creating a data dictionary that describes the purpose of each variable to make the code more understandable.

Emphasis on Top-Down Design Methodology

The book introduces a top-down design methodology in Chapter 3, and then uses it consistently throughout the rest of the book. This methodology encourages a student to think about the proper design of a program *before* beginning to code. It emphasizes the importance of clearly defining the problem to be solved and the required inputs and outputs before any other work is begun. Once the problem is properly defined, it teaches the student to break the problem down into discrete classes representing the "things" within the program, and methods representing the behavior of those "things". Finally, it teaches the importance of testing at all stages of the process, both unit testing of the component classes and methods and exhaustive testing of the final product. Examples are given of programs that work properly for some data sets, and then fail for others.

Pseudocode is introduced as a tool for use during the stepwise refinement process, and it is used consistently in all examples.

The formal design process taught by the book may be summarized as follows:

1. Clearly state the problem that you are trying to solve.
2. Define the inputs required by the program and the outputs to be produced by the program.
3. Decompose the program into classes and their associated methods. Define one or more classes, and determine how the classes interact with each other and with the outside world. Define a separate method to implement each interaction.
4. Design the algorithm that you intend to implement for each method. Stepwise decomposition and pseudocode is used to describe the methods that manipulate objects of Java classes
5. Turn the pseudocode into Java statements.
6. Test the Java program. This step includes unit testing of specific functions, and also exhaustive testing of the final program with many different data sets.

Emphasis on Java Class Libraries

One of the great advantages of Java is that it contains portable class libraries that are designed to perform many of the functions required to write working Java programs. It makes no sense to implement a feature from scratch when the compiler vendor has already provided working, tested, and portable classes and methods to implement the feature. The re-usable nature of objects derived from Java classes makes programming more rapid, simpler, and more reliable. The book emphasizes the advantages of re-use inherent in the Java language.

Supplemental Packages

Several packages containing classes of special importance to scientists and engineers have been written and supplied with this book. Package `chapman.io` contains convenience classes for reading data from files and the standard input stream, for writing data to files, and for formatting output data.

Package `chapman.graphics` contains classes for creating easy and flexible plots. Package `chapman.math` contains classes that manipulate arrays, provide an implementation of complex numbers, provide basic signal processing techniques such as FFTs, convolution, and correlation, and also provide supplemental math functions, such as `sinh`, `cosh`, `tanh`, `log10`, etc.

Good Programming Practice Boxes

These boxes highlight good programming practices when they are introduced for the convenience of the student. In addition, all good programming practices introduced in a chapter are summarized at the end of the chapter. An example Good Programming Practice Box is shown below.

GOOD PROGRAMMING PRACTICE

Always indent the body of any structure by three or more spaces to improve the readability of the code.

Programming Pitfalls Boxes

These boxes highlight common errors so that they can be avoided. An example Programming Pitfalls Box is shown below.

PROGRAMMING PITFALLS

Adding a semicolon after a `while` statement can produce a logical error. Java will compile and execute the program, but the program may go into an infinite loop.

Pedagogical Features

The book includes several features designed to aid student comprehension. An average of two quizzes appear in each chapter, with answers to all questions included in Appendix C. These quizzes can serve as a useful self-test of comprehension. In addition, there are approximately 185 end-of-chapter exercises, with the answers to selected exercises appearing at the book's Web site. Good programming practices are highlighted in all chapters with special Good Programming Practice boxes, and common errors are highlighted in Programming Pitfalls boxes. End of chapter materials include summaries, list of key terms, and summaries of good programming practice. Finally, a description of the special classes written for this book is available for download from the book's Web site.

Setting the `CLASSPATH` Environment Variable

In order to use the special packages supplied with this book, a programmer must first set the CLASSPATH environment variable on his or her computer to tell the Java compiler where to look for the packages. This variable must contain the name of the *parent directory* of the class path structure. For example, if the extra packages appear as subdirectories of directory C:\packages, then the CLASSPATH variable must include the directory c:\packages.

The manner in which the environment variable is set will vary among different types of operating systems. In Windows 95/98, the CLASSPATH environment variable is set by including the line

```
set CLASSPATH=C:\packages
```

in the `autoexec.bat` file. If a CLASSPATH already exists in the file, add a semicolon (;) followed by c:\packages to the end of the existing path.

In Windows NT, the environment variable is set through the *System* option in the *Control Panel.* See the Windows NT help system for details.

For Unix systems running the C shell, the class path is set by opening the .login file with a text editor and adding the line

```
setenv CLASSPATH $HOME/packages
```

If a CLASSPATH already exists in the file, add a colon (:) $HOME/packages to the end of the existing path.

For Unix systems running the Bourne or Korn shells, the class opening the .profile file with a text editor and adding the lines

```
CLASSPATH=$HOME/packages
export CLASSPATH
```

If a CLASSPATH already exists in the file, add a colon (:) followed by $HOME/packages to the end of the existing path.

A Final Note to the User

No matter how hard I try to proofread a document like this book, it is inevitable that some typographical errors will slip through and appear in print. If you should spot any such errors, please drop me a note via the publisher, and I will do my best to get them eliminated from subsequent printings and editions. Thank you very much for your help in this matter.

You are free to use and modify the classes distributed in this book for any non-commercial use in accordance with the license agreement included with the software. I do make one specific request, though. If you find and fix bugs, or if you enhance the functionality of some class, please send me a copy of the bug fix or enhancement, so that I can incorporate it into the basic library for the benefit of all users. My current email address should always be available through the book's Web site.

I will maintain a complete list of errata and corrections at the book's World Wide Web site, which is `http://www.prenhall.com/chapman_java`.

Please check that site for any updates and / or corrections.

Acknowledgments

I would also like to thank Alan Apt, Toni Holm, Scott Disanno, and all the crew at Prentice Hall. They have been a pleasure to work with.

Finally, I would like to thank my wife Rosa, and our children Avi, David, Rachel, Aaron, Sarah, Naomi, and Shira for being such delightful people, and the inspiration for my efforts.

Stephen J. Chapman
Melbourne, Australia
July, 1999

Contents

PREFACE VII

The Book viii
Topics Covered in This Book ix
Features of this Book ix

1 INTRODUCTION TO JAVA 1

1.1 Elements of Java 2
1.2 An Introduction to Object-Oriented Programming 3
    1.2.1 Objects 3
    1.2.2 Messages 5
    1.2.3 Classes 6
    1.2.4 Class Variables and Methods 7
    1.2.5 Class Hierarchy and Inheritance 8
    1.2.6 Java API Packages 9
1.3 Applets Versus Applications 10
1.4 A First Java Program 10
1.5 Compiling and Executing a Java Program 12

2 BASIC ELEMENTS OF JAVA 15

2.1 Introduction 15
2.2 Java Names 15
2.3 Constants and Variables 16
    2.3.1 Integer Constants and Variables 18
    2.3.2 Real Constants and Variables 18
    2.3.3 Boolean Constants and Variables 20
    2.3.4 Character Constants and Variables 20
    2.3.5 Strings 21
    2.3.6 Keeping Constants Consistent in a Program 21
2.4 Assignment Statements and Arithmetic Calculations 23
    2.4.1 Integer Arithmetic 24
    2.4.2 Floating-Point Arithmetic 25
    2.4.3 Hierarchy of Operations 26
    2.4.4 Numeric Promotion of Operands 28
    2.4.5 Assignment Conversion and Casting Conversion 29
2.5 Assignment Operators 31
2.6 Increment and Decrement Operators 32
2.7 Mathematical Methods 33
    2.7.1 Overloaded Methods 35
    2.7.2 Coercion of Arguments 35
2.8 Standard Input and Output 37
    2.8.1 Using the Standard Output Stream 37
    2.8.2 Using the Standard Input Stream 39
2.9 Program Examples 42
2.10 Debugging Java Programs 50

3 BRANCHES AND PROGRAM DESIGN 58

3.1   Introduction to Top-down Design Techniques 59
3.2   Use of Pseudocode 63
3.3   Relational and Logical Operators 64
3.4   Selection Structures 69

4 REPETITION STRUCTURES 90

4.1   The while Loop 90
4.2   The do/while Loop 97
4.3   The for Loop 98
4.4   Formatting Output Data 115
4.5   Example Problem 119
4.6   More on Debugging Java Programs 124

5 ARRAYS, FILE ACCESS, AND PLOTTING 134

5.1   Introduction to Arrays 134
5.2   Declaring Arrays 136
5.3   Using Array Elements in Java Statements 136
     5.3.1   Initializing Array Values 138
     5.3.2   Out-of-Bounds Array Subscripts 139
     5.3.3   The Use of Named Constants (Final Variables) with Array Declarations 140
5.4   Reading and Writing Data to Files 145
     5.4.1   Reading Files with Class FileIn 145
     5.4.2   Writing Files with Class FileOut 147
5.5   Example Problems 149
5.6   Introduction to Plotting 158
5.7   Two-Dimensional Arrays 161
     5.7.1   Declaring Two-Dimensional Arrays 162
     5.7.2   Initializing Two-Dimensional Arrays 164
     5.7.3   Initializing Two-Dimensional Arrays From a File 164
     5.7.4   Example Problem 165
     5.7.5   Multi-Dimensional Arrays 169

6 METHODS 178

6.1   Why Use Methods? 180
6.2   Method Definitions 181
6.3   Variable Passing in Java: The Pass-by-Value Scheme 183
6.4   Example Problem 186
6.5   Automatic Variables 189
6.6   Scope 190
6.7   Recursive Methods 191
6.8   Method Overloading 193
6.9   Class `java.util.` Arrays 200
6.10   Additional Methods Supplied with This Book 200

7 CLASSES AND OBJECT-ORIENTED PROGRAMMING 213

7.1   The Structure of a Class 215
7.2   Implementing a `Timer` Class 215
7.3   Class Scope 219
7.4   Types of Methods 220

7.5   Standard Java Packages 227
7.6   Creating Your Own Packages 229
        7.6.1   Setting the Class Path 231
        7.6.2   Using User-Defined Packages 231
7.7   Member Access Modifiers 231
7.8   Finalizers and Garbage Collection 233
7.9   Static Class Members 234
        7.9.1   Static Variables 234
        7.9.2   Static Methods 236

8 EXCEPTIONS AND COMPLEX NUMBERS 250

8.1   Exceptions and Exception Handling 250
        8.1.1   What Is an Exception? 250
        8.1.2   Creating an Exception 252
        8.1.3   Throwing an Exception 253
        8.1.4   Handling Exceptions 258
        8.1.5   The Exceptions Hierarchy and Inheritance 261
        8.1.6   Nested try/catch Structures 262
        8.1.7   Invalid Results That Do Not Produce Exceptions 265
8.2   Complex Numbers 267
        8.2.1   Using chapman.math.Complex 267
        8.2.2   Class chapman.math.SigProc 272

9 INHERITANCE, POLYMORPHISM, AND INTERFACES 276

9.1   Superclasses and Subclasses 276
9.2   Defining Superclasses and Subclasses 277
9.3   The Relationship Between Superclass Objects and Subclass Objects 282
9.4   Polymorphism 284
9.5   Abstract Classes 288
9.6   Final Methods and Classes 291
9.7   The Type-Wrapper Classes for Primitive Types 291
9.8   Interfaces 302
        9.8.1   Implementing Interfaces 302
        9.8.2   Calling Interface Methods 305
        9.8.3   Using Interfaces to Define Constants 306
        9.8.4   The Significance of Interfaces 307
9.9   The Collection and Iterator Interfaces 307

10 STRINGS 318

10.1   Creating and Initializing Strings 319
10.2   String Methods 320
        10.2.1   Substrings 320
        10.2.2   Concatenating Strings 320
        10.2.3   Comparing Strings 324
        10.2.4   Locating Characters and Substrings in a String 328
        10.2.5   Miscellaneous String Methods 329
        10.2.6   The valueOf() Method 330
10.3   Creating and Initializing StringBuffers 331
10.4   StringBuffer Methods 332
        10.4.1   The Difference between Length and Capacity 332
        10.4.2   The append and insert Methods 335

10.4.3 The reverse Method 336
10.5   The StringTokenizer Class 339
10.6   Command-Line Arguments 340

11 INTRODUCTION TO JAVA GRAPHICS 353

11.1   Containers and Components 354
    11.1.1 Creating and Displaying a Frame and a Canvas 355
    11.1.2 How to Display Graphics on a Canvas 357
    11.1.3 The Graphics Coordinate System 359
11.2   Drawing Lines 360
    11.2.1 Drawing Simple Lines 360
    11.2.2 Controlling Line Color, Width, and Style 360
    11.2.3 Eliminating Jagged Edges From Lines 363
11.3   Drawing Other Shapes 369
    11.3.1 Rectangles 369
    11.3.2 Rounded Rectangles 370
    11.3.3 Ellipses 371
    11.3.4 Arcs 372
    11.3.5 General Paths 375
11.4   Displaying Text 383
    11.4.1 Selecting and Controlling Fonts 384
    11.4.2 Getting Information About Fonts 385
11.5   The Affine Transform 388
11.6   XOR Mode 394

12 BASIC GRAPHICAL USER INTERFACES 400

12.1   How a Graphical User Interface Works 401
12.2   Creating and Displaying a Graphical User Interface 404
12.3   Events and Event Handling 406
12.4   Selected Graphical User Interface Components 407
    12.4.1 Labels 408
    12.4.2 Push Buttons and Associated Events 410
    12.4.3 Text Fields and Password Fields 415
    12.4.4 Combo Boxes 421
    12.4.5 Check Boxes and Radio Buttons 424
    12.4.6 Canvases (Blank Components) 431
12.5   Layout Managers 436
    12.5.1 BorderLayout Layout Manager 436
    12.5.2 FlowLayout Layout Manager 437
    12.5.3 GridLayout Layout Manager 438
    12.5.4 BoxLayout Layout Manager 438
    12.5.5 Combining Layout Managers to Produce a Result 440
12.6   Putting It All Together 444

13 ADDITIONAL GUI COMPONENTS AND APPLETS 465

13.1   Additional Graphical User Interface Components 465
    13.1.1 Lists 466
    13.1.2 Tables 474
13.2   Menus 475
    13.2.1 Menu Components 476
    13.2.2 Events Associated with Menu Components 478
13.3   Dialog Boxes 483
    13.3.1 Message Dialog Boxes 484

13.3.2   Confirm Dialog Boxes 485
13.3.3   Input Dialog Boxes 488
13.4   Interfaces and Adapter Classes 488
13.5   Pop-Up Menus 492
13.6   Pluggable Look and Feel 495
13.7   Introduction to Applets 504
13.7.1   The JApplet Class 504
13.7.2   Creating and Displaying an Applet 505
13.7.3   Displaying Status Information 508
13.7.4   Using Packages Within Applets 509
13.7.5   Creating an Applet That is Also an Application 510

14 INPUT AND OUTPUT 517

14.1   The Structure of the Java I/O System 519
14.2   Sequential Data Input 520
14.3   Sequential Data Output 522
14.4   Formatted Input and Output 524
14.4.1   Reading Strings from a Formatted Sequential File 524
14.4.2   Reading Numeric Data from a Formatted Sequential File 527
14.4.3   Reading Formatted Data from the Standard Input Stream 529
14.4.4   Formatted Output to a Sequential File 531
14.5   Unformatted Input and Output 533
14.5.1   Unformatted Input from a Sequential File 533
14.5.2   Unformatted Output to a Sequential File 534
14.6   Random Access Files 540
14.7   Getting Information about Files: The File class 542

APPENDIX A:
ASCII CHARACTER SET 547

APPENDIX B:
OPERATOR PRECEDENCE CHART 548

APPENDIX C:
ANSWERS TO PRACTICE BOXES 550

INDEX 562

1

Introduction to Java

Java is a relatively new but powerful programming language that it is taking the world by storm. The language has enormous appeal for many reasons. One major reason is that it is largely *platform independent,* meaning that an application written for one computer is very likely to run unchanged on another computer.[1] Thus, an engineer can write a single application that will execute across all of a company's computers, whether they are PCs, Macs, or Unix workstations. This "write once, run anywhere" philosophy means that an organization is not locked into a single type of computer hardware.

A second advantage of Java is that it is *object oriented.* As we will see, object oriented programming languages make the design and maintenance of large programs easier, by encapsulating data and the methods for modifying that data into discrete units, called **objects**. Because objects interact with each other only through well-defined interfaces, unintended side effects can be minimized, and the objects can be re-used more easily in different programs.

Another advantage of Java is that the basic language is relatively *simple.* The Java language itself has a simpler syntax than C (upon which it was based), making it easier to

SECTIONS

- 1.1 Elements of Java
- 1.2 An Introduction to Object-Oriented Programming
- 1.3 Applets Versus Applications
- 1.4 A First Java Program
- 1.5 Compiling and Executing a Java Program
- Summary
- Key Terms

OBJECTIVES

After reading this chapter, you should be able to:

- Identify the elements of Java
- Understand objects and object-oriented programming
- Know the difference between Applets and Applications
- Read a Java program
- Compile and execute a Java program

---

[1]There have been teething pains associated with achieving true platform independence, and the goal of complete platform independence has not been achieved yet. However, significant progress has been made, and if Microsoft's offerings are ignored, platform independence seems to be an achievable goal.

master. Many of the trickiest and most error-prone portions of the C language (such as pointer manipulation) simply do not exist in Java, and other features are either greatly simplified or handled automatically. For example, memory allocation and deallocation is a major source of errors in C programs. In Java, memory allocation and deallocation happens automatically.

In addition, the standard Java language includes *device-independent graphics*. While graphical output can be created in other languages such as C and Fortran, the code required is not standard, differing from computer to computer and even from device to device within the same computer. For example, the code to print the graphics on a screen will be different from that to print the same graphics on a printer. In contrast, *Java has device independent graphics built directly into the language*. A program that generates a graph on one computer will also generate the same graph when executed on another computer, even if it is a different type and has different operating system. Finally, the Java language is *free*. The Java Development Kit may be downloaded for free from `http://java.sun.com`. This kit includes a Java compiler (`javac`), a Java run-time interpreter (`java`), a debugger (`jdb`), and all of the standard Java libraries. Fancier development environments may be purchased from IBM, Symantec, Microsoft, and many others vendors, but the basic language is free.

One significant disadvantage of Java is that it is a new language which is evolving rapidly. While the basic language has been pretty much fixed, the Java Application Programming Interface (API) has changed rapidly between Java Development Kit (JDK) versions 1.0, 1.1, and 1.2 (now known as Java 2). Features of programs written with older versions of the JDK are now considered obsolescent only months after the have been created. Hopefully, the core portion of the Java API will soon mature and stabilize so that programmers can work with a consistent environment. This book teaches the Java API as it appears the JDK for Java 2.

1.1 ELEMENTS OF JAVA

Java is composed of three distinct elements:

1. The Java Programming Language
2. The Java Virtual Machine
3. The Java Application Programming Interface (API)

Java differs from other computer languages in that all Java programs are compiled to execute on a special computer known as the *Java Virtual Machine (Java VM)*. The machine language of the Java VM is known as *bytecode*. All Java compilers produce bytecodes, which can be executed directly on a Java Virtual Machine. Since the processors in real computers such as PCs and Unix workstations are not Java VMs, they cannot execute bytecode directly. Instead, each type of computer has an interpreter that converts Java VM bytecodes into the machine language of the particular computer on-the-fly as a Java program is executed. The process of compiling and executing a Java program is shown in Figure 1.1. The Java program may be created using any text editor, and is stored in a file with the special file extension `.java`. The Java compiler compiles this program into bytecode for execution on the Java VM, and stores the bytecode in a file with the special file extension `.class`. This compilation only occurs once. When the program is executed on a computer, the Java interpreter translates the Java VM bytecode on-the-fly into instructions for the actual computer executing the program. This interpretation process happens every time that the Java program is executed. Note that

Figure 1.1. A Java program is created using an editor and stored in a disk file with the file extent .java. Each program is compiled once using the java compiler, producing a file of Java bytecodes with the file extent .class. This file is interpreted by the Java interpreter each time that the program is executed.

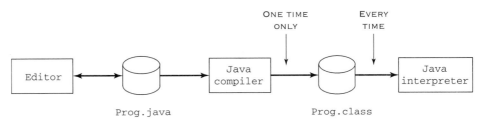

the Java bytecode is independent of any particular computer hardware, so any computer with a Java interpreter can execute the compiled Java program, no matter what type of computer the program was compiled on.

The Java API is a large collection of ready-made software components that provide many useful capabilities. These components provide standard ways to read and write files, manipulate strings, build Graphical User Interfaces, and perform many other essential functions. The components of the Java API are grouped into libraries (called *packages*) of related components. A programmer can save an enormous amount of time by using the objects in these standard packages to perform tasks instead of trying to "reinvent the wheel" each time that he or she writes a program. The components in these packages are standard across all implementations of Java, so a program that uses them to implement some function will run properly on any computer system that implements Java. In addition, the components are already debugged, so using them reduces the total effort required to write and debug a program.

We will study the Java language proper in the first seven chapters of this book. The remainder of the book will be devoted to learning about the contents of the Java API and how to use them.

We will concentrate on the study of the Java language itself in the first seven chapters. The remainder of the book will concentrate on how to use selected contents of the Java API.

1.2 AN INTRODUCTION TO OBJECT-ORIENTED PROGRAMMING

This section provides an introduction to the basic concepts of object-oriented programming. It is intended for individuals who have had prior experience with procedural programming languages such as C, Fortran, or Pascal. *Novice programmers may skip this material with no loss of continuity,* and refer back to it once Chapter 7 is reached.

Object-oriented programming (OOP) is the process of programming by modeling objects in software. The principal features of OOP are described in the following sections.

1.2.1 Objects

The physical world is full of objects: cars, pencils, trees, and so on. *Object-oriented programming* is the process of modeling the properties and behavior of real objects in software.

Any real object can be characterized by its *properties* and its *behavior*. For example, a car can be modeled as an object. A car has certain properties (color, speed, direction, fuel consumption) and certain behaviors (starting, stopping, turning and so on).

In the software world, an **object** is a software component whose structure is like that of objects in the real world. Each object consists of a combination of data (called **properties**) and behaviors (called **methods**). The properties are variables describing the essential characteristics of the object, while the methods describe how the object behaves and how the properties of the object can be modified. Thus, an object is a software bundle of variables and related methods.

A software object is often represented as shown in Figure 1.2. The object can be thought of as a cell, with a central nucleus of variables and an outer layer of methods that form an interface between the object's variables and the outside world. The nucleus of data is hidden from the outside world by the outer layer of methods. The object's variables are said to be *encapsulated* within the object, meaning that no code outside of the object can see or directly manipulate them. Any access to the object's data must be through calls to the object's methods.

The variables and methods in a Java object are formally known as **instance variables** and **instance methods** to distinguish them from class variables and class methods (described later in Section 1.2.4).

Typically, encapsulation is used to hide the implementation details of an object from other objects in the program. If the other objects in the program cannot see the internal state of an object, they cannot introduce bugs by accidentally modifying the object's state. In addition, changes to the internal operation of the object will not affect the operation of the other objects in a program. As long as the interface to the outer world is unchanged, the implementation details of an object can change at any time without affecting other parts of the program.

Encapsulation provides two primary benefits to software developers:

- **Modularity:** An object can be written and maintained independently of the source code for other objects. Therefore, the object can be easily re-used and passed around in the system.
- **Information Hiding:** An object has a public interface that other objects can use to communicate with it. However, the object's instance variables are not directly accessible to other objects. Therefore, if the public interface is not changed, an object's variables and methods that can be changed at any time without introducing side-effects in the other objects that depend on it.

Figure 1.2. An object may be represented as a nucleus of data (instance variables) surrounded and protected by methods, which implement the object's behavior and form an interface between the variables and the outside world.

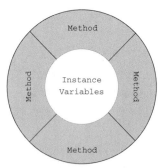

Sometimes, an object will make some of its instance variables **public** so that they can be accessed directly by other objects. This is occasionally done for reasons of efficiency if a variable has to be used very often, because invoking a method for each access will make the program be unacceptably slow. This is strictly speaking a violation of the object-oriented methodology, but it is a compromise that is sometimes made in the real world. Normally, an instance variable should *never* be made `public`.

GOOD PROGRAMMING PRACTICE:

Always make instance variables private, so that they are hidden within an object. Such encapsulation makes your programs more modular and easier to modify.

1.2.2 Messages

Objects communicate by passing messages back and forth among themselves. If Object A wants Object B to perform some action for it, it sends a message to Object B requesting the object to execute one of its methods (see Figure 1.3). The message causes Object B to execute the specified method.

Each message has three components, which provide all the information necessary for the receiving object to perform the desired method:

1. The object to whom the message is addressed.
2. The name of the method to perform on that object.
3. Any parameters needed by the method.

An object's behavior is expressed through its methods, so message passing supports all possible interactions between objects.

Note that objects don't need to be in the same process or even on the same computer to send and receive messages to each other. As long as a path to transmit messages

Figure 1.3. If object `objA` wants object `objB` to do some work for it, it sends a message to that object. The message contains three parts: the name of the object to which it is addressed, the name of the method within the object that will do the work, and required parameters. Note that the names of the object and method are separated by a period.

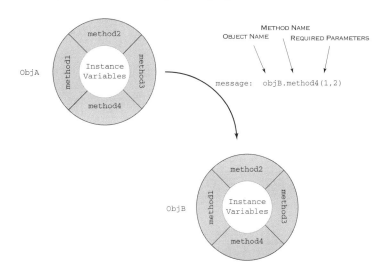

exists, the objects can interact. This characteristic makes object-oriented programs highly suited to client-server applications, in which the object sending the message resides on a different computer than the object performing the action.

1.2.3 Classes

Classes are the software blueprints from which objects are made. A class is a software construct that specifies the number and type of instance variables to be included in an object, and the instance methods that will be applied to the object. Each component of a class is known as a **member**. The two types of members are **fields**, which specify the data types defined by the class, and **methods**, which specify the operations on those fields. For example, suppose that we wish to create an object to represent a complex number. Such an object would have two instance variables, one for the real part of the number (`re`) and one for the imaginary part of the number (`im`). In addition, it would have methods describing how to add, subtract, multiply, divide, etc., with complex numbers. To create such objects, we would write a class `Complex` that defines the required fields `re` and `im`, together with their associated methods.

Note that a class is a *blueprint* for an object, not an object itself. The class describes what an object will look and behave like once it is created. Each object is created or *instantiated* in memory from the blueprint provided by a class, and many different objects can be instantiated from the same class. For example, Figure 1.4 shows a class `Complex`, and three objects a, b, and c created from that class. Each of the three

Figure 1.4.   Many objects can be instantiated from a single class. In this example, three objects a, b, and c have been instantiated from class `Complex`.

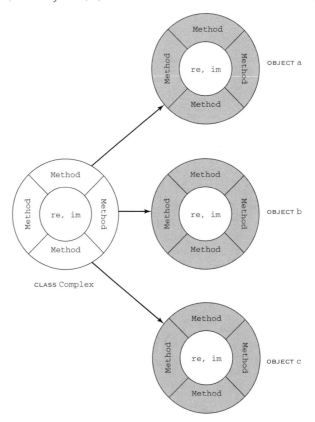

objects has its own copies of the instance variables re and im, while sharing a single set of methods to modify them.

1.2.4 Class Variables and Methods

As we described above, each object created from a class receives its own copies of all the instance variables defined in the class. The instance variables in each object are independent of the instance variables in all other objects.

In addition to instance variables, it is possible to define **class variables**. Class variables differ from instance variables in that *there is only one variable for all objects created from the class, and every object has access to it.* Class variables are effectively "common" to all of the objects created from the class in which they are defined. They are created when an object is first instantiated from a class, and remain in existence until the program finishes executing. This idea is illustrated in Figure 1.5, which shows a new version of the Complex class containing two instance variables (re and im) and one class variable (count). The instance variables re and im will contain the real and imaginary part of the complex number stored in the object, while the class variable count might contain the number of objects instantiated from this class. Every object instantiated from this class will contain a unique copy of the variables re and im, but all the objects will use a single copy of the variable count.

Class variables are typically used to keep track of data that is common across all instances of a class. For example, count could be used to count the number of objects created using class Complex. Each time that a new Complex object is created, the value stored in count would be increased by one, and that new value will be available to every Complex object.

Figure 1.5. An example class containing both instance variables and class variables. The instance variables re and im are different in objects a and b, while the class variable count is common to both objects.

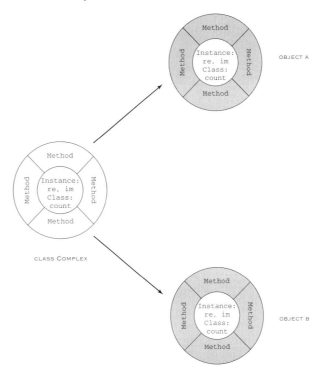

It is also possible to define **class methods**. Class methods are methods that exist independently of any objects defined from the class. These methods can access and modify class variables, but they cannot access instance variables or invoke instance methods.

1.2.5 Class Hierarchy and Inheritance

All classes in an object-oriented language are organized in a **class hierarchy**, with the highest level classes being very general in behavior and lower-level ones becoming more specific. Each lower-level class is based on and derived from a higher-level class, and the lower-level classes *inherit both the instance variables and the instance methods* of the class from which it is derived. A new class starts with all of the non-private instance variables and methods of the class on which it is based, and the programmer then adds the additional variables and methods necessary for the new class to perform its function.

The class on which a new class is based is referred to as a **superclass**, and the new class is referred to as a **subclass**. The new subclass can itself become the superclass for another new subclass. A subclass normally adds instance variables and instance methods of its own, so a subclass is generally larger than its superclass. In addition, it can **override** some methods of its superclass, changing its behavior from that of its superclass. Because a subclass is more specific than its superclass, it represents a smaller group of objects.

For example, suppose that we define a class called Vector2D to contain two-dimensional vectors. Such a class would have two instance variables x and y to

Figure 1.6. An example of inheritance. Class Vector2D has been defined to handle two-dimensional vectors. When class Vector3D is defined as a subclass of Vector2D, it inherits the instance variables x and y, as well as many methods. The programmer then adds a new instance variable z and new methods to the ones inherited from the superclass.

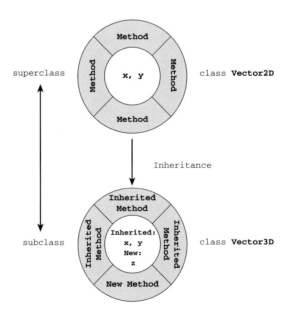

Figure 1.7.   A partial class hierarchy of the `java.util` package. Note that all classes ultimately derive from the `Object` class.

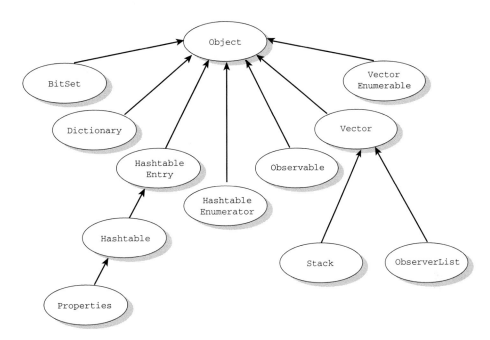

contain the x and y components of the 2D vectors, and it would need methods to manipulate the vectors such as adding two vectors, subtracting two vectors, calculating the length of a vector, etc. Now suppose that we need to create a class called `Vector3D` to contain three-dimensional vectors. If this class is based on `Vector2D`, then it will automatically inherit instance variables x and y from its superclass, so the new class will only need to define a variable z. The new class will also extend the methods used to manipulate 2D vectors to allow them to work properly with 3D vectors.

The concepts of class hierarchy and inheritance are extremely important, since inheritance allows a programmer to define certain behaviors only once in a superclass, and to re-use those behaviors over and over again in many different subclasses. This reusability makes programming more efficient.

All classses in the Java language are ultimately derived from a superclass called `Object`. For example, the class hierarchy for the `java.util` package is shown in Figure 1.7.

1.2.6 Java API Packages

Groups of related Java classes are usually collected together into special libraries called *packages*. The Java API includes many packages implementing important features of the language. A few of the more important packages in the standard Java environment are summarized in Table 1-1. Learning to use the classes and methods implemented in these packages is the largest part of learning to program in Java.

TABLE 1-1 Some Important Java API Packages

JAVA API PACKAGE	DESCRIPTION
java.applet	**The Java Applet Package** This package contains all of the classes and interfaces required to support Java Applets.
java.awt	**The Abstract Windowing Toolkit Package** This package contains many of the classes and interfaces required to support old-style Graphical User Interfaces. Portions of this package are also used with the new "Swing" Graphical User Interfaces.
java.beans	**The Java Beans Package** This package contains classes that enable programmers to create reusable software components.
java.io	**The Java Input / Output Package** This package contains classes that allow a program to input and output data.
java.lang	**The Java Language Package** This package contains the basic classes and interfaces required by most Java programs.
java.net	**The Java Networking Package** This package contains classes that allow a program to communicate via networks.
javax.swing	**The Swing Package** This package contains many of the classes and interfaces required to support the new "Swing" Graphical User Interfaces.
java.text	**The Java Text Package** This package contains classes and interfaces that allow a program to manipulate numbers, dates, characters, and strings.
java.util	**The Java Utility Package** This package contains utility classes and interfaces: data and time manipulations, random number generation, etc.

1.3 APPLETS VERSUS APPLICATIONS

Java supports two different types of programs, *applets* and *applications.* An applet is a special type of program that runs within a World Wide Web browser when an HTML document containing the applet is loaded into the browser. Applets have a graphical user interface that must follow strict rules to ensure proper integration with the browser. Applets tend to be small, so that they can be downloaded over the Internet in a small amount of time.

In contrast, applications are complete stand-alone programs designed to be loaded and executed independently within your computer. They can have either command line interfaces or graphical user interfaces, depending on the application's design. Applications are the sort of programs that are traditionally used for engineering calculations, so all of the examples in the first portion of this book are applications. We will introduce applets in Chapter 13, and also show how to design a single program that can run either as an application or as an applet.

1.4 A FIRST JAVA PROGRAM

We will begin our study of Java with an old programming tradition: a program that does nothing more than print out "Hello, World!". A program of this sort is very simple, but it illustrates many important features that we will see in more complex programs. We will analyze this program, and show how to compile and execute it in the Java development environment.

Every Java program must contain at least one class, and that class must contain at least one method. When the program is executed, the class will be used to create an object that executes the application. The execution of a Java application always begins with a method named `main` in the principal class of the program.

The "Hello, World" application is shown in Figure 1.8. Note that it contains one class (`HelloWorld`) and one method within the class (`main`). This is the simplest possible Java program.

```
1    /*
2       This program prints out "Hello, World!" on the
3       standard output stream and quits. It defines a class
4       class "HelloWorld", and a "main" method within
5       that class.
6    */
7    public class HelloWorld extends Object {
8       // Define the main method
9       public static void main(String[] args) {
10          System.out.println("Hello, World!"); //Print line
11       }
12    }
```

Figure 1.8. The "Hello, World!" program.

The first six lines of this program are *comments*. A comment is a note written by the programmer to explain what a portion of a program is doing. Comments are extremely important for understanding the purpose of a program. Every program should begin with comments describing the purpose of the program, and should include comments explaining how the various portions of the program function. The Java compiler completely ignores comments-they are for the benefit of humans looking at the code.

GOOD PROGRAMMING PRACTICE

Always begin every program with comments describing the purpose of the program. Use comments liberally throughout the program to explain how each portion of the code works.

This program illustrates two of the three types of Java comments. Multi-line comments may be created by beginning the comment with the symbol `/*` and ending the comment with the symbol `*/`. All of the text between the two symbols is a comment. Single-line comments begin with the symbol `//` and continue to the end of the line. Thus the entire block of text

```
/*
   This program prints out "Hello, World!" on the
   standard output stream and quits. It defines a class
   class "HelloWorld", and a "main" method within
   that class.
*/
```

is a comment, and the words `// Define the main method` and `//Print line` are additional comments. The third form of Java comment, a special version used with the Java documentation system, will not be covered in this text.

Line 7 defines the class `HelloWorld` as a direct subclass of class `Object`, the highest class in the Java class hierarchy. The keyword `extends` specifies that the new class being defined is a subclass of another class, so this line specifies that the new class `HelloWorld` is a subclass of `Object`. At the end of line 7, the **left brace** (**{**) begins the **body** of the class definition. The corresponding **right brace** (**}**) on line 12 ends the class definition. By convention, the left brace opening the body is always included at the end of the line declaring the class's name, and the right brace is placed on a line by itself indented at the same level as the `class` statement.

As we mentioned previously, a class can contain data (variables) and methods. This particular class does not define any variables, but it does define the method `main`. The line `public static void main(String[] args)` declares the start of the `main` method. The keyword `public` means that the method can be invoked by any caller. It must always be present in the `main` method. The keyword `static` means that this method is a class method instead of an instance method. The keyword `void` means that the method does not return a result when it finishes executing. The method's parameter list (`String[] args`) contains any command-line arguments passed to the program when it starts to execute. All of these features will be discussed in detail in later chapters.

The body of the method begins with the left brace (`{`) at the end of line 7 and ends with the corresponding right brace (`}`) on line 11. By convention, the left brace opening the method body is always included at the end of the line declaring the method's name, and the right brace is placed on a line by itself indented at the same level as the method's declaration.

The only executable statement in this method is on line 9. The statement `System.out.println("Hello, World!")` invokes method `println` on variable `out` in the `System` class. The class variable `System.out` object represents the standard output device for the computer on which the program is executing, so invoking the `println` method prints the words `"Hello, World!"` on the computer's standard output device.

Notice that the Java statement on line 10 ends in a semicolon. Every Java statement must end with a semicolon. A statement can occupy as many lines as desired, or several statements can fit on a single line. In either case, the compiler knows that the statement is complete when it sees the semicolon.

1.5 COMPILING AND EXECUTING A JAVA PROGRAM

To compile the `HelloWorld` application, it must be placed in a file called `HelloWorld.java`. Note that *the name of the class being defined must be the same as the name of the file containing the class*, with the file extension `.java` added. The name of the file must be *exactly* the same as the name of the class, including any capitalization, or the Java compiler will report an error.

PROGRAMMING PITFALLS:

Be sure that the name of file containing a class is exactly the same as the name of the class being defined, with the addition of the file extension `.java`. It is an error for the name of the file not to agree with the name of the class.

This program can be compiled with the Java compiler `javac` by typing the command "`javac HelloWorld.java`" at the command prompt:[2]

```
D:\book\java\chap1>javac HelloWorld.java
```

Note that the command `javac` is followed by the name of the file, including the file extension. If there were an error in `HelloWorld`, the compiler would list the errors after this command is entered. If there are no errors, then the compiler will compile the class into bytecode, and place the bytecode into a file called `HelloWorld.class`.

Once the program has been compiled, it may be executed using the Java interpreter or another Java Virtual Machine. This is done by invoking the Java interpreter together with the *name of the class* to execute:

```
D:\book\java\chap1>java HelloWorld
Hello, World!
```

As you can see, the program prints out the words "Hello, World!".

Note that the Java interpreter expects the name of the class to execute, *not* the name of the file containing that class. If the filename is used in the command, an error results.

```
D:\book\java\chap1>java HelloWorld.class
Can't find class HelloWorld\class
```

PROGRAMMING PITFALLS:

Always specify the *file name* (not the class name) when using the Java compiler, and specify the *class name* (not the file name) when executing the compiled program.

When a program is executed, the Java runtime system first invokes a *class loader*, which loads the bytecodes for all the required classes from disk. Once the bytecodes are loaded, a *bytecode verifier* confirms that all bytecodes are valid, and that they do not violate Java's security restrictions. After the bytecodes are verified, they are passed to the Java interpreter or just-in-time compiler for execution. All three of these steps occur when the user types the `java` command.

SUMMARY

- Java is ideally platform independent, meaning that programs written on one type of computer will run unchanged on another type of computer. This ideal has not yet been achieved, but progress is being made towards it.
- Java is object oriented.
- An object is a self-contained software component that consists of properties (variables) and methods.
- Objects communicate with each other via messages. An object uses a message to request another object to perform a task for it.

---

[2]Note that the command prompt may vary from computer to computer. Usually, a PC command prompt will begin with the drive letter followed by a colon and a blackslash and then the directory location and a greater-than sign. Possible command prompts include `C:\java>` and `D:\compilers\java>`. Unix command prompts also vary depending on the type of shell that a user is running.

- Classes are the software blueprints from which objects are made. When an object is instantiated from a class, a separate copy of each instance variable is created for the object. All objects derived from a given class share a single copy of each class variable.
- All classes reside in a class hierarchy, with the `Object` class at the top of the tree.
- All new classes are derived from (extend) some other class, and each new class inherits the non-private variables and methods of its parent class.
- The class on which a new class is based is called a superclass of the new class.
- A new class is known as a subclass of the class on which it is based.
- Groups of related Java classes are usually collected together into special libraries called packages.
- An applet is a special type of program that runs within a World Wide Web browser when an HTML document containing the applet is loaded into the browser.
- An application is a complete stand-alone program designed to be loaded and executed independently within a computer.
- Every Java application must contain a `main` method within its principal class. Program execution always starts in the `main` method.
- A comment that begins with `//` is a single-line comment.
- A comment that begins with `/*` and ends with `*/` may span multiple lines.
- The body of a class is enclosed in braces (`{ }`).
- A application's class name is used as a part of its file name (with the file extension `.java`).
- A Java statement is always terminated by a semicolon. It may stretch over multiple lines, if necessary.
- The Java compiler expects a file name as an argument, not a class name.
- The Java runtime expects a class name as an argument, not a file name.

KEY TERMS

applet	information hiding	object
application	instance method	object oriented programming
bytecode	instance variable	package
class method	instantiated	platform independent
class variable	Java Virtual Machine	properties
comments	(Java VM)	subclass
device-independent	members of a class	superclass
graphics	method	`System.out.println`
fields	modularity	method

Problems

1. Compile and execute the `HelloWorld` application on your computer. Are the results the same as shown in this chapter?

2. Delete the final `}` in the file `HelloWorld.java` and attempt to compile the program. What happens?

2

Basic Elements of Java

2.1 INTRODUCTION

The core of the Java language is relatively simple, but the Java API is extremely large and complex. In the next three chapters, we will be concentrating on the fundamental core of the Java language, while postponing the complications of the Java API until later chapters. By the end of Chapter 4, you will be able to write Java programs that perform complex calculations, including branches, loops, and disk input and output.

This chapter introduces the very basic elements of the Java language, such as Java names, the types of variables in the language, and some types of operations. By the end of the chapter, you will be able to write simple, but functional, Java programs.

2.2 JAVA NAMES

As we saw in the previous chapter, Java classes, methods, and variables all have names. A name in Java may consist of any combination of letters, numbers, and underscore characters (_), but the first character of the name must be a letter. A Java name may be as short as one character or as long as desired (there is no maximum length). The following names are legal in Java:

SECTIONS

- 2.1 Introduction
- 2.2 Java Names
- 2.3 Constants and Variables
- 2.4 Assignment Statements and Arithmetic Calculations
- 2.5 Assignment Operators
- 2.6 Increment and Decrement Operators
- 2.7 Mathematical Methods
- 2.8 Standard Input and Output
- 2.9 Program Examples
- 2.10 Debugging Java Programs
- Summary
- Key Terms

OBJECTIVES

After reading this chapter, you should be able to:

- Learn how to create Java constants and variables
- Understand how to use assignment statements
- Learn the types of operations supported in Java, and the order in which they are executed
- Learn about type conversion, including promotion of operands and casting
- Learn how to use standard Java mathematical methods
- Learn how to read from the standard input stream, and write to the standard output stream

TABLE 2-1   List of Reserved Java Keywords

RESERVED KEYWORDS				
abstract	boolean	break	byte	case
catch	char	class	continue	default
do	double	else	extends	false
final	finally	float	for	if
implements	import	instanceof	int	interface
long	native	new	null	package
private	protected	public	return	short
static	super	switch	synchronized	this
throw	throws	transient	true	try
void	volatile	while		

Reserved but Not Used by Java				
const	goto			

```
ThisIsATest
Hello
ABC
A1B2
a_12
```

and the following names are illegal:

```
1Day              // Begins with a number
_toupper          // Begins with an underscore
```

By convention, Java class names always begin with a capital letter, and Java instance methods and variables begin with a lowercase letter. For example, we capitalized the first letter of the class name `HelloWorld` in Chapter 1, and did not capitalize the first letter of method `main`. If a method or variable name consists of more than one word, such as `toUpper`, the words are joined together and each word after the first begins with an uppercase letter.

The Java language includes a number of **keywords** that have special meanings, such as `if`, `else`, `while`, and so forth. These words are **reserved**, and no Java name can be the same as one of these keywords. A complete list of these illegal names is given in Table 2-1.

GOOD PROGRAMMING PRACTICES

1. Always capitalize the first letter of a class name, and use a lowercase first letter for method and variable names.
2. If a name consists of more than one word, the words are joined together and each succeeding word should begin with an uppercase letter.

2.3 CONSTANTS AND VARIABLES

A **constant** is a data item whose value does not change during program execution, and a **variable** is a data item whose value can change during program execution. There are four basic types of data in Java (known as **primitive data types**): integer, real, bool-

TABLE 2-2 Java Primitive Data Types

TYPE	BITS	RANGE	COMMENT
boolean	1	`true` or `false`	
char	16	`'\u0000'` to `'\uFFFF'`	ISO Unicode Character set
byte	8	−128 to +127	
short	16	−32,768 to +32,767	
int	32	−2,147,483,648 to +2,147,483,648	
long	64	−9,223,372,036,854,775,808 to 9,223,372,036,854,775,807	
float	32	−3.40292347E+38 to +3.40292347E+38	IEEE 754 single-precision floating point. Numbers are represented with about 6–7 decimal digits of precision.
double	64	−1.79769313486231570E+308 to +1.79768313486231570E+308	IEEE 754 double-precision floating point. Numbers are represented with about 15–16 decimal digits of precision.

ean, and character. Integers are data types that can represent integers, such as 0, 23, and −1000. Reals are data types that can represent numbers with decimal points, such as 3.14159. Booleans are logical values that are either `true` or `false`. Characters hold a single Unicode[1] character.

There are four versions of integer data types (`byte`, `short`, `int`, and `long`) and two versions of real data types (`float` and `double`), with differing ranges and precisions. They are summarized in Table 2-2. Note that unlike other languages, *the size and range of values supported by each data type is the same on any computer running Java.* This feature helps to guarantee that a Java program written on one computer will run properly on any other computer.

Java constants are written directly into a program. For example, in the line

```
x = y + 12;
```

the characters 12 represent an integer constant.

A variable is a data item of a primitive data type that can change value during the execution of a program. Java is a *strongly typed language.* This means that every variable must be declared with an explicit type before it is used. (We will learn how to declare variables in the next few sections.) When a Java compiler encounters a variable declaration, it reserves a location in memory for the variable and then references that memory location whenever the variable is used in the program.

It is a good idea to give your variables names that describe their contents. This mnemonic aid will help you or anyone else who may be working with your program to understand what it is doing. For example, if a variable in a program contains a currency exchange rate, it could be given the name `exchangeRate`.

GOOD PROGRAMMING PRACTICE

Use meaningful variable names whenever possible to make your programs clearer.

---

[1]Unicode is an international standard character set that uses 16 bits to code each character, allowing for more than 65,000 possible characters. The Unicode character set supports the alphabets of essentially every modern world language, including Arabic, English, Chinese, Hebrew, Japanese, and Russian.

It is also important to include a **data dictionary** in the body of any classes or methods that you write. A data dictionary is a set of comments that lists the definition *each variable* used in a program. The definition should include both descriptions of the contents of the item and the units in which it is measured. A data dictionary may seem unnecessary while the program is being written, but it is invaluable when you or another person have to go back and modify the program at a later time.

GOOD PROGRAMMING PRACTICE

Create a data dictionary for each program to make program maintenance easier.

2.3.1 Integer Constants and Variables

An integer constant is an integer value written directly into a Java program. It must be written without embedded commas, and may it be preceded by a + or − sign. By default, an integer constant is of type `int`, so it is restricted to be in the range −2,147,483,648 to +2,147,483,648. If a constant is to be of type `long`, it must be concluded with a letter L. The following examples show legal literal constants:

```
12
0
-123456
9999999999L              // Type long
```

The following constants are illegal, and will produce compile-time errors:

```
1,024                    // Embedded comma
9999999999               // Value too large for int
```

When a Java compiler encounters a constant, it places the value of the constant in a specific location in memory and then references that memory location whenever the constant is used in the program. If a program uses the same constant value in more than one location, each of these constants refers to the same location in memory. This optimization helps to reduce the size of Java programs.

An integer variable is declared in a **declaration statement**. The form of a declaration statement is the name of a primitive data type followed by one or more variable names. For example, the statements

```
int var1, var2;
short var3;
```

declare two integers of type `int` and one integer of type `short`. When a declaration statement is encountered, Java automatically creates a variable of the specified type and refers to it by the specified name.

When an integer is created, its value is undefined. An initial value can be assigned to the integer by including it in the declaration:

```
int var1 = 100;     // Creates var1 and initializes it to 100
```

2.3.2 Real Constants and Variables

Real or **floating-point** numbers are values stored in the computer in a kind of scientific notation. The bits used to store a real number are divided into two separate portions, a **mantissa** and an **exponent**. A single-precision real number (type `float`) occupies 32 bits of memory, divided into a 24-bit mantissa and an 8-bit exponent, as

Figure 2.1.   Representation of a single-precision real number. The number is divided into two fields, a mantissa and an exponent.

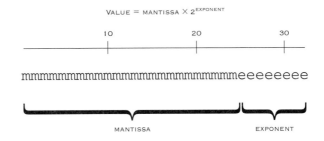

shown in Figure 2.1. The mantissa contains a number between −1.0 and 1.0, and the exponent contains the power of 2 required to scale the number to its actual value.

Real numbers are characterized by two quantities: **precision** and **range**. Precision is the number of significant digits that can be preserved in a number, and range is the difference between the largest and smallest numbers that can be represented. The precision of a real number depends on the number of bits in its mantissa, while the range of the number depends on the number of bits in its exponent. A 24-bit mantissa can represent approximately $\pm 2^{23}$ numbers, or about seven significant decimal digits, so the precision of single-precision real numbers (type `float`) is about seven significant digits. An 8-bit exponent can represent multipliers between 2^{-128} and 2^{127}, so the range of single-precision real numbers is from about 10^{-38} to 10^{38}. Note that the single-precision real data type can represent numbers much larger or much smaller than integers can, but only with seven significant digits of precision.

Similarly, a double-precision real number (type `double`) occupies 64-bits of computer memory, divided into a 53-bit mantissa and an 11-bit exponent. A 53-bit mantissa can represent approximately 15 to 16 decimal digits, so the precision of double-precision real numbers is about 15 significant digits. An 11-bit exponent can represent multipliers between 2^{-1024} and 2^{1023}, so the range of single-precision real numbers is from about 10^{-308} to 10^{308}.

When a value with more than seven digits of precision is stored in a single-precision real variable, *only the most significant seven bits of the number will be preserved*. The remaining information will be lost forever. For example, if the value 12345678.9 is stored in a `float` variable, it will be rounded off to 12345680.0. This difference between the original value and the number stored in the computer is known as **round-off error**. It is important to select a floating-point data type with enough precision to preserve the information needed to solve a particular problem.

A real constant is a literal defining a floating-point constant. It can be distinguished from an integer constant because it contains a decimal point and/or an exponent. If the constant is positive, it may be written either with or without a + sign. No commas may be embedded within a real constant. By default, a real constant is of type `double`, so it is restricted to being between −1.79769313486231570E+308 and +1.79769313486231570E+308.

A real constant *must* have either a decimal point or an exponent, and it may have both. If used, the exponent consists of the letter E or e followed by a positive or negative integer that specifies the power of ten used when the number is written in scientific notation.

The type of a real constant may be specified by appending either the letter F for `float` or the letter D for `double`. If there is no appended letter, the constant is of type `double`. The following examples show legal real constants:

```
12.                 // Type double
12E2                // Type double
12.0e2              // Type double
3.14159F            // Type float
```

The following constants are not legal real constants:

```
1.2e108F            // Too large for type float
1,234.0             // Embedded comma
1234                // An int constant, not real
```

A real variable is declared with a `float` or `double` declaration statement. For example, the statements

```
float pi = 3.14159F;
double x;
```

declare and initialize a single-precision real variable `pi` and declare a double-precision real variable `x`. The value of variable `x` is undefined.

2.3.3 Boolean Constants and Variables

The `boolean` data type contains one of only two possible values: `true` or `false`. A `boolean` constant can only have one of those two values. Thus, the following are valid `boolean` constants:

```
true
false
```

Note that the words `true` and `false` are reserved. That is, they can only be used as boolean constants. No variable, method, or class may use these names. Boolean constants are rarely used, but boolean expressions and variables are commonly used to control program execution, as we will see in Chapters 3 and 4.

A `boolean` variable is a variable containing a value of the `boolean` data type. It is declared in with a `boolean` declaration statement. For example, the statement

```
boolean test = false;
```

declares a `boolean` variable test, and automatically initializes it to a value of `false`.

2.3.4 Character Constants and Variables

All Java characters and strings use the **Unicode character set**. Unicode is a special coding system in which each character is stored in 16 bits of memory. Since 16 bits are used to represent a character there can be 65,536 possible characters. Unicode assigns a unique number to each character in almost every alphabet used on Earth, including the ideograms used in oriental languages, such as Chinese and Japanese. This support makes it possible to write Java programs that work with any language.

A character constant is a literal representing a *single* Unicode character. The literal is written between single quotes, such as `'a'` or `'0'`. Some important characters are not printable characters, but instead perform control functions. Examples include the carriage return (CR) character, which moves the cursor back to the left-hand end of a line, the line feed (LF) character, which moves the cursor down to the next line, and the tab character, which moves the cursor right by one tab stop. These characters can be represented by special **escape sequences**, as shown in Table 2-3.

A character variable is a variable containing a value of the character data type. It is declared in with a `char` declaration statement. For example, the statements

```
char ch1 = 'A';
char ch2;
```

declare and initialize character variable `ch1`, and declare character variable `ch2`.

TABLE 2-3 Table of Common Escape Sequences

SEQUENCE	COMMENT
\n	Newline. Used to position the cursor at the beginning of the next line
\t	Horizontal tab. Used to move cursor to next tab stop
\r	Carriage return. Used to position the cursor at the beginning of the current line, but not advance to the next line.
\\	Backslash. Used to represent the backslash character.
\'	Single quote. Used to represent the single quote.
\"	Double quote. Used to represent the double quote.
\u####	Unicode character specified by sequence number. Used to specify any Unicode character constant. The #### is the hexadecimal representation of the character's sequence number.

2.3.5 Strings

Strings are groups of one or more characters linked together. A string constant is defined in Java by placing the desired characters between double quotes. For example, the following expressions are all valid strings:

```
"This is a string!"
"Line1\nLine2"
"A"
```

Note that escape sequences may be embedded into strings as in the second example above.

A double quote may not appear in the middle of a string, since the double quote character will be interpreted as the end of the string, producing a compile-time error. If a double quote is needed in a string, use the escape sequence \" to represent it. For example, the statement

```
System.out.println("She said \"Hello\".");
```

will print out the string

```
She said "Hello".
```

A Java string is fundamentally different from a Java character. A Java character is a *primitive data type*, while a Java string is an *object*. We will learn much more about strings in Chapter 10, but meanwhile we will use string constants in many input/output (I/O) statements.

2.3.6 Keeping Constants Consistent in a Program

It is important to always keep your physical constants consistent throughout a program. For example, do not use the value 3.14 for π at one point in a program and 3.141593 at another point in the program. Also, you should always write your constants with as much precision as the data type you are using will accept. For example, since the float data type has seven significant digits of precision, π should be written as 3.141593, *not* as 3.14!

The best way to achieve consistency and precision throughout a program is to *assign a name to a constant and then to use that name to refer to the constant throughout the program*. If we assign the name PI to the constant 3.141593, then we can refer to PI by name throughout the program and be certain that we are getting the same value everywhere. Furthermore, assigning meaningful names to constants improves the overall readability of our programs, because a programmer can tell at a glance just what the constant represents.

By convention, the names of Java constants are written in capital letters, with underscore characters between words.

Named constants, or **final variables**, are created using the final keyword in a type declaration statement. This keyword means that the value assigned to a name is final and will never change. For example, the following program defines and uses a named constant PI containing the value of π to seven significant digits.

```
1    public class Constant {
2        public static void main(String[] args) {
3
4            // Declare constant
5            final float PI = 3.14159F;
6
7            // Print out 2*pi
8            System.out.println("2*pi = " + 2*PI);
9        }
10   }
```

When this program is executed, the results are:

```
D:\book\java\chap2>java Constant
2*pi = 6.28318
```

Any attempt to modify a final value will produce a compile-time error. For example, the following program attempts to modify the final variable PI, producing a compile-time error.

```
1    public class BadConstant {
2        public static void main(String[] args) {
3
4            final float PI = 3.14159F;
5            PI = 3.0F;
6        }
7    }
```

```
D:\book\java\rev2\chap2>javac BadConstant.java
BadConstant.java:5: Can't assign a value to a final variable: PI
        PI = 3.0F;
        ^
1 error
```

GOOD PROGRAMMING PRACTICE

Keep your physical constants consistent and precise throughout a program. To improve the consistency and understandability of your code, assign a name to any important constants, and refer to them by that name in the program.

By convention, named constants are written in capital letters, with underscores used to separate the words. This style makes constants stand out from class names, method names, and instance variables. For example, a constant describing the maximum number of values that a program can process might be written as

```
final int MAX_VALUES = 1000;
```

GOOD PROGRAMMING PRACTICE

The names of constants in your program should be in all capital letters, with underscores separating the words.

PRACTICE!

This quiz provides a quick check to see if you have understood the concepts introduced in Sections 2.1 through 2.3. If you have trouble with the quiz, reread the sections, ask your instructor, or discuss the material with a fellow student. The answers to this quiz are found in the back of the book.

Questions 1 through 8 contain a list of valid and invalid constants. State whether or not each constant is valid. If the constant is valid, specify its type. If it is invalid, say why it is invalid.

1. `10.0`
2. `-100,000`
3. `123E-5`
4. `'T'`
5. `''`
6. `3.14159`
7. `"Who are you?"`
8. `true`

Questions 9 through 11 contain two real constants each. Tell whether or not the two constants represent the same value within the computer:

9. `4650.; 4.65E+3`
10. `-12.71; -1.27E1`
11. `0.0001; 1.0e4`

Questions 12 through 15 contain a list of valid and invalid Java names. State whether or not each name is valid. If it is invalid, say why it is invalid. If it is valid, state what type of item the name represents (assuming that Java conventions are followed).

12. `isVector`
13. `MyNewApp`
14. `2ndChance`
15. `MIN_DISTANCE`

Are the following declarations correct or incorrect? If a statement is incorrect, state why it is invalid.

16. `int firstIndex = 20;`
17. `final short MAX_COUNT = 100000;`
18. `char test = "Y";`

19. Are the following statements legal or illegal? If they are legal, what is their result? If they are illegal, what is wrong with them?

```
int i, j;
final int k = 4;
i = k * k;
j = i / k;
k = i + j;
```

2.4 ASSIGNMENT STATEMENTS AND ARITHMETIC CALCULATIONS

Calculations are specified in Java with an **assignment statement** whose general form is

```
variable_name = expression;
```

The assignment operator calculates the value of the expression to the right of the equals sign and *assigns* that value to the variable named on the left of the equals sign. Note that the equals sign does not mean equality in the usual sense of the word. Instead, it means:

TABLE 2-4 Arithmetic Operators

TYPE	SYMBOL	ALGEBRAIC EXPRESSION	JAVA EXPRESSION
Addition	+	$a + b$	a + b
Subtraction	–	$a - b$	a - b
Multiplication	*	ab	a * b
Division	/	a/b or $\frac{a}{b}$ or $a \div b$	a / b
Modulus (Remainder)	%	$a \bmod b$	a % b

store the value of expression *into location* variable_name. For this reason, the equal sign is called the **assignment operator**. A statement such as

```
i = i + 10;
```

is complete nonsense in ordinary algebra, but makes perfect sense in Java. In Java, it means: Take the current value stored in variable i, add 10 to it, and store the result back into variable i.

The expression to the right of the assignment operator can be any valid combination of constants, variables, parentheses, and arithmetic or boolean operators. The standard arithmetic operators included in Java are given in Table 2-4.

Addition, subtraction, multiplication, and division will be familiar to all readers, but the **modulus** operation may be unfamiliar. The modulus operation calculates the *remainder* left after the division of a whole number has been performed. For example, $23 \div 5$ is 4 with a remainder of 3. Thus so,

```
25 % 5 = 3
```

The five arithmetic operators described in Table 2-4 are **binary operators**. This means that they should occur between and apply to two variables or constants. In addition, the + and − symbols can occur as **unary operators**, which means that they apply to one variable or constant, as shown:

```
+23
-a
```

The binary arithmetic operators are evaluated in order from left to right. Thus the expression 10 + 6 − 4 will be evaluated in the order 10 + 6 = 16 and then 16 − 4 = 12. The unary arithmetic operators are evaluated from right to left. Therefore, the expression - -z will be evaluated as - (-z).

2.4.1 Integer Arithmetic

Integer arithmetic is arithmetic involving only integer data. Integer arithmetic always produces an integer result. This is especially important to remember when an expression involves division, since there can be no fractional part in the answer. If the division of two integers is not itself an integer, the computer automatically discards the fractional part of the answer. This behavior can lead to surprising and unexpected answers. For example, integer arithmetic produces the following strange results:

$$\frac{3}{4} = 0 \qquad \frac{4}{4} = 1 \qquad \frac{5}{4} = 1 \qquad \frac{6}{4} = 1$$

$$\frac{7}{4} = 1 \qquad \frac{8}{4} = 2 \qquad \frac{9}{4} = 2$$

Because of this behavior, integers should *never* be used to calculate real-world quantities that vary continuously, such as distance, speed, time, etc. They should only be used for things that are intrinsically integer in nature, such as counters and indices.

PROGRAMMING PITFALLS

Beware of integer arithmetic. Integer division often gives unexpected results.

2.4.2 Floating-Point Arithmetic

Floating-point arithmetic is arithmetic involving floating-point constants and variables. Floating-point arithmetic always produces a floating-point result that is essentially what we would expect. For example, floating-point arithmetic produces the following results:

$$\frac{3.0}{4.0} = 0.75 \qquad \frac{4.0}{4.0} = 1.00 \qquad \frac{5.0}{4.0} = 1.25 \qquad \frac{6.0}{4.0} = 1.50$$

$$\frac{7.0}{4.0} = 1.75 \qquad \frac{8.0}{4.0} = 2.00 \qquad \frac{9.}{4.0} = 2.25 \qquad \frac{1.0}{3.0} = 0.3333333 \quad .$$

However, floating-point numbers do have peculiarities of their own. Because of the finite number of bits used to store a floating-point number, some numbers cannot be represented exactly. For example, the number 1/3 is equal to 0.33333333333. . . . But since the numbers stored in the computer have limited precision, the representation of 1/3 in the computer might be 0.3333333. As a result of this limitation in precision, some quantities that are theoretically equal will not be equal when evaluated by the computer. For example, on some computers

```
3.0 * (1.0 / 3.0) ≠ 1.0,
```

but

```
2.0 * (1.0 / 2.0) = 1.0.
```

Tests for equality must be performed very cautiously when working with real numbers. We will learn how to perform such tests safely in Chapter 3.

PROGRAMMING PITFALLS

Beware of floating-point arithmetic. Due to limited precision, two theoretically identical expressions often give slightly different results.

2.4.3 Hierarchy of Operations

Often, many arithmetic operations are combined into a single expression. For example, consider the equation for the distance traveled by an object subjected to a constant acceleration:

```
dist = d0 + v0 * time + 0.5 * acc * time * time;
```

There are four multiplications and two additions in this expression. In such an expression, it is important to know the order in which the operations are evaluated. If addition is evaluated before multiplication, this expression is equivalent to

```
dist = (d0 + v0) * (time + 0.5) * acc * time * time;
```

But if multiplication is evaluated before addition, this expression is equivalent to

```
dist = d0 + (v0 * time) + (0.5 * acc * time * time);
```

These two equations have different results, and we must be able to unambiguously distinguish between them.

To make the evaluation of expressions unambiguous, Java has established a series of rules governing the hierarchy, or order, in which operations are evaluated within an expression. The Java rules generally follow the normal rules of algebra. The order in which the arithmetic operations are evaluated is:

1. The contents of all parentheses are evaluated first, starting from the innermost parentheses and working outward.
2. All multiplications, divisions, and modulus operations are evaluated, working from left to right.
3. All additions and subtractions are evaluated, working from left to right.

Following these rules, we see that the second of our two possible interpretations is correct: The multiplications are performed before the additions.

Note that all of the above operations were applied in order from left to right across an expression. In Java, we say that the **associativity** of the operators is from left to right. Later we will see other operators whose associativity is from right to left.

EXAMPLE 2-1:

Assume that the `double` variables a, b, c, d, e, f, and g have been initialized to the following values:

```
a = 3.,    b = 2.,    c = 5.,    d = 4.,
e = 10.,   f = 2.,    g = 3..
```

Evaluate the following Java assignment statements:

```
a.  output = a*b+c%d+e/f+g;
b.  output = a*(b+c)%d+(e/f)+g;
c.  output = a*(b+c)%(d+e)/f+g;
```

SOLUTION

As we can see, the order in which operations are performed has a major effect on the final result of an algebraic expression.

a.   Expression to evaluate:

Fill in numbers:

First, evaluate multiplication,
division, and modulus operations
from left to right:

Now evaluate additions:

b.   Expression to evaluate:

Fill in numbers:

First, evaluate parentheses:

Evaluate multiplication, division and modulus
from left to right:

Evaluate additions:

c.   Expression to evaluate:

Fill in numbers:

First, evaluate parentheses:

Evaluate multiplication, division, and modulus
from left to right:

Finally, evaluate addition:

```
output = a*b+c%d+e/f+g;
output = 3.*2.+5.%4.+10./2.+3.



output = 6.+5. %4.+ 10. / 2.+3.
output = 6.+ 1.+ 10. / 2.+ 3.
output = 6.+ 1.+ 5.+ 3.
output = 15;
output = a*(b+c)%d+(e/f)+g;
output = 3.*(2.+5.)%4.+(10./2.)+3.;
output = 3. * 7. % 4.+ 5.+ 3.;

output = 21. % 4.+ 5.+ 3.;
output = 1. + 5.+ 3.;
output = 9.;
output = a*(b+c)%(d+e)/f+g;
output = 3.*(2.+5.)%(4.+10.)/2.+3.;
output = 3.*7. %14. /2.+3.;

output = 21. %14. /2.+3.;
output = 7. /2.+3.;
output = 3.5 +3.;
output = 7.5;
```

It is important that every expression in a program be made as clear as possible. Any program of value must not only be written, but also must be maintained and modified when necessary. You should always ask yourself: "Will I easily understand this expression if I come back to it in six months? Can another programmer look at my code and easily understand what I am doing?" If there is any doubt in your mind, use extra parentheses in the expression to make it as clear as possible.

GOOD PROGRAMMING PRACTICE

Use parentheses as necessary to make your equations clear and easy to understand.

If parentheses are used within an expression, then the parentheses must be balanced. That is, there must be an equal number of open parentheses and close parentheses within the expression. It is an error to have more of one type than the other type. Errors of this sort are usually typographical, and they are caught by the Java compiler. For example, the expression

```
(2. + 4.) / 2.)
```

produces an error during compilation because of the mismatched parentheses.

2.4.4 Numeric Promotion of Operands

When an arithmetic operation is performed using two `double` numbers, its immediate result is of type `double`. Similarly, when an arithmetic operation is performed using two `int` numbers, the result is of type `int`. In general, arithmetic operations are only defined between numbers of the same type. For example, the addition of two `double` numbers is a valid operation, and the addition of two `int` numbers is a valid operation, but the addition of a `double` and an `int` is *not* a valid operation. This is true because real numbers and integers are stored in completely different forms in the computer.

What happens if an operation is between a real number and an integer? Expressions containing both real numbers and integers are called **mixed-mode expressions**, and arithmetic involving both real numbers and integers is called **mixed-mode arithmetic**. In the case of an operation between a `double` and an `int`, the `int` is converted by the computer into a `double`, and real arithmetic is used to perform the operation. This automatic conversion is known as **numeric promotion**.

The rules of numeric promotion are designed to preserve as much information as possible during each calculation. The following rules apply to numeric promotion during operations involving binary operators:

1. If either operand is of type `double`, the other operand is converted to `double`.
2. Otherwise, if either operand is of type `float`, the other operand is converted to `float`.
3. Otherwise, if either operand is of type `long`, the other operand is converted to `long`.
4. Otherwise, both operands are converted to type `int`.

The rules governing numeric promotion can be confusing to beginning programmers, and even experienced programmers may trip up on them from time to time. This is especially true when the expression involves division. Consider the following expressions and their results:

	EXPRESSION	RESULT
1.	1 + 1/4	1
2.	1.0 + 1/4	1.0
3.	1 + 1.0/4	1.25

Expression 1 contains only `int`s, so it is evaluated by integer arithmetic. In integer arithmetic, `1 / 4 = 0`, and `1 + 0 = 1`, so the final result is 1 (an `int`). Expression 2 is a mixed-mode expression containing both `double`s and `int`s. However, the first operation to be performed is division, since division comes before addition in the hierarchy of operations. The division is between `int`s, so the result is `1 / 4 = 0`. Next comes an addition between the `double` `1.0` and the `int` `0`, so Java promotes the `int` `0` into a `double` `0.0` and then performs the addition. The resulting number is `1.0` (a `double`). Expression 3 is also a mixed-mode expression containing both `double`s and `int`s. The first operation to be performed is a division between a `double` and an `int`, so Java promotes the 4 into a `double` `4.0`, and then performs the division. The result is the `double` value `0.25`. The next operation to be performed is an addition between the `int` 1 and the `double` `0.25`, so Java promotes the integer 1 to a `double` `1.0`, and then performs the addition. The resulting number is `1.25` (a `double`).

The following Java program demonstrates these results:

```
// This program illustrates numeric promotion
public class TestPromotion {

    // Define the main method
    public static void main(String[] args) {

        // Demonstrate numeric promotion.
        System.out.println(1 + 1/4);
        System.out.println(1.0 + 1/4);
        System.out.println(1 + 1.0/4);
    }
}
```

When this program is compiled and executed, the results are:

```
D:\book\java\chap2>javac TestPromotion.java
D:\book\java\chap2>java TestPromotion
1
1.0
1.25
```

To summarize,

1. A binary operation between numbers of different types is called a mixed-mode operation.

2. When a mixed-mode operation is encountered, Java promotes one or both of the operands according to the rules specified above, and then performs the operation.

3. The numeric promotion does not occur until two values of different types both appear in the *same* operation. Therefore, it is possible for a portion of an expression to be evaluated in integer arithmetic, followed by another portion evaluated in real arithmetic.

Mixed-mode arithmetic can be avoided by using the *cast operator*, as we will explain in the next section.

PROGRAMMING PITFALLS

Mixed-mode expressions are dangerous, because they are hard to understand and may produce misleading results. Avoid using them whenever possible.

2.4.5 Assignment Conversion and Casting Conversion

Automatic type conversion can also occur when the variable to which the expression is assigned is of a different type than the result of the expression. Such conversion is called **assignment conversion**. There are two possible cases for assignment conversion:

1. The result of an integer expression is assigned to a floating-point variable. This is an example of a **widening conversion**, since any value that can be represented by an integer can also be represented by a floating-point variable (albeit possibly with some loss of precision). *Widening assignment conversions are legal and happen automatically*. For example, the following code is legal and results in a value of 4.0 being stored in y.

```
int x = 4;
double y;
y = x;                    // Legal: y = 4.0
```

2. The result of a double expression is assigned to an integer variable. This is an example of a **narrowing conversion**, since the possible range of floating-point values is greater than the possible range of integer values. For example, the floating-point value 1.01E38 cannot be represented as an integer. *Narrowing assignment conversions are illegal and produce a compile-time error.* For example, the following code is illegal and produces a compile time error:

```
int x;
double y = 1.25;
x = y;                    // Illegal!
```

It is possible to explicitly convert or "cast" any numeric type into any other numeric type using a **cast operator**, regardless of whether the conversion involves widening or narrowing. A cast operator is created by placing the desired data type in parentheses before the expression to be converted. For example, the statements

```
int x;
double y = 1.25;
x = (int) y;              // Legal: x = 1
```

convert the `double` value `1.25` to `int` and store the result in variable x. When a floating-point number is converted to an integer, the fractional part of the number is discarded. Thus, the value stored is the integer 1. Note that we can assign a `double` value to an `int` variable (a narrowing conversion) if we use an explicit cast operator.

The cast operator can be used to make numeric conversions explicit, and thus, it avoids possible confusion associated with mixed-mode arithmetic. The following Java program demonstrates the use of the cast operator:

```
// This program illustrates the cast operator
public class TestCast {

    // Define the main method
    public static void main(String[] args) {

        double x = 3.99, y = 1.1e38;
        System.out.println("(int) x = " + (int) x);
        System.out.println("(int) y = " + (int) y);
    }
}
```

When this program is compiled and executed, the following are the results:

```
(int) x = 3
(int) y = 2147483647
```

Note that the value of y was too large to be represented as an `int`, so the cast operator converted it into the largest possible integer. In general, if the value being cast is out of range for the new data type, Java converts it value to the closest possible number in the new data type.

GOOD PROGRAMMING PRACTICE

Use cast operators to avoid mixed-mode expressions and make your intentions clear.

PRACTICE!

This quiz provides a quick check to see if you have understood the concepts introduced in Section 2.4. If you have trouble with the quiz, reread the section, ask your instructor, or discuss the material with a fellow student. The answers to this quiz are found in the back of the book.

1. In what order are the arithmetic operations evaluated if they appear within an arithmetic expression? How do parentheses modify this order?

2. Are the following expressions legal or illegal? If they are legal, what is their result? If they are illegal, what is wrong with them?
   a. `37 / 3`
   b. `37 + 17 / 3`
   c. `28 / 3 / 4`
   d. `28 / 3 / (double) 4`
   e. `(float) 28 / 3 / 4`
   f. `(28 / 3) % 4`

3. Evaluate the following expressions:
   a. `2 + 5 * 2 - 5`
   b. `(2 + 5) * (2 - 5)`
   c. `2 + (5 * 2) - 5`
   d. `(2 + 5) * 2 - 5`

Are the following sets of statements legal or illegal? If they are legal, state the result of the calculations. If they are illegal, state why.

5.
```
int x = 16, y = 3;
double result;
result = x + y/2.0;
```

6.
```
int x = 16, y = 3;
int result;
result = x + y/2.0;
```

2.5 ASSIGNMENT OPERATORS

Java includes several special assignment operators that combine an assignment and a binary operation in a single expression. These assignment operators are convenient shortcuts that reduce the typing required in a program. For example, the assignment statement

```
a = a + 5;
```

can be abbreviated using the addition assignment operator += as

```
a += 5;
```

The += operator adds the value of the variable on the left of the operator to the value to the expression on the right of the operator and stores the result in the variable to the left of the operator.

A similar abbreviation is possible for many other binary operators, including some we have not met yet. Table 2-5 contains a list of the arithmetic assignment operators corresponding to the operators we have seen so far.

TABLE 2-5 Arithmetic Assignment Operators

ASSIGNMENT OPERATOR	SAMPLE EXPRESSION	EXPANDED EXPRESSION	RESULT
Assume: int a = 3, b = 11;			
+=	a += 3;	a = a + 3;	6 stored in a
-=	a -= 2;	a = a - 2;	1 stored in a
*=	a *= 4;	a = a * 4;	12 stored in a
/=	a /= 2;	a = a / 2;	1 stored in a
%=	b %= 3;	b = b % 3;	2 stored in b

2.6 INCREMENT AND DECREMENT OPERATORS

Java also includes a unary **increment operator** (++) and a unary **decrement operator** (--). Increment and decrement operators *increase or decrease the value stored in an integer variable by one*. For example, suppose that an integer variable c is to be increased by one. Any of the following statements will perform this operation:

```
c = c + 1;
c += 1;
c++;
```

The increment and decrement operators can be confusing to novice programmers, because they *change the value of a variable without an equals sign* appearing in the expression. However, they are commonly used, because they are so much more compact than the alternative ways of performing the same function.

If the increment or decrement operator is placed *before* a variable, it is called a **preincrement** or **predecrement** operator. The preincrement and predecrement operators cause the variable to be incremented or decremented by one, and then the new value is used in the expression in which it appears. For example, suppose that the variables i and j are defined as shown below. After these statements are executed, the value of i will be 4 and the value of k will be **8**, because the value of i will be incremented *before* the addition is performed.

```
int i = 3, j = 4, k;
k = ++i + j;                        // k = 8
```

If the increment or decrement operator is placed *after* a variable, it is called a **postincrement** or **postdecrement** operator. The postincrement and postdecrement operators cause the old value of the variable to be used in the expression in which it appears, and then the variable to be decremented or decremented by one. For example, suppose that the variables i and j are defined as shown below. After these statements are executed, the value of i will be 4 and the value of k will be **7**, because the value of i will be incremented *after* the addition is performed.

```
int i = 3, j = 4, k;
k = i++ + j;                        // k = 7
```

The operation of these operators is summarized in Table 2-6.

Increment and decrement operators can get very confusing if they are combined in complex expressions, causing unexpected or hard-to-understand results. *Never use more than one of these operators on a single variable in a single expression*—if you do, the resulting expression will be very hard to understand. An example of the misuse of these operators is shown in the following program:

TABLE 2-6   The Increment and Decrement Operators

OPERATOR	SAMPLE EXPRESSION	EXPANDED EXPRESSION RESULT
preincrement	++a	Increment a by one and then use the new value of a in the expression in which a is located.
postincrement	a++	Use the current value of a in the expression in which a is located, and then increment a by one.
predecrement	--a	Decrement a by one and then use the new value of a in the expression in which a is located.
postdecrement	a--	Use the current value of a in the expression in which a is located, and then decrement a by one.

```
 1   // This program illustrates the mis-use of pre-
 2   // incrementing and decrementing
 3   public class TestIncrement {
 4       // Define the main method
 5       public static void main(String[] args) {
 6
 7           int i = 4, k = 0;
 8           k = i-- + 2 * i * ++i;
 9           System.out.println( "i = " + i );
10           System.out.println( "k = " + k );
11
12           k = --i + 2 * i * i++;
13           System.out.println( "i = " + i );
14           System.out.println("k = " + k);
15       }
16   }
```

When this program executes, the results are as follows:

```
i = 4
k = 28
i = 4
k = 21
```

In line 8, the value of k was 28, while in line 12, the value of k was 21. The value of i was 4 at the beginning and the end of each statement. Can you determine why the two expressions produced these values of k?

Never write programs containing statements like the ones just shown. The programs will be very prone to errors and difficult to understand!

GOOD PROGRAMMING PRACTICE

Always keep expressions containing increment and decrement operators simple and easy to understand.

2.7 MATHEMATICAL METHODS

In mathematics, a *function* is an expression that accepts one or more input values and calculates a single result from them. Scientific and technical calculations usually require

Figure 2.2. When a mathematical method appears in a Java expression, the compiler generates a call to that method, and then uses the result returned by the method in the original expression. In this case, the compiler generates the call `Math.sin(1.2)`, and uses the result `0.9320390859672` in the original expression.

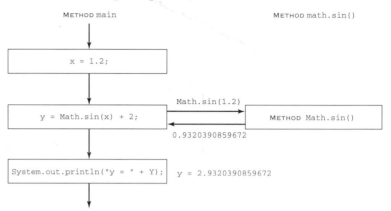

functions that are more complex than the simple addition, subtraction, multiplication, division, and modulus operations that we have discussed so far. Some of these functions are very common and are used in many different technical disciplines. Others are rarer and specific to a single problem or a small number of problems. Examples of very common functions are the trigonometric functions, logarithms, and square roots. Examples of rarer functions include the hyperbolic functions, Bessel functions, and so forth.

The Java language has mechanisms to support both the very common functions and the less common functions. Many of the common ones are implemented as methods of the `Math` class in the `java.lang` package. These methods are automatically available to any Java program. Less common functions are not included in the Java language, but they may be implemented as user-defined methods. User-defined methods are discussed in more detail in Chapter 6.

A Java mathematical method takes one or more input values and calculates a single output value from them. The input values to the method are known as **parameters**; they appear in parentheses immediately after the method name. The output of a mathematical method is a single number, which can be used together with other methods, constants, and variables in Java expressions. When a method name appears in a Java statement, the parameters of the method are passed to the method. The method calculates a result, which is used in place of the method name in the original expression. (See Figure 2.2.)

A list of the mathematical methods in class `Math` is given in Table 2-7. In addition to the methods shown in the table, the class defines two important constants, `Math.PI` (π) and `Math.E` (e, the base of the natural logarithms).

Mathematical methods are used by including them in an expression. For example, the method `Math.sin()` can be used to calculate the sine of a number as follows:

```
y = Math.sin(theta);
```

where `theta` is the parameter of the method `sin`. After this statement is executed, the variable `y` contains the sine of the value stored in variable theta. Note from Table 2-7 that the trigonometric methods expect their arguments to be in radians. If the variable `theta` is in degrees, then we must convert degrees to radians ($180° = \pi$ radians) before computing the sine. This conversion can be done in the same statement as the sine calculation:

```
y = Math.sin(theta*(3.141593/180));
```

Alternatively, we could create a named constant containing the conversion factor and refer to that constant when the method is executed:

```
final double DEG_2_RAD = Math.PI / 180;
...
y = Math.sin(theta * DEG_2_RAD);
```

PROGRAMMING PITFALLS

The parameters for all trigonometric functions must be in units of *radians*. It is very common for novice programmers to use degrees by mistake.

2.7.1 Overloaded Methods

The type of parameter required by a method and the type of value returned by it are specified in Table 2-7 for the methods listed there. Some of these methods are **overloaded methods**, which means that more than one method exists with the same name, but with different types of parameters. For example, the absolute value method `Math.abs(x)` is an overloaded method. It really consists of four methods, one each for `double`, `float`, `int`, and `long` parameters. If x is a `double`, then the `double` form of this method will be invoked, and the returned value will be of type `double`. If x is an `int`, then the integer form of this method will be invoked, and the returned value will be of type `int`, and so forth.

2.7.2 Coercion of Arguments

We can see from Table 2-7 that a method like `Math.sqrt` is only defined for input parameters of type `double`. What happens if this function is invoked with an argument of another type? The answer is that *Java automatically converts arguments of an incorrect type into arguments of the type required by the method*. This process is known as the **coercion of arguments**.

For example, suppose that we execute the following statements:

```
int i = 16;
System.out.println( Math.sqrt(i) );
```

The method `Math.sqrt` is being invoked with an `int` argument, while it needs to have a `double` argument. Therefore, Java automatically converts the integer value 16 into a double-precision floating-point value 16.0 before it passes the value to the method. The resulting output value is a `double` value 4.0.

The behavior is just the same as if we had used an explicit cast to convert the input argument to a `double`:

```
int i = 16;
System.out.println( Math.sqrt( (double) i ) );
```

TABLE 2-7   Mathematical Methods

METHOD NAME AND PARAMETERS	METHOD VALUE	PARAMETER	RESULT TYPE	COMMENTS
Math.abs(x)	$\lvert x \rvert$	float, double, int, or long	same as parameter	Absolute value of x
Math.acos(x)	$\cos^{-1} x$	double	double	Inverse cosine of x for $-1 \leq x \leq 1$ (results in *radians*)
Math.asin(x)	$\sin^{-1} x$	double	double	Inverse sine of x for $-1 \leq x \leq 1$ (results in *radians*)
Math.atan(x)	$\tan^{-1} x$	double	double	Inverse tangent of x (results in *radians* in the range $-\pi/2 \leq x \leq \pi/2$)
Math.atan2(y,x)	$\tan^{-1}\dfrac{y}{x}$	double	double	Inverse tangent of x (results in *radians* in the range $-\pi \leq x \leq \pi$)
Math.ceil(x)		double	double	Returns the smallest integer not less than x: ceil(2.2) = 3 and ceil(-2.2) = -2
Math.cos(x)	$\cos x$	double	double	Cosine of x, where x is in radians
Math.exp(x)	e^x	double	double	
Math.floor(x)		double	double	Returns the largest integer not greater than x: floor(2.2) = 2 and floor(-2.2) = -3
Math.log(x)	$\log x$ or $\ln x$	double	double	Natural logarithm of x, for $x > 0$
Math.max(x,y)		float, double, int, or long	same as parameter	Returns the larger of x or y
Math.min(x,y)		float, double, int, or long	same as parameter	Returns the smaller of x or y
Math.random()		none	double	Returns a uniformly distributed random value between 0 and 1
Math.pow(x,y)	x^y	double	double	Math.pow(2,5) = 32 Math.pow(9,.5) = 3
Math.rint(x)		double	double	Rounds floating point number to the nearest integer, and returns the result as a floating-point number.
Math.round(x)		double or float	long or int	Rounds floating point number to the nearest integer, and returns the result as an integer: round(2.2) = 2 and round(-2.2) = -2
Math.sin(x)	$\sin x$	double	double	Sine of x, where x is in radians
Math.sqrt(x)	$\sqrt{x}$	double	double	Square root of x, for $x \geq 0$
Math.tan(x)	$\tan x$	double	double	Tangent of x, where x is in radians

2.8 STANDARD INPUT AND OUTPUT

For a computer program to be useful, there must be some way to read in the data to be processed and to write out the results of the calculations. The process of reading in data and writing out results is known as **input/output (I/O)**. There are many different ways to read in and write out data in a Java program, and we will see some of them in Chapter 14. However, the simplest way to read and write data from a program is through the **standard input** and **standard output** devices of a computer. The standard input device is a special, preopened input channel that is usually connected to the computer's keyboard, so that the program can accept values that a user enters while the program is running. (This is not always true, as the standard input device can be redirected to come from a file or from the output of another program.) The standard output device is a preopened output channel that is usually displayed on the computer's monitor, so that the program can print out results for its user. (The standard output device may also be redirected.) In Java, the data from these devices are *encapsulated* inside objects, which are called **data streams**.

Every Java program has three standard I/O objects: System.in, System.out, and System.err. These objects are ready to read data from or write data to whenever the program begins executing. System.in is an object representing the **standard input stream**, which is usually the keyboard. When the program reads input data from this object, the program actually reads values typed by the user at the keyboard. System.out is an object representing the **standard output stream**, which is usually the monitor of the computer. When the program writes data to this object, the values are displayed on the monitor. Finally, System.err is a special object representing the **standard error stream**. It is a special stream used for displaying severe program errors.

All three standard I/O objects share the characteristic that *they process input or output data one byte at a time*. Sending data to the standard output stream is relatively easy, since there are standard methods that convert the data to be printed into a stream of bytes, and send those bytes to the output stream. We have already seen the println method, which performs this function.

However, reading data from the standard input stream is much harder. The standard input stream presents data to the program one byte at a time, and *it is the programmer's responsibility to clump successive bytes together to form meaningful numbers or strings* before attempting to process them. For example, if a user were to type the value 123.4, the program would have to read the characters in one byte at a time and convert the entire string into the appropriate double value after all characters had been read. Java includes standard classes to collect and buffer the input bytes until there are enough available to translate into a meaningful number or string. Unfortunately, these classes are relatively complex to use, and we will postpone a detailed explanation of their operation until Chapter 14. In this chapter, we will introduce a single "convenience class" that allows us to read data of any type from the standard input stream.

2.8.1 Using the Standard Output Stream

We have already used the System.out object in a number of programs. There are two important methods that we will learn to use with this object: print and println. The print method accepts a single parameter and prints out the value of its parameter on the standard output device. It does *not* send a newline character at the end of the value, so any additional calls to print will be displayed on the same line. By contrast, the println method accepts a single parameter, and prints out the value of its parameter *followed by a newline character*. Thus println terminates the output on a given line.

The behavior of these two methods is illustrated in the following program, which outputs two variables i and j and a string using both the print and println methods:

```
1   // This program illustrates the use of
2   // the print and println methods.
3   public class TestOutput {
4       // Define the main method
5       public static void main(String[] args) {
6
7           int i = 1; float j = 1.35F;
8           // Demonstrate output
9           System.out.print( i );
10          System.out.print( j );
11          System.out.print( "String\n" );
12
13          System.out.println( i );
14          System.out.println( j );
15          System.out.println( "String" );
16      }
17  }
```

Line 9 prints out the value "1", line 10 prints out the value "1.35", and line 11 prints out the string "String" followed by a newline character. Since these values were printed with the print method, they all appear in consecutive characters on a single line. Line 13 prints out the value "1", line 14 prints out the value "1.35", and line 15 prints out the string "String". Since these values were printed with the println method, they all appear consecutive lines. When this program is executed, the results are as follows:

```
11.35String
1
1.35
String
```

Note that there is no space between the values printed out by the print method. If you want space between the values, you must explicitly print the spaces. For example, the statements

```
System.out.print( i );
System.out.print( " " );
System.out.print( j );
System.out.print( " " );
System.out.print( "String\n" );
```

produce the output

```
1 1.35 String
```

The + operator has a special meaning when used with strings. If the + operator appears between two strings, it **concatenates** them together into one long string. Furthermore, if data of any other type is combined with a string using the + operator, *that data will automatically be converted into a string and concatenated with the other string.* For example, suppose v1 is a variable of type double containing the value 1.25. Then the statement

```
System.out.println("value = " + v1);
```

converts the contents of variable v1 into a string and concatenates it with the string "value = ". The statement prints out the line

```
value = 1.25
```

The standard error stream works exactly the same way as the standard output stream, except that the object `System.err` is substituted for `System.out`. This data stream is only used for reporting critical errors, so it is rarely used.

2.8.2 Using the Standard Input Stream

The standard input stream is used to read in data from the keyboard or some other specified source. The data in the standard input stream is presented to the program one byte at a time, and the program must combine the bytes after they are read to create the numbers or strings that the program needs to process. Reading data using standard Java methods is very complex, and we will postpone this topic until Chapter 14. Meanwhile, we will use the "convenience class" `StdIn` to read data into our programs.

Class `StdIn` allows Java to accumulate data for you until an entire line is available, and provides methods to translate the data into any primitive data type or into a `String`. For example, if method `readInt()` is called, the line is translated into an integer value, while if method `readDouble()` is called, the line is translated into a double value. (See Figure 2.3.) The `StdIn` class is located in the `chapman.io` package. To use this class, you must import package `chapman.io` into your program with the following statement:

```
import chapman.io.*;
```

`import` statements should be the first noncomment statements in your program, before the class declaration. You must also have the `CLASSPATH` environment variable set as described in the box below.

SETTING THE CLASSPATH **ENVIRONMENT VARIABLE**

In order to use the special packages supplied with this book, a programmer must first set the CLASSPATH environment variable on his or her computer to tell the Java compiler where to look for the packages. This variable must contain the name of the parent directory of the class path structure. For example, if the extra packages appear as subdirectories of directory `c:\packages`, then the CLASSPATH variable must include the directory `c:\packages`.

The manner in which the environment variable is set will vary among different types of operating systems. In Windows 95/98, the CLASSPATH environment variable is set by including the line

```
set CLASSPATH=c:\packages
```

in the `autoexec.bat` file. If a CLASSPATH already exists in the file, add a semicolon (;) followed by `c:\packages` to the end of the existing path.

In Windows NT, the environment variable is set through the System option in the Control Panel. See the Windows NT help system for details.

For Unix systems running the C shell, the class path is set by opening the `.login` file with a text editor and adding the line

```
setenv CLASSPATH $HOME/packages
```

If a CLASSPATH already exists in the file, add a colon (:) followed by `$HOME/packages` to the end of the existing path.

For Unix systems running the Bourne or Korn shells, the class path is set by opening the `.profile` file with a text editor and adding the lines

```
CLASSPATH=$HOME/packages
export CLASSPATH
```

If a CLASSPATH already exists in the file, add a colon (:) followed by `$HOME/packages` to the end of the existing path.

A `StdIn` object is created by the statement:

```
StdIn in = new StdIn();
```

Figure 2.3. An object of class `StdIn` reads a line one byte at a time from the Standard Input Stream, until an entire line has been read in. It then converts that line into an `int`, `double`, `String`, etc. value, depending on which method was called. The class automatically handles input errors, providing the user a chance to correct them.

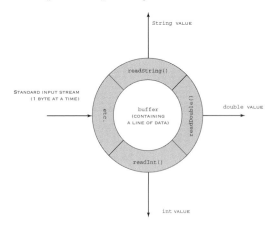

This statement creates a new `StdIn` object and makes the reference `in` refer to that object. The object automatically buffers the data coming out of the standard input stream until an entire line has been read. The `StdIn` methods `readInt()`, `readDouble()`, `readString()`, etc. then convert that line into a value of the appropriate type. The `StdIn` methods are summarized in Table 2-8, shown at the top of the next page.

The following program illustrates the use of these features to read data of various sorts from the standard input stream:

```
1    // This program tests reading values using class StdIn
2    import chapman.io.*;
3    public class ReadStdIn {
4
5       // Define the main method
6       public static void main(String[] args) {
7
8          double v1; int i1; boolean test;
9
10         // Create a StdIn object
11         StdIn in = new StdIn();
12
13         // Prompt for a double value
14         System.out.print("Enter a double value: ");
15         v1 = in.readDouble();
16         System.out.println("Value = " + v1 );
17
18         // Prompt for an int value
19         System.out.print("Enter an int value: ");
20         i1 = in.readInt();
21         System.out.println("Value = " + i1 );
22
23         // Prompt for a boolean value
24         System.out.print("Enter a boolean value: ");
25         test = in.readBoolean();
26         System.out.println("Value = " + test );
27      }
28   }
```

TABLE 2-8 Methods in Class `StdIn`

METHOD	RESULT
`readBoolean()`	Reads a line and converts it into a `boolean` result. The value is `true` if the input characters are `"true"` disregarding case, and `false` otherwise.
`readByte()`	Reads a line and converts it into a `byte` result.
`readShort()`	Reads a line and converts it into a `short` result.
`readInt()`	Reads a line and converts it into an `int` result.
`readLong()`	Reads a line and converts it into a `long` result.
`readFloat()`	Reads a line and converts it into a `float` result.
`readDouble()`	Reads a line and converts it into a `double` result.
`readString()`	Reads a line and converts it into a `String` result.

Note that this program includes an `import` statement to import the `StdIn` class from the `chapman.io` package. When this program is executed, the results are

```
D:\book\java\chap2>java ReadStdIn
Enter a double value: 45.6
Value = 45.6
Enter an int value: 45.6
Invalid format for integer-try again:
45
Value = 45
Enter a boolean value: true
Value = true
```

Note also that if a user types an incorrectly formatted character string, the `StdIn` class catches the error and allows the user to correct it. In this example, the value "45.6" was not a valid integer, so the `StdIn` object informed the user and gave him or her the chance to correct the error.

PRACTICE!

This quiz provides a quick check to see if you understand the concepts introduced in Sections 2.5 through 2.8. If you have trouble with the quiz, reread the sections, ask your instructor, or discuss the material with a fellow student. The answers to this quiz are found in the back of the book.

Convert the following algebraic equations into Java assignment statements:

1. The equivalent resistance R_{eq} of four resistors R_1, R_2, R_3, and R_4 connected in series:

$$R_{eq} = R_1 + R_2 + R_3 + R_4$$

2. The equivalent resistance R_{eq} of four resistors R_1, R_2, R_3, and R_4 connected in parallel:

$$R_{eq} = \frac{1}{\dfrac{1}{R_1} + \dfrac{1}{R_2} + \dfrac{1}{R_3} + \dfrac{1}{R_4}}$$

PRACTICE!

3. The period T of an oscillating pendulum:

$$T = 2\pi\sqrt{\frac{L}{g}} \, ,$$

where L is the length of the pendulum, and g is the acceleration due to gravity.

4. The equation for damped sinusoidal oscillation:

$$v(t) = V_M e^{-\alpha t} \cos \omega t \, ,$$

where V_M is the maximum value of the oscillation, α is the exponential damping factor, and ω is the angular velocity of the oscillation.

Convert the following Java assignment statements into algebraic equations:

5. The motion of an object in a constant gravitational field:

```
distance = 0.5 * accel * Math.pow(t,2) + vel0 * t + pos0;
```

6. The oscillating frequency of a damped *RLC* circuit:

```
freq = 1 / (2 * Math.PI * Math.sqrt(l * c));
```

7. Energy storage in an inductor:

```
energy = 1. / 2. * inductance * Math.pow(current,2);
```

8. Given the following definitions, decide whether each of the statements shown is legal or illegal? If a statement is legal, what is its result? If it is illegal, tell why it is illegal.

```
double a = 2., b = 3., c;
int i = 3, j = 2, k;
```

   a. `c = Math.sin(a * Math.PI));`
   b. `k = a / b;`
   c. `k = (int) a / b;`
   d. `b += a / i;`
   e. `c = a / ( j / i ));`

9. After the following statements are executed, what is stored in each of the variables?

```
double a = 2., b = 3., c;
int i = 3, j = 2, k;
k = ++i - j--;
c = i++/j-- + a/b;
```

2.9 PROGRAM EXAMPLES

In Chapter 2, we have presented the fundamental concepts required to write simple but functional Java programs. We will now present a few examples in which these concepts are used.

EXAMPLE 2-2:
TEMPERATURE
CONVERSION

Design a Java program that reads an input temperature in degrees Fahrenheit, converts it to an absolute temperature in kelvins, and writes out the result.

SOLUTION

The relationship between temperature in degrees Fahrenheit (°F) and temperature in kelvins (K) can be found in any physics textbook. The relationship is

$$T(\text{in kelvins}) = \left[\frac{5}{9} T(\text{in} \, °F) - 32.0 \right] + 273.15 \, . \tag{2-1}$$

The physics books also give us sample values on both temperature scales, which we can use to check the operation of our program. Two such values are

The boiling point of water:	212°F	373.15K
and		
The sublimation point of dry ice:	−110°F	194.26K.

Our program must perform the following steps:

1. Prompt the user to enter an input temperature in °F.
2. Read the input temperature.
3. Calculate the temperature in kelvins from Equation (2-1).
4. Write out the result, and stop.

The resulting program is shown in Figure 2.4.

To test the completed program, we will run it with the known input values given above. Note that user inputs appear in boldface.

```
C:\book\java\chap2>java TempConversion
Enter the temperature in deg Fahrenheit: 212
212.0 deg Fahrenheit = 373.15

C:book\java\chap2>java TempConversion
Enter the temperature in deg Fahrenheit: -110
-110.0 deg Fahrenheit = 194.2611111111111
```

The results of the program match the values from the physics book.

In the previous program, we echoed the input values and printed the output values together with their units. The results of this program only make sense if the units (degrees Fahrenheit and kelvins) are included together with their values. As a general rule, the units associated with any input value should always be printed along with the prompt that requests the value, and the units associated with any output value should always be printed along with that value.

GOOD PROGRAMMING PRACTICE

Always include the appropriate units with any values that you read or write in a program.

```
/*
    Purpose:
      To convert an input temperature from degrees Fahrenheit to
      an output temperature in kelvins.

    Record of revisions:
        Date        Programmer           Description of change
        ====        ==========           =====================
        03/22/98    S. J. Chapman        Original code
*/
import chapman.io.*;
public class TempConversion {

    // Define the main method
    public static void main(String[] args) {

        // Declare variables, and define each variable
        double tempF;          // Temperature in degrees Fahrenheit
        double tempK;          // Temperature in kelvins

        // Create a StdIn object
        StdIn in = new StdIn();

        // Prompt the user for the input temperature.
        System.out.print("Enter the temp in deg Fahrenheit: ");
        tempF = in.readDouble();

        // Convert to kelvins
        tempK = (5. / 9.) * (tempF - 32.) + 273.15;

        // Write out the result.
        System.out.println(tempF + " deg F = " + tempK + " K");
    }
}
```

Figure 2.4. Program to convert degrees Fahrenheit into kelvins

This above program exhibits many of the good programming practices that we have described in this chapter. It includes a data dictionary that defines the meanings of all of the variables in the program, it uses descriptive variable names, and appropriate units are attached to printed values.

EXAMPLE 2-3: ELECTRICAL ENGINEERING: CALCULATING REAL, REACTIVE, AND APPARENT POWER

Figure 2.5 shows a sinusoidal alternating current (AC) voltage source with voltage V supplying a load of impedance Z/θ Ω. From simple circuit theory, the rms current I, the real power P, reactive power Q, the apparent power S, and the power factor PF supplied to the load are given by the following equations

$$I = \frac{V}{Z}, \tag{2-2}$$

$$P = VI \cos \theta, \tag{2-3}$$
$$Q = VI \sin \theta, \tag{2-4}$$
$$S = VI, \tag{2-5}$$
$$PF = \cos\theta, \tag{2-6}$$

where V is the rms voltage of the power source in units of volts (V). The units of current are amperes (A), the units of real power are watts (W), the units of reactive power are volt-amperes-reactive (VAR), and of apparent power are volt-amperes (VA). The power factor has no units associated with it.

Figure 2.5. A sinusoidal AC voltage source with voltage V supplying a load of impedance Z∠ θΩ

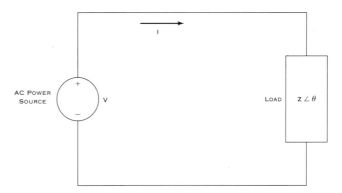

Given the rms voltage of the power source and the magnitude and angle of the impedance Z, write a program that calculates the rms current I, the real power P, the reactive power Q, the apparent power S, and the power factor PF of the load.

SOLUTION

In this program, we need to read in the rms voltage V of the voltage source and the magnitude Z and angle θ of the impedance. The input voltage source will be measured in volts, the magnitude of the impedance Z in ohms, and the angle of the impedance θ in degrees. Once the data is read, we must convert the angle θ into radians for use with the Java trigonometric functions. Next, the desired values must be calculated, and the results must be printed out.

The program must perform the following steps:

1. Prompt the user to enter the source voltage in volts.
2. Read the source voltage.
3. Prompt the user to enter the magnitude and angle of the impedance in ohms and degrees.
4. Read the magnitude and angle of the impedance.
5. Calculate the current I from Equation (2-2).
6. Calculate the real power P from Equation (2-3).
7. Calculate the reactive power Q from Equation (2-4).
8. Calculate the apparent power S from Equation (2-5).
9. Calculate the power factor PF from Equation (2-6).
10. Print out the results, and stop.

The final Java program is shown in Figure 2.6.

This program also exhibits many of the good programming practices that we have described. It includes a variable dictionary defining the uses of all of the variables in the program, it uses descriptive variable names (although the variable names are short, P, Q, S, and PF are the standard accepted abbreviations for the corresponding quantities), and it defines a named constant for the degrees-to-radians conversion factor and then uses that name everywhere throughout the program where required. Also, appropriate units are attached to all printed values.

```
/*
   Purpose:
     To calculate the current, real, reactive, and apparent power,
     and the power factor supplied to a load.

   Record of revisions:
       Date          Programmer            Description of change
       ====          ==========            =====================
     03/22/98     S. J. Chapman            Original code
*/
import chapman.io.*;
public class Power {

   // Define the main method
   public static void main(String[] args) {

      // Declare constants
      final double CONV = Math.PI / 180;    // Degrees to radians

      // Declare variables, and define each variable
      double amps;         // Current in the load (A)
      double p;            // Real power of load (W)
      double pf;           // Power factor of load
      double q;            // Reactive pwr of the load (VA)
      double s;            // Apparent pwr of the load (VAR)
      double theta;        // Impedance angle of the load (deg)
      double volts;        // Rms voltage of the power source (V)
      double z;            // Magnitude of the load impedance (ohms)

      // Create a StdIn object
      StdIn in = new StdIn();

      // Prompt the user for the rms voltage.
      System.out.print("Enter the rms voltage of the source: ");
      volts = in.readDouble();

      // Prompt the user for the magnitude of the impedance
      System.out.print("Enter the magnitude of Z (ohms): ");
      z = in.readDouble();

      // Prompt the user for the angle of the impedance
      System.out.print("Enter the angle of Z (deg): ");
      theta = in.readDouble();

      // Perform calculations
      amps = volts / z;                       // Rms current
      p = volts * amps * Math.cos(theta*CONV); // Real power
      q = volts * amps * Math.sin(theta*CONV); // React. power
      s = volts * amps;                       // App. power
      pf = Math.cos(theta * CONV);            // Power factor

      // Write out the results.
      System.out.println("Voltage      = " + volts + " volts");
      System.out.println("Impedance    = " + z + " ohms at "
                         + theta + " degrees");
      System.out.println("Current      = " + amps + " amps");
      System.out.println("Real Power   = " + p + " W");
      System.out.println("Reactive Pwr = " + q + " VAR");
      System.out.println("Apparent Pwr = " + s + " VA");
      System.out.println("Power Factor = " + pf);
   }
```

Figure 2.6.   Program to calculate the real power, reactive power, apparent power, and power factor supplied to a load.

To verify the operation of program `Power`, we will do a sample calculation by hand and compare the results with the output of the program. If the rms voltage V is 120 V, the magnitude of the impedance Z is 5 Ω, and the angle θ is 30°, then the values are as follows:

$$I = \frac{V}{Z} = \frac{120 \text{ V}}{5 \text{ } \Omega} = 24 \text{ A} , \tag{2-2}$$

$$P = VI \cos \theta = (120 \text{ V})(24 \text{ A}) \cos 30° = 2494 \text{ W} , \tag{2-3}$$

$$Q = VI \sin \theta = (120 \text{ V})(24 \text{ A}) \sin 30° = 1440 \text{ VAR} , \tag{2-4}$$

$$S = VI = (120 \text{ V})(24 \text{ A}) = 2880 \text{ VA} , \tag{2-5}$$

$$PF = \cos \theta = \cos 30° = 0.86603 . \tag{2-6}$$

When we run program **Power** with the specified input data, the results are identical to our hand calculations:

```
C:\book\java\chap2>java Power
Enter the rms voltage of the source: 120
Enter the magnitude of the impedance (ohms): 5
Enter the angle of the impedance (deg): 30
Voltage       = 120.0 volts
Impedance     = 5.0 ohms at 30.0 degrees
Voltage       = 120.0 volts
Current       = 24.0 amps
Real Power    = 2494.1531628991834 W
Reactive Power = 1439.9999999999998 VAR
Apparent Power = 2880.0 VA
Power Factor  = 0.8660254037844387
```

EXAMPLE 2-4: CARBON-14 DATING

A radioactive isotope of an element is a form of the element that is not stable. It spontaneously decays into an other element over a period of time. Radioactive decay is an exponential process. If Q_0 is the initial quantity of a radioactive substance at time $t = 0$, then the amount of the substance that will be present at any time t in the future is given by

$$Q(t) = Q_0 e^{-\lambda t} \tag{2-7}$$

where λ is the radioactive decay constant.

Because radioactive decay occurs at a known rate, it can be used as a clock to measure the time since the decay started. If we know the initial amount of the radioactive material Q_0 present in a sample, and the amount of the material Q left at the current time, we can solve for t in Equation (2-7) to determine how long the decay has been going on. The resulting equation is

$$t_{\text{decay}} = -\frac{1}{\lambda} \log \frac{Q}{Q_0} \tag{2-8}$$

Equation (2-8) has practical applications in many areas of science. For example, archaeologists use a radioactive clock based on carbon 14 to determine the time that has passed since a once-living thing died. Carbon 14 is continually taken into the body while a plant or animal is living, so the amount of it present in the body at the time of death is assumed to be known. The decay constant λ of carbon 14 is well known to be 0.00012097/year, so if the amount of carbon 14 remaining now can be

Figure 2.7.   The radioactive decay of Carbon 14 as a function of time. Notice that 50% of the original carbon 14 is left after about 5730 years have elapsed.

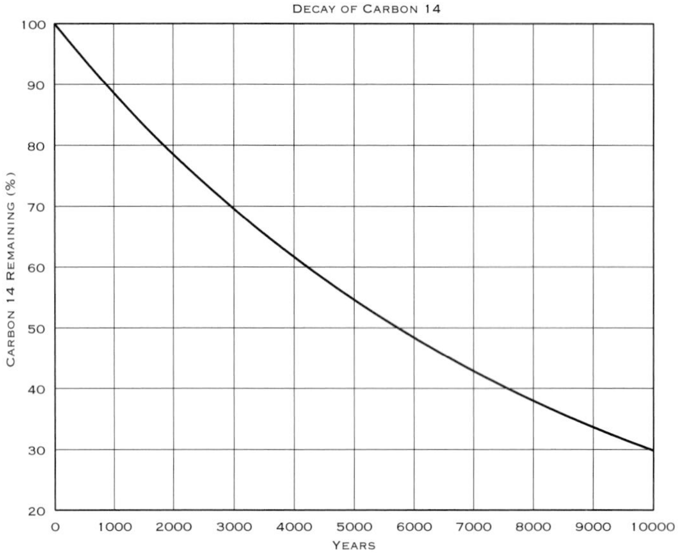

accurately measured, then Equation (2-8) can be used to determine how long ago the thing died.

Write a program that reads the percentage of carbon 14 remaining in a sample, calculates the age of the sample from it, and prints out the result with proper units.

SOLUTION

Our program must perform the following steps:

1.   Prompt the user to enter the percentage of carbon 14 remaining in the sample.
2.   Read in the percentage.
3.   Convert the percentage into the fraction Q/Q_0.
4.   Calculate the age of the sample in years using Equation (2-8).
5.   Write out the result, and stop.

The resulting code is shown in Figure 2.8.

```
/*
  Purpose:
    To calculate the age of an organic sample from the
    percentage of the original carbon 14 remaining in
    the sample.

  Record of revisions:
    Date          Programmer              Description of change
    ====          ==========              =====================
    03/22/98      S. J. Chapman           Original code
*/
import chapman.io.*;
public class C14Date {
```

Figure 2.8.   *(cont.)*

```java
// Define the main method
public static void main(String[] args) {

    // Declare constants
    final double LAMDA = 0.00012097;   // C14 decay constant (1/year)

    // Declare variables, and define each variable
    double age;         // Age of the sample (years)
    double percent;     // Percentage of carbon 14 remaining

    double ratio;       // Ratio of the Carbon 14 remaining at the time
                        // of the measurement to the original amount
                        // of Carbon 14.

    // Create a StdIn object
    chapman.io.StdIn in = new chapman.io.StdIn();

    // Prompt the user for the percentage of C-14 remaining.
    System.out.print("Enter the percentage of carbon 14 remaining:");
    percent = in.readDouble();

    // Perform calculations
    ratio = percent / 100;                          // Convert to ratio
    age = (-1.0 / LAMDA) * Math.log(ratio);  // Get age in years
    // Tell the user about the age of the sample.
    System.out.println("The age of the sample is " + age + " years.");
    }
}
```

Figure 2.8.   Program to calculate the age of a sample from the percentage of carbon 14 remaining in it

To test the completed program, we will calculate the time it takes for half of the carbon 14 to disappear. This time is known as the *half-life* of carbon 14. The program outputs the following (user input appears in boldface):

```
C:\book\java\chap2>java C14Date
Enter the percentage of carbon 14 remaining: 50
The age of the sample is 5729.90973431384 years.
```

The *CRC Handbook of Chemistry and Physics* states that the half-life of carbon 14 is 5730 years, so output of the program agrees with the reference book.

PROFESSIONAL SUCCESS: LEARNING A PROGRAMMING LANGUAGE

You are reading this book because you want to learn how to program in the Java language. What is the best way to learn to program in Java?

The simple answer is: play! The only real way to learn a programming language is to practice, experiment, and play with it. Write programs to try out the features described in this book. When you do it yourself, you will really learn the material.

Don't be afraid to try new things—the worst that could happen is that you make a mistake and your program won't compile. You won't blow the computer up—don't be afraid of it!

2.10 DEBUGGING JAVA PROGRAMS

There is an old saying that the only sure things in life are death and taxes. We can add one more certainty to that list: If you write a program of any significant size, it won't work the first time you try it! Errors in programs are known as *bugs*, and the process of locating and eliminating them is known as *debugging*. Given that we have written a program and it is not working, how do we debug it?

Three types of errors are found in Java programs. The first type of error is a **compile-time error**. Compile-time errors are errors in the Java statement itself, such as spelling errors or punctuation errors. These errors are detected by the compiler during compilation. The second type of error is the **run-time error**. A run-time error occurs when an illegal mathematical operation is attempted during program execution (e.g., attempting to divide by 0). These errors cause exceptions in Java programs. Unless the exception is caught by an exception handler, the program will abort (crash) when the execution occurs. The third type of error is a **logical error**. Logical errors occur when the program compiles and runs successfully, but produces the wrong answer.

The most common mistakes made during programming are *typographical errors*. Some typographical errors create invalid Java statements. These errors produce syntax errors that are caught by the compiler. Other typographical errors occur in variable names. For example, the letters in some variable names might have been transposed. Most of these errors will also be caught by the compiler. However, if one legal variable name is substituted for another legal variable name, the compiler cannot detect the error. This sort of substitution might occur if you have two similar variable names. For example, if variables `vel1` and `vel2` are both used for velocities in the program, then one of them might be inadvertently used instead of the other one at some point. This sort of typographical error will produce a logical error. You must check for that sort of error by manually inspecting the code, since the compiler cannot catch it.

Sometimes is it possible to successfully compile and link the program, but there are run-time errors or logical errors when the program is executed. In this case, there is something wrong with the input data or something wrong with the logical structure of the program (or both). The first step in locating this sort of bug should be to *check the input data to the program*. Verify that the input values are what you expect them to be.

If the variable names seem to be correct and the input data is correct, then you are probably dealing with a logical error. You should check each of your assignment statements

1. If an assignment statement is very long, break it into several smaller assignment statements. Smaller statements are easier to verify.
2. Check the placement of parentheses in your assignment statements. It is a very common error to have the operations in an assignment statement evaluated in the wrong order. If you have any doubts as to the order in which the variables are being evaluated, add extra sets of parentheses to make your intentions clear.
3. Make sure that you have initialized all of your variables properly.
4. Be sure that any functions you use are in the correct units. For example, the input to trigonometric functions must be in units of radians, not degrees.
5. Check for possible errors due to integer or mixed-mode arithmetic.

If you are still getting the wrong answer, place `println` statements at various points in your program to print out the results of intermediate calculations. If you can locate the point where the calculations go bad, then you know just where in the code to look for the problem, which is 95% of the battle.

If you still cannot find the problem after completing all of the above steps, explain what you are doing to another student or to your instructor, and let them look at the code. It is very common for a person to see just what he or she expects to see when they look at their own code. Another person can often quickly spot an error that you have overlooked time after time.

All modern compilers have special debugging tools called *symbolic debuggers*. A symbolic debugger is a tool that allows you to walk through the execution of your program one statement at a time, and to examine the values of any variables at each step along the way. Symbolic debuggers allow you to see all of the intermediate results without having to insert a lot of debugging `print` or `println` statements into your code. These debuggers are powerful and flexible, but unfortunately there is a different debugger for each compiler vendor. If you will be using a symbolic debugger in your class, your instructor will introduce you to the debugger appropriate for your compiler and computer.

There is a standard debugger (`jdb`) supplied with the Java Software Development Kit. This debugger is command-line oriented and much less sophisticated than the ones in the commercial packages, but it is free.

PROFESSIONAL SUCCESS: BACK UP YOUR WORK EARLY AND OFTEN

It is very important that you learn to back up your work early and often right from the start of your programming career. Anyone who has programmed for a while can tell you about the frustration of losing parts of a program and having to re-create them.

For example, suppose that you are modifying an existing program to add some new feature, and you discover that the approach you intended to take doesn't work as planned. If you don't have a copy of the original program, you will have to devote extra time removing all of the changes you made and verifying that the program works the way it used to before even thinking about a new way to modify the program.

You should make a habit of saving copies of the programs that you develop at regular "checkpoints" during the development cycle. The checkpoints should be created after any significant changes, when the program is actually functioning. Then, if you lose a file or mess up some additional modification, you an always fall back on the last checkpointed version and start over.

SUMMARY

- Java names may contain any combination of letters, numbers, and underscore characters. They may be of any length, but must begin with a letter.
- Java names may not be the same as any Java keyword. Java keywords are listed in Table 2-1.
- By convention, class names begin with a capital letter, and the first letter of each successive word is also capitalized.
- By convention, local variable and method names begin with a lowercase letter, and the first letter of each successive word is capitalized.

- By convention, named constants (final variables) are written in all capital letters, with underscores used to separate different words.

- Java includes eight primitive data types: `float`, `double`, `char`, `byte`, `short`, `int`, `long`, and `boolean`. Each type is identical on every platform supported by Java.

- Java is a strongly typed language, which means that every variable must be explicitly declared before it is used.

- A Java named constant (also known as a final variable) may be created by prefixing the keyword `final` in front of the type in a declaration statement.

- An assignment statement assigns the value to the right of the equals sign to the variable on the left of the equals sign.

- The preincrement and predecrement operators are placed before a variable, and the postincrement and postdecrement operators are placed after a variable. The preincrement and predecrement operators cause the variable to be incremented or decremented by one, and then the new value is used in the expression in which it appears. The postincrement and postdecrement operators cause the old value of the variable to be used in the expression in which it appears and then the variable to be decremented or decremented by one.

- The cast operator explicitly converts a numeric value of one data type into a numeric value of another data type.

- Java's built-in mathematical methods are contained in the `Math` class of the `java.lang` package. Since this package is automatically imported into any Java program, these methods may be used by simply naming them in a statement. The methods are summarized in Table 2-7.

- Java can include overloaded methods, which are multiple methods with the same name but different parameters. When a programmer uses an overloaded method, the Java compiler decides which actual method to use based on the number and types of the method's arguments. For example, `Math.abs(x)` is an overloaded method.

- Java automatically converts arguments of an incorrect type into arguments of the type required by the method. This process is known as the **coercion of arguments**.

- Every Java program has three standard I/O objects: `System.in`, `System.out`, and `System.err`. These objects either accept or supply data one byte at a time. *It is the programmer's responsibility to clump successive bytes together to form meaningful numbers or strings* before attempting to process them.

- Java input is a very complex subject, and it will be postponed to Chapter 14. For now, the convenience class `StdIn` will be used to read input data and convert it into values of the proper type.

- When the + operator is used between strings, it concatenates them together. If it is used between a string and another operand, it converts the other operand into a string and concatenates the two strings together.

KEY TERMS

assignment conversion
assignment operator
assignment statement
associativity
binary operator
cast operator
coercion of arguments
concatenate
constant
escape sequence
exception
exponent
declaration statement
final

final variable
hierarchy of operations
increment operator error
keyword
mantissa
named constant
narrowing conversion
numeric promotion
overloaded methods
postdecrement
postincrement
precision
predecrement
preincrement

primitive data type
range
reserved
round-off error
standard error stream
standard input stream
standard output stream
String
strongly typed language
variable
unary operator
Unicode character set
widening conversion

APPLICATIONS: SUMMARY OF GOOD PROGRAMMING PRACTICES

Every Java program should be designed so that another person who is familiar with Java can easily understand it. This is very important, since a good program may be used for a long period of time. Over that time, conditions will change, and the program will need to be modified to reflect the changes. The program modifications may be done by someone other than the original programmer. The programmer making the modifications must understand the original program well before attempting to change it.

It is much harder to design clear, understandable, and maintainable programs than it is to simply write programs. To create such clear, understandable, and maintainable programs, a programmer must develop the discipline to properly document his or her work. In addition, the programmer must be careful to avoid known pitfalls along the path to good programs. The following guidelines will help you to develop good programs:

1. Always capitalize the first letter of a class name, and use a lowercase first letter in method and variable names.
2. If a name consists of more than one word, the words should be joined together and each succeeding word should begin with an uppercase letter.
3. Use meaningful variable names whenever possible to make your programs clearer.
4. Create a data dictionary in each program that you write. The data dictionary should explicitly declare and define each variable in the program. Be sure to include the physical units associated with each variable, if applicable.
5. Keep your physical constants consistent and precise throughout a program. To improve the consistency and understandability of your code, assign a name to any important constants, and refer to them by name in the program.
6. The names of constants should be in all capital letters, with underscores separating the words.
7. Use parentheses as necessary to make your equations clear and easy to understand.
8. Use cast operators to avoid mixed-mode expressions and to make your intentions clear.
9. Always keep expressions contianing increment and decrement operators simple and easy to understand.

Problems

1. State whether each of the following Java constants is valid. If valid, state what type of constant it is. If not, state why it is invalid. (If you are not certain, try to compile the constant in a Java program to check your answer.)

    a. `3.141592`
    b. `true`
    c. `-123,456.789`
    d. `+1E-12`
    e. `"Who's coming for dinner?"`
    f. `'Hello'`
    g. `"Enter name:"`
    h. `17.0f`

2. State whether each of the Java names is valid. If a name is not valid, state why the name is invalid. If a name is valid, state what a name of that sort should represent using the Java conventions.

    a. `junk`
    b. `3rd`
    c. `executeAlgorithm`
    d. `timeToIntercept`
    e. `MyMath`
    f. `START_TIME`

3. Which of the following expressions are legal in Java? If an expression is legal, evaluate it.

    a. `5 + 10 % 3 + 2`
    b. `5 + 10 % (3 + 2)`
    c. `23 / (4 / 8)`

4. Which of the following expressions are legal in Java? If an expression is legal, evaluate it.

    a. `((58/4)*(4/58))`
    b. `((58/4)*(4/58.))`
    c. `((58./4)*(4/58.))`
    d. `((58./4*(4/58.))`

5. Assume that the variables a, b, c, i, and j are initialized as shown in the following code fragment. What is the value of each variable after these statements are executed?

    ```
    int i = 5; j = 2;
    double a = 6, b, c;
    b = ++i - j--;
    j = (int) b / 2;
    a += b / j;
    ```

6. Figure 2.9 shows a right triangle with a hypotenuse of length c and angle θ. From elementary trigonometry, the length of sides a and b are given by

    $$a = c \cos \theta ,$$

    and

    $$b = c \sin \theta .$$

    The following program is intended to calculate the lengths of sides a and b given the hypotenuse c and angle θ. Will this program run? Will it produce the correct result? Why or why not?

    ```
    import chapman.io.*;
    public class CalcTriangle {
    ```

Figure 2.9.

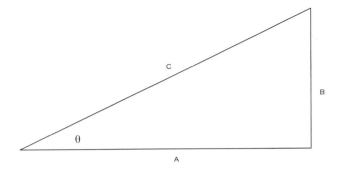

```
// Define the main method
public static void main(String[] args) {

    double a, b, c, theta;

    // Create a StdIn object
    StdIn in = new StdIn();

    // Prompt for the hypotenuse
    System.out.print("Enter the length of the hypotenuse c: ");
    c = in.readDouble();

    //Prompt for the angle
    System.out.print("Enter the angle theta in degrees: ");
    theta = in.readDouble();

    // Calculate sides
    a = c * Math.cos( theta );
    b = c * Math.sin( theta );

    // Write results
    System.out.println("Adjacent side = " + a);
    System.out.println("Opposite side = " + b);
}

}
```

7. Write a Java program that calculates an hourly employee's weekly pay. The program should ask the user for the person's pay rate and the number of hours worked during the week. It should then calculate the total pay from the formula

$$\text{Total Pay} = \text{Hourly Pay Rate} \times \text{Hours Worked} .$$

Finally, it should display the total weekly pay. Check your program by computing the weekly pay for a person earning \$7.50 per hour who worked 39 hours.

8. The potential energy of an object due to its height above the surface of the Earth is given by the equation

$$\text{PE} = mgh , \tag{2-9}$$

where m is the mass of the object, g is the acceleration due to gravity, and h is the height above the surface of the Earth. The kinetic energy of a moving object is given by the equation

$$\text{KE} = \frac{1}{2} mv^2 \tag{2-10}$$

program

to calculate

where m is the mass of the object and v is the velocity of the object. Write a Java ~~statement~~ for the total energy (potential plus kinetic) possessed by an object in the earth's gravitational field.

9. Write a Java program that calculates the percentage of carbon 14 that will be left after a given number of years. The program should read the number of years from the standard input stream.

10. If a stationary ball is released at a height h above the surface of the Earth, the velocity of the ball v when it hits the earth is given by the equation

$$v = \sqrt{2gh} ,$$ (2-11)

where g is the acceleration due to gravity, and h is the height above the surface of the Earth (assuming no air friction). Write a Java statement for the velocity of the ball when it hits the Earth.

11. **Period of a Pendulum** The period T (in seconds) of an oscillating pendulum is given by the equation

$$T = 2\pi \sqrt{\frac{L}{g}}$$ (2-12)

where L is the length of the pendulum in meters, and g is the acceleration due to gravity in meters per second squared. Write a Java program to calculate the period of a pendulum of length L. The length of the pendulum will be specified by the user when the program is run. Use good programming practices in your program. (The acceleration due to gravity at the Earth's surface is 9.81 m/s². Treat it as a constant in your program.)

12. Write a program to calculate the hypotenuse of a right triangle given the lengths of its two sides. Use good programming practices in your program.

13. The distance between two points (x_1, y_1) and (x_2, y_2) on a Cartesian coordinate plane (Figure 2.10) is given by the equation

$$d = \sqrt{(x_1 - x_2)^2 + (y_1 - y_2)^2} .$$ (2-13)

Write a Java program to calculate the distance between any two points (x_1, y_1) and (x_2, y_2) specified by the user. Use good programming practices in your program. Use the program to calculate the distance between the points (2,3) and (8,−5).

Figure 2.10.

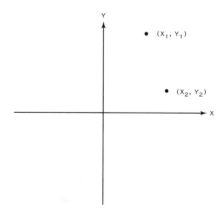

14. **Decibels** Engineers often measure the ratio of two power measurements in *decibels*, or dB. The equation for the ratio of two power measurements in dB is

$$dB = 10 \log_{10} \frac{P_2}{P_1} ,$$

Figure 2.11. A simplified representation of an AM radio set

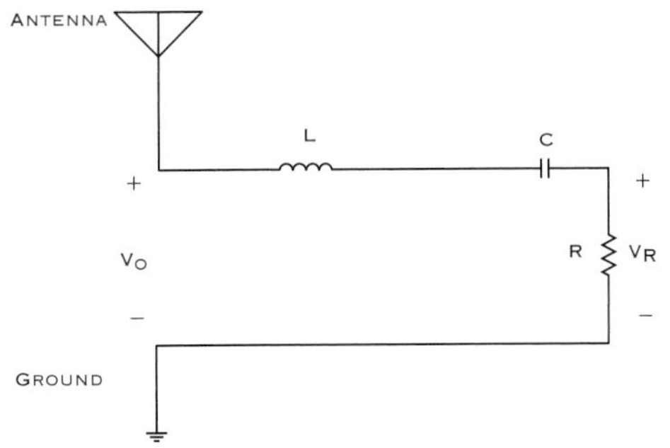

where P_2 is the power level being measured, and P_1 is some reference power level. Assume that the reference power level P_1 is 1 milliwatt, and write a program that accepts an input power P_2 and converts it into dB with respect to the 1 mW reference level.

15. **Hyperbolic cosine** The hyperbolic cosine function is defined by the equation

$$\cosh x = \frac{e^x + e^{-x}}{2} .$$

Write a Java program to calculate the hyperbolic cosine of a user-supplied value x. Use the program to calculate the hyperbolic cosine of 3.0.

16. **Radio Receiver** A simplified version of the front end of an AM radio receiver is shown in Figure 2.11. This receiver consists of an *RLC*-tuned circuit containing a resistor, capacitor, and an inductor connected in series. The *RLC* circuit is connected to an external antenna and ground, as shown in the following figure:

The tuned circuit allows the radio to select a specific station out of all the stations transmitting on the AM band. At the resonant frequency of the circuit, essentially all of the signal V_0 appearing at the antenna appears across the resistor, which represents the rest of the radio. In other words, the radio receives its strongest signal at the resonant frequency. The resonant frequency of the LC circuit is given by the equation

$$f_0 = \frac{1}{2\pi\sqrt{LC}} , \tag{2-14}$$

where L is inductance in henrys (H) and C is capacitance in farads (F). Write a program that calculates the resonant frequency of this radio set given specific values of L and C. Test your program by calculating the frequency of the radio when $L = 0.1$ mH and $C = 0.25$ nF.

3

Branches and Program Design

In the previous chapter, we developed several complete working Java programs. However, all of the programs were very simple, consisting of a single method containing a series of Java statements, which were executed one after another in a fixed order. Such programs are called *sequential* programs. They read input data, process it to produce a desired answer, print out the answer, and quit. There is no way to repeat sections of the program more than once, and there is no way to selectively execute only certain portions of the program depending on values of the input data.

In the next two chapters, we will introduce a number of Java statements that allow us to control the order in which statements are executed in a program. There are two broad categories of control statements: **selection**, or **branching**, which select specific sections of the code to execute, and **repetition**, which cause specific sections of the code to be repeated. This chapter will deal with selection structures, while Chapter 4 will cover repetition structures.

The operation of selection structures is controlled by `boolean` values (`true or false`), so before covering selection structures, we will introduce Java's relational and logical operations, which yield `boolean` results. The results of these operations will be used to control the selection structures.

SECTIONS

- 3.1 Introduction to Top-down Design Techniques
- 3.2 Use of Pseudocode
- 3.3 Relational and Logical Operators
- 3.4 Selection Structures
- Summary
- Key Terms

OBJECTIVES

After reading this chapter, you should be able to:

- To learn about the program development process and pseudocode
- To understand relational and logical operators
- To learn about the `if` and `switch` structures

Also, with the introduction of selection statements and repetition statements, our programs are going to become more complex, and it will get easier to make mistakes. To help avoid programming errors, we will introduce a formal program design procedure based upon the technique known as **top-down design**. We will also introduce a common algorithm development tool called pseudocode.

3.1 INTRODUCTION TO TOP-DOWN DESIGN TECHNIQUES

Suppose that you are an engineer working in industry and that you need to write a Java program to solve a problem. How do you begin?

When given a new problem, there is a natural tendency to sit down at a keyboard and start programming without "wasting" a lot of time thinking first. It is often possible to get away with this on-the-fly approach to programming for very small problems, such as many of the examples in this book. In the real world, however, problems are larger and more complicated, and a programmer attempting this approach will become hopelessly bogged down. For larger problems, it pays to completely think out the problem and the approach you are going to take to it before writing a single line of code.

We will introduce a formal program design process in this section and then apply that process to major applications developed in the remainder of the book. For some of the simple examples that we will be doing, the design process will seem like overkill. However, as the problems that we solve get larger and larger, the process becomes more and more essential to successful programming.

When I was an undergraduate, one of my professors was fond of saying, "Programming is easy. It's knowing what to program that's hard." His point was forcefully driven home to me after I left the university and began working in industry on larger scale software projects. I found that the most difficult part of my job was to *understand the problem* I was trying to solve. Once I really understood the problem, it became easy to break the problem apart into smaller, more easily manageable pieces with well-defined functions, and then to tackle those pieces one at a time.

In an object-oriented language such as Java, the first step in solving the problem is to break it apart by creating one or more objects that interact with the outside world in well-defined ways. It may be possible to extend a previously defined object for this purpose.

The next step is to determine how each object should interact with the outside world and to define one or more methods to describe that interaction. In general, there should be a separate method for each type of interaction.

There are several analysis techniques in common use to help a programmer decompose a problem into separate objects and methods. These object-oriented programming methods are beyond the scope of this book, since almost all of our examples can be realized as either a single class or a small number of classes. However, these methods may be encountered in advanced programming classes.

Once a problem has been decomposed into appropriate objects and methods, each method must be implemented in a structured way. This is normally done through a process of **top-down design**. Top-down design is the process of starting with a large task and breaking it down into smaller, more easily understandable pieces (subtasks) that perform a portion of the desired task. Each subtask may in turn be subdivided into smaller subtasks if necessary. Once the method is divided into small pieces, each piece can be implemented and tested independently (sometimes as a separate method). We do not attempt to combine the subtasks into a complete method until each of the subtasks has been verified to work properly by itself.

The concept of top-down design is the basis of our formal program design process. We will now introduce the details of the process, which is illustrated in Figure 3.1. The steps involved are:

1. *Clearly state the problem that you are trying to solve.* Programs are usually written to fill some perceived need, but that need may not be articulated clearly by the person requesting the program. For example, a user may ask for a program to solve a system of simultaneous linear equations. This request is not clear enough to allow a programmer to design a program to meet the need; he or she must first know much more about the problem to be solved. Is the system of equations to be solved real or complex? What is the maximum number of equations and unknowns that the program must handle? Are there any symmetries in the equations that might be exploited to make the task easier? The program designer will have to talk with the user requesting the program, and the two of them will have to come up with a clear statement of exactly what they are trying to accomplish. A clear statement of the problem will prevent misunderstandings, and it will also help the program designer to properly organize his or her thoughts. In the example we were just describing, a proper statement of the problem might have been:

Figure 3.1. The program design process used in this book

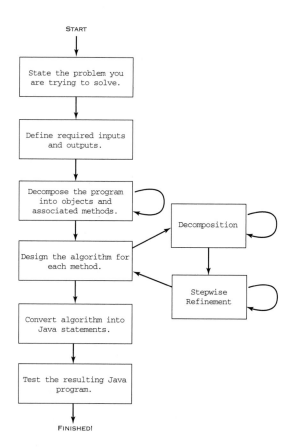

Design and write a program to solve a system of simultaneous linear equations having real coefficients and with up to 20 equations and 20 unknowns.

2. *Define the inputs required by the program and the outputs to be produced by the program.* The inputs to the program and the outputs produced by the program must be specified so that the new program will properly fit into the overall processing scheme. In the previous example, the coefficients of the equations to be solved are probably in some preexisting order, and our new program needs to be able to read them in that order. Similarly, it needs to produce the answers required by the programs that may follow it in the overall processing scheme, and it must write out those answers in the format needed by the programs following it.

3. *Decompose the program into classes and their associated methods.* Define one or more classes, and determine how the classes interact with each other and with the outside world. Define a separate method to implement each interaction.

4. *Design the algorithm that you intend to implement for each method.* An **algorithm** is a step-by-step procedure for finding the solution to a problem. It is at this stage in the process that top-down design techniques come into play. The designer looks for logical divisions within a method, and divides the method up into subtasks along those lines. This process is called **decomposition**. If the subtasks are themselves large, the designer can break them up into even smaller subsubtasks. This process continues until the problem has been divided into many small pieces, each of which does a simple, clearly understandable job. (As we shall see in later chapters, these separate pieces can become separate methods.)

    After the problem has been decomposed into small pieces, each piece is further refined through a process called **stepwise refinement**. In stepwise refinement, a designer starts with a general description of what the piece of code should do and then defines the functions of the piece in greater and greater detail until they are specific enough to be turned into Java statements. Stepwise refinement is usually done with **pseudocode**, which will be described in the next section.

    It is often helpful to solve a simple example of the problem by hand during the algorithm development process. If the designer understands the steps that he or she went through in solving the problem by hand, then he or she will be better able to apply decomposition and stepwise refinement to the problem.

5. *Turn the algorithm into Java statements.* If the decomposition and refinement process was carried out properly, this step will be very simple. All the programmer will have to do is to replace pseudocode with the corresponding Java statements on a one-for-one basis.

6. *Test the resulting Java program.* This step is the real killer. The components of the program must first be tested individually, if possible, and then the program as a whole must be tested. When testing a program, we must verify that it works correctly for *all legal input data sets.* It is very common for a program to be written, tested with some standard data set, and released for use, only to find that it produces the wrong answers (or crashes) with a different input data set. If the algorithm implemented in a program includes different branches, we must test all of the possible branches to confirm that the program operates correctly under every possible circumstance.

Large programs typically go through a series of tests before they are released for general use (see Figure 3.2). The first stage of testing is sometimes called **unit testing**. During unit testing, the individual components of the program are tested separately to confirm that they work correctly. After the unit testing is completed, the program goes through a series of *builds* during which the individual components are combined to produce the final program. The first build of the program typically includes only a few of the components. It is used to check the interactions among those components and the functions performed by their associated methods. In successive builds, more and more components are added, until the entire program is complete. Testing is performed on each build, and any errors (bugs) that are detected are corrected before moving on to the next build.

Testing continues even after the program is completed. The first complete version of the program is usually called the **alpha release**. It is used by the programmers and others very close to them in as many different ways as possible, and the bugs discovered during the testing are corrected. When the most serious bugs have been removed from the program, a new version, called the **beta release**, is prepared. The beta release is normally given to friendly outside users who have a need for the program in their normal day-to-day jobs. These users put the program through its paces under many different conditions and with many different input data sets, and they report any

Figure 3.2. A typical testing process for a large program

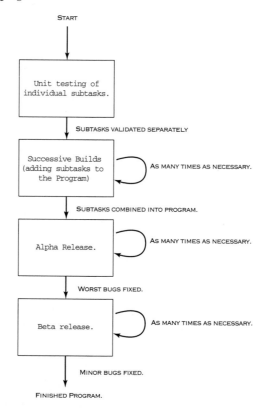

bugs that they find to the programmers. When those bugs have been corrected, the program is ready to be released for general use.

Because the programs in this book are fairly small, we will not go through the sort of extensive testing. However, we will follow the basic principles in testing all of our programs.

The program design process may be summarized as follows:

1. Clearly state the problem that you are trying to solve.
2. Define the inputs required by the program and the outputs to be produced by the program.
3. Decompose the program into classes and their associated methods.
4. Design the algorithm that you intend to implement for each method.
5. Turn the algorithm(s) into Java statements.
6. Test the Java program.

GOOD PROGRAMMING PRACTICE

Follow the steps of the program design process to produce reliable, understandable Java programs.

In a large programming project, the time actually spent programming is surprisingly small. In his book *The Mythical Man-Month*,[1] Frederick P. Brooks, Jr. suggests that in a typical large software project, 1/3 of the time is spent planning what to do (steps 1 through 3), 1/6 of the time is spent actually writing the program (step 4), and fully 1/2 of the time is spent in testing and debugging the program! Clearly, anything that we can do to reduce the testing and debugging time will be very helpful. We can best reduce the testing and debugging time by doing a very careful job in the planning phase and by using good programming practices. Using good programming practices will reduce the number of bugs in the program and will make the ones that do creep in easier to find.

Once a program has been created, it may be used over a lifetime of 20 years or more. Conditions will change during that time, and the program will have to be modified repeatedly over the course of its life. *The cost of the maintenance and modification of a program over its lifetime ususally exceeds the cost required of writing the program in the first place.* The modifications will usually be made by programmers other than the ones who originally wrote the code, and these programmers will be relatively unfamiliar with the program. It is during maintenance that good programming practices really pay off. If a program is well designed, well documented, and uses good programming practices, it will be easier (and cheaper) to modify the program without introducing new bugs.

3.2 USE OF PSEUDOCODE

As a part of the design process, it is necessary to describe the algorithm that you intend to implement. The description of the algorithm should be in a standard form that is easy for both you and other people to understand, and the description should aid you in turn-

---

[1] *The Mythical Man-Month*, by Frederick P. Brooks Jr., Addison-Wesley, 1974.

ing your concept into Java code. The standard forms that we use to describe algorithms are called **structures**, and an algorithm described using these structures is called a structured algorithm. When the algorithms in a program are implemented in a structured way, the resulting program is called a **structured program**.

The structures used to build algorithms are often described using pseudocode. Pseudocode is a hybrid mixture of Java and English. It is structured like Java, with a separate line for each distinct idea or segment of code, but the descriptions on each line are in English. Each line of the pseudocode should describe its idea in plain, easily understandable English. Pseudocode is very useful for developing algorithms, since it is flexible and easy to modify. It is especially useful, since pseudocode can be written and modified with the same text editor used to write the Java program. That is, no special graphical capabilities are required.

For example, the pseudocode for the algorithm of the `main` method in Example 2-2 is as follows:

```
Prompt user to enter temperature in degrees Fahrenheit
Read temperature in degrees Fahrenheit (tempF)
tempK in kelvins ← (5./9.) * (tempF - 32) + 273.15
Write temperature in kelvins
```

Notice that a left arrow ($\leftarrow$) is used instead of an equal sign ($=$) to indicate that a value is stored in a variable, since this avoids any confusion between assignment and equality. Pseudocode is intended to aid you in organizing your thoughts before converting them into Java code.

3.3 RELATIONAL AND LOGICAL OPERATORS

Relational operators and **logical operators** are two types of operators whose results are `boolean` `true` or `false` values. They are used to control many looping and branching structures in Java, as we shall see later in this chapter and in Chapter 4.

Relational Operators

Relational operators are operators with *two numerical operands* that yield a `boolean` (`true` or `false`) result. The result depends on the *relationship* between the two values being compared, so these operators are called relational. If the relationship expressed by the operator is true, then the result of the operation is `true`; otherwise, the result is `false`. The six relational operators are summarized in Table 3-1.

TABLE 3-1 Relational Operators

OPERATOR	SAMPLE EXPRESSION	MEANING
Relational operators:		
>	x > y	true if $x > y$
<	x < y	true if $x < y$
>=	x >= y	true if $x \geq y$
<=	x <= y	true if $x \leq y$
Equality operators:		
==	x == y	true if $x = y$
!=	x != y	true if $x \neq y$

All of these operators associate from left to right. The relational operators >, <, >=, and <= are of equal precedence, below that of the + and − operators. The equality operators == and != are also of equal precedence, just below the relational operators.

The following are some relational operations and their results:

OPERATION	RESULT
3 < 4	true
3 <= 4	true
3 == 4	false
3 > 4	false
4 <= 4	true
'A' < 'B'	true

The last logical expression is true, because characters are compared according to their positions in the Unicode character set and 'A' (sequence number 65) is less than 'B' (sequence number 66).

The equivalence relational operator is written with two equals signs, while the assignment operator is written with a single equals sign. These are very different operators, and beginning programmers often confuse them. The == symbol is a *comparison* operation that returns a boolean result, while the = symbol *assigns* the value of the expression to the right of the equal sign to the variable on the left of the equal sign. It is a very common mistake for beginning programmers to use a single equals sign when trying to do a comparison.

PROGRAMMING PITFALLS

Be careful not to confuse the equivalence relational operator (==) with the assignment operator (=).

In the hierarchy of operations, relational operators are evaluated after all arithmetic operators have been evaluated. Therefore, the following two expressions are equivalent (both are true):

```
7 + 3  <  2 + 11
(7 + 3) < (2 + 11)
```

Also, if a comparison is between two operands of differing noncharacter types, the lower ranking type is promoted to the higher ranking type. For example, if a comparison is between a double and an int value, then the int value is promoted to a double value before the comparison is performed. Comparisons between numerical data and character data are legal, with the comparison based on the collating sequence of the character:

```
4 == 4.
```
true (int is converted to double and comparison is made)

```
65 <= 'A'
```
true (The sequence value of 'A' is 65, so 65 <= 65)

Logical Operators

Logical operators are operators with *one or two boolean operands* that yield a `boolean` (`true` or `false`) result. There are six logical operators: `&&` (logical AND), `&` (boolean logical AND), `||` (logical OR), `|` (boolean logical inclusive OR), `^` (boolean logical exclusive OR), and `!` (logical NOT). These operators all accept `boolean` (`true` or `false`) operands and return a `boolean` result.

The general form of a binary logical operation is

$$l_1 \text{ op } l_2 \text{ ,}$$

where l_1 and l_2 are `boolean` expressions, variables, or constants, and op is one of the first five of the above binary logical operators.

The results of the operators are summarized in the following *truth tables*, which show the result of each operation for all possible combinations of l_1 and l_2:

TABLE 3-2(a) Truth Table for Binary Logical Operators

l_1	l_2	l_1 && l_2	l_1 & l_2	l_1 || l_2	l_1 | l_2	l_1 ^ l_2
false	false	false	false	false	false	false
false	true	false	false	true	true	true
true	false	false	false	true	true	true
true	true	true	true	true	true	false

TABLE 3-2(b) Truth Table for NOT Operator

l_1	$!l_1$
false	true
true	false

To understand these operators, consider the following expressions and their results:

```
(7 > 6) && (2 < 1)          false
(7 > 6) || (2 < 1)          true
!(7 > 6)                    false
```

Remember that relational operators produce a `boolean` result. In the first case, `7 > 6` is `true`, and `2 < 1` is `false`. Thus the result of the logical AND `(7 > 6) && (2 < 1)` is `false`, while the result of the logical OR `(7 > 6) || (2 < 1)` is `true`. Similarly, since `7 > 6` is `true`, `!(7 > 6)` is `false`.

These operators are most commonly used to combine the results of two or more relational operators to create some test. For example, suppose that we are examining pairs of (x,y) points in a Cartesian plane, and we would like to determine if a point lies in the second quadrant. For a point to lie in the second quadrant, it must have an x value less than zero and a y value greater than zero, as shown in Figure 3.3. A test to determine if the point lies in the second quadrant would be completed as shown:

```
boolean quadrant2;
...
quadrant2 = x < 0 && y > 0;
```

The result of the relational operator `x < 0` is `true` or `false`, and the result of the relational operator `y > 0` is also `true` or `false`. The logical operator then combines these two `boolean` values to calculate the result of the overall expression.

In the hierarchy of operations, logical operators are evaluated *after all arithmetic operations and all relational operators have been evaluated.* Therefore, the `boolean` results of the relational operators are calculated before the AND operator attempts to use them.

Looking at the above truth tables, it appears that the logical AND (`&&`) and the boolean logical AND (`&`) are identical, and that the logical OR (`||`) and the boolean inclusive logical OR (`|`) are identical. Why do these duplicate operators exist? This answer is that *the operators `&&` and `||` can perform partial evaluations of their operands, while the operators `&` and `|` always perform full evaluations of their operands.*

If we look at Table 3-2(*a*), we can see that the AND operators will only produce a `true` result of both operands l_1 and l_2 are true. If Java evaluates the first operand l_1 and finds that it is `false`, it already knows that the result of the AND will be `false`. Therefore, there is no need to evaluate l_2. Similarly, we can see that the inclusive OR operators will only produce a `false` result of both operands l_1 and l_2 are `false`. Therefore, if Java evaluates the first operand l_1 and finds that it is `true`, it already knows that the result of the OR will be and `true`, and there is no need to evaluate l_2.

The difference between `&&` and `||` on the one hand, and `&` and `|` on the other hand, is that `&&` and `||` permit decisions to be made if possible after evaluating only `||`, while `&` and `|` always evaluate both operands before making a decision. This difference is illustrated in the following program:

```
1   // This program illustrates the use of the AND operators
2   public class TestAnd {
3      // Define the main method
4      public static void main(String[] args) {
5
6         int i = 10, j = 9;
7         boolean test;
8
9         // Demonstrate &&
10        test = i > 10 && j++ > 10;
11        System.out.println(i);
12        System.out.println(j);
13        System.out.println(test);
14
15        // Demonstrate &
16        test = i > 10 & j++ > 10;
17        System.out.println(i);
18        System.out.println(j);
19        System.out.println(test);
20     }
21  }
```

When this program is executed, the results are as follows:

```
10
9
false
10
10
false
```

Figure 3.3.   For a point (x,y) to line in the second quadrant of a Cartesian plane, its x value must be less than zero and its y value must be greater than zero.

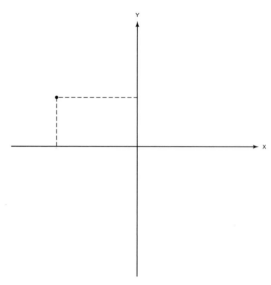

Note that the command j++ on line 10 is never executed, since the first operand is already false. Therefore, the value of j remains 9. The j++ on line 16 *is* executed, since the & operation always evaluates both operands before reaching a decision. Therefore, the value of j is increased to 10.

The hierarchy of all operations that we have seen so far is summarized in Table 3-3. In this table, all operators on the same line have equal precedence and are evaluated in the order indicated by the associativity property for that line.

TABLE 3-3   Hierarchy of Operations

OPERATORS	ASSOCIATIVITY	TYPE
( )	left to right	parentheses
++ -- + - ! (type)	right to left	unary
* / %	left to right	multiplicative
+ -	left to right	additive
< <= > >=	left to right	relational
== !=	left to right	equality
&	left to right	boolean logical AND
^	left to right	boolean logical exclusive OR
|	left to right	boolean logical inclusive OR
&&	left to right	logical AND
||	left to right	logical OR
? :	right to left	conditional (*described later in this chapter*)
= += -= *= /= %=	right to left	assignment

EXAMPLE 3-1 | Assume that the following variables are initialized with the values shown, and calculate the result of the specified expressions:

```
var1 = true;
var2 = true;
var3 = false;
```

EXPRESSION	RESULT
a. ! var1	false
b. var1 | var3	true
c. var1 && var3	false
d. var2 ^ var3	true
e. var1 && var2 || var3	true
f. var1 | var2 & var3	true
g. (var1 | var2) & var3	false

The & operator is evaluated before the | operator in Java. Therefore, the parentheses in part g of this example were required. If they had been absent, the expression in part g would have been evaluated in the order var1 | (var2 & var3).

3.4 SELECTION STRUCTURES

Selection structures are Java statements that permit us to select and execute specific sections of code (called blocks) while skipping other sections of code. They are variations of the if structure and the switch structure.

The if Structure

The if structure specifies that a statement (or a block of code) will be executed *if and only if a certain boolean expression is true.* For example, suppose that we were writing a grading program, and we wanted the program to print "Passed" if and only if the student's grade is greater than 70. If the student's grade is less than or equal to 70, then the program will not write out anything. The pseudocode for such a statement would be the following:

```
If the student's grade is greater than 70
    Print "Passed"
```

The Java if structure has the following form:

```
if (boolean_expr)
    statement;
```

or

```
if (boolean_expr) statement;
```

If the boolean expression is true, the program executes the statement. If the boolean expression is false, then the program skip the statement and executes the next statement after the if structure. The Java statement corresponding to the pseudocode above would be

```
if ( grade > 70 )
    System.out.println("Passed");
```

Figure 3.4.   An if structure consists of a control expression and a controlled statement. The controlled statement will be executed if and only if the control expression evaluates to true.

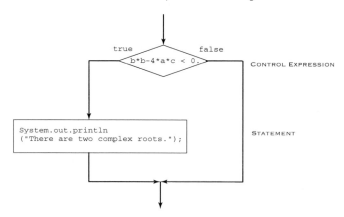

Note that the conditional statement is indented in the if structure. This is not a requirement of the Java compiler, since Java ignores *whitespace characters*, such as blanks, tabs, and newlines. However, the indenting makes the program easier for people to read. You should always indent the body of any structure to distinguish it from the surrounding code.

GOOD PROGRAMMING PRACTICE

Always indent the body of any structure by three or more spaces to improve the readability of the code.

As an example of an if structure, consider the solution of a quadratic equation of the form

$$ax^2 + bx + c = 0 \ . \tag{3-1}$$

The solution to this equation is

$$x = \frac{-b \pm \sqrt{b^2 - 4ac}}{2a} \ . \tag{3-2}$$

The term $b^2 - 4ac$ is known as the *discriminant* of the equation. If $b^2 - 4ac > 0$, then there are two distinct real roots to the quadratic equation. If $b^2 - 4ac = 0$, then there is a single repeated root to the equation, and if $b^2 - 4ac < 0$, then there are two complex roots to the quadratic equation.

Suppose that we wanted to examine the discriminant of the quadratic equation and tell a user if the equation has complex roots. In pseudocode, the if structure to do this would take the following form:

```
If b*b - 4*a*c < 0.
   Write message that equation has two complex roots.
```

In Java, the if structure is as follows:

```
if ((b*b - 4*a*c) < 0.)
   System.out.println("There are two complex roots.");
```

This structure is shown pictorially in Figure 3.4.

The `if/else` Structure

In the simple `if` structure, a statement is executed if the controlling `boolean` expression is `true`. If the controlling `boolean` expression is `false`, the statement is skipped.

Sometimes we may want to execute one statement if some condition is `true`, and a different statement if the condition is `false`. This can be accomplished with an `if/else` structure, which takes the following form:

```
if (boolean_expr)
    statement 1;
else
    statement 2;
```

If the `boolean` expression is `true`, then the program executes statement 1 and skips to the statement that follows statement 2. Otherwise, the program executes statement 2.

To illustrate the use of the `if/else` structure, let's reconsider the quadratic equation once more. Suppose that we wanted to examine the discriminant of a quadratic equation and tell a user whether the equation has real or complex roots. If the discriminant is greater than or equal to zero, there are real roots. Otherwise, the equation has complex roots. In pseudocode, this `if/else` structure would take the following form:

```
If (b*b - 4.*a*c) >= 0
    Write message that equation has real roots.
else
    Write message that equation has complex roots.
```

The Java statements to do this are as follows:

```
if ( (b*b - 4.*a*c) >= 0. )
    System.out.println("There are real roots.");
else
    System.out.println("There are complex roots.");
```

This structure is shown pictorially in Figure 3.5. Note that *the statement in the* `else` *clause of an* `if/else` *structure can be another* `if/else` *structure.* This cascading of structures allows us to make more complex selections. An example of cascaded if structures is shown:

```
if (boolean_expr_1)
    statement 1;
else if (boolean_expr_2)
    statement 2;
else
    statement 3;
```

If *boolean_expr_1* is `true`, then the program executes statement 1 and skips to the statement that follows statement 3. Otherwise, the program tests whether *boolean_expr_2* is `true`. If it is, then the program executes statement 2 and skips to the statement that follows statement 3. If both *boolean_expr_1* and *boolean_expr_2* are `false`, then the program executes statement 3. This structure might be more clearly represented as follows:

```
if (boolean_expr_1)
    statement 1;
else
    if (boolean_expr_2)
        statement 2;
    else
        statement 3;
```

Figure 3.5. An `if` structure with an `else` clause. Either statement 1 or statement 2 will be executed, depending on the result of the control expression.

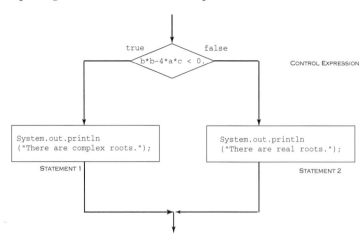

The above structure is perhaps clearer, since it emphasizes the fact that the later `if`s are inside the `else` clauses of the previous `if`s. Since Java ignores whitespace, both ways of writing this structure are equivalent.

Any number of `if/else` structures can be cascaded to produce arbitrarily complex selection structures.

To illustrate the use of cascaded `if/else` structures, let's reconsider the quadratic equation once more. Suppose that we wanted to write a program that examines the discriminant of a quadratic equation and tells the user whether the equation has two complex roots, two identical real roots, or two distinct real roots. In pseudocode, this construct would take the following form:

```
If (b*b - 4.*a*c) < 0
    Write message that equation has two complex roots.
else if (b*b - 4.*a*c) == 0.
    Write message that equation has two identical real roots.
else
    Write message that equation has two distinct real roots.
```

The Java statements to do this are as follows:

```
if ((b*b - 4.*a*c) < 0. )
    System.out.println("There are two complex roots.");
else if ( (b*b - 4.*a*c) == 0. )
    System.out.println("There are 2 identical real roots.");
else
    System.out.println("There are 2 distinct real roots.");
```

This cascaded structure is shown pictorially in Figure 3.6.

Executing Multiple Statements in an `if` Structure

The `if` and `if/else` structures are each designed to execute a *single statement* if a particular condition is `true`. What would happen if we needed to execute multiple statements in response to a condition? Java's answer to this problem is the **compound statement**.

A compound statement is a set of statements enclosed between a pair of braces ({ and }). A compound statement can be used anywhere in Java where an ordinary state-

Figure 3.6.   A cascaded `if` structure. The second control expression is executed if and only if the first control expression is false.

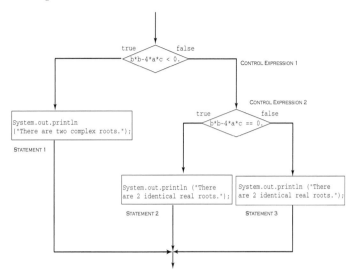

ment is expected. Thus, an `if`/`else` structure containing multiple lines takes the following form:

```
if (logical_expr) {
    statement 1;
    statement 2;
    statement 3;
}
else {
    statement 4;
    statement 5;
    statement 6;
}
```

Examples Using `if` Structures

We will now look at two examples that illustrate the use of `if` structures.

**EXAMPLE 3-2:
THE
QUADRATIC
EQUATION**

Design and write a program to solve for the roots of a quadratic equation, regardless of type.

SOLUTION

We will follow the design steps outlined earlier in the chapter.

1. **State the problem.** The problem statement for this example is very simple. We want to write a program that will solve for the roots of a quadratic equation, whether they are distinct real roots, repeated real roots, or complex roots.

2. **Define the inputs and outputs.** The inputs required by this program are the coefficients a, b, and c of the quadratic equation

$$ax^2 + bx + c = 0 .$$
(3-1)

The output from the program will be the roots of the quadratic equation, whether they are distinct real roots, repeated real roots, or complex roots.

3. **Decompose the program into classes and their associated methods**. For the next three chapters, this step will be trivial, because every program will have only one class. We will begin learning how to decompose problems into separate classes in Chapter 7, after we learn more about the structure of classes. For now, there will be a single class, and only the `main` method within that class. We will call the class `QuadraticEquation` and make it a subclass of the root class `Object`. (If no other superclass is explicitly specified in the class definition, any new class is automatically a subclass of `Object`.)

4. **Design the algorithm that you intend to implement for each method**. There is only one method in this program. The `main` method can be broken down into three major sections, whose functions are input, processing, and output:

```
Read the input data
Calculate the roots
Write out the roots
```

We will now break each of the above major sections into smaller, more detailed pieces. There are three possible ways to calculate the roots, depending on the value of the discriminant, so it is logical to implement this algorithm with an `if/else` structure. The resulting pseudocode is:

```
Prompt the user for the coefficient a.
Read a
Prompt the user for the coefficient b.
Read b
Prompt the user for the coefficient c.
Read c
discriminant ← b*b - 4. * a * c
if discriminant > 0 {
    x1 ← ( -b + Math.sqrt(discriminant) ) / ( 2 * a )
    x2 ← ( -b - Math.sqrt(discriminant) ) / ( 2 * a )
    Write message that equation has two distinct real roots.
    Write out the two roots.
}
else if discriminant == 0 {
    x1 ← -b / ( 2. * a )
    Write message that equation has two identical real roots.
    Write out the repeated root.
}
else {
    realPart ← -b / ( 2. * a )
    imagPart ← Math.sqrt ( Math.abs( discriminant ) ) / ( 2 * a )
    Write message that equation has two complex roots.
    Write out the two roots.
}
```

5. **Turn the algorithm into Java statements**. The final Java code is shown in Figure 3.7, shown at the top of the next page. Note that the `if` structure is shown in bold face.

```
/*
    Purpose:
        This program solves for the roots of a quadratic equation of the
        form a*x*x + b*x + c = 0. It calculates the answers regardless of
        the type of roots that the equation possesses.

    Record of revisions:
            Date      Programmer      Description of change
            ====      ==========      =====================
        3/27/98  S. J. Chapman   Original code

*/
import chapman.io.*;
public class QuadraticEquation {

    // Define the main method
    public static void main(String[] args) {

        // Declare variables, and define each variable
        double a;              // Coefficient of x**2 term of equation
        double b;              // Coefficient of x term of equation
        double c;              // Constant term of equation
        double discriminant;   // Discriminant of the equation
        double imagPart;       // Imag part of equation (for complex roots)
        double realPart;       // Real part of equation (for complex roots)
        double x1;             // 1st soln of equation (for real roots)
        double x2;             // 2nd soln of equation (for real roots)

        // Create a StdIn object
        StdIn in = new StdIn();

        // Prompt the user for the coefficients of the equation
        System.out.println("This program solves for the roots of a");
        System.out.println("quadratic equation of the form ");
        System.out.println("A * X*X + B * X + C = 0.");
        System.out.print("Enter the coefficient A: ");
        a = in.readDouble();
        System.out.print("Enter the coefficient B: ");
        b = in.readDouble();
        System.out.print("Enter the coefficient C: ");
        c = in.readDouble();

        // Calculate discriminant
        discriminant = b*b - 4. * a * c;

        // Solve for the roots, depending on the discriminant
        if ( discriminant > 0. ) {

            // Two real roots...
            x1 = ( -b + Math.sqrt(discriminant) ) / ( 2 * a );
            x2 = ( -b - Math.sqrt(discriminant) ) / ( 2 * a );
            System.out.println("This equation has 2 real roots:");
            System.out.println("X1 = " + x1 + ", X2 = " + x2);
        }

        else if ( discriminant == 0. ) {

            // One repeated root...
            x1 = ( -b ) / ( 2 * a );
            System.out.println("This equation has 2 identical real roots:");
            System.out.println("X1 = X2 = " + x1);
        }
```

Figure 3.7. *(cont.)*

```
              else {
                 // Complex roots...
                 realPart = ( -b ) / ( 2. * a );
                 imagPart = Math.sqrt( Math.abs ( discriminant ) ) / ( 2 * a );
                 System.out.println("This equation has complex roots:");
                 System.out.println("X1 = " + realPart + " +i " + imagPart);
                 System.out.println("X2 = " + realPart + " -i " + imagPart);
              }
          }
      }
```

Figure 3.7. Program to solve for the roots of a quadratic equation

6. **Test the program**. Next, we must test the program using real input data. Since there are three possible paths through the program, we must test all three paths before we can be certain that the program is working properly. From Equation (3-2), it is possible to verify the solutions to the following equations:

$$x^2 + 5x + 6 = 0, \qquad x = -2, \text{ and } x = -3,$$

$$x^2 + 4x + 4 = 0, \qquad x = -2,$$

$$x^2 + 2x + 5 = 0, \qquad x = -1 \pm i2.$$

If this program is compiled and run three times with the above coefficients, the results are as follows (user inputs are shown in bold face):

```
C:\book\java\chap3>jave QuadraticEquation
This program solves for the roots of a quadratic
equation of the form A * X*X + B * X + C = 0.
Enter the coefficient A: 1
Enter the coefficient B: 5
Enter the coefficient C: 6
This equation has two real roots:
X1 = -2.0, X2 = -3.0

This program solves for the roots of a quadratic
equation of the form A * X*X + B * X + C = 0.
Enter the coefficient A: 1
Enter the coefficient B: 4
Enter the coefficient C: 4
This equation has two identical real roots:
X1 = X2 = -2.0

This program solves for the roots of a quadratic
equation of the form A * X*X + B * X + C = 0.
Enter the coefficient A: 1
Enter the coefficient B: 2
Enter the coefficient C: 5
This equation has complex roots:
X1 = -1.0 +i 2.0


X2 = -1.0 -i 2.0
```

The program gives the correct answers for our test data in all three possible cases.

EXAMPLE 3-3:
EVALUATING A
FUNCTION OF
TWO
VARIABLES

Write a Java program to evaluate a function $f(x,y)$ for any two user-specified values x and y. The function $f(x,y)$ is defined as follows:

$$f(x, y) = \begin{cases} x + y & x \ge 0 \text{ and } y \ge 0 , \\ x + y^2 & x \ge 0 \text{ and } y < 0 , \\ x^2 + y & x < 0 \text{ and } y \ge 0 , \\ x^2 + y^2 & x < 0 \text{ and } y < 0 . \end{cases}$$

SOLUTION

The function $f(x,y)$ is evaluated differently depending on the signs of the two independent variables x and y. To determine the proper equation to apply, it will be necessary to check for the signs of the x and y values supplied by the user. We will use the following steps to solve the problems:

1. **State the problem**. This problem statement is very simple: Evaluate the function $f(x,y)$ for any user-supplied values of x and y.

2. **Define the inputs and outputs**. The inputs required by this program are the values of the independent variables x and y. The output from the program will be the value of the function $f(x,y)$.

3. **Decompose the program into classes and their associated methods**. Again, there will be a single class and only the `main` method within that class. We will call the class `Eval` and make it a subclass of the root class `Object`.

4. **Design the algorithm that you intend to implement for each method**. The `main` method can be broken down into three major sections, whose functions are input, processing, and output:

   ```
   Read the input values x and y
   Calculate f(x,y)
   Write out f(x,y)
   ```

   We will now break each of the above major sections into smaller, more detailed pieces. There are four possible ways to calculate the function $f(x,y)$, depending on the values of x and y, so it is logical to implement this algorithm with a four-branched `if`/`else` structure.

   ```
   Prompt the user for the value x.
   Read x.
   Prompt the user for the value x.
   Read y.
   Echo the input coefficients.
   if x >= 0 and y >= 0
       fun ← x + y
   else if x ≥ 0 and y < 0
       fun ← x + y*y
   else if x < 0 and y ≥ 0
       fun ← x*x + y
   else
       fun ← x*x + y*y
   Write out f(x,y).
   ```

5. **Turn the algorithm into Java statements**. The final Java code is shown in Figure 3.8.

```
/*
    Purpose:
      This program solves the function f(x,y) for user-specified x and
          y, where f(x,y) is defined as:


                    _
                   |
                   | x + y              x >= 0 and y >= 0,
                   | x + y*y            x >= 0 and y < 0,
        f(x,y)  =  | x*x + y            x < 0 and y >= 0,
                   | x*x + y*y          x < 0 and y < 0.
                   |_


    Record of revisions:
        Date        Programmer          Description of change
        ====        ==========          =====================
      03/27/98   S. J. Chapman          Original code
*/
import chapman.io.*;
public class Eval {

// Define the main method
   public static void main(String[] args) {

   // Declare variables, and define each variable
   double x;                 // First independent variable
   double y;                 // Second independent variable
   double fun;               // Resulting function

   // Create a StdIn object
   StdIn in = new StdIn();

   // Prompt the user for the coefficients of the equation
   System.out.print("Enter x: ");
   x = in.readDouble();
   System.out.print("Enter y: ");
   y = in.readDouble();

   // Calculate the function f(x,y) based on the sign of x and y
   if ( (x >= 0) && (y >= 0) )
      fun = x + y;
   else if ( (x >= 0) && (y < 0) )
      fun = x + y*y;
   else if ( (x < 0) && (y >= 0) )
      fun = x*x + y;
   else
      fun = x*x + y*y;

   // Write the value of the function.
   System.out.println("The value of the function is: " + fun);
   }
}
```

Figure 3.8.   Program Eval from Example 3-3

6.   **Test the program**. Next, we must test the program using real input data. Since there are four possible paths through the program, we must test all four paths before we can be certain that the program is working properly. To test all

four possible paths, we will execute the program with the four sets of input values $(x,y) = (2,3), (-2,3), (2,-3)$, and $(-2,-3)$. Calculating by hand, we see that

$$f(2, 3) = 2 + 3 = 5 \,,$$

$$f(2, -3) = 2 + (-3)^2 = 11 \,,$$

$$f(-2, 3) = (-2)^2 + 3 = 7 \,,$$

$$f(-2, -3) = (-2)^2 + (-3)^2 = 13 \,.$$

If this program is compiled, and then run four times with the previously stated values, the results are as follows:

```
C:\book\java\chap3>java Eval
Enter x: 2
Enter y: 3
The value of the function is: 5.0

C:\book\java\chap3>java Eval
Enter x: 2
Enter y: -3
The value of the function is: 11.0

C:\book\java\chap3>java Eval
Enter x: -2
Enter y: 3

The value of the function is: 7.0

C:book\java\chap3>java Eval
Enter x: -2
Enter y: -3
The value of the function is: 13.0
```

The program gives the correct answers for our test values in all four possible cases.

Testing for Equality in `if` Structures

A common problem with `if` statements occurs when *floating-point* (`float` *and* `double`) *variables are tested for equality.* Because of small round-off errors during floating-point arithmetic operations, two numbers that theoretically should be equal may differ by a tiny amount, and the test for equality will fail. This failure can cause a program to execute the wrong statement in an `if/else` structure, producing a subtle and hard-to-find bug. For example, consider the quadratic equation program of Example 3-2. In that program, we concluded that a quadratic equation had two identical real roots if the discriminant, $b^2 - 4ac = 0$. Depending on the coefficients of the equation, round-off errors might cause the discriminant to be a very small nonzero number, say 10^{-14}, when it should theoretically be zero. If this happens, then the test for identical real roots would fail.

When working with floating-point variables, it is often a good idea to replace a test for equality with a test for *near equality.* For example, instead of testing to see if the `double` value x is equal to `10.`, you might test to see if $|x - 10.| < 1e-10$. Any value of x between 9.9999999999 and 10.0000000001 will satisfy the latter test, so round-off error will not cause problems. The Java statement,

```
if ( x == 10. )
```

would be replaced by

```
if ( Math.abs(x - 10.) <= 1e-10 )
```

GOOD PROGRAMMING PRACTICE

When working with floating-point values, it is a good idea to replace test for equality with tests for near equality to avoid improper results due to cumulative round-off errors.

Nested `if` Structures

The `if` structure is very flexible. Since any number of `if` structures can be cascaded in an `if/else...if/else...if/else` structure, where each succeeding `if` lies in the `else` clause of the preceding `if`, it is possible to implement any desired selection construct. When `if` structures lie inside other if structures, they are said to be **nested**.

Nested `if` structures are very useful and flexible, but they are also a very common source of bugs in Java programs. This happens because novice programmers often make mistakes in the use of `else` clauses. *The Java compiler always associates an `else` statement with the immediately preceding `if` statement,* unless told to otherwise by the proper use of braces ({}). Bugs can occur when using `else` clauses with nested `if` structures, because the Java compiler associates the `else` clause with a different `if` than the programmer expected it to.

Let's take a simple example to illustrate this problem. Suppose that we want to test two variables x and y to determine if they are both greater than zero. If they are, we will print out the string `"x and y are > 0"`. If x is `<= 0`, we would like to print out the string `"x <= 0"` instead. A programmer might attempt to implement this function as follows:

```
if ( x > 0)
    if (y > 0)
        System.out.println("x and y are > 0");
else
    System.out.println("x <= 0");
```

At first glance, this code seems to be saying that if x > 0, then we will test to see if y > 0 and print the string if true, while if x <= 0, we will print out `"x <= 0"`. In other words, the `else` clause seems to be associated with the `if (x > 0)` statement. However, *the Java compiler associates the `else` with the immediately preceding `if` statement,* so the compiler actually interprets the structure as follows:

```
if ( x > 0)
    if (y > 0)
        System.out.println("x and y are > 0");
    else
        System.out.println("x <= 0");
```

The code will actually print out `"x <= 0"` when x > 0 and y <= 0! This sort of error is known as the **dangling-else problem**.

The dangling-else problem can be avoided by using braces to force the `else` to be associated with the proper `if`.

```
if ( x > 0) {
    if (y > 0)
        System.out.println("x and y are > 0");
}
else
    System.out.println("x <= 0");
```

The braces indicate to the compiler that the second `if` is inside the body of the first `if`, and that the `else` is matched with the first `if`. (If the `else` had been *inside* the braces, it would have been matched with the second `if`).

GOOD PROGRAMMING PRACTICE

Use braces in nested if structures to make your intentions clear and avoid dangling `else` clauses.

Another common error with cascaded `if`/`else` structures occurs when a programmer fails to carefully consider the order of tests that he or she is performing. For example, suppose that we want to write out messages depending on the current temperature in degrees Fahrenheit as follows:

```
temp < 60      "cold"
temp > 70      "warm"
temp > 90      "hot"
```

One possible structure might be the following:

```
if (temp < 60)
    System.out.println("cold");
else if (temp > 70)
    System.out.println("warm");
else if (temp > 90)
    System.out.println("hot");
```

This structure will compile and execute, but *it will not work properly.* If the temperature is greater than 90, we would like to print out "hot". However, the statement `if (temp > 70)` will be executed first, and since it is true, the message "warm" will be printed out. *The test `if (temp > 90)` will never be executed.* This is an example of a logical error in a program.

If the statements are restructured as follows, they work correctly:

```
if (temp > 90)
    System.out.println("hot");
else if (temp > 70)
    System.out.println("warm");
else if (temp < 60)
    System.out.println("cold");
```

PROGRAMMING PITFALLS

Carefully consider the order in which you perform tests in your `if` structures to avoid creating incorrect branches.

The Conditional Operator

The **conditional operator** (`?:`) is essentially a compact `if`/`else` structure. It is a **ternary operator**, which means that it takes three arguments that together form a conditional expression. The first argument is a `boolean` expression, whose result must be either `true` or `false`. The second argument, which follows the question mark (`?`), is the value of the operation if the condition is `true`. The third argument, which follows the colon (`:`), is the value of the operation if the condition is `false`. For example, the `if/else` structure

```
if ( grade > 70 )
    System.out.println( "Passed");
else
    System.out.println( "Failed");
```

could also be written with the conditional operator as follows:

```
System.out.println( grade > 70 ? "Passed" : "Failed");
```

The precedence of the conditional operator is very low, ranking after all relational and logical operators and before assignment operators, so the expression `grade > 70` is evaluated as a `boolean` result before the conditional operator is evaluated.

The `switch` Structure

The `switch` structure is another form of selection. It permits a programmer to select a particular code block to execute based on the value of a single integer or character expression. The general form of a `switch` structure is as follows:

```
switch (switch_expr) {

    case case_selector_1:
        Statement 1;          //
        Statement 2;          // Block 1
        ...                   //
        break;
    case case_selector_2:
        Statement 1;          //
        Statement 2;          // Block 2
        ...                   //
        break;
    ...
    default:
        Statement 1;          //
        Statement 2;          // Block n
        ...                   //
        break;
}
```

When a `switch` structure is encountered, Java evaluates the value of *switch_expr,* and execution jumps to the case whose selector matches the value of the expression. The program then executes statements in order from that point on until a `break` statement is encountered. When a `break` statement is encountered, execution skips to the first statement after the end of the `switch`.

If the value of *switch_expr* does not match any case expression, the execution will jump to the `default` case if such a case is present. If one is not present, execution continues with the first statement after the end of the `switch`.

For example, consider the simple `switch` structure in the following program:

```
// This program tests the switch structure
import chapman.io.*;
public class TestSwitch {

    // Define the main method
    public static void main(String[] args) {
```

```
int a;

// Create a StdIn object
StdIn in = new StdIn();

// Prompt for an integer
System.out.print("Enter an integer: ");
a = in.readInt();

// Switch
switch (a) {
   case 1:
      System.out.println("Value is 1");
      break;
   case 2:
      System.out.println("Value is 2");
      break;
   default:
      System.out.println("Other than 1 or 2");
      break;
}

System.out.println("After switch");
   }
}
```

If a value of 1 is read into this program, the switch expression a will be 1, so the statements from case 1 until the break will be executed, followed by the first statement after the switch. Similarly, if a value of 2 is read into this program, the switch expression a will be 2, so the statements from case 2 until the break will be executed, followed by the first statement after the switch. If any value other than 1 or 2 is read in, then the statements after default until the break will be executed, followed by the first statement after the switch.

```
C:\book\java\chap3>java TestSwitch
Enter an integer: 1
Value is 1
After switch

C:\book\java\chap3>java TestSwitch
Enter an integer: 2
Value is 2
After switch

C:\book\java\chap3>java TestSwitch
Enter an integer: 3
Other than 1 or 2
After switch
```

Note that the break statements are necessary for the proper operation of the switch structure. If they are missing, then execution will continue from the selected case through to the end of the switch. If the switch structure in the previous program did not have the break statements:

```
switch (a) {
   case 1:
      System.out.println("Value is 1");
   case 2:
```

```
            System.out.println("Value is 2");
        default:
            System.out.println("Other than 1 or 2");
    }
```

then the results would have been

```
C:\book\java\chap3>java TestSwitch
Enter an integer: 1
Value is 1
Value is 2
Other than 1 or 2
After switch

C:\book\java\chap3>java TestSwitch
Enter an integer: 2
Value is 2
Other than 1 or 2
After switch

C:\book\java\chap3>java TestSwitch
Enter an integer: 3
Other than 1 or 2
After switch
```

Also, note that the case selectors must be *mutually exclusive.* It is an error for the same selector to appear more than once in a single structure.

GOOD PROGRAMMING PRACTICE

The switch structure may be used to select among *mutually exclusive* options based on the results of a single integer or character expression.

The switch structure is never really necessary, since any selection that can be represented by a switch can also be represented by a cascaded if/else structure. For example, the switch in the previous program could be rewritten as follows:

```
if (a == 1)
    System.out.println("Value is 1");
else if (a == 2)
    System.out.println("Value is 2");
else
    System.out.println("Other than 1 or 2");
```

The switch structure is just a limited form of the cascaded if/else structure. However, some programmers prefer the switch structure for stylistic reasons.

PROGRAMMING PITFALLS

Be sure to include break statements in each case of a switch structure, so that only the statements in that case are executed when the case is selected.

PRACTICE!

This quiz provides a quick check to see if you have understood the concepts introduced in Sections 3.1 through 3.4. If you have trouble with the quiz, reread the sections, ask your instructor, or discuss the material with a fellow student. The answers to this quiz are found in the back of the book.

1. Suppose that the `double` variables a, b, and c contain the values -10., 0.1, and 2.1, respectively, and that the `boolean` variable b1, b2, and b3 contain the values `true`, `false`, and `false`, respectively. Is each of the following expressions legal or illegal? If an expression is legal, what will its result be?

   a. `a > b || b > c;`
   b. `(!a) || b1`
   c. `b1 & !b2`
   d. `a < b == b < c`
   e. `b1 || b2 && b3`
   f. `b1 | b2 && b3`

Write Java statements that perform the following functions:

2. If x is greater than or equal to zero, then assign the square root of x to variable `sqrtX` and print out the result. Otherwise, print out an error message about the argument of the square root function, and set `sqrtX` to zero.

3. A variable `fun` is calculated by dividing variable `numerator` by variable `denominator`. If the absolute value of `denominator` is less than 1.0e-30, write "Divide by zero error." Otherwise, calculate and print out `fun`.

4. The cost per mile for a rented vehicle is \$0.50 for the first 100 miles, \$0.30 for the next 200 miles, and \$0.20 for all miles in excess of 300 miles. Write Java statements that determine the total cost and the average cost per mile for a given number of miles (stored in variable `distance`).

Examine the following Java statements. Are they correct or incorrect? If they are correct, what is output by them? If they are incorrect, what is wrong with them?

5.
```
if (volts > 125)
    System.out.println("WARNING: High voltage on line.");
if (volts < 105)
    System.out.println("WARNING: Low voltage on line.");
else
    System.out.println("Line voltage is within tolerances.");
```

6.
```
double i = 3., j = 5., k;
k = i > j ? i / j : j / i;
System.out.println("k = " + k);
```

7.
```
double a = 2 * Math.PI;
double b;
switch( a ) {
    case 1:
        b = Math.sqrt(a);
        break;
    case 2:
        b = Math.pow(a,3);
        break;
    default
        b = a;
        break;
}
```

PRACTICE!

```
8. if (temperature > 37.)
     System.out.println("Human body temperature exceeded.");
   else if (temperature > 100.)
     System.out.println("Boiling point of water exceeded.");
```

PROFESSIONAL SUCCESS: RAPID PROTOTYPING

The program design process described in this chapter is very useful for creating well thought-out working programs. However, the process of decomposition and stepwise refinement can sometimes be very difficult. Suppose that you break a program down into classes and methods, but you don't know how to implement the function to be performed by one of the methods. What do you do then?

If you don't know how to perform some function, write a quick prototype program that performs *only* that function, and play with it until you get satisfactory results. Once you clearly understand what you want to do, go back to the stepwise refinement process of the original program and continue from there.

In the real world, such *rapid prototyping* is often faster and more efficient than trying to get everything exactly right on paper before writing the first line of code. This is especially true when the program is performing a function that you have never done before.

However, be careful not to incorporate the rapid prototype code directly into your final program. The prototype is a learning experience. When you rewrite the code for the final program, you will do a much better job because you now know exactly what you want to do.

SUMMARY

- Pseudocode is a hybrid mixture of Java and English used to express programming thoughts without worrying about the details of Java syntax.
- The relational operators (>, >=, <, <=, ==, !=) compare two numerical operands, and produce a `boolean` result based on that comparison.
- The logical operators (&&, &, ||, |, ^, !) accept one or two `boolean` operands and produce a `boolean` result based on the values of the operands. The results of the operations are given in Table 3-2.
- The hierarchy of Java operations is summarized in Table 3-3.
- Selection structures are Java statements that permit a program to select and execute specific sections of code (statements or compound statements) while skipping other sections of code.
- The `if` selection structure executes a code block if its condition is `true`, and skips the code block if its condition is `false`.
- The `if/else` selection structure executes one code block if its condition is `true`, and another code block if its condition is `false`.
- The Java compiler always associates an `else` clause with the most recent `if`, unless braces are used to force the association of the `else` clause with a specific `if` statement.
- The `switch` selection structure allows a program to select a set of statements to execute based on the value of an integer control expression.

- The conditional operator (`?:`) is essentially a compact `if/else` structure that selects the value of one of two possible expressions, depending on the result of a `boolean` control expression.

APPLICATIONS: SUMMARY OF GOOD PROGRAMMING PRACTICES

The following guidelines introduced in this Chapter will help you to develop good programs:

1. Follow the steps of the program design process to produce reliable, understandable Java programs.
2. Always indent the body of any structure by three or more spaces to improve the readability of the code.
3. When working with floating-point values, it is a good idea to replace tests for equality with tests for near equality to avoid improper results due to cumulative round-off errors.
4. Use braces in nested `if` structures to make your intentions clear, and avoid dangling `else` clauses.
5. The `switch` structure may be used to select among *mutually exclusive* options, based on the results of a single integer or character expression.
6. Be sure to include `break` statements in each `case` of a `switch` structure so that only the statements within that `case` are executed when the case is selected.

KEY TERMS

algorithm	`if/else` structure	selection
alpha release	logical operator	structure
beta release	null statement	structured program
`break` statement	pseudocode	`switch` structure
compound statement	relational operator	top-down design
`if` structure	repetition	unit testing

Problems

1. The tangent function is defined as $\tan \theta = \sin \theta / \cos \theta$. This expression can be evaluated to solve for the tangent as long as the magnitude of $\cos \theta$ is not too near to zero. (If $\cos \theta$ is 0, evaluating the equation for $\tan \theta$ will produce the non-numerical value `Inf`.) Assume that θ is given in degrees, and write Java statements to evaluate $\tan \theta$ as long as the magnitude of $\cos \theta$ is greater than or equal to 10^{-20}. If the magnitude of $\cos \theta$ is less than 10^{-20}, write out an error message instead.

2. Which of the following expressions are legal in Java? If an expression is legal, evaluate it.
   a. `5.5 >= 5`
   b. `20 > 20`
   c. `!(6 > 5)`
   d. `15 <= 'A'`
   e. `true > false`
   f. `35 / 17. > 35 / 17`
   g. `17.5 && (3.3 > 2)`

3. The following Java statements are intended to alert a user to dangerously high oral thermometer readings (values are in degrees Fahrenheit). Are they in the correct order? If they are not, explain why and correct them.

```
if ( temp < 97.5 )
    System.out.println("Temperature below normal");
else if ( temp > 97.5 )
    System.out.println("Temperature normal");
else if ( temp > 99.5 )
    System.out.println("Temperature slightly high");
else if ( temp > 103.0 )
    System.out.println("Temperature dangerously high");
```

4. The cost of sending a package by an express delivery service is $10.00 for the first two pounds and $3.75 for each pound or fraction thereof over two pounds. If the package weighs more than 70 pounds, a $10.00 excess weight surcharge is added to the cost. No package over 100 pounds will be accepted. Write a program that accepts the weight of a package in pounds and computes the cost of mailing the package. Be sure to handle the case of overweight packages.

5. Modify program `QuadraticEquation` to treat test for near equality instead of equality. The discriminant should be considered to be equal to zero if $|b^2 - 4ac| < 10^{-14}$.

6. The inverse sine method `Math.asin(x)` is only defined for the range $-1.0 \leq x \leq 1.0$. If x is outside this range, an error will occur when the function is evaluated. The following Java statements calculate the inverse sine of a number if it is in the proper range and print an error message if it is not. Assume that x and `inverseSine` are both type `double`. Is the code correct or incorrect? If it is incorrect, explain why and correct it.

```
if ( Math.abs(x) <= 1. )
    inverseSine = Math.asin(x);
else
    System.out.println(x + " is out of range!");
```

7. What is wrong with the following code segment?

```
switch (n) {
   case 1:
       System.out.println("Number is 1");
   case 2:
       System.out.println("Number is 2");
       break;
   default:
       System.out.println("Number is not 1 or 2");
       break;
}
```

8. Write a Java program to evaluate the function

$$y(x) = \ln\frac{1}{1-x}$$

for any user-specified value of x, where ln is the natural logarithm (logarithm to the base e). Note that the natural logarithm is only defined for positive values; when an illegal value of x is entered, tell the user and terminate the program.

9. **Refraction** When a ray of light passes from a region with an index of refraction n_1 into a region with a different index of refraction n_2, the light ray is bent. (See Figure 3.9.) The angle at which the light is bent is given by *Snell's Law*

$$n_1 \sin\theta_1 = n_2 \sin\theta_2 , \qquad\qquad (3\text{-}20)$$

where θ_1 is the angle of incidence of the light in the first region, θ_2 is the angle of incidence of the light in the second region, and n_1 and n_2 are the indices of refraction for the first and second regions, respectively. Using Snell's Law, it is possible to predict the angle of incidence of a light ray in Region 2 if the angle of incidence θ_1 in Region 1 and the indices of refraction n_1 and n_2 are known. The equation to perform this calculation is

Figure 3.9. A ray of light bends as it passes from one medium into another one. (a) If the ray of light passes from a region with a low index of refraction into a region with a higher index of refraction, the ray of light bends more towards the vertical. (b) If the ray of light passes from a region with a high index of refraction into a region with a lower index of refraction, the ray of light bends away from the vertical.

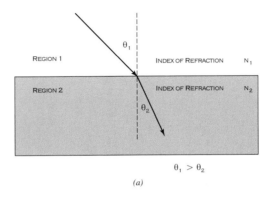

$\theta_1 > \theta_2$

(a)

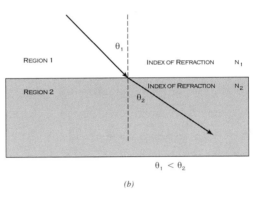

$\theta_1 < \theta_2$

(b)

$$\theta_2 = \sin^{-1}\left(\frac{n_1}{n_2}\sin\theta_1\right). \qquad (3\text{-}21)$$

Write a Java program to calculate the angle of incidence (in degrees) of a light ray in Region 2 given the angle of incidence θ_1 in Region 1 and the indices of refraction n_1 and n_2. (*Note:* If $n_1 > n_2$, then for some angles θ_1, Equation (3-20) will have no real solution, because the absolute value of the quantity $\left(\frac{n_1}{n_2}\sin\theta_1\right)$ will be greater than 1.0. When this occurs, all light is reflected back into Region 1, and no light passes into Region 2 at all. Your program must be able to recognize and properly handle this condition.) Test your program by running it for the following two cases:

a. $n_1 = 1.0, n_2 = 1.7$, and $\theta_1 = 45°$.
b. $n = 1.7, n_2 = 1.0$, and $\theta_1 = 45°$.

4

Repetition Structures

This chapter focuses on a different type of structure that allows us to control the order in which Java statements are executed: **repetition structures**, or **loops**. Repetition structures are Java structures that permit us to execute a sequence of statements more than once. There are three basic forms of repetition structures: **while** loops, **do/while** loops, and **for** loops. The first two types of loops repeat a sequence of statements an indefinite number of times until some specified control condition becomes false. In contrast, the for loops repeat a sequence of statements a specified number of times, and the number of repetitions is known before the loop starts.

4.1 THE while LOOP

A while **loop** is a statement or block of statements that are repeated indefinitely as long as some condition is satisfied. The general form of a while loop in Java is

```
while ( boolean_expr )
    statement;
```

or, with a compound statement,

```
while ( boolean_expr ) {
    statement 1;
    statement 2;
    ...
}
```

SECTIONS

- 4.1 The while Loop
- 4.2 The do/while Loop
- 4.3 The for Loop
- 4.4 Formatting Output Data
- 4.5 Example Problem
- 4.6 More on Debugging Java Programs
- Summary
- Key Terms

OBJECTIVES

After reading this chapter, you should be able to:

- To learn how to use while and do/ while loops
- To learn how to use for loops
- To learn how to use the continue and break statements
- To learn how to create formatted output using the chapman.io.Fmt class

When a while loop is encountered, Java evaluates the boolean expression. If *boolean_expr* is true, Java executes the statement(s) in the loop body. It then evaluates *boolean_expr* again. If it is still true, the statement is executed again. This process is repeated until the expression becomes false. When the expression becomes false, execution skips to the first statement after the loop. Note that if *boolean_expr* is false the first time the expression is evaluated, the statement will never be executed at all! The operation of a while loop is illustrated in Figure 4.1.

As an example of while loops, consider the following code:

```
k = 3;
while (k < 5) {
    System.out.print(" " + k);
    k++;
}
```

When this loop is first executed, k is equal to 3. The boolean expression k < 5 is true, so the statements in the block are executed, writing out k and incrementing its value to 4. Then the boolean expression evaluated again. Since k < 5 is still true, the statements in the block are executed again, writing out k and incrementing its value to 5. Then the boolean expression evaluated again. This time, k < 5 is false, so execution skips to the first statement following the loop. The resulting output is as follows:

```
3 4
```

On the other hand, the following loop is never executed at all, because the boolean expression is false when loop is first reached:

```
k = 5;
while ( k < 5 ) {
    System.out.print(" " + k);
    k++;
}
```

Figure 4.1. The structure of a while loop. Note that the boolean expression is evaluated *first*, and the statement(s) are only executed if the expression is true.

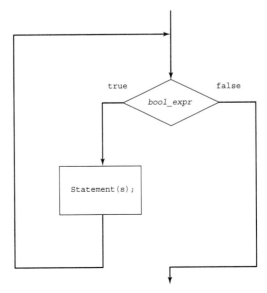

The way that `while` loops are defined in Java produces a nasty trap for programmers, one that you will probably stumble into several times as you learn the language. A typical Java `while` loop might be written as follows:

```
x = 4;
while ( x < 10 )
   x += 4;
```

Note that *there is no semicolon after the* `while`. That is, the `while` structure is not terminated until after the loop body. If we make a mistake and place a semicolon after the `while`, the statements would be:

```
x = 4;
while ( x < 10 );
   x += 4;
```

Unfortunately, this error creates a disaster. A semicolon by itself represents a **null statement**, which is a statement that does nothing. Recall that Java will happily accept multiple statements on a single line. In this case, the semicolon will create a null statement as the body of the loop, and the original statement x += 4; will be *outside* of the loop. In other words, it is as though we wrote the following code:

```
x = 4;
while ( x < 10 )
   ;
x += 4;
```

The Java compiler will compile this program with no warnings, and when the program executes, it will go into an infinite loop! Since the null statement never changes x, x will always be less than 10, and the loop will execute forever.

What makes this bug particularly dangerous is that the compiler gives no warning that anything is wrong. The program executes and runs, but produces an infinite loop. And of course, the error is very hard to spot unless you are specifically looking for it.

PROGRAMMING PITFALLS

Adding a semicolon after a `while` statement can produce a logical error. Java will compile and execute the program, but the program may go into an infinite loop.

We will now show an example statistical analysis program that is implemented using a `while` loop.

EXAMPLE 4-1: STATISTICAL ANALYSIS

It is very common in science and engineering to work with large sets of numbers, each of which is a measurement of some particular property that we are interested in. A simple example would be the grades on the first test in a college course. Each grade would be a measurement of how much a particular student has learned in the course to date.

Much of the time, we are not interested in looking closely at every single measurement that we make. Instead, we want to summarize the results of a set of measurements with a few numbers that tell us a lot about the overall data set. Two such numbers are the *average*, or *arithmetic mean*, and the *standard deviation* of the set of measurements. The average or arithmetic mean of a set of numbers is defined as

$$\bar{x} = \frac{1}{N} \sum_{i=1}^{N} x_i ,$$

(4-1)

where x_i is sample i out of N samples. The standard deviation of a set defined as

$$s = \sqrt{\frac{N \sum_{i=1}^{N} x_i^2 - \left(\sum_{i=1}^{N} x_i \right)^2}{N(N-1)}}. \qquad (4\text{-}2)$$

Standard deviation is a measure of the amount of scatter on the measurements; the greater the standard deviation is, the more scattered the points in the data set are.

Implement an algorithm that reads in a set of measurements and calculates the mean and the standard deviation of the input data set.

SOLUTION

This program must be able to read in an arbitrary number of measurements and then calculate the mean and standard deviation of those measurements. We will use a `while` loop to accumulate the input measurements before performing the calculations.

When all of the measurements have been read, we must have some way of telling the program that there are no more data to enter. For now, we will assume that all the input measurements are either positive or zero, and we will use a negative input value as a *flag* to indicate that there are no more data to read. If a negative value is entered, then the program will stop reading input values and will calculate the mean and standard deviation of the data set.

1. **State the problem**. Since we assume that the input numbers must be positive or zero, a proper statement of this problem would be to *calculate the average and the standard deviation of a set of measurements, assuming that all of the measurements are either positive or zero and that we do not know in advance how many measurements are included in the data set. A negative input value will mark the end of the set of measurements.*

2. **Define the inputs and outputs**. The inputs required by this program are an unknown number of positive or zero `double` numbers. The outputs from this program are a printout of the mean and the standard deviation of the input data set. In addition, we will print out the number of data points input to the program, since this is a useful check that the input data was read correctly.

3. **Decompose the program into classes and their associated methods**. Again, there will be a single class, and only the `main` method within that class. We will call the class `Stats` and make it a subclass of the root class `Object`.

4. **Design the algorithm that you intend to implement for each method**. The `main` method can be broken down into three major sections, whose functions are accumulating input data, processing, and output:

```
Accumulate the input data
Calculate the mean and standard deviation
Write out the mean, standard deviation, and number of points
```

The first major step of the program is to accumulate the input data. To do this, we will have to prompt the user to enter the desired numbers. When the numbers are entered, we will have to keep track of the number of values entered, plus the sum and the sum of the squares of those values. The pseudocode for these steps is as follows:

```
Initialize n, sumX, and sumX2 to 0
Prompt user for first number
Read in x
while (x >= 0)
    ++n;
    sumX ← sumX + x;
    sumX2 ← sumX2 + x*x;
    Prompt user for next number
    Read in next x
End of while
```

Note that we have to read in the first value before the `while` loop starts so that the `while` loop can have a value to test the first time it executes.

Next, we must calculate the mean and standard deviation. The pseudocode for this step is just the Java versions of Equations (4-1) and (4-2) and is the following:

```
xBar ← sumX / n
stdDev ← Math.sqrt((n*sumX2 - sumX*sumX) / (n*(n-1)))
```

Finally, we must write out the results:

```
Write out the mean value xBar
Write out the standard deviation stdDev
Write out the number of input data points n
```

5. **Turn the algorithm into Java statements**. The final Java program is shown in Figure 4.2, with the `while` loop shown in boldface.

6. **Test the program**. To test this program, we will calculate the answers by hand for a simple data set and then compare the answers to the results of the program. If we used three input values: 3, 4, and 5, then the mean and standard deviation would be the following:

$$\bar{x} = \frac{1}{N}\sum_{i=1}^{N} x_i = \frac{1}{3}\,12 = 4$$

$$s = \sqrt{\frac{N\sum_{i=1}^{N} x_i^2 - \left(\sum_{i=1}^{N} x_i\right)^2}{N(N-1)}} = 1$$

When the foregoing values are entered into the program, the results are as follows, with the input in boldface:

```
C:\book\java\chap4>java Stats
Enter first value: 3
Enter next value: 4
Enter next value: 5
Enter next value: -1
The mean of this data set is: 4.0
The standard deviation is: 1.0
The number of data points is: 3
```

The program gives the correct answers for our test data set.

```
/*
   Purpose:
      To calculate mean and the standard deviation of an input
      data set containing an arbitrary number of input values.

   Record of revisions:
      Date          Programmer        Description of change
      ====          ==========        =====================
      3/29/98       S. J. Chapman     Original code
*/
import chapman.io.*;
public class Stats {

   // Define the main method
   public static void main(String[] args) {

      // Declare variables, and define each variable
      int n = 0;            // The number of input samples.
      double stdDev = 0;  // The standard deviation of the input samples.
      double sumX = 0;    // The sum of the input values.
      double sumX2 = 0;   // The sum of the squares of the input values.
      double x = 0;       // An input data value.
      double xBar = 0;    // The average of the input samples.

      // Create a StdIn object
      StdIn in = new StdIn();

      // Get first input value
      System.out.print("Enter first value: ");
      x = in.readDouble();

      // while loop to accumulate input values.
      while (x >= 0) {

         // Accumulate sums.
         ++n;
         sumX += x;
         sumX2 += x*x;

         // Read next value
         System.out.print("Enter next value: ");
         x = in.readDouble();
      }

      // Calculate the mean and standard deviation
      xBar = sumX / n;
      stdDev = Math.sqrt((n * sumX2 - sumX*sumX) / (n * (n-1)));

      // Tell user.
      System.out.println("The mean of this data set is: " + xBar);
      System.out.println("The standard deviation is: " + stdDev);
      System.out.println("The number of data points is: " + n);
   }
}
```

Figure 4.2.   Program to calculate the mean and standard deviation of a set of nonnegative real numbers.

In the previous example, we failed to follow the design process completely. This failure has left the program with a fatal flaw! Did you spot it?

We have failed because *we did not completely test the program for all possible types of inputs.* Look at the example once again. If we enter either no numbers or only one number, then we will be dividing by zero in the equations! The division-by-zero error will cause the program to produce an `Inf` (standing for infinity) result. We need to modify the program to detect this problem, inform the user of it, and stop gracefully.

A modified version of the program called `Stats1` is shown in Figure 4.3. Here, we check to see if there are enough input values before performing the calculations. If not, the program will print out an intelligent error message and quit. Test the modified program for yourself.

```
/*
   Purpose:
      To calculate mean and the standard deviation of an input
      data set containing an arbitrary number of input values.

   Record of revisions:
      Date          Programmer            Description of change
      ====          ==========            =====================
      3/29/98    S. J. Chapman            Original code
   1. 3/29/98    S. J. Chapman            Correct divide-by-0 error if 0 or
                                          1 input values given.
*/
import chapman.io.*;
public class Stats1 {

   // Define the main method
   public static void main(String[] args) {

      // Declare variables, and define each variable
      int n = 0;              // The number of input samples.
      double stdDev = 0;   // The standard deviation of the input samples.
      double sumX = 0;        // The sum of the input values.
      double sumX2 = 0;       // The sum of the squares of the input values.
      double x = 0;           // An input data value.
      double xBar = 0;        // The average of the input samples.

      // Create a StdIn object
      StdIn in = new StdIn();

      // Get first input value
      System.out.print("Enter first value: ");
      x = in.readDouble();

      // while loop to accumulate input values.
      while (x >= 0) {

         // Accumulate sums.
         ++n;
         sumX += x;
         sumX2 += x*x;

         // Read next value
         System.out.print("Enter next value: ");
         x = in.readDouble();
      }

      // Check to see if we have enough input data.
      if (n < 2)
         System.out.println("At least 2 values must be entered!");
      else {
         // There is enough information, so
         // calculate the mean and standard deviation
         xBar = sumX / n;
         stdDev = Math.sqrt((n * sumX2 - sumX*sumX) / (n * (n-1)));
```

Figure 4.3.   (cont.)

```
        // Tell user.
        System.out.println("The mean of this data set is: " + xBar);
        System.out.println("The standard deviation is: " + stdDev);
        System.out.println("The number of data points is: " + n);
      }
    }
  }
```

Figure 4.3.   A modified statistical analysis program that avoids the divide-by-zero problems inherent in program Stats.

4.2 THE do/while LOOP

There is another form of the while loop in Java, called the **do/while loop**. The do/while structure has the following form:

```
do {
   Statement 1;
   ...
   Statement n;
} while( boolean_expr )
```

In this loop, statements 1 through n will be executed, and then the boolean expression will be tested. If the boolean expression is true, then statements 1 through n will be executed again. This process will be repeated until the boolean expression becomes false. When the bottom of the loop is reached and the boolean expression is false, the program will execute the first statement after the end of the loop. The operation of a do/while loop is illustrated in Figure 4.4.

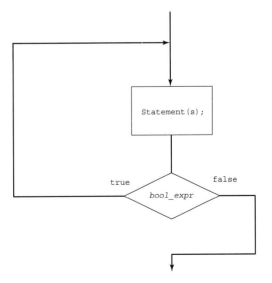

Figure 4.4.   The structure of a do/while loop. Note that the statement(s) are executed *first*, and then boolean expression is evaluated. The statement(s) in this loop will be executed *at least once* even if the boolean expression is false before the loop starts.

The major difference between the while loop and the do/while loop is that *the test for the* while *loop is executed at the **top** of the loop, while the test for the* do/ while *loop is executed at the **bottom** of the loop.* Because of this difference, the statements in a do/while loop will always be executed at least once.

GOOD PROGRAMMING PRACTICE

Use a while or do/while loop to repeat a set of statements indefinitely until a condition becomes false. Use a while loop in cases where you wish to perform the loop repetition test at the top of the loop, and use a do/while loop in cases where you wish to perform the loop repetition test at the bottom of the loop.

4.3 THE for LOOP

In the Java language, a loop that executes a block of statements a specified number of times is called a **for loop**. The for loop structure has the form

```
for ( index = initExpr; continueExpr; incrementExpr )
    Statement;
```

or

```
for ( index = initExpr; continueExpr; incrementExpr ) {
    Statement 1;
    ...
    Statement n;
}
```

where the expressions within the parentheses control the operation of the loop. The *index* is an integer whose value varies each time the loop is executed. This value is initialized to the value of *initExpr* when the loop first starts to execute. The *continueExpr* is then evaluated. If this expression is true, then the statement(s) in the body of the loop are executed. After the statement(s) are executed, the *incrementExpr* is executed to increment the value of the loop index, and *continueExpr* is reevaluated. If the expression is still true, then the statement(s) are executed again. This process is repeated until the *continueExpr* is false, at which time execution continues with the first statement following the loop. The operation of a for loop is illustrated in Figure 4.5.

A simple example of the for loop is shown below.

```
for ( int i = 1; i <= 2; i++ )
    System.out.println("i = " + i);
```

The index variable in this loop is i. When the loop first starts, i is initialized to 1, and the expression i <= 2 is evaluated. Since this expression is true, the print statement is executed. After the statement is executed, i++ is evaluated, increasing i to 2, and the expression i <= 2 is evaluated again. Since this expression is still true, the print statement is executed again. After the statement is executed, i++ is evaluated, increasing i to 3, and the expression i <= 2 is evaluated a third time. The expression is

Figure 4.5. The structure of a for loop

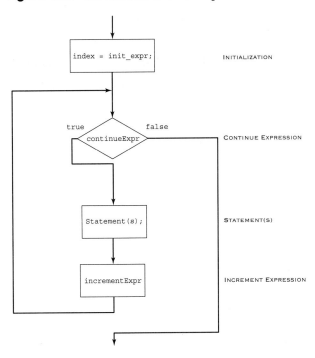

false this time, so execution transfers to the first statement after the loop. The output of this loop is the following:

```
i = 1
i = 2
```

Let's look at a number of specific examples to make the operation of the for loop clearer. First, consider the following example:

```
for ( int count = 1; count <= 10; count++ ) {
    Statement 1;
    ...
    Statement n;
}
```

In this case, statements 1 through *n* will be executed 10 times. The index variable count will be 1 the first time, 2 the second time, and so on. The index variable will be 10 on the last pass through the statements. At the end of the tenth pass, the index variable count will be increased to 11. Since the expression count <= 10 is now false, control will transfer to the first statement after the loop.

Second, consider the following example:

```
for ( int count = 1; count <= 10; count += 2 ) {
    Statement 1;
    ...
    Statement n;
}
```

In this case, statements 1 through n will be executed five times. The index variable count will be 1 the first time, 3 the second time, and so on. The index variable will be 9 on the fifth and last pass through the statements. At the end of the fifth pass, the index variable `count` will be increased to 11. Since the expression `count <= 10` is `false`, control will transfer to the first statement after the loop.

Third, consider the following example:

```
for ( int count = 10; count <= 1; count++ ) {
    Statement 1;
    ...
    Statement n;
}
```

Here, *statements 1 through* n *will never be executed*, since the expression `count <= 1` is `false` when the continue expression is first evaluated. Instead, control will transfer to the first statement after the loop.

Finally, consider the example:

```
for ( int count = 3; count >= -3; count -= 2 ) {
    Statement 1;
    ...
    Statement n;
}
```

In this case, statements 1 through n will be executed 4 times. The index variable count will be 3 the first time, 1 the second time, −1 the third time, and −3 the fourth time. At the end of the fourth pass, the index variable `count` will be decreased to −5. Since the expression `count >= -3` is now `false`, control will transfer to the first statement after the loop.

EXAMPLE 4-2: THE FACTORIAL FUNCTION

We will illustrate the operation of a `for` loop by creating one to calculate the value of factorial function. The factorial function is defined as

$$n! = \begin{cases} 1 & n = 0 \\ n \times (n-1) \times (n-2) \times \ldots \times 3 \times 2 \times 1 & n > 0 \end{cases}. \tag{4-3}$$

The Java code to calculate n factorial for positive value of n would be the following:

```
nFactorial = 1;
for (int count = 1; count <= n; count++)
    nFactorial *= count;
```

Suppose that we wish to calculate the value of 5 !. If n is 5, this loop will be executed 5 times, with the variable count taking on values of 1, 2, 3, 4, and 5 in the successive loops. The resulting value of nFactorial will be $1 \times 2 \times 3 \times 4 \times 5 = 120$.

EXAMPLE 4-3: CALCULATING THE DAY OF YEAR

The *day of year* is the number of days (including the current day) that have elapsed since the beginning of a given year. It is a number in the range 1 to 365 for ordinary years, and 1 to 366 for leap years. Write a Java program that accepts a day, month, and year and calculates the day of year corresponding to that date.

SOLUTION

To determine the day of year, this program will need to sum up the number of days in each month preceding the current month, and add that to the number of elapsed days in the current month. A `for` loop will be used to perform this sum. Since the number of days in each month varies, it is necessary to determine the correct number of days to add for each month. A `switch` structure will be used to determine the proper number of days to add for each month.

During a leap year, an extra day must be added to the day of year for any month after February. This extra day accounts for the presence of February 29 in the leap year. Therefore, to perform the day of year calculation correctly, we must determine which years are leap years. In the Gregorian calendar, leap years are determined by the following rules:

1. Years evenly divisible by 400 are leap years.
2. Years evenly divisible by 100 but *not* by 400 are not leap years.
3. All years divisible by 4 but *not* by 100 are leap years.
4. All other years are not leap years.

We will use the modulus operator (%) to determine whether a year is evenly divisible by a given number. If the result of the modulus operation is zero, then the year is evenly divisible.

1. **State the problem**. Write a Java program that accepts a day, month, and year and calculates the day of year corresponding to that date, taking into account leap years.
2. **Define the inputs and outputs**. The inputs required by this program are the month, day, and year to be translated. The output from this program is the day of year corresponding to that date.
3. **Decompose the program into classes and their associated methods**. Again, there will be a single class, and only the `main` method within that class. We will call the class `DayOfYear` and make it a subclass of the root class `Object`.
4. **Design the algorithm that you intend to implement for each method**. The `main` method can be broken down into four major sections as follows:

    ```
    Read the month, day, and year
    Check to see if this is a leap year
    Add up the days until now in current year
    Write out the day of year
    ```

    The first major step of the program is to read the month, day, and year. To do this, we will have to prompt the user to enter the desired numbers. The pseudocode for this step is the following:

    ```
    Prompt user for the month
    Read in month
    Prompt user for the day
    Read in day
    Prompt user for the year
    Read in year
    ```

    Next, we must determine if this is a leap year by using the algorithm previously described. The pseudocode for this step is:

```
      if year is divisible by 400
          leapDay ← 1;
      else if year is divisible by 100
          leapDay ← 0;
      else if year is divisible by 4
          leapDay ← 1;
      else
          leapDay ← 0;
```

Then, we must add up the days in the month so far plus all the days in all months before the current one. The pseudocode for this step is:

```
dayOfYear ← day;
for ( int i = 1; i <= month-1; i++ ) {

    switch (i) {
        case 1: case 3: case 5: case 7: case 8:
        case 10: case 12:
            dayOfYear ← dayOfYear + 31;
            break;
        case 4: case 6: case 9: case 11:
            dayOfYear ← dayOfYear + 30;
            break;
        case 2:
            dayOfYear ← dayOfYear + 28 + leapDay;
    }
  }
}
```

Finally, we must write out the results:

Write out the current day of year

5. **Turn the algorithm into Java statements**. The final Java program is shown in Figure 4.6.

```
/*
  Purpose:
      This program calculates the day of year corresponding to a speci-
          fied date. It illustrates the use for loops and the switch struc-
          ture.

  Record of revisions:
      Date        Programmer         Description of change
      ====        ==========         =====================
      3/30/98    S. J. Chapman      Original code
*/
import chapman.io.*;
public class DayOfYear {

    // Define the main method
    public static void main(String[] args) {

        // Declare variables, and define each variable
        int day;              // Day (dd)
        int dayOfYear;        // Day of year
        int leapDay;          // Extra day for leap year
        int month;            // Month (mm)
        int year;             // Year (yyyy)
```

Figure 4.6. *(cont.)*

```java
    // Create a StdIn object
    StdIn in = new StdIn();

    // Get day, month, and year to convert
    System.out.println("This program calculates the day of year");
    System.out.print("given the current date. ");
    System.out.print("Enter current month (1-12): ");
    month = in.readInt();
    System.out.print("Enter current day(1-31): ");
    day = in.readInt();
    System.out.print("Enter current year (yyyy): ");
    year = in.readInt();

    // Check for leap year, and add extra day if necessary
    if ( year % 400 == 0 )
        leapDay = 1;          // Years divisible by 400 are leap years
    else if ( year % 100 == 0 )
        leapDay = 0;          // Other centuries are not leap years
    else if ( year % 4 == 0 )
        leapDay = 1;          // Otherwise every 4th year is a leap year
    else
        leapDay = 0;          // Other years are not leap years

    // Calculate day of year
    dayOfYear = day;
    for ( int i = 1; i <= month-1; i++ ) {

        // Add days in months from January to last month
        switch (i) {
            case 1: case 3: case 5: case 7: case 8:
            case 10: case 12:
                dayOfYear = dayOfYear + 31;
                break;
            case 4: case 6: case 9: case 11:
                dayOfYear = dayOfYear + 30;
                break;
            case 2:
                dayOfYear = dayOfYear + 28 + leapDay;
        }
    }

    // Tell user
    System.out.println("Day         = " + day);
    System.out.println("Month       = " + month);
    System.out.println("Year        = " + year);
    System.out.println("day of year = " + dayOfYear);
    }
}
```

Figure 4.6. A program to calculate the equivalent day of year from a given day, month, and year.

6. **Test the program**. To test this program, we must test the program with both dates that are in leap years and dates that are not in leap years. We will use the following known results to test the program:

   1. Year 1999 is not a leap year. January 1 must be day of year 1, and December 31 must be day of year 365.

2. Year 2000 is a leap year. January 1 must be day of year 1, and December 31 must be day of year 366.

3. Year 2001 is not a leap year. March 1 must be day of year 60, since January has 31 days, February has 28 days, and this is the first day of March.

Using these test data, the program produces the following results, with inputs appearing in boldface:

```
C:\book\java\chap4>java DayOfYear
This program calculates the day of year
given the current date.  Enter current month (1-12): 1
Enter current day(1-31):     1
Enter current year (yyyy):   1999
Day        = 1
Month      = 1
Year       = 1999
day of year = 1

C:\book\java\chap4>java DayOfYear
This program calculates the day of year
given the current date.  Enter current month (1-12): 12
Enter current day(1-31):     31
Enter current year (yyyy):   1999
Day        = 31
Month      = 12
Year       = 1999
day of year = 365

C:\book\java\chap4>java DayOfYear
This program calculates the day of year
given the current date.  Enter current month (1-12): 1
Enter current day(1-31):     1
Enter current year (yyyy):   2000
Day        = 1
Month      = 1
Year       = 2000
day of year = 1

C:\book\java\chap4>java DayOfYear
This program calculates the day of year
given the current date.  Enter current month (1-12): 12
Enter current day(1-31):     31
Enter current year (yyyy):   2000
Day        = 31
Month      = 12
Year       = 2000
day of year = 366

C:\book\java\chap4>java DayOfYear
This program calculates the day of year
given the current date.  Enter current month (1-12): 3
Enter current day(1-31):     1
Enter current year (yyyy):   2001
Day        = 1
Month      = 3
Year       = 2001
day of year = 60
```

The program gives the correct answers for our test dates in all five test cases.

EXAMPLE 4-4:
STATISTICAL
ANALYSIS

Implement an algorithm that reads in a set of measurements and calculates the mean and the standard deviation of the input data set. Values in the data set can be positive, negative, or zero.

SOLUTION

This program must be able to read in an arbitrary number of measurements, and then calculate the mean and standard deviation of those measurements. Each measurement can be positive, negative, or zero.

Since we cannot use a data value as a flag this time, we will ask the user for the number of input values, and then use a `for` loop to read in those values. This program is shown in Figure 4.7. Note that the `while` loop has been replaced by a `for` loop. Verify its operation for yourself by finding the mean and standard deviation of the following 5 input values: 3., −1., 0., 1., and −2.

```
/*
   Purpose:
      To calculate mean and the standard deviation of an input data set,
      where each input value can be positive negative,or zero.

   Record of revisions:
      Date          Programmer            Description of change
      ====          ==========            =====================
      3/31/98    S. J. Chapman            Original code
*/
import chapman.io.*;
public class Stats2 {

   // Define the main method
   public static void main(String[] args) {

      // Declare variables, and define each variable
      int i;                 // Loop index
      int n = 0;             // The number of input samples.
      double stdDev = 0;     // The standard deviation of the input samples.
      double sumX = 0;       // The sum of the input values.
      double sumX2 = 0;      // The sum of the squares of the input values.
      double x = 0;          // An input data value.
      double xBar = 0;       // The average of the input samples.

      // Create a StdIn object
      StdIn in = new StdIn();

      // Get the number of points to input
      System.out.print("Enter number of points: ");
      n = in.readInt();

      // Check to see if we have enough input data.
      if (n < 2)
         System.out.println("At least 2 values must be entered!");

      else {

         // Loop to read input values.
         for (i = 1; i <= n; i++) {
```

Figure 4.7.   *(cont.)*

```
                  // Read values
                  System.out.print("Enter number: ");
                  x = in.readDouble();

                  // Accumulate sums.
                  sumX += x;
                  sumX2 += x*x;
            }

            // Calculate the mean and standard deviation
            xBar = sumX / n;
            stdDev = Math.sqrt((n * sumX2 - sumX*sumX) / (n * (n-1)));

            // Tell user.
            System.out.println("The mean of this data set is:" + xBar);
            System.out.println("The standard deviation is: " + stdDev);
            System.out.println("The number of data points is: " + n);
        }
    }
}
```

Figure 4.7.   Modified statistical analysis program that works with both positive and input values.

Details of Operation

Now that we have seen examples of a for loop in operation, we will examine some of the important details required to use for loops properly.

1. It is not necessary to indent the body of the for loop as we have just shown. The Java compiler will recognize the loop even if every statement in it starts in column 1. However, the code is much more readable if the body of the for loop is indented, so you should always indent the bodies of your loops.

GOOD PROGRAMMING PRACTICE

Always indent the body of a for loop by three or more spaces to improve the readability of the code.

2. The index variable of a for loop *must not be modified anywhere within the for loop*. Since the index variable is used to control the repetitions in the loop, changing it could produce unexpected results. In the worst case, modifying the index variable could produce an *infinite loop* that never completes. Consider the following example:

```
for ( i = 1; i <= 10; i++) {
    System.out.println("i = " + i);
    i = 5;
}
```

If i is reset to 5 every time through the loop, the loop will never end, because the index variable can never be greater than 10! This loop will run forever unless the program containing it is killed. You should *never* modify the loop index within the body of a for loop.

PROGRAMMING PITFALL

Never modify the value of a `for` loop index variable while inside the loop.

3. Never use `float` or `double` variables as the index variable in a `for` loop. If you do, roundoff errors can sometimes cause unexpected results. For example, consider the following program code:

```
// This program tests a double index in a for loop
public class TestDoubleIndex

   // Define the main method
   public static void main(String[] args) {

      // Set up for loop
      for ( double i = 0.1; i < 1.0; i += 0.1) {
         System.out.println("i = " + i);
      }
   }
}
```

This loop *should* execute nine times, with the results being i = 0.1, 0.2, ..., 0.9. In the next pass through the loop, i would be 1.0, so the condition i < 1.0 should be `false`, and the loop would terminate. However, when we execute this program the results are as follows:

```
C:\book\java\chap4>java TestDoubleIndex
i = 0.1
i = 0.2
i = 0.30000000000000004
i = 0.4
i = 0.5
i = 0.6
i = 0.7
i = 0.7999999999999999
i = 0.8999999999999999
i = 0.9999999999999999
```

The loop really executed *ten times,* because round-off errors prevented i from being exactly equal to 1.0 on the tenth pass. This sort of problem can never happen with integer loop indexes.

GOOD PROGRAMMING PRACTICE

Always use integer variables as `for` loop indexes.

4. It is a very common error to use a comma instead of a semicolon to separate the control statements in a `for` structure. This is a syntax error that will be caught by the compiler. For example, the loop

```
for (j = 1; j <= 3, j++) {
   . . .
}
```

will produce the following compiler error:

```
TestFor.java:10: ';' expected.
        for (j = 1; j \<= 3, j++) {
                      ^
1 error
```

Be sure to separate the control statements in a `for` structure with a semicolon.

5. Placing a semicolon after the `for` in a `for` loop produces a logical error. A typical Java `for` loop may be written as follows:

```
for (j = 1; j <= 10; j++)
    statement;
```

Note that *there is no semicolon after the* `for`—the `for` structure is not terminated until after the loop body. If we make a mistake and place a semicolon after the `for`, the statements would be the following:

```
for (j = 1; j <= 10; j++);
    statement;
```

Unfortunately, this creates a serious error *that is not detected by the compiler.* A semicolon by itself represents a **null statement**, which is a statement that does nothing. As with the `while` loop, the semicolon will make a null statement the body of the loop, and the original `statement` will be outside of the loop. In other words, it is as though we wrote the following:

```
for (j = 1; j <= 10; j++)
    ;
statement;
```

The Java compiler will compile this program with no warnings, and when the program executes, it will increment j from 1 to 10 while doing nothing, and afterwards execute `statement` one time only! This is the type of bug known as a logical error.

What makes this bug particularly dangerous is that the compiler gives no warning that anything is wrong. The program executes and runs, but produces the wrong answer. And of course, the error is very hard to spot unless you are specifically looking for it.

Adding a semicolon after a `for` statement can produce a logical error. Java will compile and execute the program, but the program will produce incorrect results.

6. It is possible to design `for` loops that count down as well as up. The following `for` loop executes 3 times with j being 3, 2, and 1 in the successive loops:

```
for (j = 3; j >= 1; j--) {
    . . .
}
```

The `continue` and `break` Statements

There are two additional statements that can be used to control the operation of loops: **continue** and **break**.

If the `continue` statement is executed in the body of a loop, the execution of the body will stop and control will be returned to the top of the loop. The loop index will be incremented, and execution will resume again if the continuation condition is still `true`. An example of the `continue` statement in a `for` loop is shown in the following code:

```
// This program tests the continue statement
public class TestContinue {

    // Define the main method
    public static void main(String[] args) {

        int i;

        // Set up for loop
        for ( i = 1; i <= 5; i++) {
            if ( i == 3 ) continue;
            System.out.println("i = " + i);
        }
        System.out.println("End of loop!");
    }
}
```

When this program is executed, the output is:

```
C:\book\java\chap4>java TestContinue
i = 1
i = 2
i = 4
i = 5
End of loop!
```

Note that the `continue` statement was executed on the iteration when `i` was 3 and that control returned to the top of the loop without executing the output statement.

If the `break` statement is executed in the body of a loop, the execution of the body will stop and control will be transferred to the first executable statement after the loop. An example of the `break` statement in a `for` loop is shown in the following code:

```
// This program tests the break statement
public class TestBreak {
    // Define the main method
    public static void main(String[] args) {

        int i;

        // Set up for loop
        for ( i = 1; i <= 5; i++) {
            if ( i == 3 ) break;
            System.out.println("i = " + i);
        }
        System.out.println("End of loop!");
    }
}
```

When this program is executed, the output is:

```
C:\book\java\chap4>java TestBreak
i = 1
i = 2
End of loop!
```

Note that the `break` statement was executed on the iteration when `i` was 3, and that control transferred to the first executable statement after the loop without executing the output statement.

Both the `continue` and `break` statements work with `while`, `do/while`, and `for` loops.

Nesting Loops

It is possible for one loop to be completely inside another loop. If one loop is completely inside another one, the two loops are called **nested loops**. The following example shows two nested `for` loops used to calculate and write out the product of two integers:

```
// This program tests nested for loops
public class NestedFor {

    // Define the main method
    public static void main(String[] args) {

        int i, j, product;

        for ( i = 1; i <= 3; i++) {
            for ( j = 1; j <= 3; j++) {
                product = i * j;
                System.out.println(i + " * " + j + " = " + product);
            }
        }
    }
}
```

In this example, the outer `for` loop will assign a value of 1 to index variable `i`, and then the inner `for` loop will be executed. The inner `for` loop will be executed 3 times with index variable `j` having values 1, 2, and 3. When the entire inner `for` loop has been completed, the outer `for` loop will assign a value of 2 to index variable `i`, and the inner `for` loop will be executed again. This process repeats until the outer `for` loop has executed three times. The resulting output is

```
1 * 1 = 1
1 * 2 = 2
1 * 3 = 3
2 * 1 = 2
2 * 2 = 4
2 * 3 = 6
3 * 1 = 3
3 * 2 = 6
3 * 3 = 9
```

Note that the inner `for` loop executes completely before the index variable of the outer `for` loop is incremented.

If `for` loops are nested, they must have independent index variables. Otherwise, the inner loop would be modifying the loop variable of the outer loop, causing the outer loop to behave improperly.

Labeled break and continue Statements

If a break statement appears in a nested loop structure, it breaks out of the *innermost loop* only. The outer loops will continue to execute. For example, consider the following program:

```java
public class TestBreak2 {
    // Define the main method
    public static void main(String[] args) {

        int i, j, product;

        for ( i = 1; i <= 3; i++) {
            for ( j = 1; j <= 3; j++) {
                product = i * j;
                if ( j == 3 ) break;
                System.out.println(i + " * " + j + " = " + product);
            }
        }
    }
}
```

This break statement is executed when j is 3. When the break statement is executed, only the *innermost* loop will terminate. The outer loop continues to execute, producing the following results:

```
1 * 1 = 1
1 * 2 = 2
2 * 1 = 2
2 * 2 = 4
3 * 1 = 3
3 * 2 = 6
```

To break out of more than one level of a nested structure, we must use a **labeled break statement**. We must place a **label** on the loop that we wish to break out of, and then specify that label in the break statement.

For example, suppose that we wish to modify the previous program to break out of both loops when the break statement is executed. We would place a label on the outer loop, and then refer to that label in the break statement:

```java
public class TestBreak3 {

    // Define the main method
    public static void main(String[] args) {

        int i, j, product;

        outer: for (i = 1; i <= 3; i++) {
            for (j = 1; j <= 3; j++) {
                product = i * j;
                if (j == 3) break outer;
                System.out.println(i + " * " + j + " = " + product);
            }
        }
        System.out.println("Outside nested loops.");
    }
}
```

When this program is executed, the results are

```
C:\book\java\chap4>java TestBreak3
1 * 1 = 1
1 * 2 = 2
Outside nested loops.
```

The break statement executed when j was equal to 3, and the program broke out of both loops at that time.

Similarly, if a continue statement appears in a nested loop structure, it breaks out of the *innermost* loop only. The outer loops will continue to execute. For example, consider the following program:

```
public class TestContinue2 {

    // Define the main method
    public static void main(String[] args) {

        int i, j, product;

        for ( i = 1; i <= 3; i++) {
            for ( j = 1; j <= 3; j++) {
                product = i * j;
                if ( j == 2 ) continue;
                System.out.println(i + " * " + j + " = " + product);
            }
        }
    }
}
```

This continue statement is executed when j is 2. When the continue statement is executed, the remaining statements in the *innermost* loop will be skipped, and execution continues at the top of the inner loop. The outer loop remains totally unaffected. The results of this program are

```
1 * 1 = 1
1 * 3 = 3
2 * 1 = 2
2 * 3 = 6
3 * 1 = 3
3 * 3 = 9
```

To cause a higher level loop to continue, we must use a **labeled continue statement**. We will place a label on the loop that we wish to continue and then specify that label in the continue statement. For example, the following program causes the *outer* loop to continue each time that j reaches 2 in the inner loop:

```
public class TestContinue3 {

    // Define the main method
    public static void main(String[] args) {

        int i, j, product;

        outer: for ( i = 1; i <= 3; i++) {
            inner: for ( j = 1; j <= 3; j++) {
                product = i * j;
                if ( j == 2 ) continue outer;
                System.out.println(i + " * " + j + " = " +
                product);
            }
        }
    }
}
```

When this program is executed, the results are

```
1 * 1 = 1
2 * 1 = 2
3 * 1 = 3
```

Compare this result to the result of the previous example, where the innermost loop was affected by the `continue` statement.

GOOD PROGRAMMING PRACTICE

Use labeled `break` or `continue` statements to break out of or continue outer loops in a nested loop structure.

PRACTICE!

This quiz provides a quick check to see if you have understood the concepts introduced in Sections 4.1 through 4.3. If you have trouble with the quiz, reread the sections, ask your instructor, or discuss the material with a fellow student. The answers to this quiz are found in the back of the book.

Examine the control parameters of the following `for` loops, and determine how many times each loop will be executed:

1. `for (index = 7; index <= 10; index++)`
2. `for (j = 7; j <= 10; j--)`
3. `for (index = 1; index <= 10; index += 10)`
4. `for (k = 1; k < 10; k++)`
5. `for (counter = -2; counter <= 10; counter += 2)`
6. `for (time = -2; time >= -10; time--)`
7. `for (i = -10; i <= -7; i -= 3)`

Examine the following loops, and determine the value in `ires` at the end of each of the loops. Assume that `ires`, `index`, and all loop variables are integers. How many times does each loop execute?

8.
```
ires = 0;
for (index = 1; index <= 10; index++)
    ires++;
```
9.
```
ires = 0;
for (index = 1; index <= 10; index++)
    ires += index;
```
10.
```
ires = 0; index = 0;
while ( ires < 12 )
    ires += ++index;
```
11.
```
ires = 0; index = 0;
while ( index < 5 )
    ires += ++index;
```
12.
```
ires = 0; index = 0;
do {
    ires += ++index;
} while ( index < 5 );
```
13.
```
ires = 0;
for (index = 1; index <= 6; index++) {
    if ( index == 3 )
        continue;
    ires += index;
}
```

PRACTICE!

14.
```
ires = 0;
for (index = 1; index <= 6; index++) {
   if ( index == 3 )
      break;
   ires += index;
}
```

15.
```
ires = 0;
for (index1 = 1; index1 <= 5; index1++) {
   for (index2 = 1; index2 <= 5; index2++) {
      ires++;
   }
}
```

16.
```
ires = 0;
for (index1 = 1; index1 <= 5; index1++) {
   for (index2 = index1; index2 <= 5; index2++) {
      ires++;
   }
}
```

17.
```
ires = 0;
loop1: for (index1 = 1; index1 <= 5; index1++) {
   loop2: for (index2 = 1; index2 <= 5; index2++) {
      if ( index2 == 3 )
         break loop1;
      ires++;
   }
}
```

18.
```
ires = 0;
loop1: for (index1 = 1; index1 <= 5; index1++) {
   loop2: for (index2 = 1; index2 <= 5; index2++) {
      if ( index2 == 3 )
         break loop2;
      ires++;
   }
}
```

Examine the following Java statements and state whether they are valid. If they are invalid, indicate the reason why they are invalid.

19.
```
loop1: for (i = 1; i <= 10; i++ ) {
   loop2: for (i = 1; i <= 10; i++ ) {
      . . .
   }
}
```

20.
```
x = 10;
while ( x > 0);
   x -= 3;
```

21.
```
ires = 0;
for (i = 1; i <= 10; i++ ) {
   ires += i--;
}
```

4.4 FORMATTING OUTPUT DATA

One serious limitation of the standard Java API is that there is no convenient way to format numbers for display. When Java prints out a number, it displays *all nonzero significant digits* of the number. while this is suitable under some circumstances, it is not particularly useful at other times.

For example, suppose that we were interested in creating a program that reads in the prices of a series of purchases and calculates the average price. If the average price is written out with a statement like

```
System.out.println("Average price = " + ave);
```

the result might be

```
Average price = $3.766666666666667
```

This output is not very useful, since monetary amounts are only significant to the nearest cent.

A similar problem happens if we are trying to create tables of information. If the values in the table contain different numbers of significant digits, then the columns of data in the table will not line up. For example, the following program calculates a table of the square roots and cube roots of all integers from 0 to 10.

```java
public class SquareCubeRoot {
    public static void main(String[] args) {

        // Declare variables, and define each variable
        int i;                  // Loop index
        double cubeRoot;        // Cube root of index
        double squareRoot;      // Square root of index

        // Print title
        System.out.println("Table of Square and Cube Roots:");

        // Calculate and print values
        for ( i = 0; i <= 10; i++ ) {
            squareRoot = Math.sqrt(i);
            cubeRoot = Math.pow(i,1./3.);
            System.out.println(i + " " + squareRoot + " " + cubeRoot);
        }
    }
}
```

When this program is executed, the results are:

```
Table of Square and Cube Roots:
 0   0.0   0.0
 1   1.0   1.0
 2   1.4142135623730951   1.2599210498948732
 3   1.7320508075688772   1.4422495703074083
 4   2.0   1.5874010519681994
 5   2.23606797749979   1.7099759466766968
 6   2.449489742783178   1.8171205928321397
 7   2.6457513110645907   1.912931182772389
 8   2.8284271247461903   2.0
 9   3.0   2.080083823051904
10   3.1622776601683795   2.154434690031884
```

This output looks terrible! It would be completely unacceptable for any real task.

Although Java does not include a standard formatting method, *it is possible to create a class* that will format numbers nicely. The chapman.io package that accompanies this

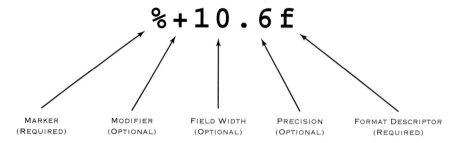

Figure 4.8.   The components of a format descriptor

TABLE 4-1   The Components of a Format Descriptor

COMPONENT	STATUS	MEANING
Marker (%)	Required	Marks the beginning of a format descriptor.
Modifier	Optional	A one-character value that modifies the behavior of the descriptor:
		+ Display a leading + for positive numbers
		0 + Show leading zeros
		- Left-align the number in the field space
		space Add a space in front of positive numbers
		# Use "alternative" format. For floating-point numbers, this modifier displays trailing zeros. For octal or hexadecimal numbers, it adds a "0" or "0x" to the front of the number.
Field Width	Optional	The number of characters to use to display the value.
Precision	Optional	A period followed by the number of places to display after the decimal point.
Format Descriptor	Required	The basic format for the value to be displayed, as shown in Table 4-2.

book includes such a class, called `Fmt`. This class contains methods that are modelled after the `printf` and `sprintf` functions of the C language and are used in a similar fashion.

The `Fmt.printf` method formats an output value according to a format string and then prints that value on the standard output stream. The `Fmt.sprintf` method is similar, except that it returns the formatted value to the calling method as a string.

The `Fmt.printf` method has the form

```
Fmt.printf (format, value);
```

where `value` is the value to be printed, and `format` is a string describing how to print the value. For example, the average price just described might be printed with the following statement:

```
Fmt.printf("Average price = $ %5.2f \n", ave);
```

The output of this statement would be:

```
Average price = $ 3.77
```

The **format string** must contain a format descriptor (which is marked by an initial % character), and may contain any number of characters before and after the format descriptor. All of the characters before and after the format descriptor will be printed unchanged, while the format descriptor is replaced by the value being printed out. The descriptor serves as a "model," describing how the value should be printed. For example, the descriptor %5.2f states that a *floating-point value* should be printed out in a field that is *five characters wide*, with *two characters after the decimal point.*

A format string may also contain **escape sequences**, which are convenient ways to include unprintable characters in the output stream. For example, the sequence \n in the foregoing example represents the **newline character**, which positions the cursor to the beginning of a new line.

The components of a format descriptor are shown in Figure 4.8, and the meanings of each component are given in Tables 4-1 and 4-2. A list of common escape sequences is given in Table 4-3.

TABLE 4-2 Format Descriptors

DESCRIPTOR	MEANING
%f	Display a floating-point number in fixed-point format (12.345).
%e, %E	Display a floating-point number in exponential format. The %e descriptor produces a lower-case e for the exponent marker (1.234500e+001), while the %E descriptor produces a upper-case E for the exponent marker (1.234500E+001).
%g, %G	Display a floating-point number in general format, which is fixed-point format for relatively small numbers and exponential format for extremely large or extremely small numbers. The %g descriptor produces a lower-case e for the exponent marker (if used), while the %G descriptor produces a upper-case E for the exponent marker (if used).
%d, %i	Display an integer in decimal format.
%x	Display an integer in hexadecimal format.
%o	Display an integer in octal format.
%c	Display a character.
%s	Display a string.

TABLE 4-3 Common Escape Sequences

DESCRIPTOR	MEANING
\n	Newline. Positions the cursor at the beginning of the next line.
\t	Horizontal tab. Moves the cursor to the next tab stop.
\r	Carriage return. Positions the cursor at the beginning of the *current* line.
\\	Backslash. Used to print the backslash character.
\'	Single quote. Used to print the single quote character.
\"	Double quote. Used to print the double quote character.
\u####	Unicode character. Used to display the Unicode character whose location in the character set is ####, where #### is a hexadecimal value between 0000 and FFFF.

EXAMPLE 4-5: If i, pi, and e are initialized as shown, then the following statements will produce the indicated results. Can you explain why each result is produced?

```
int i = 12345;
double pi = 3.14159265358979;
double e = -1.602e-19;
```

EXPRESSION	RESULT
a. Fmt.printf("i = %d\n", i);	i = 12345
b. Fmt.printf("i = %10d\n", i);	i = 12345
c. Fmt.printf("i = %010d\n", i);	i = 0000012345
d. Fmt.printf("i = %-10d\n", i);	i = 12345
e. Fmt.printf("pi = %f\n", pi);	pi = 3.141593
f. Fmt.printf("pi = %+8.4f\n", pi);	pi = +3.1416
g. Fmt.printf("pi = %12.4e\n", pi);	pi = 3.1416e+000
h. Fmt.printf("e = %12.4e\n", e);	e = -1.6020e-019

Each Fmt.printf method call can format one and only one value. If you need to print multiple values on a line, then you will have to make multiple calls to the method. This fact is illustrated by Example 4-6.

EXAMPLE 4-6: GENERATING A TABLE OF INFORMATION

Write a program to generate a table containing the square roots and cube roots of all integers between 0 and 10. Use formatted output to generate a neat table with five places after the decimal point.

SOLUTION

This program will be similar to class SquareCubeRoot, except that the output will use Fmt.printf statements to format the data. The resulting program is as follows:

```
import chapman.io.*;
public class SquareCubeRoot1 {
   public static void main(String[] args) {

      // Declare variables, and define each variable
      int i;              // Loop index
      double cubeRoot;    // Cube root of index
      double squareRoot;  // Square root of index

      // Print title
      System.out.println("Table of Square and Cube Roots:");

      // Calculate and print values
      for ( i = 0; i <= 10; i++ ) {
         squareRoot = Math.sqrt(i);
         cubeRoot = Math.pow(i,1./3.);
         Fmt.printf("%5d",i);
         Fmt.printf("      %7.5f",squareRoot);
         Fmt.printf("      %7.5f\n",cubeRoot);
      }
   }
}
```

When this program is executed, the results are as follows and are much nicer than before:

```
D:\book\java\chap4>java SquareCubeRoot1
Table of Square and Cube Roots:
     0     0.00000      0.00000
     1     1.00000      1.00000
     2     1.41421      1.25992
     3     1.73205      1.44225
     4     2.00000      1.58740
     5     2.23607      1.70998
     6     2.44949      1.81712
     7     2.64575      1.91293
     8     2.82843      2.00000
     9     3.00000      2.08008
    10     3.16228      2.15443
```

GOOD PROGRAMMING PRACTICE

Use the formatted output method `Fmt.printf` to create neat tabular output in your programs.

4.5 EXAMPLE PROBLEM

**EXAMPLE 4-7:
PHYSICS—THE
FLIGHT OF A
BALL**

If we assume negligible air friction and ignore the curvature of the earth, a ball that is thrown into the air from any point on the earth's surface will follow a parabolic flight path (see Figure 4.9a). The height of the ball at any time t after it is thrown is given by

$$y(t) = y_0 + v_{y0} + t + \frac{1}{2}g\,t^2,\tag{4-4}$$

where y_0 is the initial height of the object above the ground, v_{y0} is the initial vertical velocity of the object, and g is the acceleration due to the earth's gravity. The horizontal distance (range) traveled by the ball as a function of time after it is thrown is given by

$$x(t) = x_0 + v_{x0}\,t,\tag{4-5}$$

where x_0 is the initial horizontal position of the ball on the ground and v_{x0} is the initial horizontal velocity of the ball.

If the ball is thrown with some initial velocity v_0 at an angle of θ degrees with respect to the earth's surface, then the initial horizontal and vertical components of velocity will be the following

$$v_{x0} = v_0 \cos\theta,\tag{4-6}$$

$$v_{y0} = v_0 \sin\theta.\tag{4-7}$$

Assume that the ball is initially thrown from position $(x_0, y_0) = (0,0)$ with an initial velocity v of 20 meters per second at an initial angle of θ degrees. Design, write, and test a program that will determine the horizontal distance traveled by the ball from the time it was thrown until it touches the ground again. The program should do this for all angles θ from 0 to 90° in 1° steps. Determine the angle θ that maximizes the range of the ball.

Figure 4.9.   (a) When a ball is thrown upwards, it follows a parabolic trajectory. (b) The horizontal and vertical components of a velocity vector v at an angle θ with respect to the horizontal.

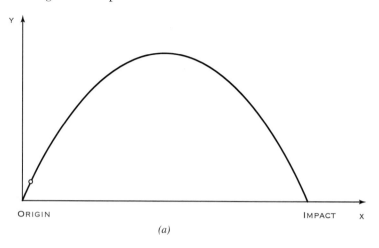

(a)

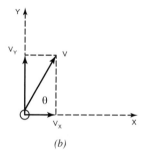

(b)

SOLUTION

In order to solve this problem, we must determine an equation for the range of the thrown ball. We can do this by first finding the time that the ball remains in the air, and then finding the horizontal distance that the ball can travel during that time.

The time that the ball will remain in the air after it is thrown may be calculated from Equation 4-4. The ball will touch the ground at the time t for which $y(t) = 0$. Remembering that the ball will start from ground level ($y(0) = 0$), and solving for t, we get

$$y(t) = y_0 + v_{y0}t + \frac{1}{2}g\ t^2 , \qquad (4\text{-}4)$$

$$0 = 0 + v_{y0}t + \frac{1}{2}g\ t^2 ,$$

$$0 = \left(v_{y0} + \frac{1}{2}g\ t\right)t .$$

So, the ball will be at ground level at time $t_1 = 0$ (when we threw it), and at time

$$t_2 = -\frac{2v_{y0}}{g} \ .$$

The horizontal distance that the ball will travel in time t_2 is found as follows:

$$\text{range} = x(t_2) = x_0 + v_{x0}t_2 , \tag{4-5}$$

$$\text{range} = 0 + v_{x0}\left(-\frac{2\ v_{y0}}{g}\right)$$

$$\text{range} = -\frac{2\ v_{x0}\ v_{y0}}{g} .$$

We can substitute Equations (4-6) and (4-7) for v_{x0} and v_{y0} to get an equation expressed in terms of the initial velocity v and initial angle θ:

$$\text{range} = -\frac{2(v_0 \cos \theta)(v_0 \sin \theta)}{g}$$

$$\text{range} = -\frac{2v_0^2}{g}\cos \theta \sin \theta \tag{4-8}$$

From the problem statement, we know that the initial velocity v_0 is 20 meters per second and that the ball will be thrown at all angles from 0° to 90° in 1° steps. Finally, any elementary physics textbook will tell us that the acceleration due to the earth's gravity is −9.81 meters per second squared.

Now let's apply our design technique to this problem.

1. **State the problem**. A proper statement of this problem would be: *Calculate the range that a ball would travel when it is thrown with an initial velocity of* v₀ *at an initial angle* θ. *Calculate this range for a* v₀ *of 20 meters per second and all angles between 0° and 90°, in 1° increments. Determine the angle* θ *that will result in the maximum range for the ball. Assume that there is no air friction.*

2. **Define the inputs and outputs**. As the problem is defined, no inputs are required. We know from the problem statement what v_0 and θ will be, so there is no need to read them in. The outputs from this program will be a table showing the range of the ball for each angle θ and the angle θ for which the range is maximum.

3. **Decompose the program into classes and their associated methods**. This step will be trivial until we learn how to write objects in Chapter 7. For now, there will be a single class, and only the `main` method within that class. We will call the class `Ball`.

4. **Design the algorithm that you intend to implement for each method**. There is only one method in this program. The `main` method can be broken down into the following major steps:

```
for theta = 0 to 90 degrees in 1 degree steps {
    Calculate the range of the ball for each angle theta.
    Determine if this theta yields the maximum range so far.
    Write out the range as a function of theta.
}
WRITE out the theta yielding maximum range
```

A `for` loop is appropriate for this algorithm, since we are calculating the range of the ball for a specified number of angles. We will calculate the range for each value of θ and compare each range with the maximum range found so far to determine which angle yields the maximum range. Note that the trigonometric functions work in radians, so the angles in degrees must be converted to radians before the range is calculated. The detailed pseudocode for this algorithm is as follows:

```
Declare variables.
Initialize v0 to 20 meters/second.
for theta = 0 to 90 degrees in 1 degree steps {
    radian ← theta * DEG_TO_RAD;    (Convert degrees to radians)
    angle ← (-2. * v0**2 / gravity) * sin(radian) * cos(radian);
    Write out theta and range.
    if range > max_range then
       max_range ← range;
       max_degrees ← theta;
    }
}
Write out max_degrees, max_range.
```

5. **Turn the algorithm into Java statements**. The final Java program is shown in Figure 4.10.

```
/*
   Purpose:
     To calculate distance traveled by a ball thrown at a specified angle
        theta and at a specified velocity V0 from a point on the surface
        of the earth, ignoring the effects of air friction and the earth's
        curvature.

   Record of revisions:
      Date         Programmer        Description of change
      ====         ==========        =====================
     3/31/98    S. J. Chapman     Original code
*/
import chapman.io.*;
public class Ball {

   // Define the main method
   public static void main(String[] args) {

      // Declare variables, and define each variable
      double gravity = -9.81; // Accel. due to gravity (m/s/s)
      final double DEG_TO_RAD = Math.PI / 180; // Deg ==> rad conv. factor
      int maxDegrees = 0;     // angle at which the max rng occurs (deg)
      double maxRange = 0;    // Max range for the ball at vel v0 (m)
      double range;           // Range of the ball at a given angle (m)
      double radian;          // Angle of throw (radians)
      int theta;              // Angle of throw (deg)
      double v0 = 20;         // Velocity of the ball (m/s)

      for (theta = 0; theta <= 90; theta++) {

         // Get angle in radians
         radian = theta * DEG_TO_RAD;

         // Calculate range in meters.
         range = (-2*v0*v0/gravity) * Math.sin(radian)* Math.cos(radian);
```

Figure 4.10. *(cont.)*

```
      // Write out the range for this angle.
      Fmt.printf("Theta = %2d deg; ", theta);
      Fmt.printf("Range = %8.4f meters\n", range);

      // Compare the range to the previous maximum range. If this
      // range is larger, save it and the angle at which it occurred.
      if (range > maxRange) {
         maxRange = range;
         maxDegrees = theta;
      }
   }

   // Skip a line, and then write out the maximum range and
   // the angle at which it occurred.
   Fmt.printf("Max range = %8.4f ", maxRange);
   Fmt.printf("at %2d degrees.\n", maxDegrees);
   }
}
```

Figure 4.10. Program `Ball` to determine the angle which maximizes the range of a thrown ball

The degrees-to-radians conversion factor is always a constant, so in the program it is declared as a named constant, and all references to the constant within the program use that name. The acceleration due to gravity at sea level can be found in any physics text. It is it is about 9.81 m/s², directed downward.

6. **Test the program**. To test this program, we will calculate the answers by hand for a few of the angles and compare the results with the output of the program:

$$\theta = 0°: \qquad \text{range} = -\frac{2(20^2)}{-9.81} = \cos 0 \sin 0 = 0 \text{ meters}$$

$$\theta = 5°: \qquad \text{range} = -\frac{2(20^2)}{-9.81} \cos\left(\frac{5\pi}{180}\right) \sin\left(\frac{5\pi}{180}\right) = 7.080 \text{ meters}$$

$$\theta = 40°: \qquad \text{range} = -\frac{2(20^2)}{-9.81} \cos\left(\frac{40\pi}{180}\right) \sin\left(\frac{40\pi}{180}\right) = 40.16 \text{ meters}$$

$$\theta = 45°: \qquad \text{range} = -\frac{2(20^2)}{-9.81} \cos\left(\frac{45\pi}{180}\right) \sin\left(\frac{45\pi}{180}\right) = 40.77 \text{ meters}$$

When program `Ball` is executed, a 90-line table of angles and ranges is produced. To save space, only a portion of the table is reproduced:

```
Theta =  0 deg; Range =   0.0000 meters
Theta =  1 deg; Range =   1.4230 meters
Theta =  2 deg; Range =   2.8443 meters
Theta =  3 deg; Range =   4.2621 meters
Theta =  4 deg; Range =   5.6747 meters
Theta =  5 deg; Range =   7.0805 meters
Theta =  6 deg; Range =   8.4775 meters
Theta =  7 deg; Range =   9.8643 meters
Theta =  8 deg; Range =  11.2390 meters
Theta =  9 deg; Range =  12.6001 meters
Theta = 10 deg; Range =  13.9458 meters

   . . .
```

```
Theta = 40 deg; Range =  40.1553 meters
Theta = 41 deg; Range =  40.3779 meters
Theta = 42 deg; Range =  40.5514 meters
Theta = 43 deg; Range =  40.6754 meters
Theta = 44 deg; Range =  40.7499 meters
Theta = 45 deg; Range =  40.7747 meters
Theta = 46 deg; Range =  40.7499 meters
Theta = 47 deg; Range =  40.6754 meters
Theta = 48 deg; Range =  40.5514 meters
Theta = 49 deg; Range =  40.3779 meters
Theta = 50 deg; Range =  40.1553 meters
...
Theta = 80 deg; Range =  13.9458 meters
Theta = 81 deg; Range =  12.6001 meters
Theta = 82 deg; Range =  11.2390 meters
Theta = 83 deg; Range =   9.8643 meters
Theta = 84 deg; Range =   8.4775 meters
Theta = 85 deg; Range =   7.0805 meters
Theta = 86 deg; Range =   5.6747 meters
Theta = 87 deg; Range =   4.2621 meters
Theta = 88 deg; Range =   2.8443 meters
Theta = 89 deg; Range =   1.4230 meters
Theta = 90 deg; Range =   0.0000 meters
Max range =   40.7747 at 45 degrees.
```

The program output matches our hand calculation for the angles calculated above to the four-digit accuracy of the hand calculation. Note that the maximum range occurred at an angle of 45°.

4.6 MORE ON DEBUGGING JAVA PROGRAMS

It is much easier to make a mistake when writing a program containing selection structures and loops than it is when writing simple sequential programs. Even after going through the full design process, a program of any size is almost guaranteed not to be completely correct the first time it is used.

Programs with many levels of `if` structures, `for` loops, etc. will contain many nested layers of braces (`{}`). One of the most common problems is to have *mismatched braces* within a program. A Java compiler will always catch this error, but the error message may not be very informative. For example, consider a portion of the program `Ball` from Figure 4.9. Suppose that by accident we leave out the opening brace of the `for` loop:

```
for (theta = 0; theta <= 90; theta++) // { missing

    // Get angle in radians
    radian = theta * deg2Rad;

    // Calculate range in meters.
    range = (-2*v0*v0/gravity) * Math.sin(radian) * Math.cos(radian);

    // Write out the range for this angle.
    System.out.print ("Theta = " + theta + " deg; ");
    System.out.println ("Range = " + range + " meters");

    // Compare the range to the previous maximum range. If this
    // range is larger, save it and the angle at which it occurred.
    if (range > max_range) {
```

```
        max_range = range;
        max_degrees = theta;
    }
}

// Skip a line, and then write out the maximum range and
// the angle at which it occurred.
System.out.println (" ");
```

If we compile this modified program with the Java compiler, the result is as follows:

```
C:\book\java\chap4>javac Ball.java
Ball.java:51: Type expected.
        System.out.println (" ");
                           ^
1 error
```

The compiler knows that something is wrong, but the resulting error message seems to be complete nonsense. In fact, the compiler has interpreted the closing brace of the `for` loop as the closing brace of the `main` method. It thinks that the next statement is a new method definition, and it says that the definition has the wrong syntax. The true error was many lines away from the point that the compiler reported an error, and it had a very different cause. If you get a problem like this, you must inspect your program *very* carefully for syntax problems such as missing braces.

Suppose that we have built and compiled a program, and after that program executes, we find that the output values are in error when it is tested. How do we go about finding the bugs and fixing them?

The best approach to locating the error is to use a symbolic debugger, if one is supplied with your compiler. You must ask your instructor or else check with your system's manuals to determine how to use the symbolic debugger supplied with your particular compiler and computer.

An alternative approach to locating the error is to insert output statements into the code to print out important variables at key points in the program. When the program is run, the output statements will print out the values of the key variables. These values can be compared with the ones you expect, and the places where the actual and expected values differ will serve as a clue to help you locate the problem. For example, to verify the operation of a `for` loop, the following output statements could be added to the program:

```
System.out.println("At loop1: ist, ien = " + ist + ", " + ien);
loop1: for (i = ist; i <= ien; i++) {
   System.out.println("In loop1: i = ", + i);
   ...
}
System.out.println("loop1 completed");
```

When the program is executed, its output listing will contain detailed information about the variables controlling the `for` loop and just how many times the loop was executed. Similar output statements could be used to debug the operation of an `if` structure:

Once you have located the portion of the code in which the error occurs, you can take a look at the specific statements in that area to locate the problem. A list of some common errors follows. Be sure to check for them in your code.

1. *If the problem is in an* `if` *structure, check to see if you used the proper relational operator in your logical expressions.* Did you use > when you really

intended >=, etc.? Logical errors of this sort can be very hard to spot, since the compiler will not give an error message for them.

2. *Another common problem with* if *statements occurs when floating-point* (float *and* double) *variables are tested for equality.* Because of small round-off errors during floating-point arithmetic operations, two numbers that theoretically should be equal will differ by a tiny amount, and the test for equality will fail. Instead of testing for equality, you shold test for *near equality,* as described in Chapter 3.

3. *Most errors in* for *loops involve mistakes with the loop parameters.* If you add output statements to the for loop as previously shown, the problem should be fairly clear. To reduce the risk of errors, ask yourself the following questions: Did the for loop start with the correct value? Did it end with the correct value? Did it increment at the proper step? If not, check the parameters of the for loop closely. You will probably spot an error in the control parameters.

4. Errors in while and do/while loops are usually related to errors in the logical expression used to control their function. These errors may be detected by examining the test expression of the loop with output statements. Errors can also be caused by using a while where a do/while is required and vice versa. In other words, confirm whether you want to test for the loop condition at the beginning or at the end of each loop.

SUMMARY

- A while loop executes a block of statements repeatedly until its boolean control expression becomes false. The control expression test occurs before the loop executes.

- A do/while loop executes a block of statements repeatedly until its boolean control expression becomes false. The control expression test occurs after the loop executes.

- A for loop executes a block of statements a specified number of times.

- The continue statement causes execution of the remaining statements within the body of a loop to be skipped, and execution resumes at the top of the loop. If the loop is a for loop, the loop increment expression is executed.

- The break statement causes execution of the remaining statements within the body of a loop to be skipped, and execution resumes at the next statement following the end of the loop.

- If while, do/while, or switch structures are nested, a break or continue statement applies to the *innermost* structure containing the statement.

- A labeled break or continue statement applies to the particular structure with that label, even if it is not the innermost one.

When I taught at various universities in the 1970s and 1980s, computer science students used to have competitions to see who could write the most difficult to understand programs. They would create working programs in C, and challenge other students to figure out what the programs did. These students got a great deal of ego gratification from writing programs that no one else could understand, but in the meantime they learned *horrible* programming practices. I have learned through bitter experience that such students often do not make good employees in industry.

A properly designed program should be understandable to any professional working in the same field, and it should be possible for such a person to modify the program without excessive pain. Java goes a long way to ensuring that by eliminating pointer arithmetic, by adding boolean data types, and by rigidly enforcing the rules of the language. However, you must do your part, too. Don't get excessively "cute" in the design of your programs. Keep things simple and well commented. This is especially important when working with loops. Make the control parameters for your loops as simple as possible, and perform your calculations within the body of the loop.

For example, the following two program fragments both read `ints` from the standard input stream and display them, until a value greater than or equal to 10 is entered.

```
StdIn in = new StdIn();
System.out.println ("Enter values:");
for (int i = in.readInt(); i < 10; i = in.readInt() ) {
   System.out.println(" i = " + i);
}
```

and

```
int i;
StdIn in = new StdIn();
System.out.println("Enter values: ");
do {
   i = in.readInt();
   System.out.println(" i = " + i);
} while(i < 10);
```

The first program fragment uses a `for` loop and performs `readInt()` calls to get each new value of `i`. Each time that the loop is executed, a value is read from the standard input stream and displayed if it is less than 10. This code compiles and works, but it is a misuse of the `for` structure. The `for` loop is designed to execute a block of code a finite number of times. Here, the loop is executing an indefinite number of times, and using a complicated loop control expression that involves reading data from the standard input stream. This is *very bad* programming practice.

The second program fragment implements the same function as a `do/while` loop. It is much clearer, and it is using the language as it is intended to be used.

APPLICATION: SUMMARY OF GOOD PROGRAMMING PRACTICES

The following guidelines introduced in this Chapter will help you to develop good programs:

1. Always indent the body of any structure by three or more spaces to improve the readability of the code.
2. Use a `while` or `do/while` loop to repeat a set of statements indefinitely until a condition becomes `false`. Use a `while` loop in cases where you wish to perform the loop repetition test at the top of the loop, and use a `do/while` loop in cases where you wish to perform the loop repetition test at the bottom of the loop.
3. Use labeled `break` or `continue` statements to break out of or continue outer loops in a nested loop structure.
4. Always use integer variables as `for` loop indexes.
5. Use the formatted output method `Fmt.printf` to create neat tabular output in your programs.

KEY TERMS

break statement	for loop	labeled continue statement
continue statement	format descriptor	nested loops
do/while loop	label	null statement
Fmt class	labeled break statement	while loop

Problems

1. Write the Java statements to calculate and print out the squares of all the even integers between 0 and 50, inclusive. Create a neat table of youre results.
2. Write a Java program to evaluate the equation $y(x) = x^2 - 3x + 2$ for all values of x between -1 and 3, inclusive, in steps of 0.1.
3. Write a Java program to calculate the factorial function, as defined in Example 4-2. Be sure to handle the special cases of 0! and of illegal input values.
4. What is the difference in behavior between a `continue` statement and a `break` statement?
5. Modify the program `Stats1` to use the `do/while` structure instead of the `while` structure currently in the program.
6. Modify the program `Stats1` to use method `Fmt.printf` for output. Display the average and standard deviation with four digits after the decimal place.
7. What is wrong with each of the following code segments?

   a.
```
x = 5;
while (x >= 0)
   x++;
```
   b.
```
x = 1;
while (x <= 5);
   x++;
```
   c.
```
for (x = 0.1; x < 1.0; x += 0.1)
   System.out.println("x = " + x);
```
   d.
```
switch (n) {
case 1:
   System.out.println("Number is 1");
case 2:
   System.out.println("Number is 2");
   break;
default:
   System.out.println("Number is not 1 or 2");
   break;
}
```

8. What does the following program do?

```java
public class Print {

    // Define the main method
    public static void main(String[] args) {

        for ( int i = 1; i <= 10; i++ ) {
            for ( int j = i; j <= 10; j++ ) {
                System.out.print("*");
            }
            System.out.println();
        }
    }
}
```

9. Examine the following for statements and determine how many times each loop will be executed. Assume that all loop index variables are integers.

    a. `for (range = -32768; range <= 32767; range++)`
    b. `for (j = 100; j >= 1; j -= 10)`
    c. `for (k = 2; k <= 3; k += 4)`
    d. `for (i = -4; i <= -7; i++)`
    e. `for (x = -10; x <= 10; x -= 10)`

10. Examine the following for loops. Determine the value of ires at the end of each of the loops and also the number of times each loop executes. Assume that all variables are integers.

    a.
    ```java
    ires = 0;
    for (index = -10; index <= 10; index++)
        ires++;
    }
    ```

    b.
    ```java
    ires = 0;
    loop1: for (idx1 = 1; idx1 <= 20; idx1 += 5) {
        if (idx1 <= 10) continue;
        loop2: for (idx2=idx1; idx2 <= 20; idx2 += 5) {
            ires = ires + idx2;
        }
    }
    ```

    c.
    ```java
    ires = 0;
    loop1: for (idx1 = 10; idx1 >= 4; idx1 -= 2) {
        loop2: for (idx2 = 2; idx2 <= idx1; idx2 += 2) {
            if (idx2 > 6) break loop2;
            ires = ires + idx2;
        }
    }
    ```

11. Examine the following while loops. Determine the value of ires at the end of each of the loops and the number of times each loop executes. Assume that all variables are integers.

    a.
    ```java
    ires = 1;
    loop1: do {
        ires = 2 * ires;
    } while (ires / 10 == 0);
    ```

    b.
    ```java
    ires = 2
    loop2: while (ires <= 512) {
        ires = ires * ires;
        if (ires == 128) break loop2;
    }
    ```

12. Modify the program Ball from Example 4-7 to read in the acceleration due to gravity at a particular location. Have the program calculate the maximum range that the ball will travel for that acceleration. After modifying the program, run it with accelerations of −9.8 m/s², −9.7 m/s², and −9.6 m/s². What effect does the reduction in gravitational attraction

have on the range of the ball? What effect does the reduction in gravitational attraction have on the best angle θ at which to throw the ball?

13. Write a program to calculate π from the following infinite series:

$$\pi = 4 - \frac{4}{3} + \frac{4}{5} - \frac{4}{7} + \frac{4}{9} - \cdots$$

Print a table showing the value of π approximated by 1 term, 2 terms, etc. from the series. The table should have three columns, showing the number of terms used, the approximate value of π, and the difference between the approximate value and the actual value. How many terms of this series are needed to get three significant digits of accuracy (3.14)?

14. Program DayOfYear in Example 4-3 calculates the day of year associated with any given month, day, and year. As written, this program does not check to see if the data entered by the user is valid. It will accept nonsense values for months and days, and it will do calculations with them to produce meaningless results. Modify the program so that it checks the input values for validity before using them. If the inputs are invalid, the program should tell the user what is wrong and quit. The year should be a number greater than zero, the month should be a number between 1 and 12, inclusive, and the day should be a number between 1 and a maximum that depends on the month, inclusive. Use a switch structure to implement the bounds checking performed on the day.

15. **Current Through a Diode** The current flowing through the semiconductor diode shown in Figure 4.11 is given by the equation

$$i_D = I_0\left(e^{\frac{qv_D}{kT}} - 1\right),$$ (4-9)

where i_D = the voltage across the diode, in volts
 v_D = the current flow through the diode, in amps
 I_0 = the leakage current of the diode, in amps
 q = the charge on an electron, 1.602×10^{-19} coulombs
 k = Boltzmann's constant, 1.38×10^{-23} joule/K
 T = temperature, in kelvins (K)

The leakage current I_0 of the diode is 2.0 μA. Write a computer program to calculate the current flowing through this diode for all voltages from −1.0 V to + 0.7 V, inclusive, in 0.1 V steps. Repeat this process for the following temperatures of 75 °F, and 100 °F, and 125 °F. Use the program of Example 2-2 to convert the temperatures from °F to kelvins.

16. **Tension on a Cable** A 200 pound object is to be hung from the end of a rigid 8-foot horizontal pole of negligible weight, as shown in Figure 4.12. The pole is attached to a wall by a pivot and is supported by an 8-foot cable that is attached to the wall at a higher point. The tension on this cable is given by the equation

$$T = \frac{W \cdot l_c \cdot l_p}{d\sqrt{l_p^2 - d^2}}$$ (4-10)

where T is the tension on the cable, W is the weight of the object, l_c is the length of the cable, l_p is the length of the pole, and d is the distance along the pole at which the cable is attached. Write a program to determine the distance d at which to attach the cable to the pole in order to minimize the tension on the cable. To do this, the program should calculate the tension on the cable at 0.1 foot intervals from $d = 1$ foot to $d = 7$ feet, inclusive, and should locate the position d that produces the minimum tension.

17. **Bacterial Growth** Suppose that a biologist performs an experiment in which he or she measures the rate at which a specific type of bacterium reproduces asexually in different culture media. The experiment shows that in Medium A the bacteria reproduce once every

Figure 4.11. A semiconductor diode

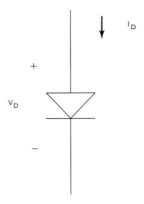

60 minutes, and in Medium B the bacteria reproduce once every 90 minutes. Assume that a single bacterium is placed on each culture medium at the beginning of the experiment. Write a Java program that calculates and writes out the number of bacteria present in each culture at intervals of three hours from the beginning of the experiment until 24 hours have elapsed. How do the numbers of bacteria compare on the two media after 24 hours?

18. **Decibels** Engineers often measure the ratio of two power measurements in *decibels*, or dB. The equation for the ratio of two power measurements in decibels is

$$dB = 10 \log_{10}\frac{P_2}{P_1}, \tag{4-11}$$

where P_2 is the power level being measured and P_1 is some reference power level. Assume that the reference power level P_1 is 1 watt (W), and write a program that calculates the decibel level corresponding to power levels between 1 W and 20 W, inclusive, in 0.5 W steps.

Figure 4.12. A 200 pound weight suspended from a rigid bar supported by a cable

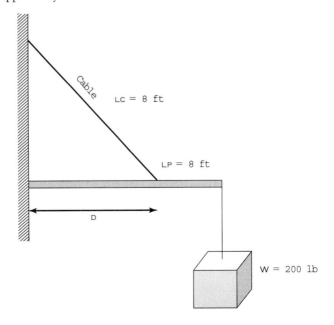

19. **Infinite Series** Trigonometric functions are usually calculated on computers by using a *truncated infinite series*. An *infinite series* is an infinite set of terms that together add up to the value of a particular function or expression. For example, one infinite series used to evaluate the sine of a number is

$$\sin x = x - \frac{x^3}{3!} + \frac{x^5}{5!} - \frac{x^7}{7!} + \frac{x^9}{9!} + \cdots \, , \qquad (4\text{-}12a)$$

or

$$\sin x = \sum_{n=1}^{\infty} (-1)^{n-1} \frac{x^{2n-1}}{(2n-1)!} \, , \qquad (4\text{-}12b)$$

where x is in units of radians.

Since a computer does not have enough time to add an infinite number of terms for every sine that is calculated, the infinite series is *truncated* after a finite number of terms. The number of terms that should be kept in the series is just enough to calculate the function to the precision of the floating point numbers on the computer on which the function is being evaluated. The truncated infinite series for $\sin x$ is

$$\sin x = \sum_{n=1}^{N} (-1)^{n-1} \frac{x^{2n-1}}{(2n-1)!} \, , \qquad (4\text{-}13)$$

where N is the number of terms to retain in the series.

Write a Java program that reads in a value for x in degrees and then calculates the sine of x using the sine intrinsic function. Next, calculate the sine of x using Equation 3-13, with $N = 1, 2, 3, \ldots, 10$. Compare the true value of $\sin x$ with the values calculated using the truncated infinite series. How many terms are required to calculate $\sin x$ to the full accuracy of your computer?

20. **Geometric Mean** The *geometric mean* of a set of numbers x_1 through x_n is defined as the nth root of the product of the numbers as follows:

$$\text{geometric mean} = \sqrt[n]{x_1 x_2 x_3 \ldots x_n} \, . \qquad (4\text{-}14)$$

Write a Java program that will accept an arbitrary number of positive input values and calculate both the arithmetic mean (i.e., the average) and the geometric mean of the numbers. Use a `while` loop to get the input values, and stop receiving inputs if the user enters a negative number. Test your program by calculating the average and geometric means of the four numbers 10, 5, 2, and 5.

21. **RMS Average** The *root-mean-square*, or *rms*, *average* is another way of calculating a mean for a set of numbers. The rms average of a series of numbers is the square root of the arithmetic mean of the squares of the numbers:

$$\text{rms average} = \sqrt{\frac{1}{N} \sum_{i=1}^{N} x_i^2} \, . \qquad (4\text{-}15)$$

Write a Java program that will accept an arbitrary number of positive input values and calculate the rms average of the numbers. Prompt the user for the number of values to be entered, and use a `for` loop to read in the numbers. Test your program by calculating the rms average of the four numbers 10, 5, 2, and 5.

22. **Harmonic Mean** The *harmonic mean* is yet another way of calculating a mean for a set of numbers. The harmonic mean of a set of numbers is given by the following equation:

$$\text{harmonic mean} = \frac{N}{\dfrac{1}{x_1} + \dfrac{1}{x_2} + \cdots + \dfrac{1}{x_N}} \, . \qquad (4\text{-}16)$$

Write a Java program that will read in an arbitrary number of positive input values and calculate the harmonic mean of the numbers. Use any method that you desire to read in the input values. Test your program by calculating the harmonic mean of the four numbers 10, 5, 2, and 5.

23. Write a single Java program that calculates the arithmetic mean (average), rms average, geometric mean, and harmonic mean for a set of positive numbers. Use any method that you desire to read in the input values. Compare these values for each of the following sets of numbers:

a.   4, 4, 4, 4, 4, 4, 4
b.   4, 3, 4, 5, 4, 3, 5
c.   4, 1, 4, 7, 4, 1, 7
d.   1, 2, 3, 4, 5, 6, 7

24. **Mean Time Between Failure Calculations** The reliability of a piece of electronic equipment is usually measured in terms of Mean Time Between Failures (MTBF), where MTBF is the average time that the piece of equipment can operate before a failure occurs in it. For large systems containing many pieces of electronic equipment, it is customary to determine the MTBFs of each component and then to calculate the overall MTBF of the system from the failure rates of the individual components. If the system is structured as is the one shown in Figure 4.13, every component must work in order for the whole system to work, and the overall system MTBF can be calculated as follows:

$$\text{MTBF}_{sys} = \frac{1}{\dfrac{1}{\text{MTBF}_1} + \dfrac{1}{\text{MTBF}_2} + \cdots + \dfrac{1}{\text{MTBF}_n}} \ . \tag{4-17}$$

Write a program that reads in the number of series components in a system and the MTBFs for each component and then calculates the overall MTBF for the system. To test your program, determine the MTBF for a radar system consisting of an antenna subsystem with an MTBF of 2000 hours, a transmitter with an MTBF of 800 hours, a receiver with an MTBF of 3000 hours, and a computer with an MTBF of 5000 hours.

Figure 4.13.   An electronic system containing three subsystems with known MTBFs

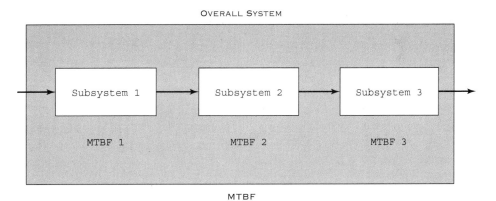

5

Arrays, File Access, and Plotting

This chapter serves as an introduction to an important data structure: the array. An **array** is a group of contiguous memory locations that all have the same name and same type. This data structure is implemented as an object in Java.

In addition, the chapter introduces convenience classes that allow a programmer to read and write data to files, and to create plots of arrays of data.

5.1 INTRODUCTION TO ARRAYS

An **array** is a special object containing (1) a group of contiguous memory locations that all have the same name and same type, and (2) a separate instance variable containing an integer constant equal to the number of elements in the array (see Figure 5.1). An individual value within the array is called an **array element**; it is identified by the name of the array together with a **subscript** in square brackets. The subscript identifies the particular location within the array. Note that *the elements of Java arrays are numbered starting with 0 and working upward.* For example, the first element shown in Figure 5.1 is referred to as a[0], and the fifth variable shown in the figure is referred to as a[4]. The subscript of an array must be an integer. Either constants or variables may be used for array subscripts.

SECTIONS

- 5.1 Introduction to Arrays
- 5.2 Declaring Arrays
- 5.3 Using Array Elements in Java Statements
- 5.4 Reading and Writing Data to Files
- 5.5 Example Problems
- 5.6 Introduction to Plotting
- 5.7 Two-Dimensional Arrays
- Summary
- Key Terms

OBJECTIVES

After reading this chapter, you should be able to:

- Understand how to create, initialize, and use arrays
- Be able to read numeric data from, and write numeric data to, disk files using the `FileIn` and `FileOut` convenience classes
- Be able plot arrays of data using the `JPlot2D` class.

The length of any Java array is included as a separate field within the array object itself, and that length can be accessed by appending the field name `.length` to the name of the array. Thus, the length of array a in Figure 5.1 can be accessed as `a.length`. The length of a Java array is specified when it is created, and it remains fixed for as long as the array exists.

PROGRAMMING PITFALLS

The elements of an n-element Java array `arr` have subscripts numbered 0, 1, 2, . . ., n − 1. Note that there is no element `arr[n]`! Novice programmers often make the mistake of trying to use this non-existant element.

As we shall see, arrays can be extremely powerful tools. They permit us to apply the same algorithm over and over again to many different data items with a simple loop. For example, suppose that we need to take the square root of 100 different real numbers. If the numbers are stored as elements of an array a consisting of 100 real values, then the code

```
for (i = 0; i < 100; i++)
    a[i] = Math.sqrt(a[i]);
```

will take the square root of each real number, and store it back into the memory location that it came from. If we wanted to take the square root of 100 numbers without using arrays, we would have to write out

```
a0 = Math.sqrt(a0);
a1 = Math.sqrt(a1);
    . . .
a99 = Math.sqrt(a99);
```

as 100 separate statements! Arrays are obviously a *much* cleaner and shorter way to handle repeated similar operations.

Figure 5.1.   An array object contains a set of elements, all of the same type, occupying successive locations in a computer's memory. It also contains an integer constant set equal to the number of elements in the array.

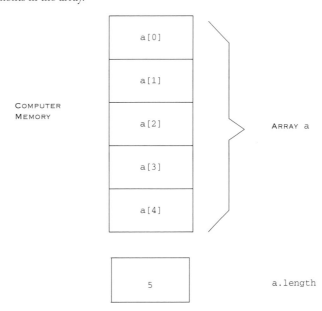

As we shall see, it is possible to manipulate and perform calculations with individual elements of arrays one by one. We will first learn how to declare arrays in Java programs. Then, we will learn how to use arrays in Java statements.

5.2 DECLARING ARRAYS

An array must be created before it can be used. This is a two-step process. First, we must declare a **reference** to an array, and then we actually create the array. A *reference* is a "handle" or "pointer" to an object that permits Java to locate the object in memory when it is needed. The declaration of a reference to an array is created by typing the object type followed by the reference name. It looks just like the declaration an `int`, `double`, or any other primitive data type, except that the name is followed by square brackets (`[]`). For example, a reference to `double` array is created by the statement

```
double x[];        // Create an array reference
```

When this statement is executed, the array reference x is created. However, the value of the reference is initially **null**, since it doesn't "point to" an array object yet. Attempting to use a `null` reference in a program will produce a run-time exception.

Once a reference is created, we can create an array object to assign to the reference using the **new** operator. This operator **instantiates** an array object of the specified size. For example, the following statement creates a new 5-element array and sets the reference x to refer to that array:

```
x = new double[5];      // Create array object
```

The `new` operator is followed by the data type of the array object to be created and square brackets containing the number of elements to be allocated. When the elements are allocated, they are automatically initialized to zero.

Note that an array reference has a type, and *the reference can only refer to array objects of that type.* Thus, the statements below are illegal, since the attempt to assign a `double` array to an `int` reference:

```
int x[];             // Create array reference
x = new double[5];   // Create array object (illegal)
```

The creation of an array reference and an array object may be written together on a single line as follows:

```
double x[] = new double[5];
```

It is also possible to create multiple reference and array objects in a single declaration. For example, the following declaration creates two `double` arrays a and b, with 5 and 10 elements respectively.

```
double a[] = new double[5], b[] = new double[10];
```

5.3 USING ARRAY ELEMENTS IN JAVA STATEMENTS

Each element of an array is a variable just like any other variable, and *an array element may be used in any place where an ordinary variable of the same type may be used.* Array elements may be included in arithmetic and logical expressions, and the results of an expression may be assigned to an array element. For example, assume that arrays `index` and `temp` are declared as:

```
int index[] = new int[5];
double temp[] = new double[4];
```

The five elements of array index would be addressed as index[0], index[1], index[2], index[3], and index[4], while the four elements of array temp would be addressed as temp[0], temp[1], temp[2], and temp[3]. With this definition, the following Java statements are perfectly valid:

```
index[0] = 1;
temp[3] = index[0] / 4.;
System.out.println("index[0] = ", index[0]);
```

Arrays are commonly used in loops to allow the same calculation to be applied to many different values stored in the array elements. For example, the simple program shown in Figure 5.2 calculates the squares of the numbers in array number, and then prints out the numbers and their squares. The for loop applies the same calculations to every element of arrays number and square.

```
// Calculates the squares of the numbers from 1 to 10
import chapman.io.*;
public class Squares {

    // Define the main method
    public static void main(String[] args) {

        double number[] = new double[10]; // Array of numbers
        double square[] = new double[10]; // Array of squares

        // Calculate squares
        for ( int i = 0; i < number.length; i++ ) {
            number[i] = i + 1;
            square[i] = number[i] * number[i];
        }

        // Write number and square
        for ( int i = 0; i < number.length; i++ ) {
            Fmt.printf("number = %4.1f ", number[i]);
            Fmt.printf("square = %5.1f\n", square[i]);
        }
    }
}
```

Figure 5.2. A program to calculate the squares of the integers from 1 to 10.

Note that the for loops performing calculations on array number use the size of the array number.length as their continuation condition. This practice makes the program more flexible, since we can change the sizes of the arrays created in the program, and the number of passes through the body of the for loops will be updated automatically. Because the elements of the array are labeled 0,1,2,...,number.length-1, the proper continuation test is i < number.length.

When this program is executed, the results are:

```
D:\book\java\chap5>java Squares
number =  1.0   square =    1.0
number =  2.0   square =    4.0
number =  3.0   square =    9.0
number =  4.0   square =   16.0
number =  5.0   square =   25.0
number =  6.0   square =   36.0
number =  7.0   square =   49.0
number =  8.0   square =   64.0
number =  9.0   square =   81.0
number = 10.0   square =  100.0
```

GOOD PROGRAMMING PRACTICE

When creating `for` loops to process the elements of an array, use the array object's `length` field in the continuation condition for the loop. This will allow the loop to adjust automatically for different sized arrays.

GOOD PROGRAMMING PRACTICE

When processing an array `arr` in a `for` loop, use a continuation condition of the form

```
for (j = 0; j < arr.length; j++)
```

The "less than" relational operator is the correct one to use, because the elements of the array are numbered $0, 1, \ldots,$ `arr.length-1`.

Although *array elements* may be used freely in Java expressions and statements, the arrays themselves cannot. For a five-element integer array, the following statements are legal:

```
for (int i = 0; i < 5; i++)
    arr[i] += 2;
```

but the statement

```
arr += 2;
```

is illegal and will produce a compilation error.

PROGRAMMING PITFALLS

It is illegal to use an unsubscripted array in a Java expression or assignment. Only individual array elements may be used in this manner.

5.3.1 Initializing Array Values

An array object may be created and initialized using an **initializer** when its reference is declared. An *initializer* is a comma-separated list of values enclosed in braces. It may only appear in an array declaration. For example, the following statement declares an array reference a, creates and assigns a 5-element array object to the reference, and initializes the array elements to 1, 2, 3, 4, and 5.

```
int a[] = {1, 2, 3, 4, 5};
```

Array initializers only work in declaration statements. They may *not* be used to initialize an object after its reference has been declared. For example, the following statements are illegal and will produce a compile-time error.

```
int a[];
a[] = {1, 2, 3, 4, 5};  // This statement is illegal
```

The simple program shown in Figure 5.3 illustrates the use of an initializer it initialize the elements of array number. When this program is executed, the output is identical to the result of the previous program.

```
// Calculates the squares of the numbers from 1 to 10
public class Square2 {

   // Define the main method
   public static void main(String[] args) {

      double number[] = {1, 2, 3, 4, 5, 6, 7, 8, 9, 10};
      double square[] = new double[10]; // Array of squares

      // Calculate squares
      for ( int i = 0; i < number.length; i++ )
         square[i] = number[i] * number[i];

      // Write number and square
      for ( int i = 0; i < number.length; i++ ) {
         Fmt.printf("number = %4.1f ", number[i]);
         Fmt.printf("square = %5.1f\n", square[i]);
      }
   }
}
```

Figure 5.3. A program illustrating the use of array initializers.

5.3.2 Out-of-Bounds Array Subscripts

Each element of an array is addressed using an integer subscript. The range of integers which can be used to address array elements depends on the declared extent of the array. For a double array declared as

```
double a[] = new double[5];
```

the integer subscripts 0 through 4 address elements in the array. *Any other integers* (less than 0 or greater than 4) *could not be used as subscripts, since they do not correspond to allocated memory locations.* Such integers subscripts are said to be **out of bounds** for the array. But what would happen if we make a mistake and try to access the out-of-bounds element a[5] in a program?

Every Java array "knows" its own length, and Java has automatic **bounds checking** built into the language. If an attempt is made to access an out-of-bounds array element, a run-time error occurs. Java calls such errors **run-time exceptions**, and the method in which the error occurs is said to **throw an exception**. We will see in Chapter 8 that Java has a special way of handling such exceptions when they occur. If an exception occurs and it is not handled, the program containing the exception will abort. The special exception produced by accessing an out-of-bounds array element is called an **ArrayIndexOutOfBoundsException**.

The program shown in Figure 5.4 illustrates the behavior of a Java program containing incorrect array references. This simple program declares a 5-element int array a. The array a is initialized with the values 1, 2, 3, 4, and 5, and then the program attempts to print out six array elements.

```
// Test array bounds checking
public class TestBounds {

    // Define the main method
    public static void main(String[] args) {

        // Declare and initialize array
        int a[] = {1,2,3,4,5};

        // Write array (with an error!)
        for (int i = 0; i <= 5; i++)
            System.out.println("a[" + i + "] = " + a[i]);
    }
}
```

Figure 5.4. A simple program to illustrate the effect of out-of-bounds array references.

When this program is compiled and executed, the results are

```
C:\book\java\chap5>java TestBounds
a[0] = 1
a[1] = 2
a[2] = 3
a[3] = 4
a[4] = 5
java.lang.ArrayIndexOutOfBoundsException: 5
        at TestBounds.main(TestBounds.java:15)
```

The program checked each array reference, and aborted when an out-of-bounds expression was encountered. Note that the error message tells us what is wrong, and even the line number at which it occurred.

5.3.3 The Use of Named Constants (Final Variables) with Array Declarations

In many Java programs, arrays are used to store large amounts of information. The amount of information that a program can process depends on the size of the arrays it contains. If the arrays are relatively small, the program will be small and will not require much memory to run, but it will only be able to handle a small amount of data. On the other hand, if the arrays are large, the program will be able to handle a lot of information, but it will require a lot of memory to run. The array sizes in such a program are frequently changed to make it run better for different problems or on different processors.

It is good practice to always declare the array sizes using named constants, which are known in Java as final variables. Named constants make it easy to re-size the arrays in a Java program. In the following code, the sizes of all arrays can be changed by simply changing the single named constant ARRAY_SIZE:

```
final int ARRAY_SIZE = 1000;
double array1[] = new double[ARRAY_SIZE];
double array2[] = new double[ARRAY_SIZE];
double array2[] = new double[2*ARRAY_SIZE];
```

Note that by convention, named constant or final variables are written in all capital letters, with underscores separating words.

This may seem like a small point, but it is *very* important to the proper maintenance of large programs. If all related array sizes in a program are declared using named constants, and if the built-in lengths of the arrays are used in any size tests in the program, then it will be much simpler to modify the program later. Imagine what it would be like if you had to locate and change every reference to array sizes within a

50,000 line program! The process could take weeks to complete and debug. By contrast, the size of a well-designed program could be modified in five minutes by changing only one statement.

GOOD PROGRAMMING PRACTICE

Declare the sizes of arrays in a Java program using named constants (final variables) to make them easy to change.

EXAMPLE 5-1: FINDING THE LARGEST AND SMALLEST VALUES IN A DATA SET

To illustrate the use of arrays, we will write a simple program that reads in data values, and finds the largest and smallest numbers in the data set. The program will then write out the values, with the word "LARGEST" printed by the largest value and the word "SMALLEST" printed by the smallest value in the data set.

SOLUTION

This program must ask the user for the number of values to read, create an array large enough to hold those values, and then read the input values into the array. Once the values are all read, it must go through the data to find the largest and smallest values in the data set. Finally, it must print out the values, with the appropriate annotations beside the largest and smallest values in the data set.

1. **State the problem**. We have not yet specified the type of data to be processed. If we are processing integer data, then the problem may be stated as follows:

   Develop a program to read a user-specified number of integer values from the standard input device, locate the largest and smallest values in the data set, and write out all of the values with the words "LARGEST" and "SMALLEST" printed by the largest and smallest values in the data set.

2. **Define the inputs and outputs**. There are two types of inputs to this program:
   (a) An integer containing the number of integer values to read. This value will come from the standard input device.
   (b) The integer values in the data set. These values will also come from the standard input device.

   The outputs from this program are the values in the data set, with the word "LARGEST" printed by the largest value, and the word "SMALLEST" printed by the smallest value.

3. **Decompose the program into classes and their associated methods**. We will not be creating multiple objects until Chapter 7, so for now, there will be a single class, and only the `main` method within that class. We will call the class `Extremes`, and make it a subclass of the root class `Object`.

4. **Design the algorithm that you intend to implement for each method**. The `main` method can be broken down into four major steps:

```
Get the number of values to read
Read the input values into an array
Find the largest and smallest values in the array
Write out the data with the words 'LARGEST' and
   'SMALLEST' at the appropriate places
```

The first two major steps of the program are to get the number of values to read in and to read the values into an input array. We must prompt the user for the number of values to read, and create an array of that size. Then we should read in the data values. The detailed pseudocode for these steps is:

```
Prompt user for the number of input values nvals
Read in nvals
Create an integer array of size nvals
for (j = 0; j < nvals; j++) {
   Read in input value
}
...
...(Further processing here)
...
```

Next we must locate the largest and smallest values in the data set. We will use variables `large` and `small` as pointers to the array elements having the largest and smallest values. The pseudocode to find the largest and smallest values is:

```
// Find largest value
temp ← input[0];
large ← 0;
for ( j = 1; j < nvals; j++ ) {
   if (input[j] > temp) {
      temp ← input[j];
      large ← j;
   }
}

// Find smallest value
temp ← input[0];
small ← 0;
for ( j = 1; j < nvals; j++ ) {
   if (input[j] < temp) {
      temp ← input[j];
      small ← j;
   }
}
```

The final step is writing out the values with the largest and smallest numbers labeled:

```
for ( j = 0; j < nvals; j++ ) {
   if (small == j)
      Write input[j] and "SMALLEST"
   else if (large == j)
      Write input[j] and "LARGEST"
   else
      Write input[j]
}
```

5. **Turn the algorithm into Java statements**. The resulting Java program is shown in Figure 5.5.

```
/*
    Purpose:
        To find the largest and smallest values in a data
        set, and to print out the data set with the
        largest and smallest values labeled.

    Record of revisions:
        Date          Programmer         Description of change
        ====          ==========         =====================
      4/02/98     S. J. Chapman             Original code
*/
import chapman.io.*;
public class Extremes {

    // Define the main method
    public static void main(String[] args) {

        // Declare variables, and define each variable
        int j;                // loop index
        int large;            // Index of largest value
        int nvals;            // Number of vals in data set
        int small;            // Index of smallest value
        int temp;             // Temporary variable

        // Create a StdIn object
        StdIn in = new StdIn();

        // Get the number of points to input
        System.out.print("Enter number of elements in
        array: "); nvals = in.readInt();

        // Create array of proper size
        int input[] = new int[nvals];

        // Get values
        for (j = 0; j < nvals; j++) {
          System.out.print("Enter value " + (j+1) + ": ");
         input[j] = in.readInt();
        }

        // Find largest value
        temp = input[0];
        large = 0;
        for ( j = 1; j < nvals; j++ ) {
            if (input[j] > temp) {
                temp = input[j];
                large = j;
            }
        }

        // Find smallest value
        temp = input[0];
        small = 0;
        for ( j = 1; j < nvals; j++ ) {
            if (input[j] < temp) {
                temp = input[j];
                small = j;
            }
        }

        // Write out results
        System.out.print("\n The values are:\n");
        for ( j = 0; j < nvals; j++ ) {
```

Figure 5.5. *(cont.)*

```
            if (small == j)
                Fmt.printf("%6d SMALLEST\n", input[j]);
            else if (large == j)
                Fmt.printf("%6d LARGEST\n", input[j]);
            else
                Fmt.printf("%6d\n", input[j]);
        }
    }
}
```

Figure 5.5.   A program to read in a data set from the standard input device, find the largest and smallest values, and print the values with the largest and smallest values labeled.

6. **Test the program**. To test this program, we will a data set with 6 values: −6, 5, −11, 16, 9, and 0.

```
D:\book\java\chap5>java Extremes
Enter number of elements in array: 6
Enter value 1: -6
Enter value 2: 5
Enter value 3: -11
Enter value 4: 16
Enter value 5: 9
Enter value 6: 0
```

The values are:
```
     -6
      5
    -11 SMALLEST
     16 LARGEST
      9
      0
```

The program correctly labeled the largest and smallest values in the data set. Thus, the program gives the correct answer for our test data set.

PRACTICE!

This quiz provides a quick check to see if you have understood the concepts introduced in Sections 5.1 through 5.3. If you have trouble with the quiz, reread the sections, ask your instructor, or discuss the material with a fellow student. The answers to this quiz are found in the back of the book.

1. What is an array? What components are found with a Java array?
2. What is a reference? How do you declare a reference to an array?
3. How is an array object created?
4. How may an array be initialized?
5. Suppose you have created an 100-element array. What range of subscripts may be used to address the elements of this array?

Determine which of the following Java statements are valid. For each valid statement, specify what will happen in the program.

6. `double arr[];`
   `arr = new double[10];`

```
7. double aaa[];
   aaa = new int[100];

8. double bbb[];
   bbb[] = {1., 2., 3., 4., 5., 6.};

9. double aaa[] = {1., 2., 3., 4., 5.};
   for (i = 1; i < aaa.length; i++)
      System.out.println("i = " + aaa[i]);

10. double aaa[] = {1., 2., 3., 4., 5.};
    for (i = aaa.length-1; i >= 0; i--)
       System.out.println("i = " + aaa[i]);
```

5.4 READING AND WRITING DATA TO FILES

Arrays are designed to hold and manipulate large amounts of data, so that we can apply the same basic calculations to many different values in just a few statements. Unfortunately, it is not quite so easy to read in and write out the large quantities of data. For example, suppose that we were working with a 10,000-element input array. Can you imagine entering all 10,000 elements by typing them one-by-one at the standard input stream?

What we really need is a convenient way to read and write data to disk files. There are two possible ways to accomplish this. One possible approach is to read data from the standard input stream and to write data to the standard output stream, but to *redirect* the standard input stream and standard output stream to disk files using **command-line redirection**. The standard input stream is redirected by typing a < followed by the file name on the command line, and the standard output stream is redirected by typing > followed by the file name on the command line.[1] If all of the inputs needed for a program are placed in the input file in the proper order, the program will be able to execute without further operator input. For example, the following command line starts program Example, which reads data from file infile and writes data to file outfile.

D:\book\java\chap5>**java Example < infile > outfile**

The other, more flexible approach is to open files and to read or write to them directly from inside a Java program. Unfortunately, the Java I/O system is very complex, and it is not easy to simply open a file, read the data you want, and close it again. We will study the details of the Java I/O system in Chapter 14, but meanwhile we will use a couple of convenience classes to simplify the reading and writing of formatted files.

The chapman.io package includes two classes called FileIn and FileOut that allow a program to easily read and write formatted files.

5.4.1 Reading Files with Class FileIn

Class FileIn is designed to read numeric data stored in formatted input files. The numbers can be arranged freely within the input file. This class contains methods readDouble(), readFloat(), readInt(), and readLong() to read double, float, int, and long values from the file, as well as a status variable readStatus to indicate the success or failure of each operation. The methods in class FileIn are summarized in Table 5-1, and the possible values of the status variable readStatus are summarized in Table 5-2.

---

[1] Command line redirection works for PC and Unix systems, but is not available on the Macintosh.

TABLE 5-1 Methods in Class `FileIn`

METHOD	DESCRIPTION
close()	Closes the file, making it available for other programs to use.
readDouble()	Reads a `double` value from the file.
readFloat()	Reads a `float` value from the file.
readInt()	Reads an `int` value from the file.
readLong()	Reads a `long` value from the file.

TABLE 5-2 Possible Values of `readStatus` for Class `FileIn`

VALUE	DESCRIPTION
READ_OK	Value read successfully from the file.
INVALID_FORMAT	The value in the file had an invalid format. For example, a string was found where numeric data was expected.
FILE_NOT_FOUND	The specified file was not found when the `FileIn` object was created.
EOF	End-of-file reached.
IO_EXCEPTION	An unspecified I/O error occurred.

To open a file with this class, we simply create a new `FileIn` object with the name of the input file. For example, the statement

```
FileIn in = new FileIn("infile");
```

creates a new `FileIn` object, sets reference `in` to refer to it, and simultaneously opens file `infile` for reading. If the file was found and opened successfully, variable `in.readStatus` will be set to value `in.READ_OK`. If the file was not found, variable `in.readStatus` will be set to value `in.FILE_NOT_FOUND`, and so forth for other types of errors.

The program in Figure 5.6 shows how to use class `FileIn` to read `double` values into an array. Note that the program checks to see if the file was opened successfully, and writes a warning message if not. Then, the program reads the input file until the end of file is reached, storing the data into array `a`.

```
// Test FileIn for double values
import chapman.io.*;
public class TestFileIn {

    // Define the main method
    public static void main(String arg[]) {

        // Declare variables and arrays
        double a[] = new double[100];   // Input array
        int i = 0;                      // Loop index
        int nvals = 0;                  // Number of values read

        // Open file
        FileIn in = new FileIn("infile");

        // Check for valid open
        if ( in.readStatus != in.FILE_NOT_FOUND ) {

            // Read numbers into array
            while ( in.readStatus != in.EOF ) {
                a[i++] = in.readDouble();
            }
            nvals = i;
```

Figure 5.6. *(cont.)*

```
                // Close file
                in.close();

                // Display the numbers read
                for ( i = 0; i < nvals; i++ ) {
                   Fmt.printf("a[%3d] = ", i);
                   Fmt.printf("%10.4f\n", a[i]);
                }
             }

             // Get here if file not found. Tell user
             else {
                System.out.println("File not found: infile");
             }
          }
       }
```

Figure 5.6. A program to read a data set from a file into an array, and then display the data.

To test this program, we will create a file `infile` containing the following data:

```
12                 34.56
3.14159265358979   45.5
1                  -7
0
```

When this program is executed, the results are:

```
D:\book\java\chap5>java TestFileIn
a[ 0] =     12.0000
a[ 1] =     34.5600
a[ 2] =      3.1416
a[ 3] =     45.5000
a[ 4] =      1.0000
a[ 5] =     -7.0000
a[ 6] =      0.0000
```

As you can see, the program read the input file successfully.

5.4.2 Writing Files with Class `FileOut`

Class `FileOut` is designed to write data to formatted output files. Its principal method is `printf`, which works identically to the `printf` to the standard output stream in the `Fmt` class. The methods in class `FileOut` are summarized in Table 5-3, and the possible values of the status variable `writeStatus` are summarized in Table 5-4.

There are two ways open a file with this class.

TABLE 5-3 Methods in Class `FileOut`

METHOD	DESCRIPTION
`close()`	Closes the file, making it available for other programs to use.
`printf(fmt,value)`	Writes data to the file using `printf` conventions.

TABLE 5-4 Possible Values of `writeStatus` for Class `FileOut`

VALUE	DESCRIPTION
`WRITE_OK`	Value written successfully to the file.
`IO_EXCEPTION`	An unspecified I/O error occurred.

```
FileOut out = new FileOut("outfile");        // Open and replace
FileOut out = new FileOut("outfile",true); // Open and append
```

The first way to open the file creates a new FileOut object, sets reference out to refer to it, and simultaneously opens file outfile for writing. If the file already exists, it will be deleted and an empty file will be opened. The second way to open the file behaves the same as the first way, except that it *appends* data to an existing file instead of deleting the file.

The program in Figure 5.7 shows how to use class FileOut to write data to a file.

```
// Test FileOut
import chapman.io.*;
public class TestFileOut {

    // Define the main method
    public static void main(String arg[]) {

        double a[] = new double[10];

        // Test open without append
        FileOut out = new FileOut("outfile");

        // Check for valid open
        if ( out.writeStatus != out.IO_EXCEPTION ) {

            // Write values
            out.printf("double = %20.14f\n",Math.PI);
            out.printf("long   = %20d\n",12345678901234L);
            out.printf("char   = %20c\n",'A');
            out.printf("String = %20s\n","This is a test.");
        }

        // Close file
        out.close();

        // Now test the append option
        out = new FileOut("outfile",true);

        // Check for valid open
        if ( out.writeStatus != out.IO_EXCEPTION ) {

            // Write values
            out.printf("double = %20.14f\n",Math.PI);
            out.printf("long   = %20d\n",12345678901234L);
            out.printf("char   = %20c\n",'A');
            out.printf("String = %20s\n","This is a test.");
        }

        // Close file
        out.close();
    }
}
```

Figure 5.7. A program to write data to an output file. Note that this program test both the replace and append options.

When this program is executed, the results are:

```
D:\book\java\chap5>java TestFileOut
D:\book\java\chap5>type outfile
double =       3.14159265358979
long   =         12345678901234
char   =                      A
String =        This is a test.
double =       3.14159265358979
long   =         12345678901234
char   =                      A
String =        This is a test.
```

As you can see, the program wrote the output successfully, appending to the existing data the second time that it opened the file.

5.5 EXAMPLE PROBLEMS

Now we will examine two example problems that illustrate the use of arrays.

EXAMPLE 5-2:
SORTING DATA

In many scientific and engineering applications, it is necessary to take a random input data set and to sort it so that the numbers in the data set are either all in *ascending order* (lowest-to-highest) or all in *descending order* (highest-to-lowest). For example, suppose that you were a zoologist studying a large population of animals, and that you wanted to identify the largest 5% of the animals in the population. The most straightforward way to approach this problem would be to sort the sizes of all of the animals in the population into ascending order, and take the top 5% of the values.

Sorting data into ascending or descending order seems to be an easy job. After all, we do it all the time. It is simple matter for us to sort the data (10, 3, 6, 4, 9) into the order (3, 4, 6, 9, 10). How do we do it? We first scan the input data list (10, 3, 6, 4, 9) to find the smallest value in the list (3), and then scan the remaining input data (10, 6, 4, 9) to find the next smallest value (4), *etc.* until the complete list is sorted.

In fact, sorting can be a very difficult job. As the number of values to be sorted increases, the time required to perform the simple sort described above increases rapidly, since we must scan the input data set once for each value sorted. For very large data sets, this technique just takes too long to be practical. Even worse, how would we sort the data if there were too many numbers to fit into the main memory of the computer? The development of efficient sorting techniques for large data sets is an active area of research, and is the subject of whole courses all by itself.

In this example, we will confine ourselves to the simplest possible algorithm to illustrate the concept of sorting. This simplest algorithm is called the **selection sort**. It is just a computer implementation of the mental math previously described. The basic algorithm for the selection sort is as follows:

1. Scan the list of numbers to be sorted to locate the smallest value in the list. Place that value at the front of the list by swapping it with the value currently at the front of the list. If the value at the front of the list is already the smallest value, then do nothing.

2. Scan the list of numbers from position 2 to the end to locate the next smallest value in the list. Place that value in position 2 of the list by swapping it with the value currently at that position. If the value in position 2 is already the next smallest value, then do nothing.

3. Scan the list of numbers from position 3 to the end to locate the third smallest value in the list. Place that value in position 3 of the list by swapping it with the value currently at that position. If the value in position 3 is already the third smallest value, then do nothing.

4. Repeat this process until the next-to-last position in the list is reached. After the next-to-last position in the list has been processed, the sort is complete.

Figure 5.8. An example problem demonstrating the selection sort algorithm.

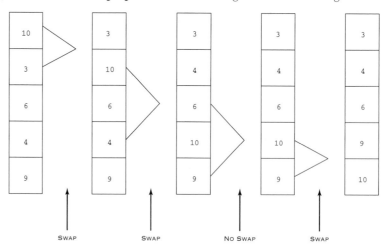

Note that if we are sorting n values, this sorting algorithm requires n−1 scans through the data to accomplish the sort. This process is illustrated in Figure 5.8. Since there are 5 values in the data set to be sorted, we will make 4 scans through the data. During the first pass through the entire data set, the minimum value is 3, so the 3 is swapped with the 10 that was in position 1. Pass 2 searches for the minimum value in positions 2 through 5. That minimum is 4, so the 4 is swapped with the 10 in position 2. Pass 3 searches for the minimum value in positions 3 through 5. That minimum is 6, which is already in position 3, so no swapping is required. Finally, pass 4 searches for the minimum value in positions 4 through 5. That minimum is 9, so the 9 is swapped with the 10 in position 4, and the sort is completed.

GOOD PROGRAMMING PRACTICE

The selection sort algorithm is the easiest sorting algorithm to understand, but it is computationally inefficient. *It should never be applied to sort really large data sets* (say, sets with more than 1000 elements). Over the years, computer scientists have developed much more efficient sorting algorithms. We will encounter one such algorithm in Chapter 6.

We will now develop a program to read a data set from the standard input stream into an array, sort it into ascending order, and display the sorted data set.

SOLUTION

This program must be able to read input data from the standard input stream, sort the data, and write out the sorted data. The first value in the standard input stream will be the number of values to be read, and the remaining numbers will be the values to sort. The design process for this problem is given below.

1. **State the problem**. We have not yet specified the type of data to be sorted. If the data is `double`, then the problem may be stated as follows:

> Develop a program to read an arbitrary number of `double` input data values from an input file, sort the data into ascending order, and write the sorted data to the standard output device.

2. **Define the inputs and outputs**. There are two types of inputs to this program:
   (a) The name of the file to open;
   (b) The values in the file, which will be the `double` values to sort. The outputs from this program are the sorted data values written to the standard output device.

3. **Decompose the program into classes and their associated methods**. There will be a single class, and only the `main` method within that class. We will call the class `SelectionSort`, and make it a subclass of the root class `Object`.

4. **Design the algorithm that you intend to implement for each method**. The `main` method can be broken down into four major steps:

```
Get file name and open input file
Read the input data into the array
Sort the data in ascending order
Write the sorted data
```

The first major steps of the program are to read the input file name, open the file, and read in the data. The pseudocode for these steps is as follows:

```
Read fileName from standard input device
Open input file
while ( in.readStatus != in.EOF ) {
   arr[i++] = in.readDouble();
}
nvals ← i;
```

Next we have to sort the data. We will need to make `nvals-1` passes through the data, finding the smallest remaining value each time. We will use a pointer to locate the smallest value in each pass. Once the smallest value is found, it will be swapped to the top of the list of it is not already there. (Note that in order to make `nvals-1` passes, the `for` loop must run from 0 to `nvals-2`.) The pseudocode for this step is as follows:

```
for ( i = 0; i <= nvals-2; i++ ) {

   // Find the minimum value in arr[i] through arr[nvals-1]
   iptr ← i;
   for ( j = i+1; j <= nvals-1; j++ ) {
      if (arr[j] < arr[iptr])
         iptr ← j;
   }

   // iptr now points to the min value, so swap arr[iptr]
   // with arr[i] if iptr != i.
   if (i != iptr) {
      temp ← arr[i];
      arr[i] ← arr[iptr];
      arr[iptr] ← temp;
   }
}
```

The final step is writing out the sorted values. No refinement of the pseudocode is required for that step. The final pseudocode is the combination of the reading, sorting and writing steps.

5. **Turn the algorithm into Java statements**. The resulting Java program is shown in Figure 5.9.

```
/*
   Purpose:
      To read in a set of double values from an input file, sort it
      into ascending order using the selection sort algorithm,
      and to write the sorted data to the standard output stream.

   Record of revisions:
       Date         Programmer        Description of change
       ====         ==========        =====================
     4/02/98     S. J. Chapman        Original code
*/
import chapman.io.*;
public class SelectionSort {

   // Define the main method
   public static void main(String[] args) {

      // Define maximum array size
      final int MAXVAL = 1000;

      // Declare variables, and define each variable
      double arr[] = new double[MAXVAL];
                             // Array of input measurements
      String fileName;   // Input file name
      int i = 0, j;      // Loop index
      int iptr;          // Pointer to smallest value
      int nvals;         // Number of data values to sort
      double temp;       // Temporary variable for swapping

      // Create StdIn object
      StdIn in = new StdIn();

      // Get input file name
      System.out.print("Enter file name: ");
      fileName = in.readString();

      // Open file
      FileIn in1 = new FileIn(fileName);

      // Check for valid open
      if ( in1.readStatus != in1.FILE_NOT_FOUND ) {

         // Read numbers into array
         while ( in1.readStatus != in1.EOF ) {
            arr[i++] = in1.readDouble();
         }
         nvals = i;

         // Close file
         in1.close();

         // Sort values
         for ( i = 0; i <= nvals-2; i++ ) {

            // Find the minimum value in arr[i] through arr[nvals-1]
            iptr = i;
```

Figure 5.9. *(cont.)*

```
                for ( j = i+1; j <= nvals-1; j++ ) {
                    if (arr[j] < arr[iptr])
                        iptr = j;
                }

                // iptr now points to the min value, so swap
                // arr[iptr] with arr[i] if iptr != i.
                if (i != iptr) {
                    temp = arr[i];
                    arr[i] = arr[iptr];
                    arr[iptr] = temp;
                }
            }

            // Write out sorted values
            for ( i = 0; i < nvals; i++ )
                System.out.println(arr[i]);
        }

        // Come here if file not found
        else {
            System.out.println("File " + fileName + " not found!");
        }
    }
}
```

Figure 5.9. A program to read values from an input file, and to sort them into ascending order.

6. **Test the program**. To test this program, we will create an input data file containing the data to sort. The data set will contain a mixture of positive and negative numbers as well as at least one duplicated value to see if the program works properly under those conditions. The following data set will be placed in file input1:

```
13.3
12.
-3.0
 0.
 4.0
 6.6
 4.
-6.
```

The first value in the file is the number of values to read, and the remaining values are the data set to sort. Running this file values through the program yields the following result:

```
D:\book\java\chap5>java SelectionSort
Enter file name: input1
-6.0
-3.0
0.0
4.0
4.0
6.6
12.0
13.3
```

The program gives the correct answers for our test data set. Note that it works for both positive and negative numbers as well as for repeated numbers.

EXAMPLE 5-3:
THE MEDIAN

In Chapter 3 we examined two common statistical measures of data: averages (or means) and standard deviations. Another common statistical measure of data is the median. The median of a data set is the value such that half of the numbers in the data set are larger than the value and half of the numbers in the data set are smaller than the value. If there are an even number of values in the data set, then there cannot be a value exactly in the middle. In that case, the median is usually defined as the average of the two elements in the middle. The median value of a data set is often close to the average value of the data set, but not always. For example, consider the following data set:

```
  1
  2
  3
  4
100
```

The average or mean of this data set is 22, while the median of this data set is 3!

An easy way to compute the median of a data set is to sort it into ascending order, and then to select the value in the middle of the data set as the median. If there are an even number of values in the data set, then average the two middle values to get the median.

In a language such as Java, where the array subscripts run from 0 to nvals-1, the median of a sorted data set is defined as:

$$\text{median} = \begin{cases} \texttt{a[nvals/2]} & \texttt{nvals odd} \\ \texttt{(a[nvals/2 - 1] + a[nvals/2])/2} & \texttt{nvals even} \end{cases} \qquad (5\text{-}1)$$

For example, in the sorted 5-element array shown below, the middle element is a[nvals/2], which is a[2], or 3.

```
a[0]              1
a[1]              2
a[2]              3
a[3]              4
a[4]            100
```

Similarly, in the sorted 4-element array shown below, the median is (a[nvals/2-1] + a[nvals/2])/2, which is (a[1] + a[2])/2, or 2.5.

```
a[0]              1
a[1]              2
a[2]              3
a[3]              4
```

Write a program to calculate the mean, median, and standard deviation of an input data set that is read from a the standard input stream.

SOLUTION

This program must be able to read input measurements from the standard input stream and calculate the mean, median, and standard deviation of the data set. Note that the data will have to be sorted in order to calculate the median. The first value in the standard input stream will be the *number* of measurements in the data set, and the remaining numbers will be the actual measurements. The design process for this problem is given below.

1. **State the problem**. Calculate the average, median, and standard deviation of a set of measurements which are read from an input file, and write those values out on the standard output device.

2. **Define the inputs and outputs**. (a) The name of the input file. (b) The input data values in the file, which will be measurements of type `double`. The outputs from this program are the average, median, and standard deviation of the input measurements. They are written to the standard output device.

3. **Decompose the program into classes and their associated methods**. There will be a single class, and only the `main` method within that class. We will call the class `Stats3`.

4. **Design the algorithm that you intend to implement for each method**. The `main` method can be broken down into five major steps:

```
Get file name and open input file
Read the input data into the array
Sort the measurements in ascending order
Calculate the average, mean, and standard deviation
Write average, median, and standard deviation
```

The detailed pseudocode for the first three steps is similar to that of the previous example:

```
Read fileName from standard input device
Open input file
while ( in.readStatus != in.EOF ) {
    arr[i++] = in.readDouble();
}
for ( i = 0; i <= nvals-2; i++ ) {

    // Find the minimum value in arr[i] through arr[nvals-1]
    iptr ← i;
    for ( j = i+1; j <= nvals-1; j++ ) {
        if (arr[j] < arr[iptr])
            iptr ← j;
    }

    // iptr now points to the min value, so swap
    // arr[iptr] with arr[i] if iptr != i.
    if (i != iptr) {
        temp ← arr[i];
        arr[i] ← arr[iptr];
        arr[iptr] ← temp;
    }
}
```

The fourth step is to calculate the required average, median, and standard deviation. To do this, we must first accumulate some statistics on the data (Σx and Σx^2), and then apply the definitions of average, median, and standard deviation given previously. The pseudocode for this step is as follows:

```
for (i = 0; i < nvals; i++) {
    sumX ← sumX + arr[i];
    sumX2 ← sumX2 + arr[i]*arr[i];
}
if (nvals >= 2) {
    xBar ← sumX / nvals;
    stdDev ← Math.sqrt((nvals*sumX2 - sumX*sumX) /(nvals*(nvals-1)));
    if nvals is an even number
        median ← (arr[nvals/2-1] + arr[nvals/2]) / 2;
    else
        median ← arr[nvals/2];
```

```
        }
        else {
            Tell user about insufficient data.
        }
```

We will decide if `nvals` is an even number by using the modulo operator `nvals%2`. If `nvals` is even, this operation will return a 0; if `nvals` is odd, it will return a 1. Finally, we must write out the results.

```
        Write out average, median, standard deviation, and no. of
        points
```

5. **Turn the algorithm into Java statements**. The resulting Java program is shown in Figure 5.10.

```
/*
   Purpose:
      To read in a set of double values from an input file, and calculate
      the mean, median, and standard deviation of the input data. The mean,
      median, and standard deviation are written to the standard output
      stream.

   Record of revisions:
      Date          Programmer        Description of change
      ====          ==========        =====================
      4/02/98       S. J. Chapman     Original code
*/
import chapman.io.*;
public class Stats3 {

   // Define the main method
   public static void main(String[] args) {

      // Define maximum array size
      final int MAXVAL = 1000;

      // Declare variables, and define each variable
      double arr[] = new double[MAXVAL];
                              // Array of input measurements
      String fileName;        // Input file name
      int i = 0, j;           // Loop index
      int iptr;               // Pointer to smallest value
      double median;          // Median of the input measurements
      int nvals;              // Number of data values to sort
      double stdDev = 0;      // The standard deviation of the input samples.
      double sumX = 0;        // The sum of the input values.
      double sumX2 = 0;       // The sum of the squares of the input values.
      double x = 0;           // An input data value.
      double xBar = 0;        // Average of the input measurements
      double temp;            // Temporary variable for swapping

      // Create a StdIn object
      StdIn in = new StdIn();

      // Get input file name
      System.out.print("Enter file name: ");
      fileName = in.readString();

      // Open file
      FileIn in1 = new FileIn(fileName);

      // Check for valid open
      if (in1.readStatus != in1.FILE_NOT_FOUND) {
```

Figure 5.10. *(cont.)*

```
          // Read numbers into array
          while (in1.readStatus != in1.EOF) {
             arr[i++] = in1.readDouble();
          }
          nvals = i;

          // Close file
          in1.close();

          // Sort values
          for (i = 0; i <= nvals-2; i++) {

             // Find the minimum value in arr[i] through arr[nvals-1]
             iptr = i;
             for (j = i+1; j <= nvals-1; j++) {
                if (arr[j] < arr[iptr])
             }

             // iptr now points to the min value, so swap a[iptr]
             // with a[i] if iptr != i.
             if (i != iptr) {
                temp = arr[i];
                arr[i] = arr[iptr];
                arr[iptr] = temp;
             }
          }


          // Calculate sums
          for (i = 0; i < nvals; i++) {
             sumX += arr[i];
             sumX2 += arr[i]*arr[i];
          }

          // Check to see if we have enough input data.
          if (nvals >= 2) {

             // There is enough information, so calculate the
             // mean, median, and standard deviation
             xBar = sumX / nvals;
             stdDev = Math.sqrt((nvals*sumX2-sumX*sumX)/(nvals*(nvals-1)));
             if (nvals%2 == 0)
                median = (arr[nvals/2-1] + arr[nvals/2]) / 2.;
             else
                median = arr[nvals/2];

             // Tell user.
             Fmt.printf("mean                 = %8.3f\n",xBar);
             Fmt.printf("median               = %8.3f\n",median);
             Fmt.printf("standard deviation = %8.3f\n",stdDev);
             Fmt.printf("No. of data points = %8d\n",nvals);
          }
          else {
             System.out.println("At least 2 values must be entered!");
          }
       }

       // Come here if file not found
       else {
          System.out.println("File " + fileName + " not found!");
       }
    }
  }
}
```

Figure 5.10.   A program to read values from an input file, and to calculate their mean, median, and standard deviation.

6. **Test the program**. To test this program, we will calculate the answers by hand for a simple data set, and then compare the answers to the results of the program. If we use five input values: 5, 3, 4, 1, and 9, then the mean and standard deviation is

$$\bar{x} = \frac{1}{N} \sum_{i=1}^{N} x_i = \frac{1}{5} 22 = 4.4,$$

$$s = \frac{\sqrt{N \sum_{i=1}^{N} x_i^2 - \left(\sum_{i=1}^{N} x_i \right)^2}}{N(N-1)} = 2.966,$$

median = 4.

If these values are placed in the file `input2` and the program is run with that file as an input, the results are

```
C:\book\java\chap5>java Stats3
Enter file name: input2
mean                = 4.400
median              = 4.000
standard deviation = 2.966
No. of data points =     5
```

The program gives the correct answers for our test data set.

5.6   INTRODUCTION TO PLOTTING

One of the great advantages of Java compared to other languages such as C and Fortran is that *device-and platform-independent graphics is built directly into the standard language*. While we will not learn the details of Java graphics until a later chapter, we will begin using Java's graphics capabilities here. The `chapman.graphics` package includes classes suitable for plotting arrays of data, and we will now learn how to use a class called **JPlot2D** to create two-dimensional plots of our data.

Java graphics are displayed in windows known as **frames**. A frame is a rectangular portion of a graphics display device that can be used to display Java graphics, including buttons, text boxes, plots, etc. A Java program can open as many frames as desired, and each frame can display different types of graphical information. The support for frames is included in Java's Abstract Windowing Toolkit, and in the Swing package. Any program that uses graphics must import packages `java.awt.*`, `javax.swing.*`, and `java.awt.event.*` from the toolkit.

For the time being, we will introduce a template that creates a frame without explaining the details of its operation, and we will use that template to display our plots.

Figure 5.11 shows a sample program that creates and displays a plot. The program creates arrays generated from the equations $y(x) = \sin x$ and $y(x) = 1.2 \cos x$ over the range $0 \leq x \leq 2\pi$, and plots the contents of those arrays.

```java
import java.awt.*;
import java.awt.event.*;
import javax.swing.*;
import chapman.graphics.JPlot2D;
public class TestPlot2D {
 /**
    * This method is an example of how to use Class JPlot2D. The
    * method creates a frame, and then places a new JPlot2D
    * object within the frame. It draws two curves on the
    * object, and also illustrates the use of line styles,
    * titles, labels, and grids.
    */
  public static void main(String s[]) {
     //*******************************************************
     //
     //   Create data to plot
     //
     //*******************************************************
     // Define arrays to hold the two curves to plot
     double x[] = new double[81];
     double y[] = new double[81];
     double z[] = new double[81];

      // Calculate a sine and a cosine wave
      for ( int i = 0; i < x.length; i++ ) {
         x[i] = (i+1) * 2 * Math.PI / 40;
         y[i] = Math.sin(x[i]);
         z[i] = 1.2 * Math.cos(x[i]);
      }

      //*******************************************************
      //
      // Create plot object and set plot information.
      //
      //*******************************************************

      JPlot2D p1 = new JPlot2D( x, y );
      p1.setPlotType ( JPlot2D.LINEAR );
      p1.setLineColor( Color.blue );
      p1.setLineWidth( 2.0f );
      p1.setLineStyle( JPlot2D.LINESTYLE_SOLID );
      p1.setMarkerState( JPlot2D.MARKER_ON );
      p1.setTitle( "Plot of sin(x) and 1.2*cos(x) vs. x" );
      p1.setXLabel( "x" );
      p1.setYLabel( "sin(x) and 1.2 cos(x)" );
      p1.setGridState( JPlot2D.GRID_ON );

      // Add a second curve to the plot.
      p1.addCurve( x, z );
      p1.setLineWidth( 3.0f );

      //*******************************************************
      //
      // Create a frame and place the plot in the center of the
      // frame. Note that the plot will occupy all of the
      // available space.
      //
      //*******************************************************

      JFrame fr = new JFrame("Plot2D ...");

      // Create a Window Listener to handle "close" events
      WindowHandler l = new WindowHandler();
```

Figure 5.11   *(cont.)*

```
                    fr.addWindowListener(l);

                    fr.getContentPane().add(pl, BorderLayout.CENTER);
                    fr.setSize(500,500);
                    fr.setVisible(true);
            }
    }


    //*************************************************************
    //
    // Create a window listener to close the program.
    //
    //*************************************************************

    class WindowHandler extends WindowAdapter {

            // This method implements a simple listener that detects
            // the "window closing event" and stops the program.
            public void windowClosing(WindowEvent e) {
                    System.exit(0);
            };
    }
```

Figure 5.11.   Program to create and plot a data set. The portions of the program in bold face must be modified to create different types of plots; the remainder of the program is Java "boilerplate."

When this program is executed, results are shown in Figure 5.12.

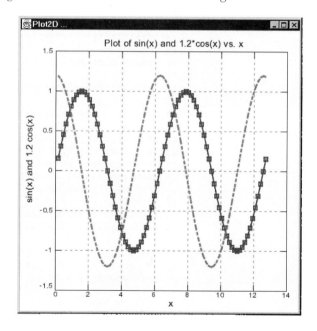

Figure 5.12.   Java plot of the equations $y(x) = \sin x$ and $y(x) = 1.2 \cos x$ over the range $0 \leq x \leq 2\pi$.

A new plot is created by instantiating a `JPlot2D` object, as shown:

```
JPlot2D pl = new JPlot2D(x,y);
```

This plot object will now automatically plot *x* versus *y* in any frame to which the object is added. Once the plot object has been created, a large number of methods may be called to

TABLE 5-5 Common Methods in Class `JPlot2D`

METHOD	DESCRIPTION
`addCurve(double[] x, double[] y)`	Add an additional curve to the plot.
`setGridState(int gs)`	Set the grid state. Legal values are `JPlot2D.GRID_OFF` (default), and `JPlot2D.GRID_ON`
`setLineColor(Color c)`	Set the line color. Legal values are any color defined in class `java.awt.Color`.
`setLineState(boolean b)`	Determines whether or not lines are to be plotted between data points on a curve. By default, lines *are* plotted. Legal values are: `JPlot2D.LINE_ON`, and `JPlot2D.LINE_OFF`.
`setLineStyle(int ls)`	Set the line style. Legal values are `JPlot2D.LINESTYLE_SOLID`, `JPlot2D.LINESTYLE_DOT`, `JPlot2D.LINESTYLE_LONGDASH`, and `JPlot2D.LINESTYLE_SHORTDASH`.
`setLineWidth(float w)`	Set the line width, in pixels.
`setMarkerColor(Color c)`	Set the marker color. Legal values are any color defined in class `java.awt.Color`.
`setMarkerState(boolean b)`	Determines whether or not markers are to be plotted at data points on a curve. By default, markers are *not* plotted. Legal values are: `JPlot2D.MARKER_ON`, and `JPlot2D.MARKER_OFF`.
`setMarkerStyle(int ms)`	Set the marker style. Legal values are as follows: `JPlot2D.MARKER_CIRCLE`, and `JPlot2D.MARKER_SQUARE`.
`setPlotType(int t)`	Set the plot type. Legal values are as follows: `JPlot2D.LINEAR` (default), `JPlot2D.SEMILOGX`, `JPlot2D.SEMILOGY`, `JPlot2D.LOGLOG`, `JPlot2D.BAR`, and `JPlot2D.POLAR`.
`setTitle(String s)`	Set the plot title.
`setXLabel(String s)`	Set the *x* label.
`setYLabel(String s)`	Set the *y* label.

modify and enhance the basic plot. Some of those methods are summarized in Table 5-5, and all of them are included in the on-line Java documentation for class `JPlot2D`.

5.7 TWO-DIMENSIONAL ARRAYS

The arrays that we have worked with so far in this chapter are **one-dimensional arrays**. These arrays can be visualized as a series of values laid out in a column, with a single subscript used to select the individual array elements (Figure 5.13*a*). Such arrays are useful to describe data that is a function of one independent variable, such as a series of temperature measurements made at fixed intervals of time.

Some types of data are functions of more than one independent variable. For example, we might wish to measure the temperature at five different locations at four different times. In this case, our 20 measurements could logically be grouped into five different columns of four measurements each, with a separate column for each location (Figure 5.13*b*). Java does not direct support two-dimensional arrays like this, but *Java arrays can be created with any type of data, including primitive data types, references to objects, or references to other arrays.* Therefore, we can declare an array, each of whose elements is a reference to another array, and the result is effectively a two-dimensional array (see Figure 5.14).

The elements of two-dimensional arrays are addressed with two subscripts, and any particular element in the array is selected by simultaneously choosing values for both of them. For example, Figure 5.15*a* shows a set of four generators whose power output has been measured at six different times. Figure 5.15*b* shows an array consisting of the six different power measurements for each of the four different generators. In

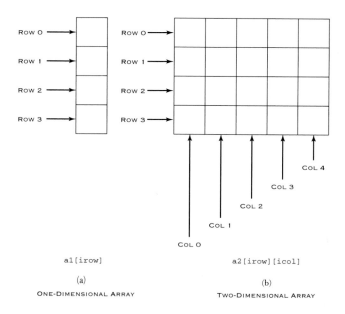

a1[irow]

(a)

ONE-DIMENSIONAL ARRAY

a2[irow][icol]

(b)

TWO-DIMENSIONAL ARRAY

Figure 5.13. Representations of one- and two-dimensional arrays.

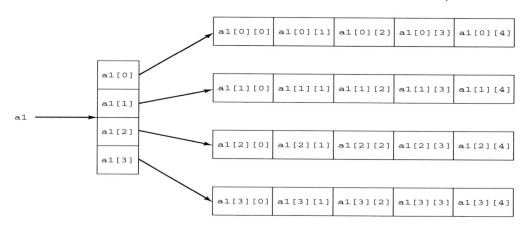

Figure 5.14. It is possible to create an array of references to other arrays.

this example, each row specifies a generator number, and each column specifies a measurement time. The array element containing the power supplied by generator 2 at time 3 would be `power[2][3]`; its value is 41.1 MW.

5.7.1 Declaring Two-Dimensional Arrays

Java implements two-dimensional arrays by creating *a one-dimensional array, each of whose elements is itself an array.* To declare a two-dimensional array, we must first declare a reference to *an array of arrays*, and afterward create the individual arrays associated with each element of that array. The declaration of a reference to an array of arrays looks similar to the examples seen earlier, except that there are *two* brackets after the array name. For example, a reference to an array of `double` arrays is created by the statement

```
double x[][];     // Create a reference to an array of arrays
```

Figure 5.15.   (*a*) A power generating station consisting of four different generators. The power output of each generator is measured at six different times. (*b*) Two-dimensional matrix of power measurements.

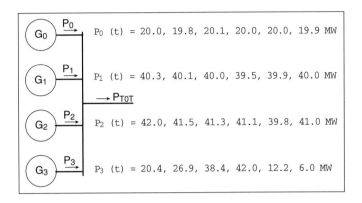

(a)

	T_0	T_1	T_2	T_3	T_4	T_5
G_0	20.0	19.8	20.1	20.0	20.0	19.9
G_1	40.3	40.1	40.0	39.5	39.9	40.0
G_2	42.0	41.5	41.3	41.1	39.8	41.0
G_3	20.4	26.9	38.4	42.0	12.2	6.0

(b)

Once the reference is created, we can create arrays to assign to the reference using the **new** operator. For example, the following statements creates an array of 3 new 5-element arrays and sets the reference x to refer to that array:

```
x = new double[3][5];   // Create array objects
```

The new operator is followed by the data type of the array object to be created and square brackets containing the number of elements to be allocated at each level. When the elements are allocated, they are automatically initialized to zero.

Note that *since a two-dimensional array is really an array of arrays, each sub-array can be declared independently.* The sub-arrays may have different lengths, but they must all have the same type. For example, the following statements create an integer array with 2 rows, with row 0 containing 5 columns and row 1 containing 3 columns.

```
int a[][];              // Declare reference
a = new int[2][];       // Create row of array references
a[0] = new int[5];      // Create columns for row 0
a[1] = new int[3];      // Create columns for row 1
```

Figure 5.16. (*a*) A two-dimensional array with two rows and three columns per row. (*b*) A two-dimensional array with an uneven number of columns per row. This array has two rows; row 0 has two columns and row 1 has three columns.

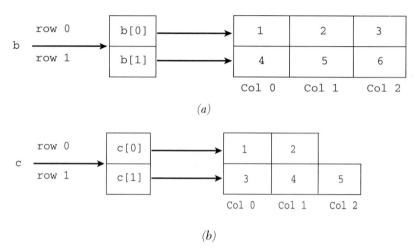

(*a*)

(*b*)

5.7.2 Initializing Two-Dimensional Arrays

A two-dimensional array may be initialized using *nested* array initializers. For example, the statement

```
int b[][] = { {1,2,3}, {4,5,6} };
```

declares a reference to a two-dimensional array b, and initializes the array with two rows, each containing three columns. The values are grouped by row in braces, so the row 0 elements b[0][0], b[0][1], and b[0][2] contain 1, 2, and 3, while the row 1 elements b[1][0], b[1][1], and b[1][2] contain 4, 5, and 6. The resulting data structure is shown in Figure 5.16*a*.

Two-dimensional arrays can also be initialized with an uneven number of columns. For example, the statement

```
int c[][] = { {1,2}, {3,4,5} };
```

declares a reference to a two-dimensional array c with two rows. Row 0 contains two columns, while row 1 contains three columns. Here, c[0][0] and c[0][1] contain 1 and 2, while c[1][0], c[1][1], and c[1][2] contain 3, 4, and 5. Note that there is no element c[0][2] for this array. The resulting data structure is shown in Figure 5.16*b*.

5.7.3 Initializing Two-Dimensional Arrays From a File

It is also possible to initialize a two-dimensional array by reading in data from a disk file. For example, a programmer might wish to initialize a 3×5 array v1 by reading the following data from a file input3:

```
2.34   14.31   5.02   5.01   -9.92
8.62   -1.01   2.01   3.55   -1.01
6.11   12.21   3.16   3.09   -7.89
```

This data can be read using the FileIn class, using a pair of nested for loops to assign the proper value to each array element. A sample program that initializes array v1 from a disk file is shown in Figure 5.17.

```
// Reading 2-D arrays from a file
import chapman.io.*;
public class Read2DArray {

    // Define the main method
    public static void main(String arg[]) {

        // Declare variables and arrays
        double v1[][] = new double[3][5]; // Input array
        int i = 0, j = 0;

        // Open file
        FileIn in = new FileIn("input3");

        // Check for valid open
        if ( in.readStatus != in.FILE_NOT_FOUND ) {

            // Read input data from the file
            for ( i = 0; i < 3; i++ ) {
                for ( j = 0; j < 5; j++ ) {
                    v1[i][j] = in.readDouble();
                }
            }

            // Close file
            in.close();

            // Display the data that we read in
            for ( i = 0; i < 3; i++ ) {
                for ( j = 0; j < 5; j++ ) {
                    Fmt.printf(" %9.4f", v1[i][j]);
                }
                System.out.println();
            }
        }

        // Get here if file not found.  Tell user
        else {
            System.out.println("File not found: input3");
        }
    }
}
```

Figure 5.17. Example program illustrating the initialization of two-dimensional arrays from a disk file.

When this program is executed with this data set, the results are:

```
D:\book\java\chap5>java Read2DArray
    2.3400   14.3100    5.0200    5.0100   -9.9200
    8.6200   -1.0100    2.0100    3.5500   -1.0100
    6.1100   12.2100    3.1600    3.0900   -7.8900
```

5.7.4 Example Problem

EXAMPLE 5-4: ELECTRIC POWER GENERATION

Figure 5.15b shows a series of electrical output power measurements at six different times for four different generators at the Acme Electric Power generating station. Write a program to read these values from a file, and to calculate the average power supplied by each generator over the measurement period, and the total power supplied by all of the generators at each time in the measurement period.

SOLUTION

1. **State the problem**. Calculate the average power supplied by each generator in the station over the measurement period, and calculate the total instantaneous power supplied by the generating station at each time within the measurement period, and the total power supplied by all of the generators at each time in the measurement period.

2. **Define the inputs and outputs**. The input to this program is a set of 24 real data values in the file, representing the power supplied by each of the 4 generators at each of 6 different times. The data in the input file must be organized so that the six values associated with generator G_0 appear on the first line, followed by the six values associated with generator G_1, *etc*.

   The outputs from this program are the average power supplied by each generator in the station over the measurement period, and the total instantaneous power supplied by the generating station at each time within the measurement period.

3. **Decompose the program into classes and their associated methods**. There will be a single class, and only the `main` method within that class. We will call the class `Generator`, and make it a subclass of the root class `Object`.

4. **Design the algorithm that you intend to implement for each method**. The `main` method can be broken down into four major steps

   ```
   Read the input data into an array
   Calculate the total instantaneous output power at each time
   Calculate the average output power of each generator
   Write the output values
   ```

   The detailed pseudocode for the method is given below:

   ```
   // Read input data from the standard input stream
   for ( igen = 0; igen < MAX_GEN; igen++ ) {
      for ( itime = 0; itime < MAX_TIME; itime++ ) {
         power[igen][itime] ← in1.readDouble();
      }
   }

   // Calculate the instantaneous output power of the station
   for ( igen = 0; igen < MAX_GEN; igen++ ) {
      for ( itime = 0; itime < MAX_TIME; itime++ ) {
         powerSum[itime] ← power[igen][itime] + powerSum[itime];
      }
   }

   // Calculate the average output power of each generator
   for ( igen = 0; igen < MAX_GEN; igen++ ) {
      for ( itime = 0; itime < MAX_TIME; itime++ ) {
         powerAve[igen] ← power[igen][itime] + powerAve[igen];
      }
      power_ave[igen] ← power_ave[igen] / MAX_TIME;
   }

   // Write out the total instantaneous power at each time
   Write out powerSum values

   // Write out the average output power of each generator
   Write out powerAve values
   ```

5. **Turn the algorithm into Java statements**. The resulting Java program is shown in Figure 5.18.

```
/*
    Purpose:
      To calculate total instantaneous power supplied by
      a generating station at each instant of time, and
      to calculate the average power supplied by each
                    generator over the period of measurement.

    Record of revisions:
        Date      Programmer         Description of change
        ====      ==========         =====================
      4/04/98   S. J. Chapman       Original code
*/
import chapman.io.*;
public class Generator {

    // Define the main method
    public static void main{String[] args) [

    // Declare variables, and define each variable
    final int MAX_GEN = 4;       // Max number of generators
    final int MAX_TIME = 6;      // Max number of times
    String fileName;             // Input file name
    int igen;                    // Loop index: generators
    int itime;                   // Loop index: time
    double power[][] = new double[MAX_GEN][MAX_TIME];
                                 // Power of each generator at each time
    double powerAve[] = new double[MAX_GEN];
                                 // Ave power of each gen over all times
    double powerSum[] = new double[MAX_TIME];
                                 // Total power of station at each time

    // Create StdIn object
    StdIn in = new StdIn();

    // Get input file name
    System.out.print("Enter file name: ");
    fileName = in.readString();

    // Open file
    FileIn in1 = new FileIn(fileName);

    // Check for valid open
    if ( in1.readStatus != in1.FILE_NOT_FOUND ) {

        // Read input data from the input file
        for ( igen = 0; igen < MAX_GEN; igen++ ) {
            for ( itime = 0; itime < MAX_TIME; itime++ ) {
                power[igen][itime] = in1.readDouble();
            }
        }

        // Close file
        in1.close();

        // Calculate the instantaneous output power of the station
        for ( igen = 0; igen < MAX_GEN; igen++ ) {
            for ( itime = 0; itime < MAX_TIME; itime++ ) {
                powerSum[itime] += power[igen][itime];
            }
        }
```

Figure 5.18   *(cont.)*

```
                    // Calculate the average output power of each generator
                    for ( igen = 0; igen < MAX_GEN; igen++ ) {
                        for ( itime = 0; itime < MAX_TIME; itime++ ) {
                            powerAve[igen] += power[igen][itime];
                        }
                        powerAve[igen] = powerAve[igen] / MAX_TIME;
                    }

                    // Tell user.
                    for ( itime = 0; itime < MAX_TIME; itime++ ) {
                        Fmt.printf("Power at time %2d = ",itime);
                        Fmt.printf("%7.2f MW\n",powerSum[itime]);
                    }
                    for ( itime = 0; itime < MAX_TIME; igen++ ) {
                        Fmt.printf("Ave Power at Gen %2d = ",igen);
                        Fmt.printf("%7.2f MW\n",powerAve[igen]);
                    }
                }
                // Come here if input file not found
                else {
                    System.out.println("File " + fileName + " not found!");
                }
            }
        }
    }
```

Figure 5.18. Program to calculate the instantaneous power produced by a generating station, and the average power produced by each generator within the station.

6. **Test the program.** To test this program, we will place the data from Figure 5.15*b* into a file called gendat. The contents of file gendat are shown below:

20.0	19.8	20.1	20.0	20.0	19.9
40.3	40.1	40.0	39.5	39.9	40.0
42.0	41.5	41.3	41.1	39.8	41.0
20.4	26.9	38.4	42.0	12.2	6.0

Note that each row of the file corresponds to a specific generator, and each column corresponds to a specific time. Next, we will calculate the answers by hand for one generator and one time, and compare the results with those from the program. At time 2 (where the first time is considered time 0), the total instantaneous power being supplied by all of the generators is

$$P_{TOT} = 20.1 \text{ MW} + 40.0 \text{ MW} + 41.3 \text{ MW} + 38.4 \text{ MW} = 139.8 \text{ MW}$$

The average power for Generator 0 is

$$P_{G1,AVE} = \frac{20.0 + 19.8 + 20.1 + 20.0 + 20.0 + 19.9}{6} = 19.97 \text{ MW}$$

The output from the program is

```
D:\book\java\chap5>java Generator
Enter file name: gendat
Power at time  0 =  122.70 MW
Power at time  1 =  128.30 MW
Power at time  2 =  139.8 MW
Power at time  3 =  142.60 MW
Power at time  4 =  111.90 MW
Power at time  5 =  106.90 MW
Ave power of Gen  0 =   19.97 MW
```

```
Ave power of Gen  1 =   39.97 MW
Ave power of Gen  2 =   41.12 MW
Ave power of Gen  3 =   24.32 MW
```

so the numbers match, and the program appears to be working correctly.

5.7.5 Multi-Dimensional Arrays

It is possible to declare an manipulate arrays with more than two dimensions in Java. This is done as a direct extension of the way Java implements two-dimensional arrays by simply adding additional subscripts and additional layers of subarrays. For example, a $2 \times 2 \times 2$ array `arr3` could be declared and initialized as:

```
int arr3[][][] = { {{1, 2}, {2,4}}, {{5, 6}, {7, 8}} };
```

Note that there are three levels of braces in this array initializer.

There is no limit to the number of subscripts that may be included with a Java array.

PRACTICE!

This quiz provides a quick check to see if you have understood the concepts introduced in Sections 5.4 through 5.7. If you have trouble with the quiz, reread the section, ask your instructor, or discuss the material with a fellow student. The answers to this quiz are found in the back of the book.

For questions 1 and 2, determine the number of elements in the array specified by the declaration statements and the valid subscript range(s) for each array.

1. `double z[][] = new double[5][7];`

2. `double z[][];`
```
z = new double[3];
z[0] = new double[2];
z[1] = new double[4];
z[2] = new double[3];
```

Determine which of the following Java statements are valid. If they are invalid, explain why they are invalid.

3. `double a[][] = { {1, 3, 2}, {-1, 2} };`

4. `int c[][];`
`c = new double[3][3];`

5. `double x[];`
`x = new double[3][3];`

SUMMARY

- An **array** is a special object containing (*1*) a group of contiguous memory locations that all have the same name and same type, and (*2*) a separate instance variable containing an integer constant equal to the number of elements in the array.

- The length of a Java array is specified when it is created, and it remains fixed for as long as the array exists.

- A *reference* is a "handle" or "pointer" to an object that permits Java to locate the object in memory when it is needed. A reference is declared by naming the object type followed by the reference name.

- Once an array reference exists, new arrays are created using the `new` operator.
- Arrays may be initialized with an array initializer, which is just a comma-separated list of valued enclosed in braces.
- Java programs always include automatic bounds checking, and any attempt to address an out-of-bounds array element will produce an exception.
- Reading from and writing to disk files can be rather complicated in Java, but the task is simplified by the use of convenience classes such as the classes `FileIn` and `FileOut` supplied with this book.
- The contents of arrays may be plotted using the `chapman.graphics.JPlot2D` class supplied with this book.
- Two-dimensional arrays are implemented in Java as arrays of arrays.

APPLICATIONS: GOOD PROGRAMMING PRACTICES

The following guidelines introduced in this chapter will help you to develop good programs:

1. When creating `for` loops to process the elements of an array, use the array object's `length` field in the continuation condition for the loop. This will allow the loop to adjust automatically for different sized arrays.
2. When processing an array `arr` in a `for` loop, use a continuation condition of the form

   ```
   for ( j = 0; j < arr.length; j++ ).
   ```

   The "less than" relational operator is the correct one to use, because the elements of the array are numbered `0,1,...,  arr.length-1`.
3. Declare the sizes of arrays in a Java program using named constants (called final variables in Java) to make them easy to change.

KEY TERMS

Abstract Windowing Toolkit (AWT)	instantiate
array	null
array element	one-dimensional array
`arrayIndexOutOfBoundsException`	out of bounds
array initializer	reference
bounds checking	token
command-line redirection	two-dimensional array
frame	

Problems

5.1. How may arrays be declared?

5.2. What is the difference between an array and an array element?

5.3. Determine if each of the following array specifications is valid or not. If it is, determine the shape and size of the arrays specified by the following declaration statements, and the valid subscript range for each dimension of each array. How many elements are there in each of the arrays?

   a. `float data[] = new float[6][6];`

   b.
```
double data1[][];
data1 = new double[3];
data1[0] = new double[3];
data1[1] = new double[2];
data1[2] = new double[4];
```

   c.
```
int data2[][][] = new int[3][4][5]
```

   d.
```
float data3[][] = new double[5][7];
```

5.4.   Determine whether or not the following Java program fragment is valid. If it is, specify what will happen in the program. If not, explain why not.

```
int b[] = new int[6][4];
int temp;
...
for ( i = 0; i < 6; i++ ) {
   for ( j = 0; j < 4; j++ ) {
      temp    = b(i,j)
      b(i,j) = b(j,i);
      b(j,i) = temp;
   }
}
```

5.5.   **Polar to Rectangular Conversion**   A *scalar quantity* is a quantity that can be represented by a single number. For example, the temperature at a given location is a scalar. In contrast, a *vector* is a quantity that has both a magnitude and a direction associated with it. For example, the velocity of an automobile is a vector, since it has both a magnitude and a direction.

Vectors can be defined either by a magnitude and a direction, or by the components of the vector projected along the axes of a rectangular coordinate system. The two representations are equivalent. For two-dimensional vectors, we can convert back and forth between the representations using the following equations.

$$\mathbf{V} = V \angle \theta = V_x \mathbf{i} + V_y \mathbf{j}$$
$$V_x = V \cos \theta$$
$$V_y = V \sin \theta$$
$$V = \sqrt{V_x^2 + V_y^2}$$
$$\theta = \tan^{-1} \frac{V_y}{V_x}$$

where **i** and **j** are the unit vectors in the *x*- and *y*-directions respectively. The representation of the vector in terms of magnitude and angle is known as *polar coordinates*, and the representation of the vector in terms of components along the axes is know as *rectangular coordinates*.

Figure 5.19.   Representations of a vector.

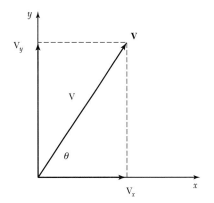

Write a program that reads the polar coordinates (magnitude and angle) of a two-dimensional vector into a two-element array `polar` (`polar[0]` will contain the magnitude V and `polar[1]` will contain the angle θ in degrees), and converts the vector from polar to rectangular form, storing the result in a two-element array `rect`. The first element of `rect` should contain the x-component of the vector, and the second element should contain the y-component of the vector. After the conversion, display the contents of array `rect`. Test your program by converting the following polar vectors to rectangular form:

a. $5\angle-36.87°$

b. $10\angle45°$

c. $25\angle233.13°$

5.6.   **Rectangular to Polar Conversion**   Write a program that reads the rectangular components of a two-dimensional vector into a two-element array `rect` (`rect[0]` will contain the component V_x, and `rect[1]` will contain the component V_y) and converts the vector from rectangular to polar form, storing the result in a two-element array `polar`. The first element of `polar` should contain the magnitude of the vector, and the second element should contain the angle of the vector in degrees. After the conversion, display the contents of array `polar`. (*Hint:* Look up method `Math.atan2`.) Test your program by converting the following rectangular vectors to polar form:

a. $3\,\mathbf{i} - 4\,\mathbf{j}$

b. $5\,\mathbf{i} + 5\,\mathbf{j}$

c. $-5\,\mathbf{i} + 12\,\mathbf{j}$

5.7.   Assume that `values` is a 101-element array containing a list of measurements from a scientific experiment, which has been declared by the statement:

```
double values[] = new double[101];
```

Write the Java statements that would count the number of positive values, negative values, and zero values in the array, and write out a message summarizing how many values of each type were found.

5.8.   Write Java statements that would print out every fifth value in the array `values` described in Exercise 5.7. Theoutput should take the form

```
values[0]  = x.xx
values[5]  = x.xx
...
values[100] = x.xx
```

5.9.   Modify the selection sort program in Example 5-2 so that it writes the sorted data set to a user-specified file.

5.10.   Write a program that can read in a two-dimensional array from a user-specified file, and calculate the sums all the data in each row and each column in the array. The size of the array to read in will be specified by two numbers on the first line in the input file, and the elements in each row of the array will be found on a single line of the input file. An example of an input data file containing a 2 row × 4 column array is shown below:

```
     2          4
 -24.0    -1121.    812.1    11.1
  35.6     8.1E3   135.23   -17.3
```

Write out the results in the form:

```
Sum of row  1 =
Sum of row  2 =
    ...
Sum of col  1 =
    ...
```

5.11.   Test the program that you wrote in Exercise 5.10 by running it on the following array:

$$\text{array} = \begin{bmatrix} 33. & -12. & 16. & 0.5 & -1.9 \\ -6. & -14. & 3.5 & 11. & 2.1 \\ 4.4 & 1.1 & -7.1 & 9.3 & -16.1 \\ 0.3 & 6.2 & -9.9 & -12. & 6.8 \end{bmatrix}$$

5.12. **Dot Product** A three-dimensional vector can be represented in rectangular coordinates as

$$\mathbf{V} = V_x\mathbf{i} + V_y\mathbf{j} + V_z\mathbf{k}$$

where V_x is the component of vector $\mathbf{V}$ in the x direction, V_y is the component of vector $\mathbf{V}$ in the y direction, and V_z is the component of vector $\mathbf{V}$ in the z direction. Such a vector can be stored in a three-element array, since there are three dimensions in the coordinate system. The same idea applies to an n-dimensional vector. An n-dimensional vector can be stored in a rank-1 array containing n elements.

One common mathematical operation between two vectors is the *dot product*. The dot product of two vectors $\mathbf{V}_1 = V_{x1}\mathbf{i} + V_{y1}\mathbf{j} + V_{z1}\mathbf{k}$ and $\mathbf{V}_2 = V_{x2}\mathbf{i} + V_{y2}\mathbf{j} + V_{z2}\mathbf{k}$ is a scalar quantity defined by the equation

$$\mathbf{V}_1 \bullet \mathbf{V}_2 = V_{x1}V_{x2} + V_{y1}V_{y2} + V_{z1}V_{z2}$$

Write a Java program that will read two vectors $\mathbf{V}_1$ and $\mathbf{V}_2$ into two one-dimensional arrays in computer memory, and then calculate their dot product according to the equation given above. Test your program by calculating the dot product of vectors $\mathbf{V}_1 = 5\,\mathbf{i} - 3\,\mathbf{j} + 2\,\mathbf{k}$ and $\mathbf{V}_2 = 2\,\mathbf{i} + 3\,\mathbf{j} + 4\,\mathbf{k}$.

5.13. **Power Supplied to an Object** If an object is being pushed by a force $\mathbf{F}$ at a velocity $\mathbf{v}$, then the power supplied to the object by the force is given by the equation

$$P = \mathbf{F} \bullet \mathbf{v}$$

where the force $\mathbf{F}$ is measured in newtons, the velocity $\mathbf{v}$ is measured in meters per second, and the power P is measured in watts. Use the Java program written in the Exercise 5-12 to calculate the power supplied by a force of $\mathbf{F} = 4\,\mathbf{i} + 3\,\mathbf{j} - 2\,\mathbf{k}$ newtons to an object moving with a velocity of $\mathbf{v} = 4\,\mathbf{i} - 2\,\mathbf{j} + 1\,\mathbf{k}$ meters per second.

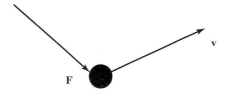

Figure 5.20. A force $\mathbf{F}$ applied to an object moving with velocity $\mathbf{v}$.

5.14. Write a set of Java statements that would search a three-dimensional array `arr` and limit the maximum value of any array element to be less than or equal to 1000. If any element exceeds 1000, its value should be set to 1000. Assume that array `arr` has dimensions $1000 \times 10 \times 30$.

5.15. **Cross Product** Another common mathematical operation between two vectors is the *cross product*. The cross product of two vectors $\mathbf{V}_1 = V_{x1}\mathbf{i} + V_{y1}\mathbf{j} + V_{z1}\mathbf{k}$ and $\mathbf{V}_2 = V_{x2}\mathbf{i} + V_{y2}\mathbf{j} + V_{z2}\mathbf{k}$ is a vector quantity defined by the equation

$$\mathbf{V}_1 \times \mathbf{V}_2 = (V_{y1}V_{z2} - V_{y2}V_{z1})\mathbf{i} + (V_{z1}V_{x2} - V_{z2}V_{x1})\mathbf{j} + (V_{x1}V_{y2} - V_{x2}V_{y1})\mathbf{k}$$

Write a Java program that will read two vectors $\mathbf{V}_1$ and $\mathbf{V}_2$ into arrays in computer memory, and then calculate their cross product according to the equation given above. Test your program by calculating the cross product of vectors $\mathbf{V}_1 = 5\,\mathbf{i} - 3\,\mathbf{j} + 2\,\mathbf{k}$ and $\mathbf{V}_2 = 2\,\mathbf{i} + 3\,\mathbf{j} + 4\,\mathbf{k}$.

5.16. **Velocity of an Orbiting Object**   The vector angular velocity ω of an object moving with a velocity $\mathbf{v}$ at a distance $\mathbf{r}$ from the origin of the coordinate system is given by the equation

$$\mathbf{v} = \mathbf{r} \times \omega$$

where $\mathbf{r}$ is the distance in meters, ω is the angular velocity in radians per second, and $\mathbf{v}$ is the velocity in meters per second. If the distance from the center of the earth to an orbiting satellite is $\mathbf{r} = 300000\,\mathbf{i} + 400000\,\mathbf{j} + 50000\,\mathbf{k}$ meters, and the angular velocity of the satellite is $\omega = -6 \times 10^{-3}\,\mathbf{i} + 2 \times 10^{-3}\,\mathbf{j} - 9 \times 10^{-4}\,\mathbf{k}$ radians per second, what is the velocity of the satellite in meters per second? Use the program written in the previous exercise to calculate the answer.

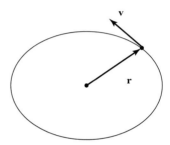

Figure 5.21.   The velocity of an orbiting object.

5.17. Plot the function $y(t) = e^{-0.8t} \cos 4\pi t$ from $t = 0$ to $t = 3$. For what fraction of the interval is $y(t) > 0.5$?

5.18. Plot the function $y(x) = 2e^{-0.8x}$ from $x = 0$ to $x = 10$ on both a linear and a semilog scale. What does this function look like on each scale?

5.19. Figure 5.22 shows an electrical load with a voltage applied to it and a current flowing into it. Assume that the voltage applied to this load is given by the equation $v(t) = 17 \sin 377\,t$ V and the current flowing into the load is given by the equation $i(t) = 1.414 \sin(377t - \pi/6)$ A. Write a Java program the performs the following actions:

   a. Create two arrays storing the voltage and current applied to the load as a function of time. There should be 1000 samples in each array, spaced at intervals of 0.1 ms.

   b. Calculate the instantaneous power supplied to the load at each time from the equation $P(t) = v(t)i(t)$, and store the power in an array.

   c. Plot the voltage, current, and power as a function of time from $t = 0$ s to $t = 0.1$ s.

   d. Calculate the average power supplied to the load over this interval.

5.20. The location of any point P in a three-dimensional space can be represented by a set of three values (x, y, z), where x is the distance along the x axis to the point, y is the distance along the y axis to the point, and z is the distance along the z axis to the point. If two points, P_1 and P_2 are represented by the values (x_1, y_1, z_1) and (x_2, y_2, z_2), then the distance between the points P_1 and P_2 can be calculated from the equation

$$distance = \sqrt{(x_1 - x_2)^2 + (y_1 - y_2)^2 + (z_1 - z_2)^2}$$

Write a Java program to read in two points (x_1, y_1, z_1) and (x_2, y_2, z_2), and to calculate the distance between them. Test your program by calculating the distance between the points $(-1, 4, 6)$ and $(1, 5, -2)$.

Figure 5.22. AC voltage and current supplied to an electrical load.

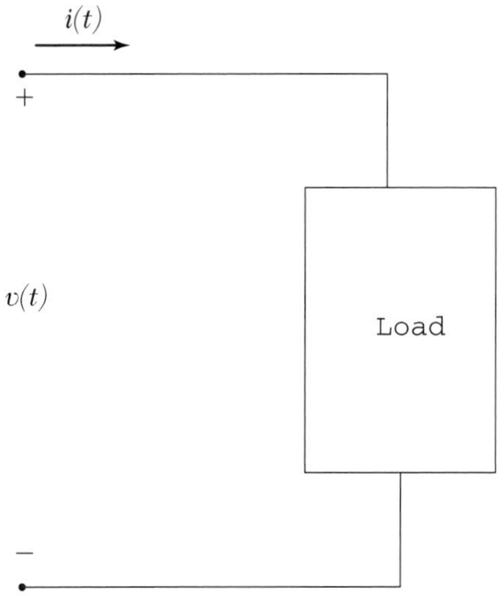

5.21.   **Average Annual Temperature**   As a part of a meterorological experiment, average annual temperature measurements were collected at 36 locations specified by latitude and longitude as shown in the chart below.

	90.0° W LONG	90.5° W LONG	91.0° W LONG	91.5° W LONG	92.0° W LONG	92.5° W LONG
30.0° N lat	68.2	72.1	72.5	74.1	74.4	74.2
30.5° N lat	69.4	71.1	71.9	73.1	73.6	73.7
31.0° N lat	68.9	70.5	70.9	71.5	72.8	73.0
31.5° N lat	68.6	69.9	70.4	70.8	71.5	72.2
32.0° N lat	68.1	69.3	69.8	70.2	70.9	71.2
32.5° N lat	68.3	68.8	69.6	70.0	70.5	70.9

Write a Java program that calculates the average annual temperature along each latitude included in the experiment, and the average annual temperature along each longitude included in the experiment. Finally, calculate the average annual temperature for all of the locations in the experiment.

5.22.   **Matrix Multiplication**   Matrix multiplication is only defined for two matrices in which *the number of columns in the first matrix is equal to the number of rows in the second matrix*. If matrix A is an $N \times L$ matrix, and matrix B is an $L \times M$ matrix, then the product $C = A \times B$ is an $N \times M$ matrix whose elements are given by the equation

$$c_{ik} = \sum_{j=1}^{L} a_{ij} b_{jk}$$

For example, if matrices A and B are 2×2 matrices

$$A = \begin{bmatrix} 3.0 & 1.0 \\ 1.0 & 2.0 \end{bmatrix} \text{ and } B = \begin{bmatrix} 1.0 & 4.0 \\ 2.0 & -3.0 \end{bmatrix}$$

then the elements of matrix C will be

$$c_{11} = a_{11}b_{11} + a_{12}b_{21} = (3.0)(1.0) + (-1.0)(2.0) = 1.0$$

$$c_{12} = a_{11}b_{12} + a_{12}b_{22} = (3.0)(4.0) + (-1.0)(3.0) = 15.0$$

$$c_{21} = a_{21}b_{11} + a_{22}b_{21} = (1.0)(1.0) + (2.0)(2.0) = 5.0$$

$$c_{22} = a_{21}b_{12} + a_{22}b_{22} = (1.0)(4.0) + (2.0)(-3.0) = -2.0$$

Write a program that can read two matrices of arbitrary size from two input disk files, multiply them if they are of compatible sizes, and write the result to a third user-specified file. If the matrices are of incompatible sizes, an appropriate error message should be printed. The number of rows and columns in each matrix will be specified by two integers on the first line in each file, and the elements in each row of the matrix will be found on a single line of the input file (this format is the same as than in Exercise 5.10). Use arrays to hold both the input matrices and the resulting output matrix. Verify your program by creating two input data files containing matrices of the compatible sizes, calculating the resulting values, and checking the answers by hand. Also, verify the proper behavior of the program if it is given two matrices are of incompatible sizes.

5.23. Use the program produces in Exercise 5.22 to calculate $C = A \times B$ where:

$$A = \begin{bmatrix} 1.0 & -5.0 & 4.0 & 2.0 \\ -6.0 & -4.0 & 2.0 & 2.0 \end{bmatrix} \quad \text{and } B = \begin{bmatrix} 1.0 & -2.0 & -1.0 \\ 2.0 & 3.0 & 4.0 \\ 0.0 & -1.0 & 2.0 \\ 0.0 & -3.0 & 1.0 \end{bmatrix}$$

How many rows and how many columns are present in the resulting matrix C?

5.24. **Relative Maxima** A point in a two-dimensional array is said to be a *relative maximum* if it is higher than any of the 8 points surrounding it. For example, the element at position (2,2) in the array shown below is a relative maximum, since it is larger than any of the surrounding points.

$$\begin{bmatrix} 11 & 7 & -2 \\ -7 & 14 & 3 \\ 2 & -3 & 5 \end{bmatrix}$$

Write a program to read a matrix a from a file, and to scan for all relative maxima within the matrix. The first line in the file should contain the number of rows and the number of columns in the matrix, and then the next lines should contain the values in the matrix, with all of the values in a given row on a single line of the input disk file. The program should only consider interior points within the matrix, since any point along an edge of the matrix cannot be completely surrounded by points lower than itself. Test your program by finding all of the relative maxima the following matrix, which can be found in file findpeak:

$$A = \begin{bmatrix} 2. & -1. & -2. & 1. & 3. & -5. & 2. & 1. \\ -2. & 0. & -2.5 & 5. & -2. & 2. & 1. & 0. \\ -3. & -3. & -3. & 3. & 0. & 0. & -1. & -2. \\ -4.5 & -4. & -7. & 6. & 1. & -3. & 0. & 5. \\ -3.5 & -3. & -5. & 0. & 4. & 17. & 11. & 5. \\ -9. & -6. & -5. & -3. & 1. & 2. & 0. & 0.5 \\ -7. & -4. & -5. & -3. & 2. & 4. & 3. & -1. \\ -6. & -5. & -5. & -2. & 0. & 1. & 2. & 5. \end{bmatrix}$$

5.25.   **Temperature Distribution on a Metallic Plate**   Under steady-state conditions, the temperature at any point on the surface of a metallic plate will be the average of the temperatures of all points surrounding it. This fact can be used in an iterative procedure to calculate the temperature distribution at all points on the plate.

Figure 5.23 shows a square plate divided in 100 squares or nodes by a grid. The temperatures of the nodes form a two-dimensional array T. The temperature in all nodes at the edges of the plate is constrained to be 20° C by a cooling system, and the temperature of the node (2,7) is fixed at 100° C by exposing to boiling water.

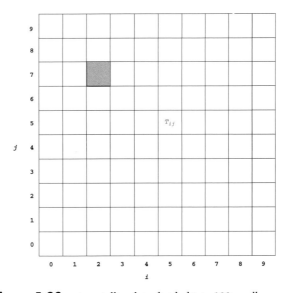

Figure 5.23.   A metallic plate divided into 100 small segments.

A new estimate of the temperature $T_{i,j}$ in any given node can be calculated from the average of the temperatures in all segments surrounding it:

$$T_{ij,new} = \frac{1}{4}\ (T_{i+1,j} + T_{i-1,j} + T_{i,j+1} + T_{i,j-1}) \tag{5-2}$$

To determine the temperature distribution on the surface of a plate, an initial assumption must be made about the temperatures in each node. Then Equation 5-2 is applied to each node whose temperature is not fixed to calculate a new estimate of the temperature in that node. These updated temperature estimates are used to calculate newer estimates, and the process is repeated until the new temperature estimates in each node differ from the old ones by only a small amount. At that point, a steady-state solution has been found.

Write a program to calculate the steady-state temperature distribution throughout the plate, making an initial assumption that all interior segments are at a temperature of 50°C. Remember that all outside segments are fixed at a temperature of 20°C and segment (2,7) is fixed at a temperature of 100°C. The program should apply Equation 5-2 iteratively until the maximum temperature change between iterations in any node is less than 0.01 degree. What will the steady-state temperature of segment (4,4) be?

6

Methods

A **method** is a separate piece of code that can be called by a main program or another method to perform some specific function. Each method must be defined within the body of some class, and many methods can be defined within a single class.

A method may be **called** or **invoked** by a main program or another method. The method is called by naming both the method and the object that it is defined within in an expression, together with a list of **parameters** in parentheses. (Parameters are values passed to the method to use in its calculations.) When the method finishes its calculations, it usually returns a *single* value to the calling program, and the calling program uses that value in its own calculations.

Figure 6.1 shows a simple program consisting of a single class containing two methods. One of these methods is the `main` method that we have seen before, and the second one is method `square`. Method `square` is defined on lines 17-21 of the program. This method accepts a single integer parameter, and calculates and returns the square of that parameter to the calling program.

To use method `square`, the main program must first create an object of the type that the method is defined

SECTIONS

- 6.1 Why Use Methods?
- 6.2 Method Definitions
- 6.3 Variable Passing in Java: The Pass-by-Value Scheme
- 6.4 Example Problem
- 6.5 Automatic Variables
- 6.6 Scope
- 6.7 Recursive Methods
- 6.8 Method Overloading
- 6.9 Class `java.util.Arrays`
- 6.10 Additional Methods Supplied With This Book
- Summary
- Key Terms

OBJECTIVES

After reading this chapter, you should be able to:

- Learn how to create and use methods
- Learn about the pass-by-value scheme used to pass parameters to methods
- Learn about variable duration and scope
- Learn about recursive methods
- Learn how to use methods in the `java.util.Arrays` class
- Learn how to use methods in the `chapman.math` package

```
1    // Calculates the squares of the numbers from 1 to 10
2    public class SquareInt {
3
4       // Define the main method
5       public static void main(String[] args) {
6
7          // Instantiate a SquareInt object
8          SquareInt sq = new SquareInt();
9
10         // Write number and square
11         for ( int i = 1; i <= 10; i++ ) {
12            System.out.print("number = " + i);
13            System.out.println(" square = " + sq.square(i));
14         }
15      }
16
17      // Definition of square method
18      public int square (int x) {
19
20         return x * x;
21      }
22   }
```

Figure 6.1. A program to calculate the squares of integers from 1 to 10. This program uses method square to calculate the squares of the integers.

within. This is done on line 8, which creates a new `SquareInt` object and assigns it to reference `sq`. Method `square` is actually called in line 13 with the expression `sq.square(i)`. Note that the program names the object containing the method, followed a period and the method name, followed by the calling parameters in parentheses. The value of integer `i` is passed to the method and stored in parameter `x`, and the method calculates and returns x^2. The `main` program then uses the returned value in the `System.out.println` function on line 13 (see Figure 6.2).

When this program is executed, the results are

```
D:\book\java\chap6>java Squares
number = 0 square = 0
number = 1 square = 1
number = 2 square = 4
number = 3 square = 9
number = 4 square = 16
number = 5 square = 25
number = 6 square = 36
number = 7 square = 49
number = 8 square = 64
number = 9 square = 81
```

Figure 6.2. When the method named square appears in the expression, the method is called with the specified parameter i. The method then calculates i^2 and returns the result to the calling method. The calling method uses that result in its println statement.

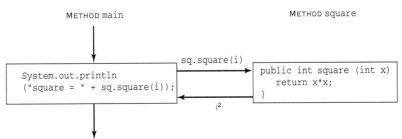

Note that method `square` was used 10 times to calculate 10 different squares. This same method could also have been used anywhere else within the program that we wanted to calculate the square of an integer.

6.1 WHY USE METHODS?

In Chapter 3, we learned the importance of good program design. The basic technique that we employed was **top-down design**. In top-down design, the programmer starts with a statement of the problem to be solved and the required inputs and outputs. Next, he or she describes the algorithm to be implemented by the program in broad outline, and applies *decomposition* to break the algorithm down into logical subdivisions called sub-tasks. Then, the programmer breaks down each sub-task until he or she winds up with many small pieces, each of which does a simple, clearly understandable job. Finally, the individual pieces are turned into Java code.

Although we have followed this design process in our examples, the results have been somewhat restricted, because we have had to combine the final Java code generated for each sub-task into a single large program. There has been no way to code, verify, and test each sub-task independently before combining them into the final program.

Fortunately, Java has two special features designed to make sub-tasks easy to develop and debug independently before building the final program: **classes** and **methods**. Classes are separately-compiled units containing data, together with the methods to manipulate that data. Methods are procedures that describe how to modify or manipulate the data contained in the class. Both classes and methods allow us to chop large programs up into smaller pieces which can be independently coded, tested, and verified. They also allow us to create *reusable* software, since a class created for one program can often be used intact in another program that needs the same features. We are studying methods in this chapter, and followed by classes in Chapter 7.

Well-designed classes and methods enormously reduce the effort required on a large programming project. Their benefits include:

1. **Independent testing of sub-tasks**. Each sub-task can be coded and compiled as an independent unit. The sub-task can be tested separately to ensure that it performs properly by itself before combining it into the larger program. This step is know as **unit testing**. It eliminates a major source of problems before the final program is even built.

2. **Reusable code**. In many cases, the same basic sub-task is needed in many parts of a program. For example, it may be necessary to sort a list of values into ascending order many different times within a program, or even in other programs. It is possible to design, code, test, and debug a *single* method to do the sorting, and then to reuse that method whenever sorting is required. This reusable code has two major advantages: it reduces the total programming effort required, and it simplifies debugging, since the sorting method only needs to be debugged once.

3. **Isolation from unintended side effects**. A caller communicates with the methods that it invokes through a list of values called an **argument list**. *The only values in the caller that are visible to the method are those in the argument list*. This is very important, since accidental programming mistakes can only affect the variables in the method in which the mistake occurred.

Once a large program is written and released, it has to be *maintained*. Program maintenance involves fixing bugs and modifying the program to handle new and unforeseen circumstances. The programmer who modifies a program during maintenance is often not the person who originally wrote it. In poorly written programs, it is common for the programmer modifying the program to make a change in one region of the code, and to have that change cause unintended side effects in a totally different part of the program. This happens because variable names are re-used in different portions of the program. When the programmer changes the values left behind in some of the variables, those values are accidentally picked up and used in other portions of the code.

The use of well-designed methods and classes minimizes this problem by **information hiding**. Except for the values in its argument list, *all of the variables within a called method are completely invisible from its calling method*, and *all of the variables in the calling method are completely invisible from the called method*. Since the variables in one method are invisible to the other method, one method cannot accidentally change the other method's variables. Thus, modifications in one of the methods will not cause unintended side-effects in the other method.

GOOD PROGRAMMING PRACTICE

Break large programming tasks into classes and methods whenever practical to achieve the important benefits of independent component testing, reusability, and isolation from unintended side effects.

6.2 METHOD DEFINITIONS

The general form of a method definition is as follows:

```
[keywords] return-value-type method-name( parameter-list ) {

    declarations and statements
    (return statement)
}
```

The *method-name* is any valid Java identifier. The *return-value-type* is the data type of the result returned from the method to the caller. If no value is returned from the method, then the *return-value-type* is **void**. A *return-value-type* must be specified for every method. If the *return-value-type* is not **void**, then a **return** statement must appear in the body of the method to specify the value to be passed back to the calling method.

The *parameter-list* is a comma-separated list containing the declarations of the parameters received by the method whenever it is called. If the method does not receive any parameters, then the *parameter-list* is empty, but the parentheses are still required. A type must be declared for every parameter in the list.

The *declarations and statements* within the braces form the **method body**. The method body is a compound statement defining the local variables and actions performed by the method.

When a method is called, execution begins at the first statement in the method body, and continues until either a **return** statement is executed or the end of the body is reached. There are two forms of the return statement. The simple statement

```
return;
```

stops execution of the method and returns control to the point at which the method was invoked *without returning a value to the calling method*. The statement

```
return expression;
```

stops execution of the method and returns control to the point at which the method was invoked *returning the value of expression to the calling method*. The first form of `return` is used with `void` methods, and the second form is used with methods that return a value to the caller.

Another example method is shown in bold face in Figure 6-3. This method calculates the hypotenuse of a right triangle from the lengths of the other two sides.

This method has two arguments in its parameter list. These arguments are placeholders for the values that will be passed to the method when it is executed. The variable `hypot` is actually defined within the method. It is used in the method, but it is not accessible to any calling program. Variables that are used within a method and that are not accessible by calling methods are called **local variables**.

After `hypot` is declared, the method calculates the hypotenuse of the right triangle from the information about the two sides. Finally, the `return` statement returns the value of `hypot` to the calling method.

To test a method, it is necessary to write a program called a **test driver**. The test driver is a small method that instantiates an object containing the method, and then

```
// Calculates the hypotenuse of a right triangle
import chapman.io.*;
public class Triangle {

   // Define the main method
   public static void main(String[] args) {

      // Declare variables
      double side1;          // Side 1 of right triangle
      double side2;          // Side 2 of right triangle

      // Create a StdIn object
      StdIn in = new StdIn();

      // Instantiate a Triangle object
      Triangle tri = new Triangle();

      // Get the two sides
      System.out.print("Enter side 1: ");
      side1 = in.readDouble();
      System.out.print("Enter side 2: ");
      side2 = in.readDouble();

      // Calculate hypotenuse and display result
      System.out.println("Hypotenuse = " + tri.hypotenuse (side1,side2));
   }
   // Definition of method hypotenuse
   public double hypotenuse (double side1, double side2) {

      double hypot;
      hypot = Math.sqrt( side1*side1 + side2*side2 );
      return hypot;
   }
}
```

Figure 6.3. A method to calculate the hypotenuse of a right triangle

invokes the new method with a sample data set for the specific purpose of testing it. The test driver for method `hypotenuse` is the `main` method of the class. When this program is executed, the results are as follows:

```
D:\book\java\chap6>java Triangle
Enter side 1: 3
Enter side 2: 4
Hypotenuse = 5.0
```

6.3 VARIABLE PASSING IN JAVA: THE PASS-BY-VALUE SCHEME

Java programs communicate with their methods using a **pass-by-value** scheme. When a method call occurs, Java *makes a copy* of each calling argument and places that copy in the corresponding parameter of the method. This scheme is called pass-by-value, because the *value* of the calling argument is placed in the corresponding parameter. Similarly, the value returned from a method is returned by value.

Note that the method has a *copy* of value of the original argument, not the argument itself. This fact means that the method cannot accidentally modify the original argument even if it modifies the parameter during its calculations. Thus the program is protected against an error caused by the method accidentally modifying data in the method that called it.

A program illustrating the pass-by-value scheme is shown in Figure 6.4. The `main` method of this program declares a variable `i`, initializes it to 5, and prints out the 5. It then calls method `test(i)`, passing the *value* of `i` to the method. Method `test` increments the value of the parameter `i` that it receives, and prints out a 6. However, it does not affect the original value in the `main` method. After execution returns from method `test`, the main method prints `i` again, and its value is still 5.

```java
// Tests the pass-by-value scheme
public class TestPassByValue {

    // Define the main method
    public static void main(String[] args) {

        // Instantiate a TestPassByValue object
        TestPassByValue t = new TestPassByValue();

        // Initialize a value and print it out
        int i = 5;
        System.out.println("Before test: i = " + i);

        // Now call method test()
        int j = t.test(i);

        // Print out value after call
        System.out.println("After test: i = " + i);

    }
    // Definition of test()
    public int test (int i) {

        int j = ++i;
        System.out.println("In test: i = " + i);
        return j;
    }
}
```

Figure 6.4. A program illustrating the pass-by-value scheme

When this program is executed, the results are as follows:

```
D:\book\java\chap6>java TestPassByValue
Before test: i = 5
In test:     i = 6
After test:  i = 5
```

GOOD PROGRAMMING PRACTICE

The pass-by-value scheme prevents a method from accidentally modifying its calling arguments.

The pass-by-value scheme also applies to objects as well, but the results are different for that case. If an object such as an array is passed as a calling argument, the program *makes a copy of the reference* to the array and places the copy of the reference in the method parameter. Because the reference was copied, the called method cannot modify the original reference in the calling method. However, it *can* use the reference that was passed to it to read or modify the actual array or other object being referred to.

A program illustrating this effect is shown in Figure 6.5. The `main` method of this program declares an array `a`, initializes it, and prints out the values. It then calls method `test(a)`, passing the *value of the reference to* `a`. Method `test` uses that reference to modify `x[3]`, prints out the results, and returns to the calling method. After execution returns from method `test`, the `main` method prints `a` again, and we can see that its value has been modified (see Figure 6.6).

```java
// Tests the pass-by-value scheme
public class TestPassByValue2 {

    // Define the main method
    public static void main(String[] args) {

        // Instantiate a TestPassByValue object
        TestPassByValue2 t = new TestPassByValue2();

        // Initialize values and print them out
        int a[] = {1, 2, 3, 4, 5};
        System.out.print("Before test: a = ");
        for ( int i = 0; i < a.length; i++ )
            System.out.print(a[i] + " ");
        System.out.println();

        // Now call method test()
        t.test(a);

        // Print out values after call
        System.out.print("After test: a = ");
        for ( int i = 0; i < a.length; i++ )
            System.out.print(a[i] + " ");
        System.out.println();

    }

    // Definition of test()
    public static void test (int x[]) {

        x[3] = -10;
        System.out.print("In test: x = ");
        for ( int i = 0; i < x.length; i++ )
            System.out.print(x[i] + " ");
        System.out.println();
    }
}
```

Figure 6.5. A program showing that a method can modify an array or other object whiose reference is passed to it by value.

Figure 6.6. Reference a in main refers to a 5-element array. When method test is called, reference a is copied into parameter x, so now method test can use and modify the same 5-element array. Note that method test cannot modify reference a in the main program, but it can modify the object that a refers to.

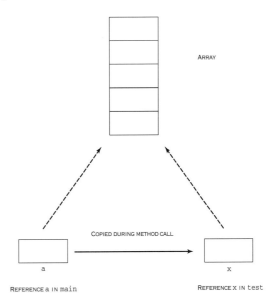

When this program is executed, the results are as follows:

```
D:\book\java\chap6>java TestPassByValue2
Before test: a = 1 2 3 4 5
In test: x = 1 2 3 -10 5
After test: a = 1 2 3 -10 5
```

There are advantages and disadvantages to passing references to arrays and objects by reference instead of copying the objects themselves. On the one hand, passing by reference weakens the security of the program, because the method can modify the calling method's data. On the other hand, the program is *much* more efficient. Imagine how much work would be involved if we attempted to pass a 10,000-element array by value! Every time that the array occurred in a method call, the program would have to make a new copy of all 10,000 elements.

A programmer must always be careful when working with arrays or other objects that are passed to methods. He or she must be certain that the method's calculations do not cause unintended modifications to the data in the arrays passed to the method. Such unintentional modifications are called **unintended side effects**, and they can create quite subtle and hard-to-find bugs.

PROGRAMMING PITFALLS

Beware of unintended side effects caused by accidentally modifying a calling method's data with references passed as parameters.

PRACTICE!

This quiz provides a quick check to see if you have understood the concepts introduced in the first three sections. If you have trouble with the quiz, reread the section, ask your instructor, or discuss the material with a fellow student. The answers to this quiz are found in the back of the book.

For questions 1 through 3, determine whether the method invocations are correct or not. If they are in error, specify what is wrong with them. If they are correct, explain what the methods do.

1.
```java
public class Test1 {
    public static void main(String[] args) {
        Test1 t = new Test1();
        int i = 5; int j[] = {1, -2, 3, -4, 5};
        t.method1(i,j);
    }
    public int method1(int i[], int j) {
        for ( int k = 0; k < j; k++ )
            System.out.println(i[k] );
    }
}
```

2.
```java
public class Test2 {
    public static void main(String[] args) {
        Test2 t = new Test2();
        double i = 5; int j = 5;
        System.out.println("Result = " + t.method2(i,j));
    }
    public void method2(double x, int y) {
        return (x / y);
    }
}
```

3.
```java
public class Test3 {
    public static void main(String[] args) {
        Test3 t = new Test3();
        int x[] = {1, -2, 3, -4, 5, -6};
        System.out.println(t.method3(x));
    }
    public double method3(int i[]) {
        int sum = 0;
        for ( int j = 0; j < i.length; j++)
            sum += i[j];
        return ( (double) sum / i.length );
    }
}
```

6.4 EXAMPLE PROBLEM

Let us now re-examine the sorting problem of Example 5-2, using methods where appropriate.

EXAMPLE 6-1:
SORTING DATA

Develop a program to read in a data set from a file, sort it into ascending order, and write the sorted data to an output file. Use methods where appropriate.

SOLUTION

The program in Example 5-2 read an arbitrary number of real input data values from an input file, sorted the data into ascending order, and wrote the sorted data to the standard output stream. The sorting process would make a good candidate for a separate method, since only the array `arr` and its length `nvals` are in common between the sorting process and the rest of the program. The other change from Example 5-2 is that we must write the sorted output to a file instead of the standard output stream.

The rewritten program using a sorting method and an output file is shown in Figure 6.7.

```
/*
   Purpose:
      To read in a set of double values from an input file, sort it into
      ascending order using the selection sort algorithm, and to write
      the sorted data to the standard output stream. The main method
      calls method  "sort" to do the actual sorting.

Record of revisions:
   Date        Programmer          Description of change
   ====        ==========          =====================
   4/06/98     S. J. Chapman       Original code
*/
import chapman.io.*;
public class SelectionSort2 {

   // Define the main method
   public static void main(String[] args) {

      // Define maximum array size
      final int MAXVAL = 1000;

      // Declare variables, and define each variable
      double arr[] = new double[MAXVAL];
                              // Array of input measurements
      String inFileName;   // Input file name
      int i = 0, j;        // Loop index
      int iptr;            // Pointer to smallest value
      int nvals;           // Number of data values to sort
      String outFileName;  // Output file name
      double temp;         // Temporary variable for swapping

      // Create StdIn object
      StdIn in = new StdIn();

      // Create a SelectionSort2 object
      SelectionSort2 s = new SelectionSort2();

      // Get input file name
      System.out.print("Enter input file name: ");
      inFileName = in.readString();

      // Get output file name
      System.out.print("Enter output file name: ");
      outFileName = in.readString();

      // Open input file
      FileIn in1 = new FileIn(inFileName);

      // Check for valid open
      if ( in1.readStatus != in1.FILE_NOT_FOUND ) {

         // Read numbers into array
         while ( in1.readStatus != in1.EOF ) {
            arr[i++] = in1.readDouble();
         }
         nvals = i;
```

Figure 6.7. *(cont.)*

```
            // Close file
            in1.close();

            // Sort values
            s.sort( arr, nvals );

            // Open output file
            FileOut out = new FileOut(outFileName);

            // Check for valid open
            if ( out.writeStatus != out.IO_EXCEPTION ) {

               // Write sorted output values
               for ( i = 0; i < nvals; i++ )
                  out.printf("%10.4f\n",arr[i]);
            }

            // Close file
            out.close();
         }

         // Come here if file not found
         else {
            System.out.println("File " + inFileName + " not found!");
         }
      }

   // Define the sort method
   public void sort(double arr[], int nvals) {

      // Declare variables, and define each variable
      int i, j;               // Loop index
      int iptr;               // Pointer to smallest value
      double temp;            // Temporary variable for swapping

      // Sort values
      for ( i = 0; i <= nvals-2; i++ ) {

         // Find the minimum value in arr[i] through arr [nvals-1]
         iptr = i;
         for ( j = i+1; j <= nvals-1; j++ ) {
            if (arr[j] < arr[iptr])
               iptr = j;
         }

         // iptr now points to the min value, so swap a[iptr]
         // with a[i] if iptr != i.
         if (i != iptr) {
            temp = arr[i];
            arr[i] = arr[iptr];
            arr[iptr] = temp;
         }
      }
   }
}
```

Figure 6.7. Program to sort real data values into ascending order using a sort method

Note that the sort method is declared to be void, meaning that it does not return a value to the calling method. Instead, it uses the reference to array arr passed by the calling method to directly manipulate the values in the array.

This new program can be tested just as the original program was, with identical results. The following data set will be placed in file `input1`:

```
13.3
12.
-3.0
 0.
 4.0
 6.6
 4.
-6.
```

Running this file through the program yields the following result:

```
D:\book\java\chap6>java SelectionSort2
Enter input file name: input1
Enter output file name: output1

D:\book\java\chap6>type output1
   -6.0000
   -3.0000
    0.0000
    4.0000
    4.0000
    6.6000
   12.0000
   13.3000
```

The program gives the correct answers for our test data set, as before.

Method `sort` performs the same function as the sorting code in the original example, but now `sort` is an independent method that we can re-use unchanged whenever we need to sort any array of `double` numbers.

Note that the array was declared in the `sort` method as

```
public static void sort(double arr[], int nvals)
```

The statement tells the Java compiler that parameter `arr` is a one-dimensional array of `double` values. It does *not* specify the length of the array, since that will not be known until the program is actually executed.

6.5 AUTOMATIC VARIABLES

Every variable in Java is characterized by a **duration** and a **scope**. The *duration* of a variable is the time during which it exists, and the *scope* of a variable is the portion of the program from which the variable can be addressed.

Variables defined with the body of a method are sometimes called **local variables**. These variables may be defined anywhere within the method, and they are automatically created and initialized when program execution reaches that point in the method. Once created, such local variables continue to exist until the program exits the block in which they were defined. When that happens, the variables are automatically destroyed.

Such variables are said to have **automatic duration**, because they are automatically created when they are needed, and automatically destroyed when they are no longer needed. Variables with automatic duration are known as **automatic variables**.

For example, consider the following example method:

```
int sum ( int array[] ) {
   int i = 0, total = 0;
   for ( int i = 0; i < array.length; i++ ) {
      total += array[i];
   return (total);
}
```

Figure 6.8. An example method declaring two automatic variables

In this method, integer variables i and total are automatic variables. They are automatically created and initialized to zero. The for loop sums up all of the elements in the input array, and the total is returned to the calling method. When the method stops executing, variables i and total are automatically destroyed. Note that if the method is called again, new variables will be created and initialized to zero, and the process will start over again.

Automatic variables are very useful, because they conserve memory in a program. If they remained in memory, the local variables of all methods not currently being executed would just be taking up space without serving a useful purpose.

GOOD PROGRAMMING PRACTICE

Automatic variables conserve memory in a program by automatically removing unused variables when they are no longer needed in memory.

It is also possible to declare variables that persist from the moment that the class defining them is first loaded into memory until the program stops executing. These variables are said to have **static duration**, and they are known as **static variables**. They can be used to preserve information between invocations of a method, or to share data between methods, as we will see in Chapter 7. We will learn how to declare static variables in Chapter 7, where we will also learn how to declare static methods.

6.6 SCOPE

The **scope** of a variable is the portion of the program from which the variable can be addressed. There are two possible scopes for Java variables: **class scope** and **block scope**.

Methods and the instance variables of a class have *class scope*. Class scope begins at the opening left brace ({) of a class definition and ends at the closing right brace (}) of the class definition. Class scope allows any method in the class to directly invoke any other method of the class (or any method inherited from a superclass), and to directly access any instance variable of the class. Instance variables are effectively *global* within a class, since they can be seen from within any method in the class. Thus, instance variables can be used to communicate between methods in a class, or to retain information between invocations of a given method in the class.

Variables defined inside a block have *block scope*. A **block** is defined as a *compound statement*, which consists of all the statements between an open brace ({) and the corresponding closing brace (}). Variables defined within a block are visible within the block and within any blocks contained within the block, but they are not visible after the block finishes executing. For example, the local variables defined at the beginning of a method have block scope. They are visible between the open brace ({) and the corresponding closing brace (}) of the method. They are also visible within any blocks contained within the block, such as within the `for` loop of Figure 6.8.

Any block may contain variable declarations which will only be valid for the duration of the block. For example, it is possible to declare a loop index within a `for` loop itself:

```
for (int j = 0; j < n; j++ ) {
    . . .
    . . .
}
```

The variable `j` in this loop is an automatic variable that is only defined while the `for` loop is executing. It is automatically destroyed when loop execution ends.

However, it is illegal to declare a variable in an inner block that has the same name as a variable in an outer block. Thus, the following code would produce a compile-time error:

```
int sum ( int array[] ) {
    int i = 0, total = 0;
    i += array[0];
    for ( int i = 0; i < array.length; i++ ) {
        total += array[i];
    return (total);
}
```

PROGRAMMING PITFALLS

It is illegal to declare a variable in an inner block that has the same name as a variable in an outer block.

It *is* legal to declare a variable within a block that has the same name as an instance variable within a class. If this is done, the instance variable is "hidden" until he block terminates execution. We will learn how to access such "hidden" instance variables in Chapter 7.

6.7 RECURSIVE METHODS

For some classes of problems, it is convenient for a Java method to invoke itself. A **recursive method** is a method that invokes itself either directly or indirectly through another method. Java methods are inherently recursive, since all local variables are automatic, and new copies of each variable are created each time that the method is invoked.

There are certain classes of problems that are easily solved recursively. For example, the factorial function can be defined as follows:

$$N! = \begin{cases} N(N-1)! & \text{for} \quad N \ge 1 \\ 1 & \text{for} \quad N = 0 \end{cases} \tag{6-1}$$

This definition can easily be implemented recursively, with the procedure that calculates $N!$ calling itself to calculate $(N-1)!$, and that procedure calling itself to calculate $(N-2)!$, etc. until finally the procedure is called to calculate $0!$.

A recursive method to calculate the factorial function is shown in Figure 6-9. Note that if n > 1, method `factorial` calls itself with the argument n-1. Method `factorial` in this class includes two `println` statements, so that we can see happens as the method calls itself recursively.

```
/*
    Purpose:
        To calculate the factorial function N! through a
        recursive method.

    Record of revisions:
        Date            Programmer          Description of change
        ====            ==========          =====================
        4/07/98         S. J. Chapman       Original code
*/
import chapman.io.*;
public class Factorial {

    // Define method factorial
    public int factorial ( int n ) {
        int answer;      // Result of calculation
        System.out.println("In factorial: n = " + n);
        if ( n >= 1 )
            answer = n * factorial(n-1);
        else
            answer = 1;
        System.out.println("In factorial: n = "
                        + n + " answer = " + answer);
        return answer;
    }

    // Define the main method
    public static void main(String[] args) {

        int n; // Integer to calculate factorial of

        // Create a StdIn object
        StdIn in = new StdIn();

        // Instantiate a Factorial object
        Factorial f = new Factorial();

        // Get number to calculate factorial of
        System.out.print("Enter int to calculate factorial of: ");
        n = in.readInt();

        // Output factorial
        System.out.print(n + "! = " + f.factorial(n));
    }
}
```

Figure 6.9. A method to recursively implement the factorial function

When this program is used to calculate the value of 5!, the results are as follows:

```
D:\book\java\chap6>java Factorial
Enter integer to calculate factorial of: 5
In factorial: n = 5
In factorial: n = 4
In factorial: n = 3
In factorial: n = 2
In factorial: n = 1
In factorial: n = 0
In factorial: n = 0 answer = 1
In factorial: n = 1 answer = 1
```

```
In factorial: n = 2 answer = 2
In factorial: n = 3 answer = 6
In factorial: n = 4 answer = 24
In factorial: n = 5 answer = 120
5! = 120
```

Note that the method was called by the main program with n = 5, and then the method called itself with n = 4, etc. It is easy to verify by hand calculation that this method produced the correct answer.

6.8 METHOD OVERLOADING

Java allows several methods to be defined with the same name, as long as the methods have different sets of parameters (based on the number, types, and order of the parameters). This is called **method overloading**. When an overloaded method is called, the Java compiler selects the proper method by examining the number, type, and order of the calling arguments. Method overload is commonly used to create several methods that perform the same function, but with different data types. For example, the program in Figure 6.10 includes two methods to calculate the square of a number, one for ints and the other for doubles. Java determines which of the two methods to call based on the argument of a particular method call.

```java
// This program illustrates method overloading
public class Overload1 {

   // Define the main method
   public static void main(String[] args) {

      int i; double x;

      // Instantiate an Overload1 object
      Overload1 ov = new Overload1();

      // Write number and square using integers
      System.out.println("Using integers:");
      for ( i = 1; i <= 5; i++ ) {
         System.out.print("number = " + i);
         System.out.println(" square = " + ov.square(i));
      }

      // Write number and square using doubles
      System.out.println("Using doubles:");
      for ( i = 1; i <= 5; i++ ) {
         x = i;
         System.out.print("number = " + x);
         System.out.println(" square = " + ov.square(x));
      }
   }

   // Definition of square method 1
   public int square (int x) {
      return x * x;
   }

   // Definition of square method 2
   public double square (double x) {
      return x * x;
   }
}
```

Figure 6.10. A Java program illustrating method overloading

When this program is executed, the results are as follows:

```
D:\book\java\chap6>java Overload1
Using integers:
number = 1 square = 1
number = 2 square = 4
number = 3 square = 9
number = 4 square = 16
number = 5 square = 25
Using doubles:
number = 1.0 square = 1.0
number = 2.0 square = 4.0
number = 3.0 square = 9.0
number = 4.0 square = 16.0
number = 5.0 square = 25.0
```

Note that Java used the first method when the method was invoked with an `int` argument, and the second method when the method was invoked with a `double` argument.

Overloaded methods are distinguished by their **signature**, which is a combination of the method name and the number, type, and order of parameters. If two methods have the same signature, then the Java compiler cannot distinguish between them. Defining two methods with the same signature produces a compile-time error. This is true *even if the two methods return different data types*. For example, the program shown in Figure 6.11 contains two methods with an identical signature but different return data types.

```
// This program contains two methods with identical
// signatures, which is an error.
class Overload2 {

   // Define the main method
   public static void main(String[] args) {

      // Instantiate an Overload2 object
      Overload2 ov = new Overload2();

      // Write number and square using integers
      for ( int i = 1; i <= 10; i++ ) {
         System.out.print("number = " + i);
         System.out.println(" square = " + ov.square(i));
      }
   }

   // Definition of square method 1
   public int square (int x) {
      return x * x;
   }

   // Definition of square method 2
   public double square (int x) {
      return (double) x * x;
   }
}
```

Figure 6.11. A Java program containing two different methods with the same signature in the same class.

When this program is compiled, the results are as follows:

```
D:\book\java\chap6>javac Overload2.java
Overload2.java:24:
Methods can't be redefined with a different return
type: double square(int) was int square(int)
   public double square (int x) {
                 ^
1 error
```

PROGRAMMING PITFALLS

It is an error to define two different methods with the same signature in a single class.

EXAMPLE 6-2:
STATISTICS
METHODS

Develop a set of reusable methods capable of determining the average and standard deviation of a data set consisting of numbers in an array. The method should work for data input arrays of `int`, `float`, and `double` types.

SOLUTION

To solve this problem, we will need to create six different methods, one each to determine the average and the standard deviation of `int`, `float`, and `double` arrays. Note that we will be using method overloading so that the same method name may be called to get the average of a data set, whether it is an `int`, a `float`, or a `double`. In addition, we will need to define a `main` method to test our six other methods.

1. **State the problem**. The problem is clearly stated above. We will write six different methods: three forms of `average` to calculate the average of the three types of data sets, and three forms of `stdDev` to calculate the standard deviation of the three types of data sets.

2. **Define the inputs and outputs**. The input to each method will be array of `int`, `float`, or `double` values. The output will be a `double` value containing either the average or the standard deviation of the data in the array. Note that we are using a `double` value in all cases, because the average and standard deviations of even the integer arrays will not in general be integer values.

3. **Decompose the program into classes and their associated methods**. We have not yet studied classes in detail, so for now there will be only one class. The class will contain six methods to calculate the average and standard deviations, plus the `main` method to contain text driver code. We will call the class `Stats`, and make it a subclass of the root class `Object`.

4. **Design the algorithm that you intend to implement for each method**. The pseudocode for the `average` methods is as follows:

```
Initialize sumX to zero
if (arr.length >= 1) {
    for ( int i = 0; i < arr.length; i++ ) {
        sumX ← sumX + arr[i];
    }
    xBar ← sumX / arr.length;
else {
    Insufficient data: set xBar to 0.
}
return xBar;
```

The pseudocode for the `stdDev` methods is:

```
Initialize sumX and sumX2 to zero.
if (arr.length >= 2) {
    for ( int i = 0; i < arr.length; i++ ) {
        sumX ← sumX + arr[i];
```

```
                        sumX2 ← sumX2 + arr[i]*arr[i];
                   }
                   stdDev ← Math.sqrt((nvals*sumX2 - sumX*sumX)
                         / (arr.length*(arr.length-1)));
              else {
                 Insufficient data: set stdDev to 0.
              }
              return stdDev;
```

The `main` method will have to test all six calculational methods, so it must define three arrays containing `int`, `float`, or `double` values, and call both `average` and `stdDev` with each array. The pseudocode for the `main` method is:

```
              int arr1 = { 8, 9, 10, 11, 12 };
              float arr2 = { 8.F, 9.F, 10.F, 11.F, 12.F };
              double arr3 = { 8., 9., 10., 11., 12. };
              System.out.println("Integer array:");
              System.out.println("Average = " + average(arr1));
              System.out.println("Standard Deviation = " + stdDev(arr1));
              System.out.println("Float array:");
              System.out.println("Average = " + average(arr2));
              System.out.println("Standard Deviation = " + stdDev(arr2));
              System.out.println("Double array:");
              System.out.println("Average = " + average(arr3));
              System.out.println("Standard Deviation = " + stdDev(arr3));
```

5. **Turn the algorithm into Java statements**. The resulting Java program is shown in Figure 6.12.

```
/*
   Purpose:
     To calculate the average and standard deviation of
     integer, float, or double arrays.  This class
     illustrates method overloading.

   Record of revisions:
     Date         Programmer            Description of change
     ====         ==========            =====================
     4/10/98      S. J. Chapman         Original code
*/
public class Stats {

   // Define the average method for integer arrays
   public double average( int arr[] ) {

      // Declare variables, and define each variable
      double sumX = 0;      // Sum of the input samples
      double xBar = 0;      // Average of input samples

      if (arr.length >= 1) {
         for ( int i = 0; i < arr.length; i++ ) {
            sumX += arr[i];
         }
         xBar = sumX / arr.length;
      }
```

Figure 6.12. *(cont.)*

```
        else {
           // Insufficient data
           xBar = 0;
        }
        return xBar;
     }

     // Define the average method for float arrays
     public double average( float arr[] ) {

        // Declare variables, and define each variable
        double sumX = 0;      // Sum of the input samples
        double xBar = 0;      // Average of input samples

        if (arr.length >= 1) {
           for ( int i = 0; i < arr.length; i++ ) {
              sumX += arr[i];
           }
           xBar = sumX / arr.length;
        }
        else {
           // Insufficient data
           xBar = 0;
        }
        return xBar;
     }

     // Define the average method for double arrays
     public double average( double arr[] ) {

        // Declare variables, and define each variable
        double sumX = 0;      // Sum of the input samples
        double xBar = 0;      // Average of input samples

        if (arr.length >= 1) {
           for ( int i = 0; i < arr.length; i++ ) {
              sumX += arr[i];
           }
           xBar = sumX / arr.length;
        }
        else {
           // Insufficient data
           xBar = 0;
        }
        return xBar;
     }

     // Define the stdDev method for integer arrays
     public double stdDev( int arr[] ) {

        // Declare variables, and define each variable
        double stdDev = 0;   // Std deviation of input samples
        double sumX = 0;      // Sum of the input samples
        double sumX2 = 0;     // Sum of squares of input samples
        double xBar = 0;      // Average of input samples

        if (arr.length >= 2) {
           for ( int i = 0; i < arr.length; i++ ) {
              sumX += arr[i];
```

Figure 6.12.   *(cont.)*

```
                            sumX2 += arr[i] * arr[i];
                    }
                    stdDev = Math.sqrt((arr.length*sumX2 - sumX*sumX)
                            / (arr.length*(arr.length-1)));
            }
            else {
                // Insufficient data
                stdDev = 0;
            }
            return stdDev;
    }

    // Define the stdDev method for float arrays
    public double stdDev( float arr[] ) {

            // Declare variables, and define each variable
            double stdDev = 0;   // Std deviation of input samples
            double sumX = 0;       // Sum of the input samples
            double sumX2 = 0;      // Sum of squares of input samples
            double xBar = 0;       // Average of input samples

            if (arr.length >= 2) {
                for ( int i = 0; i < arr.length; i++ ) {
                    sumX += arr[i];
                    sumX2 += arr[i] * arr[i];
                }
                stdDev = Math.sqrt((arr.length*sumX2 - sumX*sumX)
                        / (arr.length*(arr.length-1)));
            }
            else {
                // Insufficient data
                stdDev = 0;
            }
            return stdDev;
    }

    // Define the stdDev method for double arrays
    public double stdDev( double arr[] ) {

            // Declare variables, and define each variable
            double stdDev = 0;   // Std deviation of input samples
            double sumX = 0;       // Sum of the input samples
            double sumX2 = 0;      // Sum of squares of input samples
            double xBar = 0;       // Average of input samples

            if (arr.length >= 2) {
              for ( int i = 0; i < arr.length; i++ ) {
                    sumX += arr[i];
                    sumX2 += arr[i] * arr[i];
              }
              stdDev = Math.sqrt((arr.length*sumX2 - sumX*sumX)
                        / (arr.length*(arr.length-1)));
            }
            else {
                // Insufficient data
                stdDev = 0;
            }
            return stdDev;
    }
```

Figure 6.12. *(cont.)*

```
// Define the main method
public static void main(String[] args) {

    // Instantiate a Stats object
    Stats st = new Stats();

    // Declare test arrays
    int arr1[] = { 8, 9, 10, 11, 12 };
    float arr2[] = { 8.F, 9.F, 10.F, 11.F, 12.F };
    double arr3[] = { 8., 9., 10., 11., 12. };

    // Calculate average and standard dev of each array
    System.out.println("Integer array:");
    System.out.println("Average       = " + st.average(arr1));
    System.out.println("Std Deviation = " + st.stdDev(arr1));
    System.out.println("Float array:");
    System.out.println("Average       = " + st.average(arr2));
    System.out.println("Std Deviation = " + st.stdDev(arr2));
    System.out.println("Double array:");
    System.out.println("Average       = " + st.average(arr3));
    System.out.println("Std Deviation = " + st.stdDev(arr3));
  }
}
```

Figure 6.12. Program to calculate the average and standard deviation of int, float, or double arrays. This program illustrates method overloading.

6. **Test the resulting Java programs**. To test this program, we can calculate the average and standard deviation of the values 8, 9, 10, 11, 12 from the definitions of average and standard deviation:

$$\bar{x} = \frac{1}{N} \sum_{i=1}^{N} x_i = \frac{1}{5} \, 50 = 10.0, \qquad (6\text{-}1)$$

$$s = \sqrt{\frac{N \sum_{i=1}^{N} x_i^2 - \left(\sum_{i=1}^{N} x_i \right)^2}{N(N-1)}} = 1.5811. \qquad (6\text{-}2)$$

When the program is executed, the results are as follows:

```
D:\book\java\chap6>java Stats
Integer array:
Average       = 10.0
Standard Deviation = 1.5811388300841898
Float array:
Average       = 10.0
Standard Deviation = 1.5811388300841898
Double array:
Average       = 10.0
Standard Deviation = 1.5811388300841898
```

The results of the program agree with our hand calculations to the number of significant digits that we performed the calculation.

6.9 CLASS java.util.Arrays

Beginning with the Java Development Kit version 1.2, Java includes a special class that contains some methods designed to make manipulating arrays easier. This class is named `Arrays`, and it is located in the `java.util` package.

The `Arrays` class contains several overloaded methods designed to make working with arrays easier. Some of these methods are summarized in Table 6-1.

The quicksort method implemented in this class is much more efficient than the selection sort method that we developed in Example 5-2. You will be asked to compare the sorting speeds of these two methods in an end-of chapter exercise.

The `Arrays` class must be imported into a Java program before it can be used. The easiest way to do this is to include the statement

```
import java.util.*;        // Import Java utils package
```

before the class definition in which the methods will be used. Once the `Arrays` class has been imported, the methods can be invoked as `Arrays.sort()`, `Arrays.fill()`, and so forth.

Note that these methods are all `static`, like the ones in the `Math` class. We will explain `static` methtods in Chapter 7. For now, the importance of the `static` declaration is that the methods can be invoked directly without first instantiating an object of type `Arrays`.

GOOD PROGRAMMING PRACTICE

Use the `sort()` method in the `java.util.Arrays` class to sort arrays in practical programs. This method is very efficient, already debugged, and built right into the basic Java environment.

6.10 ADDITIONAL METHODS SUPPLIED WITH THIS BOOK

Because Java was created as a computer scientist's language, it lacks some of the functions that engineers are accustomed to using in other languages such as Fortran, Gnu C, MATLAB, etc. A number of classes have been supplied with this book to partially fill in the gap. Two of these classes (containing extended math methods and array manipulations) are described in this section, while other classes for complex numbers, signal processing, etc. are described later in the book. You should check the book's Web site (given in the Chapter 2) for the latest versions of these classes, as enhancements and bug fixes are expected throughout the life of the book.

Class `Math1` contains a collection of static methods to supplement the methods included in Java's `Math` class. These methods may be used in the same way as Java's standard math methods, but you must import package `chapman.math` into your program with the statement

```
import chapman.math.*;
```

The methods in class `Math1` are summarized in Table 6-2.

Class `Array` contains set of `static` methods designed to manipulate one- and two-dimensional arrays in a convenient fashion. These methods permit a programmer to treat an array as an entity, and to perform operations on an entire array with a single method invocation. It is also in package `chapman.math`.

Various methods in this class support data of types `int`, `long`, `float`, and `double`, although not all data types are supported for all functions. Consult the detailed online documentation accompanying the package to determine which data types are supported by each method. The methods in this class fall into several categories, as follows:

1. **Calculational Methods**. These methods perform calculations on the elements of an array. Examples include `add`, `sub`, `mul`, `div`, `sum`, `product`, `dotProduct`, `sin`, `sinc`, `sind`, `sinh`, `cos`, `cosd`, `cosh`, `tan`, `tand`, `tanh`, `asin`, `asind`, `asinh`, `acos`, `acosd`, `acosh`, `atan`, `atand`, `atanh`, `abs`, `exp`, `log`, `log10`, and `pow`.

2. **Inquiry Methods**. These methods extract information from an array. Examples include `maxAbs`, `maxAbsLoc`, `maxVal`, `maxLoc`, `minVal`, and `minLoc`.

TABLE 6-1   Selected Methods in `java.util.Arrays`

METHOD NAME	DESCRIPTION

`int binarySearch(long[] a, long key)`
`int binarySearch(int[] a, int key)`
`int binarySearch(short[] a, short key)`
`int binarySearch(char[] a, char key)`
`int binarySearch(byte[] a, byte key)`
`int binarySearch(double[] a, double key)`
`int binarySearch(float[] a, float key)`
`int binarySearch(Object[] a, Object key)`
	These overloaded methods search array a for the specified value key using the binary search algorithm. The array *must* be sorted prior to making this call. The method returns the index of the search key, if it is contained in the array, and a negative number, if it is not contained in the array.

`boolean equals(long[] a, Object o)`
`boolean equals(int[] a, Object o)`
`boolean equals(short[] a, Object o)`
`boolean equals(char[] a, Object o)`
`boolean equals(byte[] a, Object o)`
`boolean equals(double[] a, Object o)`
`boolean equals(float[] a, Object o)`
`boolean equals(Object[] a, Object o)`
	These overloaded methods test to see if array a is equal to the given object o. The array and the object are considered equal if the object is an array of the same type, both arrays contain the same number of elements, and all corresponding pairs of elements in the two arrays are equal. In other words, the two arrays are equal if they contain the same elements in the same order.

`void fill(long[] a, long val)`
`void fill(void[] a, void val)`
`void fill(short[] a, short val)`
`void fill(char[] a, char val)`
`void fill(byte[] a, byte val)`
`void fill(double[] a, double val)`
`void fill(float[] a, float val)`
`void fill(Object[] a, Object val)`
	These overloaded methods fill each element of array a with the value `val`.

`void sort(long[] a)`
`void sort(int[] a)`
`void sort(short[] a)`
`void sort(char[] a)`
`void sort(byte[] a)`
`void sort(double[] a)`
`void sort(float[] a)`
`void sort(Object[] a)`
	These overloaded methods sort the array a into ascending numerical order. The sorting algorithm is a tuned quicksort. Note that is possible to sort arrays of `Objects` as well as primitive data types, provided that the objects are mutually comparable.

TABLE 6-2 Mathematical Methods in Class `chapman.math.Math1`

METHOD NAME AND PARAMETERS	METHOD VALUE	PARAMETER TYPE	RESULT TYPE	COMMENTS
`Math1.acosd(x)`	$\cos^{-1} x$	Double	Double	Returns inverse cosine of x for $-1 \le x \le 1$ (results in *degrees*)
`Math1.acosh(x)`	$\cosh^{-1} x$	Double	Double	Returns inverse hyperbolic cosine of x
`Math1.asind(x)`	$\sin^{-1} x$	Double	Double	Returns inverse sine of x for $-1 \le x \le 1$ (results in *degrees*)
`Math1.asinh(x)`	$\sinh^{-1} x$	Double	Double	Returns inverse hyperbolic sine of x
`Math1.atand(x)`	$\tan^{-1} x$	Double	Double	Returns inverse tangent of x (results in *degrees* in the range $-90° \le x \le 90°$)
`Math1.atan2d(y,x)`	$\tan^{-1} y/x$	Double	Double	Returns inverse tangent of x (results in *degrees* in the range $-180 \le x \le 180$)
`Math1.atanh(x)`	$\tanh^{-1} x$	Double	Double	Returns inverse hyperbolic tangent of x
`Math1.cosd(x)`	$\cos x$	Double	Double	Returns cosine of x, where x is in degrees
`Math1.cosh(x)`	$\cosh x$	Double	Double	Returns hyperbolic cosine of x
`Math1.log10(x)`	$\log_{10} x$	Double	Double	Returns logarithm to the base 10 of x, for $x > 0$
`Math1.randomGaussian()`		N/A	Double	Returns a normally-distributed Gaussian random number
`Math1.randomRayleigh()`		N/A	Double	Returns a Rayleigh-distributed random number
`Math1.sinc(x)`	$\text{sinc } x$	Double	Double	Returns the value of sinc x, where sinc $x = \sin x / x$
`Math1.sind(x)`	$\sin x$	Double	Double	Returns sine of x, where x is in degrees
`Math1.sinh(x)`	$\sinh x$	Double	Double	Returns hyperbolic sine of x
`Math1.tand(x)`	$\tan x$	Double	Double	Returns tangent of x, where x is in degrees
`Math1.tanh(x)`	$\tanh x$	Double	Double	Returns hyperbolic tangent of x

3. **Relational Methods**. These methods perform relational comparisons on the data in an array, producing a `boolean` result. Examples include `isGreaterThan`, `isGreaterThanOrEqual`, `isLessThan`, `isLessThanOrEqual`, `isEqual`, and `isNotEqual`.

4. **Logical Methods**. These methods manipulate `boolean` arrays, which can be produced by the relational methods described above. Examples include `all`, `any`, `count`, `and`, `or`, `xor`, and `not`. The resulting `boolean` arrays can be used as a mask to control certain operations.

5. **Random Number Methods**. These methods return arrays of random values. Examples include `random`, `randomGaussian`, and `random-Rayleigh`.

EXAMPLE 6-3: USING ARRAY METHODS

The methods provided in class `chapman.math.Array` allow certain types of engineering problems to be solved with a relatively few statements. As a quick example, suppose that we want to determine the percentage of samples in a Rayleigh-distributed random data set that are greater than 3.0. Figure 6.13 shows a Rayleigh probability distribution. Clearly, some samples will exceed the threshold, but how many?

SOLUTION

One approach to solving this problem is by Monte Carlo simulation, which is the process of making many random trials, and determining for each trial whether the result exceeds 3.0. If we do enough trials, the average number of times that the random number exceeds 3.0 will approximate the theoretical answer.

Figure 6.13. A Rayleigh probability distribution

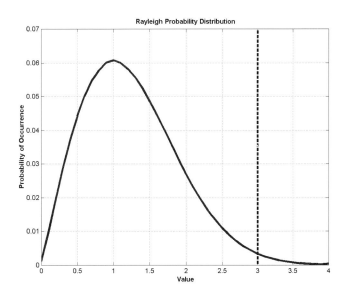

```
/*
    Purpose:
        To calculate the percentage of random samples from a
        Rayleigh distribution that exceed 3.0. This class
        demonstrates the use of methods from chapman.math.Array.

    Record of revisions:
        Date          Programmer           Description of change
        ====          ==========           =====================
        9/10/98       S. J. Chapman        Original code
*/
import chapman.io.*;
import chapman.math.*;
public class ThresholdCrossing {

    public static void main(String[] args) {

        double arr[];           // Array of random samples
        int count;              // Number of samples > 3.0

        // Get an array of 50000 random values
        arr = Array.randomRayleigh(50000);

        // Find out how many samples are > 3.0.
        count = Array.count(Array.isGreaterThan(arr, 3.));

        // Print result
        Fmt.printf("Percentage = %6.2f %", 100.*count/arr.length);
    }
```

Figure 6.14. Program to calculate the percentage of samples from a Rayleigh distribution that exceed 3.0

Figure 6.14 shows a Java program that solves this problem by Monte Carlo simulation. First, it uses method `Array.randomRayleigh` to generate an array of 50,000 samples from a Rayleigh distribution. Next the program uses method `Array.isGreaterThan` to generate a `boolean` array whose elements are `true` at any location where the sample was greater than 3, and method `Array.count` to count the number of `true` values in the `boolean` array.

When the program is executed, the results are as follows:

```
D:\book\java\chap6>java ThresholdCrossing
Percentage = 1.08 %
```

About 1% of the samples will exceed 3.0.

PRACTICE!

This quiz provides a quick check to see if you have understood the concepts introduced in Sections 6.4 through 6.10. If you have trouble with the quiz, reread the sections, ask your instructor, or discuss the material with a fellow student. The answers to this quiz are found in the back of the book.

1. What is the duration of a variable? What types of duration exist in Java?
2. What is the scope of a variable? What types of scope exist in Java?
3. What is the duration and scope of local variables defined within a Java method?
4. What is a recursive method?
5. What is method overloading?

For questions 6 and 7, determine whether there are any errors in these programs. If so, tell what the errors are. If not, tell what the output from each program will be.

6.
```java
public class Test {
    public static void main(String[] args) {
        int i = 2; int j = 3;
        while (j > 0) {
            int i = j;
            System.out.println(i*j);
            j--;
        }
    }
}
```

7.
```java
public class Test {
    public static void main(String[] args) {
        Test t = new Test();
        int a = 5, b = 10;
        System.out.println(t.m1(a,b));
    }
    public static double m1 (int i, int j) {
        return (i + 2*j);
    }

    public static double m1 (int x, int y) {
        return (x - 2*y);
    }
}
```

SUMMARY

- A **method** performs a specific function and returns (at most) a *single* value to the calling method. All methods must be defined within a Java class definition.
- A method definition includes four components: (1) optional keywords, (2) the data type of the returned value, (3) the method name, and (4) the list of parameters that the method expects to receive. This definition is followed by the body of the method within braces ({ }).
- A method calls or invokes another method by including its name, together with appropriate calling arguments in parentheses, in an expression.
- A method executes until the end of the body is reached, or until a `return` statement is executed. The value returned by the method is the value of the expression in the `return` statement.

- It is possible for a method to return no value to a calling methods. In that case, the method is declared with a `void` data type.
- Local variables are variables defined within a method and not accessible to calling methods. These variables are automatic variables, meaning that they are automatically created when the methods starts executing, and automatically destroyed when the method stops executing.
- Java uses a *pass-by-value* scheme to pass the value of calling arguments to method parameters. A *copy* of the value of each calling argument is placed in the corresponding parameters. As a result, any modifications of the parameters within the method have no effect on the calling arguments.
- When an array or object is passed to a method, Java copies the value of the *reference* to the array or object and places it in the corresponding parameter. The method can then use that reference to modify the original array or object.
- Automatic variables are created when a body is executed, and destroyed when the execution of the body is completed.
- Static variables are created when the class defining them is first loaded into memory, and persist until the program stops executing.
- The scope of a variable is the portion of the program from which the variable can be addressed.
- Variables and methods with class scope can be addressed from anywhere within the class in which they are defined. For example, instance variables have class scope.
- Variables with block scope are defined within a block, and are visible within that block and within any blocks contained within that block.
- A block is a compound statement, consisting of all the statements between an open brace (`{`) and the corresponding close brace (`}`).
- A recursive method is a method that calls itself, either directly or indirectly.
- Method overloading is the definition of two or more methods with the same name, distinguishable by the type, number, and order of their calling parameters.
- Overload methods are distinguished by their **signature**, which is a combination of the method name and the number, type, and order of parameters. No two methods in a single class may have the same signature.

APPLICATIONS: SUMMARY OF GOOD PROGRAMMING PRACTICES

The following guidelines introduced in this chapter will help you to develop good programs:

1. Break large program tasks into classes and methods whenever practical to achieve the important benefits of independent component testing, reusability, and isolation from unintended side effects.
2. The pass-by-value scheme prevents a method from accidentally modifying its calling arguments.
3. Automatic variables conserve memory in a program by automatically removing unused variables when they are no longer needed in memory.
4. Use the `sort()` method in the `java.util.Arrays` class to sort arrays in practical programs. This method is very efficient, already debugged, and built right into the basic Java environment.

KEY TERMS

argument list
automatic duration
automatic variables
block
block scope
`chapman.math.Array` class
`chapman.math.Math1` class
class scope
duration
information hiding

`java.util.Arrays` class
local variables
method
method body
method call
method invocation
method overloading
parameters
pass-by-value
recursive method

return statement
scope
signature
static duration
static variables
test driver
top-down design
unit testing
`void`

Problems

1. When a method is called, how is data passed from the calling method to the called method, and how are the results of the method returned to the calling program?

2. What are the advantages and disadvantages of the pass-by-value scheme used in Java?

3. Suppose that a fifteen-element array `a` is passed to a method as a calling argument. What will happen if the method attempts to access element `a[15]`?

4. Determine whether the following method calls are correct or not. If they are in error, specify what is wrong with them. If they are correct, describe what the program does.

   a.
```java
public class Test {
    public static void main(String[] args) {
        Test t = new Test();
        int arr[] = { 1, 2, 3, 4, 5};
        System.out.println(t.sum(arr));
    }
    public int sum (int a) {
        int sum = 0;
        for ( int i = 0; i < a.length; i++ )
            sum += a[i];
        return (sum);
    }
}
```

   b.
```java
public class Test {
    public static void main(String[] args) {
        Test t = new Test();
        int arr[] = {1, 2, 3, 4, 5};
        int i;
        // Print array
        System.out.print("Before: ");
        for (i = 0; i < arr.length; i++)
            System.out.print(arr[i] + " ");
        System.out.println();

        t.calc(arr,6);

        System.out.print("After: ");
        for (i = 0; i < arr.length; i++)
            System.out.print(arr[i] + " ");
        System.out.println();
    }
    public static void calc (int a[], int b) {
        int sum = 0;
        for ( int i = 0; i < a.length; i++ ) {
            a[i] *= b;
            sum += a[i];
        }
        return (sum);
    }
}
```

5. Modify the selection sort method developed in this chapter so that it sorts `double` values in *descending* order.

6. The mathematical method `Math.random()` returns a sample value from a uniform distribution in the range [0,1). Each time that the method is called, a random value in the range $0 \leq$ `value` < 1 is returned, with every possible value having an equal probability of occurrence. A method like `Math.random()` can be used to introduce an element of chance into a program.

    Every possible number between 0 and 1 should have an equal probability of being returned as a result from this method. Test the distribution of values returned from this method by calling it 10,000 times and calculating the number of values falling between 0 and 0.1, 0.1 and 0.2, etc. Are the values evenly distributed between 0 and 1? Plot the number of values falling in each interval using the plotting classes provided in package `chapman.graphics`.

7. Use method `Math.random()` to generate arrays containing 1000, 10,000, and 100,000 random values between 0.0 and 1.0. Then, use the statistical methods developed in this chapter to calculate the average and standard deviation of values in the arrays. The theoretical average of a uniform random distribution in the range [0,1) is 0.5, and thetheoretical standard deviation of the uniform random distribution is $1/(\sqrt{12})$. How close do the random arrays generated by `Math.random()` come to behaving like the theoretical distribution?

8. Write a method that uses method `Math.random()` to generate a random value in the range [−1.0, 1.0).

9. **Dice Simulation** It is often useful to be able to simulate the throw of a fair die. Write a Java method `dice()` that simulates the throw of a fair die by returning some random integer between 1 and 6 every time that it is called. (*Hint:* Call `Math.random()` to generate a random number. Divide the possible values out of `Math.random()` into six equal intervals, and return the number of the interval that a given random number falls into.)

10. **Road Traffic Density** Method `Math.random()` produces a number with a *uniform* probability distribution in the range [0.0, 1.0). This method is suitable for simulating random events if each outcome has an equal probability of occurring. However, in many events, the probability of occurrence is *not* equal for every event, and a uniform probability distribution is not suitable for simulating such events.

    For example, when traffic engineers studied the number of cars passing a given location in a time interval of length t, they discovered that the probability of k cars passing during the interval is given by the equation

    $$P(k,t) = e^{-\lambda t}\frac{(\lambda t)^k}{k!} \text{ for } t \geq 0, \lambda > 0, \text{ and } k = 0, 1, 2,\dots . \tag{6-2}$$

    This probability distribution is known as the *Poisson distribution;* it occurs in many applications in science and engineering. For example, the number of calls k to a telephone switchboard in time interval t, the number of bacteria k in a specified volume t of liquid, and the number of failures k of a complicated system in time interval t all have Poisson distributions.

    Write a method to evaluate the Poisson distribution for any k, t, and λ. Test your method by calculating the probability of 0, 1, 2, . . ., 5 cars passing a particular point on a highway in 1 minute, given that λ is 1.6 per minute for that highway.

11. Write three Java methods to calculate the hyperbolic sine, cosine, and tangent functions:

    $$\sinh(x) = \frac{e^x - e^{-x}}{2}, \qquad \cosh(x) = \frac{e^x + e^{-x}}{2}, \qquad \tanh(x) = \frac{e^x - e^{-x}}{e^x + e^{-x}}$$

Use your methods to calculate the hyperbolic sines, cosines, and tangents of the values between −2.0 and 2.0 in steps of 0.25. Compare your answers with the ones produced by the methods `Math1.sinh()`, `Math1.cosh()`, and `Math1.tanh()`. Create plots of the shapes of the hyperbolic sine, cosine, and tangent functions.

12. **Cross Product** Write a method to calculate the cross product of two `double` vectors $\mathbf{V}_1$ and $\mathbf{V}_2$. The cross product is defined as

$$\mathbf{V}_1 \times \mathbf{V}_2 = (V_{y1}V_{z2} - V_{y2}V_{z1})\mathbf{i} + (V_{z1}V_{x2} - V_{z2}V_{x1})\mathbf{j} + (V_{x1}V_{y2} - V_{x2}V_{y1})\mathbf{k},$$

where $\mathbf{V}_1 = V_{x1}\mathbf{i} + V_{y1}\mathbf{j} + V_{z1}\mathbf{k}$ and $\mathbf{V}_2 = V_{x2}\mathbf{i} + V_{y2}\mathbf{j} + V_{z2}\mathbf{k}$. Note that this method will return a `double` array as its result. Use the method to calculate the cross product of the two vectors $\mathbf{V}_1 = [-2, 4, 0.5]$ and $\mathbf{V}_2 = [0.5, 3, 2]$.

13. **Sort with Carry** It is often useful to sort an array `arr1` into ascending order, while simultaneously carrying along a second array `arr2`. In such a sort, each time an element of array `arr1` is exchanged with another element of `arr1`, the corresponding elements of array `arr2` are also swapped. When the sort is over, the elements of array `arr1` are in ascending order, while the elements of array `arr2` that were associated with particular elements of array `arr1` are still associated with them. For example, suppose we have the following two arrays:

Element	arr1	arr2
1.	6.	1.
2.	1.	0.
3.	2.	10.

After sorting array `arr1` while carrying along array `arr2`, the contents of the two arrays will be:

Element	arr1	arr2
1.	1.	0.
2.	2.	10.
3.	6.	1.

Write a method to sort one `double` array into ascending order while carrying along a second one. Test the method with the following two 9-element arrays:

```
double a[] = {  1., 11., -6., 17.,-23.,  0.,  5.,  1., -1. };
double b[] = { 31.,101., 36.,-17.,  0., 10., -8., -1., -1. };
```

14. **Comparing Sort Algorithms** Write a program to compare the sorting speed of the selection sort method developed in Example 6-1 with the quicksort sorting method included in the `java.util.Arrays` class. Use method `Math.random()` to generate two arrays containing 1000 and 10,000 random values between 0.0 and 1.0. Then, use both sorting methods to sort copies of these arrays. How does the sorting time compare for these two methods? (*Note:* The method `System.currentTimeMillis()` returns the current system time in milliseconds as a `double` value. You can determine the elapsed time required by a sorting algorithm by calling this method before and after the call to each sorting algorithm.)

15. **Linear Least Squares Fit** Develop a method that will calculate slope m and intercept b of the least-squares line that "best fits" an input data set. The input data points (x,y) will be passed to the method in two input arrays, x and y. The equations describing the slope and intercept of the least-squares line are

$$y = mx + b \tag{6-3}$$

$$m = \frac{(\Sigma xy) - (\Sigma x)\bar{y}}{(\Sigma x^2) - (\Sigma x)\bar{x}} \tag{6-4}$$

and

$$b = \bar{y} - m\,\bar{x} \tag{6-5}$$

where

$\quad \Sigma x$ is the sum of the x values
$\quad \Sigma x^2$ is the sum of the squares of the x values
$\quad \Sigma xy$ is the sum of the products of the corresponding x and y values
$\quad \bar{x}$ is the mean (average) of the x values
$\quad \bar{y}$ is the mean (average) of the y values

Test your method using a test driver program that calculates the least-squares fit to the following 20-point input data set, and plots both the original input data and the resulting least-squares fit line:

Sample Data to Test Least Squares Fit Method

NO.	x	y	NO.	X	Y
1	−4.91	−8.18	11	−0.94	0.21
2	−3.84	−7.49	12	0.59	1.73
3	−2.41	−7.11	13	0.69	3.96
4	−2.62	−6.15	14	3.04	4.26
5	−3.78	−5.62	15	1.01	5.75
6	−0.52	−3.30	16	3.60	6.67
7	−1.83	−2.05	17	4.53	7.70
8	−2.01	−2.83	18	5.13	7.31
9	0.28	−1.16	19	4.43	9.05
10	1.08	0.52	20	4.12	10.95

16. **Correlation Coefficient of Least Squares Fit** Develop a method that will calculate both the slope m and intercept b of the least-squares line that best fits an input data set, and also the correlation coefficient of the fit. The input data points (x,y) will be passed to the method in two input arrays, x and y. The equations describing the slope and intercept of the least-squares line are given in the previous problem, and the equation for the correlation coefficient is

$$r = \frac{n(\Sigma xy) - (\Sigma x)(\Sigma y)}{\sqrt{[(n\Sigma x^2) - (\Sigma x)^2][(n\Sigma y^2) - (\Sigma y)^2]}}, \tag{6-6}$$

where

$\quad \Sigma x$ is the sum of the x values
$\quad \Sigma y$ is the sum of the y values
$\quad \Sigma x^2$ is the sum of the squares of the x values
$\quad \Sigma y^2$ is the sum of the squares of the y values
$\quad \Sigma xy$ is the sum of the products of the corresponding x and y values
$\quad n$ is the number of points included in the fit

Test your method using a test driver program and the 20-point input data set given in the previous problem.

17. **The Birthday Problem** The Birthday Problem is: if there are a group of n people in a room, what is the probability that two or more of them have the same birthday? It is possible to determine the answer to this question by simulation. Write a method that calculates the probability that two or more of n people will have the same birthday, where n is a calling argument. (*Hint:* To do this, the method should create an array of size n and generate n birthdays in the range 1 to 365 randomly. It should then check to see if any of the n birthdays are identical. The method should perform this experiment at least 5000 times, and calculate the fraction of those times in which two or more people had the same birth-

day.) Write a program that calculates and prints out the probability that 2 or more of n people will have the same birthday for $n = 2, 3, \ldots, 40$. Then, plot the probability as a function of the number of people in the room. At what size group does the probability of having two people with the same birthday exceed 80%?

18. **Evaluating Infinite Series** The value of the exponential function can be calculated by evaluating the following infinite series:

$$e^x = \sum_{n=0}^{\infty} \frac{x^n}{n!}$$

Write a Java method that calculates using the first 12 terms of the infinite series. Compare the result of your method with the result of the intrinsic method `Math.exp(x)` for $x = -10, -5, -1, 0, 1, 5,$ and 10.

19. **Gaussian (Normal) Distribution** Method `Math.random()` returns a uniformly-distributed random variable in the range $[0,1)$, which means that there is an equal probability of any given number in the range occurring on a given call to the method. Another type of random distribution is the Gaussian Distribution, in which the random value takes on the classic bell-shaped curve shown in Figure 6.15. A Gaussian Distribution with an average of 0.0 and a standard deviation of 1.0 is called a *standardized normal distribution*, and the probability of any given value occurring in the standardized normal distribution is given by the equation

$$p(x) = \frac{1}{\sqrt{2\pi}} e^{-x^2/2}. \tag{6-7}$$

It is possible to generate a random variable with a standardized normal distribution starting from a random variable with a uniform distribution in the range $[-1, 1)$ as follows:

1. Select two uniform random variables x_1 and x_2 from the range $[-1, 1)$ such that $x_1^2 + x_2^2 < 1$. To do this, generate two uniform random variables in the range $[-1, 1)$, and see if the sum of their squares happens to be less than 1. If so, use them. If not, try again.

2. Then each of the values y_1 and y_2 in the equations below will be a normally-distributed random variable (note that "ln" is the symbol for the natural logarithm to the base e).

$$y_1 = \sqrt{\frac{-2\ln r}{r}}\, x_1, \tag{6-8}$$

Figure 6.15. A Normal probability distribution

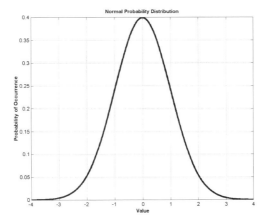

$$y_2 = \sqrt{\frac{-2 \ln r}{r}} \, x_2, \tag{6-9}$$

where
$$r = x_1^2 + x_2^2. \tag{6-10}$$

Write a method that returns a normally-distributed random value each time that it is called. Test your method by getting 1000 random values and calculating the standard deviation. How close to 1.0 was the result?

20. Use the method developed in the previous problem to generate an array of 50,000 random samples. Test the distribution of the values returned from this method by calculating the number of values falling within the ranges -4.0 to -3.9, -3.9 to -3.8, etc., up to 3.9 to 4.0. Divide the number of values in each bin by the total number of samples (50,000), and plot the resulting distribution.

21. **Gravitational Force** The gravitational force F between two bodies of masses m_1 and m_2 is given by the equation

$$F = \frac{Gm_1m_2}{r^2}, \tag{6-11}$$

where G is the gravitational constant (6.672×10^{-11} N m^2 / kg^2), m_1 and m_2 are the masses of the bodies in kilograms, and r is the distance between the two bodies. Write a method to calculate the gravitational force between two bodies given their masses and the distance between them. Test you method by determining the force on an 800 kg satellite in orbit 38,000 km above the Earth. (The mass of the Earth is 5.98×10^{24} kg.)

7

Classes and Object-Oriented Programming

This chapter expands on the definition and use of classes and objects. It is the most important chapter of this book, since it explains how to properly create and use objects.

As we said in Chapter 1, Java is an *object-oriented language*. Everything in Java (except for variables of primitive data types) is an object. Objects encapsulate data (*properties*) and methods (*behaviors*), hiding the details of their internal manipulation from the outside world. Thus objects inherently support **information hiding**. Since code outside of the object cannot directly "see" the data in an object, it cannot accidentally modify that data and introduce unintended bugs into the program. Objects interact with the outside world through well-defined *interfaces* defined and implemented by their associated methods.

In C, Fortran, and similar *procedural programming languages*, programmers tend to concentrate on writing procedures, which describe the actions to be performed by the program. The basic unit of programming in C is called a *function* (like a Java method); it describes how data is manipulated. The structure of a C program is oriented towards the *actions* to be performed, with the result that

SECTIONS

- 7.1 The Structure of a Class
- 7.2 Implementing a `Timer` Class
- 7.3 Class Scope
- 7.4 Types of Methods
- 7.5 Standard Java Packages
- 7.6 Creating Your Own Packages
- 7.7 Member Access Modifiers
- 7.8 Finalizers and Garbage Collection
- 7.9 Static Class Members
- Summary
- Key Terms

OBJECTIVES

After reading this chapter, you should be able to:

- Understand the structure of a class.
- Understand class scope and the use of references to access instance variables and methods.
- Learn how to create and use packages.
- Understand how and why to use member access modifiers.
- Understand finalizers and the garbage collection process.
- Understand `static` variables and methods.

the various components tend to be interdependent. This interdependence makes it harder to modify the program later without introducing unintentional bugs.

By contrast, the basic units in Java are **classes**, which are descriptions of the *data* in a program. Each class contains some type of data together with the specific instructions (methods) for manipulating that data. A class isolates its data from the outside world through the specific interface formed by the class's methods. This approach to programming has three critical advantages:

- **Modularity**: The source code for a class can be written and maintained independently of the source code for other classes. As long as the interface between a class and the outside world (the class's method definitions) doesn't change, the rest of the program won't care about the details of the class's implementation. Therefore, individual classes can be modified and upgraded without "breaking" the rest of the program.
- **Reusability**: Since a class is only connected to the rest of the program through well-defined interfaces, it is easy to re-use the class in other programs. Once a class has been written once, it never needs to be re-written. This leads to a "snowball effect". The first object-oriented project that you do will take a long time, since you will have to write every object from scratch. The second and subsequent projects will become quicker and easier, because you will have an ever-expanding collection of pre-defined and debugged classes to apply to your new projects.
- **Information Hiding**: A class has a public interface that other classes can use to communicate with it. But the class can maintain private information, and code outside the class cannot accidentally modify this information. This reduces the occurrence of bugs caused by unintended side-effects.

Classes are effectively new **programmer-defined types**, with each class defining data (called **fields**) and a set of methods to manipulate the data. Recall from Chapter 1 that classes are the "blueprint" or template from which objects are created. The fields in the class serve as a template for the **instance variables** that will be created when objects are instantiated (created) from that class. Each time that an object is instantiated from a class, *a new set of instance variables is created and initialized for that object*. This fact means that if two objects are created from the same class, they will have independent copies of all the instance variables defined in the class. The instance variables in a object can be modified and manipulated through calls to the object's methods.

It is important to remember that all classes from a part of a **class hierarchy**. Every class is a **subclass** of some other class, and the class inherits both instance variables and methods from its parent class. The class can add additional instance variables and methods, and can also override the behavior of methods inherited from its parent class.

Any class above a specific class in the class hierarchy is known as a **superclass** of that class. The class just above a specific class in the hierarchy is known as the **immediate superclass** of the class. Any class below a specific class in the class hierarchy is known as a subclass of that class.

Inheritance is another major advantage of object-oriented programming; once a behavior (method) is defined in a superclass, that behavior is automatically inherited by all subclasses unless it is explicitly overridden with a modified method. Thus behaviors only need to be coded *once*, and they can be used by all subclasses. A subclass need only provide methods to implement the *differences* between itself and its parent.

The highest class in the hierarchy is class `Object`; all classes inherit behaviors from this class.

7.1 THE STRUCTURE OF A CLASS

The major components (class members) of any class are:

1. **Fields**: Fields define the instance variables that will be created when an object is instantiated from a class. Instance variables are the data encapsulated inside an object. A new set of instance variables is created each time that an object is instantiated from the class.

2. **Constructors**: **Constructors** are special methods that specify how to initialize the instance variables in an object when it is created. Constructors are easy to identify, because they have the same name as the class that they are initializing, and they do not have a return data type. Constructors can be overloaded as long as the different constructors can be distinguished by their signatures.

3. **Methods**: Methods implement the behaviors of a class. Some methods may be explicitly defined in a class, while other methods may be inherited from superclasses of the class. As we learned in Chapter 6, methods may be overloaded as long as the different methods with the same name can be distinguished by their signatures.

4. **Finalizer**: Just before an object is destroyed, it makes a call to a special method called a **finalizer**. The method performs any necessary clean-up (releasing resources, etc.) before the object is destroyed. This special method is always named `finalize`. There can be at most one finalizer in a class, and many classes do not need a finalizer at all.

The members of a class, whether variables or methods, are accessed by referring to an object created from the class using the **member access operator**, also known as the **dot operator**. For example, suppose that a class `MyClass` contains an instance variable a and a method `processA`. If an object of this class is named `obj`, then the instance variable in `obj` would be accessed as `obj.a`, and the method would be accessed as `obj.processA()`.

7.2 IMPLEMENTING A Timer CLASS

When developing software, it is often useful to be able to determine how long a particular part of a program takes to execute. This measurement can help us locate the "hot spots" in the code, the places where the program is spending most of its time, so that we can try to optimize them. This is usually done with an *elapsed time calculator*.

Figure 7.1. A class consists of fields (data), one or more constructors to initialize the data, one or more methods to modify and manipulate the data, and up to one finalizer to clean up before the object is destroyed. Note that both fields and methods may be inherited from a superclass.

An elapsed time calculator needs to contain the following components:

1. A method to reset the timer to zero.
2. A method to return the elapsed time since the last reset.
3. An instance variable to store the time that the timer started running, for use by the elapsed time method.

This method must be able to determine the current time whenever one of its methods is called. Fortunately, the System class of the standard Java core API includes a method to read the current system time in milliseconds from the computer's system clock: **System.currentTimeMillis()**. This method will provide the current time information needed by the class.

The Timer class is shown in Figure 7.2.

```
1   /*
2      Purpose:
3        Object to measure the elapsed time between the most
4        recent call to method resetTimer() and the call to
5        method elapsedTime(). This class creates and starts
6        a timer when a Timer object is instantiated, and
7        returns the elapsed time in seconds whenever
8        elapsedTime() is called.
9
10     Record of revisions:
11       Date        Programmer           Description of change
12       ====        ==========           =====================
13       4/13/98     S. J. Chapman        Original code
14   */
15   public class Timer {
16
17      // Define instance variables
18      private double savedTime;    // Saved start time in ms
19
20      // Define class constructor
21      public Timer() {
22         resetTimer();
23      }
24
25      // ResetTimer() method
26      public void resetTimer() {
27         savedTime = System.currentTimeMillis();
28      }
29
30      // elapsedTime() method returns elapsed time in seconds
31      public double elapsedTime() {
32         double eTime;
33         eTime = (System.currentTimeMillis() - savedTime) / 1000;
34         return eTime;
35      }
36   }
```

Figure 7.2. The Timer class

This class contains a single instance variable savedTime, a single constructor Timer(), and two methods resetTimer() and elapsedTime().

To use this class in a program, the programmer must first instantiate a Timer object with a statement like

```
Timer t = new Timer();
```

Figure 7.3. The statement `Timer t = new Timer();` instantiates (or creates) a new `Timer` object from the template provided by the class definition, and makes reference `t` point to that object. This object has its own unique copy of the instance variable `savedTime`

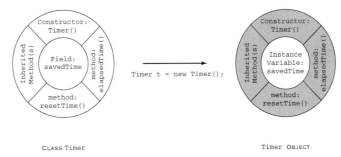

CLASS Timer   Timer OBJECT

This statement defines a reference `t` to refer to a `Timer` object, and then instantiates a new `Timer` object (See Figure 7.3). When the `Timer` object is instantiated, Java automatically calls the class constructor `Timer` to initialize the object. The constructor for this class begins on line 21; it resets the elapsed time counter so that by default it measures the elapsed time since the creation of the `Timer` object.

A program can reset the elapsed timer to zero at any time by calling method `resetTimer()`, and can get the elapsed time by calling method `elapsedTime()`. An example program that uses the `Timer` object is shown in Figure 7.4. The program tests this class by measuring the time required to perform 25,000,000 iterations of a pair of nested `for` loops.

```
/*
    Purpose:
        Class to test the operation of Timer.

    Record of revisions:
        Date        Programmer          Description of change
        ====        ==========          =====================
        4/13/98     S. J. Chapman       Original code
*/
public class TestTimer {

    // Define the main method to test this object
    public static void main(String[] args) {

        // Declare variables, and define each variable
        double arr[];          // Data array to sort
        int i, j, k;           // Loop index

        // Instantiate a Timer object
        Timer t = new Timer();

        // Start the timer running
        t.resetTimer();

        // Waste some time
        for ( i = 1; i <= 5000; i++ ) {
            for ( j = 1; j <= 5000; j++ ) {
                k = i + j;
            }
        }

        // Read and display elapsed time
        System.out.println( "Time = " + t.elapsedTime() + " s" );
    }
}
```

Figure 7.4. A program to test the `Timer` class

When this program is executed on my Pentium 133 MHz PC, the results are as follows:

```
D:\book\java\chap7>java TestTimer
Time = 0.401 s
```

The measured time will of course differ on computers of different speeds.

Note that this class saves the time of the last reset in an instance variable `savedTime`. Each time that an object is instantiated from a class, it receives its own copy of all instance variables defined in the class. This fact means that many `Timer` objects could be instantiated and used simultaneously in a program, and *they will not interfere with each other*, because each timer has its own private copy of the instance variable `savedTime`.

Notice that each class member in the program in Figure 7.2 is declared with either a **public** or **private** keyword. These keywords are known as **member access modifiers**. Any instance variable or method definition declared with the `public` member access modifier can be accessed any time that a program has access to an object of class `Timer`. Any instance variable or method declared with the `private` member access modifier is only accessible to methods of the object in which it is defined.

In this case, the instance variable `savedTime` is declared `private`, so it cannot be seen or modified by any method outside of the object in which it is defined. Since no method outside of `Timer` can see `savedTime`, it is not possible for some other method to accidentally modify the value stored there and so mess up the elapsed time measurement. The only way that a program can utilize the elapsed time measurement is through the `public` methods `resetTimer()` and `elapsedTime()`.

Every instance variable and method definition in a class should be preceded by an explicit member access modifier. It is good practice to group `public` and `private` member access modifiers together in a class for clarity and readability.

GOOD PROGRAMMING PRACTICES

Every instance variable and method definition in a class should be preceded by an explicit member access modifier.

The instance variables of a class are normally declared `private` and the methods of a class are normally declared `public`, so that the methods form an interface with the outside world, hiding the internal behavior of the class from any other parts of the program. This approach has many advantages, since it makes programs more modular. For example, suppose that we have written a program that makes extensive use of `Timer` objects. If necessary, we could completely re-design the internal behavior of the `Timer` class, and the program will continue to work properly as long as we have not changed the parameters or returned values from methods `resetTimer()` and `elapsedTime()`. This **public interface** isolates the internals of the class from rest of the program, making incremental modifications easier.

GOOD PROGRAMMING PRACTICES

The instance variables of a class should normally be declared `private`, and the class methods should be used to provide a standard interface to the class.

There are some exceptions to this general rule. Many classes contain `private` methods that perform specialized calculations in support of the `public` methods of the class. These are called **utility methods**, and since they are not intended to be called directly by users, they are declared with the `private` member access modifier. Also, some classes contain `public` instance variables that can be directly accessed by a user. This is relatively rare, but it is sometimes done for efficiency reasons.

7.3 CLASS SCOPE

The instance variables and methods of a class all have **class scope**, meaning that they can be accessed from any method within the class by name. For example, any method in class `Timer` can access the instance variable `savedTime` just by using its name. Similarly, any method in a class can call any other method in the same class by simply using its name[1].

Outside of a class's scope, those instance variables and methods that have been declared `public` can still be accessed, but *not* directly. Instead, they have to be accessed by reference to the object in which they are defined. Primitive data type instance variables would be accessed as `Reference.primitiveVariableName`, and object instance variables and methods would be accessed as `Reference.objectName` or `Reference.methodName`. For example, the program in Figure 7.4 created a `Timer` object using a reference `t`, and then invoked method `elapsedTime()` using that reference: `t.elapsedTime()`.

By contrast, variables defined within a method have **block scope**, with the block being the method body. These variables cannot be accessed from any other method, even if it is in the same class.

It is possible for a variable in a method to have the *same name* as an instance variable or method in the class in which the method is defined. If this happens, then the instance variable is *hidden* from the method by the local variable, and the method cannot access it directly even though the variable has class scope.

For example, Figure 7.5 shows a portion of a Java class defining a point in two-dimensional space. This portion of the class contains two instance variables x and y, two constructors, and a method to set the value of the point.

Notice that method `setPoint()` includes two local variables x and y, which have the same names as the class instance variables x and y. The instance variables have *class scope*, so they are accessible in any method within the class. However, the local variables in `setPoint()` that have the same names as the instance variables prevent the method from just using the names x and y to access the instance variables. Instead, *the instance variables are referred to as* `this.x` *and* `this.y`. The reference **this** always refers to the *current object*, which is the object within which the reference appears. Therefore, `this.x` refers to the instance variable x defined in the current object, and `this.y` refers to the instance variable y defined in the current object.

GOOD PROGRAMMING PRACTICE

If the name of a class member is hidden by a local variable name in a method within the same class, use the `this` reference to refer to the class member.

---

[1]This statement is not quite true for static methods, as we shall see later in the chapter.

```
public class Point {
   // Define instance data
   private double x;      // x position of point
   private double y;      // y position of point

   // Define constructors
   public void Point() {
      x = 0;
      y = 0;
   }

   public void Point(double x, double y) {
      this.x = x;
      this.y = y;
   }

   public void setPoint(double x, double y) {
      this.x = x;
      this.y = y;
   }

     . . .
     . . .
     . . .
}
```

Figure 7.5. Partial definition of a class, illustrating access to class instance variables having the same name as method variables.

7.4 TYPES OF METHODS

Since instance variables are usually hidden within a class, the only way to work with them is through the interface formed by the class's methods. The methods are the public face of the class, providing a standard way to work with the information while hiding the unnecessary details of the implementation from the user.

A class's methods must perform certain common "housekeeping" functions, as well as the specific actions required by the class. These housekeeping functions fall into a few broad categories, and they are common to most classes regardless of their specific purpose. A class must usually provide a way to store data into its instance variables, read data from its instance variables, test the status of its instance variables, and display the contents of its instance variables in a human-readable form.

Since the instances variables in a class cannot be used directly, classes must define methods to store data into the instance variables and to read data from them. By Java convention, the names of methods that store data begin with "set" and are called **set methods**, while the names of methods that read data begin with "get" and are called **get methods**.

Set methods take information from the outside world and store the data into the class's instance variables. In the process, they *should also check the data for validity and consistency*. This checking prevents the instance variables of the class from being set into an illegal state.

For example, suppose that we have created a class Date containing instance variables day (with a range of 1–31), month (with a range of 1–12), and year (with a range of 1900–2100). If these instance variables were declared public, then any method in the program could modify them directly. For example, assume that a Date object was declared as

```
Date d1 = new Date();
```

With this declaration, any method in the program could directly set the day to an illegal value.

```
d1.day = 32;
```

Set methods and private instance variables prevent this sort of illegal behavior by testing the input parameters. If the parameters are valid, the method stores them in the appropriate instance variables. If the parameters are invalid, the method either modifies the inputs to be legal, or by raises an exception if it is not possible to modify the illegal values into acceptable ones. (We will learn about exceptions in Chapter 8.)

Get methods are used to retrieve information from the instance variables and to format it properly for presentation to the outside world. For example, our Date class might include methods getDay(), getMonth(), and getYear() to recover the day, month, and year respectively.

Another type of method tests for the truth or falsity of some condition. These methods are called **predicate methods**. These methods typically begin with the word is, and they return a boolean (true/false) result. For example, a Date class might include a method isLeapYear(), which would return true if the specified year is a leap year, and false otherwise. In could also include methods like isEqual(), isEarlier(), and isLater() to compare two dates chronologically.

GOOD PROGRAMMING PRACTICE

1. Use set methods to check the validity and consistency of input data before it is stored in an object's instance variables.
2. Define predicate methods to test for the truth or falsity of conditions associated with any classes you create.

Another very important function of methods is to display the contents of the object in human-readable form. This is accomplished with a special method called toString(). The toString() method is defined for every Java class, since it is defined in the Object class, and every class is a subclass of Object. It is used to convert the data stored in an object into a form suitable for printing out. Every class should include a customized toString() method to properly format its data for display. The toString() method is automatically called whenever an object is concatenated with a string. For example, in the statement

```
System.out.println( "Date = " + d1);
```

the data in object d1 is converted into a string and printed on the standard output stream. If d1 is an object of the Date class, and if the Date class defines a toString() method, then that method will be used to convert the date into a string. The result might be something like

```
Date = 1/5/1999
```

GOOD PROGRAMMING PRACTICE

Override the toString() method of any classes that you define to create a reasonable display of the class's data.

EXAMPLE 7-1:
CREATING A
Date CLASS

We will illustrate the concepts described in this chapter by creating a Date class designed to hold and manipulate dates on the Gregorian calendar.

This class should be able to hold the day, month, and year of a date in instance variables that are protected from outside access. The class must include constructors to create dates, set and get methods to retrieve the stored information, predicate methods to recover information about date objects and to allow two Date objects to be compared, and a toString method to allow the information in a Date object to be displayed easily.

SOLUTION

The Date class will need three instance variables, day, month, and year. They will be declared private to protect them from direct manipulation by outside methods. The day variable should have a range of 1–31, corresponding to the days in a month. The month variable should have a range of 1–12, corresponding to the months in a year. The year variable will be greater than or equal to zero.

We will define two constructors for our class. One constructor will have no input parameters, and will initialize the date to January 1, 1900. The other constructor will have a day, month, and year as input arguments, and will initialize the date to the appropriate values.

We will also define a method setDate() to set a new date into a Date object, and three methods getDay(), getMonth(), and getYear() to return the day, month, and year from a given Date object.

The supported predicate methods will include isLeapYear() to test if a year is a leap year. This method will use the leap year test described in Example 4-2. In addition, we will create three methods isEqual(), isEarlier(), and isLater() to compare two Date objects. (For the purposes of comparison, an expression like d1.isEarlier(d2) should return true if d1 is an earlier date than d2.) Finally, method toString() will format the date as a string in the normal US style: dd/mm/yyyy.

The resulting class is shown in Figure 7.6.

```
/*
    Purpose:
       This class stores and manipulates dates on the
       Gregorian calendar.  It implements constructors,
       set methods, get methods, and predicate methods,
       and overrides the toString method.

    Method list:
       Date()                    Date constructor
       Date(day,month,year)      Date constructor
       setDate(day,month,year)   Set Date
       getDay()                  Get day
       getMonth()                Get month
       getYear()                 Get year
       isLeapYear()              Test for leap year
       isEqual()                 Test for equality
       isEarlier()               Is chronologically earler
       isLater()                 Is chronologically later
       toString()                Convert to string for display

  Record of revisions:
     Date           Programmer           Description of change
     ====           ==========           =====================
     4/16/98     S. J. Chapman           Original code
```

Figure 7.6. (*cont.*)

```
*/
public class Date {

   // Define instance variables
   private int year;        // Year (0 - xxxx)
   private int month;       // Month (1 - 12)
   private int day;         // Day (1 - 31)

   // Default constructor is January 1, 1900
   public Date() {
      year = 1900;
      month = 1;
      day = 1;
   }

   // Constructor for specified date
   public Date(int day, int month, int year) {
      setDate( day, month, year );
   }

   // Method to set a date
   public void setDate(int day, int month, int year) {
      this.year  = year;
      this.month = month;
      this.day   = day;
   }

    // Method to get day
   public int getDay() {
      return day;
   }

   // Method to get month
   public int getMonth() {
      return month;
   }

   // Method to get year
   public int getYear() {
      return year;
   }

   // Method to check for leap year
   public boolean leapYear() {
      boolean leapYear;
      if ( year % 400 == 0 )
         leapYear = true;
      else if ( year % 100 == 0 )
         leapYear = false;
      else if ( year % 4 == 0 )
         leapYear = true;
      else
         leapYear = false;
      return leapYear;
   }
```

Figure 7.6. *(cont.)*

```
                           // Method to check for equality
                           public boolean isEqual( Date d ) {
                              boolean equal;
                              if ( year == d.year && month == d.month && day == d.day )
                                 equal = true;
                              else
                                 equal = false;
                              return equal;
                           }

                           // Method to check if the date stored in this
                           // object is earlier than the Date d.
                           public boolean isEarlier( Date d ) {
                              boolean earlier;

                              // Compare years
                              if ( year > d.year )
                                 earlier = false;
                              else if ( year < d.year )
                                 earlier = true;
                              else {

                                 // Years are equal.  Compare months
                                 if ( month > d.month )
                                    earlier = false;
                                 else if ( month < d.month )
                                    earlier = true;
                                 else {

                                    // Months are equal.  Compare days.
                                    if ( day >= d.day )
                                       earlier = false;
                                    else
                                       earlier = true;
                                 }
                              }
                              return earlier;
                           }

                           // Method to check if the date stored in this
                           // object is later than the Date d.
                           public boolean isLater( Date d ) {
                              boolean later;

                              // Compare years
                              if ( year > d.year )
                                 later = true;
                              else if ( year < d.year )
                                 later = false;
                              else {

                                 // Years are equal.  Compare months
                                 if ( month > d.month )
                                    later = true;
                                 else if ( month < d.month )
                                    later = false;
                                 else {
```

Figure 7.6. *(cont.)*

```
                    // Months are equal.  Compare days.
                    if ( day > d.day )
                        later = true;
                    else
                        later = false;
                }
            }
            return later;
        }

        // Method to convert a date to a string.
        public String toString() {

            return (month + "/" + day + "/" + year);
        }
    }
```

Figure 7.6. The Date class

We must create a test driver class to test the Date class. Such a class is shown in Figure 7.7. Class TestDate instantiates four Date objects, and initializes them using both constructors. It then exercises all of the methods defined in the class (note that the toString() method is implicitly exercised by the System.out.println() statements).

```
/*
    Purpose:
        This class tests the Date class.

    Record of revisions:
        Date          Programmer         Description of change
        ====          ==========         =====================
        4/16/98     S. J. Chapman        Original code
*/
public class TestDate {

    // Define the main method to test class Date
    public static void main(String[] args) {

        // Declare variables, and define each variable
        Date d1 = new Date(4,1,1996);    // Date 1
        Date d2 = new Date(1,3,1998);    // Date 2
        Date d3 = new Date();            // Date 3
        Date d4 = new Date();            // Date 4

        // Set d3
        d3.setDate(3,1,1996);

        // Print out dates
        System.out.println ("Date 1 = " + d1);
        System.out.println ("Date 2 = " + d2);
        System.out.println ("Date 3 = " + d3);
        System.out.println ("Date 4 = " + d4);

        // Check isLeapYear
        if ( d1.isLeapYear() )
            System.out.println (d1.getYear() + " is a leap year.");
```

Figure 7.7. (cont.)

```
              else
                 System.out.println (d1.getYear() + " is not a leap year.");
              if ( d2.isLeapYear() )
                 System.out.println (d2.getYear() + " is a leap year.");
              else
                 System.out.println (d2.getYear() + " is not a leap year.");

              // Check isEqual
              if ( d1.isEqual(d3) )
                 System.out.println (d3 + " is equal to " + d1);
              else
                 System.out.println (d3 + " is not equal to " + d1);

              // Check isEarlier
              if ( d1.isEarlier(d3) )
                 System.out.println (d1 + " is earlier than " + d3);
              else
                 System.out.println (d1 + " is not earlier than " + d3);

              // Check isLater
              if ( d1.isLater(d3) )
                 System.out.println (d1 + " is later than " + d3);
              else
                 System.out.println (d1 + " is not later than " + d3);

        }
    }
```

Figure 7.7.   Class TestDate to test the Date class

When this program is executed, the results are as follows:

```
D:\book\java\chap7>java TestDate
Date 1 = 1/4/1996
Date 2 = 3/1/1998
Date 3 = 1/3/1996
Date 4 = 1/1/1900
1996 is a leap year.
1998 is not a leap year.
1/3/1996 is not equal to 1/4/1996
1/4/1996 is not earlier than 1/3/1996
1/4/1996 is later than 1/3/1996
```

Note that the date strings are being written out in the order month/day/year. From the test results, this class appears to be functioning correctly.

This class works, but it could be improved. For example, there is no validity checking performed on the input values in the setDate() method, and the toString() method could be modified to produce dates with explicit month names such as "January 1, 1900".

PROFESSIONAL SUCCESS: RETURNING MULTIPLE VALUES FROM JAVA METHODS

In other programming languages such as Fortran, a single subroutine (which corresponds to a Java method) can calculate many different results and return them all to the calling program. Unfortunately, Java methods are designed to only return a *single value* to the calling program. This limitation can be quite severe, requiring multiple methods to perform the same function that a single subroutine can perform in another language.

For example, suppose we wanted to write a function to calculate the average, standard deviation, minimum, and maximum in a data set. In Fortran, we could create a single subroutine `calc_stats`, and that subroutine could calculate and return all four values. In contrast, Java would require four different methods to return the four values, resulting in duplicate calculations and taking more time.

It is possible to get around this limitation of Java by creating a class containing the four instance variables `average`, `stdDev`, `min`, and `max`, and designing the `calcStats` method to return an object of that class. The method is returning a *single* object, but it is actually calculating and returning all four values!

```
public class StatValues {
   double average;
   double stdDev;
   double min;
   double max;

// Constructor that does nothing
   public StatValues()
}
```

and the statements shown below define a method `calcStats` that returns a `StatValues` object.

```
public StatValues calcStats( double[] data ) {
   StatValues result;
   ...
   (Insert calculations here)
   ...
   return result;
}
```

7.5 STANDARD JAVA PACKAGES

Every program that we have written has used classes and methods imported from the Java API. These pre-defined classes make programming much easier by allowing us to take advantage of other people's work instead of having to "reinvent the wheel" each time that we set out to write a program.

The Java API consists of literally hundreds of pre-defined classes containing thousands of pre-defined methods. These classes and methods are organized into related groups called **packages**. A package consists of a set of classes and methods that share some related purpose. For example, we could use classes from the `java.io` package to read data into our programs. This package is a set of classes that allow programs to input or output data.

The standard Java API packages as of Java 1.1.x are summarized in Table 7-1. A large number of additional packages have been added in Java 2, mostly to do with graphics. We will discuss some of the additional packages in Chapters 8 and 9.

TABLE 7-1   The Java API Packages

JAVA API PACKAGE	EXPLANATION
java.applet	The Java Applet Package.
	This package contains the Applet class and several interfaces that allow programmers to create applets and control their interactions with a browser.
java.awt	The Abstract Windowing Toolkit (AWT) Package.
	This package contains the classes and interfaces required to create Graphical User Interfaces. The term "abstract" is applied to this packages because in can create GUI windows on any type of computer regardless of the underlying operating system type.
java.awt.datatransfer	The Java Data Transfer Package.
	This package contains classes and interfaces that allow a program to transfer data between a Java program and a computer's clipboard (a temporary storage area used for cut and paste operations).
java.awt.event	The Java AWT Event Package.
	This package contains classes and interfaces that support event handling for GUI components.
java.awt.image	The Java AWT Event Package.
	This package contains classes and interfaces that enable storing and manipulating images in a program.
java.awt.peer	The Java AWT Peer Package.
	This package contains interfaces that allow Java's GUI components to interact with their platform-specific versions (for example, a button is actually implemented differently on a Macintosh than it is on a Windows or X-Windows machine). This package should never be used directly by Java programmers.
java.beans	The Java Beans Package.
	This package contains classes and interfaces that enable programmers to create reusable software components.
java.io	The Java Input/Output Package.
	This package contains classes that enable programs to input and output data.
java.lang	The Java Language Package.
	This package contains the basic classes and interfaces required to make Java programs work. It is automatically imported into all Java programs.
java.lang.reflect	The Java Core Reflection Package.
	This package contains classes and interfaces that allow a program to discover the accessible methods and variables of a class dynamically during the execution of a program.
java.net	The Java Networking Package.
	This package contains classes that enable a program to communicate over a network (the Internet or an intranet).
java.rmi java.rmi.dgc java.rmi.registry java.rmi.server	The Java Remote Method Invocation Packages. These packages contains classes and interfaces that enable a programmer to create distributed Java programs. A program can use RMI to call methods in other programs, whether they are located on the same computer or on another computer somewhere else on the network.

TABLE 7-1 (continued)

JAVA API PACKAGE	EXPLANATION
java.security java.security.acl java.security.inter- faces	The Java Security Packages These packages contains classes and interfaces that enable a program to encrypt data, and to control the access privileges provided to a Java program for security purposes.
java.sql	The Java Database Connectivity Package. This package contains classes and interfaces that enable a Java program to communicate with a database.
java.text	The Java Text Package. This package contains classes and interfaces that enable a Java program to manipulate numbers, dates, characters, and strings. This package provides many of Java's internationalization capabilities. For example, date and time strings can be automatically displayed in the proper format for the country in which a Java program is running.
java.util	The Java Utilities Package. This package contains classes and interfaces that perform important utility functions in a program. Examples include: date and time manipulations, random number generation, storing an processing large amounts of data, and certain string manipulations.
java.util.zip	The Java Utilities Zip Package. This package contains classes and interfaces that allow a Java program to create and read compressed archives called Java Archive (JAR) files. These archives can hold pre-compiled .class files as well as audio and image information.

A Java API class must be **imported** before it can be used in a program. There are two ways to import a Java class. The most common way is to include an **import** statement in the program before the class definition in which the API class will be used. For example, to use the Arrays class from the java.util package, we would include the line

```
import java.util.Arrays; // import java.util.Array class
```

at the start of the class in which it is used. It is also possible to import all of the classes and interfaces in an entire package with a statement of the form

```
import java.util.*; // import entire java.util package
```

The package java.lang contains classes that are fundamental to the operation of all Java programs, and it is automatically imported into every program. No import statement is required for this package.

A detailed description of all of the classes in the Java API can be found in the Java Development Kit (JDK) documentation. The JDK may be downloaded for free from http://java.sun.com, and the documentation may be viewed with any Web browser.

7.6 CREATING YOUR OWN PACKAGES

One of the great strengths of Java is the ability to re-use classes written for one project on other projects. Packages are a very useful way to bundle groups of related classes and to make them easy to re-use. If a set of useful classes is created and placed in a package, then those classes can be re-used on other projects by simply importing them into your new programs in the same manner as you import the packages built into the Java API. In fact, we have already been doing this with the `chapman.io`, `chapman.graphics`, and `chapman.math` packages, which were written for this book.

It is easy for a programmer to create his or her own packages. Any class that a programmer writes can be included in a package by adding a **package statement** to the file defining the class. For example, the class `Class1` shown in Figure 7-8 can be placed in package `chapman.testpackage` by including a `package` statement in the file before the beginning of the class definition. This statement indicates that the class defined in this file is a part of the specified package. (Note that the `package` and `import` statements are the only two statements in Java that can occur outside of a class definition.)

```
// Class to test creating and using a package
package chapman.testpackage;    // Place in testpackage
public class Class1 {

   // Method mySum
   public int mySum(int a, int b) {
      return a + b;
   }
}
```

Figure 7.8. A sample class containing a `package` statement

When a class containing a `package` statement is compiled, the resulting `.class` file is automatically placed in the directory indicated by the `package` statement. The series of names separated by periods in the statement is actually the directory hierarchy leading to the directory in which the file will be placed. Thus, the compiled output of this file will be placed in directory `<classroot>\chapman\testpackage` on a PC system, or directory `<classroot>/chapman/testpackage` on a Unix system. The `<classroot>` is the starting directory for the package directory structure on a particular computer, as described in Section 7.6.1.

When a class containing a `package` statement is compiled with the compiler in the Java Development Kit, the root directory for the package structure `<classroot>` must be specified using the `-d` compiler option. For example, the statement

```
javac -d c:\packages Class1.java
```

specifies that the root directory of the package structure is `c:\packages`. The root directory must already exist when the file is compiled. When this command is executed, the file `Class1.java` will be compiled, and the resulting `.class` file will be placed in directory `c:\packages\chapman\testpackage`. If necessary, the subdirectories will be created to hold the package. Other classes can be added to this package in the same way.

7.6.1 Setting the Class Path

Before a user-defined package can be used, the root directory of the package directory structure `<classroot>` must be inserted into your computer's **class path**. The class path is defined by an environment variable called CLASSPATH. When the Java compiler or Java interpreter needs to locate a class in a package, it looks at each directory defined in CLASSPATH to see if directory tree containing the package can be found there.

On a PC running Windows 95/98 the class path can be defined by adding the following line to the `autoexec.bat` file:

```
set CLASSPATH=c:\packages
```

If the CLASSPATH variable already exists in the file, add a semicolon followed by `c:\packages` to the end of the existing path. You will need to restart your computer before this change takes effect.

On a Windows NT computer, the class path is set through the System option of the Control Panel. On a Unix machine, the class path is set in different ways depending on the particular shell that you are using. If necessary, see you instructor for help in setting the class path on these computers.

7.6.2 Using User-Defined Packages

Once a package is created and the class path has been set, the package can be imported into any class desiring to use the package. For example, the class in Figure 7.9 imports package `testpackage`, and then uses `Class1` from it.

```
// Class to test using a package
import chapman.testpackage.*;
public class TestClass1 {

   // Define the main method to test Class1
   public static void main(String[] args) {

      // Declare variables
      int i = 8, j = 6;

      // Instantiate a Class1 object
      Class1 c = new Class1();

      // Use the object
      System.out.println("i + j = " + c.mySum(i,j));
   }
}
```

Figure 7.9.   Importing and using a class from a user-defined package

This class can be compiled and executed just like any other class. The computer automatically searches the specified class path to locate `testpackage` and import it.

```
C:\book\java\chap7>javac TestClass1.java
C:\book\java\chap7>java TestClass1
i + j = 14
```

7.7 MEMBER ACCESS MODIFIERS

There are four types of member access modifiers in Java: `public`, `private`, `protected`, and package. The first three are defined by explicit keywords in an instance variable or method definition, and the last is the default access that results if no access modifier is explicitly selected.

We have already seen the two member access modifiers `public` and `private`. A class member that is declared `public` may be accessed by any method anywhere within a program. A class member that is declared `private` may only be accessed by methods within the same class as the class member.

If no access modifiers are included in a definition, then the class member has **package access**. The member may be accessed by methods in all classes within the same package (that is, within the same directory) as the class in which the member is defined, but not by methods in other classes. This type of access is often convenient, because the classes in a package are usually related and must work closely together, while the details of their interactions will be hidden from methods outside the package.

This type of access is illustrated in Figure 7.10. Note that we are able to modify the instance variables `a.x` and `a.s` directly, because classes `TestPackageAccess` and `AccessTest` both reside in the same directory.

```
// Class to test package access
public class TestPackageAccess {

    // Define the main method to test Class1
    public static void main(String[] args) {

        // Instantiate a AccessTest object
        AccessTest a = new AccessTest();

        // Write out the value of the instance variable
        System.out.println(a.toString());

        // Modify the instance variables of class
        // AccessTest directly
        a.x = 3;
        a.s = "After: ";

        // Write out the value of the instance variable
        System.out.println(a.toString());
    }
}

// Define class AccessTest. Note that this class has
// package access.
class AccessTest {

    // Instance variables
    int x = 1;
    String s = "Before: ";

    // Method toString()
    public String toString() {
    return (s + x);
    }
}
```

Figure 7.10. A program illustrating package access

When this program is compiled and executed, the results are as follows:

```
C:\book\java\chap7>javac TestPackageAccess.java
C:\book\java\chap7>java TestPackageAccess
Before: 1
After: 3
```

Package access is inherently dangerous, since the methods of one class may be modifying the members of another class directly. If the class whose members are being modified directly is changed, then that modification may "break" the other classes that are accessing the class members directly. Thus, package access weakens the information hiding and the inherent modifiability of Java classes.

On the other hand, package access is efficient, because the classes' instance variables are being used and set without going through the overhead of `get` and `set` methods. This reduction in overhead allows the whole package to execute faster, while still hiding implementation details from the outside world. If a package only contains a few closely-related classes that can be modified and maintained together, then package access can provide an acceptable compromise between speed and safety.

GOOD PROGRAMMING PRACTICE

Package access is inherently dangerous, since it weakens information hiding in Java. Do not use it unless it is absolutely necessary for performance reasons. If it is necessary, restrict the package to a few closely-related classes.

The final access modifier is **`protected`**. Members declared with a `protected` modifier can be accessed by methods in all classes within the same package as the class in which the member is defined, and also by all *subclasses* of the class.

PRACTICE!

This quiz provides a quick check to see if you have understood the concepts introduced in Sections 7.1 through 7.7. If you have trouble with the quiz, reread the section, ask your instructor, or discuss the material with a fellow student. The answers to this quiz are found in the back of the book.

1. Name the major components of a class, and describe their purposes.
2. What types of member access modifiers may be defined in Java, and what access does each type give? What member access modifier should normally be used for instance variables? for methods?
3. What is the difference between class scope and block scope?
4. What happens in a program if a method contains a local variable with the same name as an instance variable in the method's class?
5. What statement(s) do you have to include in a program before you can use classes in Java API packages other than `java.lang`?
6. How do you create a user-defined package? How do you use the package?
7. What is the function of the `CLASSPATH` environment variable?
8. Explain the difference between `public`, `private`, `protected`, and package access.

7.8 FINALIZERS AND GARBAGE COLLECTION

Just before an object is destroyed, it makes a call to a special method called a **finalizer**, which performs any necessary clean-up (releasing resources, etc.) before the object is destroyed. This special method is always named `finalize`. There can be at most one finalizer in a class, and many classes do not need a finalizer at all.

When a class is instantiated with the `new` operator, the class constructor creates a new object. The constructor allocates memory for defined instance variables and objects, and may acquire other system resources such as open files, network sockets, etc. These resources are used by the object for as long as it is needed in the program.

When an object is no longer needed, it should be destroyed and its resources should be returned to the system for re-use. This function is performed automatically in Java by the **garbage collector**. The garbage collector is a low-priority thread[2] within the Java interpreter that normally runs in the background whenever the interpreter is executing. It constantly scans the list of objects created by the program. Any object that no longer has a reference pointing to it is a candidate for garbage collection, *because once all references to an object are gone, the object can no longer be used in any way by the program*. When the garbage collector spots such an object, it makes a call to the object's `finalize` method, and then destroys the object, releasing its memory to the system.

A program can force the garbage collector to run at high priority by making an explicit call to the `System.gc()` method. We might want to do this to ensure that garbage collection occurs at a specific time in a program.

The call to the object's `finalize` method is an opportunity for the object to close any files that it might have open and to perform any other required terminal housekeeping. Once the `finalize` method completes, the object is destroyed by the garbage collector.

The `finalize` method is normally declared `protected`, so that it is protected against accidental calls from outside methods. We will illustrate the use of `finalize` methods in Example 7-2.

7.9 STATIC CLASS MEMBERS

It is possible for both variables and methods in a class to be declared `static`. Such variables and methods have special properties, which are explained in this section.

7.9.1 Static Variables

Each object of a class has its own copy of all of the instance variables defined in the class. If a class defines an instance variable x, and two objects a and b are created from the class, then `a.x` and `b.x` will be two separate variables.

However, it is sometimes useful to have a particular variable in a class shared by all of the objects created from the class. If a variable is declared **static**, then one copy of that variable will be created the first time that a class is loaded, and that copy will remain in existence until the program stops running. Any objects instantiated from that class will share the single copy of that variable. Static variables are also known as **class variables**.

This concept is illustrated in Figure 7.11, which shows a class A defining two fields x and y and a `static` or class variable z. Two objects a1 and a2 are instantiated from this class. These two objects contain separate instance variables x and y, but they share a single copy of `static` variable z.

---

[2]A *thread* or *thread of execution* is a part of a program that can execute in parallel with other parts of the same program. Java supports multithreading as a part of its basic structure, but the discussion of that topic is beyond the scope of this book.

Figure 7.11. Two objects `a1` and `a2` instantiated from a single class `A`. These two objects have their own instance variables `x` and `y`, but share a single copy of the static variable `z`.

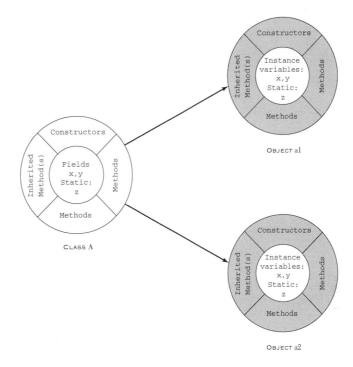

`Static` variables are useful for keeping track of global information such as the number of objects instantiated from a class, or the number of those objects still surviving at any given time. They are also useful for defining single copies of final variables that will be shared among all objects of the class. For example, the speed of light in a vacuum is $c = 2.99792458 \times 10^8$ meters per second. This value could be declared in a class as

```
static final double C = 2.99792458e8;
```

and a single copy of this constant will be created and shared among all of the objects instantiated from the class.

GOOD PROGRAMMING PRACTICE

Use `static` class variables to share a single copy of a variable among all of the objects instantiated from the class.

The *duration* of a `static` variable is different from the duration of an instance variable. Instance variables are created each time that an object is instantiated, and destroyed when the object is destroyed by the garbage collector. In contrast, `static` variables are created as soon as the class is loaded into memory, and persist until program execution ends.

Although `static` variables are global in the sense that they are shared among all of the objects instantiated from a class, they still have *class scope*. They are only visible outside of the class by reference to the class in which they are defined.

If a `static` variable is declared `public`, it may be accessed through any object of the class, or directly through the class name using the dot operator. For example, suppose that a class `Class1` defines a `public static` variable z, and an object c is instantiated from that class. Then the variable z can be accessed by other objects in the program either by `Class1.z` or by `c.z`.

Note that *the* `static` *variables in a class can be accessed without first creating an object from that class.* A good example of a `static` variable is `out` in the `System` class. We have used `System.out` in all of our programs since Chapter 1 without having to first instantiate a `System` object.

7.9.2 Static Methods

Static methods are methods that are declared `static` within a class. These methods can directly access the `static` variables in the class, but *cannot* directly access instance variables. Static methods are also known as **class methods**.

`Static` methods are commonly used to perform calculations that are independent of any instance data that might be defined in a class. For example, the method `sqrt()` in the `Math` class calculates the square root of any value passed to it, and returns the result. This method is independent of any data stored in the `Math` class, so it is declared `static`.

`Static` methods may be accessed by reference to a class's name without first creating an object from the class. Thus, we are able to use `Math.sqrt()` in any program without first instantiating an object from the `Math` class.

Every method in Java must be defined within a class, but some methods like `sqrt()`, `sin()`, `cos()`, etc. are not closely tied to any data within the class. These methods are usually declared `static` so that they can be accessed without having to instantiate an object first.

A very famous `static` method is `main`, the starting point of any Java application. The `main` method must be `static` so that it can be executed without first instantiating any object.

GOOD PROGRAMMING PRACTICE

Utility methods that perform functions independent of the instance data within a class may be declared `static` to make them easier to access and use.

EXAMPLE 7-2: USING STATIC VARIABLES AND FINALIZERS

To illustrate the use of `static` variable and finalizers, we will create a class containing two `static` variables. One of the variables will keep track of the number of times that an object is instantiated from the class, and the other one will keep track of the number of those objects still in existence. We will make these variables `private` so that no outside methods can tamper with them, and will provide `static` get methods to recover their current values when necessary.

In addition, the class will contain a single instance variable, which will contain an integer value, and a method to recover that value.

The resulting class is shown in Figure 7.12.

```
/*
    Purpose:
      This class illustrates the use of static variables to keep track of
      the number of objects created from the class.

    Record of revisions:
       Date        Programmer          Description of change
       ====        ==========          =====================
      4/20/98    S. J. Chapman        Original code
*/
public class Widget {

   // Define class variables
   private int value;         // Instance variable containing a value
   private static int created; // Total number of objects created
   private static int alive;   // Total number of objects still alive

   // Constructor
   public Widget(int value) {
      this.value = value;
      created++;
      alive++;
   }

   // Method to get number of Widgets created
   public static int getCreated() {
      return created;
   }

   // Method to get number of Widgets still alive
   public static int getAlive() {
      return alive;
   }

   // Method to get value of object
   public int getValue() {
      return value;
   }

   // Finalizer
   protected void finalize() {
      alive--;
      System.out.println("Finalizer running ...");
   }
}
```

Figure 7.12. The Widget class

We must create a test driver class to test the Widget class. Such a class is shown in Figure 7.13.

This class creates three objects of type Widget, initializing them to 10, 20, and 30 respectively. It then calls the static methods Widget.getCreated() and Widget.getAlive() to show how many objects of this type have been created, and how many objects are still alive.

Next the method calls the method getValue() for each object, showing that the instance variables in each object are unique to that object.

Next, the program nullifies the references to objects w1 and w2. Once these references are gone, the objects are inaccessible, and they become candidates for garbage collection. In theory, the two objects could disappear at any time after this point in the program. However, the garbage collector is a low priority thread, so the objects are not likely to disappear until we explicitly force the garbage collector to run.

When the garbage collector runs, it calls the finalizers for the objects being destroyed before actually destroying them. After starting the garbage collector running,

```
/*
    Purpose:
      This class tests the Widget class.

    Record of revisions:
      Date          Programmer            Description of change
      ====          ==========            =====================
      4/20/98       S. J. Chapman         Original code
*/
public class TestWidget {

        // Define the main method to test class Widget
        public static void main(String[] args) {

         // Create three new Widgets
         Widget w1 = new Widget(10);    // Widget 1
         Widget w2 = new Widget(20);    // Widget 2
         Widget w3 = new Widget(30);    // Widget 3

         // Check to see how many Widget are created and alive
         System.out.println (Widget.getCreated() + " Widgets created");
         System.out.println (Widget.getAlive() + " Widgets alive");

         // Print values of widgets
         System.out.println ("Widget 1 = " + w1.getValue());
         System.out.println ("Widget 2 = " + w2.getValue());
         System.out.println ("Widget 3 = " + w3.getValue());

         // Nullify references to two Widgets
         w1 = null;
         w2 = null;

         // Check to see how many Widget are created and alive
         System.out.println (Widget.getCreated() + " Widgets created");
         System.out.println (Widget.getAlive() + " Widgets alive");

         // Run the garbage collector
         System.gc();

         // Check to see how many Widget are created and alive
         System.out.println (Widget.getCreated() + " Widgets created");
         System.out.println (Widget.getAlive() + " Widgets alive");
    }
 }
```

Figure 7.13. Test driver for the Widget class

the main program continues executing and calls the static methods Widget.get-Created() and Widget.getAlive() again to show the status of the Widget objects.

Note that the garbage collector is running at the *same time* as the main program. If the garbage collector has had time to destroy the two objects with nullified references before the main program calls Widget.getAlive(), the call will show only one object left. However, the timing of the garbage collector will vary from run to run.

When this program was executed twice on my computer, the results were:

```
C:\book\java\chap7>java TestWidget
3 Widgets created
3 Widgets alive
Widget 1 = 10
Widget 2 = 20
Widget 3 = 30
3 Widgets created
3 Widgets alive
Finalizer running...
Finalizer running...
3 Widgets created
```

```
1 Widgets alive
D:\book\java\chap7>java TestWidget
3 Widgets created
3 Widgets alive
Widget 1 = 10
Widget 2 = 20
Widget 3 = 30
3 Widgets created
3 Widgets alive
3 Widgets created
3 Widgets alive
Finalizer running...
Finalizer running...
```

Note that each object's finalizer ran before the object was destroyed. On the first execution, the garbage collector destroyed the two objects *before* the second call to `Widget.getAlive()`. On the second execution, the garbage collector destroyed the two objects *after* the second call to `Widget.getAlive()`. Since the garbage collector and the main program are "racing", the number of objects left can vary from run to run.

EXAMPLE 7-3:
EXTENDED
MATH
METHODS

Class `Math` in package `java.lang` contains a number of common mathematical functions such as `abs()`, `sin()`, `cos()`, `sqrt()`, and so forth. While these functions are useful, the list is limited compared to the elementary functions available in other languages such as Fortran. Write an extended mathematics class `ExMath` containing static methods implementing the following additional functions:

Hyperbolic sine: $\quad\quad\quad\quad\quad\quad \sinh(x) = \dfrac{e^x - e^{-x}}{2},$

Hyperbolic cosine: $\quad\quad\quad\quad\quad \cosh(x) = \dfrac{e^x + e^{-x}}{2},$

Hyperbolic tangent: $\quad\quad\quad\quad \tanh(x) = \dfrac{e^x - e^{-x}}{e^x + e^{-x}},$

Log to the base 10: $\quad\quad\quad\quad \log_{10}(x) = \dfrac{\log_e x}{\log_e 10}.$

Insert the class into package `chapman.math`.

SOLUTION

This class will contain only `static` methods and the `static` final variable $\log_e 10$, so that the methods in it can be called without first instantiating an object.

1. **State the problem**. The problem is clearly stated above. We will write four different methods, implementing the four functions just described.
2. **Define the inputs and outputs**. The input to each method will be a single value of type `double`, and the result will be of type `double`. Numeric promotion will allow these methods to be used with data of other types.
3. **Decompose the program into classes and their associated methods**. There will be a single class, with four methods to calculate the hyperbolic sine, hyperbolic cosine, hyperbolic tangent, and logarithm to the base 10. We will call the class `ExMath`, and make it a subclass of the root class `Object`.

4. **Design the algorithm that you intend to implement for each method.**
   The pseudocode for the `sinh()` method is:

   ```
   return ( (Math.exp(x) - Math.exp(-x)) / 2 );
   ```

   The pseudocode for the `cosh()` method is:

   ```
   return ( (Math.exp(x) + Math.exp(-x)) / 2 );
   ```

   The pseudocode for the `tanh()` method is:

   ```
   double exp = Math.exp(x);
   double exm = Math.exp(-x);
   return ( (exp - exm) / (exp + exm) );
   ```

   The pseudocode for the `log10(x)` method is:

   ```
   return ( Math.log(x) / LOGE_10 );
   ```

   where `LOGE_10` is the constant $\log_e 10$.

5. **Turn the algorithm into Java statements.** The resulting Java methods are
   shown in Figure 7.14.

```
/*
   Purpose:
      This class defines an extended library of mathematical func-
      tions beyond those built into the java.lang.Math class.

   Record of revisions:
      Date          Programmer       Description of change
      ====          ==========       ======================
      4/22/98       S. J. Chapman    Original code
*/

// Specify package for class
package chapman.math;

public class ExMath {

   // Define class variables
   final static private double LOGE_10 = 2.302585092994046;

   // Hyperbolic sine method
   public static double sinh ( double x ) {
      return ( (Math.exp(x) - Math.exp(-x)) / 2 );
   }

   // Hyperbolic cosine method
   public static double cosh ( double x ) {
      return ( (Math.exp(x) + Math.exp(-x)) / 2 );
   }

   // Hyperbolic tangent method
   public static double tanh ( double x ) {
      double exp = Math.exp(x);
      double exm = Math.exp(-x);
      return ( (exp - exm) / (exp + exm) );
   }

   // Logarithm to the base 10
   public static double log10 ( double x ) {
      return ( Math.log(x) / LOGE_10 );
   }
}
```

Figure 7.14. Class ExMath

6. **Test the resulting Java program**. To test this program, we can manually calculate the values of the hyperbolic sine, hyperbolic cosine, hyperbolic tangent, and logarithm to the base 10 for $x = 1$ and $x = 10$, and compare the results with the output of a test driver program. The results of calculations on a scientific hand calculator are as follows:

X	SINH(X)	COSH(X)	TANH(X)	LOG10(X)
1	1.175201193	1.543080634	0.7615941559	0.0
10	11013.23287	11013.23292	0.9999999959	1.0

An appropriate test driver program is shown in Figure 7.15.

```
/*
   Purpose:
     This class tests the ExMath class.

   Record of revisions:
     Date         Programmer         Description of change
     ====         ==========         =====================
     4/22/98    S. J. Chapman        Original code
*/

import chapman.math.*;   // Get ExMath class

public class TestExMath {

   // Define the main method to test class Date
   public static void main(String[] args) {

      // Call the various methods
      System.out.println("sinh( 1)  = " + ExMath.sinh( 1));
      System.out.println("sinh(10)  = " + ExMath.sinh(10));
      System.out.println("cosh( 1)  = " + ExMath.cosh( 1));
      System.out.println("cosh(10)  = " + ExMath.cosh(10));
      System.out.println("tanh( 1)  = " + ExMath.tanh( 1));
      System.out.println("tanh(10)  = " + ExMath.tanh(10));
      System.out.println("log10( 1) = " + ExMath.log10( 1));
      System.out.println("log10(10) = " + ExMath.log10(10));
   }
}
```

Figure 7.15. Test driver for class ExMath

When this program is executed, the results are as follows:

```
C:\book\java\chap7>java TestExMath
sinh( 1)  = 1.1752011936438014
sinh(10)  = 11013.232874703397
cosh( 1)  = 1.5430806348152437
cosh(10)  = 11013.232920103328
tanh( 1)  = 0.7615941559557649
tanh(10)  = 0.9999999958776926
log10( 1) = 0.0
log10(10) = 1.0
```

The results of the program agree with our hand calculations to the number of significant digits that we performed the calculation.

PRACTICE!

This quiz provides a quick check to see if you have understood the concepts introduced in Sections 7.8 and 7.9. If you have trouble with the quiz, reread the section, ask your instructor, or discuss the material with a fellow student. The answers to this quiz are found in the back of the book.

1. What is the garbage collector? How does it operate? When are objects eligible for garbage collection?
2. What are `static` variables? What are they typically used for?
3. What are `static` methods typically used for?

SUMMARY

- The members of a class are instance variables and methods. Members of a class are accessed using the member access operator—the dot operator.
- Class definitions begin with the keyword `class`. The body of a class definition is included within braces (`{}`).
- An instance variable or method that is declared `public` is visible to any method with access to an object of the class.
- An instance variable or method that is declared `private` is only visible to other members of the class.
- An instance variable or method that is declared `protected` is visible to any method in the same package with access to an object of the class, and also to any method of a subclass of the class.
- An instance variable or method that has no member access modifier is visible to any method in the same package with access to an object of the class.
- A constructor is a special method used to initialize a new object. Constructors may be overloaded to provide multiple ways to initialize a new object.
- A finalizer is a special method used to release resources just before an object is destroyed.
- Within a class's scope, class members may be referenced by their names alone. Outside a class's scope, accessible class members are referenced through a reference to an object plus the dot operator.
- The instance variables in a class are normally declared `private`, and `public` set and get methods are used to control access to them.
- Predicate methods are methods used to test the truth or falsity of some condition relating to an object.
- Java packages are convenient ways to create libraries of reusable software. Classes are placed in packages using the `package` statement, and are imported from packages using the `import` statement.
- The `CLASSPATH` environment variable must be set properly before user-defined packages can be imported into programs.
- The `this` reference may be used to reference both methods and instance variables from within an object.
- A `static` variable is a variable that is common to all objects created from a given class. `Static` variables are created when the class is first loaded, and

remain in existence until the program terminates. `Static` class variables have class scope.

- A `static` method cannot access non-`static` class members. `Static` methods and variables exist independently of any objects instantiated from a class. `Static` methods are commonly used for utility operations that are basically independent of objects, such as `Math.sqrt()`.

APPLICATIONS: SUMMARY OF GOOD PROGRAMMING PRACTICES

The following guidelines introduced in this chapter will help you to develop good programs:

1. Every instance variable and method definition in a class should be preceded by an explicit member access modifier.
2. The instance variables of a class should normally be declared private, and the class methods should be used to provide a standard interface to the class.
3. If the name of a class member is hidden by a local variable name in a method within the same class, use the this reference to refer to the class member.
4. Use set methods to check the validity and consistency of input data before it is stored in an object's instance variables.
5. Define predicate methods to test for the truth or falsity of conditions associated with any classes you create.
6. Override the toString() method of any classes the you define to create a reasonable display of the class's data.
7. Create packages containing of groups of related classes to make it easy to re-use those classes in other programs.
8. Package access is inherently dangerous, since it weakens information hiding in Java. Do not use it unless it is absolutely necessary for performance reasons. If it is necessary, restrict the package to a few closely-related classes
9. Use static class variables to share a single copy of a variable among all of the objects instantiated from the class.
10. Utility methods that perform functions independent of the instance data within a class may be declared static to make them easier to access and use.

KEY TERMS

block scope	garbage collector	programmer-defined types
CLASSPATH	immediate superclass	public
class hierarchy	inheritance	set methods
class members	information hiding	System.currentTimeMillis()
class methods	instance variables	static method
class scope	member access operator	static variable
class variables	method	subclass
constructor	package access	superclass
dot operator	package statement	utility method
finalizer	private	

Problems

1. List and describe the major components of a class.

2. What is the difference between instance variables and methods and `static` variables and methods? When should instance variables and methods be used? When should `static` variables and methods be used?

3. What types of member access modifiers exist in Java? What restriction does each modifier place on access to a class member?

4. **Complex Data Type** Create a class called `Complex` to perform arithmetic with complex numbers. The class should have two `private` instance variables for the real and imaginary parts of the number. In addition, it should have class constructors, a set method to store a complex value, two get methods to recover the real and imaginary parts of the complex number, and methods for addition, subtraction, multiplication, division, and the absolute value function. In addition, the class should override the `toString()` method to print a complex number as a string of the form $a + b\ i$, where a is the real part of the number and b is the imaginary part of the number.

   If complex numbers c_1 and c_2 are defined as $c_1 = a_1 = b_1 i$ and $c_2 = a_2 + b_2 i$, then the addition, subtraction, multiplication, and division of c_1 and c_2 are defined as:

$$c_1 + c_2 = (a_1 + a_2) + (b_1 + b_2)i, \tag{7-1}$$

$$c_1 - c_2 = (a_1 - a_2) + (b_1 - b_2)i, \tag{7-2}$$

$$c_1 \times c_2 = (a_1 a_2 - b_1 b_2) + (a_1 b_2 + b_1 a_2)i, \tag{7-3}$$

$$\frac{c_1}{c_2} = \frac{a_1 a_2 + b_1 b_2}{a_2^2 + b_2^2} + \frac{b_1 a_2 - a_1 b_2}{a_2^2 + b_2^2}i. \tag{7-4}$$

   The absolute value of c_1 is defined as

$$|c_1| = \sqrt{a_1^2 + b_1^2}. \tag{7-5}$$

   Create a test driver program to test your class and confirm that all methods are working properly.

5. Determine whether the following class is correct or not. If it is in error, specify what is wrong with it. If it is correct, describe what the program does.

```
public class Norm {

    // Define instance data
    private double x;      // x position of point
    private double y;      // y position of point

    // Define constructor
    public void Norm(double x, double y) {
        this.x = x;
        this.y = y;
    }
    public void calcNorm() {
        return Math.sqrt(x*x + y*y);
    }

    public static void main(String s[]) {
        x = 3;
        y = 4;
        System.out.println("The norm is " + Norm.calcNorm () );
    }
}
```

6. **Extended Math Class** Expand the extended math class created in this chapter to include the following additional functions:

$$\text{Inverse hyperbolic sine: } \text{asinh}(x) = \log_e[x + \sqrt{x^2 + 1}]$$

for all x, (7-6)

$$\text{Inverse hyperbolic cosine: } \text{acosh}(x) = \log_e[x + \sqrt{x^2 - 1}]$$

$x \geq 1$, (7-7)

$$\text{Inverse hyperbolic tangent: } \text{atanh}(x) = \frac{1}{2} \log_e\left(\frac{1 + x}{1 - x}\right) -1 < x < 1 \quad (7-8)$$

Create a test driver program to verify that these functions work properly. The program should verify that the inverse functions work by showing that the inverse of a function undoes the action of the function itself. For example, it could show that asinh(sinh x) is just x.

7. Enhance the `Date` class created in this chapter by adding:

   1. A method to calculate the day-of-year for the specified date.
   2. A method to calculate the number of days since January 1, 1900 for the specified date.
   3. A method to calculate the number of days between the date in the current `Date` object and the date in another `Date` object.

   Also, convert the `toString` method to generate the date string in the form Month dd, yyyy. Generate a test driver program to test all of the methods in the class.

8. **Comparing Sort Algorithms** Write a program to compare the sorting speed of the selection sort method developed in Example 6-1 with the quicksort sorting method included in the `java.util.Arrays` class. Use method `Math.random()` to generate two arrays containing 1000 and 10,000 random values between 0.0 and 1.0. Then, use both sorting methods to sort copies of these arrays. How does the sorting time compare for these two methods? Use the `Timer` class to compare the times of the two sorting algorithms.

9. **Three-Dimensional Vectors** The study of the dynamics of objects in motion in three dimensions is an important area of engineering. In the study of dynamics, the position and velocity of objects, forces, torques, and so forth are usually represented by three-component vectors $\mathbf{v} = x\,\hat{\mathbf{i}} + y\,\hat{\mathbf{j}} + z\,\hat{\mathbf{k}}$, where the three components (x, y, z) represent the projection of the vector $\mathbf{v}$ along the x-, y-, and z- axes respectively, and $\hat{\mathbf{i}}$, $\hat{\mathbf{j}}$, and $\hat{\mathbf{k}}$ are the unit vectors along the x-, y-, and z- axes respectively (see Figure 7.16). The solutions of many mechanical problems involve manipulating these vectors in specific ways. The most common operations performed on these vectors are:

   1. **Addition.** Two vectors are added together by separately adding their x-, y-, and z- components. If

   $$\mathbf{v}_1 = x_1\,\hat{\mathbf{i}} + y_1\,\hat{\mathbf{j}} + z_1\,\hat{\mathbf{k}} \quad (7-9)$$

   and

   $$\mathbf{v}_2 = x_2\,\hat{\mathbf{i}} + y_2\,\hat{\mathbf{j}} + z_2\,\hat{\mathbf{k}} \quad (7-10)$$

   then

   $$\mathbf{v}_1 + \mathbf{v}_2 = (x_1 + x_2)\hat{\mathbf{i}} + (y_1 + y_2)\hat{\mathbf{j}} + (z_1 + z_2)\hat{\mathbf{k}}. \quad (7-11)$$

   2. **Subtraction.** Two vectors are subtracted by separately subtracting their x-, y-, and z- components. If

   $$\mathbf{v}_1 = x_1\,\hat{\mathbf{i}} + y_1\,\hat{\mathbf{j}} + z_1\,\hat{\mathbf{k}} \quad (7-12)$$

Figure 7.16. A three-dimensional vector

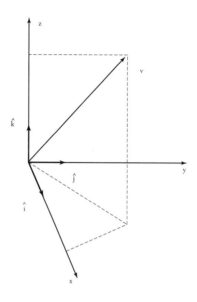

and

$$\mathbf{v}_2 = x_2\,\hat{\mathbf{i}} + y_2\,\hat{\mathbf{j}} + z_2\,\hat{\mathbf{k}} \tag{7-13}$$

then

$$\mathbf{v}_1 - \mathbf{v}_2 = (x_1 - x_2)\hat{\mathbf{i}} + (y_1 - y_2)\hat{\mathbf{j}} + (z_1 - z_2)\hat{\mathbf{k}}. \tag{7-14}$$

3. **Multiplication by a Scalar**. A vector is multiplied by a scalar by separately multiplying each component by the scalar. If

$$\mathbf{v} = x\,\hat{\mathbf{i}} + y\,\hat{\mathbf{j}} + z\,\hat{\mathbf{k}} \tag{7-15}$$

then

$$a\mathbf{v} = ax\,\hat{\mathbf{i}} + ay\,\hat{\mathbf{j}} + az\,\hat{\mathbf{k}}. \tag{7-16}$$

4. **Division by a Scalar**. A vector is divided by a scalar by separately dividing each component by the scalar. If

$$\mathbf{v} = x\,\hat{\mathbf{i}} + y\,\hat{\mathbf{j}} + z\,\hat{\mathbf{k}}, \tag{7-17}$$

then

$$\frac{\mathbf{v}}{a} = \frac{x}{a}\,\hat{\mathbf{i}} + \frac{y}{a}\,\hat{\mathbf{j}} + \frac{z}{a}\,\hat{\mathbf{k}}. \tag{7-18}$$

5. **The Dot Product**. The dot product of two vectors is one form of multiplication operation performed on vectors. It produces a scalar which is the sum of the products of the vector's components. If

$$\mathbf{v}_1 = x_1\,\hat{\mathbf{i}} + y_1\,\hat{\mathbf{j}} + z_1\hat{\mathbf{k}} \tag{7-19}$$

and

$$\mathbf{v}_2 = x_2\,\hat{\mathbf{i}} + y_2\,\hat{\mathbf{j}} + z_2\hat{\mathbf{k}}, \tag{7-20}$$

then the dot product of the vectors is

$$\mathbf{v}_1 \cdot \mathbf{v}_2 = x_1 x_2 + y_1 y_2 + z_1 z_2 \tag{7-21}$$

6. **The Cross Product**. The cross product is another multiplication operation that appears frequently between vectors. The cross product of two vectors is another vector whose direction is perpendicular to the plane formed by the two input vectors. If

$$\mathbf{v}_1 = x_1 \,\hat{\mathbf{i}} + y_1 \,\hat{\mathbf{j}} + z_1 \,\hat{\mathbf{k}} \tag{7-22}$$

and

$$\mathbf{v}_2 = x_2 \,\hat{\mathbf{i}} + y_2 \,\hat{\mathbf{j}} + z_2 \,\hat{\mathbf{k}}, \tag{7-23}$$

then the cross product of the two vectors is defined as

$$\mathbf{v}_2 \times \mathbf{v}_2 = (y_1 z_2 - y_2 z_1)\hat{\mathbf{i}} + (z_1 x_2 - z_2 x_1)\hat{\mathbf{j}} + (x_1 y_2 - x_2 y_1)\hat{\mathbf{k}}. \tag{7-24}$$

Create a class called `Vector3D`, having three components x, y, and z. Define methods to create vectors from three-element arrays, to convert vectors to arrays, and to perform the six vector operations defined above. Define a `toString` method that creates an output string of the form $x\,\mathbf{i} + y\,\mathbf{j} + z\,\mathbf{k}$. Then, create a program to test all of the functions of your new class.

10. **Derivative of a Sampled Function** The *derivative* of a continuous function $f(x)$ is defined by the equation

$$\frac{d}{dx} f(x) = \lim_{\Delta x \to 0} \frac{f(x + \Delta x) - f(x)}{\Delta x} \tag{7-25}$$

In a sampled function, this definition becomes

$$f'(x_i) = \frac{f(x_{i+1}) - f(x_i)}{\Delta x}, \tag{7-26}$$

where $\Delta x = x_{i+1} - x_i$. Assume that an array `samples` contains a series of samples of a function taken at a spacing of dx per sample. Create a class `Derivative`, and write a method that will calculate the derivative of this array of samples from Equation 7-7.

To check your method, you should generate a data set whose derivative is known, and compare the result of the method with the known correct answer. A good choice for a test function is sin x. From elementary calculus, we know that d/d_x (sin x) = cos x. Generate an input array containing 100 values of the function sin x starting at $x = 0$, and using a step size Δx of 0.05. Take the derivative of the vector with your method, and plot the function and its derivative on the same set of axes. Compare the derivative calculated by your method to the known correct answer. How close did your method come to calculating the correct value for the derivative?

11. **Derivative in the Presence of Noise** We will now explore the effects of input noise on the quality of a numerical derivative. First, generate an input array containing 100 values of the function sin x starting at $x = 0$, and using a step size Δx of 0.05, just as you did in the previous problem. Next, use method `Math.random()` to generate a small amount of uniform random noise with a maximum amplitude of ±0.02, and add that random noise to the samples in your input vector. Note that the peak amplitude of the noise is only 2% of the peak amplitude of your signal, since the maximum value of sin x is 1.0 (see Figure 7.17). Now take the derivative of the function using the `derivative` method that you developed in the last problem. Plot the derivative with and without noise on the same set of axes. How close to the theoretical value of the derivative did you come?

12. **Histograms** A *histogram* is a plot that shows how many times a particular measurement falls within a certain range of values. For example, consider the students in this class. Suppose that there are 30 students in the class, and that their scores on the last exam had a spread described by the following table:

Figure 7.17. (*a*) A plot of sin *x* as a function of *x* with no noise added to the data. (*b*) A plot of sin *x* as a function of *x* with a 2% peak amplitude uniform random noise added to the data.

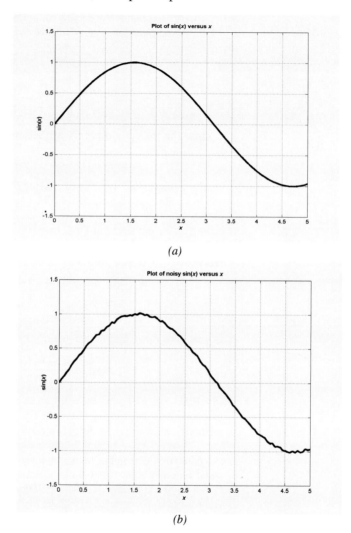

(a)

(b)

RANGE	NO. OF STUDENTS
100 – 95	3
94 – 90	6
89 – 85	9
84 – 80	7
79 – 75	4
74 – 70	2
69 – 65	1

Figure 7.18 is a histogram plot of the number of students scoring in each range of numbers.

Figure 7.18.   Histogram of Student Scores on Last Test

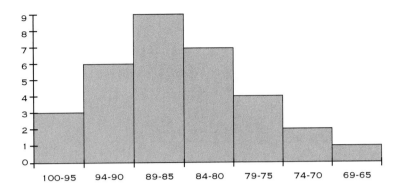

To create this histogram, we started with a set of data consisting of 30 student grades. We divided the range of possible grades on the test (0 to 100) into 20 bins, and then counted how many student scores fell within each bin. Then we plotted the number of grades in each bin. (Since no one scored below 65 on the exam, we didn't bother to plot all of the empty bins between 0 and 64 in Figure 7.8.)

Create a `Histogram` class that contains an instance array of bins to accumulate data in. The number of bins should be specified in the class constructor. The class should include a method `hist` that accepts an array of double values, determines the bin each value falls in, and increments the count in the appropriate bin. It should also include two methods `getBins()` and `getCount()` to return arrays containing the centers of each bin and the number of counts in each bin respectively.

Finally, create a test driver program that reads input data from a user-specified disk file, calculates a histogram from the data using the `Histogram` class, and uses the plotting classes in package `chapman.graphics` to create a plot of the histogram.

8

Exceptions and Complex Numbers

This chapter covers two disparate topics: exceptions and complex numbers. They are grouped together here for convenience because each topic is relatively short.

8.1 EXCEPTIONS AND EXCEPTION HANDLING

Java differs from most other computer languages in the way that it handles errors. For example, suppose that we would like to open a disk file in a program and read data from it. In Fortran or C, if the disk file does not exist, the open statement will return a value in a status variable indicating that the file could not be found. The program must check that status variable and deal with the error at that point in the program.

By contrast, when Java finds an error like this, it creates or "throws" an **exception**. The exception can be handled by the program either in the class where it occurred, or in any superclass of the class in which the error occurred. Thus, Java's error-handling mechanism is much more general than that in other languages. In this chapter, we learn how to generate (throw) and handle (catch) exceptions.

8.1.1 What Is an Exception?

Just what is an exception? An exception is an event that interrupts the normal processing flow of a program. This event is usually an error of some sort. For example, an attempt to divide an integer value by zero will produce a runtime exception called `ArithmeticException`.

Whenever a Java method cannot complete its normal processing, it **throws an exception**. Like everything else in Java, an exception is an object. Exceptions are objects of the

SECTIONS

- 8.1 Exceptions and Exception Handling
- 8.2 Complex Numbers
- Summary
- Key Terms

OBJECTIVES

After reading this chapter, you should be able to:

- Explain what an exception is
- Create exceptions
- Handle exceptions using a `try`/`catch` structure
- Use class `chapman.math.Complex` to create and manipulate complex numbers

`Exception` class or of some subclass of the `Exception` class. If an exception is **thrown** by a method and not **caught** by an exception handler, the program generating the exception will abort.

Exceptions are primarily intended as a way to handle errors that must be dealt with in a different scope (a different level of the program) from the one that detected the error. For example, the Java API includes many standard classes that can be utilized by a programmer when he or she is writing a new program. If an error occurs in a method in one of the Java API classes, *the error must be dealt with by the programmer* in his/her own code, since there is no way the original writers of the Java API could possibly guess what the programmer would want to do about the error. The method in the Java API throws an exception, which may be caught and handled in the programmer's code (see Figure 8.1).

There are two fundamental types of exceptions in Java, **runtime exceptions** and **checked exceptions**. Runtime exceptions are those exceptions that occur within the Java runtime system, including arithmetic exceptions (such as integer division by zero), pointer exceptions (such as trying to access an object through a null reference), and indexing exceptions (such as attempting to access an array element through an index that is either too large or too small). These sorts of exceptions can occur *anywhere* in a program, so Java does not force a programmer to list every possible runtime exception that can occur in every method.

All other exceptions in a Java program are known as **checked exceptions**, because the compiler checks that these exceptions are either caught or explicitly ignored by any method in which the exception could possibly occur. If an exception is to be ignored by a method, the method must explicitly "throw" the exception in it's method declaration, so that a method higher up the calling tree can have a chance to "catch" it.

Figure 8.1.   When a program calls a method in the Java API, the API method usually executes to completion, and program flow returns to the next statement following the one where the API method was called. This normal program flow is represented by the solid arrows in the diagram. If an error occurs in the API method, it throws an exception, which must be caught by a user-written exception handler. This abnormal program flow is shown by the dashed arrow in the diagram. Note that the exception handler does *not* have to be in the method that made to API call.

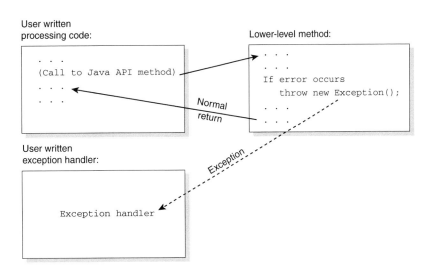

Every Java method has a **catch or specify requirement** for any checked exceptions that can be thrown *within the scope of that method*. This means that the exception must be explicitly caught and handled by the method, or else the method must explicitly declare that it throws the exception. The words "within the scope of the method" imply that the method must either catch or throw exceptions that were thrown by the method itself or by any other method directly or indirectly called by the method.

GOOD PROGRAMMING PRACTICE

Use exceptions to trap and correct errors in Java programs, especially if the errors occur in lower-level general-purpose classes that manipulate files or data.

8.1.2 Creating an Exception

An exception is an object of the `Exception` class or one of its subclasses. The `Exception` class includes two constructors of the forms shown below:

```
public Exception()
public Exception( String s )
```

The first form of the constructor creates a new `Exception` object with no arguments. The second form creates a new object and specifies an error message string that will be stored in the object. The `Exception` class includes two important methods that are useful in building exception handlers and debugging programs. Method `getMessage()` returns the error message stored in the `Exception` object so that it can be displayed. Method `printStackTrace()` prints a listing of the sequence of method calls that led up to the exception, which can help to identify the cause of the error. We will see examples of both of these methods later in the chapter.

The Java language includes a hierarchy of exception classes organized under the general `Exception` class. There are many direct subclasses of `Exception`, and most of them have further subclasses, with each subclass representing a specific type of exception. Figure 8.2 shows a portion of the exception class hierarchy. The root of the hierarchy is class `Exception`, which could represent any type of exception in a program. One subclass of `Exception` is `IOException`, which is the type of exception produced by input/output failures. Subclasses of `IOException` include `EOFException`, `FileNotFoundException`, and so forth. These subclasses are specific types of I/O exceptions. Notice that each subclass in the exception hierarchy is more specific than the superclass above it. A complete list of the pre-defined exception classes can be found in the Java Development Kit documentation.

Any Java method can throw any of the pre-defined exception classes. You may find that one of the pre-defined exceptions will be a good description of a problem that you encounter, in which case you can throw that exception in your code.

If none of the pre-defined exceptions meet your exact needs, then you can create your own exception class as a subclass of any existing class in the exception hierarchy. For example, let's reconsider the `Date` class that we created in Chapter 7. What would happen in that class if a user passes an invalid date to a `Date` object using the `setDate` method? At the moment, nothing would happen, since the values passed to `setDate` are

Figure 8.2.   Partial exception class hierarchy.

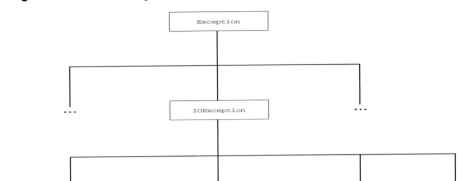

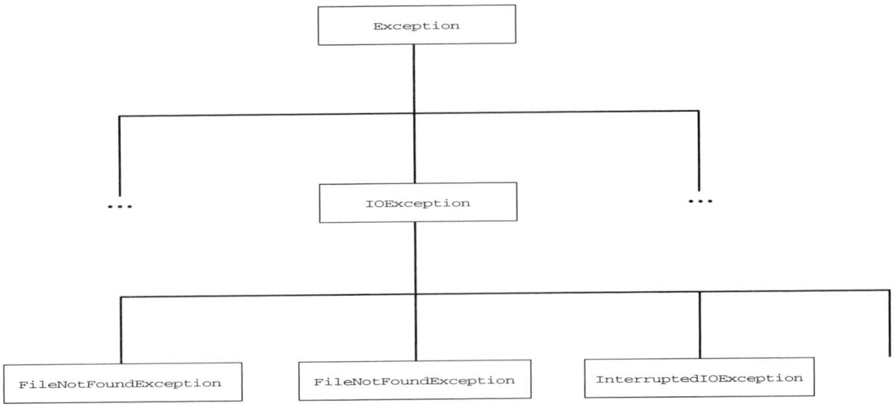

stored without validity checking. It would be better if we checked for the validity of the date, and threw an exception if an invalid date was passed to the method. We can create a special subclass of Exception called InvalidDateException for this purpose.

A possible InvalidDateException class is defined in Figure 8.3. Note that the expression "InvalidDateException extends Exception" means that our new class is a direct subclass of class Exception. This new class contains a single constructor, which initializes the class. The super method is a call to the constructor of the superclass Exception. It specifies the error string that will be available for display whenever this exception occurs.

```
// InvalidDateException
public class InvalidDateException extends Exception {

    // Define a constructor for this class
    public InvalidDateException() {
        super("Invalid date: please try again...");
    }
}
```

Figure 8.3.   Class InvalidDateException.

8.1.3 Throwing an Exception

Now that we have created an InvalidDateException, how would the method setDate throw the exception? This can be done by including a **throw statement** at any desired point within the method. The throw statement must consist of the keyword throw followed by an object of the Exception class or one of its subclasses. The location of the throw statement is known as the **throw point**.

A version of the setDate method that throws an InvalidDateException is shown in Figure 8.4. This method checks to see if the year, month, and day specified in the call are valid. If they are, it saves the information in the Date object. If not, it creates a new object of the InvalidDateException class, and throws that object.

```
                    // Method to set a date
                    public void setDate(int day, int month, int year)
                                      throws InvalidDateException {

                       int maxDays = 0;    // Max days in a month

                       // Determine if year is valid
                       if ( year < 0 )
                          throw new InvalidDateException();
                       else
                          this.year  = year;

                       // Determine if month is valid
                       if ( month < 1 || month > 12 )
                          throw new InvalidDateException();
                       else
                          this.month = month;

                       // Determine if day is valid.  This
                       // depends on the month.
                       switch ( month ) {
                          case 1:  case 3:  case 5:  case 7:
                          case 8:  case 10: case 12:
                             maxDays = 31;
                             break;
                          case 4: case 6: case 9: case 11:
                             maxDays = 30;
                             break;
                          case 2:
                             if ( isLeapYear() )
                                maxDays = 29;
                             else
                                maxDays = 28;
                       }

                       if ( day < 1 || day > maxDays )
                          throw new InvalidDateException();
                       else
                          this.day = day;
                    }
```

Figure 8.4. A version of method setDate that throws an InvalidDateException.

A complete version of the Date class that contains methods capable of throwing an InvalidDateException is shown in Figure 8.5. Note that the constructor Date(day,month,year) throws an InvalidDateException, because it calls method setDate, which throws that exception.

```
    /*
       Purpose:
          This class stores and manipulates dates on the
          Gregorian calendar.  It implements constructors,
          set methods, get methods, and predicate methods,
          and overrides the toString method.

       Method list:
          Date()                    Date constructor
          Date(day,month,year)      Date constructor
          setDate(day,month,year)   Set Date
          getDay()                  Get day
```

Figure 8.5. (cont.)

```
          getMonth()              Get month
          getYear()               Get year
          isLeapYear()            Test for leap year
          isEqual()               Test for equality
          isEarlier()             Is chronologically earler
          isLater()               Is chronologically later
          toString()              Convert to string for display

   Record of revisions:
      Date       Programmer        Description of change
      ====       ==========        =====================
      4/16/98    S. J. Chapman     Original code
   1. 4/22/98    S. J. Chapman     Modified to throw
                                     InvalidDateException
*/
public class Date {

   // Define instance variables
   private int year;       // Year (0 - xxxx)
   private int month;      // Month (1 - 12)
   private int day;        // Day (1 - 31)

   // Default date is January 1, 1900
   public Date() {
      year = 1900;
      month = 1;
      day = 1;
   }

   // Constructor for specified date
   public Date(int day, int month, int year)
                     throws InvalidDateException {
      setDate( day, month, year );
   }

   // Method to set a date
   public void setDate(int day, int month, int year)
                     throws InvalidDateException {

      int maxDays = 0;    // Max days in a month

      // Determine if year is valid
      if ( year < 0 )
         throw new InvalidDateException();
      else
         this.year  = year;

      // Determine if month is valid
      if ( month < 1 || month > 12 )
         throw new InvalidDateException();

      else
         this.month = month;

      // Determine if day is valid.  This
      // depends on the month.
      switch ( month ) {
         case 1:  case 3:  case 5:  case 7:
         case 8:  case 10: case 12:
            maxDays = 31;
            break;
```

Figure 8.5. *(cont.)*

```
            case 4: case 6: case 9: case 11:
               maxDays = 30;
               break;
            case 2:
               if ( isLeapYear() )
                  maxDays = 29;
               else
                  maxDays = 28;
         }

      if ( day < 1 || day > maxDays )
         throw new InvalidDateException();
      else
         this.day = day;
   }

   // Method to get day
   public int getDay() {
      return day;
   }

   // Method to get month
   public int getMonth() {
      return month;
   }

   // Method to get year
   public int getYear() {
      return year;
   }

   // Method to check for leap year
   public boolean isLeapYear() {
      boolean leapYear;
      if ( year % 400 == 0 )
         leapYear = true;
      else if ( year % 100 == 0 )
         leapYear = false;
      else if ( year % 4 == 0 )
         leapYear = true;
      else
         leapYear = false;
      return leapYear;
   }

   // Method to check for equality
   public boolean isEqual( Date d ) {
      boolean equal;
      if ( year == d.year && month == d.month && day == d.day )
         equal = true;
      else
         equal = false;
      return equal;
   }

   // Method to check if d is earlier than the
   // value stored in the object.
   public boolean isEarlier( Date d ) {
      boolean earlier;
```

Figure 8.5.   *(cont.)*

```
         // Compare years
         if ( d.year > year )
            earlier = false;
         else if ( d.year < year )
            earlier = true;
         else {

            // Years are equal.  Compare months
            if ( d.month > month )
               earlier = false;
            else if ( d.month < month )
               earlier = true;
            else {

               // Months are equal.  Compare days.
               if ( d.day >= day )
                  earlier = false;
               else
                  earlier = true;
            }
         }
         return earlier;
   }

   // Method to check if d is later than the
   // value stored in the object.
   public boolean isLater( Date d ) {
      boolean later;

      // Compare years
      if ( d.year > year )
         later = true;
      else if ( d.year < year )
         later = false;
      else {

         // Years are equal.  Compare months
         if ( d.month > month )
            later = true;
         else if ( d.month < month )
            later = false;
         else {

            // Months are equal.  Compare days.
            if ( d.day > day )
               later = true;
            else
               later = false;
         }
      }
      return later;
   }

   // Method to convert a date to a string.
   public String toString() {

      return (month + "/" + day + "/" + year);
   }
}
```

Figure 8.5. An improved Date class that contains methods which check for invalid dates and throws an InvalidDateException when an invalid input is supplied.

8.1.4 Handling Exceptions

Any exception that is thrown by a method must be either caught or re-thrown by every method above that method in the calling tree. The Java compiler enforces this requirement. However, it does *not* force some method to catch and handle the exception—it is possible for every method all the way back to main to simply re-throw the exception.

If an exception is *not* caught by some method in the user's program, then the exception will cause the program to abort. For example, the program shown in Figure 8.6 attempts to create a new Date object with an invalid date.

```
/*
   Purpose:
     This class attempts to create a Date object with an
     invalid date.

   Record of revisions:
      Date          Programmer          Description of change
      ====          ==========          =====================
      4/22/98       S. J. Chapman       Original code
*/
public class BadDate {

    // Define the main method
    public static void main(String[] args)
                throws InvalidDateException {

        // Create a new Date object
        Date d = new Date(29,2,1998);

        // Print out date
        System.out.println ("Date = " + d);

    }
}
```

Figure 8.6. A program that attempts to create a new Date object with an invalid date.

When this method is executed, the program aborts with a trace showing the type of exception and the calling true to the location where the exception occurred.

```
D:\book\java\chap8>java BadDate
InvalidDateException: Invalid date: please try again...
        at Date.setDate(Date.java:84)
        at Date.<init>(Date.java:45)
        at BadDate.main(BadDate.java:18)
```

It is possible for a method to **catch** an exception and handle the error that caused the problem. This is done with a **try/catch structure**. The form of a try/catch structure is

```
try {
    ...
}
catch(exception1) {
    ...
}
catch(exception2) {
    ...
}
    ...
finally {
    ...
}
```

where the `try` block contains a set of statements to be executed, and the `catch` block(s) contain the **exception handlers**, which are sets of statements to be executed if the specified exceptions occur while the statements in the `try` block are being executed. There can be more than one `catch` block, with each one catching a different type of exception. In addition there can be a single `finally` block. The code in this block will be executed regardless of whether or not an exception occurs. It is typically used to release resources allocated by the `try` block so that they may be returned to the system.

Figure 8.7 illustrates the use of `try`/`catch` blocks for exception handling. This class contains two `try`/`catch` blocks surrounding statements that attempt to create new `Date` objects. The first new `Date` object is invalid, while the second new `Date` object is valid.

When this program is executed, the first attempt to create a new `Date` object produces an `InvalidDateException`, which is caught by the `catch` block. This block prints out information about the exception using the `getMessage()` and `printStackTrace()` methods, and then allows execution to continue. Next, the `finally` block is executed whether an error occurs or not.

The second attempt to create a new `Date` object is valid, so the code in the `try` block is executed completely, and the `catch` block is skipped. Again, the `finally` block is executed whether an error occurs or not.

```
/*
   Purpose:
     This class attempts to create a Date object with an
     invalid date, and catches the error in an exception
     handler.

   Record of revisions:
       Date          Programmer           Description of change
       ====          ==========           =====================
     4/22/98        S. J. Chapman         Original code
*/
public class CatchBadDate {

   // Define the main method
   public static void main(String[] args) {

      // Try to create an invalid date
      System.out.println("\nFirst try/catch block:");
      try {

         // Create a new Date object
         Date d1 = new Date(29,2,1998);

         // Print out date
         System.out.println ("Date = " + d1);
      }

      catch (InvalidDateException e) {

         // Tell user
         System.err.println("The exception is:\n  " + e.getMessage());
         System.err.println("\nThe stack trace is:");
         e.printStackTrace();
      }
      finally {
```

Figure 8.7. *(cont.)*

```
                              System.out.println("Finally always executes...");
                          }

                          // Try to create a valid date
                          System.out.println("\nSecond try/catch block:");
                          try {

                              // Create a new Date object
                              Date d2 = new Date(29,2,1996);

                              // Print out date
                              System.out.println ("Date = " + d2);
                          }

                          catch (InvalidDateException e) {

                              // Tell user
                              System.err.println("The exception is:\n  " + e.getMessage());
                              System.err.println("\nThe stack trace is:");
                              e.printStackTrace();
                          }
                          finally {
                              System.out.println("Finally always executes...");
                          }
                      }
                  }
```

Figure 8.7. A class that illustrates the use of try/catch blocks for exception handling.

When this program is executed, the results are:

```
D:\book\java\chap8>java CatchBadDate

First try/catch block:
The exception is:
  Invalid date: please try again...

The stack trace is:
InvalidDateException: Invalid date: please try again...
        at Date.setDate(Date.java:84)
        at Date.<init>(Date.java:45)
        at CatchBadDate.main(CatchBadDate.java:22)
Finally always executes...

Second try/catch block:
Date = 2/29/1996
Finally always executes...
```

GOOD PROGRAMMING PRACTICE

Use try/catch structures to trap and handle exceptions without causing the program producing the exception to abort.

8.1.5 The Exceptions Hierarchy and Inheritance

All exceptions inherit either directly or indirectly from the superclass `Exception`. Exception types form a tree or hierarchy, with the upper levels being very general and the lower levels being more specific.

Because all exceptions inherit from the superclass `Exception`, every exception, regardless of subclass, is also an `Exception` and will respond to a `catch` block set to catch objects of type `Exception`. Thus the following `try`/`catch` structure would catch every possible exception that could occur, regardless of its specific class:

```
try {
   ...
}
catch ( Exception e ) {
    System.err.println("An exception occurred!);
    System.err.println("The stack trace is:");
    e.printStackTrace();
}
{
```

If this single `catch` block can catch every possible exception, then why do we bother to create an elaborate structure of different exceptions? The answer is that the lower the level of an exception, the more detail that we have about what went wrong in the program. For example, if we set up a `catch` block that traps a `FileNotFound-Exception`, we would know very specifically that a specified file was not found during an I/O operation. If instead we set up a `catch` block that traps an `IOException`, the block would also trap the `FileNotFoundException`, but the code would only know that a general I/O error occurred, not specifically that a file was not found. The lower the level at which we trap the exception, the more specific our correction of the problem can be.

GOOD PROGRAMMING PRACTICE

Try to catch exceptions at the lowest exception subclass possible, in order to have as much information as possible about what went wrong.

On the other hand, it can be very tedious to trap every possible error. It may be convenient to trap exceptions at some higher level to reduce the effort required. For example, in some programs, it might be convenient to trap all I/O exceptions with a `catch (IOException e)` block. A compromise is often made between creating a long list of low-level `catch` blocks with very specific information and creating a single `catch` block to trap all exceptions. This trade-off must be made on a case-by-case method.

It is usual to have the most important exceptions for a specific application explicitly listed in their own `catch` blocks, with all other possible exceptions handled by a single higher level `catch` block. For example, if we were opening a file, there might be a specific `catch` block for the `FileNotFoundException`, and an additional `catch` block for `Exception`. The second `catch` block will handle all exceptions that are not `FileNotFoundExceptions`. If this design is used, the more general `catch` block must occur *after* the specific catch blocks in a `try`/`catch` structure. The following try/catch structure specifically tests for a FileNotFoundException and processes it separately, and then catches any other exceptions in a generic catch block.

```
try {
   ...
}
catch ( FileNotFoundException e ) {
   ...
}
catch ( Exception e ) {
   ...
}
```

8.1.6 Nested try/catch Structures

Exceptions can occur at any level in a program, and try/catch blocks can occur at any level as well. Thus the main method of a program may include a try/catch block covering a major part of the program, while a lower-level class within the scope of that try block may include another try/catch block associated with opening a file for the program. In this case, the two try/catch blocks are effectively *nested* inside each other.

If an exception occurs inside a set of nested try/catch blocks, it is presented to the *innermost* set of catch blocks first. Those blocks will catch the exception if it is of a type that they are set to trap. If not, the exception is presented to the next innermost set of catch blocks. Those blocks will catch the exception if it is of a type that they are set to trap. This process repeats until the outermost set of catch blocks are reached. If they cannot process the exception, then the program will abort.

It is possible for an exception to be caught and handled on more than one level. An inner catch block can catch the exception and perform partial processing on it, and then re-throw it so that a higher-level catch block can finish the processing. This behavior is illustrated in the sample program in Figure 8.8.

The program in Figure 8.8 contains two methods, method main and method throwsException. Method main calls method throwsException within a try/catch structure, and method throwsException throws an exception within a try/catch structure of its own. Since the innermost try/catch structure has a catch block for this type of exception, it is processed there first. Since that catch block re-throws the exception, it is also processed by the catch block in the outer structure.

```
/*
   Purpose:
      This class illustrates the way that exceptions can
      be caught and re-thrown at multiple levels.

   Record of revisions:
      Date          Programmer              Description of change
      ====          ==========              =====================
      4/23/98       S. J. Chapman           Original code
*/
public class CatchException {

   // Define the main method
   public static void main(String[] args) {

      try {
         throwsException();
      }
      catch (Exception e) {
```

Figure 8.8. *(cont.)*

```
            // Tell user
            System.err.println("\nException caught in main.");
            System.err.println("The stack trace is:");
            e.printStackTrace();
        }
    }

    public static void throwsException() throws Exception {

        // Throw an exception and catch it
        try {
            System.out.println("In method throwsException...");
            throw new Exception("New exception!");
        }

        catch (Exception e) {
            // Tell user
            System.err.println("Exception caught in throwsException.");
            System.err.println("The stack trace is:");
            e.printStackTrace();

            // Re-throw the exception for further processing
            throw e;
        }
    }
}
```

Figure 8.8. A program illustrating nested `try/catch` structures, with the inner structure partially processing and re-throwing an exception.

When this program executes, the results are:

```
D:\book\java\chap8>java CatchException
In method throwsException...
Exception caught in throwsException.
The stack trace is:
java.lang.Exception: New exception!
    at CatchException.throwsException (CatchException.java:35)

    at CatchException.main(CatchException.java:17)

Exception caught in main.
The stack trace is:
java.lang.Exception: New exception!
    at CatchException.throwsException (CatchException.java:35)
    at CatchException.main(CatchException.java:17)
```

**EXAMPLE 8-1
USING A
TRY/CATCH
STRUCTURE
TO TRAP
INPUT ERRORS**

One possible way to use a `try/catch` structure to trap input errors is to place the entire structure inside a `do/while` loop, with the `try` and `catch` blocks setting the control boolean for the loop. If this is done properly, the loop will repeat until a valid set of input data is entered.

To illustrate this point, we will create a program that prompts the user to enter a date and creates a new object of the `Date` class. This will be done inside a `do/while` loop and a `try/catch` structure so that we can trap `InvalidDateExceptions` if they are generated, and prompt the user to try again.

SOLUTION
This program must have an outer `do/while` loop whose loop continuation condition is only set to `false` when a valid date is entered. This is accomplished by setting the bool-ean as the last statement in the `try` block. This statement will only be executed if a valid

date has been set into the `Date` object. Otherwise, an `InvalidDateException` will occur, the `catch` block print out an error message, and the loop will run again.

```
/*
    Purpose:
      This class prompts a user to enter a date, and
      reads the date from the standard input stream.
      If the user enters an invalid date, it tries again.

    Record of revisions:
        Date         Programmer           Description of change
        ====         ==========           =====================
        4/25/98      S. J. Chapman        Original code
*/
import chapman.io.*;
public class GetDate {

    // Define the main method
    public static void main(String[] args) {

        // Declare variables
        int day, month, year;     // Day, month, and year
        Date d = new Date();      // New Date object
        boolean valid = false;    // Valid date flag

        // Create a StdIn object
        StdIn in = new StdIn();

        // while loop to get date
        do {

            // Get information to create a date object
            try {

                // Get day
                System.out.print("Enter day (dd):    ");
                day = in.readInt();

                // Get month
                System.out.print("Enter month (mm):  ");
                month = in.readInt();

                // Get year
                System.out.print("Enter year (yyyy): ");
                year = in.readInt();

                // Set Date into object
                d.setDate(day,month,year);

                // Set valid flag
                valid = true;
            }

            catch ( InvalidDateException e) {

                System.err.println("Invalid date entered--try again!\n");
                valid = false;

            }
        } while ( !valid );

        // Display final date
        System.out.println("\nThe date is: " + d);
    }
}
```

Figure 8.9. A program that uses a `try`/`catch` structure to trap and correct input errors.

When this program executes, the results are:

```
D:\book\java\chap8>java GetDate
Enter day (dd):     30
Enter month (mm):   13
Enter year (yyyy): 1998
Invalid date entered--try again!

Enter day (dd):     29
Enter month (mm):   2
Enter year (yyyy): 1998
Invalid date entered--try again!

Enter day (dd):     29
Enter month (mm):   2
Enter year (yyyy): 1996

The date is: 2/29/1996
```

Note that the program keeps prompting the user until a valid date is entered.

8.1.7 Invalid Results That Do Not Produce Exceptions

There is one major part of the Java language that does *not* throw an exception when an error occurs: the floating-point math library. Java uses IEEE Standard 754 floating-point arithmetic, which defines two special bit patterns to handle errors: NaN and Infinite. NaN stands for "Not a Number", and it is produced whenever a mathematical operation cannot produce a real result. For example, the result of the method call Math.sqrt(-1) is NaN, since $\sqrt{-1}$ has no valid real answer. Infinite is produced as the result of a floating-point division by zero. In either case, the program continues to run without generating an exception.

Java provides methods to detect NaN and Infinite results in floating-point variables. The Java methods Double.isNan(d) or Double.isInfinite(d) return a true result if the value of the double variable d is a NaN or Infinite respectively. Similarly, methods Float.isNan(f) or Float.isInfinite(f) return a true result if the value of the float variable f is a NaN or Infinite.

Interestingly, errors in integer arithmetic *do* produce exceptions. For example, integer division by zero produces an ArithmeticException. A program to illustrate floating-point and integer error handling is shown in Figure 8.10.

```
/*
   Purpose:
     This class illustrates the use of isNaN and isInf
     to check for floating-point math errors, and also
     the exception thrown for integer math errors.

   Record of revisions:
       Date        Programmer            Description of change
       ====        ==========            =====================
       9/15/98     S. J. Chapman         Original code
*/
import chapman.io.*;
public class MathError {

    // Define the main method
    public static void main(String[] args) {
```

Figure 8.10.   *(cont.)*

```
            double a, b, c;
            int i,j, k;


            // Create a new StdIn object
            StdIn in = new StdIn();


            // Get input for square root
            System.out.print("Enter value for sqrt: ");
            a = in.readDouble();
            b = Math.sqrt(a);
            if ( Double.isNaN(b) )
               System.out.println("Error!  Result = " + b);
            else
               System.out.println("sqrt("+a+") = " + b);


            // Get input for floating-point division
            System.out.println("\nFloating-point division:");
            System.out.print("Enter numerator:    ");
            a = in.readDouble();
            System.out.print("Enter denomenator: ");
            b = in.readDouble();
            c = a / b;
            if ( Double.isInfinite(c) )
               System.out.println
                    ("Division by 0!  Result = " + c);
            else
               System.out.println("a/b = " + c);


            // Get input for integer division
            System.out.println("\nInteger division:");
            System.out.print("Enter numerator:    ");
            i = in.readInt();
            System.out.print("Enter denomenator: ");
            j = in.readInt();
            k = i / j;
            System.out.println("i/j = " + k);
      }
}
```

Figure 8.10.   A program to illustrate floating-point and integer error handling in Java.

When this program is executed, the results are:

```
D:\book\java\chap8>java MathError
Enter value for sqrt: -1
Error! Result = NaN

Floating-point division:
Enter numerator:    5
Enter denomenator: 0
Division by 0! Result = Infinity

Integer division:
Enter numerator:    5
Enter denomenator: 0
Exception in thread "main" java.lang.ArithmeticException: / by zero
        at MathError.main(MathError.java:53)
```

Note that the floating-point math errors did not create an exception, but the integer math error did. Also, note that `ArithmeticException` is a runtime exception, so it did not have to be declared in a `throws` clause.

PRACTICE!

This quiz provides a quick check to see if you have understood the concepts introduced in Sections 8.1 through 8.5. If you have trouble with the quiz, reread the section, ask your instructor, or discuss the material with a fellow student. The answers to this quiz are found in the back of the book.

1. What is an exception?
2. What is the difference between a runtime exception and a checked exception?
3. What is meant by Java's catch or specify requirement?

8.2 COMPLEX NUMBERS

Many practical engineering problems involve working with complex numbers. For example, determining the voltages and currents in a circuit, calculating the behavior of a control system, and analyzing simple harmonic motion in a mechanical system all involve complex numbers.

Java does not have native support for complex numbers, but it is an extensible object-oriented language. As we mentioned in Chapter 7, each class is effectively a user-defined data type, with its instance variables representing the type's data and its methods representing the types of manipulations that can be performed on the data. Therefore, we can create our own complex data type as a `Complex` class.

Class `chapman.math.Complex` defines a complex data type with two `double` instance variables: `re` for the real part and `im` for the imaginary part of the complex number. In addition, it defines instance methods to add, subtract, multiply, and divide complex numbers, and static methods to calculate the sine, cosine, etc. of complex numbers.

8.2.1 Using `chapman.math.Complex`

A `Complex` object is created with a constructor of one of the three forms shown below.

```
Complex c1 = new Complex();                  // Value (0,0)
Complex c2 = new Complex(double a);          // Value (a,0)
Complex c3 = new Complex(double a, double b); // Value (a,b)
```

The first form of constructor creates a new `Complex` object with the value (0,0). The second form of constructor creates a new `Complex` object with the specified real part and a zero imaginary part `(a,0)`. The third form of constructor creates a new `Complex` object with the specified real and imaginary parts `(a,b)`.

Once created, `Complex` objects may be added, subtracted, multiplied, and divided using instance methods. Unfortunately, Java will not allow us to use the +, *, and / symbols to perform those operations, but we can do the equivalent operations with method names. For example, the following statement would add complex numbers `c1` and `c2`, and store the result in `c3`.

```
c3 = c1.add(c2);
```

More complex expressions can be created by concatenating several operations together, *with the resulting operations evaluated from left to right.* If the hierarchy of mathematical operations requires a different order of evaluation, we must use parentheses to enforce the proper order. An example of several mathematical operations and their `Complex` equivalents is shown below:

OPERATION	JAVA STATEMENT
c4 = c1 + c2 − c3	`c4 = c1.add(c2).sub(c3);`
c4 = c1 * c2 + c3	`c4 = c1.mul(c2).add(c3);`
c4 = c1 + c2 * c3	`c4 = c1.add( c2.mul(c3) );`

Note that in the third case we used parentheses to force the multiplication to occur before the addition.

A summary of some instance methods included in this class appears in Table 8-1, and a summary of selected static methods appears in Table 8-2. Consult the on-line documentation for a complete listing of complex methods.

TABLE 8-1 Selected Instance Methods in Class `chapman.math.Complex`

METHOD NAME AND PARAMETERS	MEANING	COMMENTS
In the following method definitions, assume that c1, c2, and c3 are references to Complex objects, and that d1 and d2 are double values.		
`c1.abs()`	$\|c1\|$	Calculate the absolute value of c1 as a double value.
`c1.add(c2)`	c1 + c2	Add c1 and c2, and store the result in a new Complex object.
`c1.conj()`		Calculate complex conjugate of c1, and store the result in a new Complex object.
`c1.div(c2)`	c1 / c2	Divide c1 by c2, and store the result in a new Complex object.
`c1.im()`		Return imaginary part of c1 as a double.
`c1.inv()`	1 / c1	Return the reciprocal of c1.
`c1.mul(c2)`	c1 * c2	Multiply c1 from c2, and store the result in a new Complex object.
`c1.neg()`		Calculate negative of c1, and store the result in a new Complex object.
`c1.phase()`		Calculate the phase angle of c1 as a double value.
`c1.pow(c2)`	$c_1^{c_2}$	Calculate the c1 to the power of c2.
`c1.re()`		Return real part of c1 as a double.
`c1.rect(d1,d2)`		Store d1 as the real part of c1 and d2 as the real part of c1.
`c1.sub(c2)`	c1 − c2	Subtract c2 from c1, and store the result in a new Complex object.

TABLE 8-2 Selected Static Methods in Class `chapman.math.Complex`

METHOD NAME AND PARAMETERS	METHOD VALUE	PARAMETER TYPE	RESULT TYPE	COMMENTS
`Complex.abs(c)`	$\|c\|$	Complex	double	Calculate magnitude of a complex value.
`Complex.acos(c)`	$\cos^{-1}c$	Complex	Complex	Inverse hyperbolic cosine of x
`Complex.acosh(c)`	$\cosh^{-1}c$	Complex	Complex	Inverse hyperbolic cosine of x
`Complex.asin(c)`	$\sin^{-1}c$	Complex	Complex	Inverse sine of c
`Complex.asinh(c)`	$\sinh^{-1}c$	Complex	Complex	Inverse hyperbolic sine of c
`Complex.atan(c)`	$\tan^{-1}c$	Complex	Complex	Inverse tangent of c

TABLE 8-2   Selected Static Methods in Class `chapman.math.Complex`

METHOD NAME AND PARAMETERS	METHOD VALUE	PARAMETER TYPE	RESULT TYPE	COMMENTS
`Complex.atanh(c)`	$\tanh^{-1} c$	Complex	Complex	Inverse hyperbolic tangent of c
`Complex.cos(c)`	$\cos c$	Complex	Complex	Cosine of c
`Complex.cosh(c)`	$\cosh c$	Complex	Complex	Hyperbolic cosine of c
`Complex.inv(c)`	$1/c$	Complex	Complex	Inverse of c
`Complex.log(c)`	$\log_e c$	Complex	Complex	Natural logarithm of c
`Complex.phase(c)`		Complex	double	Calculate the principal angle of a complex value, in radians.
`Complex.sin(c)`	$\sin c$	Complex	Complex	Sine of c
`Complex.pow(c1,c2)`	$c_1^{c_2}$	Complex	Complex	Exponentiation
`Complex.sinh(c)`	$\sinh c$	Complex	Complex	Hyperbolic sine of c
`Complex.tan(c)`	$\tan c$	Complex	Complex	Tangent of c
`Complex.tanh(c)`	$\tanh c$	Complex	Complex	Hyperbolic tangent of c

To illustrate the use of complex numbers, we will revisit the solution to the quadratic equation.

EXAMPLE 8-2 THE QUADRATIC EQUATION (REVISITED)

Write a general program to solve for the roots of a quadratic equation, regardless of type. Use `Complex` objects so that no branches will be required based on the value of the discriminant.

SOLUTION
The quadratic equation was originally solved in Example 3-2. We will deliberately solve this problem in a manner as similar as possible to the program in Example 3-2 so that you can do a direct comparison between the two programs.

1. **State the problem**. Write a program that will solve for the roots of a quadratic equation, whether they are distinct real roots, repeated real roots, or complex roots, without requiring tests on the value of the discriminant.

2. **Define the inputs and outputs**. The inputs required by this program are the coefficients a, b, and c of the quadratic equation

$$ax^2 + bx + c = 0 \qquad (3\text{-}1)$$

The output from the program will be the roots of the quadratic equation, whether they are real, repeated, or complex.

3. **Decompose the program into classes and their associated methods**. Because we are keeping this program as similar as possible to the one in Example 3-2, we will use a single class `Quad` and a single method `main` to solve the problem.

4. **Design the algorithm that you intend to implement for each method**. There is only one method in this program. The pseudocode for the `main` method is shown below. Note that there are no branches in this solution, unlike the previous quadratic equation solver.

```
Prompt the user for the coefficient a.
Read a
Prompt the user for the coefficient b.
Read b
Prompt the user for the coefficient c.
Read c
discr ← b1.mul(b1).sub( a.mul(c).mul(4) );
x1 ← (b.neg().add( Complex.sqrt(discr)) ). div( a.mul(2) );
x2 ← (b.neg().sub( Complex.sqrt(discr)) ).div( a.mul(2) );
Write out the two roots.
```

5. **Turn the algorithm into Java statements**. The final Java code is shown in Figure 8.11. Note that unlike Example 3-2, there are no if structures in this program.

```
/*
Purpose:
  This program solves for the roots of a quadratic equation
  of the form a*x*x + b*x + c = 0. It calculates the answers
  regardless of the type of roots that the equation
  possesses.

  Record of revisions:
      Date          Programmer          Description of change
      ====          ==========          =====================
      3/27/98       S. J. Chapman       Original code
  1.  9/23/98       S. J. Chapman       Original code
*/
import chapman.io.*;
import chapman.math.Complex;
public class Quad {

  // Define the main method
  public static void main(String[] args) {

    // Declare variables, and define each variable
    Complex a;          // Coefficient of x**2 term of equation
    Complex b;          // Coefficient of x term of equation
    Complex c;          // Constant term of equation
    Complex discr;      // Discriminant of the equation
    double temp;        // Temp variable
    Complex x1;         // 1st soln of equation
    Complex x2;         // 2nd soln of equation

    // Create a StdIn object
    StdIn in = new StdIn();

    // Prompt the user for the coefficients of the equation
    System.out.println("This program solves for the roots of a");
    System.out.println("quadratic equation of the form ");
    System.out.println("A * X*X + B * X + C = 0.");
    System.out.print("Enter the coefficient A: ");
    temp = in.readDouble();
    a = new Complex(temp);
    System.out.print("Enter the coefficient B: ");
    temp = in.readDouble();
    b = new Complex(temp);
    System.out.print("Enter the coefficient C: ");
    temp = in.readDouble();
    c = new Complex(temp);
```

Figure 8.11. *(cont.)*

```
// Calculate discriminant
discr = b.mul(b).sub( a.mul(c).mul(4) );

// Solve for the roots
x1 = (b.neg().add( Complex.sqrt(discr)) ).div ( a.mul(2) );
x2 = (b.neg().sub( Complex.sqrt(discr)) ).div ( a.mul(2) );

// Write out answers
System.out.println("The roots are:");
System.out.println("x1 = " + x1);
System.out.println("x2 = " + x2);
        }
}
```

Figure 8.11. Program to solve for the roots of a quadratic equation using `Complex` numbers.

6. **Test the program**. Next, we must test the program using real input data. Since there are three possible paths through the program, we must test all three paths before we can be certain that the program is working properly. From Equation (3-2), it is possible to verify the solutions to the equations given below:

$$x^2 + 5x + 6 = 0 \qquad x = -2, \text{ and } x = -3$$
$$x^2 + 4x + 4 = 0 \qquad x = -2$$
$$x^2 + 2x + 5 = 0 \qquad x = -1 \pm i2$$

If this program is compiled, and then run three times with the above coefficients, the results are as shown below (user inputs are shown in bold face):

```
D:\book\java\chap8>java Quad
This program solves for the roots of a
quadratic equation of the form
A * X*X + B * X + C = 0.
Enter the coefficient A: 1
Enter the coefficient B: 5
Enter the coefficient C: 6
The roots are:
x1 = (-2.0 + i 0.0)
x2 = (-3.0 + i 0.0)

D:\book\java\chap8>java Quad
This program solves for the roots of a
quadratic equation of the form
A * X*X + B * X + C = 0.
Enter the coefficient A: 1
Enter the coefficient B: 4
Enter the coefficient C: 4
The roots are:
x1 = (-2.0 + i 0.0)
x2 = (-2.0 + i 0.0)

D:\book\java\chap8>java Quad
This program solves for the roots of a
quadratic equation of the form
A * X*X + B * X + C = 0.
Enter the coefficient A: 1
Enter the coefficient B: 2
Enter the coefficient C: 5
The roots are:
x1 = (-1.0 + i 2.0)
x2 = (-1.0 - i 2.0)
```

The program gives the correct answers for our test data in all three possible cases. Note how much simpler this program is compared to the quadratic root solver found in Example 3-2. The use of the `Complex` objects has greatly simplified our program.

8.2.2 Class `chapman.math.SigProc`

Class `chapman.math.SigProc` implements several of the most common signal processing algorithms used by engineers. It builds on the `Complex` class, and allows a programmer to perform fast Fourier transforms (FFTs), convolutions, correlations, and so forth. The static methods in this class permit engineers to solve many common engineering problems.

Some of the methods in this class are summarized in Table 8-3. Examples of how to use these classes can be found among the supplemental materials posted at the book's Web site.

TABLE 8-3   Selected Static Methods in Class`chapman.math.SigProc`

METHOD NAME AND PARAMETERS	RESULT TYPE	COMMENTS
`calcFreq(double fs,int fftSize)`	`double[]`	This method calculates the frequency associated with each element of the output array from an FFT, taking into account the ambiguities above the Nyquist frequency.
`conv(Complex[] za,Complex[] zb)`	`Complex[]`	This method calculates the convolution of two arrays of arbitrary length, returning the result in an array of length `za.length + zb.length - 1`.
`correl(Complex[] za,Complex[] zb)`	`Complex[]`	This method calculates the cross-correlation between two arrays.
`correl(Complex[] za,Complex[] zb, boolean norm)`	`Complex[]`	This method calculates the cross-correlation between two arrays, with optional normalization.
`fft(Complex[] c)`	`Complex[]`	Calculate fast Fourier transform of complex array `c`. The length of `c` must be a power of 2, (32, 64, 128, etc.) This method throws an `InvalidArraySizeException` if the length is not a power of 2.
`fftswap(double[] z)`	`double[]`	This method shifts the output of an FFT so that the dc component appears in the middle of the spectrum.
`fftswap(Complex[] z)`	`Complex[]`	This method shifts the output of an FFT so that the dc component appears in the middle of the spectrum.
`ifft(Complex[] c)`	`Complex[]`	Calculate inverse fast Fourier transform of complex array `c`. The length of `c` must be a power of 2, (32, 64, 128, etc.) This method throws an `InvalidArraySize-Exception` if the length is not a power of 2.
`NextMul(int arraySize)`	`int`	This method calculates the power of two greater than or equal to a given input size. It is useful for determining the size of FFT required by a given input array.

SUMMARY

- Exceptions are objects created when an error occurs during normal processing. They are typically used when the error occurs in a different scope from that where the malfunction was detected.
- Exception handling should be used to process exceptions from software components such as libraries of classes that are likely to be widely used, since the writer of the classes cannot anticipate what the final user would like to do about each exception.
- When a Java method encounters an error that it cannot handle, it creates and throws an exception.
- There are two types of exceptions-runtime exceptions and checked exceptions.
- Programmers must catch or specifically throw any checked exception that may be produced with the scope of a method.
- Exceptions can be caught and handled by enclosing code within a `try/catch` structure.
- The catch block `catch (Exception e)` will catch all exceptions, since the `Exception` class is at the top of the exception class hierarchy.
- Exception handlers are searched in order from innermost to outermost looking for an handler capable of dealing with the exception type. The first handler capable of dealing with the exception is executed.
- A `catch` block may re-throw an exception to an outer `try/catch` structure.
- The `finally` block is always executed in a `try/catch` structure. It may be used to release allocated resources.
- Class `chapman.math.Complex` implements a complex data type for Java, which is very useful for solving many practical engineering problems.

APPLICATION: GOOD PROGRAMMING PRACTICES

The following guidelines introduced in this chapter will help you to develop good programs:

1. Use exceptions to trap and correct errors in Java programs, especially if the errors occur in lower-level general-purpose classes that manipulate files or data.
2. Use `try/catch` structures to trap and handle exceptions without causing the program producing the exception to abort.
3. Try to catch exceptions at the lowest exception subclass possible, in order to have as much information as possible about what went wrong.

KEY TERMS

catch or specify requirement
`chapman.math.Complex` class
`chapman.math.SigProc` class
checked exception
exception

`Exception` class
exception handling
`finally` clause
runtime exception

throw an exception
`throw` statement
throw point
`try/catch` structure

Problems

8.1. What is an exception? What is the difference between a runtime exception and a checked exception?

8.2. Why are exceptions especially useful for dealing with errors within Java API methods?

8.3. If no exceptions are thrown within a `try` block, where does execution continue after the `try` block is finished? If an exception is thrown within a `try` block and caught in a `catch` block, where does execution continue after the `catch` block is finished?

8.4. Write a class that creates a fifteen-element array a and initializes its elements to the values 1 through 15. Include a method in the class that attempts to take the square root of 16 elements in the array. What exception occurs when this happens? Is this exception a runtime exception or a checked exception? Write a `try`/`catch` structure that traps this exception.

8.5. What sort of exception occurs if a modulo operation is evaluated with zero as the second operand (for example, `4 % 0`)?

8.6. Write a program that reads two `int` values and calculates and displays the sum, difference, product, quotient, and modulus of the numbers. Include a `try`/`catch` structure to trap and report any possible runtime exceptions.

8.7. Write a class that prompts the user to enter two complex numbers (as separate real and imaginary components), and an operation to apply to them (addition, subtraction, multiplication, or division). The program should read the numbers, perform the operation, and display the complex result. In addition, it should plot the two input vectors and the result vector on a Cartesian coordinate system.

8.8. Create a class `Polar` that stores a complex number in polar in (amplitude, phase) format. Write a class containing a method that will accept a complex number $c = a + ib$ stored in a `Complex` object, and returns an equivalent `Polar` object. (*Hint*: Use method `Math.atan2`.)

8.9. If two complex numbers are expressed polar form, the two numbers may be multiplied by multiplying their magnitudes and adding their angles. That is, if $P_1 = z_1 \angle \theta_1$ and $P_2 = z_2 \angle \theta_2$, then $P_1 \times P_2 = z_1 z_2 \angle \theta_1 + \theta_2$. Add a method to your `Polar` class that multiplies two objects of type "polar" using this expression, and returns a result in polar form. Note that the resulting angle θ should be in the range $-\pi/2 < \theta \leq \pi/2$.

8.10. If two complex numbers are expressed polar form, the two numbers may be divided by dividing their magnitudes and subtracting their angles. That is, if $P_1 = z_1 \angle \theta_1$ and $P_2 = z_2 \angle \theta_2$, then $\dfrac{P_1}{P_2} = \dfrac{z_1}{z_1} \angle \theta_1 - \theta_2$. Write a function that divides two variables of type "polar" together using this expression, and returns a result in polar form. Note that the resulting angle θ should be in the range $-\pi/2 < \theta \leq \pi/2$.

8.11. **Euler's Equation** Euler's equation defines e raised to an imaginary power in terms of sinusoidal functions as follows:

$$e^{i\theta} = \cos \theta + i \sin \theta \qquad (8\text{-}4)$$

Write a method to evaluate $e^{i\theta}$ for any θ using Euler's equation, returning the result as a `Complex` object. Also, evaluate $e^{i\theta}$ using the static method `Complex.pow`. Compare the answers that you get by the two methods for the cases where $\theta = 0$, $\dfrac{\pi}{2}$, and π.

8.12. **Synchronization Sequences** Modern satellite communications encode data as a series of bits, each having a value of 0 or 1. These bits are grouped together into bytes or larger units and interpreted as characters or numbers. The bit stream is transmitted by a ground station to a satellite as a radio signal, and then retransmitted by the satellite to another ground station. When the second ground station receives the signal, it decodes the bit stream into the original message.

A major problem faced by the receiving station is knowing just when a new message begins. The ground station receives a continuous stream of random bits before the message starts, and it is hard to distinguish those random bits from an actual message. To mark the start of a message, each message is prefaced by a *synchronization sequence,* which is a special pattern of 0's and 1's. The receiving ground station continually correlates the input bit stream with a replica of the synchronization sequence, and a peak in the output marks the start of the new message so that it can be decoded.

Simulate the operation a synchronization sequence by creating an array of 1,000 values, each randomly selected to be a 1 or a 0. Next, insert the synchronization sequence 01110001010110100001100100111110 in 32 consecutive values somewhere within the array, and then cross-correlate the entire array with a replica of the synchronization sequence. Plot the resulting cross correlation. Do you see a peak at the location of the synchronization sequence? (*Note:* You can cross correlate two arrays using method Sig-Proc.correl.)

9

Inheritance, Polymorphism, and Interfaces

This chapter explains how inheritance allows Java to treat objects from different subclasses as a single unit by referring to them as objects of their common superclass. It also explains how, when working with a collection of superclass objects, Java is able to automatically apply the proper methods to each object, regardless of the subclass the object came from. This ability is known as **polymorphism**. Finally, it introduces **interfaces**, and shows how interfaces reduce duplication in programming effort.

9.1 SUPERCLASSES AND SUBCLASSES

All classes form a part of a class hierarchy. Every class except `Object` is a subclass of some other class, and the class inherits both instance variables and methods from its parent class. The class can add additional instance variables and methods, and can also override the behavior of methods inherited from its parent class.

    Any class above a specific class in the class hierarchy is known as a superclass of that class. The class just above a specific class in the hierarchy is known as the *immediate superclass* of the class. Any class below a specific class in the class hierarchy is known as a subclass of that class.

    Inheritance is major advantage of object-oriented programming; once a behavior (method) is defined in a superclass, that behavior is automatically inherited by all

SECTIONS

- 9.1 Superclasses and Subclasses
- 9.2 Defining Superclasses and Subclasses
- 9.3 The Relationship Between Superclass Objects and Subclass Objects
- 9.4 Polymorphism
- 9.5 Abstract Classes
- 9.6 Final Methods and Classes
- 9.7 The Type-Wrapper Classes for Primitive Types
- 9.8 Interfaces
- 9.9 The `Collection` and `Iterator` Interfaces
- Summary
- Key Terms

OBJECTIVES

After reading this chapter, you should be able to:

- Understand the concepts of inheritance, superclasses and subclasses
- Understand polymorphism, and be able to create polymorphic behavior
- Be able to create and use abstract classes
- Create `final` methods and classes, and explain why we would wish to use them
- Use the type-wrapper classes to manipulate primitive data types as objects
- Be able to create and use interfaces

subclasses unless it is explicitly overridden with a modified method. Thus, behaviors only need to be coded *once,* and they can be used by all subclasses. A subclass need only provide methods to implement the *differences* between itself and its parent.

9.2 DEFINING SUPERCLASSES AND SUBCLASSES

For example, suppose that we were to create a class `Employee`, describing the characteristics of the employees of a company. This class would contain the name, social security number, address, etc. of the employee, together with pay information. However, most companies have two different types of employees, those on a salary and those paid by the hour. Therefore, we could create two subclasses of `Employee`, `Salaried Employee` and `HourlyEmployee`, with different methods for calculating monthly pay. Both of these subclasses would inherit all of the common information and methods from `Employee` (name, etc.), but would override the method used to calculate pay.

Objects of either the `SalariedEmployee` *or* `HourlyEmployee` *classes may be treated as objects of the* `Employee` *class,* and so forth for any additional classes up the inheritance hierarchy. This fact is very important since objects of the two subclasses can be grouped together and treated as a *single* collection of objects of the superclass `Employee`.

For all practical purposes, any object of class `SalariedEmployee` or `Hourly-Employee` *is* an object of class `Employee`. In object-oriented programming terms, we say that these classes have an "isa" relationship with `Employee`, because an object of either class "is an" object of class `Employee`.

The Java code for the `Employee` class is shown in Figure 9.2. This class includes four instance variables, `firstName`, `lastName`, `ssn`, and `pay`. Notice that these instance variables are declared to have **protected access**, meaning that they can be accessed by the methods of this class and also the methods of any subclass of this class. The class also defines two constructors and seven methods to manipulate the instance variables of the class.

Figure 9.1.   A simple inheritance hierarchy. Both `SalariedEmployee` and `HourlyEmployee` inherit from `Employee`, and an object of either of their classes is also an object of the `Employee` class.

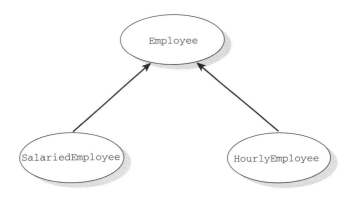

```
1   /*
2      Purpose:
3        This class defines an employee record.  It defines
4        basic employee information (first name, last name,
5        and social security number), and provides two
6        constructors and the following methods:
7          setName
8          setSsn
9          getFirstName
10         getLastName
11         getSsn
12         toString
13         calcPay
14
15     Record of revisions:
16        Date          Programmer            Description of change
17        ====          ==========            =====================
18        4/27/98       S. J. Chapman         Original code
19   */
20
21   public class Employee {
22
23      // Define instance variables
24      protected String firstName;      // First name
25      protected String lastName;       // Last name
26      protected String ssn;            // Social security number
27      protected double pay;            // Monthly pay
28
29      // Constructors
30      public Employee() {
31         firstName = " ";
32         lastName = " ";
33         ssn = "000-00-0000";
34         pay = 0;
35      }
36
37      public Employee(String first, String last, String ssn) {
38         firstName = first;
39         lastName = last;
40         this.ssn = ssn;
41         pay = 0;
42      }
43
44      // Set name
45      public void setName( String first, String last ) {
46         firstName = first;
47         lastName = last;
48      }
49
50      // Set social security number
51      public void setSsn( String ssn ) {
52         this.ssn = ssn;
53      }
54
55      // Get first name
56      public String getFirstName() {
57         return firstName;
58      }
59
```

Figure 9.2. *(cont.)*

```
60      // Get last name
61      public String getLastName() {
62         return lastName;
63      }
64
65      // Get social security number
66      public String getSsn() {
67         return ssn;
68      }
69
70      // Convert to string (this method will be
71      // overridden by different subclasses)
72      public String toString() {
73         String s = lastName + ", " + firstName + "   ("
74               + ssn + ") ";
75         return s;
76      }
77
78      // Method to calculate pay (this method will
79      // be overridden by different subclasses)
80      public double calcPay( double hours ) {
81         pay = 0;
82         return pay;
83      }
84   }
```

Figure 9.2.   The Employee class.

The method calcPay in this class returns a zero instead of calculating a valid pay, since the method of calculating the pay will depend on the type of employee, and we don't know that information yet in this class.

The Java code for the SalariedEmployee subclass is shown in Figure 9.3. This class *inherits* the four instance variables, firstName, lastName, ssn, and pay, and adds an additional instance variable salary. Notice that instance variable salary is declared to have private access, because it will not need to be accessed by any subclasses. It also defines a new method setSalary, and overrides the methods toString and calcPay from the superclass.

```
1    /*
2       Purpose:
3          This class defines an salaried employee record.
4          It overrides toString and calcPay from class
5          Employee.
6
7       Record of revisions:
8          Date          Programmer           Description of change
9          ====          ==========           =====================
10         4/27/98       S. J. Chapman        Original code
11   */
12   import chapman.io.Fmt;
13   public class SalariedEmployee extends Employee {
14
15      // Define instance variables
16      private double salary;          // Monthly salary
17
18      // Constructors
19      public SalariedEmployee() {
20         salary = 0;                 // Implicit call to Employee()
21      }
```

Figure 9.3.   *(cont.)*

```
22
23     public SalariedEmployee( String first, String last,
24                               String ssn, double salary) {
25        // Explicit call to Employee(first, last, ssn)
26        super(first, last, ssn);
27        this.salary = salary;
28        pay = this.salary;
29     }
30
31     // Method setSalary
32     public void setSalary( double salary ) {
33        this.salary = salary;
34        pay = this.salary;
35     }
36
37     // Convert to string
38     public String toString() {
39        String s = lastName + ", " + firstName + "   ("
40                 + ssn + "): Salary = $"
41                 + Fmt.sprintf("%.2f",salary);
42        return s;
43     }
44
45     // Method to calculate pay
46     public double calcPay( double hours ) {
47        pay = salary;
48        return pay;
49     }
50  }
```

Figure 9.3. The `SalariedEmployee` class.

Class `SalariedEmployee` defines two constructors to build objects of this class. Note that when an object of a subclass is instantiated, *a constructor for its superclass is called either implicitly or explicitly before any other initialization is performed.* In the constructor on line 19 of class `SalariedEmployee`, the superclass constructor is called implicitly to initialize `firstName`, `lastName`, `ssn`, and `pay` to their default values. (Any implicit call to a superclass constructor is always to the **default constructor**, the one with no input parameters.) In the constructor on line 23 of class `SalariedEmployee`, the superclass constructor is called explicitly to initialize `firstName`, `lastName`, `ssn`, and `pay` to the values provided by the user. The superclass *must* be initialized either implicitly or explicitly before any subclass initialization can occur. Thus, the following statements would produce an error:

```
public SalariedEmployee( String first, String last,
                          String ssn, double salary) {
   this.salary = salary;
   pay = this.salary;
   super(first, last, ssn); // Explicit call to Employee()
}
...
```

GOOD PROGRAMMING PRACTICE

When writing a subclass, call the superclass's constructor either implicitly or explicitly *as the first action in the subclass constructor.* Failure to do so will produce a compile-time error.

Similarly, if a subclass has a finalizer, the *last* statement of the subclass's finalizer should be a call to the superclass's finalizer, so that the superclass can perform cleanup on the resources allocated by the superclass constructor. The form of the subclass's finalize method should be

```
protected void finalize() {
   ...
   super.finalize();
}
```

GOOD PROGRAMMING PRACTICE

When writing a subclass, call the superclass's finalizer explicitly *as the last action in the subclass finalizer.* Failure to do so may result in resources such as files, network sockets, etc. not being released properly.

The Java code for the HourlyEmployee subclass is shown in Figure 9.4. This class *inherits* the four instance variables, firstName, lastName, ssn, and pay, and adds an additional instance variable rate. Notice that instance variable rate is declared to have private access, because it will not need to be accessed by any subclasses. It also defines a new method setRate, and overrides the methods toString and calcPay from the superclass.

```
1  /*
2     Purpose:
3       This class defines an hourly employee record.
4       It overrides toString and calcPay from class
5       Employee.
6
7     Record of revisions:
8        Date        Programmer          Description of change
9        ====        ==========          ======================
10       4/27/98     S. J. Chapman       Original code
11 */
12 import chapman.io.Fmt;
13 public class HourlyEmployee extends Employee {
14
15    // Define instance variables
16    private double rate;         // Hourly rate
17
18    // Constructors
19    public HourlyEmployee() {
20       rate = 0;                 // Implicit call to Employee()
21       pay = 0;
22    }
23
24    public HourlyEmployee( String first, String last,
25                           String ssn, double rate) {
26       // Explicit call to Employee(first, last, ssn)
27       super(first, last, ssn);
28       this.rate = rate;
29       pay = 0;
30    }
31
32    // Method setRate
33    public void setRate( double rate ) {
```

Figure 9.4. *(cont.)*

```
34          this.rate = rate;
35       }
36
37       // Convert to string
38       public String toString() {
39          String s = lastName + ", " + firstName + "    ("
40                     + ssn + "): Monthly Pay = $"
41                     + Fmt.sprintf("%.2f",pay);
42          return s;
43       }
44
45       // Method to calculate pay
46       public double calcPay( double hours ) {
47          pay = hours * rate;
48          return pay;
49       }
50    }
```

Figure 9.4.   The `HourlyEmployee` class.

Class `HourlyEmployee` defines two constructors to build objects of this class, and also overrides methods `toString` and `calcPay` to provide appropriate implementations for this subclass.

9.3 THE RELATIONSHIP BETWEEN SUPERCLASS OBJECTS AND SUBCLASS OBJECTS

Note that an object of a subclass has all of the non-private instance variables and methods of its superclass. In fact, *an object of any subclass may be treated as ("is") an object of its superclass.* This fact implies that we can manipulate objects with either subclass references or superclass references. Figure 9.5 illustrates this point.

```
1    /*
2       Purpose:
3          This class tests access to an objects of class
4          SalariedEmployee and HorulyEmployee using both
5          references to the subclasses and references to
6          the superclass Employee.
7
8       Record of revisions:
9          Date          Programmer          Description of change
10         ====          ==========          =====================
11         4/27/98       S. J. Chapman       Original code
12    */
13
14   public class TestEmployee {
15
16       // Define the main method to test class Employee
17       public static void main(String[] args) {
18
19          // Create a SalariedEmployee object
20          SalariedEmployee s1 = new SalariedEmployee(
21                  "John","Jones","111-11-1111",3000);
22
```

Figure 9.5.   *(cont.)*

```
23          // Create an HourlyEmployee object
24          HourlyEmployee h1 = new HourlyEmployee(
25                  "Jane","Jones","222-22-2222",12.50);
26
27          // Create an array of Employee objects
28          Employee e[] = new Employee[2];
29          e[0] = s1;
30          e[1] = h1;
31
32          // Calculate pay using subclass references
33          System.out.println("Calculation with subclass refs:");
34          System.out.println("Pay = " + s1.calcPay(160));
35          System.out.println("Pay = " + h1.calcPay(160));
36
37          // Calculate pay using superclass references
38          System.out.println("\nCalculation with superclass refs:");
39          for ( int i = 0; i < e.length; i++ )
40              System.out.println("Pay = " + e[i].calcPay(160));
41
42          // List employee info with superclass refs
43          System.out.println("\nEmployee information:");
44          for ( int i = 0; i < e.length; i++ )
45              System.out.println("Info: " + e[i].toString());
46
47      }
48  }
```

Figure 9.5. A program that illustrates the manipulation of objects with superclass references.

This test program creates one SalariedEmployee object and one Hourly-Employee object, and assigns them to references of the same types. Then it creates an array of Employee references, and assigns references to the two objects to the elements of that array. Normally, it is illegal to assign an object of one type to a reference of another type. However, it is ok here because *the objects of the subtypes* SalariedEmployee *and* HourlyEmployee *are also objects of the supertype* Employee.

Once the program assigns the references to the array, it uses both the original references and the array of Employee references to access some methods. When this program executes, the results are:

```
D:\book\java\chap9>java TestEmployee
Calculation with subclass refs:
Pay = 3000.0
Pay = 2000.0

Calculation with superclass refs:
Pay = 3000.0
Pay = 2000.0

Employee information:
Info: Jones, John    (111-11-1111): Salary = $3000.00
Info: Jones, Jane    (222-22-2222): Monthly Pay = $2000.00
```

Notice that the pay calculated with the subclass references is identical to the pay calculated with the superclass references.

It is possible to freely assign an object of a subclass to a reference of a superclass type, since the object of the subclass is also an object of the superclass. However, the converse is *not* true. An object of a superclass type is *not* an object of its subclass types.

Thus, if `e` is an `Employee` reference and `s` is a `SalariedEmployee` reference, then the statement

```
e = s
```

is perfectly legal, and the `SalariedEmployee` reference is said to be **upcast** to an `Employee` reference. In contrast, the statement

```
s = e
```

is illegal and will produce a compile time error.

It is possible to explicitly **downcast** a superclass type into a subclass type, as shown below:

```
s = (SalariedEmployee) e
```

This statement is legal and will compile correctly. However, the superclass reference `e` must actually refer to a subclass `SalariedEmployee` object when the program executes, or Java will throw a **ClassCastException**.

PROGRAMMING PITFALLS

It is illegal to assign a superclass reference to a subclass reference. However, you may *cast* a superclass reference into a subclass reference, as long as the object referred to really is a member of that subclass. If it is not, Java will throw a `ClassCastException` at runtime.

9.4 POLYMORPHISM

Let's look at the program in Figure 9.5. Pay was calculated using superclass references on line 40, and string conversions were performed using superclass references on line 45. Note that the methods `calcPay(160)` and `toString()` differed for `e[0]` and `e[1]`. The object referred to by `e[0]` was really a `SalariedEmployee`, so Java used the `SalariedEmployee` versions of `calcPay` and `toString` to calculate the appropriate values for it. On the other hand, the object referred to by `e[1]` was really an `HourlyEmployee`, so Java used the `HourlyEmployee` versions of `calcPay` and `toString` to calculate the appropriate values for it. The versions of `calcPay` and `toString` defined in class `Employee` were never used at all.

Note that we were working with an array of `Employee` objects, but *this program automatically selected the proper method to apply to each given object based on the subclass that it also belonged to.* This ability to automatically vary methods depending on the subclass that an object belongs to is known as **polymorphism** (meaning "many forms").

Polymorphism is an incredibly powerful feature of object-oriented languages. It makes them very easy to change. For example, suppose that we wrote a program using arrays of `Employee`s to work out a company payroll, and then later the company wanted to add a new type of employee, one paid by the piece. We could define a new subclass called `PieceworkEmployee` as a subclass of `Employee`, overriding the `calcPay` and `toString` methods appropriately, and create employees of this type. *The rest of the program will not have to be changed,* since the program manipulates arrays of class `Employee`, and polymorphism allows Java to automatically select the proper version of a method to apply whenever an object belongs to a particular subclass.

GOOD PROGRAMMING PRACTICE

Polymorphism allows multiple objects of different subclasses to be treated as objects of a single superclass, while automatically selecting the proper methods to apply to a particular object based on the subclass that it belongs to.

Note that for polymorphism to work, the methods to be used must be *defined in the superclass and overridden in the various subclasses.* Polymorphism will *not* work if the method you want to use is only defined in the subclasses. Thus a polymorphic method call like `e[1].toString()` is legal, because method `toString()` is defined in class `Employee` and overridden in subclasses `SalariedEmployee` and `HourlyEmployee`. On the other hand, a method call like `e[1].setRate()` is illegal, because method `setRate()` is only defined in class `HourlyEmployee`, and we cannot use an `Employee` reference to refer to an `HourlyEmployee` method.

It *is* possible to access a subclass method by casting the superclass reference into a subclass reference, such as

```
((HourlyEmployee) e[1]).setRate(14);
```

However, if `e[1]` does not really refer to an object of this subclass, the cast will throw a `ClassCastException`.

GOOD PROGRAMMING PRACTICE

To create polymorphic behavior, define all polymorphic methods in a common superclass, and then override the behavior of the methods in each subclass that inherits from the superclass.

**EXAMPLE 9-1:
POLYMORPHIC
BEHAVIOR**

To illustrate polymorphic behavior, let's create a superclass `Color`, and three subclasses `Red`, `Green`, and `Blue`. Class `Color` should have a single instance variable containing the intensity of a particular color on a scale of 0 to 255, plus a constructor and method `toString()`. Classes `Red`, `Green`, and `Blue` should override the `toString()` method in the `Color` class. We will include `println` statements in each method and constructor to print out a message whenever the method or constructor is executed.

Also, create a test program that creates an array of `Color` objects of various types, and executes the `toString()` method for each object in the array.

SOLUTION
Class `Color` is shown in Figure 9.6, and subclass `Red` is shown in Figure 9.7 (only subclass `Red` is shown, as subclasses `Green` and `Blue` are identical except for their names). Note the `println` statements in each constructor and method.

```
1   /*
2      Purpose:
3        This class defines the strength of a generic color.
4
5      Record of revisions:
6         Date          Programmer            Description of change
7         ====          ==========            =====================
8         9/27/98       S. J. Chapman         Original code
9   */
10
11  public class Color {
12
13     // Define instance variables
14     protected int intensity;         // Intensity of color
15
16     // Constructors
17     public Color() {
18        System.out.println("In constructor Color():");
19        intensity = 0;
20     }
21
22     public Color(int intensity) {
23        System.out.println("In constructor Color(int intensity):");
24        this.intensity = intensity;
25     }
26
27     // Convert to string
28     public String toString() {
29        System.out.println("In Color.toString():");
30        String s = "Color: intensity = " + intensity;
31        return s;
32     }
33  }
```

Figure 9.6. Class Color.

```
1   /*
2      Purpose:
3        This class defines the intensity of the color Red.
4
5      Record of revisions:
6         Date          Programmer            Description of change
7         ====          ==========            =====================
8         9/27/98       S. J. Chapman         Original code
9   */
10
11  public class Red extends Color {
12
13     // Constructors
14     public Red() {
15        System.out.println("In constructor Red():");
16     }
17
18     public Red(int intensity) {
19        super(intensity);
20        System.out.println("In constructor Red(int intensity):");
21     }
22
23     // Convert to string
24     public String toString() {
25        System.out.println("In Red.toString():");
26        String s = "Red: intensity = " + intensity;
27        return s;
28     }
29  }
```

Figure 9.7. Class Red.

The class `TestColor` is shown in Figure 9.8. It defines an array of `Color` references, and creates `Red`, `Green`, and `Blue` objects with them. Note that two of the new objects are created with specific intensity values, whereas one of them uses the default constructor. After creating the objects, the program prints out their contents in a `for` loop using the `toString()` method.

```
1   /*
2      Purpose:
3         This class tests class Color and its subclasses.
4
5      Record of revisions:
6         Date        Programmer          Description of change
7         ====        ==========          =====================
8         9/27/98     S. J. Chapman       Original code
9   */
10
11  public class TestColor {
12
13      public static void main(String[] args) {
14
15          // Create an array of Colors
16          Color c[] = new Color[3];
17          c[0] = new Red(120);
18          c[1] = new Green(255);
19          c[2] = new Blue();
20
21          // Display color values
22          System.out.println("\nColor values:");
23          for ( int i = 0; i < c.length; i++ )
24              System.out.println("Color = " + c[i]);
25      }
26  }
```

Figure 9.8. Class `TestColor`.

When this program is executed, the results are

```
D:\book\java\chap9>java TestColor
In constructor Color(int intensity):
In constructor Red(int intensity):
In constructor Color(int intensity):
In constructor Green(int intensity):
In constructor Color():
In constructor Blue():

Color values:
In Red.toString():
Color = Red: intensity = 120
In Green.toString():
Color = Green: intensity = 255
In Blue.toString():
Color = Blue: intensity = 0
```

Note that when each `Red`, `Green`, and `Blue` object was created, the constructor for that object called the constructor for the superclass `Color` as its first action. Also, when the `toString()` method was invoked with a `Color` reference, the `toString()` method in class `Color` was *not* used. Instead, the `toString()` method the appropriate subclass was invoked polymorphically.

9.5   ABSTRACT CLASSES

Look at the `Employee` class again. Note that we defined methods `calcPay` and `toString` in that class, but *neither method is ever used.* Since we only ever instantiate members of the subclasses `SalariedEmployee` and `HourlyEmployee`, these methods are *always* overridden polymorphically by the corresponding methods in the two subclasses. If these methods are never going to be used, why did we bother to write them at all? The answer is that in order for polymorphism to work, the polymorphic methods must be declared in both the parent class and in all of the subclasses.

However, the *bodies* of the polymorphic methods in the parent class will never be used if no objects are ever instantiated from that class, so Java allows us to declare the headers only without writing the body of the methods. Such methods are called **abstract methods**, and classes containing abstract methods are known as **abstract classes** (as opposed to ordinary classes, which are called **concrete classes**).

Abstract methods are declared using the `abstract` keyword in the method header, with no method body. For example, an abstract method `calcPay` would be declared as

```
public abstract double calcPay( double hours );
```

Any class containing an abstract method, or failing to override an abstract method inherited from its superclass, is an abstract class. Abstract classes must also be declared with the `abstract` keyword. For example, if class `Employee` contained any abstract methods, it would be declared as

```
abstract public class Employee {
```

An abstract version of the `Employee` class is shown in Figure 9.9.

```
1  /*
2     Purpose:
3       This class defines an employee record.  It defines
4       basic employee information (first name, last name,
5       and social security number), and provides two
6       constructors and the following methods:
7           setName
8           setSsn
9           getFirstName
10          getLastName
11          getSsn
12          toString
13          calcPay
14
15     Record of revisions:
16        Date          Programmer           Description of change
17        ====          ==========           =====================
18       4/27/98    S. J. Chapman         Original code
19  */
20
21  public abstract class Employee {
22
23     // Define instance variables
24     protected String firstName;        // First name
25     protected String lastName;         // Last name
26     protected String ssn;              // Social security number
27     protected double pay;              // Monthly pay
28
```

Figure 9.9.   *(cont.)*

```
29      // Constructors
30      public Employee() {
31         firstName = " ";
32         lastName = " ";
33         ssn = "000-00-0000";
34         pay = 0;
35      }
36
37      public Employee(String first, String last, String ssn) {
38         firstName = first;
39         lastName = last;
40         this.ssn = ssn;
41         pay = 0;
42      }
43
44      // Set name
45      public void setName( String first, String last ) {
46         firstName = first;
47         lastName = last;
48      }
49
50      // Set social security number
51      public void setSsn( String ssn ) {
52         this.ssn = ssn;
53      }
54
55      // Get first name
56      public String getFirstName() {
57         return firstName;
58      }
59
60      // Get last name
61      public String getLastName() {
62         return lastName;
63      }
64
65      // Get social security number
66      public String getSsn() {
67         return ssn;
68      }
69
70      // Convert to string (this method will be
71      // overridden by different subclasses)
72      public abstract String toString();
73
74      // Method to calculate pay (this method will
75      // be overridden by different subclasses)
76      public abstract double calcPay( double hours );
77   }
```

Figure 9.9. An abstract `Employee` class.

Abstract classes define the list of methods that will be available to subclasses of the class, and can provide partial implementations of those methods. For example, the abstract class `Employee` in Figure 9.9 provides implementations of `setName` and `setSsn` that will be inherited by the subclasses of `Employee`, but does *not* provide implementations of `calcPay` and `toString`.

Any subclasses of an abstract class must override all abstract methods of the superclass, or they will be abstract themselves. Thus classes `SalariedEmployee` and

`HourlyEmployee` must override methods `calcPay` and `toString`, or they will be abstract themselves.

Unlike concrete classes, *no objects may be instantiated from an abstract class.* Because an abstract class does not provide a complete definition of the behavior of an object, no object may be created from it. The class serves as a template for concrete subclasses, and objects may be instantiated from those concrete subclasses. An abstract class defines the types of polymorphic behaviors that can be used with subclasses of the class, but does not define the details of those behaviors.

PROGRAMMING PITFALLS

No objects may be instantiated from an abstract class.

Abstract classes often appear at the top of an object-oriented programming class hierarchy, defining the broad types of actions possible with objects of all subclasses of the class. Concrete classes appear at lower levels in a hierarchy, providing implementations details for each subclass.

GOOD PROGRAMMING PRACTICE

Use abstract classes to define broad types of behaviors at the top of an object-oriented programming class hierarchy, and use concrete classes to provide implementation details in the subclasses of the abstract classes.

In summary, to create polymorphic behavior in a program:

1. **Create a parent class containing all methods that will be needed to solve the problem**. The methods that will change in different subclasses can be declared `abstract`, if desired, and we will not have to define a method body for them in the superclass. Note that this makes the superclass `abstract`—no objects may be instantiated directly from it.

2. **Define subclasses for each type of object to be manipulated**. The subclasses must implement a specific method for each abstract method in the superclass definition.

3. **Create objects of the various subclasses, and refer to them using superclass references**. When a method call appears with a superclass reference, Java automatically executes the method of the object's actual subclass.

The trick to getting polymorphism right is to determine what behaviors that objects of the superclass must exhibit, and to make sure that there is a method to represent every behavior in the superclass definition.

9.6 FINAL METHODS AND CLASSES

In Chapter 2, we saw that variables can be declared `final` to indicate that they cannot be modified once they are declared and initialized. Effectively, `final` variables become named constants.

It is also possible to define **final methods** and **final classes**. A method that is declared `final` cannot be overridden in a subclass, so it can never exhibit polymorphic behavior. Since a `final` method's definition will never change, Java can perform compiler optimizations on the code to speed up execution. This can be especially useful for "utility methods" that are executed many times, since the optimizations can speed up the overall execution of the program.

Methods that are declared `static` or `private` are automatically `final`, since they can never be overridden in a subclass.

A class that is declared `final` cannot be a superclass, since no portion of the class may be overridden. All methods in a `final` class are automatically `final`, and the Java compiler is free to optimize them just like any other `final` method.

Many of the classes in the Java API are declared final to ensure that their behavior cannot be overridden. This practice helps to ensure that the Java API behaves in a consistent fashion at all times.

GOOD PROGRAMMING PRACTICE

You may declare commonly-used methods that do not need to be inherited to be `final`. This practice allows the Java compiler to optimize the method calls and speed up program execution. Note that `static` methods are automatically final.

9.7 THE TYPE-WRAPPER CLASSES FOR PRIMITIVE TYPES

The discussions of classes in Chapter 7 and this chapter describe how Java manipulates objects. Many Java classes are designed to polymorphically manipulate objects of type `Object`, which means that they can manipulate any object in Java, since ultimately all classes inherit from `Object`.

The odd men out in this whole structure are the primitive data types: `byte`, `short`, `int`, `long`, `char`, `float`, `double`, and `boolean`. They alone do not inherit from class `Object`, and so cannot be manipulated by many Java classes.

To get around this problem, Java defines a **type-wrapper class** for each primitive data type. These classes are called `Byte`, `Short`, `Integer`, `Character`, `Long`, `Float`, `Double`, and `Boolean`. Each class contains a single instance variable of the primitive type indicated by its name, along with methods to manipulate that variable. These classes enable a program to manipulate variables of primitive data types as objects of class `Object`, and so combine them with other objects in a program.

All of the numeric type wrapper classes inherit from the abstract class `Number`, which defines basic methods that can be applied polymorphically to all of the numeric subclasses. This class structure is shown in Figure 9.10.

The type-wrapper classes are all `final` classes, and many of the methods in the type-wrapper classes are declared `static`. They are commonly used to process primitive data types. For example, type-wrapper classes can be used to convert a string s con-

Figure 9.10. The class hierarchy of the type-wrapper classes.

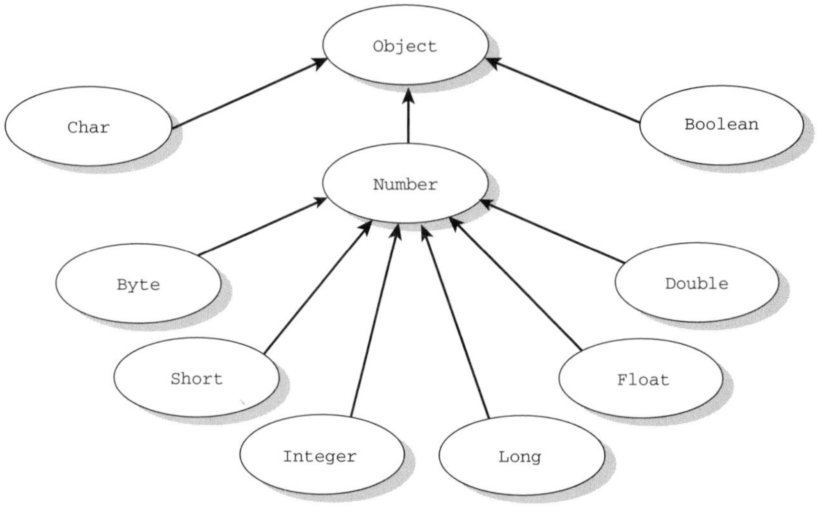

taining the character representation of a number into a value of a primitive data type. In the statement

```
v1 = Double.valueOf(s).doubleValue();
```

the valueOf(s) method converts the character representation in string s into an object of type Double, and then the doubleValue() method extracts the value contained in the Double object so that it can be stored in variable v1. The overall effect is to translate the string of characters into a double value.

If you need to manipulate primitive data types in your program, refer to the JDK documentation for the type-wrapper classes. They may fill your need without having to write your own custom classes.

EXAMPLE 9-2: ABSTRACT CLASSES AND POLYMORPHIC BEHAVIOR

To illustrate the concepts of abstract classes and polymorphic behavior, let's consider generic two-dimensional shapes. There are many types of shapes, including circles, triangles, squares, rectangles, pentagons, and so forth. All of these shapes have certain characteristics in common, since they are closed two-dimensional shapes having an enclosed area and a perimeter of finite length.

Create a generic Shape class having methods to determine the area and perimeter of a shape, and then create an appropriate class hierarchy for the following specific shapes: circles, equilateral triangles, squares, rectangles, and pentagons. The Shape class should also include a static variable to keep track of the number of shapes that have been instantiated at any time. Then, illustrate polymorphic behavior by creating shapes of each type and determining their area and perimeter using references to the generic shape class.

SOLUTION

To solve this problem, we should create a general Shape class and a series of subclasses below it. The Shape class should be abstract, since we will never directly instantiate any objects of that class, and since the methods to determine area and perimeter will be different for each subclass.

The listed shapes fall into a logical hierarchy based on their relationships. Circles, equilateral triangles, rectangles, and pentagons are all specific types of shapes, so they should be subclasses of our general `Shape` class. A square is a special kind of rectangle, so it should be a subclass of the `Rectangle` class. These relationships are shown in Figure 9.11.

A circle can be completely specified by it radius r, and the area A and perimeter (circumference) P of a circle can be calculated from the equations:

$$A = \pi r^2 \tag{9-1}$$
$$P = 2\pi r \tag{9-2}$$

An equilateral triangle can be completely specified by the length of one side s, and the area A and perimeter P of the equilateral triangle can be calculated from the equations:

$$A = \frac{\sqrt{3}}{4}s^2 \tag{9-3}$$
$$P = 3s \tag{9-4}$$

A rectangle can be completely specified by its length l and its width w, and the area A and perimeter P of the rectangle can be calculated from the equations:

$$A = lw \tag{9-5}$$
$$P = 2(l + \omega) \tag{9-6}$$

A square is a special rectangle whose length is equal to its width, so it can be completely specified by setting the length and width of a rectangle to the same size s. The area A and perimeter P of the square can then be calculated from the Equations (9-5) and (9-6).

A pentagon can be completely specified by the length of one side s, and the area A and perimeter P of the pentagon can be calculated from the equations:

Figure 9.11. The Shape class hierarchy.

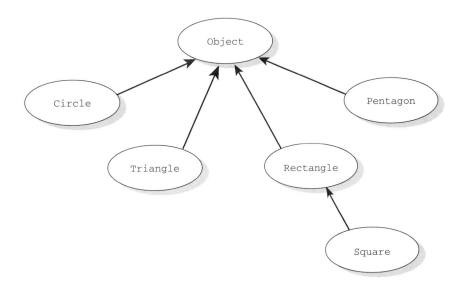

$$A = \frac{5}{4} s^2 \cot \frac{\pi}{5} \tag{9-7}$$

$$P = 5s \tag{9-8}$$

where cot is the cotangent, which is the reciprocal of the tangent.

1. **State the problem**. Define and implement a generic class `Shape` with methods to calculate the area and perimeter of a specified shape. Define and implement appropriate subclasses for circles, equilateral triangles, rectangles, squares, and pentagons, with the area and perimeter calculations appropriate for each shape.

2. **Define the inputs and outputs**. Each class will need constructors capable of creating the appropriate objects. For circles, the constructor will need the radius r. For equilateral triangles, the constructor will need the length of a side s. For rectangles, the constructor will need the length l and width w. For squares, the constructor will need the length of a side s. For pentagons, the constructor will need the length of a side s.

   Each of these classes will contain `area`, `perimeter`, and `toString` methods, returning the area, perimeter, and a string representation of the shape respectively.

3. **Decompose the program into classes and their associated methods**. The classes required for this problem are `Shape`, `Circle`, `Triangle`, `Rectangle`, `Square`, and `Pentagon`. `Shape` is an abstract superclass representing a closed, two-dimensional object with a finite area and perimeter. `Circle`, `Triangle`, `Rectangle`, and `Pentagon` are special kinds of shapes, so they should be subclasses of `Shape`. `Square` is special kinds of rectangle, so it should be a subclass of `Rectangle`. The methods in each class will be the class constructor, `area`, `perimeter`, `toString`, and `finalize`. In addition, the `Shape` class itself must have a static method to return the number of shapes that have been created.

   Note that `Shape` will be an `abstract` class, since we will not implement the methods `area` and `perimeter` in that class.

4. **Design the algorithm that you intend to implement for each method**. The constructor of the `Shape` class must increment the `static` shape counter, but it does not have to do anything else. The constructors of the individual subclasses will initialize objects of the specified types, and call the superclass constructor to increment the shape counter.

   The finalizer of the `Shape` class must decrement the `static` shape counter, but it does not have to do anything else. The finalizers of the individual subclasses will call the superclass finalizer to decrement the shape counter.

   The pseudocode for the `area()` method in the `Circle` class is:

   ```
   return ( Math.PI * r*r );
   ```

   The pseudocode for the `perimeter()` method in the `Circle` class is:

   ```
   return ( 2 * Math.PI * r );
   ```

   The pseudocode for the `area()` method in the `Triangle` class is:

   ```
   return ( Math.sqrt(3.)/4 * s*s );
   ```

   The pseudocode for the `perimeter()` method in the `Triangle` class is:

   ```
   return ( 3 * s );
   ```

The pseudocode for the `area()` method in the `Rectangle` class is:

```
return ( l * w );
```

The pseudocode for the `perimeter()` method in the `Rectangle` class is:

```
return ( 2 * (l + w) );
```

The pseudocode for the `area()` and `perimeter()` methods in the `Square` class is the same as for the `Rectangle` class. These methods may be directly inherited from the `Rectangle` class.

The pseudocode for the `area()` method in the `Pentagon` class is:

```
return ( 1.25 * s*s / Math.tan( Math.PI / 5 ) );
```

The pseudocode for the `perimeter()` method in the `Pentagon` class is:

```
return ( 5 * s );
```

5. **Turn the algorithm into Java statements**. The abstract class `Shape` is shown in Figure 9.12. Note that this class defines abstract methods `area()` and `perimeter()`, so that all subclasses will be required to implement these methods, and they may be used polymorphically with objects of type `Shape`. The method `toString()` does not appear in this class, but it is present because it is inherited from class `Object`. Thus, `toString()` will also exhibit polymorphic behavior.

The class also provides a concrete implementation of method `get-Counter()`, so this method will be inherited by all subclasses.

```
/*
   Purpose:
      This abstract class defines a generic shape, and
      abstract methods to calculate the area and
      perimeter of the shape.  It also includes a
      shape counter.

   Record of revisions:
      Date          Programmer              Description of change
      ====          ==========              =====================
      4/29/98       S. J. Chapman           Original code
*/

public abstract class Shape {

   // Define instance variables
   private static int counter;    // Shape counter

   // Constructor
   public Shape() {
      counter++;
   }

   // Calculate area
   public abstract double area( );

   // Calculate perimeter
   public abstract double perimeter( );
```

Figure 9.12. *(cont.)*

```
   // Get number of shapes
   public int getCount() {
      return counter;
   }

   // Finalizer
   protected void finalize() {
      counter--;
   }
}
```

Figure 9.12.   Abstract class Shape.

The class Circle is shown in Figure 9.13. This class defines an instance variable r for the radius of the circle, and provides concrete implementations of area(), perimeter(), and toString().

```
/*
   Purpose:
     This class defines the shape Circle, with
     methods to calculate the area and perimeter
     of the shape.

   Record of revisions:
       Date          Programmer            Description of change
       ====          ==========            =====================
       4/29/98     S. J. Chapman           Original code
*/

public class Circle extends Shape {

   // Define instance variables
   private double r;         // Radius of circle

   // Constructor
   public Circle(double r) {
      super();
      this.r = r;
   }

   // Calculate area
   public double area( ) {
      return ( Math.PI * r*r );
   }

   // Calculate perimeter
   public double perimeter( ) {
      return ( 2 * Math.PI * r );
   }

   // Convert to string
   public String toString() {
      return ("Circle of radius " + r);
   }

   // Finalizer
   protected void finalize() {
      super.finalize();
   }
}
```

Figure 9.13.   Class Circle.

The class `Triangle` is shown in Figure 9.14. This class defines an instance variable s for the length of the side of the triangle, and provides concrete implementations of `area()`, `perimeter()`, and `toString()`.

```
/*
   Purpose:
     This class defines the shape Triangle, with
     methods to calculate the area and perimeter
     of the shape.

   Record of revisions:
      Date        Programmer          Description of change
      ====        ==========          =====================
      4/29/98     S. J. Chapman       Original code
*/

public class Triangle extends Shape {

   // Define instance variables
   private double s;        // Length of side

   // Constructor
   public Triangle(double s) {
      super();
      this.s = s;
   }
   // Calculate area
   public double area( ) {
      return ( Math.sqrt(3.)/4 * s*s );
   }

   // Calculate perimeter
   public double perimeter( ) {
      return ( 3 * s );
   }

   // Convert to string
   public String toString() {
      return ("Equilateral triangle of side " + s);
   }

   // Finalizer
   protected void finalize() {
      super.finalize();
   }
}
```

Figure 9.14. Class `Triangle`.

The class `Rectangle` is shown in Figure 9.15. This class defines instance variables l and w for the length and width of the rectangle, and provides concrete implementations of `area()`, `perimeter()`, and `toString()`. Note that the instance variables l and w are declared protected instead of private, because they must be inherited by subclass `Square`.

```
/*
   Purpose:
      This class defines the shape Rectangle, with
      methods to calculate the area and perimeter
      of the shape.

   Record of revisions:
      Date         Programmer          Description of change
      ====         ==========          =====================
      4/29/98    S. J. Chapman         Original code
*/

public class Rectangle extends Shape {

   // Define instance variables
   protected double l;          // Length of rectangle
   protected double w;          // Width of rectangle

   // Constructor
   public Rectangle(double l, double w) {
      super();
      this.l = l;
      this.w = w;
   }

      // Calculate area
   public double area( ) {
      return ( l * w );
   }

   // Calculate perimeter
   public double perimeter( ) {
      return ( 2 * (l + w) );
   }

   // Convert to string
   public String toString() {
      return ("Rectangle of length " + l + " and width " + w);
   }

   // Finalizer
   protected void finalize() {
      super.finalize();
   }
}
```

Figure 9.15.   Class `Rectangle`.

The class `Square` is shown in Figure 9.16. Since a square is just a rectangle with its length equal to its width, this class *inherits* its instance variables `l` and `w` from class `Rectangle`, as well as concrete implementations of `area()` and `perimeter()`. The class overrides method `toString()`.

```
/*
   Purpose:
     This class defines the shape Square, with
     methods to calculate the area and perimeter
     of the shape.

   Record of revisions:
       Date         Programmer              Description of change
       ====         ==========              =====================
       4/29/98      S. J. Chapman           Original code
*/

public class Square extends Rectangle {

   // All instance variables are inherited from Rectangle

   // Constructor
   public Square(double s) {
      super(s,s);
   }

   // Convert to string
   public String toString() {
      return ("Square of side " + l);
   }

   // Finalizer
   protected void finalize() {
      super.finalize();
   }
}
```

Figure 9.16.   Class Square.

The class Pentagon is shown in Figure 9.17. This class defines an instance variable s for the length of the side of the pentagon, and provides concrete implementations of area(), perimeter(), and toString().

```
/*
   Purpose:
     This class defines the shape Pentagon, with
     methods to calculate the area and perimeter
     of the shape.

   Record of revisions:
       Date         Programmer              Description of change
       ====         ==========              =====================
       4/29/98      S. J. Chapman           Original code
*/

public class Pentagon extends Shape {

   // Define instance variables
   private double s;          // Length of side

   // Constructor
   public Pentagon(double s) {
      super();
      this.s = s;
   }
```

Figure 9.17.   (cont.)

```
   // Calculate area
   public double area( ) {
       return ( 1.25 * s*s / Math.tan( Math.PI / 5 ) );
   }

   // Calculate perimeter
   public double perimeter( ) {
       return ( 5 * s );
   }

   // Convert to string
   public String toString() {
       return ("Pentagon of side " + s);
   }

   // Finalizer
   protected void finalize() {
       super.finalize();
   }
}
```

Figure 9.17. Class `Pentagon`.

6. **Test the resulting Java program**. To test this program, we will calculate the area and perimeter of several shapes by hand, and compare the results with those produced by a test driver program.

SHAPE	AREA	PERIMETER
Circle of radius 2:	$A = \pi r^2 = 12.5664$	$P = 2\pi r = 12.5664$
Triangle of side 2:	$A = \dfrac{\sqrt{3}}{4} s^2 = 1.7321$	$P = 3s = 6$
Rectangle of length 2 and width 1:	$A = lw = 2$	$P = 2(l+w) = 6$
Square of side 2:	$A = lw = 2 \times 2 = 4$	$P = 2(l+w) = 8$
Pentagon of side 2:	$A = \dfrac{5}{4} s^2 \cot \dfrac{\pi}{5} = 6.8819$	$P = 5s = 10$

An appropriate test driver program is shown in Figure 9.18. Note that this program creates an array of references of type `Shape[]`, and then creates objects of various subclasses, assigning them to elements of the array. It then uses method `getCount()` to report the number of `Shape` objects created, and uses the methods `toString()`, `area()`, and `perimeter()` on each object in array s.

```
/*
   Purpose:
      This class tests class Shape and its subclasses.

   Record of revisions:
      Date        Programmer           Description of change
      ====        ==========           =====================
      4/29/98     S. J. Chapman        Original code
*/

public class TestShape {
```

Figure 9.18. *(cont.)*

```
    // Define the main method to test class Shape
    public static void main(String[] args) {

        // Create an array of Shapes
        Shape s[] = new Shape[5];

        // Create objects
        s[0] = new Circle(2);
        s[1] = new Triangle(2);
        s[2] = new Rectangle(2,1);
        s[3] = new Square(2);
        s[4] = new Pentagon(2);

        // Print out number of shapes created
        System.out.println(s[0].getCount() + " shapes created.");

        //Print out information about the shapes
        for (int i = 0; i < s.length; i++ ) {
            System.out.println("\n" + s[i].toString());
            System.out.println("Area      = " + s[i].area());
            System.out.println("Perimeter = " + s[i].perimeter());
        }
    }
}
```

Figure 9.18. Program to test class Shape and its subclasses.

When this program is executed, the results are:

```
D:\book\java\chap9>java TestShape
5 shapes created.
Circle of radius 2.0
Area      = 12.566370614359172
Perimeter = 12.566370614359172

Equilateral triangle of side 2.0
Area      = 1.7320508075688772
Perimeter = 6.0

Rectangle of length 2.0 and width 1.0
Area      = 2.0
Perimeter = 6.0

Square of side 2.0
Area      = 4.0
Perimeter = 8.0

Pentagon of side 2.0
Area      = 6.881909602355868
Perimeter = 10.0
```

The results of the program agree with our hand calculations to the number of significant digits that we performed the calculation. Note that the program called the correct polymorphic version of each method. Also, note that each time an object of any subclass was created, the total count of Shapes increased by one. This happened because each subclass constructor called its superclass constructor, and the Shape constructor increased the total count of shapes.

9.8 INTERFACES

An **interface** is a special kind of block containing method signatures (and possibly constants) only. Interfaces define the signatures of a set of methods, without the method bodies that would implement their functionality. Method declarations in an interface are essentially the same as method declarations in abstract classes.

Interfaces have no direct inherited relationship with any particular class-they are defined independently. An example interface is shown in Figure 9.19.

```
/*
   Purpose:
     This interface defines the relationship between
     two objects, according to the "natural order"
     of the objects.

   Record of revisions:
      Date        Programmer          Description of change
      ====        ==========          =====================
      4/30/98    S. J. Chapman        Original code
*/

public interface Relation {

    // Returns true if a > b, where a is the current object
    public boolean isGreater( Object b );

    // Returns true if a < b, where a is the current object
    public boolean isLess( Object b );

    // Returns true if a == b, where a is the current
    public boolean isEqual( Object b );
}
```

Figure 9.19.   An example of an interface. Interface `Relation` defines the method signatures of three methods that can be used to compare two objects.

9.8.1 Implementing Interfaces

Any class may choose to **implement** an interface by adding an `implements` clause to its class definition. If a class chooses to implement an interface, then it guarantees that it will provide an implementation for *every* method in the interface, and the methods will have the same sequence of calling arguments as shown in the interface definition. If these conditions are not met, the Java compiler will generate an error.

A class that implements an interface has an "isa" relationship with that interface, just as a subclass has an "isa" relationship with its superclass. Just as an object of a subclass can be treated as an object of its superclass type, an object of a class that implements an interface can be treated as a object of the interface type, and can be used by any method that uses objects of the interface type (see Figure 9.20).

What is the big deal about interfaces? Interfaces are a standard and public way of defining the communication between classes. They allow classes, regardless of their locations in the class hierarchy, to implement common behaviors. For example, suppose that we were to create 10 different classes of different types, and we would like to be

Figure 9.20.   Classes that implement an interface bear the same relationship to the interface as the subclasses of an abstract class bear to their parent class. Just as an object of SubClass1 is an ("isa") object of AbstractClass , so an object of Class3 is an ("isa") object of MyInterface.

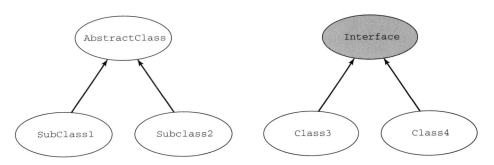

able to sort objects of each of these classes into ascending order. Without an interface, we would have to implement a sort method for each class separately, requiring us to write the same basic code 10 times! On the other hand, if each of the 10 classes implements the Relation interface defined in Figure 9.19, we can write a *single* method to sort objects of the Relation type, and that method will work for *any* of the classes implementing the Relation interface.

Note that interfaces exhibit **polymorphism**, since a program may call an interface method, and the proper version of that method will be executed depending on the type of object passed to the interface method in the call.

GOOD PROGRAMMING PRACTICE

Use interfaces to create the same standard method definitions in many different classes. Once a set of standard method definitions is created, you can write a *single* method to manipulate (sort, search, etc.) all of the classes that implement the interface.

If a class implements an interface, *it must implement all of the methods specified in the interface*, since the methods calling that interface will rely on the existence of those methods.

A sample class Line that implements the interface Relation is shown in Figure 9.21. This class defines a line segment by its two endpoints (x_1, y_1) and (x_2, y_2), and provides a method length() to calculate the length of the line segment. This class implements interface Relation, so it must define methods isGreater(), isLess(), and isEqual() *with exactly the same calling sequence as in the interface.* Note that this interface requires Objects to be passed to the methods. Inside the methods, these Objects are cast to Lines so that the length() method can be used to compare them, and the appropriate boolean value is returned to the calling method.

```
/*
   Purpose:
     This class defines line segment in terms of
     two (x,y) endpoints.  It provides a method
     to calculate the length of the line segment,
     and implements interface Relation so that
     the lines can be sorted by length.

   Record of revisions:
       Date          Programmer           Description of change
       ====          ==========           =====================
       4/30/98       S. J. Chapman        Original code
*/
public class Line implements Relation {

   // Instance variables
   private double x1;         // First x value
   private double x2;         // Second x value
   private double y1;         // First y value
   private double y2;         // Second y value

   // Constructor
   public Line(double x1, double y1, double x2, double y2) {
      this.x1 = x1;
      this.x2 = x2;
      this.y1 = y1;
      this.y2 = y2;
   }

   // Calculate length
   public double length( ) {
      return Math.sqrt( (x2-x1)*(x2-x1) + (y2-y1)*(y2-y1) );
   }

   // Returns true if current object > b
   public boolean isGreater( Object b) {
      return length() > ((Line)b).length();
   }

   // Returns true if current object < b
   public boolean isLess( Object b ) {
      return length() < ((Line)b).length();
   }

   // Returns true if current object == b
   public boolean isEqual( Object b ) {
      return length() == ((Line)b).length();
   }

   // toString()
   public String toString( ) {
      String s;
      s = "Line from (" + x1 + "," + y1 + ") to ("
        + x2 + "," + y2 + "): Length = " + length();
      return s;
   }
}
```

Figure 9.21.   Class Line, which implements interface Relation.

9.8.2 Calling Interface Methods

A `static` method that uses the `Relation` interface to sort objects is shown in Figure 9.22. This method accepts any array of class `Object`, and sorts the array using the methods defined in the `Relation` interface. Note that *in order to sort the objects using the methods in the* `Relation` *interface, the objects must be cast into type* `Relation` *when the methods are invoked.* An example of this manipulation is

```
((Relation) o[j]).isLess( (Relation) o[iptr] );
```

The expression `(Relation)  o[j]` casts the object reference `o[j]` into a `Relation` type, which can be used with the method `isLess()` defined in the interface. If the object `o[j]` is of a class that does not support the `Relation` interface, this expression will cause a runtime exception.

This method will sort arrays of any class that implements the `Relation` interface, so we only need to write one sort method to work with many different classes.

```
/*
    Purpose:
        This class contains a static method to sort objects using
        the selection sort algorithm.  It supports any class that
        implements the Relation interface.  Note that this is not
        a particularly efficient sorting technique--it is used
        here only because it is easy to understand.

    Record of revisions:
        Date        Programmer          Description of change
        ====        ==========          =====================
        4/30/98     S. J. Chapman       Original code
*/
public class SortObj {

    // Define the sort method
    public static Object[] sort ( Object[] o ) {

        // Declare variables, and define each variable
        int i, j;              // Loop index
        int iptr;              // Pointer to "smallest" value
        Object temp;           // Temporary variable for swapping

        // Sort values
        for ( i = 0; i < o.length-1; i++ ) {

            // Find the minimum value in o[i] through o[nvals-1]
            iptr = i;
            for ( j = i+1; j < o.length; j++ ) {
              if ( ((Relation)o[0]).isLess( (Relation) o[j], (Relation) o[iptr] ))
                  iptr = j;
            }

            // iptr now points to the min value, so swap o[iptr]
            //with o[i] if iptr != i.
            if (i != iptr) {
                temp = o[i];
                o[i] = o[iptr];
                o[iptr] = temp;
            }
        }

        // Return sorted objects
        return o;
    }
}
```

Figure 9.22. A method to sort objects that implement interface `Relation` into ascending order using the selection sort.

A test driver program that creates `Line` objects and sorts them using the `SortObj.sort()` method is shown in Figure 9.23. This method creates an array of `Object` references, and assigns five new `Line` objects to that array. It then sorts the array into ascending order of length using method `SortObj.sort()`.

```
/*
    Purpose:
      This class tests class Line and the Relation
      interface.

    Record of revisions:
        Date          Programmer            Description of change
        ====          ==========            =====================
        4/30/98    S. J. Chapman            Original code
*/

public class TestLine {

    // Define the main method
    public static void main(String[] args) {

        // Create an array of Objects
        Object o[] = new Line[5];

        // Create objects
        o[0] = new Line(0,0,2,1);
        o[1] = new Line(0,0,1,-1);
        o[2] = new Line(-1,1,1,1);
        o[3] = new Line(2,0,0,0);
        o[4] = new Line(0,2,-2,0);

        // Sort the objects in ascending order
        SortObj.sort( o );

        // Print out information about the Lines
        for (int i = 0; i < o.length; i++ ) {
            System.out.println(o[i].toString());
        }
    }
}
```

Figure 9.23.   A test driver program for classes `Line` and `SortObj`.

When this program is executed, the results are:

```
D:\book\java\chap9>java TestLine
Line from (0.0,0.0) to (1.0,-1.0): Length = 1.4142135623730951
Line from (-1.0,1.0) to (1.0,1.0): Length = 2.0
Line from (2.0,0.0) to (0.0,0.0): Length = 2.0
Line from (0.0,0.0) to (2.0,1.0): Length = 2.23606797749979
Line from (0.0,2.0) to (-2.0,0.0): Length = 2.8284271247461903
```

9.8.3 Using Interfaces to Define Constants

An interface may contain constants only, with no method definitions. An example of such an interface is shown in Figure 9.24. An interface like this defines constants that can be used in many class definitions. Any class that implements this interface can use these constants anywhere within the class definition.

```
interface Constants {

    public static final double PI = 3.14159265358979;
    public static final double E = 2.71828182845905;

}
```

Figure 9.24. An interface containing only constants.

9.8.4 The Significance of Interfaces

A class that implements an interface is almost identical in behavior to a subclass of an abstract class that defines the same abstract methods. If this is so, why bother to define interfaces at all? Why not just use abstract classes for everything?

The basic reason for interfaces is that *a class can only inherit from one immediate parent class, but it can implement many different interfaces.* Interfaces permit a single class to implement many different types of standard behaviors, and so make the class more flexible and easier to use.

PRACTICE!

This practice box provides a quick check to see if you have understood the concepts introduced in Sections 9.1 through 9.8. If you have trouble with the quiz, reread the section, ask your instructor, or discuss the material with a fellow student. The answers to this quiz are found in the back of the book.

1. What is inheritance?

2. What is polymorphism?

3. What are abstract classes and abstract methods? Why would you wish to use an abstract classes and methods in your programs?

4. What are the advantages of declaring methods or classes to be `final`? What are the disadvantages?

5. What is an interface? How do interfaces save programming effort?

9.9 THE COLLECTION AND ITERATOR INTERFACES

The `Collection` and `Iterator` interfaces are new features of JDK 1.2. They can serve as good example of how interfaces are used in Java. The `Collection` interface defines a standard set of methods to access to all the different types of collections implemented by Java, while the `Iterator` interface defines a standard way of stepping through the collection on an element-by-element basis.

A "collection" in data structure terms is a group of data elements. Some types of collections that are supported by Java include the following:

- `List`—a collection containing an ordered sequence of elements
- `Set`—a collection containing a mathematical set of elements, with no duplication
- `Map`—a collection that maps keys into values

`List`, `Set`, and `Map` are sub-interfaces of the `Collection` interface. Similarly, `ListIterator` is a sub-interface of the `Iterator` interface. We will now consider

Figure 9.25. *(a)* A Vector consists of an array of references, each element of which points to a specific object. Vectors are very efficient for random access, since locating a specific array element is very quick. However, it takes a long time to add elements to the middle of a vector, because all of the higher values in the array of references must be shifted upward when a new value is inserted.

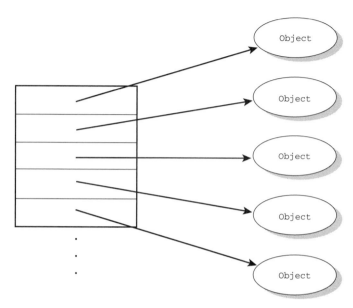

the List and ListIterator interfaces in more detail. Information about the Set and Map interfaces may be found in the Java API documentation.

Examples of Lists implemented by Java include Vectors and LinkedLists. A **vector** is a list of objects that can be accessed in random order by an index (see Figure 9.25*a*). It is like an array, except that the size of a vector can grow and shrink while the size of an array is fixed. A **linked list** is a list of objects, each containing a data element and a reference to the next object in the list (see Figure 9.25*b*). It is easy to add and remove elements in a linked list, but the data in the list can only be accessed sequentially.

Linked lists and vectors have very different properties. It is easy to add and remove data from the middle or the ends of a linked list, but random access to the data in the linked list is very hard, since the program has to perform a linear search from the beginning or the end of the list to find a particular element. On the other hand, it is hard to add or delete elements from a vector, since the remaining elements must be physically moved each time something is added or deleted. However, it is very easy to randomly access elements in a vector in any order. Thus, lists that will have frequent additions and deletions and that are always searched sequentially might be best implemented as linked lists, while lists whose values will be accessed randomly might be best implemented as vectors.

Even though these types of lists are very different, they both implement the List and ListIterator interfaces, so *the two types of lists can be used in exactly the same way* by other methods in a program. The details of the list implementation are hidden from the user. This fact is very significant, because a program can be written using one form of list, and then the list can be replaced by a different form with *no other change* in

Figure 9.25. (b) A `LinkedList` is a series of objects, each containing two references. One reference points to the next item in the linked list (the dashed line), and the other reference points to the object stored at that location in the list (the solid line). It is very efficient to add a new element in the middle of a linked list, because only the reference values in the new element and in the element just before the new element need to be changed. However, it is very inefficient to access elements randomly, since locating an element requires a sequential search from the top of the list.

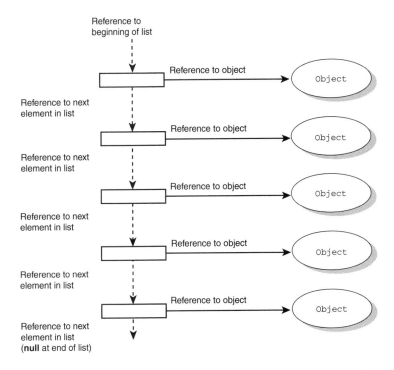

the program. We might want to make such a switch while optimizing the execution speed of a program.

The following example illustrates the use of linked lists and vectors through the `List` interface.

EXAMPLE 9-3: USING LINKED LISTS AND VECTORS

To illustrate the use of interfaces in Java, create a linked list and a vector (both are types of lists), store 10,000 `Double` objects in each list, and then access the objects both in sequential order using `ListIterator` interface methods and in random order using the `List` interface methods. Compare the time required to perform each operation for each type of list.

SOLUTION
To solve this problem, we will create a linked list and a vector, using a reference of type `Object` to refer to each of them. We will then add elements to the lists using `List` interface methods, access the elements sequentially using `ListIterator` interface methods, and access the elements randomly using `List` interface methods. We will use the `Timer` class developed in Chapter 7 to time each operation.

Some selected `List` interface methods are shown in Table 9-1, and some selected `ListIterator` methods are shown in Table 9-2. A complete list of `List` and `ListIterator` methods may be found in the Java API Documentation. We will

TABLE 9-1 Selected `List` Interface Methods

METHOD	DESCRIPTION
boolean **add**(object o)	Appends the specified element to the end of this `List`.
void **add**(int index, Object element)	Inserts the specified element at the specified position in this `List`. Shifts the element currently at that position and any subsequent elements to the right (adds one to their indices).
Object **get**(int index)	Returns the element at the specified position in this `List`.
ListIterator **listIterator**()	Returns a `ListIterator` of the elements in this `List` (in proper sequence). This object can be used to walk through the list sequentially using the methods in the `ListIterator` interface.
Object **remove**(int index)	Removes the element at the specified position in this `List`. Shifts any subsequent elements to the left (subtracts one from their indices). Returns the element that was removed from the `List`.
Object **set**(int index, Object element)	Replaces the element at the specified position in this `List` with the specified element.
int **size**()	Returns the number of elements in this `List`.

use the `add` method in the `List` interface to add elements to each list, the `next` method in the `ListIterator` interface to recover elements in sequential order, and the `get` method on the `List` interface to recover elements in random order.

We will use the `new` operator to create each list:

```
o = new LinkedList();
```

or

```
o = new Vector();
```

where o is a reference to an arbitrary `Object`.

We will use the `add` method from the `List` interface to add elements to each list. In order to do this, we will have to cast the object reference o into a `List`:

```
((List)o).add(new Double(temp));
```

Similarly, we will use the `get` method from the `List` interface to get the elements from the list in random order.

```
d = ((List)o).get(index);
```

Finally, we will use the `next` method from the `ListIterator` interface to step through the elements in sequential order.

```
d = it.next();
```

The resulting program is shown in Figure 9.26. This program creates a new `List` and adds 10,000 `Double` objects to it using the `add` method. It then creates a `ListIterator` and uses it to step through the list sequentially. Finally, it uses the `get` method to recover 10,000 randomly-ordered values from the list. It calculates the elapsed time required in each case.

TABLE 9-2 Select `ListIterator` Interface Methods

METHOD	DESCRIPTION
boolean **hasNext()**	Returns true if this `ListIterator` has more elements when traversing the `List` in the forward direction.
boolean **hasPrevious()**	Returns true if this `ListIterator` has more elements when traversing the `List` in the reverse direction.
Object Object **next()**	Returns the next element in the `List`. This method may be called repeatedly to iterate through the `List`, or intermixed with calls to previous to go back and forth.
Object **previous()**	Returns the previous element in the `List`.

```
/*
   Purpose:
      This class tests classes Vector and LinkedList, using
      interfaces List and ListIterator to access each class.
      Note that the code to build the list and access the
      lists is completely identical in each case, because we
      are using the common interface List and ListIterator.

   Record of revisions:
        Date        Programmer          Description of change
        ====        ==========          =====================
       5/1/98      S. J. Chapman        Original code
*/
import java.util.*;
public class TestList {

   // Define the main method
   public static void main(String[] args) {

      // Define variables
      Object d;                    // Temp Double object
      int index;                   // Index
      ListIterator it;             // ListIterator
      double temp;                 // Scratch variable

      // Instantiate timer
      Timer t = new Timer();

      //**********************************************
      //   This portion of the code creates a new
      //   vector of Double values, stores 10,000
      //   elements in it, and accesses the elements
      //   10,000 times in random order.
      //**********************************************

      Object o = new Vector();
      System.out.println("Vector:");

      // Reset timer
      t.resetTimer();
```

Figure 9.26. (cont.)

```
                // Add random values in successive locations
                for (int i = 0; i < 10000; i++) {
                   temp = 1000 * Math.random();
                   ((List)o).add(new Double(temp));
                }

                // Get elapsed time to add elements
                System.out.println( "Time to add elements = " +
                                    t.elapsedTime() );

                // Reset timer
                t.resetTimer();

                // Access elements in sequential order
                it = ((List)o).listIterator();
                for (int i = 0; i < 10000; i++) {
                   d = it.next();
                   temp = ((Double) d).doubleValue();
                }

                // Get elapsed time to access elements
                System.out.println(
                   "Time to get sequential elements = " +
                   t.elapsedTime() );

                // Reset timer
                t.resetTimer();

                // Access elements in random order
                for (int i = 0; i < 10000; i++) {
                   index = (int) (1000 * Math.random());
                   if ( index == 1000 ) index = 0;
                   d = ((List)o).get(index);
                   temp = ((Double) d).doubleValue();
                }

                // Get elapsed time to access elements
                System.out.println(
                   "Time to get random elements = " +
                   t.elapsedTime() );

                //*********************************************
                //  This portion of the code creates a new
                //  LinkedList of Double values, stores 10,000
                //  elements in it, and accesses the elements
                //  10,000 times in random order.
                //*********************************************
                o = new LinkedList();
                System.out.println("Linked list:");

                // Reset timer
                t.resetTimer();

                // Add random values in successive location
                for (int i = 0; i < 10000; i++) {
                   temp = 1000 * Math.random();
                   ((List)o).add(new Double(temp));
                }
```

Figure 9.26.   *(cont.)*

```
                 // Get elapsed time to add elements
                 System.out.println( "Time to add elements = " +
                                     t.elapsedTime() );

                 // Reset timer
                 t.resetTimer();

                 // Access elements in sequential order
                 it = ((List)o).listIterator();
                 for (int i = 0; i < 10000; i++) {
                     d = it.next();
                     temp = ((Double) d).doubleValue();
                 }

                 // Get elapsed time to access elements
                 System.out.println(
                     "Time to get sequential elements = " +
                     t.elapsedTime() );

                 // Reset timer
                 t.resetTimer();

                 // Access elements in random order
                 for (int i = 0; i < 10000; i++) {
                     index = (int) (1000 * Math.random());
                     if ( index == 1000 ) index = 0;
                     d = ((List)o).get(index);
                     temp = ((Double) d).doubleValue();
                 }

                 // Get elapsed time to access elements
                 System.out.println(
                     "Time to get random elements = " +
                     t.elapsedTime() );
             }
     }
```

Figure 9.26. A program to create and manipulate linked lists and vectors using the
`List` and `ListIterator` interfaces.

When this program is executed, the results are:

```
D:\book\java\chap9>java TestList
Vector:
Time to add elements = 0.461
Time to get sequential elements = 0.1
Time to get random elements = 0.25
Linked list:
Time to add elements = 1.122
Time to get sequential elements = 0.05
Time to get random elements = 7.08
```

The results of the program agree with our previous discussion about the nature of
linked lists and vectors. Vectors are faster for random access, while linked lists are faster
for sequential access.

The most important point of this example is that *both linked lists and vectors can be
accessed using identically the same statements,* because they both support the `List` and

TABLE 9-3 Select `ListIterator` Interface Methods

METHOD	DESCRIPTION
boolean **hasNext()**	Returns true if this `ListIterator` has more elements when traversing the `List` in the forward direction.
boolean **hasPrevious()**	Returns true if this `ListIterator` has more elements when traversing the `List` in the reverse direction.
Object Object **next()**	Returns the next element in the `List`. This method may be called repeatedly to iterate through the `List`, or intermixed with calls to `previous` to go back and forth.
Object **previous()**	Returns the previous element in the `List`.

`ListIterator` interfaces. This design allows us to change the type of list we are using in a program after the program has been written with almost no impact on the rest of the code.

SUMMARY

- Through inheritance, a new subclass inherits the instance variables and methods of its previously defined superclass. The subclass only needs to provide instance variables and methods to implement the *differences* between itself and its parent.
- An object of a subclass may be treated as an object of its corresponding superclass. Thus an object of a subclass may be freely assigned to a superclass reference.
- An *object* of a superclass type may not be assigned to a reference of a subclass type. However, a *reference* of a superclass type may be cast into a reference of a subclass type. If the object pointed to by the reference is really of this subclass, this operation will work. Otherwise, it will throw a `ClassCastException`.
- A subclass's constructor must make an explicit or implicit call to its superclass's constructor as the *first* action in the subclass constructor.
- A subclass's finalizer must make an explicit call to its superclass's finalizer as the *last* action in the subclass finalizer.
- Polymorphism is the ability to automatically vary methods depending on the subclass that an object belongs to.
- To create polymorphic behavior, define all polymorphic methods in the common superclass, and override the behavior of the methods in each subclass that inherits from the superclass.
- An abstract method is a method whose heading is declared without an associated body. It defines the calling sequence of the method, but not how it will be implemented. An abstract method is declared by prefixing the method definition with the keyword `abstract`.
- An abstract class is a class containing one or more abstract methods.
- Each subclass of an abstract class must provide an implementation of all abstract methods, or the subclass will remain abstract.
- Methods and classes can be declared `final` to indicate that they cannot be overridden in a subclass. Final methods are usually more efficient than ordinary methods, because the Java compiler can perform extra optimizations on them.
- All of the methods in a `final` class are implicitly `final`.

demonstrate that the proper methods are called polymorphically when Vec references are passed to the addition and subtraction methods.

9.8.   Create an interface called Vec, which defines methods to add and subtract two vectors. Create two classes, Vec2D and Vec3D, that implement this interface for two-dimensional and three-dimensional vectors respectively. Class Vec2D must define instance variables x and y. Class Vec3D must define instance variables x, y, and z. Write a test program to demonstrate that the proper methods are called polymorphically when the interface methods are called.

10

Strings

A **string** is a group of one or more characters treated as a single unit. For example, in the statement

```
System.out.println("Value = " + value);
```

the term `"Value = "` is a string. The principal importance of strings in our programs is that *they represent information in a form easily readable by humans* and so are regularly used to enter information into a program and to display the results of the program.

It is important to understand the difference between a string representing a value and the value itself as it is stored inside a computer. For example, let's compare the integer value 123 and the string `"123"`. The integer value 123 is stored as the binary pattern 01111011 in a memory location inside the computer. It is in the form that the computer can use directly in its calculations, but it *cannot* be displayed on a computer screen in that form. In contrast, the string `"123"` consists of three Unicode characters encoding the characters 1, 2, and 3, respectively. A computer cannot use the string `"123"` directly in numerical calculations, but humans can easily recognize the number that it represents.

SECTIONS

- 10.1 Creating and Initializing `Strings`
- 10.2 `String` Methods
- 10.3 Creating and Initializing `StringBuffers`
- 10.4 `StringBuffer` Methods
- 10.5 The `StringTokenizer` Class
- 10.6 Command-Line Arguments
- Summary
- Key Terms

OBJECTIVES

After reading this chapter, you should be able to:

- Create `Strings`
- Understand `String` Methods
- Create `StringBuffers`
- Understand `StringBuffer` Methods
- Use the `StringTokenizer` Class
- Utilize Command-Line Arguments

Because humans enter data for computer programs and read the results of the programs, most input and output from programs is in the form of character strings. On the other hand, most internal calculations are performed with the binary representations of numbers. Thus, we must be able to convert from strings to numbers when data are read into a program, as well as convert from numbers to strings when data are printed out of a program. The ability to work with strings is vital if we humans are to actually use computers. This chapter teaches us how to manipulate character strings in Java.

There are two types strings in Java: `Strings` and `StringBuffers`. Both types are implemented as objects. The fundamental difference between the two classes is that the `String` class consists of strings that *never change* once they are created, while the `StringBuffer` class consists of modifiable strings.

Java distinguishes between these two types of strings for efficiency reasons. Java knows that any object of the `String` class can never be changed once it is created, so the compiler and run-time system can use a single object for all strings containing the same set of characters, thus reducing program size.

10.1 CREATING AND INITIALIZING Strings

A reference to a `String` object is created by a statement such as

```
String str1;          // Create a String reference
```

When this statement is executed, reference `str1` is created and set to `null`, since it does not yet point to a `String` object. Attempting to use a null reference in a program will produce a run-time exception.

`String` objects may be created and assigned to a `String` reference in several ways. The easiest way is with a **String literal**. `String` literals (which are also known as `String` constants or **anonymous String objects**) are written as a string of characters between quotation marks. For example, the following is a `String` object:

```
"This is a test."
```

A `String` reference can be created and a `String` literal can be assigned to that reference in a single statement:

```
String str1 = "This is a test.";
```

`String` objects can also be created using `String` constructors. `String` constructors can create new strings from other strings, from `StringBuffers`, from arrays of bytes, and from arrays of characters. Some examples of `String` constructors are shown below:

```
String str1 = new String("This is a test.");  / From anotherstring
String str2 = new String( buffer );           / From a StringBuffer
String str3 = new String( charArray );        / From a char array
String str4 = new String( byteArray );        / From a byte rray
String str5 = new String( );                  / New empty string
```

Once it has been created, each `String` object contains a fixed number of characters. The number of characters in any `String` can always be found using the `length` method. For example, the expression `str1.length()` returns a value of 15 for the string `str1` defined above.

10.2 `String` METHODS

There are many methods available for manipulating strings in Java programs. Some of the more important string methods are summarized in Table 10-1. All of the `String` methods are described in the Java API documentation in class `java.lang.String`.

10.2.1 Substrings

A **substring** is a portion of a string. The method `substring` allows a substring to be extracted from a Java string. There are two forms of this method. The first form is

```
s.substring( int st )
```

It takes one integer argument that specifies the starting index of the substring only and returns a new string containing the characters from that index to the end of the original string. The second form is

```
s.substring( int st, int en )
```

It takes two integer arguments and specifies both the starting and ending indexes of the substring. (The actual string returned consists of the characters from position `st` to position `en-1`.) If the indexes specified in either case are less than zero or greater than the number of characters in the string, then a `StringIndexOutOfBounds` exception will occur.

The class shown below illustrates both types of `substring` methods.

```
// Substrings
public class Substring {

    public static void main(String[] args) {
        String s = "abcdefghijABCDEFGHIJabcdefghij";

        // Test substring methods
        System.out.println("String = \"" + s + "\"");
        System.out.println("Substring starting at 18 = "
            + "\"" + s.substring(18) + "\"");

        System.out.println("Substring from 18 to 24  = "
            + "\"" + s.substring(18,24) + "\"");
    }
}
```

When this program is executed, the results are as follows:

```
D:\book\java\chap10>java Substring
String = "abcdefghijABCDEFGHIJabcdefghij"
Substring starting at 18 = "IJabcdefghij"
Substring from 18 to 24 = "IJabcd"
```

10.2.2 Concatenating Strings

Two strings may be **concatenated** (joined end-to-end) using the `concat` method. The expression

```
s1.concat( s2 )
```

TABLE 10-1 Select `String` Methods

METHOD	DESCRIPTION
`char charAt(int index)`	Returns the character at a specified index in the string.
`int compareTo(String s)`	Compares the `String` object to another `String` lexicographically. Returns 0 if string is equal to `s`, a negative number if string is less than `s`, a positive number if string is greater than `s`
`String concat(String s)`	Concatenates `s` to the end of the string.
`boolean endsWith(String suffix)`	Returns `true` if this string ends with the specified suffix.
`boolean equals(Object o)`	Returns `true` if `o` is a `String`, and `o` contains exactly the same characters as the string.
`boolean equalsIgnoreCase(String s)`	Returns `true` if `s` contains exactly the same characters as the string, disregarding case.
`void getChars(int i1, int i2, char[] dst, int i3)`	Copies the characters in the string from position `i1` to position `i2` into character array `dst`, starting at index `i3`.
`int IndexOf(char ch)`	Returns the index of the *first* location of `ch` in the string.
`int IndexOf(char ch, int start)`	Returns the index of the *first* location of `ch` at or after position `start` in the string.
`int IndexOf(String s)`	Returns the index of the *first* location of substring `s` in the string.
`int IndexOf(String s, int start)`	Returns the index of the *first* location of substring `s` at or after position `start` in the string.
`int LastIndexOf(char ch)`	Returns the index of the *last* location of `ch` in the string.
`int LastIndexOf(char ch, int start)`	Returns the index of the *last* location of `ch` at or before position `start` in the string.
`int LastIndexOf(String s)`	Returns the index of the *last* location of substring `s` in the string.
`int LastIndexOf(String s, int start)`	Returns the index of the *last* location of substring `s` at or before position `start` in the string.
`boolean regionMatches(int off1,String s, int off2, int len)`	This method compares `len` characters of the string starting at index `off1` with `len` characters of `s` starting at index `off2`. If they match, the method returns true. Otherwise, the method returns false.
`boolean regionMatches(boolean ignoreCase, int off1, String s, int off2, int len)`	This method compares `len` characters of the string starting at index `off1` with `len` characters of `s` starting at index `off2`. If `ignoreCase` is true and the substrings match *ignoring case*, the method returns `true`. If `ignoreCase` is `false` and the substrings match *exactly*, the method returns `true`. Otherwise, the method returns `false`.
`String replace(char old, char new)`	Returns a new string with every occurrence of character `old` replaced by character `new`.
`boolean startsWith(String p)`	Returns `true` if the beginning of the string matches `p` exactly.
`boolean startsWith(String p, int off1)`	Returns `true` if the beginning of the substring starting at index `off1` exactly matches `p`.
`String substring(int st)`	Returns the substring starting at index `st` and going to the end of the string.
`String substring(int st, int en)`	Returns the substring starting at index `st` and going to index `en-1`.
`String toLowerCase()`	Converts the string to lowercase.
`String toUpperCase()`	Converts the string to uppercase.
`String trim()`	Removes white space from either end of the string.
`static String valueOf(boolean b)`	Returns the string representation of a `boolean` argument.
`static String valueOf(char c)`	Returns the string representation of a character argument.
`static String valueOf(int i)`	Returns the string representation of an integer argument.

TABLE 10-1 *(cont.)*

METHOD	DESCRIPTION
static String **valueOf**(long l)	Returns the string representation of a long argument.
static String **valueOf**(float f)	Returns the string representation of a float argument.
static String **valueOf**(double d)	Returns the string representation of a double argument.
static String **valueOf**(Object o)	Returns the string representation of an Object.

creates a new string by appending the characters in s2 to the end of s1. The original String objects s1 and s2 are not affected. The class shown below illustrates the use of concat.

```
1   // Concatenation
2   public class Concatenate {
3
4       public static void main(String[] args) {
5           String s1 = "abc";
6           String s2 = "def";
7
8           // Test concatenation method
9           System.out.println("Test concatenation:");
10          System.out.println("s1 = " + s1);
11          System.out.println("s2 = " + s2);
12          System.out.println("s1.concat(s2) = "
13              + s1.concat(s2));
14
15          // Watch what happens here!
16          System.out.println("\nBefore assignment:");
17          System.out.println("s1 = " + s1);
18          System.out.println("s2 = " + s2);
19          s1 = s1.concat(s2);
20          System.out.println("\nAfter assignment:");
21          System.out.println("s1 = " + s1);
22          System.out.println("s2 = " + s2);
23      }
24  }
```

When this program is executed, the results are as follows:

```
D:\book\java\chap10>java Concatenate
Test concatenation:
s1 = abc
s2 = def
s1.concat(s2) = abcdef

Before assignment:
s1 = abc
s2 = def

After assignment:
s1 = abcdef
s2 = def
```

Note that the concat method concatenated string s1 with string s2.

The second part of the program illustrates a common source of confusion of novice Java programmers. We stated at the beginning of this chapter that Strings never

Figure 10.1. (*a*) Initially reference s1 points to the String object containing "abc", and reference s2 points to the String object containing "def". (*b*) After line 19 is executed, reference s1 points to the String object containing "abcdef", and reference s2 points to the String object containing "def". The object containing "abc" no longer has a reference, and it will be garbage collected.

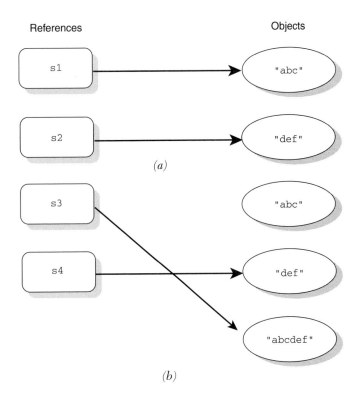

change once they are created, and yet s1 changes value between lines 17 and 21 in the above program! What is happening here?

The answer is very simple. Remember that s1 and s2 are *references to strings,* not strings themselves. Lines 5 and 6 of the program create two String objects containing the strings "abc" and "def" and set references s1 and s2 to refer to them. Therefore, lines 17 and 18 print out s1 = "abc" and s2 = "def". The concat method in line 19 creates a *new* String object containing the string "abcdef" and sets the reference s1 to point to the new object. Therefore, line 21 prints out s1 = "abcdef". This process is illustrated in Figure 10.1.

What happened to the original String object pointed to by s1? It is still present, but there is no longer any reference to it. This object can never be used again, and it will be destroyed the next time that the garbage collector runs.

10.2.3 Comparing Strings

Two strings may be compared using methods `equals`, `equalsIgnoreCase`, `compareTo`, and `regionMatches`. When two strings are compared, they are compared according to the **lexicographic sequence** of the characters in the strings. This is the sequence in which the characters appear within the Unicode character set. Appendix A shows the order of the first 127 letters according to the Unicode character set. In this set, the letter 'A' is character 64 and the letter 'a' is 96, so 'A' is lexicographically less than 'a'. *Note that capital letters are not the same as lowercase letters* when they are compared lexicographically.

If the strings being compared are more than one character long, then the comparison starts with the first character in each string. If the two characters are equal, then the comparison moves to the second character in the strings, and so on, until the first difference is found. If there is no difference between the two strings, then they are considered equal.

The method `equals` compares two strings and returns `true` if they contain identically the same value. For example, if

```
s1 = new String("Hello");
s2 = new String("Hello");
s3 = new String("hello");
```

then the expression `s1.equals( s2 )` will be `true`, because the two strings are identically the same, while the expression `s1.equals( s3 )` will be `false`, because the two strings are differ in the first position.

Note that *comparing two strings with the method* `equals` *is not the same as comparing two strings with the* `==` *operator*. When the `==` operator compares two object references, *it checks to see if the two references point to the same object*. If you are comparing two objects with the `==` operator, they will not be equal, even if they have identically the same contents. For example, if `s1` and `s2` are as defined above, the expression

```
s1.equals(s2)
```

will return `true`, because the contents of the two objects are equal, but the expression

```
s1 == s2
```

will return `false`, because `s1` and `s2` are two different objects.

PROGRAMMING PITFALLS

Never attempt to compare two objects for equality with the `==` operator. This operator checks to see if two references point to the same object, and not to see if two objects have equal values.

The method `equalsIgnoreCase` is similar to `equals`, except that it ignores the case of letters when comparing the two strings. Thus, the expression `s1.equals IgnoreCase(s3)` will be `true`, because the two strings are only differ in the case of the letter 'H'.

The method `s1.compareTo(s2)` compares two strings `s1` and `s2` and returns an integer equal to the *difference in lexicographic position* between the corresponding letters at the first differing location in the strings. This difference will be negative if

Figure 10.2. The difference between `s1.equals(s2)` and `s1 == s2`. (*a*) In this case, `s1` and `s2` point to *two different objects* whose contents are equal. Here, `s1.equals(s2)` is true, and `s1 == s2` is false. (*b*) In this case, `s1` and `s2` point to the same object. Here, `s1.equals(s2)` is true, and `s1 == s2` is also true.

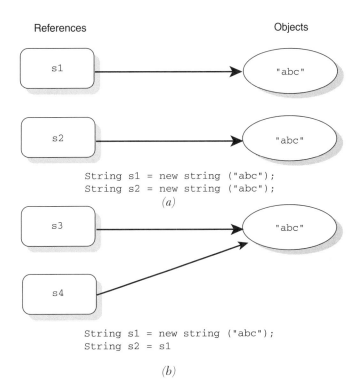

References   Objects

```
String s1 = new string ("abc");
String s2 = new string ("abc");
```
(*a*)

```
String s1 = new string ("abc");
String s2 = s1
```

(*b*)

and the letter 'e' appears 32 characters after 'E' in the Unicode character set. Finally, the expression `s3.compareTo(s4)` will be zero, since the strings are equal.

The method `regionMatches` compares two strings `s1` and `s2` to determine if two regions within the strings are equal to each other. There are two forms of this method. The first form is

```
s1.regionMatches( i1, s2, i2, len)
```

where `i1`, `i2`, and `len` are all integers. The value `i1` is the index in `s1` to start the comparison at, `i2` is the index in `s2` at which to start the comparison, and `len` is the number of characters to compare. This method returns `true` if the two regions match exactly, including case.

The second form of `regionMatches` is

```
s1.regionMatches( ignoreCase, i1, s2, i2, len)
```

The second form of `regionMatches` is

```
s1.regionMatches( ignoreCase, i1, s2, i2, len)
```

where `ignoreCase` is a `boolean` and all other arguments have the same meaning as before. If `ignoreCase` is `true`, this method compares the two regions *ignoring case*. Otherwise, it acts exactly like the first form of the method. For example, if

```
s1 = new String("started");
s2 = new String("starting");
s3 = new String("nowStarting");
```

then the method call

```
s1.regionMatches(0, s2, 0, 5)
```

will return a `true` value, because the first five characters in the two strings are identical (remember that Java indexes start at 0). The method call

```
s1.regionMatches(0, s3, 3, 5)
```

will return a `false` value, because `"start"` is not equal to `"Start"`. However, the method call

```
s1.regionMatches(true, 1, s3, 4, 5)
```

will return a `true` value, because `"start"` is equal to `"Start"` when ignoring case.

The methods `startsWith` and `endsWith` can be used to determine whether or not a string starts with or ends with a particular substring. For example, if

```
s1 = new String("started");
```

then the method call

```
s1.startsWith("st")
```

would return `true`, because `"started"` does start with `"st"`. Similarly, the method call

```
s1.endsWith("ed")
```

would return `true`, because `"started"` does end with `"ed"`.

All of these comparison methods are illustrated in the Java program shown below.

```
// Comparisons
public class Compare {

    public static void main(String[] args) {

        String s1, s2, s3, s4;  // Declare references

        // Test equality and inequality
        System.out.println("Test equality:");
        s1 = new String("Hello");
        s2 = new String("Hello");
        s3 = new String("hello");

        System.out.println("s1 = \"" + s1 + "\"");
        System.out.println("s2 = \"" + s2 + "\"");
        System.out.println("s3 = \"" + s3 + "\"");
        System.out.println("s1.equals(s2) = " + s1.equals(s2));
        System.out.println("s1.equals(s3) = " + s1.equals(s3));
        System.out.println("s1.equalsIgnoreCase(s3) = " + s1.equalsIgnoreCase(s3));
        System.out.println("s1 == s2 = " + (s1 == s2) );
```

```
                   // Test comparison
                   System.out.println("\nTest compare:");
                   s1 = new String("Good");
                   s2 = new String("Help");
                   s3 = new String("HELP");
                   s4 = new String("HELP");

                   System.out.println("s1 = \"" + s1 + "\"");
                   System.out.println("s2 = \"" + s2 + "\"");
                   System.out.println("s3 = \"" + s3 + "\"");
                   System.out.println("s4 = \"" + s4 + "\"");
                   System.out.println("s1.compareTo(s2) = " + s1.compareTo(s2));
                   System.out.println("s2.compareTo(s3) = " + s2.compareTo(s3));
                   System.out.println("s3.compareTo(s4) = " + s3.compareTo(s4));

                   // Test regionMatches
                   System.out.println("\nTest regionMatches:");
                   s1 = new String("started");
                   s2 = new String("starting");
                   s3 = new String("nowStarting");

                   System.out.println("s1 = \"" + s1 + "\"");
                   System.out.println("s2 = \"" + s2 + "\"");
                   System.out.println("s3 = \"" + s3 + "\"");
                   System.out.println("s1.regionMatches(0, s2, 0, 5) = "
                       + s1.regionMatches(0, s2, 0, 5));
                   System.out.println("s1.regionMatches(0, s3, 3, 5) = "
                       + s1.regionMatches(0, s3, 3, 5));
                   System.out.println("s1.regionMatches(true, 0, s3, 3, 5) = "
                       + s1.regionMatches(true, 0, s3, 3, 5));

                   // Test startsWith and endsWith
                   System.out.println("\nTest startsWith & endsWith:");
                   s1 = new String("started");
                   s2 = new String("starting");

                   System.out.println("s1 = \"" + s1 + "\"");
                   System.out.println("s2 = \"" + s2 + "\"");
                   System.out.println("s1.startsWith(\"st\") = "
                       + s1.startsWith("st"));
                   System.out.println("s1.endsWith(\"ed\") = "
                       + s1.endsWith("ed"));
                   System.out.println("s2.endsWith(\"ed\") = "
                       + s2.endsWith("ed"));

           }
   }
```

When this program is executed, the results agree with our previous discussions:

```
   D:\book\java\chap10>java Compare
   Test equality:
   s1 = "Hello"
   s2 = "Hello"
   s3 = "hello"
   s1.equals(s2) = true
   s1.equals(s3) = false
   s1.equalsIgnoreCase(s3) = true
   s1 == s2 = false
   Test compare:
   s1 = "Good"
   s2 = "Help"
```

```
s3 = "HELP"
s4 = "HELP"
s1.compareTo(s2) = -1
s2.compareTo(s3) = 32
s3.compareTo(s4) = 0

Test regionMatches:
s1 = "started"
s2 = "starting"
s3 = "nowStarting"
s1.regionMatches(0, s2, 0, 5) = true
s1.regionMatches(0, s3, 3, 5) = false
s1.regionMatches(true, 0, s3, 3, 5) = true

Test startsWith & endsWith:
s1 = "started"
s2 = "starting"
s1.startsWith("st") = true
s1.endsWith("ed") = true
s2.endsWith("ed") = false
```

10.2.4 Locating Characters and Substrings in a String

A substring can be located inside another string using the `indexOf` and `lastIndexOf` methods. The `indexOf` method takes one of the following forms:

```
s1.indexOf(String s2);
s1.indexOf(String s2, int start);
s1.indexOf(char c);
s1.indexOf(char c, int start);
```

This method starts at the starting index (or at 0 if the starting index is not specified), and searches string `s1` from *left to right* until it locates an occurrence of the specified substring or character. It returns the index where that substring or character was found or −1 if it was not found. For example, if

```
s1 = new String("This is a test.");
```

then the expression `s1.indexOf("is")` will return a 2, because the `"is"` in `"This"` starts at index 2. Similarly, the expression `s1.indexOf("is",3)` will return a 5, because this expression begins searching at index 3 in the string, and the first occurrence of `"is"` that it finds will be at index 5. Finally, the expression `s1.indexOf("is",6)` will return a −1, because this is no occurrence of `"is"` after that point in the string.

The `lastIndexOf` method takes one of the forms

```
s1.lastIndexOf(String s2);
s1.lastIndexOf(String s2, int start);
s1.lastIndexOf(char c);
s1.lastIndexOf(char c, int start);
```

This method starts at the starting index (or at the end of the string if the starting index is not specified) and searches string `s1` from *right to left* until it locates an occurrence of the specified substring or character. It returns the index where that substring or character was found or −1 if it was not found.

The `indexOf` and `lastIndexOf` methods are illustrated in the Java program shown below.

```
// IndexOf
public class Find {

    public static void main(String[] args) {

        // Test indexOf
        System.out.println("Test indexOf:");
        String s1 = new String("This is a test.");
        System.out.println("s1 = \"" + s1 + "\"");
        System.out.println("s1.indexOf(\"is\") = "
            + s1.indexOf("is"));
        System.out.println("s1.indexOf(\"is\",3) = "
            + s1.indexOf("is",3));
        System.out.println("s1.indexOf(\"is\",6) = "
            + s1.indexOf("is",6));
        System.out.println("s1.indexOf(\'s\') = "
            + s1.indexOf('s'));

        // Test lastIndexOf
        System.out.println("\nTest lastIndexOf:");
        System.out.println("s1.lastIndexOf(\"is\") = "
            + s1.lastIndexOf("is"));

    }
}
```

When this program is executed, the results are:

```
D:\book\java\chap10>java Find
Test indexOf:
s1 = "This is a test."
s1.indexOf("is") = 2
s1.indexOf("is",3) = 5
s1.indexOf("is",6) = -1
s1.indexOf('s') = 3

Test lastIndexOf:
s1.lastIndexOf("is") = 5
```

10.2.5 Miscellaneous String Methods

This section discusses four miscellaneous string methods: replace, toUpperCase, toLowerCase, and trim.

Method replace creates a new string with every occurrence of a specified character in the original string replaced with a different character. The form of this method is

```
s1.replace(old, new)
```

where s1 is a string, old is the character to replace, and new is the replacement character. For example, if

```
s1 = "This is a test.";
```

then the expression s1.replace('i','I') will return the string "ThIs Is a test.".

Methods toUpperCase and toLowerCase return strings with all characters shifted to uppercase and lowercase letters, respectively. Thus, s1.toUpperCase() will return the string "THIS IS A TEST.", and s1.toLowerCase() will return the string "this is a test.".

Method trim returns a string that is identical to the original string, except that *the leading and trailing whitespace has been removed.* For example, consider the following statements:

```
s1 = "   Hello   ";
s1.length()
s2 = s1.trim;
s2.length()
```

String `s1` is 11 characters long, and the expression `s1.length()` will return a value of 11. String `s2` will be the same as string `s1` with the leading and trailing whitespace removed, so `s2.length()` will be 5.

These methods are illustrated in the program below:

```
// Miscellaneous methods
public class Misc {

    public static void main(String[] args) {

        String s1 = new String("This is a test.");
        String s2;

        System.out.println("Test replace:");
        System.out.println("s1 = \"" + s1 + "\"");
        System.out.println("s1.replace(\'i\',\'I\') = "
            + s1.replace('i','I'));

        System.out.println("\nTest toUpperCase:");
        System.out.println("s1.toUpperCase() = "
            + s1.toUpperCase());

        System.out.println("\nTest toLowerCase:");
        System.out.println("s1.toLowerCase() = "
            + s1.toLowerCase());

        System.out.println("\nTest trim:");
        s1 = new String("   Hello   ");
        s2 = s1.trim();
        System.out.println("s1 = \"" + s1 + "\"");
        System.out.println("s2 = \"" + s2 + "\"");
    }
}
```

When this program is executed, the results are as follows:

```
D:\book\java\chap10>java Misc
Test replace:
s1 = "This is a test."
s1.replace('i','I') = ThIs Is a test.

Test toUpperCase:
s1.toUpperCase() = THIS IS A TEST.

Test toLowerCase:
s1.toLowerCase() = this is a test.

Test trim:
s1 = " Hello "
s2 = "Hello"
```

10.2.6 The `valueOf()` Method

Data are stored and used inside a computer in binary format, but before they can be displayed for human use, they must be converted into a `String` representation. One technique available for this conversion is the `String.valueOf` method.

The static method String.valueOf returns a string representation of the value of its argument, whether the argument is a primitive data type or an object. There are separate versions of this method for each primitive data type and for objects. (The version for objects uses the object's toString() method to create a string representation of the object's value.)

Since this is a static method, it can be used without first instantiating a String object. The following program illustrates the use of the valueOf() method, using the Date class from Chapter 8 as the example object:

```
// This program tests String.valueOf().  It uses
// class Date from Chapter 8.
public class ValueOf {

    public static void main(String[] args)
                            throws InvalidDateException {

        // Test valueOf
        System.out.println("Test valueOf:");
        int i = 123456;
        float f = 1.2345f;
        double d = Math.PI;
        Object o = new Date(1,1,2000);

        System.out.println("int    = " + String.valueOf(i) );
        System.out.println("float  = " + String.valueOf(f) );
        System.out.println("double = " + String.valueOf(d) );
        System.out.println("object = " + String.valueOf(o) );
    }
}
```

When this program is executed, the results are as follows:

```
C:\book\java\chap10>java ValueOf
Test valueOf:
int    = 123456
float  = 1.2345
double = 3.141592653589793
object = 1/1/2000
```

10.3 CREATING AND INITIALIZING StringBuffers

The **StringBuffer class** consists of modifiable strings. The contents of a String-Buffer may be freely changed, and the size of StringBuffer can grow or shrink during program execution.

A reference to a StringBuffer is created by the following statement:

```
StringBuffer buf1; // Create a StringBuffer reference
```

When this statement is executed, reference buf1 is created and set to null, since it does not yet point to a StringBuffer object. Attempting to use a null reference in a program will produce a runtime exception.

StringBuffer objects are created using StringBuffer constructors. There are three forms of StringBuffer constructors. A constructor with no arguments creates an empty StringBuffer object with a capacity of 16 characters. A constructor with an integer argument creates an empty StringBuffer object with a capacity specified by the integer. A constructor with a String argument creates a StringBuffer initialized to the value of the string, with a capacity equal to the number of characters in the string plus 16. Some examples of `StringBuffer` constructors are shown below:

```
StringBuffer buf1, buf2, buf3
buf1 = new StringBuffer();           / 16 char capacity
buf2 = new StringBuffer(50);         / 50 char capacity
buf3 = new StringBuffer("Hello");    / 21 char capacity
```

10.4 `StringBuffer` METHODS

There are many methods available for manipulating `StringBuffers` in Java programs. Some of the more important methods are summarized in Table 10-2. All of the `StringBuffer` methods are described in the Java API documentation in class `java.lang.StringBuffer`.

10.4.1 The Difference between Length and Capacity

Every `StringBuffer` is characterized by two parameters, a **length** and a **capacity**. The **length** of a `StringBuffer` is the number of characters *actually stored* in the `StringBuffer`, while the **capacity** is the number of characters that *can be* stored without allocating additional memory. (See Figure 10.3.) These two values are independent of each other, except that the capacity of a buffer must always be greater than or equal to the length of the actual characters stored in the buffer. If a method call makes the length of the buffer larger than its current capacity, that capacity is automatically extended so that all of the characters will fit.

The length of a `StringBuffer` object can be determined using `length` method, and the capacity of a `StringBuffer` object can be determined using the `capacity` method. These methods return the length or capacity of the buffer in units of characters.

The `ensureCapacity` method can be used to force a `StringBuffer` object to have at least a minimum capacity. The form of this method is

```
buf.ensureCapacity(cap)
```

where `cap` is an integer specifying the minimum capacity of the buffer `buf`. Java may choose to allocate more than this capacity, but it guarantees that the buffer will be able to hold at least `cap` characters.

The actual number of characters stored in a buffer can be set using the `length` method. The form of this method is

```
buf.length(len)
```

where `len` is an integer specifying the number of actual characters in the buffer. If `len` is less than the current number of characters in the buffer, the number of characters is truncated to `len`. If `len` is greater than the current number of characters in the buffer, the characters are padded with null characters (Unicode character `'u0000'`).

The following program illustrates the use of these methods.

```
// This program tests StringBuffer capacity and length
public class StringBufferCapLen {

    public static void main(String[] args) {
        StringBuffer buf;
        buf = new StringBuffer("This is a test string.");
```

TABLE 10-2   Selected `StringBuffer` Methods

METHOD	DESCRIPTION
StringBuffer **append**(Object o)	Appends the string representation of the `Object` argument to this string buffer.
StringBuffer **append**(String s)	Appends the string to this string buffer.
StringBuffer **append**(Char[] c)	Appends the string representation of the `char` array c to this string buffer.
StringBuffer **append**(boolean b)	Appends the string representation of the `boolean` argument to this string buffer.
StringBuffer **append**(char c)	Appends the string representation of the `char` argument to this string buffer.
StringBuffer **append**(int i)	Appends the string representation of the `int` argument to this string buffer.
StringBuffer **append**(long l)	Appends the string representation of the `long` argument to this string buffer.
StringBuffer **append**(float f)	Appends the string representation of the `float` argument to this string buffer.
StringBuffer **append**(double d)	Appends the string representation of the `double` argument to this string buffer.
int **capacity**()	Returns the current capacity, which is the number of characters that may be inserted before more memory must be allocated.
char **charAt**(int index)	Returns the character at the specified index.
void **ensureCapacity**(int min)	Ensures that the capacity of the buffer is at least equal to the specified minimum.
StringBuffer **insert**(int n, Object o)	Inserts the string representation of the `Object` argument at index n in this string buffer.
StringBuffer **insert**(int n, String s)	Inserts the string at index n in this string buffer.
StringBuffer **insert**(int n, Char[] c)	Inserts the string representation of the `char` array c at index n in this string buffer.
StringBuffer **insert**(int n, boolean b)	Inserts the string representation of the `boolean` argument at index n in this string buffer.
StringBuffer **insert**(int n, char c)	Inserts the string representation of the `char` argument at index n in this string buffer.
StringBuffer **insert**(int n, int i)	Inserts the string representation of the `int` argument at index n in this string buffer.
StringBuffer **insert**(int n, long l)	Inserts the string representation of the `long` argument at index n in this string buffer.
StringBuffer **insert**(int n, float f)	Inserts the string representation of the `float` argument at index n in this string buffer.
StringBuffer **insert**(int n, double d)	Inserts the string representation of the `double` argument at index n in this string buffer.
int **length**()	Returns the number of characters in this string buffer.
StringBuffer **reverse**()	Reverse the sequence of characters in this string buffer
void **setLength**(int len)	Sets the length (the number of characters) in this buffer. If `len` is less than the current string buffer length, the string buffer is truncated. If `len` is greater, then the string buffer is padded with null characters (`\u0000`).
String **toString**()	Convert the contents of this string buffer into a string.

Figure 10.3. The difference between length and capacity in a `StringBuffer`. The length of this `StringBuffer` is 6, while its capacity is 11.

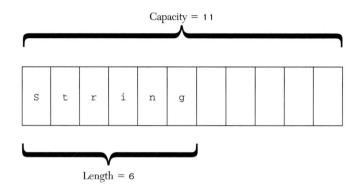

```
// Get length and capacity
System.out.println("Initial conditions:");
System.out.println("buf      = " + buf );
System.out.println("Capacity = " + buf.capacity() );
System.out.println("Length   = " + buf.length() );

// Increase capacity
System.out.println("\nAfter ensureCapacity:");
buf.ensureCapacity(75);
System.out.println("buf      = " + buf );
System.out.println("Capacity = " + buf.capacity() );
System.out.println("Length   = " + buf.length() );

// Truncate length
System.out.println("\nAfter setLength:");
buf.setLength(10);
System.out.println("buf      = " + buf );
System.out.println("Capacity = " + buf.capacity() );
System.out.println("Length   = " + buf.length() );

    }
}
```

When this program is executed, the results are as follows:

```
C:\book\java\chap10>java StringBufferCapLen
Initial conditions:
buf      = This is a test string.
Capacity = 38
Length   = 22

After ensureCapacity:
buf      = This is a test string.
Capacity = 78
Length   = 22

After setLength:
buf      = This is a
Capacity = 78
Length   = 10
```

Note that the initial length of the buffer was 22 characters, and the initial capacity of the buffer was 38 characters (= 22 + 16 extra). After the `buf.ensureCapacity(76)` method was executed, the new capacity of the buffer was 78. Java ensured that the capacity was at least 76 characters. Finally, after the `buf.setLength(10)` method was executed, the number of characters in the buffer decreased to 10, while the capacity of the buffer remained at 78.

10.4.2 The `append` and `insert` Methods

The most important `StringBuffer` methods are `append` and `insert`. Java allows you insert or append string representations of just about anything (`boolean`, `char`, `int`, `long`, `float`, `double`, `String`, or a general `Object`) at any point in a string buffer.

In fact, Java uses the `StringBuffer` append method to implement the + and += operators for concatenating strings. A string concatenation expression like

```
String s = "value = " + 1.234;
```

is actually implemented by the Java expression

```
String s = new StringBuffer("value = ").append(1.234).toString();
```

which creates a new `StringBuffer` containing the characters `"value   =   "`, appends a string representation of the double value 1.234 to it, and then converts the entire `StringBuffer` into a `String`.

The append method appends a character representation of a primitive data type or object to an existing `StringBuffer`. It takes the form

```
buf.append( value );
```

where `value` can be any `boolean`, `char`, `int`, `long`, `float`, `double`, `String`, or a general `Object`.

The `insert` method inserts a character representation of a primitive data type or object into the middle of an existing `StringBuffer`. It takes the form

```
buf.insert( index, value );
```

where `index` is the index at which to insert the characters, and `value` can be any `boolean`, `char`, `int`, `long`, `float`, `double`, `String`, or a general `Object`.

The following program illustrates the use of these methods. First, it creates a new buffer `buf`, and then it *appends* an `int`, `String`, `double`, `char`, and `Object` to `buf`. The program prints out the resulting string buffer. Next, it resets the length of `buf` to zero, and then *inserts* the same values starting at index zero each time. The program then prints out the new string buffer. Note that the order of the values is reversed between the two strings.

```
// This program tests StringBuffer append and insert.
// It uses class Date from Chapter 8.
public class StringBufferInsApp {
    public static void main(String[] args)
                        throws InvalidDateException {

        // Define variables
        StringBuffer buf = new StringBuffer();
        int i = 123456;
        double d = Math.PI;
        Object o = new Date(1,1,2000);
        // Test append
        System.out.println("Test append:");
        buf.append(i);              // int
        buf.append(" ");            // String
        buf.append(d);              // double
        buf.append(' ');            // char
```

```
        buf.append(o);              // Object
        System.out.println("buf = " + buf );

        // Test insert
        System.out.println("\nTest insert:");
        buf.setLength(0);           // Clear buffer
        buf.insert(0,i);            // int
        buf.insert(0," ");          // String
        buf.insert(0,d);            // double
        buf.insert(0,' ');          // char
        buf.insert(0,o);            // Object
        System.out.println("buf = " + buf );
    }
}
```

When this program is executed, the results are as follows:

```
C:\book\java\chap10>java StringBufferInsApp
Test append:
buf = 123456 3.141592653589793 1/1/2000

Test insert:
buf = 1/1/2000 3.141592653589793 123456
```

10.4.3 The reverse Method

One other useful `StringBuffer` method is `reverse`. This method reverses the order of the characters stored in a buffer. The form of this method is

```
buf.reverse();
```

The following program illustrates the use of this method:

```
// This program tests the StringBuffer reverse method.
public class StringBufferReverse {

    public static void main(String[] args) {

        // Define variables
        StringBuffer buf = new StringBuffer("1234567890");

        // Test append
        System.out.println("Test reverse:");
        System.out.println("Before: buf = " + buf );
        buf.reverse();
        System.out.println("After:  buf = " + buf );
    }
}
```

When this program is executed, the results are as follows:

```
C:\book\java\chap10>java StringBufferReverse
Test reverse:
Before: buf = 1234567890
After:  buf = 0987654321
```

EXAMPLE 10-1:
COMPARING
Strings AND
StringBuffers

Java `Strings` are more efficient for operations such as comparison and matching, while `StringBuffers` are more efficient for operations such as appending or inserting. However, it is possible to do many operations with either `Strings` or `StringBuffers`. For example, we can add a string to the end of another string with the `String concat` method, or with the `StringBuffer append` method.

To compare the performance of these two approaches, create a new string by concatenating the string `"ab"` 1000 times with either the `concat` method or the `append` method. Use the `Timer` class to calculate the elapsed time required to concatenate the string using each method.

SOLUTION

The code required to create a string `s` by concatenating the string `"ab"` 1000 times using the `concat` method is as follows:

```
String s = new String();
for ( i = 1; i <= 1000; i++ ) {
   s = s.concat("ab");
}
```

The code required to create a string `s` by concatenating the string `"ab"` 1000 times using the `append` method is the following:

```
String s;
StringBuffer buf = new StringBuffer();
for ( i = 1; i <= 1000; i++ ) {
   buf.append("ab");
}
s = buf.toString();
```

A program implementing these two approaches is shown in Figure 10.4.

```
/*
   Purpose:
      This class tests concatenation using both the
      String method concat and the StringBuffer method
      append.

   Record of revisions:
      Date          Programmer          Description of change
      ====          ==========          =====================
      5/03/98    S. J. Chapman          Original code
*/

public class TestConcat {

   // Define the main method
   public static void main(String[] args) {

      // Definitions of variables
      StringBuffer buf;                  // String buffer
      double elapsedTime;                // Elapsed time (s)
      String s;                          // String
      Timer t;                           // Timer object

      // Start a Timer
      t = new Timer();

      // Concatenate the data using string
      s = new String();
      for ( int i = 1; i <= 1000; i++ ) {
         s = s.concat("ab");
      }

      // Get elapsed time
      elapsedTime = t.elapsedTime();
```

Figure 10.4. *(cont.)*

```
                              // Display results
                              System.out.println("Results with s.concat():");
                              System.out.println("String begins: "
                                                      + s.substring(0,8) + "...");
                              System.out.println("String length = " + s.length());
                              System.out.println("Time = " + elapsedTime + " s");

                              // Reset Timer
                              t.resetTimer();

                              // Concatenate the data using StringBuffer
                              buf = new StringBuffer();
                              for ( int i = 1; i <= 1000; i++ ) {
                                 buf.append("ab");
                              }
                              s = buf.toString();

                              // Get elapsed time
                              elapsedTime = t.elapsedTime();

                              // Display results
                              System.out.println("Results with buf.append():");
                              System.out.println("String begins: "
                                                      + s.substring(0,8) + "...");
                              System.out.println("String length = " + s.length());
                              System.out.println("Time = " + elapsedTime + " s");
                           }
                       }
```

Figure 10.4. A program comparing concatenation with String objects to appending with String-Buffer objects.

When this program is executed, the result are as follows:

```
C:\book\java\chap10>java TestConcat
Results with s.concat():
String begins: abababab...
String length = 2000
Time = 0.12 s
Results with buf.append():
String begins: abababab...
String length = 2000
Time = 0.01 s
```

The append method was about 10 times quicker than the concat method. This is true because every time s.concat() was executed, the program had to create a *new* String object two characters longer than the previous one, and then it had to copy the contents of the old object into the new one before adding on the two new characters. This process is very inefficient in both time and memory. Note that it left 1000 String objects in limbo waiting to be destroyed by the garbage collector!

For insert and append operations, StringBuffers are much more efficient than Strings.

GOOD PROGRAMMING PRACTICE

Use the `StringBuffer` insert and append methods instead of the `String` concat method for combining strings. The `StringBuffer` methods are much more efficient, and they produce fewer "waste" objects for garbage collection.

10.5 THE `StringTokenizer` CLASS

Java includes a special class called **`StringTokenizer`** to break the contents of a string apart into separate units, called **tokens**. A *token* is a connected group of characters separated by from other tokens by **delimiters**, which are usually whitespace characters such as blanks, tabs, or newlines. For example, the string `"This is a test"` contains the four tokens `"This"`, `"is"`, `"a"`, and `"test"`. Class `StringTokenizer` allows us to chop strings up into such bite-sized pieces for further processing.

Class `StringTokenizer` has the following three constructors:

```
new StringTokenizer( String s );
new StringTokenizer( String s, String delim );
new StringTokenizer( String s, String delim, boolean returnTokens);
```

where s is the string to split into tokens. If `delim` is included, it is a string containing all of the characters that mark the boundaries between tokens. By default, the delimiter list is `" \t\n\r\f"`, which is the space character, the tab character, the newline character, the carriage-return character, and the form-feed character. If `returnTokens` is `true`, the delimiters between tokens are also returned as tokens. If it is `false` or if it is not present, the delimiters between tokens are not returned.

The class includes a method `countTokens()` to return the number of tokens in the string, a method `hasMoreTokens()` indicate that there are still tokens to recover, and a method `nextToken()` to recover the next token.

The program shown below illustrates the use of `StringTokenizer`.

```
/*
   Purpose:
     This class tests StringTokenizer.

   Record of revisions:
      Date        Programmer           Description of change
      ====        ==========           =====================
     5/03/98    S. J. Chapman         Original code
*/
import java.util.*;
public class TestStringTokenizer {

   // Define the main method
   public static void main(String[] args) {

      // Definitions of variables
      String s = "Test-case 1, test case 2";
      StringTokenizer st;

      // Create a StringTokenizer with the default options
      st = new StringTokenizer(s);
      System.out.print("Default case:");
      System.out.println("the " + st.countTokens() + " tokens are:");
      while (st.hasMoreTokens()) {
```

```
                              System.out.println(st.nextToken());
                }
                // Create a StringTokenizer that recognizes "-" and "," as
                // delimeters
                st = new StringTokenizer(s," -,\t\n\r\f");
                System.out.print("\nWith - and ': ");
                System.out.println("the " + st.countTokens() + " tokens are:");
                while (st.hasMoreTokens()) {
                              System.out.println(st.nextToken());

                }
        }
}
```

When this program is executed, the results are:

```
C:\book\java\chap10>java TestStringTokenizer
Default case:the 5 tokens are:
Test-case
1,
test
case
2

With - and ': the 6 tokens are:
Test
case
1
test
case
2
```

GOOD PROGRAMMING PRACTICE

Use the `StringTokenizer` methods to break strings up into separate tokens for further processing.

10.6 COMMAND-LINE ARGUMENTS

Since the very first `HelloWorld` application in Chapter 1, we have defined the main method of a program with the sequence

```
public static void main(String[] args) {
```

Along the way, we have learned the meanings of most of this definition. The keyword `public` means that the method is visible anywhere in the Java program. The keyword `static` means that the method can be called directly without first instantiating an object of its class. The keyword `void` means that the methods does not return a value to its caller, and `main` is the name of the method. So what about the `String` array `args`? We have never mentioned it.

`String` array `args` is an array containing the arguments typed on the command line after the name of the class to be executed. These arguments are copied into an array of `Strings` and made available for the program to use. **Command-line arguments** are a convenient way to pass parameters such as file names, options, etc. to a program as it begins executing. For example, it is possible to pass a file name on the command line, and then open the file using a `FileIn` object. We shall see this usage in Example 10-2 below.

A program illustrating the use of command-line arguments is shown below:

```
/*
    Purpose:
      This class tests command-line arguments.

    Record of revisions:
        Date        Programmer          Description of change
        ====        ==========          =====================
        5/03/98    S. J. Chapman        Original code


*/
public class TestArgs {

    // Define the main method
    public static void main(String[] args) {

        // List arguments
        System.out.println("There are " + args.length
                        + " command-line arguments.");
        System.out.println("The command-line arguments are:");
        for ( int i = 0; i < args.length; i++ )
            System.out.println( args[i] );
    }
}
```

When this program is executed, the command-line arguments are broken up into tokens and stored as separate strings in array `args`. For example,

```
C:\book\java\chap10>java TestArgs Hello! 1 3.14159 "1 2 3"
There are 4 command-line arguments.
The command-line arguments are:
Hello!
1
3.14159
1 2 3
```

Note that all characters within double quotes on the command line are treated as a single string.

GOOD PROGRAMMING PRACTICE

Parameter `args` in the `main` method of a program is an array of `Strings` containing information from the command line that is passed to the program at startup. It can include information such as file names, options, and so forth.

PRACTICE!

This quiz provides a quick check to see if you have understood the concepts introduced in Sections 10.1 through 10.6. If you have trouble with the quiz, reread the section, ask your instructor, or discuss the material with a fellow student. The answers to this quiz are found in the back of the book.

1. What is the difference between a `String` and a `StringBuffer`? When would you want to use a `StringBuffer`?

   Determine which of the following Java statements are valid. For each valid statement, specify what will happen in the program. For invalid statements, explain why the are invalid.

2. ```
   String s1 = new String("abcdefg");
   String s2 = s1.substring(1,8);
   ```

3. ```
   String s1, s2, s3;
   s1 = new String("abcdefg");
   s2 = new String("123");
   s3 = s1.substring(1,3);
   s3 = s3.concat(s2);
   System.out.println(s3);
   ```

4. ```
   StringBuffer s1, s2, s3;
   s1 = new StringBuffer("abcdefg");
   s2 = new StringBuffer("123");
   s3 = s1.substring(1,3);
   s3 = s3.concat(s2);
   System.out.println(s3);
   ```

5. ```
   String s1 = new String("Hello");
   String s2 = new String("hello");
   System.out.println(s1.equals(s2));
   System.out.println(s1.equalsIgnoreCase(s2));
   ```

6. ```
   String s1 = new String("Hello");
   String s2 = new String("Hello");
   System.out.println(s1 == s2);
   ```

7. Write the Java code to locate the index of every s in the string `"Sassafras"`, first considering case and then ignoring case.

8. What is the difference between the length and the capacity of a `StringBuffer`?

9. What are command-line arguments? How are they accessed?

EXAMPLE 10-2: ALPHABETIZING LISTS OF STRINGS

It is very common to alphabetize lists of names, index entries, and so forth. Create a `SortString` class containing a method `sort` that will sort a collection of `Strings` into either ascending or descending alphabetical order *disregarding case*. Use the selection sort algorithm that we introduced in Chapter 5 as the basis of the `sort` method. Include an instance variable in the `SortString` class to specify whether the sorting is to be in ascending or descending order.

Also, create a `TestSortString` class containing a `main` method that reads the strings to be sorted from an input file. The name of the input file should be supplied as a command line argument to the program. In addition, the `main` method should support a command line switch "`-r`" to force the sort to be in the reverse direction.

SOLUTION
To solve this problem, we need to sort a collection of strings alphabetically in either ascending or descending order disregarding case. Unfortunately, Java does not have
   ```

a `compareToIgnoreCase` method, so we must perform a case-insensitive comparison in some other way. One approach is to convert both strings to upper case before the comparison, so that the `compareTo` method will provide a result in alphabetical order.

A second problem is that we do not know in advance how many strings will be read from the input file, so we cannot size an array to hold the strings. The solution to this problem is to use the `Vector` class to hold the strings, since this class can grow as large as necessary to accommodate the input data.

1. **State the problem**. Create a class `SortString` containing a method `sort` that sorts a collection of `Strings` into either ascending or descending alphabetical order disregarding case. Use the selection sort algorithm as the basis of the `sort` method. Include an instance variable int the `SortString` class to specify whether the sorting is to be in ascending or descending order. Create a class `TestSortString` to reads the strings to be sorted from an input file specified as a command-line argument. The `main` method should support a command line switch "`-r`" to force the sort to be in the reverse direction.

2. **Define the inputs and outputs**. The inputs to the `main` method will be an input file name plus possibly the "`-r`" switch on the command line. If the "`-r`" switch is specified, it should *precede* the file name according to the Unix convention. The other inputs to the method are a series of strings in the input file specified on the command line. The output from the `main` method will be the sorted list of strings send to the standard output stream.

   The input to the `sort` method in the `SortString` class will be an object of class `Vector` containing the strings to be sorted. The output from the sort method will be a reference to the sorted `Vector`.

3. **Decompose the program into classes and their associated methods**. This program will require two classes, `SortString` and `TestSortString`. Since class `SortString` can be used to sort data in either forward or reverse order, we will need to create two constructors for the class. The default constructor will not include a sort-order flag, and it will automatically create an object that sorts alphabetically in ascending order. The second constructor will include a `boolean` flag to specify the sort order. If the `boolean` value is `true`, it will create an object that sorts alphabetically in *descending* order. If the `boolean` value is `false`, it will create an object that sorts alphabetically in *ascending* order like the default constructor.

   The class must also contain method `sort` to do the actual sorting, and a method `comp` to compare two strings in a case-independent manner, taking into account the desired sorting direction.

   Class `TestSortString` will contain a single `main` method to read the input strings and store them into a `Vector`, create a `SortString` object, sort the strings into the specified order, and write them to the standard output stream.

4. **Design the algorithm that you intend to implement for each method**. Class `SortString` is the heart of this problem. The pseudocode for the selection sort algorithm used by method `sort` is the same as that presented in Chapter 5, and it will not be repeated here. The only change is that the > relational operators will be replaced by a call to method `comp`.

   Method `comp` must accept two `Strings` s1 and s2 as input parameters. The selection sort attempts to identify the smallest items first and place them at the top of the list. Thus, if the sort order is *ascending,* the method must return a `true` value if `s1` is lexicographically *less than* `s2` disregarding case, and `false` otherwise. If the sort order is *descending,* the method must return a `true` value if `s1` is lexicographically *greater than* `s2` disregarding case, and `false` otherwise. The pseudocode for this method is:

```
if ( !reverse ) {
   // Normal sort order
   if ( (s1.toUpperCase()).compareTo(s2.toUpperCase()) < 0 )
      return true;
   else
      return false;
}
else {
   // Reverse sort order
   if ( (s1.toUpperCase()).compareTo(s2.toUpperCase()) > 0 )
      return true;
   else
      return false;
}
```

The `main` method must read the arguments, open the input file, create a `Vector` and add each string to the `Vector` as it is read. The strings must be read from the input file, and we will not know in advance how many strings there are. Each string must be stored in an element of type `Vector` using the `add` method. We will use the convenience class `chapman.io.FileInLines` to read the lines from the input file.

Then the method must create a `SortString` object with the proper sorting direction, and pass the `Vector` to it for sorting. Finally, it must print out the sorted strings. The pseudocode for these steps is:

```
(Read file name and open file)

// Create new vector
Object v = new Vector;

// Open file for reading lines
FileInLines in = new FileInLines(fileName);

// Check for valid open
if ( in.readStatus != in.FILE_NOT_FOUND ) {

   // Read numbers into array
   while ( in.readStatus != in.EOF ) {
      s = in.readLine();
      v.add(s);
   }

   // Close file
   in.close();

   Create SortString object
   Call sort method
   Print out sorted strings
}

// Get here if file not found. Tell user
else {
   System.out.println("File not found: "+ fileName);
}
```

Before creating a `SortString` object, `main` must check to see if there is a "`-r`" command-line option. The pseudocode for this step is:

```
reverse = false;
if any arguments are present {
   if ( args[0].equals("-r") ) {
      reverse = true;
   }
}
```

5. **Turn the algorithm into Java statements**.

Class `SortString` is shown in Figure 10.5. Note that the comparison and swapping operations in the selection sort method that we studied in Chapter 5 have been replaced by `Vector` get and set methods.

```
/*
   Purpose:
     This class sorts a list of strings into ascending
     or descending lexccographic order, depending on
     the value of the reverse instance variable.

   Record of revisions:
       Date       Programmer         Description of change
       ====       ==========         =====================
       5/05/98    S. J. Chapman      Original code
*/
import java.util.*;
public class SortString {

   // Define instance variables
   private boolean reverse;    // Reverse order flag

   // Constructors
   public SortString() {
      reverse = false;
   }

   public SortString( boolean reverse ) {
      this.reverse = reverse;
   }

   // comp method.  This method compares two Objects,
   // assuming that the two Objects are really Strings.
   // Note that it converts the strings to uppercase
   // before performing the comparison.
   private boolean comp( Object o1, Object o2 ) {
      String s1 = (String) o1;
      String s2 = (String) o2;
      if ( !reverse ) {

         // Normal sort order
         if ( (s1.toUpperCase()).compareTo(s2.toUpperCase()) < 0 )
            return true;
         else
            return false;
      }
      else {

         // Reverse sort order
         if ( (s1.toUpperCase()).compareTo(s2.toUpperCase()) > 0 )
            return true;
```

Figure 10.5. *(cont.)*

```
            else
                return false;
        }
    }

    // Define the sort method.  This method sorts the
    // elements of Vector v.
    public void sort( Vector v ) {

        // Declare variables, and define each variable
        int i, j;               // Loop index
        int iptr;               // Pointer to smallest value
        int nvals;              // Number of values to sort
        Object temp;            // Temporary object ref for swapping

        // Get size of list
        nvals = v.size();

        // Sort values
        for ( i = 0; i <= nvals-2; i++ ) {

            // Find the minimum value in v(i) through v(nvals-1)
            iptr = i;
            for ( j = i+1; j <= nvals-1; j++ ) {
                if ( comp(v.get(j), v.get(iptr)) )
                    iptr = j;
            }

            // iptr now points to the min value, so swap v(iptr) with
            // v(i) if iptr != i.
            if (i != iptr) {
                temp = v.get(i);
                v.set( i, v.get(iptr) );
                v.set( iptr, temp );
            }
        }
    }
}
```

Figure 10.5.   Class SortString.

Class TestSortString is shown in Figure 10.6.

```
/*
   Purpose:
     This class reads a collection of strings from the
     an input file and stores them in a Vector.  The input
     file name is specified as a command line argument
     when the program is started.  It passes the Vector
     to the sort method of the SortString class to sort
     the strings into ascending or descending lexicographical
     order.  Note that this class looks for a command-line
     switch to specify the sorting order.  If the "-r" switch
     is present, it must precede the file name.

   Record of revisions:
       Date          Programmer            Description of change
       ====          ==========            =====================
     5/05/98      S. J. Chapman          Original code
```

Figure 10.6.   *(cont.)*

```
*/
import chapman.io.*;
import java.util.*;
public class TestSortString {

    // Define the main method
    public static void main(String[] args) {

        // Define variables
        String fileName = ""; // Input file name
        boolean reverse;      // Reverse sort switch
        String s;             // Input string

        // Get command line arguments.  Note that
        // there may be one or two arguments.
        reverse = false;
        if ( args.length == 1 ) {
            fileName = args[0];
        }
        else if ( args.length == 2 ) {
            if ( args[0].equals("-r") ) {
                reverse = true;
            }
            fileName = args[1];
        }

        else {
            System.out.println
                ("Usage: java TestSortString -r fileName");
            return;
        }
        // Open input file for reading lines
        FileInLines in = new FileInLines(fileName);

        // Create a Vector to store the strings
        Vector v = new Vector();

        // Check for valid open
        if ( in.readStatus != in.FILE_NOT_FOUND ) {

            // Read numbers into array
            while ( in.readStatus != in.EOF ) {
                s = in.readLine();
                v.add(s);
            }

            // Close file
            in.close();

            // Create the SortString object.
            SortString ss = new SortString ( reverse );

            // Sort the strings
            ss.sort( v );

            // Print out the resulting strings
            System.out.println("\nThe sorted output is:");
            for ( int i = 0; i < v.size(); i++ ) {
                System.out.println( v.get(i) );
            }
        }
```

Figure 10.6. *(cont.)*

```
                    // Get here if file not found.  Tell user
                    else {
                       System.out.println("File not found: "+ fileName);
                    }
                }
            }
        }
```

Figure 10.6. Class `TestSortString`.

6. **Test the resulting Java program**. To test this program, we will create an input data file containing a series of names. The following information will be placed in a file called `input`:

```
deBrincat, Charles
Chapman, Stephen
Johnson, James
Chapman, Rosa
Anderson, William
Johnston, Susan
Johns, Joe
```

When this program is executed *without* the "-r" command-line option, the results are:

```
D:\book\java\chap10>java TestSortString input

The sorted output is:
Anderson, William
Chapman, Rosa
Chapman, Stephen
deBrincat, Charles
Johns, Joe
Johnson, James
Johnston, Susan
```

When this program is executed *with* the "-r" command-line option, the results are:

```
D:\book\java\chap10>java TestSortString -r input

The sorted output is:
Johnston, Susan
Johnson, James
Johns, Joe
deBrincat, Charles
Chapman, Stephen
Chapman, Rosa
Anderson, William
```

The program appears to be functioning correctly. Note that "deBrincat" appears in proper order, even though it begins with a lowercase "d". This indicates that we are indeed sorting the strings properly disregarding case.

SUMMARY

- Strings are groups of one or more characters treated as a single unit. Objects of type `String` never change once they are created.
- `String` method `length` returns the number of characters in a `String`.
- `String` method `s1.concat(s2)` returns a new `String` that is the concatenation of strings `s1` and `s2`.
- `String` method `s1.equals(s2)` returns `true` if the contents of strings `s1` and `s2` are identical.
- `String` method `s1.equalsIgnoreCase(s2)` returns `true` if the contents of strings `s1` and `s2` are identical ignoring case.
- The operator `s1 == s2` returns `true` if references `s1` and `s2` point to identically the same object in memory.
- `String` method `s1.compareTo(s2)` returns 0 if `s1` and `s2` are equal, a negative number if `s1` is lexicographically less than `s2`, and a negative number if `s1` is lexicographically greater than `s2`.
- Other common `String` methods are summarized in Table 10-1.
- `StringBuffer` method `length` returns the number of characters currently stored in `StringBuffer`. Method `capacity` returns the number of characters that can be stored in `StringBuffer` without allocating more memory.
- `StringBuffer` method `append` appends the character description of a primitive data type, `String`, or `Object` to the end of a `StringBuffer`.
- `StringBuffer` method `insert` inserts the character description of a primitive data type, `String`, or `Object` at a specified point in a `StringBuffer`.
- Other common `StringBuffer` methods are summarized in Table 10-2.
- Class `StringTokenizer` can be used to chop a character string up into separate blocks called tokens. The delimiters used to separate the tokens can be specified when the `StringTokenizer` is created.
- The `String[]` array `args` in the `main` method can be used to pass command-line arguments to a Java program.

APPLICATIONS: SUMMARY OF GOOD PROGRAMMING

The following guidelines introduced in this chapter will help you to develop good programs:

1. Use the `StringBuffer` `insert` / `append` methods instead of the `String` `concat` method for combining strings. The `StringBuffer` methods are much more efficient, and they produce fewer "waste" objects for garbage collection.
2. Use the `StringTokenizer` methods to break strings up into separate tokens for further processing.
3. Parameter `args` in the `main` method of a program is an array of `Strings` containing information from the command line that is passed to the program at startup. It can include information such as file names, options, and so forth.

KEY TERMS

anonymous `String` object
command-line arguments
concatenate
delimiter
lexciographic sequence

`String` class
`String` literal
`StringBuffer` capacity
`StringBuffer` class

`StringBuffer` length
`StringTokenizer` class
substring
token

Problems

10.1. Assume that `s1` and `s2` are `Strings` and that

```
String s = "abcdefghijABCDEFGHIJabcdefghij";
```

What will be the contents of `s1` and `s2` after the following statements are executed?

```
g.  s1 = s.substring(10);
    s2 = s.substring(10,12);
h.  s1 = s.substring(1,3);
    s2 = s.substring(7,9);
    s1 = s1.concat(s2);
```

10.2. Assume the definitions

```
String s1 = "Test1";
String s2 = "test1";
String s3 = "Test1";
String s4 = "Test2";
String s5 = s1;
```

What will be the results of the following expressions?

```
a.  s1.equals(s2);
h.  s1.equals(s3);
i.  s1.equalsIgnoreCase(s2);
j.  s1 == s3;
k.  s1 == s5;
l.  s1.compareTo(s2);
m.  s1.compareTo(s4);
n.  s1.regionMatches(1, s2, 1, 3);
o.  s1.regionMatches(true, 1, s2, 1, 3);
p.  s1.startsWith("Te");
q.  s4.endsWith("1");
```

10.3. Assume the definitions

```
String s1 = " The first string ";
```

What will be the results of the following expressions?

```
a.  s1.indexOf("st");
b.  s1.indexOf("st",14);
c.  s1.lastIndexOf("st");
d.  s1.indexOf('i');
e.  s1.replace('s','S');
f.  s1.toUpperCase();
g.  s1.trim();
```

10.4. Assume the definitions

```
StringBuffer b1 = new StringBuffer("1234567890");
String s1;
```

What will be the results of the following expressions?

```
a.  s1 = new String( b1.append('X') );
```

b. `s1 = new String( b1.insert(3, 'X') );`

10.5. Modify the class `TestSortString` of Example 10-2 to check for invalid command-line arguments. If any command-line argument other than "`-r`" or the file name is found, or if the "`-r`" argument is out of order, the program should display the invalid argument(s), provide a list of legal arguments, and shut down.

10.6. Write a method `caps` that searches for all of the words within a `String` and capitalizes the first letter of each word, while shifting the remainder of the word to lower case. Use `StringTokenizer` to identify each word, modifying the delimiter list to include punctuation (e.g., periods, commas, question marks, and exclamation marks), as well as the default delimiters. Then use `indexOf` to locate the position of that word in the string, and replace it by its capitalized equivalent.

10.7. **Input Parameter File** A common feature of large programs is an *input parameter file* in which the user can specify certain values to be used during the execution of the program. In most programs, default values are defined for the input parameters in the file, and *only the input parameters whose defaults need to be modified will be included in the input file*. Furthermore, the values that do appear in the input file may occur in any order. Each parameter in the input file is recognized by a corresponding *keyword* indicating what that parameter is for.

For example, a numerical integration program might include default values for the starting time of the integration, the ending time of the integration, the step size to use, and whether or not to plot the output. These default values could be overridden by lines in the input file. An input parameter file for this program might contain the following items:

```
start = 0.0
stop = 10.0
dt = 0.2
plot off
```

These values could be listed in any order, and some of them could be omitted if the default values are acceptable. In addition, the keywords might appear in uppercase, lowercase, or mixed case. The program will read this input file a line at a time, and update the variables specified by the keyword with the value on the line.

Write a class `TestFile` that tests reading an input parameter file. The class should include the following `private` instance variables, with the defaults as given in the following code block:

```
private double start = 0.0;
private double stop = 1.0;
private double dt = 0.1;
private boolean plot = false;
```

The class should also include a `main` method that reads the name of the input parameter file from the command line. It should read the file, and call a separate method to interpret each line, displaying the updated parameter values. The separate method should accept a `String` containing a line from the input parameter file, determine the keyboard on the line (regardless of case), and update the appropriate private instance variable. It should throw an exception if an unrecognized keyword is found.

Test your program using a variety of input files, containing keywords in various orders, in differing cases, and with invalid keywords added.

10.8. **Filters** Filters are programs the read input data from the standard input stream, process it in some fashion, and write it out to the standard output stream. Effectively, they filter the input data stream in some specified manner. Write a Java filter that reads lines of data as `String`s from the input stream, looks for and removes repeated words (tokens) from the lines and writes the lines out to the standard output stream. The program can use `StringTokenizer` to identify successive tokens. (Be sure the modify the `StringTokenizer` delimiter list so that it recognizes punctuation marks as a delimiter.) Test your filter on the following data:

```
Paris in the the Spring.
same same, Same same
123 123, 123 456
```

10.9. **Word Count** Write a program that reads input data from an input file and counts the number of words in the data set. Write the number of words to the standard output device. For these purposes, a word is defined as a set of characters separated by whitespace. (*Hint:* Use class `StringTokenizer`.)

10.10. Write a program that accepts a `String` containing an international telephone number of the form +55-555-555-5555, where the digits before the first dash are the country code, the digits between the first and second dashes are the city code (or area code), and the digits after the second dash are the phone number. Parse the string and print the country code, city code, and phone number separately with appropriate labels. (Note that international phone numbers can have anywhere from five to eight digits and may or may not have a dash in the middle of the number, so you can't design your program to work with fixed number of digits.) Test your program with the following phone numbers:

a. +1-800-555-1212

b. +61-3-9999-9999

c. +44-1289-555555

11

Introduction to Java Graphics

We will now begin our discussion of one of Java's most interesting and important features—its built-in device- and platform-independent graphics. Java's graphics system has evolved rapidly from Java Development Kit 1.0 through JDK 1.1 to JDK 1.2 (now renamed Java 2), expanding dramatically in terms of power, flexibility, and capability. This growth has been accomplished while maintaining backward compatibility with earlier versions of the graphics system, which has unfortunately resulted in a complex mishmash of old and new graphics classes and interfaces.

In this book, we will restrict ourselves to a small fraction of Java's graphics classes and methods, concentrating on only the most recent and capable techniques, which use the Java 2D geometry package and the Swing Graphical User Interface (GUI). The Java 2D geometry package is an improved set of classes for creating high-quality 2D graphics. It is the principal topic of this chapter. The Swing GUI is a new, more efficient, and more flexible graphical user-interface system that is the preferred way to create GUIs in Java 2. It will be discussed in detail beginning in the next chapter.

Note that if you are modifying older preexisting programs, you will need to consult other texts or the on-line JDK documentation for the details of how the earlier GUI and graphics systems worked.

SECTIONS

- 11.1 Containers and Components
- 11.2 Drawing Lines
- 11.3 Drawing Other Shapes
- 11.4 Displaying Text
- 11.5 The Affine Transform
- 11.6 XOR Mode
- Summary
- Key Terms

OBJECTIVES

After reading this chapter, you should be able to:

- Understand how to create and display Java graphics
- Draw lines, rectangles, rounded rectangles, ellipses, and arc
- Control the line style and color used to draw objects
- Fill objects with selected colors
- Create objects of arbitrary shape with `GeneralPath` objects
- Display text in various fonts
- Use affine transforms to shift, rotate, and skew graphics objects

TABLE 11-1 Selected Java GUI and Graphics Packages

JAVA API PACKAGE	EXPLANATION
`java.awt`	*The Abstract Windowing Toolkit (AWT) Package.* This package contains the classes and interfaces required to create graphical user interfaces. The term "abstract" is applied to this packages, because it can create GUI windows on any type of computer, regardless of the underlying operating system type.
`java.awt.datatransfer`	*The Java Data Transfer Package.* This package contains classes and interfaces that allow a program to transfer data between a Java program and a computer's clipboard (a temporary storage area used for cut and paste operations).
`java.awt.dnd`	*The Java Drag and Drop Package.* This package provides interfaces and classes for supporting drag-and-drop operations.
`java.awt.event`	*The Java AWT Event Package.* This package contains classes and interfaces that support event handling for GUI components.
`java.awt.font`	*The Java AWT Font Package.* This package contains classes and interfaces relating to fonts.
`java.awt.geom`	*The Java AWT Geometry Package.* Provides the Java 2D classes for defining and performing operations on objects related to two-dimensional geometry.
`java.awt.image`	*The Java AWT Image Package.* This package contains classes and interfaces that enable storing and manipulating images in a program.
`java.awt.peer`	*The Java AWT Peer Package.* This package contains interfaces that allow Java's GUI components to interact with their platform-specific versions. (For example, a button is actually implemented differently on a Macintosh than it is on a Windows or a unix based X-Windows machine.) This package should never be used directly by Java programmers.
`java.awt.print`	*The Java AWT Printing Package.* This package contains classes and interfaces that support a general-purpose printing API.
`javax.swing`	*The Swing Package.* This package contains many of the classes and interfaces required to support the newer Swing Graphical User Interface.

Java's graphics system can be found in the Abstract Windowing Toolkit (AWT) Package, the Swing Package, and in several subordinate packages, the most important of which are summarized in Table 11-1.

In this chapter, we will learn about the basic graphics concepts of a **container** and a **component** and then concentrate on learning how to draw graphical elements on the computer screen. In the following two chapters, we will expand on this beginning by learning how to create a Graphical User Interface (GUI), complete with buttons, sliders, text boxes, etc., that can respond to input from the keyboard or the mouse.

11.1 CONTAINERS AND COMPONENTS

Two of the most important graphics objects are components and containers. A **component** is a visual object containing text or graphics, which can respond to keyboard or mouse inputs. All Swing components are subclasses of class `javax.swing.JComponent`. Examples of components include buttons, labels, text boxes, check boxes, and lists. A completely blank component is known as a **canvas** (like an artist's canvas). A canvas can be used as a drawing area for text or graphics.[1] All components inherit a common set of methods, the most important of which is **paintComponent**. The paintComponent method causes a component to be drawn or re-drawn whenever it is called. This method is called automatically whenever a component is made visible, or in response to such actions as dragging or resizing with a mouse.

A **container** is a graphical object that can hold components or other containers. The most important type of container is a **frame**, which is an area of the computer screen surrounded by borders and a title bar. Frames are implemented by class javax.swing. JFrame. The inheritance hierarchy of these classes is shown in Figure 11.1.

11.1.1 Creating and Displaying a Frame and a Canvas

The basic steps required to display graphics in Java are as follows:

1. Create the component or components to display.
2. Create a frame to hold the component(s), and place the component(s) into the frame(s).
3. Create a listener object to detect and respond to mouse clicks, and assign the listener to the frame.

In this chapter, the only container that we will use is JFrame, and the only component that we will use is a JCanvas or a subclass of JCanvas. Additional components will be

Figure 11.1. A portion of the graphics class inheritance hierarchy, showing the classes JCanvas and JFrame.

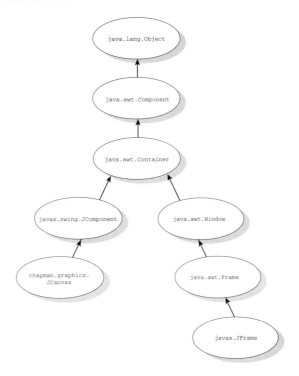

---

[1] There is a standard Canvas class in the older Java AWT GUI, but there is no equivalent JCanvas class in the Swing GUI. The chapman.graphics package includes a JCanvas class, and we will use that class to create all of the graphical examples in this chapter.

introduced in Chapters 12 and 13. The listener object will monitor the mouse, and respond if a click occurs while the cursor is pointing at the frame. The listener is very important, because without it we could never close a frame once it is created.

Figure 11.2 shows a simple program that displays the basic skeleton required to create Java graphics. This program creates a new blank yellow JCanvas, creates a new JFrame, places the canvas within the frame, and displays the frame on the computer's display. It also includes a listener to respond to mouse clicks.

```
1    import java.awt.*;
2    import java.awt.event.*;
3    import javax.swing.*;
4    import chapman.graphics.JCanvas;
5    public class TestJCanvas {
6
7        // This method illustrates how to create graphics in Java.
8        // It creates a new JFrame, attaches a blank JCanvas to it,
9        // and makes the frame and canvas visible on the screen.
10       public static void main(String s[]) {
11
12           // Create a Window Listener to handle "close" events
13           MyWindowListener l = new MyWindowListener();
14
15           // Create a blank yellow JCanvas
16           JCanvas c = new JCanvas();
17           c.setBackground( Color.yellow );
18
19           // Create a frame and place the canvas in thecenter
20           // of the frame.
21           JFrame f = new JFrame("Test JCanvas ...");
22           f.addWindowListener(l);
23           f.add(c, BorderLayout.CENTER);
24           f.setSize(400,400);
25           f.setVisible(true);
26       }
27   }
```

```
1
2    class MyWindowListener extends WindowAdapter {
3
4        // This method implements a simple listener that detects
5        // the "window closing event" and stops the program.
6        public void windowClosing(WindowEvent e) {
7            System.exit(0);
8        };
9    }
```

Figure 11.2. A program that creates a frame, places a blank canvas within the frame, and displays the result. This is the basic core structure required to display Java graphics.

Lines 16 and 17 of this program create a new JCanvas, which is the component on which graphics output will be drawn. The background color of the canvas is set to yellow. Line 21 creates a new JFrame, and sets its title bar to display the words "Test JCanvas ...". Line 23 adds the JCanvas to the center of the frame. The statement "f.set-Size(400,400)" sets the size of the frame in pixels, with the first number being the width and the second number being the height of the frame. Finally, the statement "f.setVisible(true)" makes the frame visible on your computer screen.

Line 13 creates a MyWindowListener object, whose job is to listen for mouse clicks within the frame, and to perform an action if such a mouse click

Figure 11.3. The output of program `TestCanvas`. It consists of a 400 × 400 pixel frame containing a blank yellow canvas.

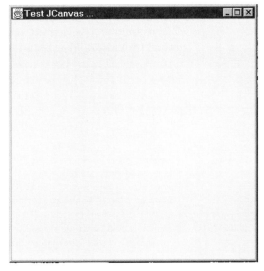

occurs. The definition of the `MyWindowListener` class appears at the bottom of the figure. Such listener classes will be discussed in Chapter 12. In this case, the class listens for a mouse click in the "close window" box of the frame and closes the frame when the click is detected. Line 22 adds this listener to the `JFrame`, so that it will monitor mouse clicks that happen within the frame.

When this program is executed, the result is a frame with a blank yellow canvas, as shown in Figure 11.3. Note that a mouse click in the "close window" box will close the frame, because the listener executes the statement "`System.exit(0)`" when the mouse click occurs.

GOOD PROGRAMMING PRACTICE

To display Java graphics:

1. Create a component or components to display.
2. Create a `JFrame` to hold the component(s), and place the component(s) into the frame.
3. Create a "listener" object to detect and respond to mouse clicks, and assign the listener to the `JFrame`.

11.1.2 How to Display Graphics on a Canvas

Every Swing component has a special **`paintComponent` method** associated with it. When this method is called, the component issues graphics commands to draw or redraw itself. By default, the `paintComponent` method of a `JCanvas` sets the background color and exits without doing anything useful. The way to create useful graphics is to create a *subclass* of `JCanvas` and then override the `paintComponent` method in the subclass to display the data you are interested in.

The `paintComponent` method always has the calling sequence

```
public void paintComponent ( Graphics g );
```

where g is a reference to the java.awt.Graphics object used to draw lines, figures, text, etc. To use the modern Java graphics features, this Graphics object must be immediately downcast to a java.awt.Graphics2D object, and then all of the tools in the java.awt.geom package can be applied to draw graphics on the screen.[2]

A sample class that extends JCanvas and draws a single line on a white background is shown in Figure 11.4, together with the resulting output. Note that this class immediately casts the Graphics reference to a Graphics2D reference and uses that reference to draw the line on the screen. Also note that the class imports package java.awt.geom. All of Java's 2D drawing tools are in this package, so you must always import it into your graphics programs.

```java
import java.awt.*;
import java.awt.event.*;
import java.awt.geom.*;
import javax.swing.*;
import chapman.graphics.JCanvas;
public class DrawLine extends JCanvas {

    // This method extends JCanvas and draws a line on the canvas.
    public void paintComponent ( Graphics g ) {

        // Cast the graphics object to Graph2D
        Graphics2D g2 = (Graphics2D) g;

        // Set background color
        Dimension size = getSize();
        g2.setColor( Color.white );
        g2.fill(new Rectangle2D.Double(0,0,size.width, size.height));

        // Draw line
        g.setColor( Color.black );
        Line2D line = new Line2D.Double (10., 10., 360., 360.);
        g2.draw(line);
    }

    public static void main(String s[]) {

        // Create a Window Listener to handle "close" events
        MyWindowListener l = new MyWindowListener();

        // Create a DrawLine object
        DrawLine c = new DrawLine();

        // Create a frame and place the object in the center
        // of the frame.
        JFrame f = new JFrame("Test Line ...");
        f.addWindowListener(l);
        f.getContentPane().add(c, BorderLayout.CENTER);
        f.setSize(400,400);
        f.setVisible( true );
    }
}
```

Figure 11.4. (a) Class DrawLine extends JCanvas and draws a single line on a white background.

---

[2] This rather silly business of forcing every paintComponent method to accept a Graphics object and immediately casting it to a Graphics2D object is for backward compatibility with earlier versions of Java. The first JDK had rather primitive graphics and only supported Graphics objects—if the paintComponent method were changed to pass the new Graphics2D objects as parameters, all of those older programs would no longer work.

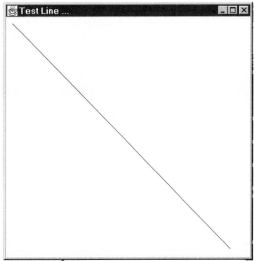

Figure 11.4. *(b)* The output produced by class `DrawLine`.

11.1.3 The Graphics Coordinate System

Java employs a coordinate system whose origin is in the upper left hand corner of the screen, with positive *x* values to the right and positive *y* values down. (See Figure 11.5.) By default, the units of the coordinate system are **pixels,** with 72 pixels to an inch. However, we shall see later that this mapping can be changed.

Figure 11.5.   The graphics coordinate system begins in the upper left-hand corner of the dis play device, with the *x*-axis extending horizontally and the *y*-axis extending downward.

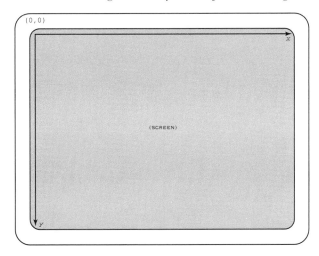

In class `DrawLine`, we drew a line from (10,10) to (360,360). The resulting line extended from the upper left-hand corner of the `JCanvas` (10,10) to the lower right-hand corner of the `JCanvas` (360,360).

11.2 DRAWING LINES

In this section, we will learn how to draw lines on a graphics device. In the process of doing so, we will learn about controlling line color, line width, and line style, all of which will apply to other shapes as well. Finally, we will learn how to eliminate jagged edges from lines using Java's antialiasing technology.

11.2.1 Drawing Simple Lines

The basic class used to draw a line in Java is **`java.awt.geom.Line2D`**. This is an abstract class with two concrete subclasses: `Line2D.Double` and `Line2D.Float`. The only difference between these two classes is that one expects `double` input parameters, while the other expects `float` input parameters.

The most common constructors for a `Line2D` object have the form

```
Line2D.Double( double x1, double y1, double x2, double y2 )
Line2D.Float( float x1, float y1, float x2, float y2 )
```

where the line is defined from point (x_1, y_1) to point (x_2, y_2) on the display. Once a line object is created, the actual line can be drawn by calling the `Graphics2D` draw method with a reference to the line object. For example, the following statements create a line going from (10,10) to (360,360) and draw the line on the current graphics object, as we saw in Figure 11.4:

```
Line2D line = new Line2D.Double (10., 10., 360., 360.);
g2.draw(line);
```

11.2.2 Controlling Line Color, Width, and Style

The color, width, and style of any line (or any other Java2D object) may be easily controlled. The color of a line is set by a call to the `Graphics2D` method **`setColor`**. The form of this method call is

```
g2.setColor(color)
```

where `color` is any object of class `java.awt.Color`. This class includes many predefined color constants (see Table 11-2), and you can also create your own custom colors. (To create your own custom colors, use the methods in class `java.awt.Color`. They are described in the JDK on-line documentation.)

The width, style, and ends of a line are controlled by a special class called **`java.awt.BasicStroke`**. This class defines four basic attributes of lines:

- Line width in pixels
- The shape of line end caps

TABLE 11-2 Predefined Java Colors

Color.black	Color.magneta
Color.blue	Color.orange
Color.cyan	Color.pink
Color.darkGray	Color.red
Color.green	Color.white
Color.lightGray	Color.yellow

TABLE 11-3 BasicStroke Parameters

PARAMETER	DESCRIPTION
width	A float value representing the width of the line in pixels.
cap	An int value representing the type of caps to draw on the ends of the lines. Possible choices are CAP_BUTT, CAP_SQUARE (default), and CAP_ROUND.
join	An int value representing the connection to be made between line segments. Possible choices are JOIN_BEVEL, JOIN_MITER (default), and JOIN_ROUND.
dash	A float array representing the dashing pattern in pixels. Even-numbered ([0], [2], ...) elements in the array represent the lengths of visible segments, in pixels, and odd-numbered ([1], [3], ...) elements in the array represent the lengths of transparent segments, in pixels.
dashPhase	A float value containing the offset in pixels at which to start the dash pattern.

- The shape of decorations where two line segments meet
- The style of the line (solid, dashed, dotted, etc.)

The two most common constructors for a `BasicStroke` object have the following form:

```
BasicStroke(float width);
BasicStroke(float width, int cap, int join, float miterlimit,
        float[] dash, float dashPhase);
```

The meanings of these parameters are listed in Table 11-3.

The program in Figure 11.6 illustrates the use of these features to control the way a line is displayed. This program creates and displays two lines. The first line is red, solid, and 2 pixels wide, while the second line is blue, dashed, and 4 pixels wide.

```
import java.awt.*;
import java.awt.event.*;
import java.awt.geom.*;
import javax.swing.*;
import chapman.graphics.JCanvas;
public class DrawLine2 extends JCanvas {

    // This method draws two lines with color and styles.
    public void paintComponent ( Graphics g ) {

        BasicStroke bs;                    // Ref to BasicStroke
        Line2D line;                       // Ref to line
        float[] solid = {12.0f,0.0f};      // Solid line style
        float[] dashed = {12.0f,12.0f};    // Dashed line style

        // Cast the graphics object to Graph2D
        Graphics2D g2 = (Graphics2D) g;

        // Set background color
        Dimension size = getSize();
        g2.setColor( Color.white );
        g2.fill(new Rectangle2D.Double(0,0,size.width,size.height));

        // Set the Color and BasicStroke
        g2.setColor(Color.red);
        bs = new BasicStroke( 2.0f, BasicStroke.CAP_SQUARE,
                              BasicStroke.JOIN_MITER, 1.0f,
                              solid, 0.0f );
        g2.setStroke(bs);
```

Figure 11.6. *(cont.)*

```
                        // Draw line
                        line = new Line2D.Double (10., 10., 360., 360.);
                        g2.draw(line);

                         // Set the Color and BasicStroke
                        g2.setColor(Color.blue);
                        bs = new BasicStroke( 4.0f, BasicStroke.CAP_SQUARE,
                                              BasicStroke.JOIN_MITER, 1.0f,
                                              dashed, 0.0f );
                        g2.setStroke(bs);

                        // Draw line
                        line = new Line2D.Double (10., 300., 360., 10.);
                        g2.draw(line);
                    }

                    public static void main(String s[]) {

                        // Create a Window Listener to handle "close" events
                        MyWindowListener l = new MyWindowListener();

                        // Create a DrawLine2 object
                        DrawLine2 c = new DrawLine2();

                        // Create a frame and place the object in the center
                        // of the frame.
                        JFrame f = new JFrame("DrawLine2 ...");
                        f.addWindowListener(l);
                        f.getContentPane().add(c, BorderLayout.CENTER);
                        f.setSize(400,400);
                        f.setVisible(true);
                    }
```

Figure 11.6. (*a*) Class DrawLine2.

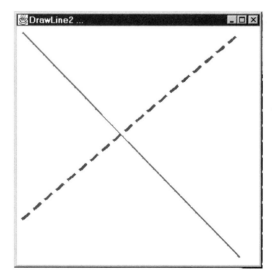

Figure 11.6. (*b*) The output created by class DrawLine2.

PROFESSIONAL SUCCESS: DESIGNING EFFECTIVE GRAPHICS FOR PRINTING

The `BasicStroke` class allows a programmer to customize the color and linestyle of Java 2D objects such as lines, rectangles, and other shapes. This flexibility allows a programmer to display multiple types of data on a single plot, while keep the data items distinct from each other.

When a novice programmer first starts creating graphics with this flexibility, there is a tendency to rely heavily on color to distinguish the many lines on the graph. Unfortunately, color is usually not preserved when a graph is printed, so a display that is very effective on the computer screen may appear confusing when printed on a monochrome printer.

As a programmer, you should always consider both the display on a screen and the printed out version of the display when designing your graphics. Use combinations of color, linestyle, and line width to distinguish your lines, so that they will still appear different when printed on a monochrome printer.

11.2.3 Eliminating Jagged Edges From Lines

If you look closely at the lines drawn in Figure 11.6, you may notice that the edges of the lines have a slightly jagged appearance. This jaggedness happens because the canvas on which the lines are drawn has only a finite number of pixels, and each pixel is either fully on or off. When a line jumps over by one pixel, the jump can leave a rough edge.

Java graphics includes a special technology know as **antialiasing** to eliminate these rough edges. When it is turned on, it allows pixels at the edges of the line to be partially on or off, causing the edge of the line to appear smooth to a human observer. This technology is controlled by a `Graphics2D` method called `setRendering-Hints`. The command to turn on antialiasing is the following:

```
// Set rendering hints to improve display quality
g2.setRenderingHint(RenderingHints.KEY_ANTIALIASING,
                    RenderingHints.VALUE_ANTIALIAS_ON);
```

When this command is included in the `paintComponent` method of class `DrawLine2`, the results are as shown Figure 11.7. Note how much smoother and cleaner the lines appear to be in that figure compared to Figure 11.6.

GOOD PROGRAMMING PRACTICE

To draw lines in Java:

1. Select a line color using the Graphics2D `setColor` method.
2. Select a line width and line style using a `BasicStroke` object, and associate that basic stroke with the line using the Graphics2D `setBasicStroke` method.
3. Set the endpoints of the line using a `Line2D.Double` or `Line2D.Float` method, and draw the line with a call to the Graphics2D `draw` method.

Figure 11.7. The output of program `DrawLine2` with antialiasing turned on. Note how much smoother the edges of the lines are here compared to Figure 11.6.

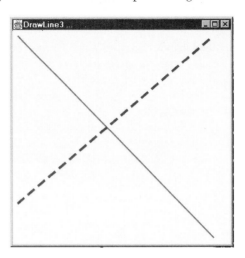

GOOD PROGRAMMING PRACTICE

Eliminate jagged edges from your lines by turning on antialiasing with the Graphics2D method `setRenderingHints`.

**EXAMPLE 11-1:
PLOTTING THE
FUNCTION
SIN θ**

The `Line2D.Double` class can be used to plot curves of arbitrary shape by breaking each curve into small, straight line segments, and plotting each segment separately. To illustrate this operation, we will create a plot of the function sin θ over the range $0 \leq \theta \leq 2\pi$. The plotted curve should be a solid blue line four pixels wide. Use antialiasing to smooth the edges of the curve.

SOLUTION

To create an overall sinusoidal shape, we will divide this curve into 40 separate line segments and plot each segment separately. The code required to generate the 41 points bounding the 40 line segments is

```
double theta[] = new double[41];
double sin[] = new double[41];
delta = 2 * Math.PI / 40;
for ( i = 0; i < theta.length; i++ ) {
   theta[i] = delta * i;
   sin[i] = Math.sin(theta[i]);
}
```

Once we have the ends of the line segments, it is necessary to plot them in the space provided. If we assume that the space available for the plot is about 380 × 380 pixels, then the range of possible values of θ must be mapped into 380 horizontal pixels, and the range of possible values of sin θ must be mapped into about 360 vertical pixels (the extra 20 vertical pixels allows space for the title bar at the top of the frame). The range of θ is $0 \leq \theta \leq 2\pi$, so $\theta = 0$ should correspond to pixel 0, and $\theta = 2\pi$ should correspond to pixel 380. A suitable mapping function would be the following:

$$xpos = \left(\frac{380}{2\pi}\right)\theta = \left(\frac{190}{\pi}\right)\theta \qquad (11\text{-}1)$$

Similarly, the range of possible value of $\sin\theta$ is $-1 \leq \sin\theta \leq 1$, so the 360 vertical pixels must be mapped to that range. The y-axis mapping is trickier, though, because y values *start at zero at the top of the display and increase downward.* To make the plot come out right, we must make $y = -1$ correspond to pixel 360, and $y = +1$ correspond to pixel 0. A suitable mapping function would be

$$ypos = 180 - 180\sin\theta. \qquad (11\text{-}2)$$

Note that this function produces 0 when $\sin\theta = 1$, and 360 when $\sin\theta = -1$. The code required to apply these mappings to the function can be displayed is:

```
for ( i = 0; i < theta.length; i++ ) {
    theta[i] = (190/Math.PI) * theta[i];
    sin[i] = 180 - 180 * sin[i];
}
```

Finally, the code required to plot the 40 line segments is:

```
for ( i = 0; i < theta.length-1; i++ ) {
    line = new Line2D.Double (theta[i], sin[i],
                              theta[i+1], sin[i+1]);
    g2.draw(line);
}
```

The paintComponent method required to generate this curve is shown in Figure 11.8. The rest of the program is not shown, because it is essentially the same as the previous two programs.

```
// This method plots one cycle of a sine wave.
public void paintComponent ( Graphics g ) {

    BasicStroke bs;                        // Ref to BasicStroke
    double delta;                          // Step between points
    int i;                                 // Loop index
    Line2D line;                           // Ref to line
    double sin[] = new double[41];         // sin(theta)
    float[] solid = {12.0f,0.0f};          // Solid line style
    double theta[] = new double[41];       // Angles in radians

    // Cast the graphics object to Graph2D
    Graphics2D g2 = (Graphics2D) g;

    // Set rendering hints to improve display quality
    g2.setRenderingHint(RenderingHints.KEY_ANTIALIASING,
                        RenderingHints.VALUE_ANTIALIAS_ON);

    // Set background color
    Dimension size = getSize();
    g2.setColor( Color.white );
    g2.fill(new Rectangle2D.Double(0,0,size.width,size.height));
```

Figure 11.8. *(cont.)*

```
      // Set the Color and BasicStroke
      g2.setColor(Color.blue);
      bs = new BasicStroke( 4.0f, BasicStroke.CAP_SQUARE,
                            BasicStroke.JOIN_MITER, 1.0f,
                            solid, 0.0f );
      g2.setStroke(bs);
      // Calculate points on curve
      delta = 2 * Math.PI / 40;
      for ( i = 0; i < theta.length; i++ ) {
         theta[i] = delta * i;
         sin[i] = Math.sin(theta[i]);
      }
      // Translate curve position to pixels
      for ( i = 0; i < theta.length; i++ ) {
         theta[i] = (190/Math.PI) * theta[i];
         sin[i] = 180 - 180 * sin[i];
      }

      // Plot curve
      for ( i = 0; i < theta.length-1; i++ ) {
         line = new Line2D.Double (theta[i], sin[i],
                                   theta[i+1], sin[i+1]);
         g2.draw(line);
      }
   }
```

Figure 11.8. The `paintComponent` method from a program to plot the function
$\sin \theta$ for $0 \leq \theta \leq 2\pi$

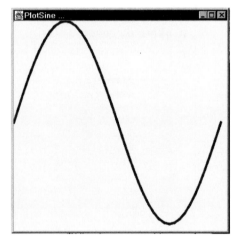

Figure 11.9. The output of program `PlotSine`

When this program is executed, the results are as shown in Figure 11.9.

EXAMPLE 11-2:
AUTOMATIC
SCALING OF
PLOTS

The program in Example 11-1 contains a serious flaw. Note that we designed the plot to occupy a space of 380 × 360 pixels. What would happen to this plot if we changed the size of the frame it was plotted in? For example, suppose that we used the mouse to make the frame larger or smaller. What would we see? If the frame is made smaller, then only a portion of the curve will be displayed. If the frame is made larger, then the curve will only occupy a portion of the available space. These problems are illustrated in Figure 11.10.

What we need is a way to determine the size of the canvas that we a plotting on, so that the plot can automatically re-scale whenever the size changes. Fortunately, every Java `Component` includes a method **`getSize()`** to recover the size of the `Component`. Since `JCanvas` is a subclass of `Component`, it automatically inherits the `getSize()` method.

The method `getSize()` is used as follows:

```
Dimension size = getSize();
```

This method returns a `Dimension` object, which has two `public` instance variables `height` and `width`. Thus the height of the component in pixels will be `size.height` and the width of the component in pixels will be `size.width`.

We can use this information to create a `paintComponent` method that automatically re-sizes whenever its container re-sizes by changing the mappings to be

$$xpos = \left(\frac{\texttt{size.width}}{2\pi}\right)\theta \tag{11-3}$$

and

$$ypos = \frac{\texttt{size.height}}{2} - \frac{\texttt{size.height}}{2}\sin\theta \tag{11-4}$$

Figure 11.10.   When the frame containing the sinusoidal plot is resized, the plot does not change size to match: (a) small frame, (b) large frame.

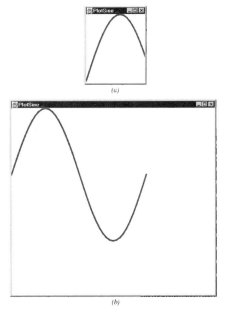

```java
// This method plots one cycle of a sine wave.
public void paintComponent ( Graphics g ) {

    BasicStroke bs;                    // Ref to BasicStroke
    double delta;                      // Step between points
    int i;                             // Loop index
    Line2D line;                       // Ref to line
    double sin[] = new double[41];     // sin(theta)
    float[] solid = {12.0f,0.0f};      // Solid line style
    double theta[] = new double[41];   // Angles in radians

    // Cast the graphics object to Graph2D
    Graphics2D g2 = (Graphics2D) g;

    // Set rendering hints to improve display quality
    g2.setRenderingHint(RenderingHints.KEY_ANTIALIASING,
                        RenderingHints.VALUE_ANTIALIAS_ON);

    // Get plot size
    Dimension size = getSize();

    // Set background color
    g2.setColor( Color.white );
    g2.fill(new Rectangle2D.Double
    (0,0,size.width,size.height));

    // Set the Color and BasicStroke
    g2.setColor(Color.blue);
    bs = new BasicStroke( 4.0f, BasicStroke.CAP_SQUARE,
                        BasicStroke.JOIN_MITER, 1.0f,
                        solid, 0.0f );

    g2.setStroke(bs);

    // Calculate points on curve
    delta = 2 * Math.PI / 40;
    for ( i = 0; i < theta.length; i++ ) {
        theta[i] = delta * i;
        sin[i] = Math.sin(theta[i]);
    }

    // Translate curve position to pixels
    for ( i = 0; i < theta.length; i++ ) {
        theta[i] = (size.width/(2*Math.PI)) * theta[i];
        sin[i] = size.height/2 - size.height/2 * sin[i];
    }

    // Plot curve
    for ( i = 0; i < theta.length-1; i++ ) {
        line = new Line2D.Double (theta[i], sin[i],
                                theta[i+1], sin[i+1]);
        g2.draw(line);
    }
}
```

Figure 11.11. The `paintComponent` method to plot sin θ with automatic re-sizing

The `paintComponent` method with automatic resizing is shown in Figure 11.11.

Execute this program and re-size its frame with a mouse. Notice how the plot changes size to take advantage of the available space.

11.3 DRAWING OTHER SHAPES

The `java.awt.geom` package includes classes to draw several other shapes, including rectangles, rounded rectangles, ellipses, arcs, and quadratic and cubic curves. All of these shapes function in a manner basically similar to the `Line2D` class that we saw in the previous section. They all use the same techniques to set color, line width, and line style, so we already know most of what we need to know to use them.

11.3.1 Rectangles

The basic class used to draw a rectangle is **`java.awt.geom.Rectangle2D`**. This is an abstract class with two concrete subclasses: `Rectangle2D.Double` and `Rectangle2D.Float`. The only difference between these two classes is that one expects `double` input parameters and the other expects `float` input parameters.

The most common constructors for a `Rectangle2D` object have the form

```
Rectangle2D.Double( double x, double y, double w, double h )
Rectangle2D.Float( float x, float y, float w, float h )
```

where the upper left-hand corner of the rectangle is a point (x,y), and the rectangle is w pixels wide and h pixels high. For example, the following statements create a rectangle starting at position (30,40) that is 200 pixels wide and 150 pixels high and draw the rectangle on the current graphics device:

```
Rectangle2D rect = new Rectangle2D.Double (30., 40., 200., 150.);
g2.draw(rect);
```

Unlike a line, a rectangle is a closed shape that has an interior and a border. The method `g2.draw(rect)` draws the *border* of the rectangle, but leaves the interior empty. It is also possible to fill the interior of a rectangle with the `Graphics2D` method `fill`. For example, the following statements create a 200 × 150 rectangle object, fill its interior with yellow, and draw a black border around it.

```
bs = new BasicStroke( 3.0f, BasicStroke.CAP_SQUARE,
                      BasicStroke.JOIN_MITER, 1.0f,
                      solid, 0.0f );
g2.setStroke(bs);
Rectangle2D rect = new Rectangle2D.Double (30., 40., 200., 150.);
g2.setColor(Color.yellow);
g2.fill(rect);
g2.setColor(Color.black);
g2.draw(rect);
```

The resulting shape is shown in Figure 11.12.

GOOD PROGRAMMING PRACTICE

Use the `Rectangle2D` classes to create rectangles.

Figure 11.12. A yellow rectangle with a black border.

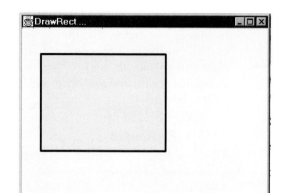

11.3.2 Rounded Rectangles

The class used to draw a rectangle with rounded corners is **java.awt.geom. RoundRectangle2D**. This is an abstract class with two concrete subclasses: RoundRectangle2D.Double and RoundRectangle2D.Float. The only difference between these two classes is that one expects double input parameters, while the other expects float input parameters.

The simplest constructor for a RoundRectangle2D object has the form

```
RoundRectangle2D.Double( double x, double y, double w,
                         double h, double arcw, double arch )
RoundRectangle2D.Float( float x, float y, float w, float h,
                        float arcw, float arch )
```

where the upper left-hand corner of the rectangle is a point (x,y), and the rectangle is w pixels wide and h pixels high. The values arcw and arch specify the width and height, respectively, of the arcs that round off the corners of the rectangle. For example, the following statements create a rounded rectangle starting at position (30,40) that is 200 pixels wide and 150 pixels high, with 40-pixel-wide arcs at the corners:

```
RoundRectangle2D rect
rect = new RoundRectangle2D.Double(30.,40.,200.,150.,40.,40.);
g2.draw(rect);
```

Similarly, the following statements create a 200 × 150 rounded rectangle object with 40-pixel arcs in both height and width, fill its interior with pink, and draw a dashed black border around it:

```
bs = new BasicStroke( 3.0f, BasicStroke.CAP_SQUARE,
                      BasicStroke.JOIN_MITER, 1.0f,
                      dashed, 0.0f );
g2.setStroke(bs);
RoundRectangle2D rect = new RoundRectangle2D.Double
               (30., 40., 200., 150., 40., 40.);
g2.setColor(Color.pink);
g2.fill(rect);
g2.setColor(Color.black);
g2.draw(rect);
```

Figure 11.13. A pink rounded rectangle with a dashed black border.

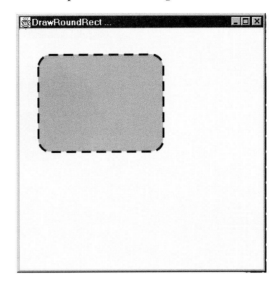

The resulting shape is shown in Figure 11.13.

11.3.3 Ellipses

The class used to draw circles and ellipses is **java.awt.geom.Ellipse2D**. This is an abstract class with two concrete subclasses: Ellipse2D.Double and Ellipse2D.Float. The only difference between these two classes is that one expects double input parameters, while the other expects float input parameters.

The constructor for an Ellipse2D object has the form

```
Ellipse2D.Double( double x, double y, double w, double h);
Ellipse2D.Float( float x, float y, float w, float h);
```

where the upper left-hand corner of the rectangular box in which the ellipse is drawn is point (x,y), and the ellipse is w pixels wide and h pixels high. Note that if w and h are equal, this class draws a circle. For example, the following statements create an ellipse starting at position (30,40) that is 200 pixels wide and 150 pixels high:

```
Ellipse2D ell
ell = new Ellipse2D.Double (30.,40.,200.,150.);
g2.draw(ell);
```

Similarly, the following statements create a 200 × 150 ellipse object and fill its interior with black:

```
Ellipse2D rect = new Ellipse2D.Double (30., 40., 200., 150.);
g2.setColor(Color.black);
g2.fill(rect);
```

Figure 11.14. An ellipse.

The resulting shape is shown in Figure 11.14.

11.3.4 Arcs

An *arc* is a portion of an ellipse. An arc is drawn from a *starting angle* and covers an *extent*, both of which are given in degrees. The starting angle is the angle at which the arc begins, and the extent is the is the number of degrees covered by the arc. For this purpose, angles are defined as they are on a Cartesian coordinate plane, positive counterclockwise from the positive *x*-axis. (See Figure 11.15) Arcs with a positive extent sweep clockwise from the starting angle, while arcs with a negative extent sweep counterclockwise from the starting angle.

The class used to draw arcs is **Arc2D**. This is an abstract class with two concrete subclasses: `Arc2D.Double` and `Arc2D.Float`. The only difference between these two classes is that one expects `double` input parameters, while the other expects `float` input parameters. The constructors for `Arc2D` objects have the form

```
Arc2D.Double( double x, double y, double w, double h,
              double start, double extent, int type );
Arc2D.Float( float x, float y, float w, float h,
             float start, float extent, int type );
```

where the upper left-hand corner of the rectangular box in which the arc is drawn is point (x,y) and the arc is w pixels wide and h pixels high. The starting angle of the arc is `start` degrees, measured counterclockwise from the positive *x*-axis, and the extent of

Figure 11.15. Arc starting angles are measured in degrees from the positive *x*-axis, and are considered to be positive counterclockwise. Arc extents are positive if they are counterclockwise, and negative if they are clockwise.

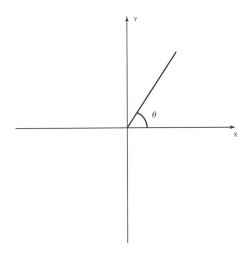

the arc is extent degrees. Finally, type is the closure type for the arc. There are three possible closure types: Arc2D.OPEN, Arc2D.CHORD, and Arc2D.PIE. The Arc2D.OPEN type leaves the end of the arc open, while the Arc2D.CHORD type connects the ends with a straight line, and the Arc2D.PIE type connects the end with a pie slice.

For example, the following statements create an ellipse starting at position (30,40) that is 200 pixels wide and 150 pixels high. The starting angle is 0°, and the extent is 90°. The closure type for this arc is Arc2D.OPEN.

```
Arc2D arc = new Arc2D.Double (30.,40.,200.,150.,
                              0., 90., Arc2D.OPEN);
g2.draw(arc);
```

It is also possible to fill an arc with the fill method.

Figure 11.16 shows the paintComponent method of a program that illustrates more of the arc options. This method creates four arcs with various combinations of starting angles, extents, fills, and closures.

The resulting arcs are shown in Figure 11.17.

GOOD PROGRAMMING PRACTICE

Use the Arc2D classes to create elliptical and circular arcs.

PROGRAMMING PITFALLS

The angles in class Arc2D are given in *degrees*, while the angles in almost every other Java class are given in *radians*. Be careful not to confuse the angle units when using Arc2D.

```java
// This method draws several arcs with different options.
public void paintComponent ( Graphics g ) {

    BasicStroke bs;                      // Ref to BasicStroke
    Arc2D.Double arc;                    // Ref to arc
    float[] solid = {12.0f,0.0f};        // Solid line style

    // Cast the graphics object to Graph2D
    Graphics2D g2 = (Graphics2D) g;

    // Set rendering hints to improve display quality
    g2.setRenderingHint(RenderingHints.KEY_ANTIALIASING,
                        RenderingHints.VALUE_ANTIALIAS_ON);

    // Set background color
    Dimension size = getSize();
    g2.setColor( Color.white );
    g2.fill(new Rectangle2D.Double(0,0,size.width,size.height));

    // Set the basic stroke
    bs = new BasicStroke( 3.0f, BasicStroke.CAP_SQUARE,
                        BasicStroke.JOIN_MITER, 1.0f,
                        solid, 0.0f );
    g2.setStroke(bs);

    // Define arc1
    arc = new Arc2D.Double (20., 40., 100., 150.,
                        0., 60., Arc2D.PIE);

    g2.setColor(Color.yellow);
    g2.fill(arc);
    g2.setColor(Color.black);
    g2.draw(arc);

    // Define arc2
    arc = new Arc2D.Double (10., 200., 100., 100.,
                        90., 180., Arc2D.CHORD);
    g2.setColor(Color.black);
    g2.draw(arc);

    // Define arc3
    arc = new Arc2D.Double (220., 10., 80., 200.,
                        0., 120., Arc2D.OPEN);
    g2.setColor(Color.lightGray);
    g2.fill(arc);
    g2.setColor(Color.black);
    g2.draw(arc);

    // Define arc4
    arc = new Arc2D.Double (220., 220., 100., 100.,
                        -30., -300., Arc2D.PIE);
    g2.setColor(Color.orange);
    g2.fill(arc);
}
```

Figure 11.16. A paintComponent method to draw four arcs

Figure 11.17. Miscellaneous arcs created with `Arc2D`.

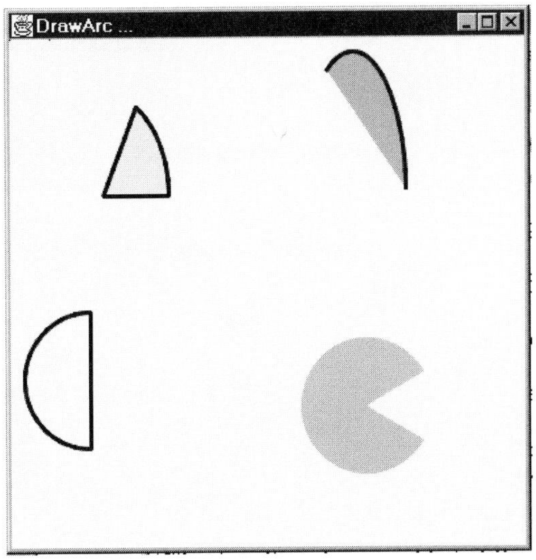

11.3.5 General Paths

In addition to the specific shapes described above, Java includes a **java.awt.geom. GeneralPath** class to allow the construction of completely arbitrary shapes. This class is much more complex than the shapes we have examined so far, but it is very powerful and deserves careful attention.

The most common constructor for a `GeneralPath` object has the form

```
GeneralPath();
```

Once a `GeneralPath` object has been created, a programmer can add as many points to the object as he or she wishes, and the points may optionally be connected by straight lines or curves. Table 11-4 contains a summary of the more important methods associated with this class.

As a simple example, suppose that we want to construct an equilateral triangle. The statements required to construct and plot an equilateral triangle with vertices at (100,300), (300,300), and (200,127) are as follows:

TABLE 11-4   `GeneralPath` Methods

METHOD	DESCRIPTION
`closePath()`	Closes the current subpath by drawing a straight line from the current point back to the last `moveTo` position.
`curveTo(float x1, float y1, float x2, float y2,` `    float x3, float y3);`	Adds a point to the path by drawing a Bezier curve from the current point through (x_1,y_1) and (x_2,y_2) to (x_3,y_3).
`lineTo(float x,float y);`	Adds a point to the path by drawing a straight line from the current coordinates to the newly specified coordinates.
`moveTo(float x,float y);`	Adds a point to the path by moving to the specified coordinates *without drawing a line*.
`quadTo(float x1,float y1, float x2, float y2);`	Adds a point to the path by drawing a quadratic curve from the current point through (x_1,y_1) to (x_2, y_2).
`setWindingRule(int rule);`	Sets a winding rule to determine the interior regions of the path. The options are `WIND_NON_ZERO` (default) or `WIND_EVEN_ODD`.

Figure 11.18.   A equalilateral triangle created with a `GeneralPath`.

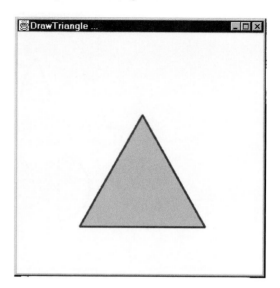

```
GeneralPath p = new GeneralPath();
p.moveTo(100.0f,300.0f);
p.lineTo(300.0f,300.0f);
p.lineTo(200.0f,127.0f);
p.closePath();
g2.setColor( Color.lightGray );
g2.fill(p);
g2.setColor( Color.blue );
g2.draw(p);
```

The resulting shape is shown in Figure 11.18. Note that `GeneralPath` methods work with `float` parameters, not `double`. Be sure to cast any `double` values to `float` before using them to construct a `GeneralPath`.

It is possible for a single `GeneralPath` to create multiple overlapping closed paths by using multiple `moveTo` methods. For example, the following statements produce two overlapping equilateral triangles:

```
GeneralPath p = new GeneralPath();

// First triangle
p.moveTo( 50.0f,300.0f);
p.lineTo(250.0f,300.0f);
p.lineTo(150.0f,127.0f);
p.closePath();

// Second triangle
p.moveTo(150.0f,250.0f);
p.lineTo(350.0f,250.0f);
p.lineTo(250.0f, 77.0f);
p.closePath();

g2.setColor( Color.lightGray );
g2.fill(p);
g2.setColor( Color.black );
g2.draw(p);
```

The resulting overlapping triangles are shown in Figure 11.19.

Figure 11.19. Two overlapping triangles drawn with a single `GeneralPath` and the default Winding Rule.

Figure 11.20. Two overlapping triangles drawn with a single `GeneralPath` and Winding Rule `WIND_EVEN_ODD`.

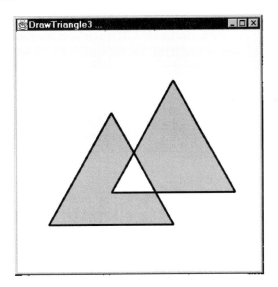

The triangles in Figure 11.19 are filled with a light gray color, including the region common to both triangles. There might actually some confusion about the overlapping region. Did we intend that region to be inside both shapes, or did we intend to draw to nonoverlapping shapes with the common region outside of both? To resolve this ambiguity, Java provides two "Winding Rules" to determine the interior regions to fill. The default Winding Rule is `GeneralPath.WIND_NON_ZERO`. It treats overlapping regions as inside the shapes, and so it fills them, as we saw in Figure 11.19. If the Winding Rule is set to `GeneralPath.WIND_EVEN_ODD` with the `setWindingRule`

method, the overlapping area will be treated as outside the shapes. Figure 11.20 shows the result when the Winding Rule is WIND_EVEN_ODD.

GOOD PROGRAMMING PRACTICE

Use class GeneralPath to create arbitrarily complex graphics shapes.

GOOD PROGRAMMING PRACTICE

If a GeneralPath object includes two or more overlapping shapes, specify a Winding Rule to determine how to treat the overlapping regions. The default Winding Rule treats overlapping regions as interior to the shape, while the WIND_EVEN_ODD rule treats overlapping regions as outside to the shape.

EXAMPLE 11-3: CREATING STARS

To test the general shape class, create a five-pointed star and plot it three times: once as a line drawing only, once with a fill using the WIND_NON_ZERO winding rule, and once with a fill using the WIND_EVEN_ODD winding rule.

SOLUTION

A five-pointed star has five vertices located at the vertices of a regular pentagon. (See Figure 11.21a). The star is created by drawing straight lines that connect *every other vertex* until the lines close on themselves. The vertices can be calculated from the knowledge that a pentagon has five equal sides and that the outside angles of each vertex are spaced 72° apart.

The location of each vertex can be found from the following equations:

$$x_1 = (length) \cos \theta, \tag{11-5}$$
$$y_1 = (length) \sin \theta, \tag{11-6}$$

where *length* is the length of a side. If θ increases by 72° at each step around the circle, we can find each of the vertices in succession. Since we know one vertex is straight up, we can start at $\theta = 90°$ and work around the circle. Therefore, the Java code to calculate the vertices of a pentagon centered on the origin would be as follows:

```
double[] x = new double[5];
double[] y = new double[5];
...
theta = 90 * Math.PI/180;
delta = 72 * Math.PI/180;
for ( i = 0; i < x.length; i++ ) {
   x[i] = length * Math.cos(theta);
   y[i] = length * Math.sin(theta);
   theta += delta;
}
```

Now we know where the vertices of the pentagon are when it is centered on the origin, but the display is *not* centered on the origin, so we must translate the vertices to the center of the display, and also reverse the y values to account for the fact that the y-axis is positive downward. The Java code for this step is:

Figure 11.21. *(a)* A five-pointed star is formed by drawing lines between every other vertex of a regular pentagon. *(b)* The vertices are at equal distances from the origin, and spaced 72° apart.

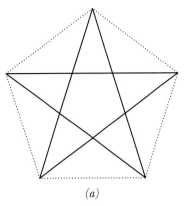

(a)

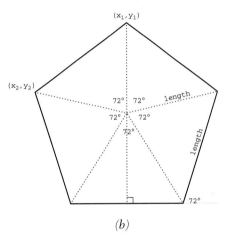

(b)

```
// Get plot size
Dimension size = getSize();

// Shift the reference position to the center of
// the display. The center of the display is
// size.width/2 and size.height/2.
for ( i = 0; i < x.length; i++ ) {
   x[i] = size.width/2 + x[i];
   y[i] = size.height/2 - y[i];
}
```

At this point, we can draw the star by placing line segments between every other vertex with a GeneralPath object.

```
GeneralPath p = new GeneralPath();
p.moveTo((float) x[0],(float) y[0]);
p.lineTo((float) x[2],(float) y[2]);
p.lineTo((float) x[4],(float) y[4]);
p.lineTo((float) x[1],(float) y[1]);
p.lineTo((float) x[3],(float) y[3]);
p.closePath();
```

We will actually draw three stars offset from each other so that they do not over-lap, leaving one in outline only and filling the other two. The program to draw the three stars is shown in Figure 11.22.

```java
import java.awt.*;
import java.awt.event.*;
import java.awt.geom.*;
import javax.swing.*;
import chapman.graphics.JCanvas;
public class DrawStar extends JCanvas {

   // This method draws three stars.
   public void paintComponent ( Graphics g ) {

      BasicStroke bs;              // Ref to BasicStroke
      double delta;                // Delta angle (radians)
      int i;                       // Loop index
      double length = 80;          // Length of a side of
                                   // pentagon
      GeneralPath p;               // Ref to GeneralPath
      float[] solid = {12.0f,0.0f}; // Solid line style
      double theta;                // Angle (radians)
      double[] x = new double[5];   // Vertices of reference pentagon
      double[] y = new double[5];   // Vertices of reference pentagon
      double[] x1 = new double[5];  // Vertices of shifted pentagon
      double[] y1 = new double[5];  // Vertices of shifted pentagon

      // Cast the graphics object to Graph2D
      Graphics2D g2 = (Graphics2D) g;

      // Get plot size
      Dimension size = getSize();

      // Set rendering hints to improve display quality
      g2.setRenderingHint(RenderingHints.KEY_ANTIALIASING,
                     RenderingHints.VALUE_ANTIALIAS_ON);

      // Set background color
      g2.setColor( Color.white );
      g2.fill(new Rectangle2D.Double(0,0,size.width,size.height));

      // Set the basic stroke
      bs = new BasicStroke( 3.0f, BasicStroke.CAP_SQUARE,
                        BasicStroke.JOIN_MITER, 1.0f,
                        solid, 0.0f );
      g2.setStroke(bs);

      // Calculate the locations of the vertices of the
      // pentagon surrounding the star.
      theta = 90 * Math.PI/180;
      delta = 72 * Math.PI/180;
      for ( i = 0; i < x.length; i++ ) {
         x[i] = length * Math.cos(theta);
         y[i] = length * Math.sin(theta);
         theta += delta;
      }
```

Figure 11.22. *(cont.)*

```
// Shift the reference position to the center of
// the display.  The center of the display is
// size.width/2 and size.height/2.
for ( i = 0; i < x.length; i++ ) {
   x[i] = size.width/2 + x[i];
   y[i] = size.height/2 - y[i];
}

// Create a star in the top center and draw
// lines only
for ( i = 0; i < x.length; i++ ) {
   x1[i] = x[i];
   y1[i] = y[i] - size.height/4;
}
p = new GeneralPath();
p.moveTo((float) x1[0],(float) y1[0]);
p.lineTo((float) x1[2],(float) y1[2]);
p.lineTo((float) x1[4],(float) y1[4]);
p.lineTo((float) x1[1],(float) y1[1]);
p.lineTo((float) x1[3],(float) y1[3]);
p.closePath();

 // Set color and draw
g2.setColor(Color.black);
g2.draw(p);

// Create a star in the lower left and draw
// with the default winding rule
for ( i = 0; i < x.length; i++ ) {
   x1[i] = x[i] - size.width/4;
   y1[i] = y[i] + size.height/4;
}
p = new GeneralPath();
p.moveTo((float) x1[0],(float) y1[0]);
p.lineTo((float) x1[2],(float) y1[2]);
p.lineTo((float) x1[4],(float) y1[4]);
p.lineTo((float) x1[1],(float) y1[1]);
p.lineTo((float) x1[3],(float) y1[3]);
p.setWindingRule(GeneralPath.WIND_NON_ZERO);
p.closePath();

// Set color and draw
g2.setColor(Color.yellow);
g2.fill(p);
g2.setColor(Color.black);
g2.draw(p);

// Create a star in the lower right and draw
// with the WIND_EVEN_ODD winding rule
for ( i = 0; i < x.length; i++ ) {
   x1[i] = x[i] + size.width/4;
   y1[i] = y[i] + size.height/4;
}
p = new GeneralPath();
p.moveTo((float) x1[0],(float) y1[0]);
p.lineTo((float) x1[2],(float) y1[2]);
p.lineTo((float) x1[4],(float) y1[4]);
p.lineTo((float) x1[1],(float) y1[1]);
p.lineTo((float) x1[3],(float) y1[3]);
p.setWindingRule(GeneralPath.WIND_EVEN_ODD);
p.closePath();
```

Figure 11.22. *(cont.)*

```
        // Set color and draw
        g2.setColor(Color.green);
        g2.fill(p);
        g2.setColor(Color.black);
        g2.draw(p);
    }

    public static void main(String s[]) {

        // Create a Window Listener to handle "close" events
        MyWindowListener l = new MyWindowListener();

        // Create a DrawStar object
        DrawStar c = new DrawStar();

        // Create a frame and place the object in the center
        // of the frame.
        JFrame f = new JFrame("DrawStar ...");
        f.addWindowListener(l);
        f.getContentPane().add(c, BorderLayout.CENTER);
        f.setSize(400,400);
        f.setVisible( true );
    }
}
```

Figure 11.22. The paintComponent method to draw three stars using General-Path objects.

The display produced when this program is executed is shown in Figure 11.23.

Figure 11.23. The output of program DrawStar.

11.4 DISPLAYING TEXT

Text may be displayed on a graphics device using the Graphics2D method **drawString**. The most common forms of this methods are

```
drawString(String s, int x, int y);
drawString(String s, float x, float y);
```

where s is the string to display, and (x,y) is the *lower left-hand corner* of region where the String will be displayed. When this method is executed, the characters in s will be displayed on the screen in the current color, and using the current Font.

The paintComponent method from an example program that displays a String is shown in Figure 11.24, together with the result produced on the display.

```
// This method displays a string on the graphics device.
public void paintComponent ( Graphics g ) {

    // Cast the graphics object to Graph2D
    Graphics2D g2 = (Graphics2D) g;

    // Set rendering hints to improve display quality
    g2.setRenderingHint(RenderingHints.KEY_ANTIALIASING,
                        RenderingHints.VALUE_ANTIALIAS_ON);

    // Set background color
    Dimension size = getSize();
    g2.setColor( Color.white );
    g2.fill(new Rectangle2D.Double(0,0,size.width, size.height));

    // Display string
    g2.setColor( Color.black );
    g2.drawString("This is a test!",20,40);
}
```

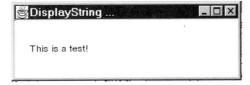

Figure 11.24. Method demonstrating how to write a String to a graphics device.

Note that if you specify a *y* value of 0, no text will be visible, since 0 corresponds to the *top* of the display area, and it also marks the *bottom* of the region where the String will be displayed! This is a common mistake made by novice Java programmers.

PROGRAMMING PITFALLS

Do not to display text at an (*x, y*) position with a *y* value of 0. It will be displayed above the top of the display window, and so will be invisible!

TABLE 11-5 Standard Font Names

FONT NAME	DESCRIPTION
Serif	This is the standard serif font for a particular system. Examples are Times and Times New Roman.
SansSerif	This is the standard sansserif font for a particular system. Examples are Helvetica and Arial.
Monospaced	This is the standard monospaced font for a particular system. Examples are Courier and Courier New.
Dialog	This is the standard font for dialog boxes on a particular system.
DialogInput	This is the standard font for dialog inputs on a particular system.

11.4.1 Selecting and Controlling Fonts

The font used to display text on a graphics device can be controlled by defining a **java.awt.Font** object and then specifying that object to be the current font. A Font object is declared with a constructor of the form

```
Font( String s, int style, int size );
```

where s is the name of the font to use, `style` is the style of the font (plain, italic, bold, or bold italic), and `size` is the point size of the font. There may be many fonts available on a system, but Java guarantees that the fonts shown in Table 11-5 will *always* be available on every Java implementation.

The font style may be specified by one or more of the constants `Font.PLAIN`, `Font.BOLD`, and `Font.ITALIC`. Note that it is possible to use the BOLD and ITALIC styles at the same time by simply adding the two constants together. The font size may be any integer point size. For example, the statement shown below creates a 14-point bold italic monospaced font.

```
Font font1 = new Font( "Monospaced", Font.BOLD+Font.ITALIC, 14);
```

Once a font has been created, it can be set to be the current font with the Graphics2D method **setFont**. The form of this method is

```
g2.setFont( font1 );
```

After this method is executed, any subsequent text will be displayed in the specified font.

The program in Figure 11.25 illustrates various combinations of font names, styles, and sizes.

```
// This method tests various fonts
public void paintComponent ( Graphics g ) {

    // Cast the graphics object to Graph2D
    Graphics2D g2 = (Graphics2D) g;

    // Set rendering hints to improve display quality
    g2.setRenderingHint(RenderingHints.KEY_ANTIALIASING,
                        RenderingHints.VALUE_ANTIALIAS_ON);

    // Set background color
    Dimension size = getSize();
    g2.setColor( Color.white );
    g2.fill(new Rectangle2D.Double(0,0,size.width,size.height));

    // Define several fonts...
    Font f1 = new Font("Serif",Font.PLAIN,12);
    Font f2 = new Font("SansSerif",Font.ITALIC,16);
    Font f3 = new Font("Monospaced",Font.BOLD,14);
    Font f4 = new Font("Serif",Font.BOLD+Font.ITALIC,20);
```

Figure 11.25. *(cont.)*

```
        // Display fonts
        g2.setColor( Color.black );
        g2.setFont(f1);
        g2.drawString("12-point plain Serif",20,40);
        g2.setFont(f2);
        g2.drawString("16-point italic SansSerif",20,80);
        g2.setFont(f3);
        g2.drawString("14-point bold Monospaced",20,120);
        g2.setFont(f4);
        g2.drawString("20-point bold italic Serif",20,160);
    }
```

(a)

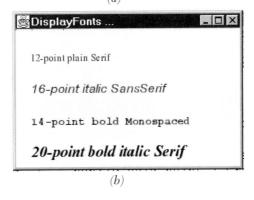

(b)

Figure 11.25. *(a)* Method displaying various fonts. *(b)* The resulting output.

A summary of useful methods in the `java.awt.Font` class can be found in Table 11-6.

TABLE 11-6 Methods in the `java.awt.Font` Class

FONT NAME	DESCRIPTION
`public int getStyle()`	Returns an integer value containing the current font style.
`public int getSize()`	Returns an integer value containing the current font size.
`public String getName()`	Returns the current font name as a `String`.
`public String getFamily()`	Returns the current font family as a `String`.
`isBold()`	Returns `true` if the font is bold.
`isItalic()`	Returns `true` if the font is italic.
`isPlain()`	Returns `true` if the font is plain.

11.4.2 Getting Information About Fonts

It is sometimes necessary to get precise information about a font that it being used in an application. For example, we may need to place two or more lines of text under each other at a comfortable spacing. How can we tell precisely how tall and long a particular line is, so that we can place other information above, below, or to the side of it? Java contains a special class called **`java.awt.FontMetrics`** to provide this information about any specified font.

There are several types of metrics associated with a font. These metrics include the font's *height*, *ascent* (the amount a normal character rises above the baseline), *descent* (the amount a character dips below the baseline), and *leading* (the amount

Figure 11.26. Font metrics.

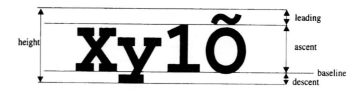

above the ascent line occupied by especially tall characters). These quantities are illustrated in Figure 11.26.

A new `FontMetrics` object can be declared with a constructor of the following form:

```
FontMetrics fm = new FontMetrics( Font f );
```

In addition, a `FontMetrics` object for the current font can be created using the following `getFontMetrics()` method of the `Graphics2D` class:

```
FontMetrics fm = g2.getFontMetrics();
```

Once the object has been created by one of these techniques, information about the font can be retrieved with any of the methods in Table 11-7.

TABLE 11-7 Methods in the `FontMetrics` Class

METHOD NAME	DESCRIPTION
`public int getAscent()`	Returns the ascent of a font in pixels.
`public int getDescent()`	Returns the descent of a font in pixels.
`public int getHeight()`	Returns the height of a font in pixels.
`public int getLeading()`	Returns the leading of a font in pixels.

The `paintComponent` method in Figure 11.27 illustrates the use of these methods to recover information about the current font.

```
// This method illustrates the use of FontMetrics
public void paintComponent ( Graphics g ) {

    // Cast the graphics object to Graph2D
    Graphics2D g2 = (Graphics2D) g;

    // Define a font...
    Font f1 = new Font("Serif",Font.PLAIN,14);

    // Set font
    g2.setFont(f1);
    // Get information about the font
    FontMetrics fm = g2.getFontMetrics();

    // Get information about the current font
    System.out.println("Font metrics:");
    System.out.println("Font height  = " + fm.getHeight());
    System.out.println("Font ascent  = " + fm.getAscent());
    System.out.println("Font descent = " + fm.getDescent());
    System.out.println("Font leading = " + fm.getLeading());
}
```

Figure 11.27. Method displaying font metrics.

When this program is executed, the results are as follows:

```
D:\book\java\chap11>java ShowFontMetrics
Font metrics:
Font height  = 20
Font ascent  = 15
Font descent = 4
Font leading = 1
```

Thus, the spacing between successive line of this font must be greater than 20 pixels.

**EXAMPLE 11-4:
DISPLAYING
MULTIPLE
LINES OF TEXT**

Write a program that will display three lines of text, leaving the proper vertical spacing between lines. Calculate the proper spacing using the FontMetrics methods.

SOLUTION
The program in Figure 11.28 displays the required data. Note that it uses the height returned from the getHeight() method to set the spacing between successive lines.

```
import java.awt.*;
import java.awt.event.*;
import java.awt.geom.*;
import javax.swing.*;
import chapman.graphics.JCanvas;
public class DisplayStrings extends JCanvas {

    // This method illustrates the use of FontMetrics
    // to automatically set the proper spacing between
    // lines.
    public void paintComponent ( Graphics g ) {

        // Cast the graphics object to Graph2D
        Graphics2D g2 = (Graphics2D) g;

        // Set rendering hints to improve display quality
        g2.setRenderingHint(RenderingHints.KEY_ANTIALIASING,
                            RenderingHints.VALUE_ANTIALIAS_ON);

        // Set background color
        Dimension size = getSize();
        g2.setColor( Color.white );
        g2.fill(new Rectangle2D.Double(0,0,size.width,size.height));

        // Define a font...
        Font f1 = new Font("Serif",Font.BOLD,16);

        // Set font
        g2.setFont(f1);

        // Get font height
        int height = g2.getFontMetrics().getHeight();

        // Display the text
        g2.setColor( Color.black );
        g2.drawString("This is line 1.",20,  height+20);
        g2.drawString("This is line 2.",20,2*height+20);
        g2.drawString("This is line 3.",20,3*height+20);
    }
```

Figure 11.28. *(cont.)*

```
        public static void main(String s[]) {

            // Create a Window Listener to handle "close" events
            MyWindowListener l = new MyWindowListener();

            // Create a DisplayStrings object
            DisplayStrings c = new DisplayStrings();

            // Create a frame and place the object in the center
            // of the frame.
            JFrame f = new JFrame("DisplayStrings ...");
            f.addWindowListener(l);
            f.getContentPane().add(c, BorderLayout.CENTER);
            f.setSize(300,200);
            f.setVisible( true );
        }
    }
```

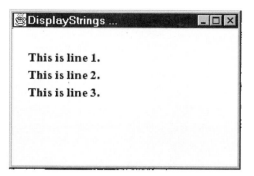

Figure 11.28. A program to display three lines of text with proper spacing.

The display produced when this program is executed is also shown in Figure 11.28.

11.5 THE AFFINE TRANSFORM

An **affine transform** is a user-specified combination of translations, scalings, rotations, and shears that is automatically applied to any Graphics2D object whenever it is rendered on a graphics device. (The term *affine transform* refers to a transformation that converts an input shape into an output shape while preserving parallel lines.) The types of transformations that may be applied include the following:

- **Translations**—Moving from one place to another within the display window without changing the shape of the object.
- **Scalings**—Making the object larger or smaller.
- **Rotations**—Rotating the object about a user-specified axis.
- **Shears**—Causing one side of the object to be displaced relative to the other side, so that it appears "slanted".

Any combination of these transformations may be applied in any desired order.

TABLE 11-8   Selected Methods in the `AffineTransform` Class

METHOD NAME	DESCRIPTION
`public void rotate(double theta)`	Rotates data by `theta` radians. A positive angle corresponds to a *clockwise* rotation.
`public void rotate(double theta,double x, double y)`	Rotates data by `theta` radians about point (x,y). A positive angle corresponds to a *clockwise* rotation.
`public void scale(double sx,double sy)`	Scales (multiplies) *x*- and *y*-axes by the specified amounts.
`public void shear(double shx,double shy)`	Shears *x*- and *y*-axes by the specified amounts. The equations applied are $x' = x + (\text{shx})\,y$ and $y' = y + (\text{shy})\,x$.
`Public void translate(double tx,double ty)`	Moves data by `tx` pixels on the *x*-axis and `ty` pixels on the *y*-axis.

When a new `Graphics2D` object is created, an affine transform is automatically associated with the object. The default affine transform is a 1-to-1 mapping, meaning that any shape or text created by a Java 2D class is displayed without modification on the graphics device. However, a programmer can modify this mapping at any time while displaying text or graphics on the device.

A new **`java.awt.geom.AffineTransform`** object can be created with a constructor of the form

```
AffineTransform at = new AffineTransform();
```

Once the object has been created, the methods in Table 11-8 can be used to add translations, scalings, rotations, and shears to the data will be displayed on a graphics device. *Note that the effects of each method call will be added to the effects of all previous calls*, so it possible to build very complex behaviors with these methods. Finally, after all transformations have been added, the affine transform object must be associated with a specific `Graphics2D` object using the `Graphics2D` method `setTransform`.

```
g2.setTransform(at);
```

The program in Figure 11.29 illustrates how to use the affine transform. It writes out the string "Hello, World!" eight times, rotating the string by 45° ($\pi/4$) each time that the text is printed out. Note that the effect of the calls to rotate are cumulative, so the text rotates by a total of 360°.

```
// This method tests an affine transform by displaying
// rotated text.
public void paintComponent ( Graphics g ) {

    AffineTransform at;            // Ref to ffine transform
    int i;                         // Loop index

    // Cast the graphics object to Graph2D
    Graphics2D g2 = (Graphics2D) g;

    // Get plot size
    Dimension size = getSize();

    // Set rendering hints to improve display quality
    g2.setRenderingHint(RenderingHints.KEY_ANTIALIASING,
                    RenderingHints.VALUE_ANTIALIAS_ON);

    // Set background color
    g2.setColor( Color.white );
    g2.fill(new Rectangle2D.Double(0,0,size.width,size.height));

    // Get the affine transform
    at = new AffineTransform();
```

Figure 11.29.   *(cont.)*

```
                    // Define and set font
                    Font f1 = new Font("Serif",Font.BOLD,18);
                    g2.setFont(f1);

                    //
                    Color colorArray[] = new Color[10];
                    colorArray[0] = Color.blue;
                    colorArray[1] = Color.green;
                    colorArray[2] = Color.magenta;
                    colorArray[3] = Color.black;
                    colorArray[4] = Color.blue;
                    colorArray[5] = Color.green;
                    colorArray[6] = Color.magenta;
                    colorArray[7] = Color.black;

                    for ( i = 0;  i < 8; i++) {
                       at.rotate(Math.PI/4, 180, 200);
                       g2.setTransform(at);
                       g2.setColor(colorArray[i]);
                       g2.drawString("Hello, World!", 200, 200);
                    }
                 }
```

Figure 11.29. A program to test the affine transform by rotating a text string.

PROGRAMMING PITFALLS:

Use `AffineTransforms` to translate, scale, rotate, or shear your `Graphics2D` shapes and text.

EXAMPLE 11-5: APPLYING THE AFFINE TRANSFORM

Illustrate the use of the Affine Transform by displaying a single `Rectangle2D` object in four different ways on a single canvas:

1. Display the original rectangle in the upper left-hand quadrant of the canvas.
2. Display the rectangle rotated by 45° in the upper right-hand quadrant of the canvas.
3. Display the rectangle at 1/2 size and rotated by 90° in the lower left-hand quadrant of the canvas.

4. Display the rectangle with a 30° horizontal shear in the lower right-hand quadrant of the canvas.

SOLUTION

To display the rectangle four times as specified, we must first create a `Rectangle2D.Double` object. For simplicity, we will create the object centered at the origin (0,0) and then translate it to the desired quadrant with an affine transform each time that it is displayed.

```
// Define rectangle centered about (0,0)
rect = new Rectangle2D.Double (-75., -40., 150., 80.);
```

The display in the upper left-hand corner is very simple, since all we have to do is to shift the center of the shape from the origin to the middle of that quadrant. The affine transform to perform this shift is

```
at = new AffineTransform();
at.translate(100.,120.);
g2.setTransform(at);
```

The display in the upper right-hand corner is more complex, since we must both shift the rectangle and rotate it by 45°. Remember that rotation angles are specified in *radians*, with a positive number corresponding to a clockwise rotation. Therefore, the affine transform to perform the shift to the upper right-hand quadrant and the 45° rotation is

```
at = new AffineTransform();
at.translate(300.,120.);
at.rotate(Math.PI/4);
g2.setTransform(at);
```

The display in the lower left-hand corner requires us to shift the rectangle to that corner, rotate it by 90° ($\pi/2$), and reduce it to half size. Therefore, the affine transform to create this display is

```
at = new AffineTransform();
at.translate(100.,280.);
at.rotate(Math.PI/2);
at.scale(0.5,0.5);
g2.setTransform(at);
```

The display in the lower right-hand corner requires us to shift the rectangle to that corner and apply a 30° shear. The shear angle can be determined from basic trigonometry. Figure 11.30 shows the relationship between the shear value specified in the transform and the resulting shear angle. By simple trigonometry,

$$\tan \theta = \frac{\Delta x}{y} = \frac{(\text{shx})y}{y} = \text{shx},$$

so an angle of 30° would require a value of `shx` = 0.577. Therefore, the affine transform to create this display is

```
at = new AffineTransform();
at.translate(280.,280.);
at.shear(0.577,0.);
g2.setTransform(at);
```

The final `paintComponent` method is shown in Figure 11.31, together with the resulting graphics output.

Figure 11.30.   The relationship between the sheer angle θ and the `sheer` method parameter shx.

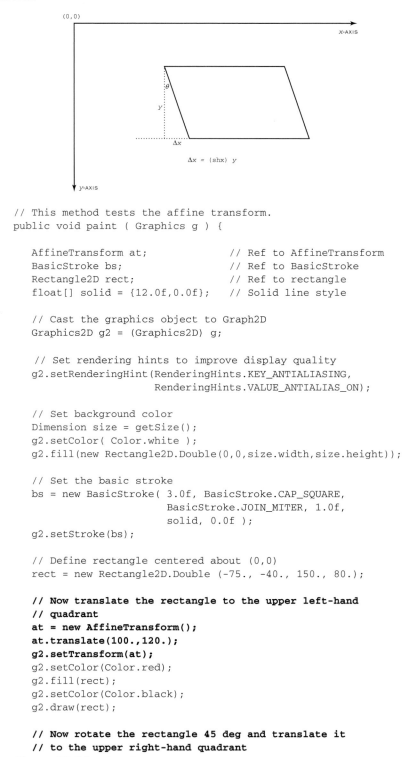

$$\Delta x = (shx)\ y$$

```
// This method tests the affine transform.
public void paint ( Graphics g ) {

   AffineTransform at;               // Ref to AffineTransform
   BasicStroke bs;                   // Ref to BasicStroke
   Rectangle2D rect;                 // Ref to rectangle
   float[] solid = {12.0f,0.0f};     // Solid line style

   // Cast the graphics object to Graph2D
   Graphics2D g2 = (Graphics2D) g;

    // Set rendering hints to improve display quality
   g2.setRenderingHint(RenderingHints.KEY_ANTIALIASING,
                  RenderingHints.VALUE_ANTIALIAS_ON);

   // Set background color
   Dimension size = getSize();
   g2.setColor( Color.white );
   g2.fill(new Rectangle2D.Double(0,0,size.width,size.height));

   // Set the basic stroke
   bs = new BasicStroke( 3.0f, BasicStroke.CAP_SQUARE,
                  BasicStroke.JOIN_MITER, 1.0f,
                  solid, 0.0f );
   g2.setStroke(bs);

   // Define rectangle centered about (0,0)
   rect = new Rectangle2D.Double (-75., -40., 150., 80.);

   // Now translate the rectangle to the upper left-hand
   // quadrant
   at = new AffineTransform();
   at.translate(100.,120.);
   g2.setTransform(at);
   g2.setColor(Color.red);
   g2.fill(rect);
   g2.setColor(Color.black);
   g2.draw(rect);

   // Now rotate the rectangle 45 deg and translate it
   // to the upper right-hand quadrant
```

Figure 11.31.   *(cont.)*

```
at = new AffineTransform();
at.translate(300.,120.);
at.rotate(Math.PI/4);
g2.setTransform(at);
g2.setColor(Color.red);
g2.fill(rect);
g2.setColor(Color.black);
g2.draw(rect);

// Now display at half size, rotated 90 deg in the
// lower left-hand quadrant
at = new AffineTransform();
at.translate(100.,280.);
at.rotate(Math.PI/2);
at.scale(0.5,0.5);
g2.setTransform(at);
g2.setColor(Color.red);
g2.fill(rect);
g2.setColor(Color.black);
g2.draw(rect);

// Now apply a 30 deg horizontal sheer and display
// in the lower right-hand quadrant
at = new AffineTransform();
at.translate(280.,280.);
at.shear(0.577,0.);
g2.setTransform(at);
g2.setColor(Color.red);
g2.fill(rect);
g2.setColor(Color.black);
g2.draw(rect);
}
```

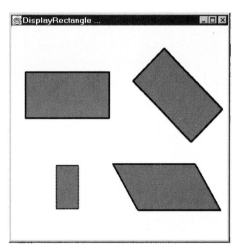

Figure 11.31.   A program that displays the same rectangular shape in four different locations with varying scales, rotations, and shears.

11.6 XOR MODE

When two overlapping objects are drawn on a graphics device, the second object will normally cover up the underlying object in the region of overlap, making it impossible to determine the exact shape of the first object in the region that is covered up. However, it is sometimes useful to see the full outlines of both shapes, even if they overlap. For those circumstances, Java includes a special paint mode know as XOR (exclusive OR) mode.

In XOR mode, the outlines of both objects are visible, and the region of overlap is painted in a special color to make it obvious. XOR mode is set by the `Graphics2D` method `setXORmode`. The calling sequence for this method is

```
g2.setXORMode( Color c );
```

where g2 is a `Graphics2D` device and c is a `Color` object. When overlapping objects are drawn in the *same* color, then the XOR mode color is used to draw the overlapping region.

The `paintComponent` method in Figure 11.32 illustrates the use of XOR mode to display overlapping regions of both objects. Note that the XOR color is only used when both overlapping objects have the same color.

```
// This method tests XOR mode.
public void paintComponent ( Graphics g ) {


    AffineTransform at;              // Ref to AffineTransform
    BasicStroke bs;                  // Ref to BasicStroke
    Ellipse2D ell1, ell2;            // Ref to ellipse
    float[] solid = {12.0f,0.0f};    // Solid line style


    // Cast the graphics object to Graph2D
    Graphics2D g2 = (Graphics2D) g;


    // Set rendering hints to improve display quality
    g2.setRenderingHint(RenderingHints.KEY_ANTIALIASING,
                    RenderingHints.VALUE_ANTIALIAS_ON);


    // Set background color
    Dimension size = getSize();
    g2.setColor( Color.white );
    g2.fill(new Rectangle2D.Double(0,0,size.width,
    size.height));


    // Define two ellipses and plot them in normal mode
    ell1 = new Ellipse2D.Double (30., 30., 150., 80.);
    ell2 = new Ellipse2D.Double (130., 30., 150., 80.);
    g2.setColor(Color.green);
    g2.fill(ell1);
    g2.setColor(Color.orange);
    g2.fill(ell2);


    // Define two ellipses with different colors and
    // plot them in XOR mode
    ell1 = new Ellipse2D.Double (70., 140., 150., 80.);
    ell2 = new Ellipse2D.Double (170., 140., 150., 80.);
```

Figure 11.32. *(cont.)*

```
                    g2.setXORMode(Color.white);
                    g2.setColor(Color.green);
                    g2.fill(ell1);
                    g2.setColor(Color.orange);
                    g2.fill(ell2);


                    // Define two ellipses with the same color and
                    // plot them in XOR mode
                    ell1 = new Ellipse2D.Double (110., 250., 150., 80.);
                    ell2 = new Ellipse2D.Double (210., 250., 150., 80.);
                    g2.setXORMode(Color.white);
                    g2.setColor(Color.green);
                    g2.fill(ell1);
                    g2.setColor(Color.green);
                    g2.fill(ell2);
                }
```

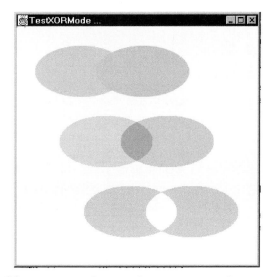

Figure 11.32.   A program that tests the XOR paint mode.

GOOD PROGRAMMING PRACTICE

Use the `Graphics2D` method `setXORMode` to make the overlapping regions of objects visible.

PRACTICE!

This quiz provides a quick check to see if you understand the concepts introduced in Sections 11.1 through 11.6. If you have trouble with the quiz, reread the sections, ask your instructor, or discuss the material with a fellow student. The answers to this quiz are found in the back of the book.

1. What is a container? Which type of container are we using in this chapter?
2. What is a component? Which type of component(s) arewe using in this chapter?
3. What steps are required to display graphics in Java?
4. What coordinate systems is used to display graphics in Java? Where is the point (0,0) in this system?
5. What class does the method `getSize()` belong to? How is it used?
6. What class controls the style of lines and borders in Java?
7. How is text displayed on a Java graphics device? What classes are used to set and get information about the font being used?
8. What is an affine transform? How is it used?

SUMMARY

- The `java.awt` and `java.awt.geom` packages contain the classes necessary to work with graphics. The `javax.swing` package contains the classes necessary to create Swing GUIs.
- A component is a visual object containing text or graphics, which can respond to keyboard or mouse inputs. In the Swing GUI, components are implemented as subclasses of class `JComponent`.
- A canvas is a special component that is a blank area for drawing text or graphics.
- A container is a graphical object that can hold components or other containers.
- A frame is a container with borders and a title bar. In the Swing GUI, frames are implemented by class `JFrame`.
- Every subclass of `JComponent` includes a `paintComponent` method, which is called whenever the object is to be displayed on a graphics device. Every `paintComponent` method has a single parameter, which is an object of the `java.awt.Graphics` class.
- Every `paintComponent` method should immediately downcast the `Graphics` object to a `Graphics2D` object, so that the "2D" classes can be used with it.
- The `Graphics2D` methods `draw` and `fill` are used to draw and fill the interior of an object on a graphics device.
- The abstract class `Line2D` is used to draw lines on a graphics device. There are two concrete subclasses of this class: `Line2D.Double` and `Line2D.Float`.
- The abstract class `Rectangle2D` is used to draw rectangles on a Java graphics device. There are two concrete subclasses of this class: `Rectangle2D.Double` and `Rectangle2D.Float`.
- The abstract class `Ellipse2D` is used to draw circles and ellipses on a Java graphics device. There are two concrete subclasses of this class: `Ellipse2D.Double` and `Ellipse2D.Float`.
- The abstract class `Arc2D` is used to draw arcs on a Java graphics device. There are two concrete subclasses of this class: `Arc2D.Double` and `Arc2D. Float`.

- The class `GeneralPath` is used to create arbitrary shapes on a Java graphics device. It includes `moveTo`, `lineTo`, `curveTo`, and `quadTo` methods, which allow a user to connect arbitrary points with straight lines, quadratic curves, or Bezier curves.
- The width, style, and ends of a "2D" line or border are controlled by an object of the `BasicStroke` class.
- The color of an object displayed on a graphics device may be controlled with the `Graphics2D` method `setColor`. This method has a single parameter, which is an object of the `java.awt.Color` class.
- Antialiasing may be used to eliminate jagged edges from objects displayed on a Java graphics device. Antialiasing is controlled with the `Graphics2D` method `setRenderingHints`.
- Text may be displayed on a graphics device with the `Graphics2D` method `drawString`. The font used to display the text is set with the `Graphics2D` method `setFont`.
- Class `Font` is used to specify the characteristics of a particular font.
- Class `Metrics` is used get information about the characteristics of a particular font.
- Class `AffineTransform` is used to translate, scale, rotate, or shear objects before they are displayed on a Java graphics device. It is applied to a graphics device by calling the `Graphics2D` method `setTransform` before calling the methods `draw` or `drawString`.
- Normally, when two objects overlap on a graphics device, the later object covers up the earlier one. The `Graphics2D` method `setXORMode` can be used to modify this behavior so that both objects are visible.
- A summary of the `Graphics2D` methods discussed in the chapter is presented in Table 11-9.

TABLE 11-9   Summary of `Graphics2D` Methods Discussed in Chapter 11

PARAMETER	DESCRIPTION
`draw(Shape s);`	Draws the outline of a `Shape` object, such as `Rectangle2D`, `Arc2D`, etc.
`drawString(String s, float x, float y);`	Draws the specified text at location (x,y), using the current color and font.
`fill(Shape s);`	Fills the interior of a `Shape` object, such as `Rectangle2D`, `Arc2D`, etc.
`getFontMetrics();`	Returns a `FontMetrics` object containing the current font metrics.
`setColor(Color c)`	Sets the color with which to draw objects on this graphics device.
`setFont(Font f)`	Sets the specified font as the current font to use when rendering text on this graphics device.
`setRenderingHint(String hintKey,Object hintValue)`	Sets the preferences for the rendering algorithms. Used to specify the use of antialiasing algorithms.
`setStroke(BasicStroke b)`	Sets the basic stroke to use when drawing the outlines of objects.
`setTransform(AffineTransform at)`	Sets the affine transform to apply to objects drawn on this graphics device.
`setXORMode(Color c)`	Sets the paintComponent mode to XOR mode, so that if shapes overlap, both of their outlines are visible.

APPLICATIONS: GOOD PROGRAMMING PRACTICES

The following guidelines introduced in this chapter will help you to develop good programs:

1. To display Java graphics, *(1)* create a component to display; *(2)* create a `JFrame` to hold the component, and place the component into the frame; and *(3)* create a "listener" object to detect and respond to mouse clicks, and assign the listener to the `JFrame`.
2. To create Java graphics, write a class that extends `JCanvas` and overrides the `paintComponent` method to produce the desired output.
3. To draw lines in Java: *(1)* select a line color using the `Graphics2D setColor` method; *(2)* Select a line width and line style using a `BasicStroke` object; *(3)* Set the endpoints of the line using a `Line2D.Double` or `Line2D.Float` method, and draw the line with a call to the `Graphics2D draw` method.
4. Eliminate jagged edges from your lines by turning on antialiasing with the `Graphics2D` method `setRenderingHints`.
5. Use the `Rectangle2D` classes to create rectangles.
6. Use the `RoundRectangle2D` classes to create rectangles with rounded edges.
7. Use the `Ellipse2D` classes to create circles and ellipses.
8. Use the `Arc2D` classes to create elliptical and circular arcs.
9. Use class `GeneralPath` to create arbitrarily complex graphics shapes.
10. If a `GeneralPath` object includes two or more overlapping shapes, specify a Winding Rule to determine how to treat the overlapping regions. The default Winding Rule treats overlapping regions as interior to the shape, while the `WIND_EVEN_ODD` rule treats overlapping regions as outside to the shape.
11. Use `AffineTransforms` to translate, scale, rotate, or shear your `Graphics2D` shapes and text.
12. Use the `Graphics2D` method `setXORMode` to make the overlapping regions of objects visible.

KEY TERMS

affine transform
`chapman.graphics.JCanvas` class
component
container
draw method
drawString method
fill method
`java.awt.BasicStroke` class
`java.awt.Container` class
`java.awt.Font` class
`java.awt.FontMetrics` class
`java.awt.geom.AffineTransform` class
`java.awt.geom.Arc2D` class
`java.awt.geom.Ellipse2D` class

`java.awt.geom.GeneralPath` class
`java.awt.geom.Line2D` class
`java.awt.geom.Rectangle2D` class
`java.awt.geom.RoundRectangle2D` class
`java.awt.Graphics2D` class
`javax.swing.JComponent` class
`javax.swing.JFrame` class
paintComponent method
setColor method
setRenderingHints method
setStroke method
setTransform method
setXORMode method
XOR paint mode

Problems

11.1.   Explain the steps required to generate graphics in Java.

11.2.   Write a program that draws a series of 5 concentric circles. The radii of the circles should differ by 20 pixels, with the innermost circle having a 20 pixel radius and the outer circle having a 100 pixel radius. Fill each circle with a different color.

11.3.   Modify the program of Exercise 11.2 so that each circle is surrounded by a 2-pixel-wide black border. Be sure to use antialiasing to make the borders smooth.

11.4.   Create a program that plots the function e^x over the range $-1 \le x \le 1$. Use a solid 4-pixel-wide blue line to plot the curve, and use solid 1-pixel-wide black curves for the x and y axes.

11.5.   Modify the program created in Exercise 11.3 so that it automatically re-scales whenever the frame containing it is re-sized.

11.6.   Write a program that plots a two-pixel-wide red dashed spiral. A spiral can be specified by two values r and θ, where r is the distance from the origin to a point and θ is the angle counterclockwise from the positive x axis to the point. In these terms, the spiral will be specified by the equation

$$r = \frac{\theta}{2\pi}, \text{ for } 0 \le \theta \le 6\pi$$

11.7.   Create a plot of $\cos x$ versus x for $-2\pi \le x \le 2\pi$. Use a solid 6-pixel-wide line for the plot. Add a thin black box around the plot, and create a title and x- and y-axis labels. Note that you will need to use an affine transform to rotate the text for the y-axis label.

11.8.   Modify the plot in Exercise 11.7 to add thin dotted grid lines in both the horizontal and vertical directions.

11.9.   Modify the plot in Exercise 11.7 to re-size properly whenever the frame containing the plot is re-sized.

11.10.   Create a program that displays samples of all the standard Java fonts on your computer.

11.11.   What is the height of a line of 24-point `SansSerif` text? What class and method did you use to learn this information?

11.12.   Create a program that plots four ellipses of random size and shape. Each ellipse should be a distinct color.

11.13.   Modify the previous program to use the XOR paint mode? How does the output of the program change?

11.14.   Write a program that creates a bar plot, using `Rectangle2D` objects to create each bar.

11.15.   Write a program that displays a line of text, and then displays the same text upside down.

12

Basic Graphical User Interfaces

A Graphical User Interface (GUI) is a pictorial interface to a program. A good GUI can make programs easier to use by providing them with a consistent appearance, and with intuitive controls like push buttons, sliders, pull-down lists, menus, etc. The GUI should behave in an understandable and predictable manner, so that a user knows what to expect when he or she performs an action. For example, when a mouse click occurs on a pushbutton, the GUI should initiate the action described on the label of the button.

The Java API contains two different graphical user interfaces. The old GUI is generally known as the Abstract Windowing Toolkit (AWT) GUI; it was introduced with JDK 1.0. The new GUI is known as the Swing GUI; it became a part of the standard JDK with the release of Java 2. The Swing GUI consists of additional classes built on top of the older AWT classes. It is faster and more flexible than the AWT GUI and is recommended for all new program development. This book teaches the Swing GUI only. If you must work with older programs containing the AWT GUI, please refer to the JDK on-line documentation. This chapter contains an introduction to the basic elements of the Swing GUIs. It does *not* contain a complete description of GUI features, but it does provide us with the basics

SECTIONS

- 12.1 How a Graphical User Interface Works
- 12.2 Creating and Displaying a Graphical User Interface
- 12.3 Events and Event Handling
- 12.4 Selected Graphical User Interface Components
- 12.5 Layout Managers
- Summary
- Key Terms

OBJECTIVES

After reading this chapter, you should be able to:

- Understand the operation of Graphical User Interfaces
- Build basic Graphical User Interfaces
- Understand the role events and event handlers play in GUI operation
- Understand `ActionEvent`s and the `ActionListener` interface
- Able to create and manipulate labels, buttons, checkboxes, radio buttons, text fields, password fields, combo boxes, and panels
- Understand and be able to use layout managers

required to create functional GUIs for our programs. Additional features of GUIs are covered in Chapter 13.

12.1 HOW A GRAPHICAL USER INTERFACE WORKS

A graphical user interface provides the user with a familiar environment in which to work. It contains push buttons, drop down lists, menus, text fields, and so forth, all of which are already familiar to the user, so that he or she can concentrate on the purpose of the application instead of the mechanics involved in doing things. However, GUIs are harder for the programmer, because a GUI-based program must be prepared for mouse clicks (or possibly keyboard input) for any GUI element at any time. Such inputs are known as **events**, and a program that responds to events is said to be *event driven*. The four principal elements required to create a Java Graphical User Interface are the following:

1. **Components**. Each item on a Java Graphical User Interface (push buttons, labels, text fields, etc.) is a **component,** meaning that the item inherits from the JComponent class introduced in Chapter 11. Regardless of their function, components all share a common set of methods, because the methods are defined in the superclass JComponent.

2. **Container**. The components of a GUI must be arranged within a **container**, which is a class ultimately derived from class Container. In this chapter, we will work with two types of containers: **JPanel** and **JFrame**. A JPanel is a very simple container that lays out the components left to right and top to bottom. A JFrame is a more complex container with borders and a title bar.

3. **Layout Manager**. When the components of a GUI are added to a container, a **layout manager** controls the location at which they will be placed within the container. Java provides six standard layout managers, each of which lays out components in a different fashion. A layout manager is automatically associated with each container when it is created, but the programmer can freely change the layout manager, if desired.

4. **Event Handlers**. Finally, there must be some way to perform an action if a user clicks a mouse on a button or types information on a keyboard. A mouse click or a key press creates an **event**, which is an object, like everything else in Java. Events are handled by creating **listener classes**, which listen for a specific type of event, and execute a specific method (called an **event handler**) if the event occurs. Listener classes implement **listener interfaces**, which specify the names of the event handler methods required to handle specific types of events. The standard listener interfaces can be found in package **java.awt.event**.

A subset of the basic GUI elements are summarized in Table 12-1. We will be studying examples of these elements in the next two chapters, and then build working GUIs from them. Figure 12.1 shows the inheritance hierarchy for some of the component, container, and layout classes in the java.awt and javax.swing packages.

TABLE 12-1 Some Basic GUI Elements

ELEMENT	DESCRIPTION
Components	
JButton	A graphical object that implements a pushbutton. It triggers an event when clicked with a mouse.
JCheckBox	A graphical object that is either selected or not selected. This object creates checkboxes.
JComboBox	A drop-down list of items, one of which may be selected. Single-clicking an item selects it, while double-clicking an item generates an action event.
JDialog	Creates a dialog window to display messages, warnings, etc., to the user.
JLabel	An area to display a label (text and/or images that a user cannot change).
JList	An area where a list of items is displayed. Single-clicking an item selects it, while double-clicking an item generates an action event.
JTable	An area where a table of items is displayed.
JPasswordField	Displays a text field that can be used to enter passwords. Asterisks are printed out in the field as characters are entered.
JRadioButton	A graphical object that implements a radio button: a set of buttons, only one of which can be selected at a time.
JTextField	An area (surrounded by a box) where a program can display text data and a user can optionally enter text data.
Containers	
Box	A simple container with no borders or title bar that uses the BoxLayout manager.
JDialog	A simple container for warning, error, and information messages.
JFrame	A container with borders and a title bar.
JPanel	A simple container with no borders or title bar that uses the FlowLayout manager.
Layout Managers	
BorderLayout	A layout manager that lays out elements in a central region and four surrounding borders. This is the default layout manager for a JFrame.
BoxLayout	A layout manager that allows multiple components to be laid out either vertically or horizontally, without wrapping. This is the default layout manager for a Box.
CardLayout	A layout manager that stacks components like a deck of cards, only the top one of which is visible.
FlowLayout	A layout manager that lays out elements left-to-right and top-to-bottom within a container. This is the default layout manager for a JPanel.
GridBagLay	A layout manager that lays out elements in a flexible grid, where the size of each element can vary.
GridLayout	A layout manager that lays out elements in a rigid grid.
Menu Components	
JMenu	A class to create menus.
JMenuBar	A container for menus. This is the bar running across the top of a container, and containing one or more menus.
JMenuItem	A single item within a menu.
JCheckBoxMenu	A single item within a menu that has a toggled on/off state.
JPopUpMenu	A menu that can be accessed by right-clicking the mouse.

Figure 12.1.   (*a*) Inheritance hierarchy for the container classes discussed in this book. (*b*) Inheritance hierarchy for the component classes discussed in this book. (Box and all classes with names starting with J are in package javax.swing. The other classes are in package java.awt.)

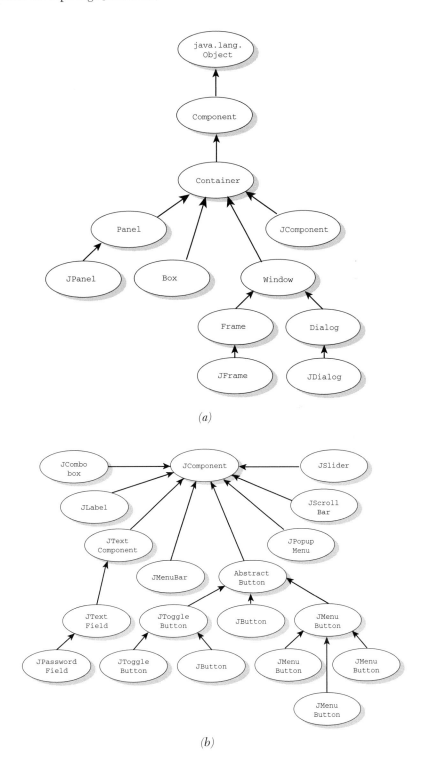

(*a*)

(*b*)

12.2 CREATING AND DISPLAYING A GRAPHICAL USER INTERFACE

The following basic steps are required required to create a Java GUI:

1. Create a container class to hold the GUI components. In this chapter, we will use subclasses of JPanel as the basic container.
2. Select a layout manager for the container if the default layout manager is not acceptable.
3. Create components and add them to the container.
4. Create listener objects to detect and respond to the events expected by each GUI component, and register the listeners with appropriate components.
5. Create a JFrame object, and place the completed container in the center of **content pane** associated with the frame. (The content pane is the location where GUI objects are attached to a JFrame or JApplet container. The method getContentPane() returns a reference to a container's content pane.)

Figure 12.2 shows a program that creates a simple GUI with a single button and a single label field. The label field contains the number of times that the button has been pressed since the program started. Note that class FirstGUI extends JPanel, and this class serves as the container for our GUI components (step 1 above).

```
1   // A first GUI.  This class creates a label and
2   // a button.  The count in the label is incremented
3   // each time that the button is pressed.
4   import java.awt.*;
5   import java.awt.event.*;
6   import javax.swing.*;
7   public class FirstGUI extends JPanel {
8
9      // Instance variables
10     private int count = 0;         // Number of pushes
11     private JButton pushButton;    // Push button
12     private JLabel label;          // Label
13
14     // Initialization method
15     public void init() {
16
17        // Set the layout manager
18        setLayout( new BorderLayout() );
19
20        // Create a label to hold push count
21        label = new JLabel("Push Count: 0");
22        add( label, BorderLayout.NORTH );
23        label.setHorizontalAlignment( label.CENTER );
24
25        // Create a button
26        pushButton = new JButton("Test Button");
27        pushButton.addActionListener( new ButtonHandler (this) );
28        add( pushButton, BorderLayout.SOUTH );
29     }
30
31     // Method to update push count
32     public void updateLabel() {
33        label.setText( "Push Count: " + (++count) );
34     }
```

Figure 12.2. *(cont.)*

```
35   }
36
37       // Main method to create frame
38       public static void main(String s[]) {
39
40           // Create a frame to hold the application
41           JFrame fr = new JFrame("FirstGUI ...");
42           fr.setSize(200,100);
43
44           // Create a Window Listener to handle "close" events
45           WindowHandler l = new WindowHandler();
46           fr.addWindowListener(l);
47
48           // Create and initialize a FirstGUI object
49           FirstGUI fg = new FirstGUI();
50           fg.init();
51
52           // Add the object to the center of the frame
53           fr.getContentPane().add(fg, BorderLayout.CENTER);
54
55           // Display the frame
56           fr.setVisible( true );
57       }
58
59   class ButtonHandler implements ActionListener {
60       private FirstGUI fg;
61
62       // Constructor
63       public ButtonHandler ( FirstGUI fg1 ) {
64           fg = fg1;
65       }
66
67       // Execute when an event occurs
68       public void actionPerformed( ActionEvent e ) {
69           fg.updateLabel();
70       }
71   }
```

Figure 12.2. A program that creates a container, sets a layout manager for the container, adds components and listeners for the components, and places the whole container within a JFrame. This is the basic core structure required to create Java GUIs.

This program contains two classes: class FirstGUI to create and display the GUI, and class ButtonHandler to respond to mouse clicks on the button.

Class FirstGUI contains three methods: init(), updateLabel(), and main. Method init() initializes the GUI.[1] It specifies which layout manager to use with the container (line 18), creates the JButton and JLabel components (lines 21 and 26), and adds them to the container (lines 22 and 28). In addition, it creates a listener object of class ButtonHandler to listen for and handle events generated by mouse clicks and assigns that object to monitor mouse clicks on the button (line 27).

Method updateLabel() (lines 32–34) is the method that should be called every time that a button click occurs. It updates the label with the number of button clicks that have occurred.

---

[1] It is customary (but not required) to use the name init() for the method that sets up a GUI in a Java application. It *is* required to use the name init() for the method that sets up a GUI in a Java applet.

The main method creates a new JFrame (line 41), creates and initializes a FirstGUI object (lines 49–50), places the FirstGUI object in the center of the frame (line 53), and makes the frame visible (line 56).

Class ButtonHandler is a listener class designed to listen for and handle mouse clicks on the button. It implements the ActionListener interface, which guarantees that the class will have a method called actionPerformed. If an object of this class is associated (registered) with a GUI button, then *the actionPerformed method in the object will be called every time that a user clicks on the button with the mouse.* An object of this class is registered to handle events from the button in class FirstGUI (line 27), so whenever this button is clicked, the ButtonHandler method actionPerformed is called. Since that method calls the FirstGUI method updateLabel(), each mouse click causes the count displayed by the label to increase by one.

When this program is executed, the main method creates a new JFrame, creates and initializes a FirstGUI object, places the object in the center of the content pane associated with the frame, and makes the frame visible. The First-GUI object creates a label and a button, as well as an ButtonHandler to listen for button clicks. At this point, program execution stops, and it will *only* resume if an external event such as a mouse click occurs. If a mouse click occurs on the button, Java automatically calls method actionPerformed, because the ButtonHandler object was set to listen for mouse clicks on the button. This method calls method updateLabel(), which increases the button click count and updates the display.

12.3 EVENTS AND EVENT HANDLING

An **event** is an object that is created by some external action, such as a mouse click, key press, etc. When an event such as a mouse click occurs, *Java automatically sends that event to the GUI object that was clicked on.* For example, if a mouse click occurs over a button, Java sends the event to the GUI object that created that button.

When the mouse click event is received, the button checks to see if an object has *registered* with it to receive mouse events, and it forwards the event to the action-Performed method of that object. The actionPerformed method is known as an **event handler** because it performs whatever steps are required to process the event. In many cases, this event handler makes a call to a **callback method** in the object that created the GUI, since such methods can update instance variables within the object directly.

This process is illustrated in Figure 12-3 for the FirstGUI program. When a mouse click occurs on the button, an event is created and sent to the JButton object. Since the ButtonHandler object is registered to handle mouse clicks on the button, the JButton object calls the actionPerformed method of the ButtonHandler object. This method makes a callback to FirstGUI method updateLabel, which actually performs the required work (updating the instance variable count and the label text).

This basic procedure works for all types of Java events, but the name of the event handling method will differ for different types of events.

Figure 12.3. Event handling in program `FirstGUI`. When a user clicks on the button with the mouse, an event is sent to the `JButton` object. The `JButton` object calls the `actionPerformed` method of the `ButtonHandler` object, because that object is registered to handle the button's mouse click events. The `actionPerformed` method calls the `update` method of the `FirstGUI` object, which in turn calls the `setText` method of the `JLabel` object to change the push count.

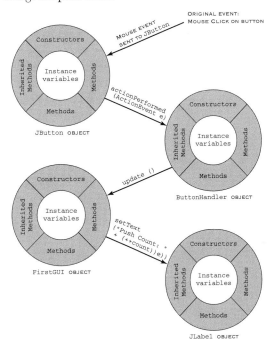

Figure 12.4. The display produced by program `First-GUI` after three button clicks.

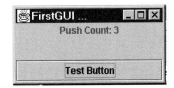

12.4 SELECTED GRAPHICAL USER INTERFACE COMPONENTS

This section summarizes the basic characteristics of some common graphical user interface components. It describes how to create and use each component, as well as the types of events each component can generate. The components discussed in this section are:

- Labels
- Push Buttons
- Text Fields and Password Fields
- Combo Boxes (Drop-down Lists)

- Check boxes
- Radio Buttons
- Canvases

12.4.1 Labels

A **label** is an object that displays a single line of *read-only text and/or an image.* A JLabel object can display either text, or an image, or both. You can specify how the text and image are aligned in the display area by setting the vertical and horizontal alignment, and you can specify whether the text is placed left, right, above, or below the image. By default, text-only labels are left-aligned, and image-only labels are horizontally centered. If both text and image are present, text is to the right of the image by default.

A label is created with the JLabel class using one of the following constructors:

```
public JLabel();
public JLabel(String s);
public JLabel(String s, int horizontalAlignment);
public JLabel(Icon image);
public JLabel(Icon image, int horizontalAlignment);
public JLabel(String s, Icon image, int horizontalAlignment);
```

In these constructors, s is a string containing the text to display on the label, image is the image to display on the label, and horizontalAlignment is the alignment of the text and image within the label. Possible alignment values are JLabel.LEFT, JLabel.RIGHT, and JLabel.CENTER. Note that the first constructor creates a label containing neither text nor an image.

Some of the methods in class JLabel are described in Table 12-2. Note that JLabels do not generate any events, so there are no listener interfaces or classes associated with them.

The following program shows how to create labels both with images and without images. The first label consists of an image followed by text, left justified in its field. The second label consists of text followed by an image, right justified in its field. The third label consists of text only, centered in its field. Note that the images may be stored in **GIF** or **JPEG** files, which can be read by creating an ImageIcon object.

TABLE 12-2   JLabel Methods

METHOD	DESCRIPTION
public Icon getIcon()	Returns the image from a JLabel.
public String getText()	Returns the text from a JLabel.
public void setIcon(Icon image)	Sets the JLabel image.
public void setText(String s)	Sets the JLabel text.
public void setHorizontalAlignment(int alignment)	Sets the horizontal alignment of the JLabel text and image. Valid values are LEFT, CENTER, and RIGHT.
public void setHorizontalTextPosition(int textPosition)	Sets the position of the text relative to the image. Valid values are LEFT, CENTER, and RIGHT.
public void setVerticalAlignment(int alignment)	Sets the vertical alignment of the JLabel text and images. Valid values are TOP, CENTER, and BOTTOM.
public void setVerticalTextPosition(int textPosition)	Sets the position of the text relative to the image. Valid values are TOP, CENTER, and BOTTOM.

```
// Test labels.  This program creates a GUI containing
// three labels, with and without images.
import java.awt.*;
import java.awt.event.*;
import javax.swing.*;
public class TestLabel extends JPanel {

    // Instance variables
    private JLabel l1, l2, l3;   // Labels

    // Initialization method
    public void init() {

        // Set the layout manager
        setLayout( new BorderLayout() );

        // Get the images to display
        ImageIcon right = new ImageIcon("BlueRightArrow.gif");
        ImageIcon left = new ImageIcon("BlueLeftArrow.gif");

         // Create a label with icon and text
        l1 = new JLabel("Label 1", right, JLabel.LEFT);
        add( l1, BorderLayout.NORTH );

        // Create a label with text and icon
        l2 = new JLabel("Label 2", left, JLabel.RIGHT);
        add( l2, BorderLayout.CENTER );
        l2.setHorizontalTextPosition( JLabel.LEFT );

        // Create a label with text only
        l3 = new JLabel("Label 3 (Text only)", JLabel.CENTER);
        add( l3, BorderLayout.SOUTH );
    }

    // Main method to create frame
    public static void main(String s[]) {

        // Create a frame to hold the application
        JFrame fr = new JFrame("TestLabel ...");
        fr.setSize(200,100);

        // Create a Window Listener to handle "close" events
        MyWindowListener l = new MyWindowListener();
        fr.addWindowListener(l);

        // Create and initialize a TestLabel object
        TestLabel tl = new TestLabel();
        tl.init();

        // Add the object to the center of the frame
        fr.getContentPane().add(tl, BorderLayout.CENTER);

        // Display the frame
        fr.setVisible( true );
    }
}
<
```

Figure 12.5. A program illustrating the use of labels, with and without images.

When this program is executed, the results are as shown in Figure 12.6.

Figure 12.6. The display produced by program `TestLabel`.

12.4.2 Push Buttons and Associated Events

A **push button** is a component that a user can click on to trigger a specific action. Push buttons are created by the **JButton** class. Each JButton has a label and/or icon printed on its face to identify the purpose of the button. A GUI can have many buttons, but each button label should be unique, so that a user can tell them apart.

Swing buttons are very flexible. Each button may be labeled with text, an image, or both, and the location of the text and image on the button can be controlled. Buttons may be enabled and disabled during program execution; when a button is disabled, it is grayed out and cannot be pressed. The icon displayed by a button can be automatically changed whenever it is pressed or disabled. In addition, **keyboard shortcuts** (mnemonic keys) can be defined to allow a user to activate the button via the keyboard. Finally, Java buttons support **tool tips**, which are messages that are displayed in pop-up windows when the cursor rests over the top of the button. Tool tips are used to explain the function of the button to the program's user.

A push button is created with one of the following constructors:

```
public JButton();
public JButton(String s);
public JButton(Icon image);
public JButton(String s, Icon image);
```

These constructors create new buttons with a text label, an image, or both. Note that the first constructor creates a button containing neither text nor an image. Some of the methods in class `Button` are described in Table 12-3.

Events Associated with Buttons   When the mouse button is *both pressed and released* while the cursor is over a button, the button generates an `ActionEvent` and sends that event to any objects that have been registered with it as listeners. An **ActionEvent** is a special kind of event that means that the usual action associated with the component has occurred. For example, buttons are meant to be clicked on, so an `ActionEvent` from a button means that the button has been clicked on. (`ActionEvents` from other components will have different meanings.)

ActionEvents include several methods that allow a program to recover information about the triggering event. The most important of these methods are listed in Table 12-4.

The `ActionListener` Interface   ActionEvents are processed by classes that implement the **ActionListener interface**, which defines the single event handling method **actionPerformed**. When an `ActionListener` object is registered with a button using the JButton method `addActionListener`, the ActionListener method `actionPerformed` will be automatically called whenever a click occurs on that button.

TABLE 12-3 JButton Methods

METHOD	DESCRIPTION
public void addActionListener(ActionListener l)	Adds the specified action listener to receive action events from this button.
public Icon getIcon()	Returns the image from a JButton.
public String getLabel()	Returns the label of the button.
public void setActionCommand(String s)	Sets the action command string generated by this button when it is pressed.
public void setDisabledIcon(Icon icon)	Sets the icon to display when the button is disabled.
public void setEnabled(boolean b)	Enables or disables the button.
public void setHorizontalAlignment(int alignment)	Sets the horizontal alignment of the text and images. Valid values are LEFT, CENTER, and RIGHT.
public void setHorizontalTextPosition(int textPosition)	Sets the position of the text relative to the images. Valid values are LEFT, CENTER, and RIGHT.
public void setLabel(String s)	Sets the label of this button to the specified String.
public void setIcon(Icon icon)	Sets the default icon for this button.
public void setMnemonic(char mnemonic)	Set the keyboard character combination used to activate the button from the keyboard.
public void setPressedIcon(Icon icon)	Sets the icon to display when the button is pressed.
public void setToolTipText(String text)	Sets the tool tip text to display when the cursor rests over the button.
public void setVerticalAlignment(int alignment)	Sets the vertical alignment of the text and images. Valid values are TOP, CENTER, and BOTTOM.
public void setVerticalTextPosition(int textPosition)	Sets the position of the text relative to the images. Valid values are TOP, CENTER, and BOTTOM.

TABLE 12-4 ActionEvent Methods

METHOD	DESCRIPTION
public String getActionCommand()	Returns the command string associated with this action. By default, this method returns the *text label printed on the button.*
public int getModifiers()	Returns the modifier keys held down during this action event. Possible modifiers are ALT_MASK, CTRL_MASK, META_MASK, and SHIFT_MASK.
public String paramString()	Returns a parameter string identifying this action event. This method is useful for logging events and for debugging.

TABLE 12-5 ActionListener Interface Method

METHOD	DESCRIPTION
void actionPerformed(ActionEvent e)	Method invoked when an ActionEvent occurs.

Chapter 12 Basic Graphical User Interfaces

The following program illustrates the use of push buttons. It defines three buttons, with text and images on each button. The left button enables the center button when it is clicked, and the right button disables the center button when it is clicked. If the center button is enabled, each click on the button will increment the displayed count by one. Note that disabled buttons are "grayed out" and that mouse clicks on them are ignored.

Each button has a keyboard shortcut (mnemonic) assigned to it, so the key combination ALT+e will press the left button, ALT+c will press the center button, and ALT+d will press the right button.

This application also illustrates the display of multiple images depending on the state of a button. When the middle button is disabled, it displays a red ball. When it is enabled, it displays a green ball. Finally, when the button is clicked, the ball turns yellow.

This program also shows how a class can handle its own events. Note that the TestPushButtons class implements the ActionListener interface, and this class is registered with each button using the method addActionListener(this). When an enabled button is clicked, it sends an ActionEvent to the actionPerformed method of the TestPushButtons class. This method checks to see which button generated the event, using the string returned by the ActionEvent method getActionCommand() to distinguish among them. Note that for buttons the default string returned by getActionCommand() is the text on the label of the button. As long as this text is different for every button, we can use that label to tell which button was pressed.

When the left button is pressed, the actionPerformed method is called automatically and the result of e.getActionCommand() will be "Enable". When the right button is pressed, the actionPerformed method is called automatically, and the result of e.getActionCommand() will be "Disable". When the center button is pressed, the actionPerformed method is called automatically, and the first five letters returned by e.getActionCommand() will be "Count". An if structure can test the value of string button and perform the proper action depending on which button was pressed.

```
// This program tests push buttons.
import java.awt.*;
import java.awt.event.*;
import javax.swing.*;
public class TestPushButtons extends JPanel
                     implements ActionListener {

    // Instance variables
    private int c = 0;                  // Count
    private JButton b1, b2, b3;     // Buttons

    // Initialization method
    public void init() {

        // Set the layout manager
        setLayout( new FlowLayout() );

        // Get the images to display
        ImageIcon right = new ImageIcon("RightArrow.gif");
        ImageIcon left = new ImageIcon("LeftArrow.gif");
        ImageIcon green = new ImageIcon("green-ball.gif");
        ImageIcon red = new ImageIcon("red-ball.gif");
        ImageIcon yellow = new ImageIcon("yellow-ball.gif");
```

Figure 12.7. (cont.)

```
      // Create buttons
      b1 = new JButton("Enable",right);
      b1.addActionListener( this );
      b1.setMnemonic('e');
      b1.setToolTipText("Enable middle button");
      add(b1);

      String s = "Count = " + c;
      b2 = new JButton(s,green);
      b2.addActionListener( this );
      b2.setMnemonic('c');

      b2.setEnabled(false);
      b2.setToolTipText("Press to increment count");
      b2.setPressedIcon(yellow);
      b2.setDisabledIcon(red);
      add(b2);

      b3 = new JButton("Disable",left);
      b3.addActionListener( this );
      b3.setMnemonic('d');
      b3.setEnabled(false);
      b3.setToolTipText("Disable middle button");
      add(b3);
   }

   // Event handler to handle button pushes
   public void actionPerformed(ActionEvent e) {
      String button = e.getActionCommand();

      if (button.equals("Enable")) {
         b1.setEnabled(false);
         b2.setEnabled(true);
         b3.setEnabled(true);
      }
      else if (button.substring(0,5).equals("Count")) {
         b2.setText("Count = " + (++c));
      }
      else if (button.equals("Disable")) {
         b1.setEnabled(true);
         b2.setEnabled(false);
         b3.setEnabled(false);
      }
   }

   // Main method to create frame
   public static void main(String s[]) {

      // Create a frame to hold the application
      JFrame fr = new JFrame("TestPushButtons ...");
      fr.setSize(400,80);

      // Create a Window Listener to handle "close" events
      MyWindowListener l = new MyWindowListener();
      fr.addWindowListener(l);

      // Create and initialize a TestPushButtons object
      TestPushButtons ob = new TestPushButtons();
      ob.init();
```

Figure 12.7. *(cont.)*

```
            // Add the object to the center of the frame
            fr.getContentPane().add(ob, BorderLayout.CENTER);

            // Display the frame
            fr.setVisible( true );
        }
    }
```

Figure 12.7. A program to test the operation of push buttons.

Figure 12.8a shows the initial state of the program, with the center button disabled. Figure 12.8b shows the program after the center button has been enabled and pressed twice.

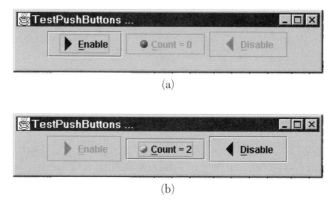

(a)

(b)

Figure 12.8. (a) The display produced by program `TestPushButtons` when it is first started. (b) The display produced by the program after one button click on the left button and two clicks on the center button.

GOOD PROGRAMMING PRACTICE

Buttons generate `ActionEvents` when pressed. To handle button events, use a class that implements the `Action Listener` interface, and contains an `actionPerformed` method. Register an object from this class with each button, and code the `actionPerformed` method to do whatever is required when the button is pressed.

GOOD PROGRAMMING PRACTICE

One `ActionListener` object can monitor many buttons, using the result of the `getActionCommand` method to determine the button that created a particular event.

12.4.3 Text Fields and Password Fields

A text field is a single-line area in which text can be entered by a user from the keyboard. When a user types information into a `JTextField` and presses the Enter key, an `ActionEvent` is generated. If an `ActionListener` has been registered with the text field, then the event will be handled by the `actionPerformed` method, and the data typed by the user is available for use in the program. A `JTextField` may also be used to display read-only text that a user cannot modify. A `JPasswordField` field is identical to a text field, except that asterisks are displayed instead of the characters that are typed on the keyboard.

A text field or password is created with one of the following constructors:

```
public JTextField();
public JTextField(int cols);
public JTextField(String s);
public JTextField(String s, int cols);
public JPasswordField();
public JPasswordField(int columns);
public JPasswordField(String s);
public JPasswordField(String s, int cols);
```

The first form of constructor creates a new blank `JTextField` or `JPasswordField`, while the second form of constructor creates a new blank `JTextField` or `JPasswordField` large enough to contain `cols` characters. The third form of the constructor creates a new `JTextField` or `JPasswordField` initialized with the specified string, and the fourth form of the constructor creates a new `JTextField` or `JPasswordField` large enough to contain `columns` characters and initialized with the specified string. Some of the methods in these classes are described in Table 12-6.

An `ActionEvent` object is created whenever a user presses Enter on the keyboard after typing data into a text field. By default, The `getActionCommand()` method of the `ActionEvent` object will return a string containing the data that was typed in. As before, this event may be handled by the `actionEvent` method of an `ActionListener`.

The program shown in Figure 12.9 illustrates the use of editable and read-only text fields, plus a password field. The first text field in this program is an ordinary text field in which the data that a user types is visible. The second field is a `JPasswordField`, in which the data that a user types is replaced by asterisks. The third text field is a "read-only" text field. It is used to display the data returned by the event handler after a user presses the Enter key on one of the other text fields.

TABLE 12-6 `JTextField` and `JPasswordField` **Methods**

METHOD	DESCRIPTION
`public String getText()`	Gets the text currently displayed in this component.
`public String getSelectedText()`	Gets the selected text from the text currently displayed in this component.
`public void setActionCommand(String s)`	Sets the action command string generated by this text field when it is pressed.
`public void setEditable(boolean b)`	Sets the editability status of the field. If `true`, a user can change the data in the field. If `false`, the user cannot change the data in the field.
`public void setText(String t)`	Displays the text in string `t`.
`public void setToolTipText( String text)`	Sets the tool tip text to display when the cursor rests over the text field.

```
// This program tests text fields.
import java.awt.*;
import java.awt.event.*;
import javax.swing.*;
public class TestTextField extends JPanel {

    // Instance variables
    private JLabel l1, l2, l3;          // Labels
    private JTextField t1, t3;          // Text Fields
    private JPasswordField t2;          // Password Field
    private TextFieldHandler handler;   // ActionEvent handler

    // Initialization method
    public void init() {

        // Set background color
        setBackground( Color.lightGray );

        // Set the layout manager
        setLayout( new FlowLayout() );

        // Create ActionEvent handler
        handler = new TextFieldHandler( this );

        // Create first Text Field
        l1 = new JLabel("Visible text here:",JLabel.RIGHT);
        add( l1 );
        t1 = new JTextField("Enter Text Here",25);
        t1.addActionListener( handler );
        add( t1 );

        // Create Password Field
        l2 = new JLabel("Hidden text here:",JLabel.RIGHT);
        add( l2 );
        t2 = new JPasswordField("Enter Text Here",25);
        t2.addActionListener( handler );
        add( t2 );

        // Create third Text Field
        l3 = new JLabel("Results:",JLabel.RIGHT);
        add( l3 );
        t3 = new JTextField(25);
        t3.setEditable( false );
        add( t3 );
    }

    // Method to update t3
    public void updateT3( String s ) {
        t3.setText( s );
    }

    // Main method to create frame
    public static void main(String s[]) {
        // Create a frame to hold the application
        JFrame fr = new JFrame("TestTextField ...");
        fr.setSize(400,130);
        (rest of main is the same as previous examples...)
    }
}
```

Figure 12.9. *(cont.)*

```
class TextFieldHandler implements ActionListener {
   private TestTextField ttf;

   // Constructor
   public TextFieldHandler ( TestTextField t ) {
      ttf = t;
   }

   // Execute when an event occurs
   public void actionPerformed( ActionEvent e ) {
      ttf.updateT3(e.getActionCommand());
   }
}
```

Figure 12.9. A program to test `JTextField` and `JPasswordField` objects.

When information is typed in Text Field 1 and the Enter key is pressed, an `Action-Event` is generated and handled by the `actionPerformed` method. This method makes a call back to method `updateT3` to display the typed information in the read-only field.

When this program is executed, the results after information is typed into Text Field 1 are shown in Figure 12.10a, and the results after information is typed into Text Field 2 are shown in Figure 12.10b.

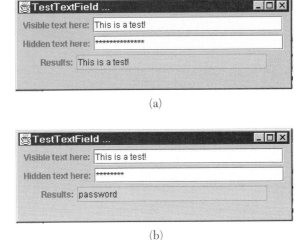

(a)

(b)

Figure 12.10. Results when information is typed in the text and password fields.

EXAMPLE 12-1:
TEMPERATURE
CONVERSION

Write a program that converts temperature from degrees Fahrenheit to degrees Celsius, and vice versa, using a GUI to accept data and display results.

SOLUTION

To create this program, we will need a label and text field for the temperature in degrees Fahrenheit and another label and text field for the temperature in degrees Celsius. We will also need a method to convert degrees Fahrenheit to degrees Celsius and a method to convert degrees Celsius to degrees Fahrenheit. Finally, we will need two event handlers to accept text entry in the two text fields.

The `init()` method for this program must create two labels and two text fields to hold the temperature in degrees Celsius and degrees Fahrenheit. In addition, it must create `ActionListener` objects for both text fields. The code for these steps is as follows:

```
// Create ActionEvent handlers
cHnd = new DegCHandler( this );
fHnd = new DegFHandler( this );

// Create degrees Celsius field
l1 = new JLabel("deg C:", JLabel.RIGHT);
add( l1 );
t1 = new JTextField("0.0",15);
t1.addActionListener( cHnd );
add( t1 );

// Create degrees Celsius field
l2 = new JLabel("deg F:", JLabel.RIGHT);
add( l2 );
t2 = new JTextField("32.0",15);
t2.addActionListener( fHnd );
add( t2 );
```

Method `toC` will convert temperature from degrees Fahrenheit to degrees Celsius. It must implement the equation

$$\deg C = \frac{5}{9}\,(\deg F - 32) \tag{12-1}$$

and must update the text fields with this information. The pseudocode for these steps is:

```
degC ← (5. / 9.) * (degF - 32);
t1.setText( Fmt.sprintf("%5.1f",degC) );
t2.setText( Fmt.sprintf("%5.1f",degF) );
```

Note that we are using the `Fmt.sprintf` method from the `chapman.io` package to format the temperatures for display. Method `toF` will convert temperature from degrees Celsius to degrees Fahrenheit. It must implement the equation

$$\deg F = \frac{9}{5}\,\deg C + 32 \tag{12-2}$$

and must update the text fields with this information. The pseudocode for these steps is

```
degF ← (9. / 5.) * degC + 32;
t1.setText( Fmt.sprintf("%5.1f",degC) );
t2.setText( Fmt.sprintf("%5.1f",degF) );
```

The `ActionListeners` must listen for inputs in a text field, convert the input `String` into a `double` value, and call the appropriate `toC` or `toF` method. For example, the code for the `actionPerformed` method that monitors the degrees Celsius text field would be:

```
public void actionPerformed( ActionEvent e ) {
    String input = e.getActionCommand();
    double degC = Double.parseDouble( input );
    tc.toF( degC );
}
```

The final program is shown in Figure 12.11.

```
/*
    Purpose:
      This GUI-based program converts temperature in
      degrees Fahrenheit to degrees Celsius, and vice versa.

    Record of revisions:
        Date        Programmer          Description of change
        ====        ==========          =====================
      10/14/98   S. J. Chapman          Original code
*/
import java.awt.*;
import java.awt.event.*;
import javax.swing.*;
import chapman.io.*;
class TempConversion extends JPanel {

    // Instance variables
    private JLabel l1, l2;       // Labels
    private JTextField t1, t2;   // Text Fields
    private DegCHandler cHnd;     // ActionEvent handler
    private DegFHandler fHnd;     // ActionEvent handler

    // Initialization method
    public void init() {
        // Set the layout manager
        setLayout( new FlowLayout() );

        // Create ActionEvent handlers
        cHnd = new DegCHandler( this );
        fHnd = new DegFHandler( this );

        // Create degrees Celsius field
        l1 = new JLabel("deg C:", JLabel.RIGHT);
        add( l1 );

        t1 = new JTextField("0.0",15);
        t1.addActionListener( cHnd );
        add( t1 );

        // Create degrees Celsius field
        l2 = new JLabel("deg F:", JLabel.RIGHT);
        add( l2 );
        t2 = new JTextField("32.0",15);
        t2.addActionListener( fHnd );
        add( t2 );
    }

    // Method to convert deg F to deg C
    // and display result
    public void toC( double degF ) {
        double degC = (5. / 9.) * (degF - 32);
        t1.setText( Fmt.sprintf("%5.1f",degC) );
        t2.setText( Fmt.sprintf("%5.1f",degF) );
    }
```

Figure 12.11. *(cont.)*

```
        // Method to convert deg C to deg F
        // and display result
        public void toF( double degC ) {
            double degF = (9. / 5.) * degC + 32;
            t1.setText( Fmt.sprintf("%5.1f",degC) );
            t2.setText( Fmt.sprintf("%5.1f",degF) );
        }

        // Main method to create frame
        public static void main(String s[]) {

            // Create a frame to hold the application
            JFrame fr = new JFrame("TempConversion ...");
            fr.setSize(250,100);

            // Create a Window Listener to handle "close" events
            MyWindowListener l = new MyWindowListener();
            fr.addWindowListener(l);

            // Create and initialize a TempConversion object
            TempConversion tf = new TempConversion();
            tf.init();
            // Add the object to the center of the frame
            fr.getContentPane().add(tf, BorderLayout.CENTER);

            // Display the frame
            fr.setVisible( true );
        }
    }

    class DegCHandler implements ActionListener {
        private TempConversion tc;

        // Constructor
        public DegCHandler( TempConversion t ) { tc = t; }

        // Execute when an event occurs
        public void actionPerformed( ActionEvent e ) {
            String input = e.getActionCommand();
            double degC = Double.parseDouble( input );
            tc.toF( degC );
        }
    }

    class DegFHandler implements ActionListener {
        private TempConversion tc;

        // Constructor
        public DegFHandler( TempConversion t ) { tc = t; }

        // Execute when an event occurs
        public void actionPerformed( ActionEvent e ) {
            String input = e.getActionCommand();
            double degF = Double.parseDouble( input );
            tc.toC( degF );
        }
    }
```

Figure 12.11. A GUI-based temperature conversion program.

When this program is executed, the results are as shown in Figure 12.12. Try this program for yourself with several different temperature values.

Figure 12.12.   (a) Result when the user enters 100° C. (b) Result when the user enters 72° F.

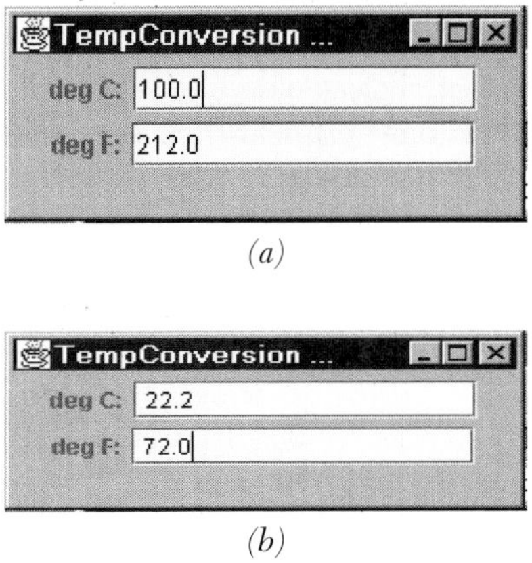

(a)

(b)

12.4.4 Combo Boxes

A **combo box** is a field in which a user can either type an entry or select an entry from a *drop-down list* of choices. If desired, the combo box can be restricted so that only choices in the drop-down list may be selected. The selected choice is displayed in the combo box field after a selection has been made.

Combo boxes are implemented by the JComboBox class. A JComboBox is created with the following constructor:

```
public JComboBox();
public JComboBox( Object[] );
public JComboBox( Vector );
```

The first constructor creates an empty combo box. The second constructor builds a new combo box with the array of objects (such as Strings) used to initialize the choices in the box. The last constructor builds a new combo box with a Vector of objects (such as Strings) used to initialize the choices in the box. Some of the methods in class JComboBox are described in Table 12-7.

TABLE 12-7   Selected JComboBox Methods

METHOD	DESCRIPTION
public void addActionListener(ActionListener l)	Adds the specified listener to receive ActionEvents from this JComboBox list. These events happen when selection is complete.
public void addItem(Object o)	Adds an item to the JComboBox list.
public Object getItemAt(int index)	Returns the JComboBox item at location index.
public int getItemCount()	Returns the number of items in this JComboBox list.
public int getSelectedIndex()	Returns the index of the selected JComboBox item.
public Object getSelectedItem()	Returns the selected JComboBox item.
public boolean isEditable()	Returns the editable state of the JComboBox.
public void insertItemAt(Object o, int i)	Inserts an item ant position i in the JComboBox list.
public void removeItem(Object o)	Removes the specified JComboBox item.
public void removeItemAt(int index)	Removes the JComboBox item at location index.
public void setEditable(boolean b)	If b is true, a user can type in the combo box (default is false).
public void setToolTipText(String text)	Sets the tool tip text to display when the cursor rests over the text field.

Class JComboBox implements the ActionListener interface, which means that it generates ActionEvents. When an item is accepted in a JComboBox field, the JComboBox generates an ActionEvent and sends that event to any objects that have been registered with it as listeners.

The program in Figure 12.13 shows how to create a JComboBox and to implement choices based on selections in that field. This class creates a combo box and a read-only text field. The user selects a font name from the choice list (Serif, SansSerif, Monospaced, or Dialog), and the sample text is displayed with appropriate formatting in the text field. (Note that this example uses an *uneditable* combo box, because only the valid font names supplied should be selectable.)

```java
// This program tests combo boxes.
import java.awt.*;
import java.awt.event.*;
import javax.swing.*;
public class TestComboBox extends JPanel {

    // Instance variables
    private JComboBox c1;             // Combo box
    private JTextField t1;            // TextField
    private ComboHandler handler;     // ActionEvent handler

    // Initialization method
    public void init() {

        // Set background color
        setBackground( Color.lightGray );

        // Set the layout manager
         setLayout( new FlowLayout() );

        // Create ActionEvent handler
        handler = new ComboHandler( this );

        // Create the JComboBox
        String[] s = {"Serif","SansSerif","Monospaced","Dialog"};
        c1 = new JComboBox(s);
        c1.addActionListener( handler );
        add( c1 );

        // Create the text field with default font
        Font font = new Font(c1.getItemAt(0).toString(),
                            Font.PLAIN, 14);
        t1 = new JTextField("Test string",30);
        t1.setEditable( false );
        t1.setFont( font );
        add( t1 );
    }

    // Method to update font
    public void updateFont() {
        int valBold, valItalic;

        // Get current font info
        int fontStyle  = t1.getFont().getStyle();
        int fontSize   = t1.getFont().getSize();
```

Figure 12.13. *(cont.)*

```
        // Get new font name
        String fontName = (String) c1.getSelectedItem();

        // Set new font
        t1.setFont( new Font(fontName, fontStyle, fontSize) );

        // Repaint the JTextField
        t1.repaint();
    }

    // Main method to create frame
    public static void main(String s[]) {

        // Create a frame to hold the application
        JFrame fr = new JFrame("TestComboBox ...");
        fr.setSize(400,100);

        (rest of main is the same as previous examples...)
    }
}


class ComboHandler implements ActionListener {
    private TestComboBox tcb;

    // Constructor
    public ComboHandler( TestComboBox t ) { tcb = t; }

    // Execute when an event occurs
    public void actionPerformed( ActionEvent e ) {

        // State has changed, so call updateFont
        tcb.updateFont();
    }
}
```

Figure 12.13. A program showing how different fonts can be selected with a
JcomboBox.

When the combo box is clicked, a drop-down list appears with the four possible font names. When the user selects one of these font names by clicking on the name, an ActionEvent is created and the actionPerformed method is called. This method in turn calls updateFont() to display the new font. Method updateFont() gets the new font name from the choice list using the getSelectedItem() method, which returns an Object reference. This reference is downcast to a String, and that font name is used to create a new font with that name and the original font style (PLAIN, BOLD, etc.) and size. Finally, the JTextField is repainted to display the new font.

When this program is executed, the results are as shown in Figure 12.14.

GOOD PROGRAMMING PRACTICE

Use JComboBoxes to make a single selection from a list of mutually exclusive choices.

Figure 12.14.   The results of program `TestComboBox` as different fonts are selected from the choice list.

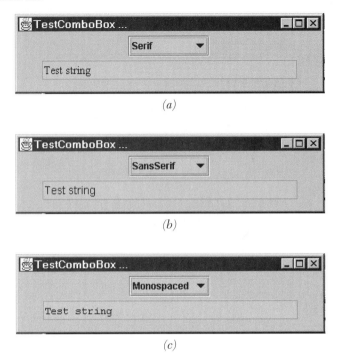

(a)

(b)

(c)

12.4.5 Check Boxes and Radio Buttons

A **check box** is a type of button that toggles between two possible states: on/off, or `true/false`. When the check box is on, a small check mark appears in it, and when the check box is off, the mark is removed. Each time that the mouse clicks on a check box, the check box toggles to the opposite state. Check boxes look like small square boxes with check marks in them, but they are in fact full-fledged buttons with all of the features that we learned about when studying pushbuttons. For example, it is possible to include both text and images on a check box, and it is possible to define keyboard shortcuts for them. Checkboxes are implemented by the **JCheckBox** class.

A JCheckBox is created with one of the following constructors:

```
public JCheckBox( String s );
public JCheckBox( String s, boolean state );
public JCheckBox( Icon Image );
public JCheckBox( Icon image, boolean state );
public JCheckBox( String s, Icon image );
public JCheckBox( String s, Icon image, boolean state );
```

In these constructors, s is the text label for the checkbox, image is the image to display on the check box, and state is the initial on/off state of the check box. If state is absent from a constructor, then the new checkbox defaults to off. Some of the methods in class JCheckBox are described in Table 12-8.

Class JCheckBox implements the `ActionListener` interface, which means that it generates `ActionEvents`. When a Checkbox is clicked, the Checkbox gen-

TABLE 12-8 Selected `JCheckBox` and `JRadioButton` Methods

METHOD	DESCRIPTION
`public String addActionListener(ActionListener l)`	Adds the specified listener to receive `ActionEvents` from this `JCheckBox`.
`public Icon getIcon()`	Returns the image from a `JCheckBox` or `JRadioButton`.
`public String getLabel()`	Returns the label from the `JCheckBox` or `JRadioButton`.
`public boolean isSelected()`	Returns the state of the `JCheckBox` (`true` or `false`).
`public void setLabel(String s)`	Sets a new label into the `JCheckBox` or `JRadioButton`.
`public void setActionCommand(String s)`	Sets the action command string generated by this `JCheckBox` or `JRadioButton` when it is clicked.
`public void setDisabledIcon(Icon icon)`	Sets icon to display when the check box / radio button is disabled.
`public void setEnabled(boolean b)`	Enables or disables this `JCheckBox` or `JRadioButton`.
`public void setHorizontalAlignment(int alignment)`	Sets the horizontal alignment of the text and images. Legal values are LEFT, CENTER, and RIGHT.
`public void setHorizontalTextPosition(int textPosition)`	Sets the position of the text relative to the images. Legal values are LEFT, CENTER, and RIGHT.
`public void setLabel(String s)`	Sets the label of this check box / radio button to the specified `String`.
`public void setIcon(Icon icon)`	Sets the default icon for this check box / radiobutton.
`public void setMnemonic(char mnemonic)`	Set the keyboard character combination used to activate the \check box / radio button from the keyboard.
`public void setPressedIcon(Icon icon)`	Sets the icon to display when the check box / radio button is pressed.
`public void setSelected(boolean b)`	Sets a new state into the `JCheckBox` or `JRadioButton`.
`public void setToolTipText(String text)`	Sets the tool tip text to display when the cursor rests over the check box or button.
`public void setVerticalAlignment(int alignment)`	Sets the vertical alignment of the text and images. Legal values are TOP, CENTER, and BOTTOM.
`public void setVerticalTextPosition(int textPosition)`	Sets the position of the text relative to the images. Legal values are TOP, CENTER, and BOTTOM.

erates an `ActionEvent` and sends that event to any objects that have been registered with it as listeners.

The program in Figure 12.15 shows how to create `JCheckBoxes` and to implement choices based on the state of the `JCheckBox`. This class expands on the previous program by adding two check boxes to select bold and/or italic font types for display.

```
// This program tests check boxes.
import java.awt.*;
import java.awt.event.*;
import javax.swing.*;
public class TestCheckBox extends JPanel {

    // Instance variables
    private JCheckBox cb1, cb2;     // Check boxes
    private JComboBox c1;           // Combo box
    private JTextField t1;          // TextField
    private ActionHandler h1;       // ActionEvent handler
```

Figure 12.15. *(cont.)*

```
                 // Initialization method
                 public void init() {

                     // Set the layout manager
                     setLayout( new FlowLayout() );

                     // Create ActionEvent handler
                     h1 = new ActionHandler( this );

                     // Create the JComboBox for font names
                     String[] s = {"Serif","SansSerif","Monospaced",
                                   "Dialog"};
                     c1 = new JComboBox(s);
                     c1.addActionListener( h1 );
                     add( c1 );

                     // Create the text field with default font
                     Font font = new Font( c1.getItemAt(0).toString(),
                                           Font.PLAIN, 14);
                     t1 = new JTextField("Test string",20);
                     t1.setEditable( false );
                     t1.setFont( font );
                     add( t1 );

                     // Create check boxes for bold and italic
                     cb1 = new JCheckBox("Bold");
                     cb1.addActionListener( h1 );
                     cb1.setMnemonic('b');
                     add( cb1 );
                     cb2 = new JCheckBox("Italic");
                     cb2.addActionListener( h1 );
                     cb2.setMnemonic('i');
                     add( cb2 );
                 }

                 // Method to update font
                 public void updateFont() {
                     int valBold, valItalic;

                     // Get current font info
                     int fontStyle   = t1.getFont().getStyle();
                     int fontSize    = t1.getFont().getSize();

                     // Get new font name
                     String fontName = (String) c1.getSelectedItem();

                     // Get new font style
                     valBold   = cb1.isSelected() ? Font.BOLD   : Font.PLAIN;
                     valItalic = cb2.isSelected() ? Font.ITALIC : Font.PLAIN;
                     fontStyle = valBold + valItalic;

                     // Set new font
                     t1.setFont( new Font(fontName, fontStyle, fontSize) );

                     // Repaint the JTextField
                     t1.repaint();
                 }
```

Figure 12.15. *(cont.)*

```
        // Main method to create frame
        public static void main(String s[]) {
            // Create a frame to hold the application
            JFrame fr = new JFrame("TestCheckBox ...");
            fr.setSize(380,100);

            (rest of main is the same as previous examples...)
        }
    }


    class ActionHandler implements ActionListener {
        private TestCheckBox tcb;

        // Constructor
        public ActionHandler( TestCheckBox t ) { tcb = t; }

        // Execute when an event occurs
        public void actionPerformed( ActionEvent e ) {

            // State has changed, so call updateFont
            tcb.updateFont();
        }
    }
```

Figure 12.15.   A program using JCheckBoxes to select bold and italic font styles.

When a check box is clicked (or activated by the proper keyboard combination), an ActionEvent is created and the actionPerformed method in class Action-Handler is called. This method in turn calls updateFont() to display the new font. Method updateFont() gets the status of the bold and italic check boxes using the isSelected() method, and it creates a new font with that style.

When this program is executed, the results are as shown in Figure 12.16.

Radio buttons are a group of check boxes in which *at most one check box can be on at a time*. Radio buttons look like small circles with a dot inside the selected one, but otherwise have the same characteristics as any button. Radio buttons are implemented by the **JRadioButton** class.

A JRadioButton is created with one of the following constructors:

```
public JRadioButton( String s );
public JRadioButton( String s, boolean state );
public JRadioButton( Icon Image );
public JRadioButton( Icon image, boolean state );
public JRadioButton( String s, Icon image );
public JRadioButton( String s, Icon image, boolean state );
```

In these constructors, s is the text label for the radio button, image is the image to display on the radio button, and state is the initial on/off state of the radio button. If state is absent from a constructor, then the new radio button defaults to off. The methods in class JRadioButton are the same as those in class JCheckBox and are described in Table 12-8.

A group of radio buttons is made mutually exclusive (only one can be on at a time) by placing them in a **ButtonGroup**. The ButtonGroup ensures that when one of the JRadioButtons is turned on, the others are all off.

A ButtonGroup is created with the following constructor:

```
public ButtonGroup();
```

Some of the methods in class ButtonGroup are described in Table 12-9.

Figure 12.16. The results of program `TestCheckBox` as different combinations of the bold and italic checkboxes are turned on.

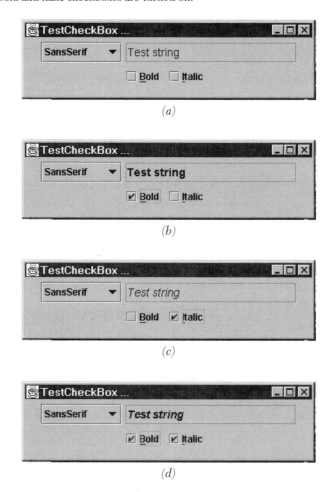

The program in Figure 12.17 shows how to create a set of radio buttons using `JRadioButtons` in a `ButtonGroup`. This class modifies the previous program by using four radio buttons instead of two check boxes to select bold and/or italic font types for display.

TABLE 12-9 Selected `ButtonGroup` Methods

METHOD	DESCRIPTION
`public void add(AbstractButton b)`	Adds a button to the `ButtonGroup`.
`public void remove(AbstractButton b)`	Removes a button from the `ButtonGroup`.

```java
// This program tests radio buttons.
import java.awt.*;
import java.awt.event.*;
import javax.swing.*;
public class TestRadioButton extends JPanel {

    // Instance variables
    private ButtonGroup bg;                // ButtonGroup
    private JRadioButton b1, b2, b3, b4;   // Check boxes
    private JComboBox c1;                  // Combo box
    private JTextField t1;                 // TextField
    private ActionHandler h1;              // ActionEvent handler

    // Initialization method
    public void init() {

        // Set the layout manager
        setLayout( new FlowLayout() );

        // Create ActionEvent handler
        h1 = new ActionHandler( this );

        // Create the JComboBox for font names
        String[] s = {"Serif","SansSerif","Monospaced","Dialog"};
        c1 = new JComboBox(s);
        c1.addActionListener( h1 );
        add( c1 );

        // Create the text field with default font
        Font font = new Font( c1.getItemAt(0).toString(),
                              Font.PLAIN, 14);
        t1 = new JTextField("Test string",20);
        t1.setEditable( false );
        t1.setFont( font );
        add( t1 );

        // Create radio buttons
        b1 = new JRadioButton("Plain", true );
        b1.addActionListener( h1 );
        add( b1 );
        b2 = new JRadioButton("Bold", false );
        b2.addActionListener( h1 );
        add( b2 );
        b3 = new JRadioButton("Italic", false );
        b3.addActionListener( h1 );
        add( b3 );
        b4 = new JRadioButton("Bold Italic", false );
        b4.addActionListener( h1 );
        add( b4 );

        // Create button group, and add radio buttons
        bg = new ButtonGroup();
        bg.add( b1 );
        bg.add( b2 );
        bg.add( b3 );
        bg.add( b4 );
    }
```

Figure 12.17. *(cont.)*

```
            // Method to update font
            public void updateFont() {
                int valBold, valItalic;

                // Get current font info
                int fontStyle  = t1.getFont().getStyle();
                int fontSize   = t1.getFont().getSize();

                // Get new font name
                String fontName = (String) c1.getSelectedItem();

                // Get new font style
                if ( b1.isSelected() )
                   fontStyle = Font.PLAIN;
                else if ( b2.isSelected() )
                   fontStyle = Font.BOLD;
                else if ( b3.isSelected() )
                   fontStyle = Font.ITALIC;
                else if ( b4.isSelected() )
                   fontStyle = Font.BOLD + Font.ITALIC;

                 // Set new font
                t1.setFont( new Font(fontName, fontStyle, fontSize) );

                // Repaint the JTextField
                t1.repaint();
            }

            // Main method to create frame
            public static void main(String s[]) {

                // Create a frame to hold the application
                JFrame fr = new JFrame("TestRadioButton ...");
                fr.setSize(380,100);

                (rest of main is the same as previous examples...)
            }
        }

        class ActionHandler implements ActionListener {
            private TestRadioButton tcb;

            // Constructor
            public ActionHandler( TestRadioButton t ) { tcb = t; }

            // Execute when an event occurs
            public void actionPerformed( ActionEvent e ) {

                // State has changed, so call updateFont
                tcb.updateFont();
            }
        }
```

Figure 12.17. A program using radio buttons to select font styles.

When a radio button is clicked, an `ActionEvent` is created, and the `actionPerformed` method in class `ActionHandler` is called. This method in turn calls `updateFont()` to display the new font. Method `updateFont()` determines which radio button is selected using the `isSelected()` method and creates a new font with

Figure 12.18. The results of program `TestRadioButton` as different radio buttons are turned on.

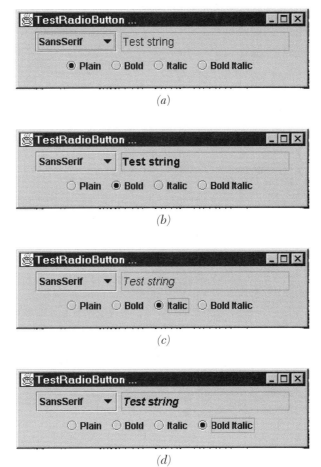

(a)

(b)

(c)

(d)

that style. Note that the `ButtonGroup` ensures that only one of the radio buttons will be selected at a time.

When this program is executed, the results are as shown in Figure 12.18.

GOOD PROGRAMMING PRACTICE

Use `JradioButton`s to select the state of a set of items represented by `boolean` variables, only one of which can be `true` at any time.

12.4.6 Canvases (Blank Components)

As we learned in Chapter 11, a **canvas** is a blank component that can be used for drawing. The older AWT GUI had a special class called `Canvas` for this purpose, but the Swing GUI does not have a corresponding blank class. The `chapman.graphics` package includes a `JCanvas` class that can be used for this purpose, but it is just as easy for a user to subclass `JComponent` directly to produce a blank canvas.

TABLE 12-10 Selected `JComponent` Methods

METHOD	DESCRIPTION
`public void setMinimumSize(Dimension d)`	Sets the minimum size of the component in pixels. The dimension object used to set the size is created with the constructor: `new Dimension(int width, int height);`
`public void setMaximumSize(Dimension d)`	Sets the maximum size of the component in pixels. The dimension object used to set the size is created with the constructor: `new Dimension(int width, int height);`
`public void paintComponent(Graphics g)`	Paints text and graphics on the component.
`public void repaint()`	Repaints text and graphics on the component.
`public void setPreferredSize(Dimension d)`	Sets the preferred size of the component in pixels. The dimension object used to set the size is created with the constructor: `new Dimension(int width, int height).`

A blank canvas can be created using a subclass of either `JComponent` or `chapman.graphics.JCanvas`. To create custom graphics, a program should create a subclass of one of these classes, and override the `paintComponent` method in that subclass. To redraw the component after a change has occurred, a programmer should call the component's `repaint()` method. Some common methods associated with canvases are given in Table 12-10.

Blank components can be used to add graphics to a Graphical User Interface. They can be added to the GUI just like any other component. For example, the program in Figure 12.19 creates a canvas that displays an ellipse, and adds the canvas to a `JPanel` that also includes labels and text fields. The program changes the size of the ellipse based on values input into the text fields. Note that the program calls the `redraw()` method to redraw the ellipse whenever its size has changed.

```
// This class tests drawing and redrawing a canvas
// as part of a GUI.
import java.awt.*;
import java.awt.event.*;
import java.awt.geom.*;
import javax.swing.*;
public class TestCanvas extends JPanel {

    // Instance variables
    private DrawEllipse dr;        // DrawEllipse object
    private JLabel l1, l2;         // Labels
    private JTextField t1, t2;     // TextFields
    private HeightHandler h1;      // ActionEvent handler
    private WidthHandler h2;       // ActionEvent handler
    private double height = 100;   // Height
    private double width = 150;    // Width

    // Initialization method
    public void init() {

        // Set background color
        setBackground( Color.lightGray );

        // Set the layout manager
        setLayout( new FlowLayout() );
```

Figure 12.19. *(cont.)*

```
        // Create height and width handlers
        h1 = new HeightHandler( this );
        h2 = new WidthHandler( this );

        // Create drawing area
        dr = new DrawEllipse( width, height );
        dr.setPreferredSize(new Dimension(400,300));
        add ( dr );

        // Create height JTextField
        l1 = new JLabel("Height:");
        add( l1 );
        l1.setHorizontalAlignment( JLabel.RIGHT );
        t1 = new JTextField("100",10);
        t1.addActionListener( h1 );
        add( t1 );

        // Create width JTextField
        l2 = new JLabel("Width:");
        add( l2 );
        l2.setHorizontalAlignment( JLabel.RIGHT );
        t2 = new JTextField("150",10);
        t2.addActionListener( h2 );
        add( t2 );
    }

    // Method to update height
    public void updateHeight( double height ) {
        this.height = height;
        dr.setHeight(height);
        dr.repaint();
    }

    // Method to update width
    public void updateWidth( double width ) {
        this.width = width;
        dr.setWidth(width);
        dr.repaint();
    }

    // Main method to create frame
    public static void main(String s[]) {

        // Create a frame to hold the application
        JFrame fr = new JFrame("TestCanvas ...");
        fr.setSize(400,370);

        // Create a Window Listener to handle "close" events
        MyWindowListener l = new MyWindowListener();
        fr.addWindowListener(l);

        // Create and initialize a TestCanvas object
        TestCanvas tc = new TestCanvas();
        tc.init();

        // Add the object to the center of the frame
        fr.getContentPane().add(tc, BorderLayout.CENTER);
```

Figure 12.19.   *(cont.)*

```
                    // Display the frame
                    fr.setVisible( true );
                }
            }

class HeightHandler implements ActionListener {
    private TestCanvas tc;

    // Constructor
    public HeightHandler( TestCanvas t ) { tc = t; }

    // Execute when an event occurs
    public void actionPerformed( ActionEvent e ) {
        double height = Double.parseDouble(e.getActionCommand());
        tc.updateHeight(height);
    }
}

class WidthHandler implements ActionListener {
    private TestCanvas tc;

    // Constructor
    public WidthHandler( TestCanvas t ) { tc = t; }

    // Execute when an event occurs
    public void actionPerformed( ActionEvent e ) {
        double width = Double.parseDouble(e.getActionCommand());
        tc.updateWidth(width);
    }
}

// This class extends JComponent and draws an ellipse
class DrawEllipse extends JComponent {

    // Instance variables
    private double height;         // Ellipse height
    private double width;          // Ellipse width

    // Constructor
    public DrawEllipse( double width, double height ) {
        this.height = height;
        this.width = width;
    }

    public void paintComponent( Graphics g ) {

        BasicStroke bs;                    // Ref to BasicStroke
        Ellipse2D ell;                     // Ref to Ellipse

        // Cast the graphics object to Graph2D
        Graphics2D g2 = (Graphics2D) g;

        // Set background color
        Dimension size = getSize();
        g2.setColor( Color.white );
        g2.fill(new Rectangle2D.Double(0,0,size.width,size.height))

        // Set rendering hints to improve display quality
        g2.setRenderingHint(RenderingHints.KEY_ANTIALIASING,
                             RenderingHints.VALUE_ANTIALIAS_ON);
```

Figure 12.19. *(cont.)*

```
          // Define Ellipse
          ell = new Ellipse2D.Double (30., 40., width, height);
          g2.setColor(Color.yellow);
          g2.fill(ell);
          g2.setColor(Color.black);
          g2.draw(ell);
      }

      public void setHeight ( double height ) {
          this.height = height;
      }

      public void setWidth ( double width ) {
          this.width = width;
      }
}
```

Figure 12.19. A program that uses a canvas to add graphics to a GUI.

When a user types a height or width into the appropriate text field, an `Action-Event` is created, and the corresponding event handler is called. This event handler get the `String` typed by the user with the `getActionCommand()` method and converts the `String` into a `double` value. The event handler calls the method `update-Height` or `updateWidth`, which, in turn, sets the height or width of the ellipse. A typical output from this program is shown in Figure 12.20.

GOOD PROGRAMMING PRACTICE

Use subclasses of `JComponent` or `chapman.graphics.JCanvas` to add graphical displays to a GUI.

Figure 12.20. Output from the program `TestCanvas`.

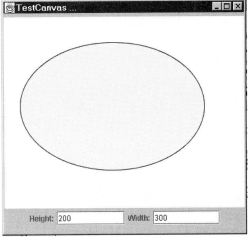

12.5 LAYOUT MANAGERS

A **layout manager** is a helper class that is designed to automatically arrange GUI components within a container for presentation purposes. The layout managers allows a user to add components to a container without worry over the specifics of how to place them within the container. They are especially useful for cross-platform applications, because the size of a particular component may vary slightly from platform to platform, and the layout manager will automatically adjust the spacing of components to accommodate these differences.

The six standard layout managers in Java are summarized in Table 12-11. Only the BorderLayout, BoxLayout, FlowLayout, and GridLayout managers will be described in this book. Refer to the JDK documentation for information about the CardLayout and GridBagLayout managers.

12.5.1 BorderLayout Layout Manager

The BorderLayout layout manager arranges components in five regions, known as *North, South, East, West,* and *Center* (with North being the top of the container). A BorderLayout is created with one of the following constructors:

```
public BorderLayout();
public BorderLayout(int horizontalGap, int vertical Gap);
```

The first constructor creates a BorderLayout with no pixel gaps between components, while the second constructor creates a BorderLayout with the programmer-specified gaps between components.

After a layout object has been created, it is associated with a container by the container's **setLayout** method. For example, the statement required to create a new BorderLayout object and to associate it with the current container is

```
setLayout( new BorderLayout() );
```

Objects should be added to a BorderLayout using the add method qualified by one of the constants NORTH, SOUTH, EAST, WEST, or CENTER. For example, the following statements produce a GUI containing five buttons, one in each region:

TABLE 12-11   Standard Layout Managers

ELEMENT	DESCRIPTION
BorderLayout	A layout manager that lays out elements in a central region and four surrounding borders. This is the default layout manager for a JFrame.
BoxLayout	A layout manager that lays out elements in a row horizontally or vertically. Unlike FlowLayout, the elements in a BoxLayout do not wrap around. This is the default layout manager for a Box.
CardLayout	A layout manager that stacks components like a deck of cards, only the top one of which is visible.
FlowLayout	A layout manager that lays out elements left-to-right and top-to-bottom within a container. This is the default layout manager for a JPanel.
GridBagLayout	A layout manager that lays out elements in a flexible grid, where the size of each element can vary.
GridLayout	A layout manager that lays out elements in a rigid grid.

Figure 12.21. A typical `Border Layout`.

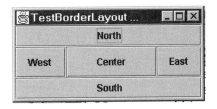

Figure 12.22. A typical `Flow Layout`.

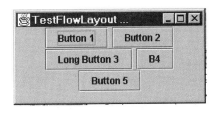

```
setLayout(new BorderLayout());
add(new Button("North"), BorderLayout.NORTH);
add(new Button("South"), BorderLayout.SOUTH);
add(new Button("East"), BorderLayout.EAST);
add(new Button("West"), BorderLayout.WEST);
add(new Button("Center"), BorderLayout.CENTER);
```

and these statements will produce the GUI shown in Figure 12.21.

In a `BorderLayout`, the component in the center expands to use up all remaining space in the container. `BorderLayout` is the default layout manager for `JFrame`, and all of our frames have used it. Examine the `main` method in any of the programs in this chapter. Note that the `JPanels` that we have created were added to the `CENTER` section of the `Frame`, and none of the other sections were used. Since the center section of a `BorderLayout` expands to use all available space, the `JPanels` have completely filled their frames.

Programs `FirstGUI` in Figure 12.2 and `TestLabel` in Figure 12.5 also illustrate the use of the `BorderLayout` layout manager.

12.5.2 `FlowLayout` Layout Manager

The `FlowLayout` layout manager arranges components in order from left to right and top to bottom across a container. Components are added to a line until there is no more room, and then they are added to the next line. The components that do fit into a line are displayed centered horizontally on the line. A `FlowLayout` is created with one of the following constructors:

```
public FlowLayout();
public FlowLayout(int align);
public FlowLayout(int align, int horizontalGap, int verticalGap);
```

The first constructor creates a `FlowLayout` with no pixel gaps between components and with the components centered on each line, while the second constructor creates a `FlowLayout` with no pixel gaps between components and with the specified alignment. Possible alignments are `LEFT`, `RIGHT`, and `CENTER`. The third constructor allows the programmer to specify both the alignment on each line and the horizontal and vertical gap between components.

Objects should be added to a `FlowLayout` using the `add` method. For example, the following statements produce a GUI containing five buttons, centered on each line, with a five-pixel gap between buttons:

```
setLayout(new FlowLayout(FlowLayout.CENTER,5,0));
add(new JButton("Button 1"));
add(new JButton("Button 2"));
add(new JButton("Long Button 3"));
add(new JButton("B4"));
add(new JButton("Button 5"));
```

and these statements will produce the GUI shown in Figure 12.22.

Most of the programs in the chapter have used `FlowLayout` to lay out the components on their panels. `FlowLayout` is the default layout manager for `JPanel` and for applets (class `JApplet`).

12.5.3 `GridLayout` Layout Manager

The `GridLayout` layout manager arranges components in a rigid rectangular grid structure. The container is divided into equal-sized rectangles, and one component is placed in each rectangle. A `GridLayout` is created with one of the following constructors:

```
public GridLayout(int rows, int cols);
public GridLayout(int rows, int cols, int horizGap, int
vertGap);
```

The first constructor creates a `GridLayout` with `rows` rows and `cols` columns, and no pixel gaps between components. The second constructor creates a `GridLayout` with `rows` rows and `cols` columns, and with the specified horizontal and vertical gaps between components.

Objects are be added to a `GridLayout` using the `add` method. For example, the following statements produce a GUI containing six buttons in a 3 × 2 grid.

```
setLayout(new GridLayout(3,2));
add(new JButton("1"));
add(new JButton("2"));
add(new JButton("3"));
add(new JButton("4"));
add(new JButton("5"));
add(new JButton("6"));
```

and these statements will produce the GUI shown in Figure 12.23.

Figure 12.23. A typical `Grid Layout`.

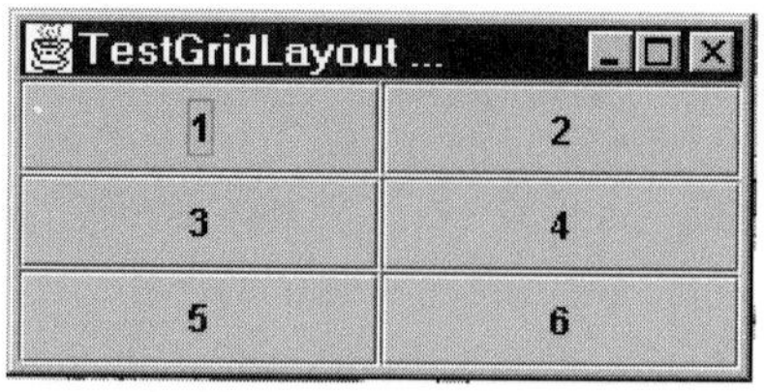

12.5.4 `BoxLayout` Layout Manager

The `BoxLayout` layout manager arranges components within a container in a single row or a single column. It is more flexible than the other layout managers that we have discussed, since the spacing and alignment of each element on each row or column can be individually controlled. Containers using `BoxLayout` layout managers can be

Figure 12.24. A typical vertical BoxLayout.

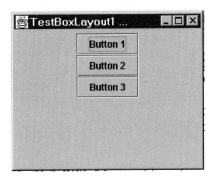

TABLE 12-12 Methods to Control Spacing in a BoxLayout

METHOD	DESCRIPTION
Box.createRigidArea(Dimension d)	Creates a rigid spacing in pixels between two components in a BoxLayout. The Dimension object specifies the vertical and horizontal spacing between the two components.
Box.createHorizontalGlue()	Creates a "virtual component" that uses up all the extra horizontal space in a container.
Box.createVerticalGlue()	Creates a "virtual component" that uses up all the extra vertical space in a container.

nested inside each other to produce arbitrarily complex structures that do not change shape when the size of a component or container is changed.

A BoxLayout is created with the following constructor:

```
public BoxLayout(Container c, int direction);
```

The first parameter in the constructor specifies the container that the layout manager will control, and the second component specifies the axis along which the components will be laid out (legal values are BoxLayout.X_AXIS and BoxLayout.Y_AXIS).

Objects are added to a BoxLayout using the add method. For example, the following statements produce a GUI containing three buttons arranged vertically.

```
// Create a new panel
JPanel p = new JPanel();

// Set the layout manager
p.setLayout(new BoxLayout(p, BoxLayout.Y_AXIS));

// Add buttons
p.add( new JButton("Button 1") );
p.add( new JButton("Button 2") );
p.add( new JButton("Button 3") );

// Add the new panel to the existing container
add( p );
```

These statements will produce the GUI shown in Figure 12.24.

The flexibility of the BoxLayout manager is enhanced by two additional constraints that can be added to the layout process: rigid areas and glue regions. **Rigid areas** are fixed horizontal and/or vertical spacings between components that can be individually specified between any two adjacent components. **Glue regions** are regions that expand or contract to absorb any extra space present when a container changes size. Rigid areas and glue regions are created using the methods in Table 12-12.

Figure 12.25. A `BoxLayout` illustrating the use of rigid areas to control spacing between components.

To illustrate the use of these components, we will create a new GUI that lays out the same three buttons vertically as before, but places a fixed 20-pixel vertical spacing between Button 1 and Button 2, and a fixed 5-pixel spacing between Button 2 and Button 3. The code for this example is

```
// Create a new panel
JPanel p = new JPanel();

// Set the layout manager
p.setLayout(new BoxLayout(p, BoxLayout.Y_AXIS));

// Add buttons
p.add( new JButton("Button 1") );
p.add( Box.createRigidArea(new Dimension(0,20)) );
p.add( new JButton("Button 2") );
p.add( Box.createRigidArea(new Dimension(0,5)) );
p.add( new JButton("Button 3") );

// Add the new panel to the existing container
add( p );
```

These statements will produce the GUI shown in Figure 12.25.

12.5.5 Combining Layout Managers to Produce a Result

It is often difficult to create exactly the GUI that we want using a standard layout manager, and this fact can be very frustrating. However, it is sometimes possible to *combine* layout managers to achieve a desired appearance. Only one layout manager can be used with a given container at any time, but one container can be placed inside another container, and the two containers can have different layout managers.

To understand how multiple layout managers can be better than a single one, let's reconsider the temperature conversion program of Example 12-1. That program used a `FlowLayout`, which means that the components of the program were laid out horizontally until the end of a line, and then starting over on the next line. Unfortunately, such as design will fail if a user resizes the application, or if the size of the components differs significantly from platform to platform. Figure 12.26 illustrates this problem, showing how the appearance of the application changes as the program frame is resized.

Instead of using a `FlowLayout` with a single container, we can create the same interface using three containers and `BoxLayouts`. The first container (`pHoriz`) will use a horizontal `BoxLayout`, and the other two containers (`pVertL` and `pVertR`) will be placed inside the first one and use vertical `BoxLayouts`. The labels will be placed in container `pVertL` and the text fields will be placed in container `pVertR`. The horizon-

Figure 12.26. (*a*) The `TempConversion` program laid out with the default width and height. (*b*) The program after the frame width has been increased.

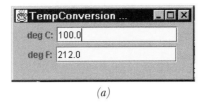

(*a*)

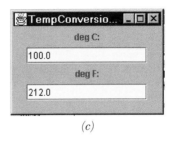

(*b*)

(*c*)

tal space between these two containers will be set by adding a rigid area to the top-level container. The code to build this structure is shown below:

```
// Create a new high-level panel
JPanel pHoriz = new JPanel();
pHoriz.setLayout(new BoxLayout(pHoriz, BoxLayout.X_AXIS));
add( pHoriz );

// Create two subordinate panels
JPanel pVertL = new JPanel();
JPanel pVertR = new JPanel();
pVertL.setLayout(new BoxLayout(pVertL, BoxLayout.Y_AXIS));
pVertR.setLayout(new BoxLayout(pVertR, BoxLayout.Y_AXIS));

// Add to pHoriz with a horizontal space between panels
pHoriz.add( pVertL );
pHoriz.add( Box.createRigidArea(new Dimension(20,0)) );
pHoriz.add( pVertR );

// Create degrees Celsius field
l1 = new JLabel("deg C:", JLabel.RIGHT);
pVertL.add( l1 );
t1 = new JTextField("0.0",15);
t1.addActionListener( cHnd );
pVertR.add( t1 );

// Create degrees Fahrenheight field
l2 = new JLabel("deg F:", JLabel.RIGHT);
pVertL.add( l2 );
t2 = new JTextField("32.0",15);
t2.addActionListener( fHnd );
pVertR.add( t2 );
```

Figure 12.27. *(a)* The `Temp Conversion2` program laid out with the default width and height. *(b)* The program after the frame width has been increased. Note that the relative positions of the labels and text fields have been preserved.

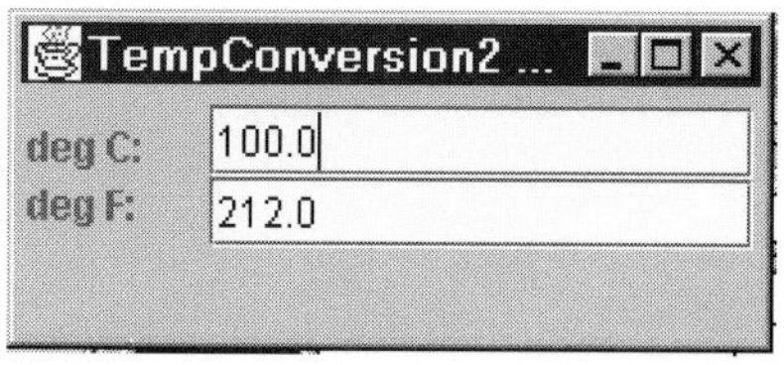

(a)

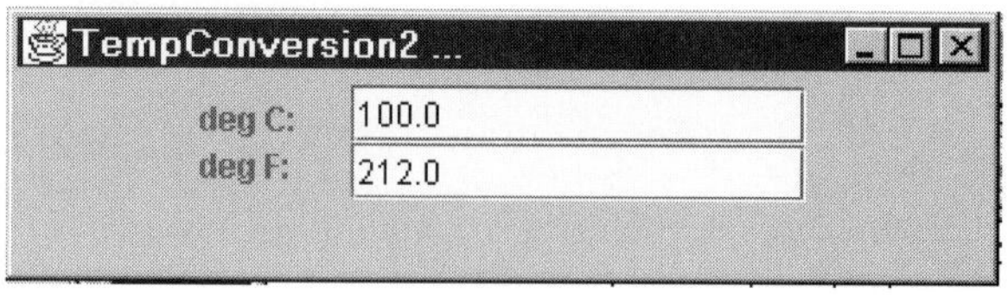

(b)

Figure 12.27 shows the behavior of this program as the frame containing the GUI is resized. This time, the GUI preserves its shape despite changes in frame size.

EXAMPLE 12-2:
CREATING A
CALCULATOR
GUI

Write a program that creates the Graphical User Interface for a calculator.

SOLUTION
A calculator GUI should have a display window for results all across the top, with a rectangular grid of buttons below it. We cannot create such a display with a `BorderLayout` manager, `FlowLayout` manager, a `GridLayout` manager, or a `BoxLayout` manager by itself, but we *can* create it if we can combine a `BorderLayout` manager with a `GridLayout` manager.

The code shown in Figure 12.28 creates two containers, both `JPanel`s. The outer container uses the `BorderLayout` manager, and the inner container uses the `GridLayout` manager. The inner container p2 uses the `GridLayout` manager to lay out a keypad, and then the entire inner container is placed in the center region of the outer container. The results window is placed in the `NORTH` region of the outer container. The resulting GUI is shown in Figure 12.29.

```
// Create a GUI for a calculator.
import java.awt.*;
import java.awt.event.*;
import javax.swing.*;
public class CalculatorGUI extends JPanel {

    // Initialization method
    public void init() {

        // Set the layout manager
        setLayout( new BorderLayout() );

        // Add the result field to the panel
        JTextField t1 = new JTextField(10);
        t1.setEditable( false );
        t1.setBackground( Color.white );
        add( t1, BorderLayout.NORTH );
```

Figure 12.28. *(cont.)*

```
        // Create another Panel for the keypad, and place it
        // in the high-level panel
        JPanel p2 = new JPanel();
        p2.setLayout( new GridLayout(4,5) );
        add( p2, BorderLayout.CENTER );

        // Add keys to the panel
        p2.add( new JButton("7") );
        p2.add( new JButton("8") );
        p2.add( new JButton("9") );
        p2.add( new JButton("/") );
        p2.add( new JButton("sqrt") );
        p2.add( new JButton("4") );
        p2.add( new JButton("5") );
        p2.add( new JButton("6") );
        p2.add( new JButton("*") );
        p2.add( new JButton("%") );
        p2.add( new JButton("1") );
        p2.add( new JButton("2") );
        p2.add( new JButton("3") );
        p2.add( new JButton("-") );
        p2.add( new JButton("1/x") );
        p2.add( new JButton("0") );
        p2.add( new JButton("+/-") );
        p2.add( new JButton(".") );
        p2.add( new JButton("+") );
        p2.add( new JButton("=") );
    }
```

Figure 12.28. Creating a calculator GUI by combining two different containers with different layout managers.

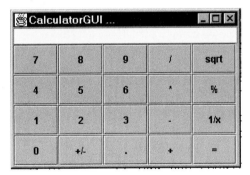

Figure 12.29. A calculator GUI.

PRACTICE!

This quiz provides a quick check to see if you have understood the concepts introduced in Sections 12.1 through 12.5. If you have trouble with the quiz, reread the section, ask your instructor, or discuss the material with a fellow student. The answers to this quiz are found in the back of the book.

1. What is a container? Which type of containers(s) are we using in this chapter?
2. What is a component? Which type of components are we using in this chapter?
3. What is a layout manager? What does it do?
4. Why would you wish to use more than one layout manager in a single program?
5. What is an event handler? How are events handled in Java?
6. What listener interface(s) were introduced in this chapter? What does each one do, and which components produce it?

PROFESSIONAL SUCCESS: CREATING EFFECTIVE GUIS

The purpose of a GUI is to make it easy for a user to execute a program or to get some sort of information. You should never forget this simple fact.

When a programmer first learns how to create GUIs, there is a tendency to create flashy, complicated displays that positively get in the way of program usage, just because he or she knows how to do it. We all see examples of such trashy design every time we use the World Wide Web. People create web sites with animations, flashing objects, sounds, etc. that convey no information, take a long time to download, and get in the way of information transfer. Don't fall into this trap!

In general, you should follow a few simple guidelines in creating a GUI:

1. Place the information that a user will most want in a prominent location on the GUI. Don't bury it in meus or in lower-level displays.
2. Keep the GUI as uncluttered as possible. Relegate infrequently used options to menus, where they will not be in the way.
3. Do not clutter a GUI up with useless animations, images, etc. just because you think they are cute.

12.6 PUTTING IT ALL TOGETHER

We will now put together the material that we have discussed in the last two chapters to produce two sample applications with working GUIs.

EXAMPLE 12-3: PLOTTING DATA

Create a program that plots sin x, cos x, or both depending on the values of two checkboxes. The curves should be plotted for the range $0 \leq x \leq 2\pi$. Use BoxLayout so that the locations of the components will be preserved when the application changes size.

SOLUTION
We can plot the data using chapman.graphics.JPlot2D, which is a Swing component just like any other component. This program will require one JPlot2D object and two checkboxes, as well as an ActionListener to monitor the state of the checkboxes.

1. **State the problem**. Create a GUI-based program that plots sin x, cos x, or both depending on the values of two checkboxes. Ensure that the layout of the components does not change as the window is resized.

2. **Define the inputs and outputs**. The inputs to this program are the status of the two checkboxes "Plot sine" and "Plot cosine". The output from the program is a plot of the sine and/or cosine, depending on the status of the checkboxes.

3. **Decompose the program into classes and their associated methods**. This program requires two classes to function properly, if we make the principal class also function as an `ActionListener`. The principal class (called `PlotSinCos`) must contain the following methods: *(1)* a method `init()` to generate the GUI display, *(2)* a method `display()` to display the desired curve(s), *(3)* a method `actionListener` to respond to mouse clicks on the checkboxes, and *(4)* a `main` method to start up the application. The second required class is a `WindowListener` class to shut down the program when it is running as an application and the user clicks on the "Close Window" box.

4. **Design the algorithm that you intend to implement for each method**. The `init()` method of the `PlotSinCos` class must create the GUI. It must lay out the graphical elements. We would like to arrange the GUI so that the plot appears on top of the display, and the two checkboxes appear side-by-side below it. One way to achieve this design is with nested panels using `BoxLayouts`, as shown in Figure 12.30. The top-level panel `pVert` will use a vertical `BoxLayout`, and the `JPlot2D` object and a horizontal panel `pHoriz` will be added to it. Then, the two checkboxes can be added to the horizontal panel.

   The code required to create this GUI is shown below.

Figure 12.30.   The structure of containers and layout managers required to create the GUI for the `PlotSinCos` program.

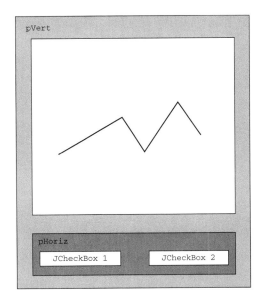

```
// Create a new high-level panel
JPanel pVert = new JPanel();
pVert.setLayout(new BoxLayout(pVert, BoxLayout.Y_AXIS));
add( pVert );

// Add a blank plot
pl = new JPlot2D();
pl.setPreferredSize(new Dimension(400,400));
pVert.add( pl );

// Create a subordinate panel for the bottom
JPanel pHoriz = new JPanel();
pHoriz.setLayout(new BoxLayout(pHoriz, BoxLayout.X_AXIS));
pVert.add( pHoriz );

// Create the "Add sine" checkbox
b1 = new JCheckBox("Add sine");
b1.addActionListener( this );
pHoriz.add( b1 );
pHoriz.add( Box.createRigidArea(new Dimension(40,0)) );

// Create the "Add cosine" checkbox
b2 = new JCheckBox("Add cosine");
b2.addActionListener( this );
pHoriz.add( b2 );
```

Method `init()` must also create the data to plot when a plot is requested. The code required for this step is

```
for ( int i = 0; i < x.length; i++ ) {
    x[i]  = (i+1) * 2 * Math.PI / 40;
    y1[i] = Math.sin(x[i]);
    y2[i] = Math.cos(x[i]);
}
```

Method `display()` must display the requested curves. To do this, it must first remove any existing curves on the plot with the `JPlot2D` method `removeAll()`, and then add the requested curves back into the plot. The method can check the state of each checkbox using the `isSelected()` method. This code is shown in the complete program below.

Method `actionListener()` is very simple. It must listen for any change in either checkbox, and call method `display()` when one occurs. Method `display()` does all the hard work.

Finally, method `main()` and the `MyWindowListener` class are essentially identical to the ones shown in earlier applications.

5. **Turn the algorithm into Java statements**. The resulting Java program is shown in Figure 12.31.

```
/*
   Purpose:
     This program plots sin x and/or cos x for 0 <= x <= PI
     depending on the state of two checkboxes.

   Record of revisions:
       Date          Programmer            Description of change
       ====          ==========            =====================
       12/16/98     S. J. Chapman          Original code
*/
import java.awt.*;
import java.awt.event.*;
import javax.swing.*;
import chapman.graphics.JPlot2D;
public class PlotSinCos extends JPanel
                    implements ActionListener {
```

Figure 12.31. *(cont.)*

```
    // Instance variables
    private JCheckBox b1, b2;      // Check boxes
    private JPlot2D p1;            // Plot
    double[] x, y1, y2;           // Data to plot

    // Initialization method
    public void init() {

        // Create a new high-level panel
        JPanel pVert = new JPanel();
        pVert.setLayout(new BoxLayout(pVert, BoxLayout.Y_AXIS));
        add( pVert );

        // Add a blank plot
        p1 = new JPlot2D();
        p1.setPreferredSize(new Dimension(400,400));
        pVert.add( p1 );

        // Create a subordinate panel for the bottom
        JPanel pHoriz = new JPanel();
        pHoriz.setLayout(new BoxLayout(pHoriz,BoxLayout.X_AXIS));
        pVert.add( pHoriz );

        // Create the "Add sine" checkbox
        b1 = new JCheckBox("Add sine");
        b1.addActionListener( this );
        pHoriz.add( b1 );
        pHoriz.add( Box.createRigidArea(new Dimension(40,0)) );

        // Create the "Add cosine" checkbox
        b2 = new JCheckBox("Add cosine");
        b2.addActionListener( this );
        pHoriz.add( b2 );

        // Define arrays to hold the two curves to plot
        x  = new double[41];
        y1 = new double[41];
        y2 = new double[41];

        // Calculate a sine and a cosine wave
        for ( int i = 0; i < x.length; i++ ) {
            x[i]  = (i+1) * 2 * Math.PI / 40;
            y1[i] = Math.sin(x[i]);
            y2[i] = Math.cos(x[i]);
        }
    }

    // Method to display sine and cosine plots
    public void display() {
        // Remove old curves
        p1.removeAll();

        // Add sine curve
        if ( b1.isSelected() ) {
            p1.addCurve(x, y1);
            p1.setLineColor( Color.blue );
            p1.setLineWidth( 2.0f );
            p1.setLineStyle( JPlot2D.LINESTYLE_SOLID );
        }
```

Figure 12.31.   *(cont.)*

```
                         // Add cosine curve
                         if ( b2.isSelected() ) {
                             pl.addCurve(x, y2);
                             pl.setLineColor( Color.red );
                             pl.setLineWidth( 2.0f );
                             pl.setLineStyle( JPlot2D.LINESTYLE_LONGDASH );
                         }

                         // Turn on grid
                         pl.setGridState( JPlot2D.GRID_ON );

                         // Repaint plot
                         pl.repaint();
                     }

                     // Execute when an event occurs
                     public void actionPerformed( ActionEvent e ) {
                         String input = e.getActionCommand();

                         if ( input.equals("Add sine") )
                             display();

                         else if ( input.equals("Add cosine") )
                             display();

                         // Update display
                         display();
                     }

                     // Main method to create frame
                     public static void main(String s[]) {

                         // Create a frame to hold the application
                         JFrame fr = new JFrame("PlotSinCos ...");
                         fr.setSize(400,460);

                         // Create a Window Listener to handle "close" events
                         MyWindowListener l = new MyWindowListener();
                         fr.addWindowListener(l);

                         // Create and initialize a PlotSinCos object
                         PlotSinCos ps = new PlotSinCos();
                         ps.init();
                         // Add the object to the center of the frame
                         fr.getContentPane().add(ps, BorderLayout.CENTER);

                         // Display the frame
                         fr.setVisible( true );
                     }
                 }
```

Figure 12.31. The PlotSinCos application.

6. **Test the resulting Java program**. To test this program, we will execute it both as an application and as an applet, and observe the results. Figure 12.32 shows the appearance of the final program. Execute the program youself to veryify that it functions properly. Also, re-size the application and see if the GUI components preserve their relative locations.

Figure 12.32. Output of program PlotSinCos.

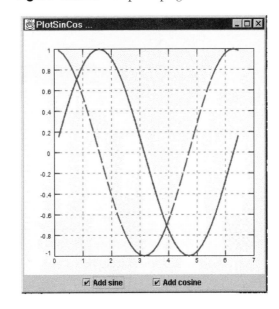

Create a GUI-based program that generates and displays a time-domain signal consisting of two sinusoids plus optional random noise, and determines and displays the frequency spectrum of that signal. The program should display the time signal and the corresponding frequency spectrum, and it should include GUI elements to allow the user to change the frequency, amplitude, and phase of each sinusoid. It should also allow the user to select whether or not to include noise on the signal, and to choose the noise distribution (uniform or Gaussian) and average amplitude.

SOLUTION
We will first discuss the algorithms required to solve this problem, and afterwards the details of the GUI.

The required time-domain signal consists of two sinusoids plus optional random noise. In, other words, the signal will be

$$v(t) = A_1 \sin(2\pi f_1 t + \theta_1) + A_2 \sin(2\pi f_2 t + \theta_2) + \text{noise} \tag{12-1}$$

where A_1, A_2, f_1, f_2, θ_1, θ_2, and the noise are all user-settable values. This signal must be sampled at some sampling frequency f_s for display and processing. The time step Δt between successive samples will be $1/f_s$, so the sampled signal can be represented by an array, each of whose elements is calculated from the equation

$$v_i = A_1 \sin\left(\frac{2\pi f_1}{f_s} i + \theta_1\right) + A_2 \sin\left(\frac{2\pi f_2}{f_s} i + \theta_2\right) + \text{noise}_i \tag{12-2}$$

How can we determine the frequency content of this signal? The standard way to determine the frequency content of a time signal is to calculate the *discrete Fourier transform* (DFT) of that signal. The DFT is defined by the equation

$$F_n = \sum_{k=0}^{N-1} t_k e^{2\pi i k n T / f_s} \tag{12-3}$$

where

t_k = the kth time sample of the signal being analyzed;
N = the total number of samples in the signal being analyzed;
T = the duration of the signal being analyzed in seconds;
f_s = the sampling frequency of the signal being analyzed;
F_n = the nth frequency component of the output spectrum (a complex number). There will be N components in the complete output spectrum.

The relationship between the length of the signal being analyzed T, the sampling frequency f_s, and number of samples N is

$$N = f_s T \tag{12-4}$$

There is also a fixed relationship between the sampling frequency f_s and the spacing ΔF between components of the output frequency spectrum. This relationship is

$$\Delta F = \frac{f_s}{N} = \frac{1}{T} \tag{12-5}$$

Therefore, the longer the signal being analyzed, the greater the density of samples in the resulting spectrum.

The detailed theory of the DFT is far beyond the scope of this book. It is normally discussed during senior- or graduate-level digital signal processing courses. Fortunately, we don't have to worry about that! The beauty of having reusable Java packages is that *someone else* studied the theory and wrote and checked the method implementing the DFT algorithm. All that we users have to know is the calling sequence of the method, and just enough theory to use it intelligently.

Package `chapman.math.SigProc` contains an implementation of the DFT known as the *Fast Fourier Transform* (FFT). The FFT is just a fast implementation of the DFT algorithm given in Equation 12-3. It has the special restriction that the number of samples in the time series being analyzed must be a power of 2 (16, 32, 64, 128, 256, etc.). If the number of samples in the series is not a power of 2, then trailing zeros must be added at the end of the series until the total number of samples is a power of 2. This process is called zero-padding. If the length of the array supplied to `SigProc.fft` is not a power of 2, the method will throw a runtime `InvalidArraySize` exception.

Table 12-13 shows the calling sequence of the `fft` method. Notice that it requires an array of `Complex` objects containing the time-domain data, and returns an array of `Complex` objects containing the resulting frequency spectrum. With this background, we can now solve this problem.

1. **State the problem**. Create a GUI-based program that generates and displays a time-domain signal consisting of two sinusoids plus optional random noise, and determines and displays the frequency spectrum of that signal.

TABLE 12-13   Selected `chapman.math.SigProc` Methods

METHOD	DESCRIPTION
`public static double[] calcFreq(double fs, int fftSize)`	This method calculates the frequency of each element of the output array from an FFT, taking into account the negative frequencies in the upper half of the array.
`public static Complex[] fft(Complex[] z)`	Calculate the FFT of a time-domain signal stored in a `Complex` array. The positive frequencies of the resulting frequency spectrum are stored in the lower half of the array, with the negative frequencies stored in the upper half of the array.
`public static Complex[] ifft(Complex[] z)`	Calculate the inverse FFT of a frequency spectrum stored in a `Complex` array.

2. **Define the inputs and outputs**. This program has two outputs, which are displays of the time-domain signal and the frequency spectrum. These displays can be implemented with the `JPlot2D` class in package `chapman.graphics`.

   The inputs to this program must be:

   a. The amplitude of the first sinusoid. A `JTextField` is appropriate for this element.

   b. The frequency of the first sinusoid (a `JTextField`).

   c. The phase of the first sinusoid (a `JTextField`).

   d. The amplitude of the second sinusoid (a `JTextField`).

   e. The frequency of the second sinusoid (a `JTextField`).

   f. The phase of the second sinusoid (a `JTextField`).

   g. A noise on/off switch. Since the possible states are on and off, a `JCheckBox` is appropriate for this element.

   h. A noise distribution type (uniform or Gaussian). A `JComboBox` is appropriate for this element.

   i. The average amplitude of the noise (a `JTextField`).

3. **Decompose the program into classes and their associated methods**. This program requires many classes to function properly. The principal class (called `Spectrum`) must contain separate methods (*1*) to generate the GUI display, (*2*) to calculate the time-domain signal and frequency spectrum, (*3*) to update the values of each GUI component (nine methods), and (*4*) a `main` method to start the program.

   In addition, the program must contain nine event-handling classes to handle the events generated by the nine input GUI elements. The program must also import and use methods from classes `chapman.math.Complex`, `chapman.math.SigProc`, and `chapman.graphics.JPlot2D`.

4. **Design the algorithm that you intend to implement for each method**. The `init()` method of the `Spectrum` class must create the GUI. It must lay out 19 graphical elements consisting of eight labels, seven text boxes, one checkbox, one combo box, and two output displays. The two output displays will occupy the top left- and right-hand portions of the GUI, with the input elements arranged below them.

   The size of this GUI should be restricted to 640 × 480 pixels, so that the display will fit on any computer that has VGA resolution or better. There is no way to get a single layout manager to produce a neat-looking display of

Figure 12.33.   The nested set of containers used to create the `Spectrum` GUI.

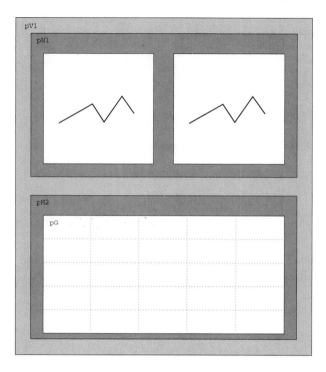

the sort that we want, so we will have to use a combination of nested panels with different layout managers to create the GUI.

How can we design the GUI for this program? If you have access to an interactive GUI builder in your Java compiler, then you can use it to "drag and drop" components onto the display until you are satisfied with the layout, and the GUI builder will automatically generate the code required to place the elements in the proper locations. If you do *not* have a GUI builder because you are using the free JDK, then get out a piece of graph paper and sketch the layout you would like. After you are satisfied with the GUI, try to figure out some combination of panels and layout managers that will create the desired layout.

Figure 12.33 shows a possible arrangement for GUI elements, with the two displays on the top and the input values organized in a grid below. As the figure shows, this type of structure requires a total of *four* nested containers to create. The highest level panel (pV1) uses a vertically-oriented `BoxLayout`. That panel contains two additional panels (pH1 and pH2) that use a horizontally-oriented `BoxLayout`. The two graphs can be placed directly into pH1, and a fourth panel (pG) with a `GridLayout` can be placed into pH2.

The portion of the code in the `init()` method that creates the required panels and layout managers is shown below:

```
// Create a new top-level vertical panel
JPanel pV1 = new JPanel();
pV1.setLayout(new BoxLayout(pV1, BoxLayout.Y_AXIS));
add( pV1 );

// Create two horizontal panels within the vertical one
JPanel pH1 = new JPanel();
JPanel pH2 = new JPanel();
pH1.setLayout(new BoxLayout(pH1, BoxLayout.X_AXIS));
```

```
pH2.setLayout(new BoxLayout(pH2, BoxLayout.X_AXIS));
pV1.add( pH1 );
pV1.add( Box.createRigidArea(new Dimension(0,5)) );
pV1.add( pH2 );

// Now create a GridLayout manager within the lower
// horizontal one
JPanel pG = new JPanel();
pG.setLayout(new GridLayout(5,4,10,5));
pH2.add( pG );
```

Once the layout has been created, the GUI components can be created and assigned to the proper container. Note that the proper container for the two plots is pH1, while the proper container for all the other elements is pG.

```
// Create time domain plot
pl1 = new JPlot2D();
pl1.setPlotType ( JPlot2D.LINEAR );
pl1.setLineColor( Color.blue );
pl1.setLineWidth( 2.0f );
pl1.setLineStyle( JPlot2D.LINESTYLE_SOLID );
pl1.setTitle( "Time Domain" );
pl1.setXLabel( "Time (s)" );
pl1.setYLabel( "Amplitude" );
pl1.setGridState( JPlot2D.GRID_ON );
pl1.setPreferredSize(new Dimension(290,290));

pH1.add( pl1 );
pH1.add( Box.createRigidArea(new Dimension(10,0)) );

// Create frequency domain plot
pl2 = new JPlot2D();
pl2.setPlotType ( JPlot2D.LINEAR );
pl2.setLineColor( Color.blue );
pl2.setLineWidth( 2.0f );
pl2.setLineStyle( JPlot2D.LINESTYLE_SOLID );
pl2.setTitle( "Frequency Domain" );
pl2.setXLabel( "Frequency (Hz)" );
pl2.setYLabel( "Amplitude" );
pl2.setGridState( JPlot2D.GRID_ON );
pl2.setPreferredSize(new Dimension(290,290));
pH1.add( pl2 );

// Create signal 1 frequency field
l1 = new JLabel("Signal 1 Frequency (Hz):");
pG.add( l1 );
tf1 = new JTextField(12);
tf1.addActionListener( ht1 );
pG.add ( tf1 );

// Create signal 2 frequency field
l2 = new JLabel("Signal 2 Frequency (Hz):");
pG.add( l2 );
tf2 = new JTextField(12);
tf2.addActionListener( ht2 );
pG.add ( tf2 );

// Create the signal 1 amplitude field
l3 = new JLabel("Signal 1 Amplitude:");
pG.add( l3 );
tf3 = new JTextField(12);
tf3.addActionListener( ht3 );
pG.add ( tf3 );
```

```
// Create the signal 2 amplitude field
l4 = new JLabel("Signal 2 Amplitude:");
pG.add( l4 );
tf4 = new JTextField(12);
tf4.addActionListener( ht4 );
pG.add ( tf4 );

// Create the signal 1 phase field
l5 = new JLabel("Signal 1 Phase (deg):");
pG.add( l5 );
tf5 = new JTextField(12);
tf5.addActionListener( ht5 );
pG.add ( tf5 );

// Create the signal 2 phase field
l6 = new JLabel("Signal 2 Phase (deg):");
pG.add( l6 );
tf6 = new JTextField(12);
tf6.addActionListener( ht6 );
pG.add ( tf6 );

// Create the noise type Combo Box
l7 = new JLabel("Noise distribution:");
pG.add( l7 );
String[] s = {"Uniform","Gaussian"};
c1 = new JComboBox(s);
c1.addActionListener( hc1 );
pG.add( c1 );

// Create the noise amplitude field
l8 = new JLabel("Noise Amplitude:");
pG.add( l8 );
tf7 = new JTextField(12);
tf7.addActionListener( ht7 );
pG.add ( tf7 );

// Create noise on/off checkbox
b1 = new JCheckBox("Add Noise to Signal");
b1.addActionListener( hcb1 );
pG.add( b1 );
```

The other important task of the `init()` method is to create event handlers for each input GUI element, and to associate those handlers with the elements.

Method `updatePlot()` in class `Spectrum` must calculate the time-domain signal and the corresponding frequency spectrum, and display the results. The procedure to calculate the time series and the resulting frequency spectrum will be:

a. Calculate the time-domain series from Equation (12-2). Note that there are three options associated with the noise: it can be uniformly distributed, Gaussian distributed, or absent.

b. Convert the time-domain samples into a `Complex` array whose length is a power of 2.

c. Call method `SigProc.fft` to calculate the frequency spectrum of the time-domain signal.

d. Create a double array containing the magnitude of each point in the frequency spectrum for later display.

e. Display the time-domain and frequency-domain data on the two `JPlot2D` objects.

The portion of the code required to implement these steps is shown below:

```
// Build signal plus noise
for ( int i = 0; i < time.length; i++ ) {
    double temp = 0;
    double fac1 = 2 * Math.PI * sig1Freq / fs;
    double fac2 = 2 * Math.PI * sig2Freq / fs;
    double ph1 = sig1Phase * Math.PI / 180;
    double ph2 = sig1Phase * Math.PI / 180;
    if ( noiseFlag ) {
        if ( noiseType == 0 )
            temp = 2 * (Math.random() - 0.5);
        else if ( noiseType == 1 )
            temp = Math1.randomGaussian();
    }
    time[i] = new Complex(
            sig1Amp * Math.sin(fac1*i + ph1)
        + sig2Amp * Math.sin(fac2*i + ph2)
        + noiseAmp * temp, 0);
}

// Calculate frequency steps
double freqArray[] = new double[time.length];
freqArray = SigProc.calcFreq( fs, time.length );

// call fft
spec = SigProc.fft(time);

// Create time domain data to plot
double x1[] = new double[time.length];
double y1[] = new double[time.length];
for ( int i = 0; i < time.length; i++ ) {
    x1[i] = dt * i;
    y1[i] = Complex.re(time[i]);
}

// Update time domain plot
pl1.setValues( x1, y1 );

// Create freq domain data to plot
double x2[] = new double[spec.length/2];
double y2[] = new double[spec.length/2];
for ( int i = 0; i < spec.length/2; i++ ) {
    x2[i] = freqArray[i];
    y2[i] = Complex.abs(spec[i]);
}

// Update frequency domain plot
pl2.setValues( x2, y2 );
```

There must also be methods to update the display when the user supplies new input values. These methods are in two parts: nine event handling methods in listener classes to capture the input events, and nine methods in Spectrum to do the actual updating. The event handler classes are essentially identical to those in previous programs, so they won't be discussed here. The update methods in class Spectrum must be called by an event handler when the appropriate event occurs, and they must update the appropriate value, re-calculate the time-domain signal and the frequency spectrum, and update the displays. An example method to update the sinusoid 1 frequency is shown below. Note that this method saves the new frequency in an instance variable, updates the plot information, and calls repaint() to update the two output plots.

```
                        // Update signal 1 frequency
                        public void updateSignal1Freq ( double f ) {
                            sig1Freq = Math.max(Math.min(f,FREQ_MAX), FREQ_MIN);
                            tf1.setText( Fmt.sprintf("%.2f",sig1Freq) );
                            updatePlot();
                            pl1.repaint();
                            pl2.repaint();
                        }
```

Finally, there must be a `main` method so that the program can be executed. The `main` method must create a `JFrame` and place the `Spectrum` object within it. This method is not shown, since it is similar to that in all our previous programs.

5. **Turn the algorithm into Java statements**. The resulting Java program is shown in Figure 12.34.

```
/*
   Purpose:
     This program displays the time- and frequency-domain
     representations of a signal consisting of two sinusoids
     and noise.  The noise is optional, and it may come from
     either a uniform or a Gaussian distribution.


   Record of revisions:
       Date         Programmer            Description of change
       ====         ==========            =====================
     10/21/98    S. J. Chapman           Original code
*/
import java.awt.*;
import java.awt.event.*;
import javax.swing.*;
import chapman.graphics.*;
import chapman.io.*;
import chapman.math.*;
class Spectrum extends JPanel {


    // Declare constants
    private final double AMP_MAX = 10;      // Max amp
    private final double AMP_MIN = 0;       // Min amp
    private final double FREQ_MAX = 8;      // Max = 8 Hz
    private final double FREQ_MIN = 0;      // Min = 0 Hz


    // Declare instance variables
    private JPlot2D pl1, pl2;               // 2D Plots
    private Complex time[]
            = new Complex[256];            // Time Signal
    private Complex spec[]
            = new Complex[256];            // Freq Spectrum
    private double sig1Freq = 1.05;        // Signal 1 Freq (Hz)
    private double sig2Freq = 2.70;        // Signal 2 Freq (Hz)
    private double fs = 16;                // Sampling Freq (Hz)
    private double dt = 1 / fs;            // dt (s)
    private double df = fs/time.length;    // Freq step size (Hz)
    private double sig1Amp = 1;            // Signal 1 amp
    private double sig2Amp = 0.4;          // Signal 2 amp
    private double sig1Phase = 30;         // Signal 1 phase (deg)
    private double sig2Phase = 90;         // Signal 2 phase (deg)
```

Figure 12.34. *(cont.)*

```
private double noiseAmp = 0.4;        // Noise amp
private boolean noiseFlag = true;     // Noise on/off flag
private int noiseType = 0;            // Noise type
                                      //   (0=Uniform;1=Gaussian)
// GUI Objects
JCheckBox b1;                         // CheckBox
JComboBox c1;                         // Combo box
JLabel 11,12,13,14,15,16,17,18;       // Labels
JTextField tf1,tf2,tf3,tf4,tf5,tf6,tf7; // Text fields


// Event handlers
private TextField1Handler ht1;        // Sig 1 Freq
private TextField2Handler ht2;        // Sig 2 Freq
private TextField3Handler ht3;        // Sig 1 Amp
private TextField4Handler ht4;        // Sig 2 Amp
private TextField5Handler ht5;        // Sig 1 Phase
private TextField6Handler ht6;        // Sig 2 Phase
private TextField7Handler ht7;        // Noise Amp
private Combo1Handler hc1;            // Noise type
private CheckBox1Handler hcb1;        // Add noise checkbox


//***********************************************
//   Initialization method
//***********************************************
public void init() {

   // Create a new top-level vertical panel
   JPanel pV1 = new JPanel();
   pV1.setLayout(new BoxLayout(pV1, BoxLayout.Y_AXIS));
   add( pV1 );

   // Create two horizontal panels within the vertical one
   JPanel pH1 = new JPanel();
   JPanel pH2 = new JPanel();
   pH1.setLayout(new BoxLayout(pH1, BoxLayout.X_AXIS));
   pH2.setLayout(new BoxLayout(pH2, BoxLayout.X_AXIS));
   pV1.add( pH1 );
   pV1.add( Box.createRigidArea(new Dimension(0,5)) );
   pV1.add( pH2 );

   // Now create a GridLayout manager within the lower
   // horizontal one
   JPanel pG = new JPanel();
   pG.setLayout(new GridLayout(5,4,10,5));
   pH2.add( pG );

   // Create Event handlers
   ht1  = new TextField1Handler( this );
   ht2  = new TextField2Handler( this );
   ht3  = new TextField3Handler( this );
   ht4  = new TextField4Handler( this );
   ht5  = new TextField5Handler( this );
   ht6  = new TextField6Handler( this );
   ht7  = new TextField7Handler( this );
   hc1  = new Combo1Handler( this );
   hcb1 = new CheckBox1Handler( this );
```

Figure 12.34. *(cont.)*

```
                             // Create time domain plot
                             pl1 = new JPlot2D();
                             pl1.setPlotType ( JPlot2D.LINEAR );
                             pl1.setLineColor( Color.blue );
                             pl1.setLineWidth( 2.0f );
                             pl1.setLineStyle( JPlot2D.LINESTYLE_SOLID );
                             pl1.setTitle( "Time Domain" );
                             pl1.setXLabel( "Time (s)" );
                             pl1.setYLabel( "Amplitude" );
                             pl1.setGridState( JPlot2D.GRID_ON );
                             pl1.setPreferredSize(new Dimension(290,290));
                             pH1.add( pl1 );
                             pH1.add( Box.createRigidArea(new Dimension(10,0)) );

                             // Create frequency domain plot
                             pl2 = new JPlot2D();
                             pl2.setPlotType ( JPlot2D.LINEAR );
                             pl2.setLineColor( Color.blue );
                             pl2.setLineWidth( 2.0f );
                             pl2.setLineStyle( JPlot2D.LINESTYLE_SOLID );
                             pl2.setTitle( "Frequency Domain" );
                             pl2.setXLabel( "Frequency (Hz)" );
                             pl2.setYLabel( "Amplitude" );
                             pl2.setGridState( JPlot2D.GRID_ON );
                             pl2.setPreferredSize(new Dimension(290,290));
                             pH1.add( pl2 );

                             // Create signal 1 frequency field
                             l1 = new JLabel("Signal 1 Frequency (Hz):");
                             pG.add( l1 );
                             tf1 = new JTextField(12);
                             tf1.addActionListener( ht1 );
                             pG.add ( tf1 );

                             // Create signal 2 frequency field
                             l2 = new JLabel("Signal 2 Frequency (Hz):");
                             pG.add( l2 );
                             tf2 = new JTextField(12);
                             tf2.addActionListener( ht2 );
                             pG.add ( tf2 );

                             // Create the signal 1 amplitude field
                             l3 = new JLabel("Signal 1 Amplitude:");
                             pG.add( l3 );
                             tf3 = new JTextField(12);
                             tf3.addActionListener( ht3 );
                             pG.add ( tf3 );

                             // Create the signal 2 amplitude field
                             l4 = new JLabel("Signal 2 Amplitude:");
                             pG.add( l4 );
                             tf4 = new JTextField(12);
                             tf4.addActionListener( ht4 );
                             pG.add ( tf4 );
                             // Create the signal 1 phase field
                             l5 = new JLabel("Signal 1 Phase (deg):");
                             pG.add( l5 );
                             tf5 = new JTextField(12);
                             tf5.addActionListener( ht5 );
                             pG.add ( tf5 );
```

Figure 12.34. *(cont.)*

```
    // Create the signal 2 phase field
    l6 = new JLabel("Signal 2 Phase (deg):");
    pG.add( l6 );
    tf6 = new JTextField(12);
    tf6.addActionListener( ht6 );
    pG.add ( tf6 );

    // Create the noise type Combo Box
    l7 = new JLabel("Noise distribution:");
    pG.add( l7 );
    String[] s = {"Uniform","Gaussian"};
    c1 = new JComboBox(s);
    c1.addActionListener( hc1 );
    pG.add( c1 );

    // Create the noise amplitude field
    l8 = new JLabel("Noise Amplitude:");
    pG.add( l8 );
    tf7 = new JTextField(12);
    tf7.addActionListener( ht7 );
    pG.add ( tf7 );

    // Create noise on/off checkbox
    b1 = new JCheckBox("Add Noise to Signal");
    b1.addActionListener( hcb1 );
    pG.add( b1 );

    // Update plot information
    updatePlot();

    // Fill in the initial values in all fields
    tf1.setText( Fmt.sprintf("%.2f",sig1Freq) );
    tf2.setText( Fmt.sprintf("%.2f",sig2Freq) );
    tf3.setText( Fmt.sprintf("%.2f",sig1Amp) );
    tf4.setText( Fmt.sprintf("%.2f",sig2Amp) );
    tf5.setText( Fmt.sprintf("%.2f",sig1Phase) );
    tf6.setText( Fmt.sprintf("%.2f",sig2Phase) );
    tf7.setText( Fmt.sprintf("%.2f",noiseAmp) );
    b1.setSelected( noiseFlag );
}

//***********************************************
//  Method to update plot information
//***********************************************
public void updatePlot() {

    // Build signal plus noise
    for ( int i = 0; i < time.length; i++ ) {
        double temp = 0;
        double fac1 = 2 * Math.PI * sig1Freq / fs;
        double fac2 = 2 * Math.PI * sig2Freq / fs;
        double ph1 = sig1Phase * Math.PI / 180;
        double ph2 = sig1Phase * Math.PI / 180;

        if ( noiseFlag ) {
            if ( noiseType == 0 )
                temp = 2 * (Math.random() - 0.5);
            else if ( noiseType == 1 )
                temp = Math1.randomGaussian();
        }
```

Figure 12.34. *(cont.)*

```
            time[i] = new Complex(
                    sig1Amp * Math.sin(fac1*i + ph1)
                + sig2Amp * Math.sin(fac2*i + ph2)
                + noiseAmp * temp, 0);
        }

        // Calculate frequency steps
        double freqArray[] = new double[time.length];
        freqArray = SigProc.calcFreq( fs, time.length );

        // call fft
        spec = SigProc.fft(time);

        // Create time domain data to plot
        double x1[] = new double[time.length];
        double y1[] = new double[time.length];
        for ( int i = 0; i < time.length; i++ ) {
          x1[i] = dt * i;
          y1[i] = Complex.re(time[i]);
        }

        // Update time domain plot
        pl1.setValues( x1, y1 );

        // Create freq domain data to plot
        double x2[] = new double[spec.length/2];
        double y2[] = new double[spec.length/2];
        for ( int i = 0; i < spec.length/2; i++ ) {
          x2[i] = freqArray[i];
          y2[i] = Complex.abs(spec[i]);
        }

        // Update frequency domain plot
        pl2.setValues( x2, y2 );
    }

    //*************************************************
    //  Methods to update variables from events
    //*************************************************

    // Update signal 1 frequency
    public void updateSignal1Freq ( double f ) {
        sig1Freq = Math.max(Math.min(f,FREQ_MAX), FREQ_MIN);
        tf1.setText( Fmt.sprintf("%.2f",sig1Freq) );
        updatePlot();
        pl1.repaint();
        pl2.repaint();
    }

    // Update signal 2 frequency
    public void updateSignal2Freq ( double f ) {
        sig2Freq = Math.max(Math.min(f,FREQ_MAX), FREQ_MIN);
        tf2.setText( Fmt.sprintf("%.2f",sig2Freq) );
        updatePlot();
        pl1.repaint();
        pl2.repaint();
    }
```

Figure 12.34. *(cont.)*

```
// Update signal 1 amplitude
public void updateSignal1Amp ( double amp ) {
   sig1Amp = Math.max(Math.min(amp,AMP_MAX),AMP_MIN);
   tf3.setText( Fmt.sprintf("%.2f",sig1Amp) );
   updatePlot();
   pl1.repaint();
   pl2.repaint();
}

// Update signal 2 amplitude
public void updateSignal2Amp ( double amp ) {
   sig2Amp = Math.max(Math.min(amp,AMP_MAX),AMP_MIN);
   tf4.setText( Fmt.sprintf("%.2f",sig2Amp) );
   updatePlot();
   pl1.repaint();
   pl2.repaint();
}

// Update signal 1 phase
public void updateSignal1Phase ( double phase ) {
   sig1Phase = phase;
   tf5.setText( Fmt.sprintf("%.2f",sig1Phase) );
   updatePlot();
   pl1.repaint();
   pl2.repaint();
}

// Update signal 2 phase
public void updateSignal2Phase ( double phase ) {
   sig2Phase = phase;
   tf6.setText( Fmt.sprintf("%.2f",sig2Phase) );
   updatePlot();
   pl1.repaint();
   pl2.repaint();
}

// Update noise amplitude
public void updateNoiseAmp ( double amp ) {
   noiseAmp = Math.max(Math.min(amp,AMP_MAX),AMP_MIN);
   tf7.setText( Fmt.sprintf("%.2f",noiseAmp) );
   updatePlot();
   pl1.repaint();
   pl2.repaint();
}

// Update noise type
public void updateNoiseType( ) {
   noiseType = c1.getSelectedIndex();
   updatePlot();
   pl1.repaint();
   pl2.repaint();
}

// Update noise amplitude
public void updateNoiseFlag( ) {
   noiseFlag = b1.isSelected();
   updatePlot();
   pl1.repaint();
   pl2.repaint();
}
```

Figure 12.34.   *(cont.)*

```
//************************************************
//   Main method
//************************************************

(not shown to save space)

//************************************************
//   Event handlers
//************************************************

(not shown to save space)
```

Figure 12.34. GUI-based program to display a time–domain signal and the corresponding spectrum.

6. **Test the resulting Java program**. To test this program, we will execute it and examine the results. Figure 12.35 shows a typical result of a combination of two sinusoids plus noise. Execute the program for yourself and examine the displays for various input values.

Figure 12.35. Output of program Spectrum.

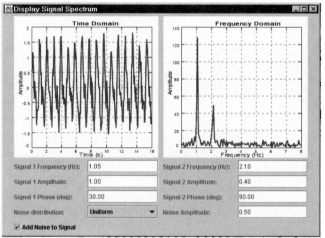

SUMMARY

- The principal elements required to create a Java GUI are components, a container to hold them, a layout manager, and event handlers.
- The JLabel class creates a GUI component that displays read-only text.
- The JButton class creates a GUI component that implements push buttons. This class generates an ActionEvent containing the button label when a button is clicked.
- The JTextField class creates a GUI component that allows a user to display and edit text. This class generates an ActionEvent containing the field's text when the Enter key is pressed.
- The JPasswordField class is identical to the JTextField class, except that asterisks are displayed in the field instead of the typed text.
- The JComboBox class creates a drop-down list of choices, and allow the user to select one of the by clicking with the mouse. It may optionally be set to

allow the user to type text directly into the combo box. This class generates an `ActionEvent` when a selection is made.

- The `JCheckBox` class creates a check box, which is a type of button that is either on or off. This class generates an `ActionEvent` when a state change occurs.
- The `JRadioButton` class creates a radio button, which a type of checkbox designed to be grouped into sets. A `ButtonGroup` object is used to group together all the radio buttons that form a set. Only *one* button within a set of radio buttons may be on at any given time.
- A canvas is a blank component that can be used to display custom graphics. It can be created by subclassing `JComponent` or `chapman.graphics. JCanvas`.
- A layout manager is a helper class that is designed to automatically arrange GUI components within a container for presentation purposes. There are six standard layout managers: `BorderLayout`, `CardLayout`, `FlowLayout`, `BoxLayout`, `GridLayout`, and `GridBagLayout`.

APPLICATIONS: GOOD PROGRAMMING PRACTICES

The following guidelines introduced in this chapter will help you to develop good programs:

1. To handle button events, use a class that implements the `ActionListener` interface, and contains an `actionPerformed` method. Register an object from this class with each button, and code the `action-Performed` method to do whatever is required when the button is pressed.
2. One `ActionListener` object can monitor many buttons, using the result of the `getActionCommand` method to determine the button that created a particular event.
3. Use `JTextFields` to accept single lines of input data from a user, or to display single lines of read-only data to the user.
4. Use `JPasswordFields` to accept input data from a user that you do not wish to have echoed to the screen, such as passwords.
5. Use `JComboBoxes` fields to make a single selection from a list of mutually-exclusive choices.
6. Use `JCheckBoxes` to select the state of items represented by boolean variables, which can only be `true` or `false`.
7. Use `JRadioButtons` to select the state of a set of items represented by boolean variables, only one of which can be `true` at any time.
8. Use subclasses of `JComponent` or `chapman.graphics.JCanvas` to add graphical displays to a GUI.

KEY TERMS

`ActionEvent` class	container	`JLabel` class
`ActionListener` interface	event handler	`JPanel` class
`actionPerformed` method	`FlowLayout` class	`JPasswordField` class
`BorderLayout` class	`GridBagLayout` class	`JRadioButton` class
`BoxLayout` class	`GridLayout` class	`JTextField` class
`ButtonGroup` class	`java.awt.event` package	keyboard shortcut
`CardLayout` class	`JButton` class	layout manager
callback method	`JCheckBox` class	radio button
checkbox	`JComboBox` class	`setLayout` method
component	`JFrame` class	tool tips

Problems

12.1. Explain the steps required to create a GUI in Java.

12.2. Modify the temperature conversion GUI of Example 12-1 to add a "thermometer". The thermometer should be a canvas with a drawing of a thermometer shape and a fluid level corresponding to the current temperature in degrees Celsius. The range of the thermometer should be 0°–100° C.

12.3. Convert the calculator GUI of Figure 12.31 into a fully functional calculator.

12.4. Create a GUI that uses a JcomboBox to select the background color displayed by the GUI.

12.5. Write a class that displays a circle of random size and color, and calculates and displays the radius, diameter, area, and circumference of the circle. Use a canvas to draw the circle, and use read-only JtextFields to display the information about the circle. Include a button that can be clicked to cause the program to generate a new randomly-selected circle. (*Note:* In determining the size of the circle, assume that there are 72 pixels per inch.)

12.6. Write a GUI program that plots the equation $y(x) = ax^2 + bx + c$. The program should use class JPlot2D for the plot, and should have GUI elements to read the values of a, b, c, and the minimum and maximum x to plot.

12.7. Modify the spectral analysis program of Example 12-4 to support four or more input sinusoids. This change should be accomplished by creating a combo box for the current sinusoid, and having a single set of frequency, amplitude, and phase text fields that refer to whichever sinusoid is currently selected. There should also be a GUI element that allows the user to select the number of sinusoids to use in the input. The range of this input value should be 0-4.

12.8. Modify the spectral analysis program of Example 12-4 to support different types of input waveforms. The possible types of waveforms should include sinusoids, square waves, triangular waves, and sawtooth waves.

12.9. Create three GUIs that place five buttons into a JPanel using the BorderLayout, FlowLayout, GridLayout, and BoxLayout layout managers. What do the resulting GUIs look like?

12.10. Create an GUI that displays a user-selected image. The GUI should contain a combo box (drop-down list) to select the desired image, and a label display the image. The Chapter 12 files available at the book's Web site include GIF files containing pictures of a dog, a cat, a cow, a pig, and a rabbit. The user should be able to select one of these pictures in the drop-down list, and the appropriate picture should be displayed.

12.11. Modify the GUI created in Exercise 12.10 to use a set of five radio buttons to select the image to display. The radio buttons should be lined up along the left-hand side of the GUI, with the image on the right-hand side of the GUI. What sort of layout manager(s) are required to create this GUI?

12.12. Write an application that draws ten randomly-sized shapes in randomly-selected colors. The type of shape to draw (square, circle, ellipse, *etc.*) should be selectable through a JComboBox, and the display should be redrawn whenever the user presses a "Go" button on the GUI.

12.13. **Least Squares Fit** Write a GUI-based application that reads a series of (x,y) values from a disk file, performs a linear least squares fit on the values, and displays both the points and the least-squares fit line using class JPlot2D. The least-squares fit algorithm is described in Exercise 6.16, and the method developed there can be used with this application.

The GUI elements in the program should include a JtextField for the input file name, a Jbutton to read the file, two read-only JtextFields for the slope and intercept of the fitted line, and class JPlot2D to display the input points and the fitted results. Use class schapman.io.FileIn to actually read the data.

How many containers and which layout managers are required to create this GUI?

13

Additional GUI Components and Applets

This chapter continues the study of graphical user interfaces. Here we learn about some additional GUI components, plus how to create menus and dialog boxes for our applications. Next, we will learn more about mouse events and event handling, including the use of adapter classes.

The chapter concludes with a study of applets, explaining the differences between applets and applications, and showing how to create a single program that can run as either an application or an applet.

13.1 ADDITIONAL GRAPHICAL USER INTERFACE COMPONENTS

The Swing GUI contains an extremely rich set of GUI components, more than can possibly be covered in this brief text. This section introduces two additional GUI components. It describes how to create the components, as well as the types of events they can generate. The additional components discussed in this section are:

- Lists
- Tables

All of the components that we studied in Chapter 12 implemented the `ActionListener` interface and generated `ActionEvents`, so event handling was essentially the same in all cases. The components that we are introducing now implement different interfaces and generate different

SECTIONS

- 13.1 Additional Graphical User Interface Components
- 13.2 Menus
- 13.3 Dialog Boxes
- 13.4 Interfaces and Adapter Classes
- 13.5 Pop-up Menus
- 13.6 Pluggable Look and Feel
- 13.7 Introduction to Applets
- Summary
- Key Terms

OBJECTIVES

After reading this chapter, you should be able to:

- Create and manipulate lists, tables, menus, and dialog boxes
- Understand events, event interfaces, and adapter classes
- Understand pluggable look and feel
- Create applets, including applets that can also run as applications

types of events, so the event handling for these components will be slightly different than what we learned about in Chapter 12.

13.1.1 Lists

A list is a class that displays a list of `Objects` (usually `Strings`) in a box, and allows the user to select one or more of the items. Depending on the list initialization options, a user can select one or many items from the list. Lists are implemented by the `JList` class, which also provides methods to determine which items are selected at any given time.

`JList` objects can operate in three possible modes: *single selection mode, single interval selection mode,* or *multiple interval selection mode.* Single selection mode is the default. In this mode, clicking on an object in the list automatically deselects the previously selected object in the list. Single interval selection mode allows a user to select starting and ending objects, and all of the ones in between will be automatically selected. The user selects the first object in the interval by clicking on it, and he or she selects the last object in the interval by clicking on it while pressing the space bar. Multiple interval selection mode allows a user to select any number of items from the list in any order. The user selects the first object by clicking on it and then selects each other object of interest by clicking on it while pressing the CTRL key.

A `JList` is created with one of the following constructors:

```
public JList();
public JList(Object[] o);
public JList(Vector v);
```

The first constructor creates an empty list. The second and third constructors create new lists containing either the elements in the `Object` array or the elements of the `Vector`. Selected methods from class `JList` are described in Table 13-1.

By itself, a `JList` has no ability to scroll, so if the list of objects to be displayed is longer than the space available to display them, the objects that don't fit on the screen will not be visible or selectable. To make a list scrollable, you must wrap a `JScrollPane` around it.

A scrollable `JList` may be created using a `JScrollPane` by first creating the `JList` and then creating the `JScrollPane` with the `JList` as an argument of the constructor. Finally, the `JScrollPane` may be added to the container. These steps are accomplished with the following code:

```
JList list = new JList(Object[] o);
JScrollPane scrollPane = new JScrollPane(list);
add( scrollPane );
```

The following code fragment illustrates how to create both nonscrollable and scrollable lists. The results of this program are shown in Figure 13.1.

```
// Partial list of states
String[] states = { "Alabama", "Alaska",
    "Arizona", "Arkansas", "California", "Colorado",
    "Connecticut", "Delaware", "Florida", "Georgia"};

// Create a non-scrollable JList
JList l1 = new JList(states);
l1.setPreferredSize(new Dimension(200,100));
add( l1 );

// Add space between the two lists
add( Box.createRigidArea(new Dimension(15,0)) );
```

TABLE 13-1   Selected `JList` Methods

METHOD	DESCRIPTION
`void addListSelectionListener(ListSelectionListener)`	Adds the specified listener to receive `ListSelectionEvents` from this `JList`.
`public void clearSelection()`	Clears all items selections.
`public int getMaxSelectionIndex()`	Gets the index of the last selected value.
`public int getMinSelectionIndex()`	Gets the index of the first selected value.
`public int getSelectedIndex()`	Gets the first selected index.
`public int[] getSelectedIndices()`	Gets all selected indices.
`public Object getSelectedValue()`	Gets the first selected value.
`public Object[] getSelectedValues()`	Gets all of the selected value.
`public int getSelectionMode()`	Gets the selection mode for this `JLIST`. Valid values are `SINGLE_SELECTION`, `SINGLE_INTERVAL_SELECTION`, or `MULTIPLE_INTERVAL_SELECTION`.
`public boolean isSelectedIndex(int i)`	Returns `true` if the specified index is selected.
`public boolean isSelectionEmpty()`	Returns `true` if not selection has been made.
`public void setPreferredSize(Dimension d)`	Sets the preferred size of the list in pixels.
`public void setSelectedIndex(int i)`	Sets the selected index.
`public void setSelectedIndices(int[] i)`	Sets all of the selected indices.
`public void setSelectedInterval(int i1, int i2)`	Selects the specified interval from the list.
`public void setSelectedValue(Object o, boolean scroll)`	Selects the specified value from the list. If the boolean is `true`, the list will scroll to make the selection visible.
`public void setSelectionMode(int m)`	Sets the selection mode for this `JList`. Valid values are the constants `SINGLE_SELECTION`, `SINGLE_INTERVAL_SELECTION`, or `MULTIPLE_INTERVAL_SELECTION`. These constants are found in class `ListSelectionModel`.

```
// Create a scrollable JList
JList l2 = new JList(states);
JScrollPane scrollPane = new JScrollPane(l2);
scrollPane.setPreferredSize(new Dimension(200,100));
add( scrollPane );
```

Lists often vary in size in different runs of a program, and sometimes may grow to be very large. To ensure that you will always be able to access all parts of your lists, you should always use scrollable lists on all of you programs.

Figure 13.1.   Sample `JLists` with and without scrollbars. Note that for the `JList` on the left, none of the states below California may be selected.

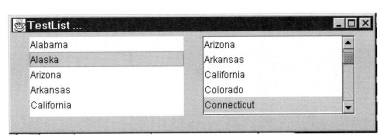

> **GOOD PROGRAMMING PRACTICE**
>
> Use class `JList` to create lists of objects for display and selection in a GUI.

> **GOOD PROGRAMMING PRACTICE**
>
> Always use scrollable `JLists` in all of your programs to ensure that a user can see all of the values in the list.

Events Associated with `JLists`   Class `JList` generates `ListSelectionEvents`. A `ListSelectionEvent` is produced each time that a user selects or de-selects any item in the list. `ListSelectionEvents` include several methods that allow a program to recover information about the triggering event. The most important of these methods are listed in Table 13-2.

TABLE 13-2 `ListSelectionEvent` Methods

METHOD	DESCRIPTION
`public int getFirstIndex()`	Returns the index of the first item whose selection may have changed.
`public int getLastIndex()`	Returns the index of the last item whose selection may have changed.
`public Object getSource()`	Returns the `Object` from which this event originated.
`public boolean getValueIsAdjusting()`	Returns `true` if the event is one of a rapid series of events. This flag lets a program ignore the events until the last one in the series, and only process the final result.
`public String paramString()`	Returns a parameter string identifying this event. This method is useful for event logging and for debugging.

The `ListSelectionListener` *Interface*   `ListSelectionEvents` are processed by classes that implement the `ListSelectionListener` **interface**, which is defined in package `javax.swing.event`. This interface defines the single event-handling method `valueChanged`. When a `ListSelectionListener` object is registered with a `JList` using the method `addListSelectionListener`, the method `value Changed` will be called automatically whenever a selection or deselection occurs in the list.

TABLE 13-3 `ListSelectionListener` Interface Method

METHOD	DESCRIPTION
`public void valueChanged(ListSelectionEvent e)`	Method invoked when a `ListSelectionEvent` occurs.

EXAMPLE 13-1: USING LISTS

Create a program that contains a list of all the states in the USA. The program should allow for single selection, single interval selection, and multiple interval selection. The program should display the total 1980 population of all selected states in a text field.

SOLUTION
This program will require a `JList` to hold the state names, a `JComboBox` to select the list selection mode, a `JTextField` to display the total population, and a `JLabel` to label the resulting display. It will also be necessary to create listeners for the `JList` and `JComboBox` events.

1. **State the problem**. Create a GUI-based program that displays all US states in a list and sums the total population of the selected states. Use the 1980 census figures for the population of the states.

2. **Define the inputs and outputs**. The inputs to this program are the names of the states and their population in 1980, plus a combo box specifying the selection mode of the list. These inputs will be hard coded into arrays in the program. The output from the program is the sum of the population of all selected states.

3. **Decompose the program into classes and their associated methods**. This program requires three classes to function properly. The principal class (called `TestList1`) must contain separate methods (1) to generate the GUI display, (2) to update the selection mode when the user changes it, and (3) to add up the total population in all selected states.

   In addition, the program must contain two event-handling classes to handle the events generated by the `JList` and `JComboBox` input GUI elements. The `JList` will require a `ListSelectionListener` and the `JComboBox` will require an `ActionListener`.

4. **Design the algorithm that you intend to implement for each method**. The `init()` method of the `TestList1` class must create the GUI. It must lay out four graphical elements consisting of one list, one combo box, one label, and one read-only text field. The elements should be organized with the list on top, the combo box below it, and the label and text field side by side below the combo box.

   This type of layout requires a total of two nested containers to create. The highest level panel (`pV1`) uses a vertically oriented `BoxLayout`. That panel contains the list, the combo box, and a panel with a horizontally oriented `BoxLayout`. The label and the text field can be placed in the horizontally oriented panel. The code to create this structure is shown below.

```
// Create a top-level vertical panel
JPanel pV = new JPanel();
pV.setLayout(new BoxLayout(pV, BoxLayout.Y_AXIS));
add( pV );

(Create and add scrollable list to vertical panel)
(Create and add combo box to vertical panel)

// Create a horizontal panel
JPanel pH = new JPanel();
pH.setLayout(new BoxLayout(pH, BoxLayout.X_AXIS));
pV.add( pH );

(Create and add JLabel to horizontal panel)
(Create and add JTextField to horizontal panel)
```

The code to create the four graphical elements is shown in Figure 13.2.

Method `updateMode()` must update the `JList` selection mode whenever the user changes it. This code must get the index of the selected selection mode and use method `setSelectionMode` to enable that mode. The code for this method is:

```
int[] vals={ListSelectionModel.SINGLE_SELECTION,
            ListSelectionModel.SINGLE_INTERVAL_SELECTION,
            ListSelectionModel.MULTIPLE_INTERVAL_SELECTION };
list.setSelectionMode( vals[c1.getSelectedIndex()] );
```

Method `updatePopulation()` must add up the population for each state that is selected. The code for this method is:

```
int sum = 0;
for (int i = 0; i < states.length; i++ ) {
    if (list.isSelectedIndex(i)) {
        sum += pop[i];
    }
}
```

The two event handlers should detect events on the `JComboBox` and the `JList` and call the methods `updateMode()` and `updatePopulation()`. Note that the `ListSelectionListener` should not respond if a series of rapid changes are occurring. Instead, it should only respond to the final result when things settle down. This is done by only updating the GUI when the method `getValueIsAdjusting()` returns `false`.

```
if ( ! e.getValueIsAdjusting() ) {
    t1.updatePopulation();
}
```

5. **Turn the algorithm into Java statements**. The resulting Java program is shown in Figure 13.2.

```
/*
   Purpose:
     This program sums the total 1980 population of all
     selected states, and displays the results in a GUI.

   Record of revisions:
       Date        Programmer          Description of change
       ====        ==========          =====================
     12/21/98    S. J. Chapman        Original code
*/
import java.awt.*;
import java.awt.event.*;
import javax.swing.*;
import javax.swing.event.*;
public class TestList1 extends JPanel {

   // Instance variables
   JComboBox c1;                 // Selection mode combo box
   JLabel l1;                    // Label for total
   JList list;                   // List of states
   JScrollPane scrollPane;       // Scrollpane for list
   JTextField t1;                // Text field to display total
   ListHandler h1;               // List handler
   ComboHandler h2;              // Combo box handler

   // List of states
   String[] states = { "Alabama", "Alaska",
      "Arizona", "Arkansas", "California", "Colorado",
      "Connecticut", "Delaware", "District of Columbia",
      "Florida", "Georgia", "Hawaii", "Idaho", "Illinois",
      "Indiana", "Iowa", "Kansas", "Kentucky", "Louisiana",
      "Maine", "Maryland", "Massachusetts", "Michigan",
      "Minnesota", "Mississippi", "Missouri", "Montana",
      "Nebraska", "Nevada", "New Hampshire", "New Jersey",
      "New Mexico", "New York", "North Carolina",
      "North Dakota", "Ohio", "Oklahoma", "Oregon",
```

Figure 13.2.   *(cont.)*

```
          "Pennsylvania", "Rhode Island", "South Carolina",
          "South Dakota", "Tennessee", "Texas", "Utah",
          "Vermont", "Virginia", "Washington", "West Virginia",
          "Wisconsin", "Wyoming" };

      // 1980 population
      int[] pop = {3893888,    401851,  2718425,  2286435,  23667565,
                   2889735,  3107576,   594317,   638432,   9746342,
                   5463105,   964691,   944038, 11426596,   5490260,
                   2913808,  2364236,  3660257,  4206312,   1125027,
                   4216975,  5737037,  9262078,  4075970,   2520638,
                   4916759,   786690,  1569825,   800493,    920610,
                   7364823,  1302981, 17558072,  5881813,    652717,
                  10797624,  3025290,  2633149, 11863895,    947154,
                   3121833,   690768,  4591120, 14229288,   1461037,
                    511456,  5346818,  4132180,  1950279,   4705521,
                    469557 };

      // Initialization method
      public void init() {

         // Create event handlers
         h1 = new ListHandler( this );
         h2 = new ComboHandler( this );

          // Create a top-level vertical panel
         JPanel pV = new JPanel();
         pV.setLayout(new BoxLayout(pV, BoxLayout.Y_AXIS));
         add( pV );

         // Create a scrollable JList
         list = new JList(states);
         list.addListSelectionListener( h1 );
         scrollPane = new JScrollPane(list);
         scrollPane.setPreferredSize(new Dimension(200,100));
         pV.add( scrollPane );

         // Add space
         pV.add( Box.createRigidArea(new Dimension(0,10)) );

         // Create a Combo Box specifying the mode of the list
         String[] s = {"Single Selection","Single Interval Selection",
                       "Multiple Interval Selection"};
         c1 = new JComboBox(s);
         c1.addActionListener( h2 );
         pV.add( c1 );

         // Add space
         pV.add( Box.createRigidArea(new Dimension(0,10)) );

         // Create a horizontal panel
         JPanel pH = new JPanel();
         pH.setLayout(new BoxLayout(pH, BoxLayout.X_AXIS));
         pV.add( pH );

         // Add a text field for the results
         l1 = new JLabel("Total");
         pH.add( l1 );
```

Figure 13.2.   *(cont.)*

```
                pH.add( Box.createRigidArea(new Dimension(5,0)) );
                t1 = new JTextField(10);
                t1.setEditable( false );
                pH.add( t1 );
            }

            // Method to set selection mode
            public void updateMode() {

                int[] vals={ListSelectionModel.SINGLE_SELECTION,
                            ListSelectionModel.SINGLE_INTERVAL_SELECTION,
                            ListSelectionModel.MULTIPLE_INTERVAL_SELECTION };
                list.setSelectionMode( vals[c1.getSelectedIndex()] );
                updatePopulation();
            }

            // Method to add up all selected states
            public void updatePopulation() {

                int sum = 0;
                for (int i = 0; i < states.length; i++ ) {
                    if (list.isSelectedIndex(i)) {
                        sum += pop[i];
                    }
                }
                t1.setText("" + sum );
                t1.repaint();
            }

            // Main method to create frame
            (not shown to save space)

        class ComboHandler implements ActionListener {
            private TestList1 t1;

            // Constructor
            public ComboHandler( TestList1 t ) { t1 = t; }

            // Execute when an event occurs
            public void actionPerformed( ActionEvent e ) {

                // List mode has changed
                t1.updateMode();
            }
        }

        class ListHandler implements ListSelectionListener {
            private TestList1 t1;

            // Constructor
            public ListHandler( TestList1 t ) { t1 = t; }

            // Execute when an event occurs
            public void valueChanged( ListSelectionEvent e ) {

                // Update after value stabilizes
                if ( ! e.getValueIsAdjusting() ) {
                    t1.updatePopulation();
                }
            }
        }
    }
```

Figure 13.2. GUI-based program to calculate the total 1980 population of all selected states.

6.   **Test the resulting Java program**.

        To test this program, we will execute it and examine the results. Figure 13.3 shows typical results for single selection mode, single interval mode, and multiple interval mode. Execute this program for yourself and experiment with the operation of the list.

Figure 13.3.   (*a*) Example results for single selection mode. (*b*) Example results for single interval selection mode. (*c*) Example results for multiple interval selection mode.

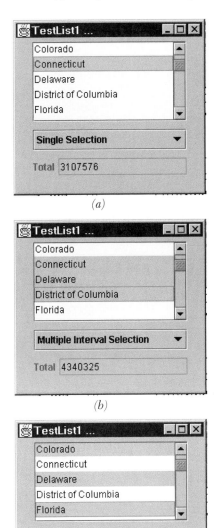

13.1.2 Tables

A table is a class that displays a table of `Objects`. The class can be customized to allow the objects in different columns to be displayed in different formats and to allow the values in the table to be dynamically edited by the user. These details may be found in the JDK documentation. In this text, we restrict ourselves to using a table as a way to display data only, not modify it. Be aware that tables have many more capabilities than are demonstrated here.

A Java table is implemented by class `JTable`. Some of the simpler constructors for this class are shown below.

```
public JTable();
public JList(Object[][] data, Object[] headings);
public JList(Vector data, Vector headings);
```

The first constructor creates a new empty table. The second and third constructors create new tables containing either the elements in the `Object` two dimensional array `data` or the elements of the `Vector` `data`. The array headings, or the `Vector` headings, contains the column headings for each column of the table. Selected methods from class `JTable` are described in Table 13-4.

By itself, a `JTable` has no ability to scroll, so if the list of objects to be displayed is longer than the space available to display them, the objects that don't fit on the screen will not be visible. To make a list scrollable, you must wrap a `JScrollPane` around it.

A scrollable `JTable` may be created using a `JScrollPane` by first creating the `JTable`, and then creating the `JScrollPane` with the `JTable` as an argument of the constructor. Finally, the `JScrollPane` may be added to the container.

```
JTable table = new JTable(data, columnNames);
JScrollPane scrollPane = new JScrollPane(table);
add( scrollPane );
```

The following code fragment illustrates how to create a scrollable table containing State names and population figures. The results of this program are shown in Figure 13.4.

```
// Initialization method. This method creates a
// table of 1980 population by state.
public void init() {

    // Convert population figures into objects
    String[] popString = new String[ pop.length ];
    for ( int i = 0; i < pop.length; i++ ) {
        popString[i] = Fmt.sprintf("%10d", pop[i]);
    }

    // Create the two-dimensional array of objects
    // to pass to the table
    Object[][] data = new Object[states.length][2];
    for ( int i = 0; i < states.length; i++ ) {
        data[i][0] = states[i];
        data[i][1] = popString[i];
    }

    // Create column headers
    String[] headers = { "State", "1980 Population" };

    // Create a scrollable JTable
    table = new JTable(data,headers);
    scrollPane = new JScrollPane(table);
    scrollPane.setPreferredSize(new Dimension(250,200));
    add( scrollPane );
}
```

Figure 13.4. A simple table showing 1980 population by state.

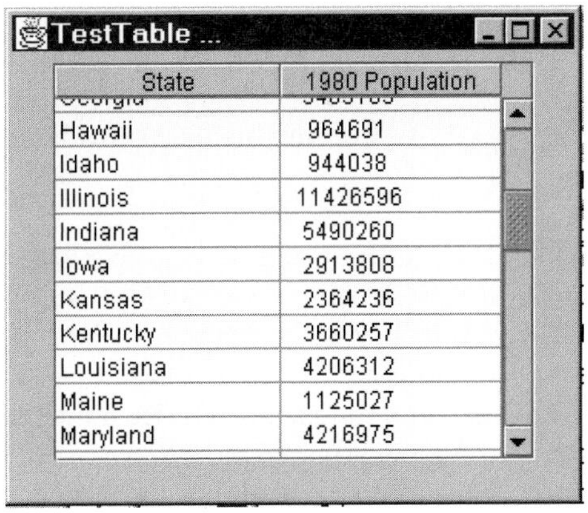

TABLE 13-4   Selected `JTable` Methods

METHOD	DESCRIPTION
`public void setPreferredScrollableViewportSize(Dimension d)`	Set the preferred size when viewed through a `JScrollPlane`.
`public void setPreferredSize(Dimension d)`	Sets the preferred size of the list in pixels.

Tables can be greatly enhanced by modifying the `TableModel` used to represent the data displayed in the table. For example, a custom `TableModel` would allow the table in Figure 13.4 to display the population numbers right aligned. Refer to the `JTable` and `TableModel` descriptions in the JDK for details about creating custom table models.

GOOD PROGRAMMING PRACTICE

Use `JTables` to display tabular data.

13.2 MENUS

Menus can be added to Java GUIs. In general, a menu allows a user to select actions without additional components appearing on the GUI display. They are useful for selecting less commonly used options without cluttering up the GUI with a lot of extra buttons.

There are two type of menus, drop-down menus and pop-up menus. Drop-down menus are attached to a bar at the top of a container, and they open downward whenever a user clicks on the menu. By contrast, pop-up menus are menus that "pop up" over a component when a user right-clicks the mouse over that component.

The items in a Java menu are just specially shaped buttons that become visible when you click on a menu bar. Because they are buttons, we already know most of what we need to know to use them. Like all buttons, they generate `ActionEvents` when a mouse click activates them. Also, it is possible to define a keyboard accelerator for a menu item.

There are three types of menu items, corresponding to the three types of buttons:

- **Menu Items:** These behave just like pushbuttons.
- **Check Box Menu Items:** These behave just like check boxes.
- **Radio Button Menu Items:** These behave just like radio buttons.

13.2.1 Menu Components

Menus are composed of five basic components: `JMenuBars`, `JMenus`, `JMenuItems`, `JCheckBoxMenuItems`, and `JradioButtonMenuItems`. (See Figures 13.5 and 13.6) A **menu bar** is the bar across the top of the frame to which the menus are attached. A **menu** is an individual list of items that is pulled down from the menu bar when the user clicks on the menu name. A **menu item** is an object inside a menu that, when selected, causes an action to be performed. (Note that a menu item can be a **submenu**, which contains menu items of its own.) Finally, **check box menu items** and **radio button menu items** are menu items that function like check boxes and radio buttons, respectively.

A menu bar is created with class `JMenuBar`. The default constructor is

```
public JMenuBar();
```

This constructor creates a blank menu bar across the top of a compatible container (a `JFrame`, `JApplet`, `JDialog`, `JRootPane`, or `JInternalFrame`). The menu bar is attached to the container using the container's `setJMenuBar` method. Selected methods from class `JMenuBar` are described in Table 13-5.

A `JMenu` is created with the constructor

```
public JMenu(String label);
```

This constructor creates a new empty menu with the name `label`. The menu is attached to the menu bar using the menu bar's `add` method. Selected methods from class `JMenu` are described in Table 13.6.

A `JMenuItem` works like a pushbutton. It generates an `ActionEvent` when a mouse click occurs on it. It is created with one of the following constructors:

```
public JMenuItem(String label);
public JMenuItem(Icon image);
public JMenuItem(String label, Icon image);
public JMenuItem(String label, int mnemonic);
```

The first constructor creates a new menu item with a text label. The second constructor creates a new menu item with an image label. The third constructor creates a new menu item with both text and an image on the label. The final constructor creates a new menu item with a text label, and it also creates a keyboard shortcut for the menu item. The menu item is attached to a menu using the menu's `add` method. The most important methods for `JMenuItem` are the same as those for `JButton`, which are given in Table 12-3.

TABLE 13-5   Selected `JMenuBar` Methods

METHOD	DESCRIPTION
`public void add(JMenu m)`	Adds a `JMenu` to the `JmenuBar`.
`public JMenu getHelpMenu()`	Gets the help menu on the menu bar.
`public JMenu getMenu(int i)`	Gets the specified menu.
`public int getMenuCount()`	Gets the number of menus on the menu bar.
`public void setHelpMenu(JMenu m)`	Sets the help menu on this menu bar to be the specified menu.

Figure 13.5. The inheritance hierarchy of Swing menu components. Note that menu items inherit from AbstractButton, so they are effectively buttons that appear when the menu bar is clicked.

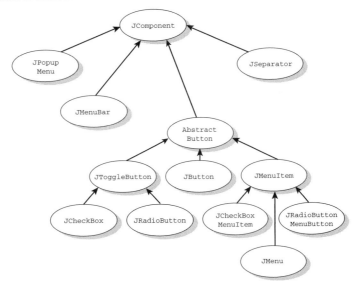

Figure 13.6. A Java GUI with menus, showing a menu bar, menus, sub-menus, and menu items.

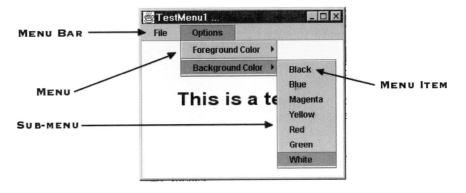

TABLE 13-6 Selected JMenu Methods

METHOD	DESCRIPTION
public JMenuItem add (JMenuItem mi)	Adds the specified menu item to this menu. (*Note:* This could be another menu.)
public void addSeparator()	Adds a separator line to the menu at the current position.
public JMenuItem getItem (int index)	Gets the item located at the specified index of this menu.
public int getItemCount()	Gets the number of items in this menu.
public JMenuItem insert (JMenuItem mi, int pos)	Insert the specified menu item at the given position.
public String paramString()	Gets the parameter string representing the state of this menu.
public void remove(Component c)	Removes the specified component from this menu.

A `JCheckBoxMenuItem` works like a `JCheckBox`. It has two states (on/off or true/false), and the state is toggled whenever a mouse click occurs on it. Note that this component generates an `ActionEvent` when a mouse click occurs on it, just as a `JcheckBox` does. It is created with one of the following constructors:

```
public JCheckBoxMenuItem( String s );
public JCheckBoxMenuItem( String s, boolean state );
public JCheckBoxMenuItem( Icon Image );
public JCheckBoxMenuItem( Icon image, boolean state );
public JCheckBoxMenuItem( String s, Icon image );
public JCheckBoxMenuItem( String s, Icon image, boolean state);
```

In these constructors, s is the text label for the check box menu item, image is the image to display on the check box menu item, and state is the initial on/off state of the check box menu item. If state is absent from a constructor, then the new check box menu item defaults to off. The methods in class `JCheckBoxMenuItem` are essentially identical to those in `JCheckBox`, and described in Table 12-8.

A `JRadioButtonMenuItem` works like a `JRadioButton`. Each radio button menu item has two states (on/off or true/false), and many radio button menu items are grouped together into a `ButtonGroup`. Only one of the radio button menu items in a `ButtonGroup` may be on at any given time. If one is turned on, the others are automatically turned off. Note that this component generates an `ActionEvent` when a mouse click occurs on it, just as a `JRadioButton` does. It is created with one of the following constructors:

```
public JRadioButtonMenuItem( String s );
public JRadioButtonMenuItem( String s, boolean state );
public JRadioButtonMenuItem( Icon Image );
public JRadioButtonMenuItem( Icon image, boolean state );
public JRadioButtonMenuItem( String s, Icon image );
public JRadioButtonMenuItem( String s, Icon image, booleans state );
```

In these constructors, s is the text label for the radio button menu item, image is the image to display on the radio button menu item, and state is the initial on/off state of the radio button menu item. If state is absent from a constructor, then the new radio button defaults to off. The methods in class `JRadioButtonMenuItem` are the same as those in class `JRadioButton`, and are described in Table 12-8.

13.2.2 Events Associated with Menu Components

All menu item classes generate ActionEvents, just like buttons. An ActionEvent is produced each time that a user clicks the mouse button on a menu item. This event can be handled by a class that implements the **ActionListener** interface. When the menu item is selected, the **actionPerformed** method of the listener class is called.

Figure 13.7 shows a simple application with menus. This application displays a test string and allows the user to change the foreground and background colors of the string using menu selections.

This application has two menus on a menu bar, a "File" menu and an "Options" menu. The "File" menu contains two menu items labeled "Enable Options" and "Exit." The "Enable Options" menu item is a `JCheckBoxMenuItem` that controls whether or not the "Options" menu is enabled. When the "Enable Options" menu item is selected, the program generates an `ActionEvent` that is handled by the `actionPerformed` method of `EnableHandler`, which in turn calls `updateOptionsMenuState()` to update the "Options" menu state. When the "Exit" menu item is selected, the program generates an `ActionEvent` that is handled by the `ExitHandler`, and the `Exit- Handler` shuts down the program.

The "Options" menu contains two sub-menus: one for the foreground color and one for the background color. If one of these menu items is selected, the corresponding sub-menu is displayed, and the user can select a color. When a color is selected, the menu item generates an `ActionEvent`, which is handled by the `actionPerformed` method of `fgColorHandler` or `bgColorHandler`, and the corresponding handler updates the display colors.

Note that this program also demonstrates the use of keyboard shortcuts, as well as the ability to enable and disable menus.

```java
// This program tests menus.
import java.awt.*;
import java.awt.geom.*;
import java.awt.event.*;
import javax.swing.*;
public class TestMenu1 extends JPanel {

    // Instance variables
    private String colorNames[] = {"Black", "Blue",
        "Magenta", "Yellow", "Red", "Green", "White"};

    private Color colorValues[] = {Color.black,
        Color.blue, Color.magenta, Color.yellow,
        Color.red, Color.green, Color.white};

    private ActionListener hBg, hFg, hEnable, hExit;
                                    // Action listeners
    private JMenuBar bar;           // Menu bar
    private JMenu fileMenu;         // File Menu
    private JMenu optionsMenu;      // Options Menu
    private JMenu fgColorMenu;      // Foreground Color Menu
    private JMenu bgColorMenu;      // Background Color Menu
    private JCheckBoxMenuItem enable; // Enable Options menu
    private JMenuItem exit;         // Exit "menu" item
    private JMenuItem fgColors[];   // Foreground colors menu items
    private JMenuItem bgColors[];   // Background colors menu items

    // Initialization method
    public void init() {

        // Create event handlers
        hBg     = new BgColorHandler( this );
        hFg     = new FgColorHandler( this );
        hEnable = new EnableHandler( this );
        hExit   = new ExitHandler();

        // Set foreground color
        setForeground( Color.black );

        // Set background color
        setBackground( Color.white );
```

Figure 13.7. *(cont.)*

```
                        // Create menu bar
                        bar = new JMenuBar();

                        // Create "File" menu
                        fileMenu = new JMenu("File");
                        fileMenu.setMnemonic('f');

                        // Create and add "Enable Options" checkbox menu item
                        enable = new JCheckBoxMenuItem("Enable Options", true);
                        enable.addActionListener(hEnable);
                        fileMenu.add( enable );

                        // Create and add "Exit" menu item
                        exit = new JMenuItem( "Exit" );
                        exit.addActionListener(hExit);
                        exit.setMnemonic('x');
                        fileMenu.add ( exit );

                        // Create "Options" menu
                        optionsMenu = new JMenu("Options");
                        fileMenu.setMnemonic('o');

                        // Create color sub-menus and add to Options menu
                        fgColorMenu = new JMenu("Foreground Color");
                        bgColorMenu = new JMenu("Background Color");
                        optionsMenu.add ( fgColorMenu );
                        optionsMenu.addSeparator();
                        optionsMenu.add ( bgColorMenu );

                        // Create foregroud colors list
                        fgColors = new JMenuItem[ colorNames.length ];
                        for ( int i = 0; i < colorNames.length; i++ ) {
                           fgColors[i] = new JMenuItem( colorNames[i] );
                           fgColorMenu.add ( fgColors[i] );
                           fgColors[i].addActionListener(hFg);
                        }

                        // Create background colors list
                        bgColors = new JMenuItem[ colorNames.length ];
                        for ( int i = 0; i < colorNames.length; i++ ) {
                           bgColors[i] = new JMenuItem( colorNames[i] );
                           bgColorMenu.add ( bgColors[i] );
                           bgColors[i].addActionListener(hBg);
                        }

                        // Add the menus to the menu bar
                        bar.add ( fileMenu );
                        bar.add ( optionsMenu );
                     }

                     //Method to update foreground color
                     public void updateFgColor( String color ) {

                        for ( int i = 0; i < colorNames.length; i++ ) {
                           if ( color.equals( colorNames[i]) ) {
                              setForeground ( colorValues[i] );
                           }
                        }
                        repaint();
                     }
```

Figure 13.7. *(cont.)*

```
// Method to update background color
public void updateBgColor( String color ) {

   for ( int i = 0; i < colorNames.length; i++ ) {
      if ( color.equals( colorNames[i]) ) {
         setBackground ( colorValues[i] );
      }
   }
   repaint();
}

// Method to update options menu state
public void updateOptionsMenuState() {

   if (enable.isSelected() )
      optionsMenu.setEnabled(true);
   else
      optionsMenu.setEnabled(false);
}

public void paintComponent ( Graphics g ) {

   // Cast the graphics object to Graph2D
   Graphics2D g2 = (Graphics2D) g;

   // Set rendering hints to improve display quality
   g2.setRenderingHint(RenderingHints.KEY_ANTIALIASING,
                       RenderingHints.VALUE_ANTIALIAS_ON);

   // Set background color
   Dimension size = getSize();
   g2.setColor( getBackground() );
   g2.fill(new Rectangle2D.Double(0,0,size.width, size.height));

   // Define a font ...
   Font f = new Font("SansSerif",Font.BOLD,24);

   // Display fonts
   g2.setFont(f);
   g2.setColor( getForeground() );
   g2.drawString("This is a test!",50,90);
}

// Main method to create frame
public static void main(String s[]) {

   // Create a frame to hold the application
   JFrame fr = new JFrame("TestMenu1 ...");
   fr.setSize(300,220);

   // Create a Window Listener to handle "close" events
   MyWindowListener l = new MyWindowListener();
   fr.addWindowListener(l);

   // Create and initialize a TestMenu1 object
   TestMenu1 tm = new TestMenu1();
   tm.init();
```

Figure 13.7. *(cont.)*

```
            // Add the menu bar to the frame
            fr.setJMenuBar( tm.bar );

            // Add the object to the center of the frame
            fr.getContentPane().add(tm, BorderLayout.CENTER);

            // Display the frame
            fr.setVisible( true );
        }
    }

class FgColorHandler implements ActionListener {
    private TestMenu1 tm1;

        // Constructor
        public FgColorHandler( TestMenu1 t ) {tm1 = t;}

        // Execute when an event occurs
        public void actionPerformed( ActionEvent e ) {
            tm1.updateFgColor(e.getActionCommand());
        }
    }

class BgColorHandler implements ActionListener {
    private TestMenu1 tm1;

        // Constructor
        public BgColorHandler( TestMenu1 t ) {tm1 = t;}

      // Execute when an event occurs
       public void actionPerformed( ActionEvent e ) {
           tm1.updateBgColor(e.getActionCommand());
       }
    }

class EnableHandler implements ActionListener {
    private TestMenu1 tm1;

        // Constructor
        public EnableHandler( TestMenu1 t ) {tm1 = t;}

        // Execute when an event occurs
        public void actionPerformed( ActionEvent e ) {
          tm1.updateOptionsMenuState();
        }
    }

class ExitHandler implements ActionListener {

        // Execute when an event occurs
        public void actionPerformed( ActionEvent e ) {
            System.exit(0);
        }
    }
```

Figure 13.7. A simple application that supports menus.

When this program is executed, it produces the GUI shown in Figure 13.8. Execute the program and try changing the foreground and background colors with the menu selections.

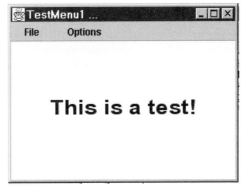

Figure 13.8. The GUI produced by the TestMenu1 application.

13.3 DIALOG BOXES

A **dialog box** is a special type of container that is used to get information from a user or to provide error or warning messages. It is a separate window similar to a frame, but is much easier to use. Dialog boxes are normally displayed for some specific purpose, and then they are made invisible or destroyed immediately after they are used.

Dialog boxes may be **modal** or non-modal. A modal dialog box does not allow any other window in the application to be accessed until it is dismissed, while a non-modal dialog box does not block access to other windows. All dialog boxes that we will discuss are modal dialog boxes. They are typically used for warning and error messages that need urgent attention and cannot be ignored.

Dialogs may be created with the JDialog class, but Java pre-defines several easy-to-use dialog box types as static methods in the JOptionPane class. These standard dialog boxes are very easy to use, so generally you should use them instead of working with JDialog directly. There are several different standard dialog boxes that can be used to display information or ask for input information. The standard types of dialogs include:

- ShowMessageDialog—This dialog displays a modal dialog box with one button, which is labeled "OK". You can easily specify the message, icon, and title that the dialog displays.
- ShowConfirmDialog—This dialog displays a modal dialog box with two buttons, labeled "Yes" and "No", or three buttons labeled "Yes", "No", and "Cancel".

- `ShowInputDialog`—This dialog displays a modal dialog box that gets a string from the user. An input dialog either displays a text field in which the user may enter text, or it displays a fixed set of options in an uneditable combo box.

- `ShowOptionDialog`—This dialog displays a modal dialog box with the specified buttons, icons, message, title, and so on. With this method, you can change the text that appears on the buttons of standard dialogs. You can also perform many other kinds of customization. It is the most flexible dialog box option.

Only the first three types of dialog boxes are discussed here, since they are usually sufficient for simple programs. However, the details of all types of dialog boxes may be found in the description of class `JOptionPane` in the JDK documentation.

13.3.1 Message Dialog Boxes

Message dialog boxes are used to display a message only. The `static` methods used to create a message dialog box are

```
static void JOptionPane.showMessageDialog(Component parentComponent,
              Object message, String title, int messageType);
static void JOptionPane.showMessageDialog(Component parentComponent,
              Object message, String title, int messageType,
              Icon icon);
```

The meanings of each parameter in these methods are defined in Table 13-7.

TABLE 13-7 Parameters for showXxxxDialog methods

METHOD	DESCRIPTION
`Component parentComponent`	Determines the frame in which the dialog will be displayed. If `null` is specified for this component, a default frame will be created.
`Object message`	The message to display (usually a `String`).
`String title`	The title string for the dialog box.
`int messageType`	The type of message to be displayed. Valid values are: `ERROR_MESSAGE`, `INFORMATION_MESSAGE`, `WARNING_MESSAGE`, `QUESTION_MESSAGE`, or `PLAIN_MESSAGE`. (All constants are defined in class `JOptionPane`)
`int optionType`	The type of options to be offered to the user. Valid values are: `YES_NO_OPTION`, or `YES_NO_CANCEL_OPTION`.
`Icon icon`	An icon to display in the dialog box. If not present, appropriate default icons are displayed for error, information, warning, and question message boxes.
`Object[] selectionValues`	An array of possible choices.
`Object initialSelectionValue`	The default choice in the input box.

The program shown in Figure 13.9 creates sample message dialog boxes. The results are shown in Figure 13.10. (Note that the Question Message Box is rather stupid. It asks a question but does not allow the user to reply. There appears to be no real use for this particular option.)

```java
// This program tests message dialog boxes.
import javax.swing.JOptionPane;
public class TestMessageDialog {

    // Main method to create frame
    public static void main(String s[]) {

        // Create error message.
        JOptionPane.showMessageDialog(null,
                "This is an error message!", "Error",
                JOptionPane.ERROR_MESSAGE);

        // Create warning message.
        JOptionPane.showMessageDialog(null,
                "This is a warning message!", "Warning",
                JOptionPane.WARNING_MESSAGE);

        // Create information message.
        JOptionPane.showMessageDialog(null,
                "This is an information message!", "Information",
                JOptionPane.INFORMATION_MESSAGE);

        // Create question message.
        JOptionPane.showMessageDialog(null,
                "Are you sure?", "Question",
                JOptionPane.QUESTION_MESSAGE);

         // Create question message.
        JOptionPane.showMessageDialog(null,
                "This is a plain message.", "Plain",
                JOptionPane.PLAIN_MESSAGE);

        System.exit(0);
    }
}
```

Figure 13.9. A program to test message dialog boxes.

13.3.2 Confirm Dialog Boxes

Confirm dialog boxes allow a user to confirm or reject an action. The `static` methods used to create a confirm dialog box are:

```java
static int JOptionPane.showConfirmDialog(Component parentComponent,
                Object message, String title, int optionType);
static int JOptionPane.showConfirmDialog(Component parentComponent,
                Object message, String title, int optionType,
                int messageType);
static int JOptionPane.showConfirmDialog(Component parentComponent,
                Object message, String title, int optionType,
                int messageType, Icon icon);
```

The meanings of each parameter in these methods are defined in Table 13-7. These methods return an `int` to the calling method, which will have one of the following values: YES_OPTION, NO_OPTION, CANCEL_OPTION, or CLOSED_OPTION. The YES_OPTION is returned if the user clicks the "Yes" button, and so forth. The CLOSED_OPTION is returned if the user closes the dialog box without making a selection; it should usually be treated as a "Cancel" or "No".

Figure 13.10. *(a)* Error Dialog Box. *(b)* Warning Dialog Box. *(c)* Information Dialog Box. *(d)* Question Dialog Box. *(e)* Plain Dialog Box..

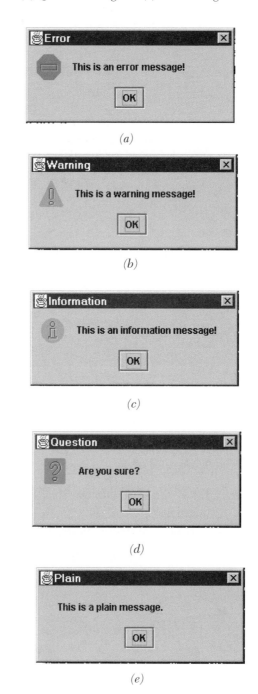

(a)

(b)

(c)

(d)

(e)

The program shown in Figure 13.11 creates example confirmation dialog boxes. The results are shown in Figure 13.12.

```java
// This program tests confirm dialog boxes.
import javax.swing.JOptionPane;
public class TestConfirmDialog {

   // Main method to create frame
   public static void main(String s[]) {

      int res;        // Result

      // Create YES/NO message
      res = JOptionPane.showConfirmDialog(null,
            "Are you sure you want to delete this file?",
            "Confirm File Delete",
            JOptionPane.YES_NO_OPTION,
            JOptionPane.QUESTION_MESSAGE);

      // What happened?
      if ( res == JOptionPane.YES_OPTION )
         System.out.println("Result = YES");
      else if ( res == JOptionPane.NO_OPTION )
         System.out.println("Result = NO");
      else if ( res == JOptionPane.CANCEL_OPTION )
        System.out.println("Result = Cancel");
      else if ( res == JOptionPane.CLOSED_OPTION )
        System.out.println("Result = Closed Window");
      else
          System.out.println("Unknown Result = " + res);

      // Create YES/NO/CANCEL message
      res = JOptionPane.showConfirmDialog(null,
             "Overwrite the existing file?",
            "Warning",
            JOptionPane.YES_NO_CANCEL_OPTION,
            JOptionPane.WARNING_MESSAGE);

      // What happened?
      if ( res == JOptionPane.YES_OPTION )
         System.out.println("Result = YES");
      else if ( res == JOptionPane.NO_OPTION )
         System.out.println("Result = NO");
      else if ( res == JOptionPane.CANCEL_OPTION )
         System.out.println("Result = Cancel");
      else if ( res == JOptionPane.CLOSED_OPTION )
         System.out.println("Result = Closed Window");
      else
         System.out.println("Unknown Result = " + res);

      System.exit(0);
   }
}
```

Figure 13.11   A program to test confirmation dialog boxes.

Figure 13.12. *(a)* Yes/No Confirmation Dialog Box. *(b)* Yes/No/Cancel Confirmation Dialog Box.

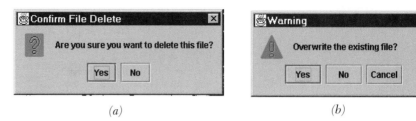

(a)   *(b)*

13.3.3 Input Dialog Boxes

Input dialog boxes allow a user to input values into a text field, or to select an option from a combo box. The `static` methods used to create an input dialog box are:

```
static String JOptionPane.showInputDialog(Object message);
static String JOptionPane.showInputDialog(Component parentComponent,
                Object message);
static String JOptionPane.showInputDialog(Component parentComponent,
                Object message, String title, int messageType);
static Object JOptionPane.showInputDialog(Component parentComponent,
                Object message, String title, int messageType,
                Icon icon, Object[] selectionValues,
                Object initialSelectionValue );
```

The meanings of each parameter in these methods are defined in Table 13-5. The first three of these methods return a `String`, and the last method returns an `Object`. The use of these methods is demonstrated in end-of-chapter Exercise 13.2.

GOOD PROGRAMMING PRACTICE

Use dialog boxes to display error and warning messages to the user, to confirm irrevocable actions such as overwriting files, and to get input values from a user.

13.4 INTERFACES AND ADAPTER CLASSES

In the last two chapters, we have learned that the Java event model is based on specifically-defined interfaces. For each type of event, Java includes an interface that *defines the names and parameters* of the methods that will be called to handle that event. For example, a `JButton` creates an `ActionEvent` when it is clicked, and the `ActionEvent` is handled by a class that implements the `ActionListener` interface, which must contain an `actionPerformed` method. Similarly, a `JList` creates a `ListSelectionEvent` when it is clicked, and the `ListSelectionEvent` is handled by a class that implements the `ListSelectionListener` interface, which must contain a `valueChanged` method.

There are many types of events and corresponding interfaces in Java, and a very brief summary of some them can be found in Table 13-8. This table lists the two high-level events that we have used so far, plus mouse and window events. The

TABLE 13-8   Selected Java Events and Interfaces

EVENT	INTERFACE	METHOD(S)	DESCRIPTION
ActionEvent	ActionListener	actionPerformed	Indicates that a high-level event has been performed, such as a button click.
ListSelectionEvent	ListSelectionListener	valueChanged	Indicates that a selection has been made from a list.
MouseEvent	MouseListener	mousePressed mouseClicked mouseReleased mouseEntered mouseExited	Indicates that the specific mouse selection actions have occurred.
MouseEvent	MouseMotionListener	mouseDragged mouseMoved	Indicates that the specific mouse motion actions have occurred.
WindowEvent	WindowListener	windowActivated windowClosed windowClosing windowDeactivated windowDeiconified windowIconified windowOpened	Indicates that the specific window actions have occurred. This interface is implemented by JFrame.

Figure 13.13. Inheritance hierarchy for selected event interfaces and adapter classes. The ListSelectionListener interface is found in package javax.swing.event; all others are found in package java.awt.event.

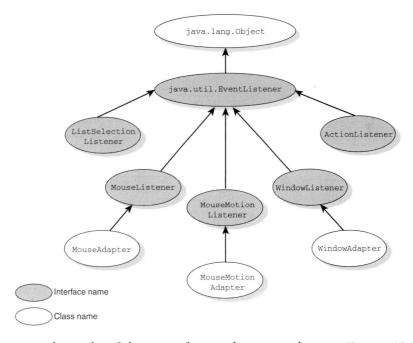

inheritance hierarchy of these interfaces and events is shown in Figures 13.13 and 13.14, respectively.

Note that some interfaces include many different methods to represent different actions that can be performed on an object. A very important example is the Window-Event, which is can be created by objects of the Window class and its subclasses, includ-

Figure 13.14.   Inheritance hierarchy for selected events. The ListSelectionEvent is found in package javax.swing.event; the others are found in package java.awt.event.

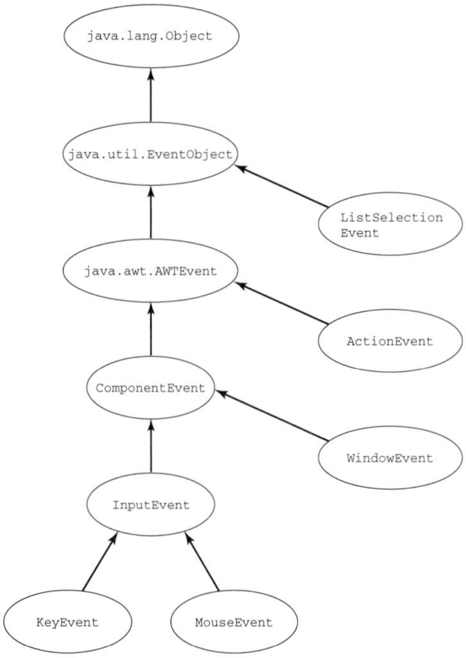

ing JFrame. Note that there are separate methods for all of the different actions that can be performed with a window, including activating, deactivating, opening, closing, iconifying, and deiconifying.

Complex interfaces such as the WindowListener interface present a problem for a programmer, because *if a class implements an interface, it must implement every method in the interface,* even if the programmer has no intention of ever using some of the methods. For example, suppose that a programmer needs to use the windowClosing method of the WindowListener interface to ensure that a program shuts down properly. In order to do so, he or she must actually implement all seven methods in the interface, even though six of the methods will do nothing! An example of such a listener class is shown in Figure 13.15.

Java includes special **adapter classes** to avoid the wasted effort involved in writing useless methods like the ones in Figure 13.15. An adapter class is a class that implements all of the methods in an interface, *with each method doing absolutely nothing.* We can write a new class that extends an adapter class, overriding *only* the methods that we wish to implement, and the adapter class will take care of all the "useless" interface method declarations.

For example, the adapter class that implements the WindowListener interface is called WindowAdapter. If we create our WindowHandler class as a subclass of WindowAdapter, only the methods that we which to change have to be implemented in the class. (See Figure 13.16 and compare Figure 13.15 to Figure 13.17.) All of the other required methods will be inherited from WindowAdapter.

```
import java.awt.event.*;
class WindowHandler implements WindowListener {

   // This method implements a simple listener that detects
   // the "window closing event" and stops the program.
   public void windowClosing(WindowEvent e) {
      System.exit(0);
   };

   // Methods that do nothing, but must be here to
   // implement the interface.
   public void windowActivated(WindowEvent e) {};
   public void windowClosed(WindowEvent e) {};
   public void windowDeactivated(WindowEvent e) {};
   public void windowDeiconified(WindowEvent e) {};
   public void windowIconified(WindowEvent e) {};
   public void windowOpened(WindowEvent e) {};
}
```

Figure 13.15.   A class that implements the WindowListener interface, showing that every method in the interface must be implemented, even if they will not be used.

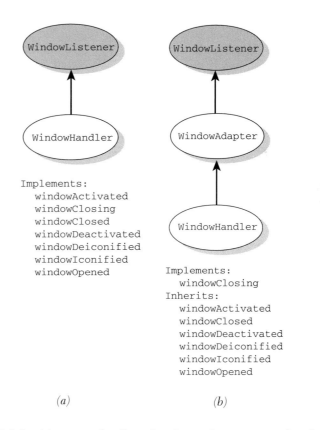

(a)   (b)

Figure 13.16.   (a) An event handling class that implements in interface directly must implement every method in the interface. (b) An event handling class that extends an adapter class only has to override the methods whose behavior must be changed.

```
import java.awt.event.*;
public class WindowHandler extends WindowAdapter {

    // This method implements a simple listener that detects
    // the "window closing event" and stops the program.
    public void windowClosing(WindowEvent e) {
        System.exit(0);
    };
}
```

Figure 13.17. A class that implements the WindowListener interface by extending WindowAdapter. Only the method that we wish to use has to be included in the class, since all of the "useless" methods in the interface are inherited from WindowAdapter.

GOOD PROGRAMMING PRACTICE

Extend adapter classes to create event handling classes. If you extend existing adapter classes, you will not have to add empty methods to your event handlers.

13.5 POP-UP MENUS

Pop-up menus are menus that "pop-up" on the screen when a user right-clicks the mouse over a component. Pop-up menus can be attached to any component in a GUI, and different pop-up menus can be created for each GUI component.

A pop-up menu is created by class JPopupMenu. This class is very similar to class JMenu in its function and methods. The constructors for this class are:

```
public JPopupMenu();
public JPopupMenu(String label);
```

The first constructor creates a pop-up menu without a title, while the second constructor creates a pop-up menu with the title string label as a title. Some of the methods in class JPopupMenu are described in Table 13-9.

TABLE 13-9 Selected JPopupMenu Methods

METHOD	DESCRIPTION
public JMenuItem add(JMenuItem mi)	Adds the specified menu item to this menu. (*Note:* This could be another menu.)
public void addSeparator()	Adds a separator line to the menu at the current position.
public JMenuItem getItem(int index)	Gets the item located at the specified index of this menu.
public int getItemCount()	Gets the number of items in this menu.
public void insert(Component component, int index)	Inserts the specified component into the menu at a given position in the menu.
public String paramString()	Gets the parameter string representing the state of this menu.
public void remove(Component comp)	Removes the specified component from this pop-up menu.
public void setPopupSize(Dimension d)	Sets the pop-up window size.
public void setPopupSize(int width, int height)	Sets the pop-up window size.
public void show(Component invoker, int x, int y)	Display the pop-up menu at the position (x,y) in the coordinate space of the specified component.

TABLE 13-10 MouseEvent Methods

METHOD	DESCRIPTION
`public int getClickCount()`	Returns the number of mouse clicks associated with this event.
`public Component getComponent()`	Returns the originator of this event.
`public int getX()`	Returns the horizontal position of the mouse click in pixels, relative to the source component.
`public int getY()`	Returns the vertical position of the mouse click in pixels, relative to the source component.
`public boolean isPopupTrigger()`	Returns `true` if this event is a pop-up menu trigger.
`public String paramString()`	Returns a `String` describing this event.

Since pop-up menus are triggered by mouse events, we must write a mouse handler to use a pop-up menu. This handler must implement the `MouseListener` interface described in the previous section and must receive `MouseEvents`. `MouseEvents` include several methods that allow a program to recover information about the triggering event, including whether or not the event was a pop-up trigger. The most important of these methods are listed in Table 13-10.

The program in Figure 13.18 shows how to create a pop-up menu and attach it to a component. This program creates a JLabel and adds a pop-up menu to the JLabel to set the color of the text being displayed. The pop-up menu is created and then added to the JLabel that it is supposed to trigger on. Note that a mouse event handler must also be added to that component, so that a pop-up event can be detected. The mouse event handler is called **MouseHandler**. It extends **MouseAdapter**, so we only have to implement the `MouseListener` methods that we need to detect pop-up events.

Figure 13.19 shows the program running with the popup menu visible.

```
// Test popup menus.  This program changes the
// color of a JLabel based a popup menu.
import java.awt.*;
import java.awt.event.*;
import javax.swing.*;
public class TestPopupMenu extends JPanel
                 implements ActionListener {

   // Instance variables
   private JLabel l1;                  // Labels
   private JMenuItem mi1, mi2, mi3;  // Menu items
   private JPopupMenu popup;           // Popup menu
   private MouseHandler h1;            // Popup listener

   // Initialization method
   public void init() {

      // Create a label with icon and text
      l1 = new JLabel("Label 1", JLabel.LEFT);
      l1.setFont(new Font("SansSerif",Font.BOLD,20));
      l1.setForeground( Color.black );
      add( l1, BorderLayout.CENTER );

      // Create a popup menu and add to label
      popup = new JPopupMenu();
      l1.add( popup );
```

Figure 13.18.   *(cont.)*

```
                           // Create a popup handler
                           h1 = new MouseHandler(popup);
                           l1.addMouseListener( h1 );

                           // Create three menu items specifying colors
                           mi1 = new JMenuItem("Black");
                           mi1.addActionListener(this);
                           popup.add( mi1 );
                           mi2 = new JMenuItem("Blue");
                           mi2.addActionListener(this);
                           popup.add( mi2 );
                           mi3 = new JMenuItem("Red");
                           mi3.addActionListener(this);
                           popup.add( mi3 );
                     }

                     public void actionPerformed( ActionEvent e) {

                           if ( e.getActionCommand().equals("Black") )
                              l1.setForeground( Color.black );
                           else if ( e.getActionCommand().equals("Blue") )
                              l1.setForeground( Color.blue );
                           if ( e.getActionCommand().equals("Red") )
                              l1.setForeground( Color.red );
                     }

                     (main method not shown to save space)
              }

              class MouseHandler extends MouseAdapter {

                     private JPopupMenu popup;
                     public MouseHandler(JPopupMenu p) { popup = p; }

                     public void mousePressed(MouseEvent e) {
                           if (e.isPopupTrigger())
                              popup.show(e.getComponent(), e.getX(), e.getY());
                     }

                     public void mouseReleased(MouseEvent e) {
                           if (e.isPopupTrigger())
                              popup.show(e.getComponent(), e.getX(), e.getY());
                     }
              }
```

Figure 13.18.   A class that demonstrates the use of pop-up menus.

Figure 13.19.   The Test PopupMenu program in operation.

13.6 PLUGGABLE LOOK AND FEEL

One of the special features of the Swing GUI is support for Pluggable Look and Feel. The **look and feel** of a program is a combination of the appearance of the windows and the way that the program responds to mouse clicks, keyboard inputs, etc. The idea of a "pluggable" look and feel is that a Java program can be written just once, and its appearance can be adjusted with a single method call to match the appearance of programs on the computer on which it is executed.

Java programs can appear as if they are Unix programs (the Motif Look and Feel), or as if they are windows programs (the Windows Look and Feel). Alternatively, they can be written to look identical across all platforms (the Java Look and Feel).

All programs that we have seen so far have used the Java Look and Feel, which is the default for Swing GUI components. This Look and Feel has the advantage of being exactly the same across all platforms, but it makes Java programs appear different from native programs on any particular computer. A programmer can choose to write programs that automatically adopt the Look and Feel of whatever computer they are running on, making them appear to be native programs.

The Look and Feel settings of a program are controlled by class **UIManager** in the javax.swing package. Selected **UIManager** methods are shown in Table 13-11, and the standard Look and Feels in the Java Development Kit are shown in Table 13-12.

To specify that the local computer's Look and Feel should be used for a program, a programmer would include the following lines in the `init()` method for the program:

```
try {
    UIManager.setLookAndFeel(
        UIManager.getCrossPlatformLookAndFeelClassName());
}
catch (Exception e) {
    System.err.println("Couldn't use the cross-platform "
                        + "look and feel: " + e);
}
```

Note that these statement should be included in a `try/catch` structure in case the Java Look and Feel is not available on some computer running the program.

TABLE 13-11 Selected `UIManager` Methods

METHOD	DESCRIPTION
public static String getCrossPlatformLookAndFeelClassName()	Returns a String containing the name of the cross-platform look and feel (the Java Look and Feel).
public static UIManager.LookAndFeelInfo[] getInstalledLookAndFeels()	Returns an array containing all of the looks and feels available on a particular computer.
public static String getSystemLookAndFeelClassName()	Returns a String containing the standard look and feel for the system that the program is executing on.
public static void setLookAndFeel(String name)	Sets the specified look and feel for use by this program. The name is the class name of the desired Look and Feel class.

TABLE 13-12   Standard Look and Feels

CLASS	DESCRIPTION
Javax.swing.plaf.metal.MetalLookAndFeel	The cross-platform (Java) Look and Feel.
com.sun.java.swing.plaf.motif.MotifLookAndFeel	Unix (Motif) Look and Feel
com.sun.java.swing.plaf.windows.WindowsLookAndFeel	Windows Look and Feel

To specify that the local computer's Look and Feel should be used for a program, a programmer would include the following lines in the `init()` method for the program:

```
try {
    UIManager.setLookAndFeel(
        UIManager.getSystemLookAndFeelClassName());
}
catch (Exception e) {
    System.err.println("Couldn't use the " + "look and feel: " + e);
}
```

Figure 13.20 illustrates the effect of setting the Look and Feel on the appearance of a program. It displays the Spectrum program of the last chapter with two different Look and Feels.

Figure 13.20.   Program Spectrum with two different Look and Feel settings. *(a)* Java Look and Feel.

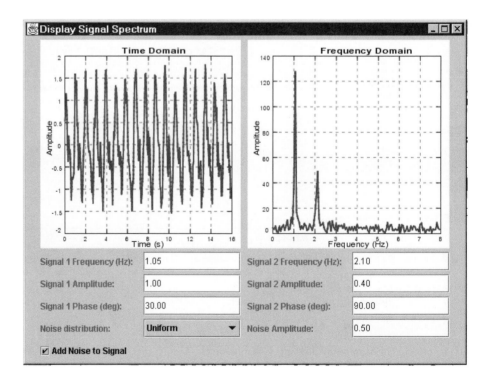

(a)

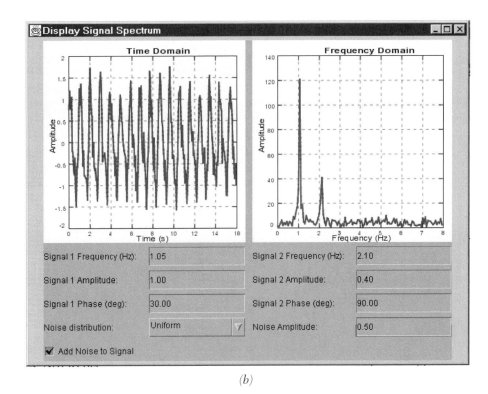

(b)

Figure 13.20. *(b)* Windows Look and Feel.

EXAMPLE 13-2: DISPLAYING A HISTOGRAM

Create a GUI-based program reads in a numeric data set from a file and displays a histogram of the data. The program should include a "File" menu with options to open a data set and to exit the program. It should use dialogs to get the name of the file to read and also to inform the user if the file does not exist. Finally, it should automatically set the program's Look and Feel to match the system on which the program is executing.

SOLUTION

This program will require a menu containing two menu items, "Open" and "Exit". In addition, it will require an object of class chapman.graphics.JHist to create and display the histogram. Documentation for class JHist is available on line in standard JDK format.

1. **State the problem**. Create a GUI-based program reads in a numeric data set from a file and displays a histogram of the data.

2. **Define the inputs and outputs**. The inputs to this program are the name of the file containing the data set and the data in the file. The data in the file must be in numeric format. The output from the program is a plot of the histogram of the data.

3. **Decompose the program into classes and their associated methods**. This program requires three classes to function properly. The principal class (called Histogram) must contain the following separate methods: (1) a method init() to generate the GUI display, (2) a method to read a file when the user clicks on the "Open" menu item, and (3) a main method to start up the application.

In addition, the program must contain two event-handling classes to handle the events generated by the Open and Exit menu items.

4. **Design the algorithm that you intend to implement for each method**. The init() method of the Histogram class must create the GUI. It must set the desired Look and Feel, create the menu, and lay out the graphical elements. Since there is only one graphical element occupying the entire display, it is logical to use a BorderLayout and place the element in the center region. To create the menu, we will need one JMenuBar, one JMenu, and two JMenuItems. We should also add keyboard accelerators to the menu items and a tool tip to the graphical element to help the user. The code required to create the single JHist object and the menu and is shown below.

```
// Set local system look and feel
try {
    UIManager.setLookAndFeel(
        UIManager.getSystemLookAndFeelClassName());
}
catch (Exception e) {
    System.err.println("Couldn't use the "
                    + "look and feel: " + e);
}

// Set layout manager
setLayout( new BorderLayout() );

// Create event handlers
hExit   = new ExitHandler();
hOpen   = new OpenHandler(this);

// Create and add histogram object
hist = new JHist(21);
hist.setTitle( "Histogram" );
hist.setXLabel( "Distribution" );
hist.setYLabel( "Count" );
hist.setToolTipText("Displays Histogram");
add( hist, BorderLayout.CENTER );

// Create menu bar
bar = new JMenuBar();

// Create "File" menu
fileMenu = new JMenu("File");
fileMenu.setMnemonic('f');

// Create and add "Open" menu item
open = new JMenuItem( "Open" );
open.addActionListener(hOpen);
open.setMnemonic('o');
fileMenu.add ( open );

// Add separator
fileMenu.addSeparator();

// Create and add "Exit" menu item
exit = new JMenuItem( "Exit" );
exit.addActionListener(hExit);
exit.setMnemonic('x');
fileMenu.add ( exit );

// Add the menu to the menu bar
bar.add ( fileMenu );
```

Method openFile() must prompt the user for a file name and open the file. If the file exists, it should read in the data, send the data to the JHist object, and paint the new histogram. The method will use an input dialog box to get the file name and will open the file with the convenience method `chapman.io.FileIn`. If the file does not exist, it will display an error dialog box to tell the user. The code required for these steps is:

```
// Get name of file to open
fileName = JOptionPane.showInputDialog(null,
        "Enter file to open", "Open Dialog",
        JOptionPane.PLAIN_MESSAGE);

// Open file to read
FileIn in = new FileIn(fileName);

// Check for valid open
if ( in.readStatus == in.FILE_NOT_FOUND ) {
   String s = "File " + fileName + " not found!";
   JOptionPane.showMessageDialog(null, s,
           "I/O Error", JOptionPane.ERROR_MESSAGE);
}
else {
   (Read in data here)
}
```

If the file *does* exist, we will have to read in an unknown number of data values from the file, so we must store the values in a data structure that can grow to accommodate any number of elements. A `Vector` (see Section 9.9) is a good choice, since it can hold any number of objects. Note that `Vectors` hold `Objects`, so we will have to convert the numeric values to `Double` objects to store them in the `Vector`. The code to read the values and store them in a `Vector` is:

```
data = new Vector();
while ( in.readStatus != in.EOF ) {
   data.add(new Double(in.readDouble()));
}
```

Once all of the data have been read, they must be stored in a `double` array to send to the histogram object. The data can be fetched one element at a time from the `Vector` using the `get` method, as shown below:

```
data1 = new double[ data.size() ];
for (int i = 0; i< data1.length; i++ ) {
   Object o = data.get(i);
   data1[i] = ((Double)o).doubleValue();
}
```

Finally, the data will be sent to the histogram object:

```
hist.setData( data1 );
hist.repaint();
```

The two event handlers should detect events on the "Open" and "Exit" menu items. The "File" event handler should call the method `openFile()`, while the "Exit" event handler should shut down the program.

5. **Turn the algorithm into Java statements**. The resulting Java program is shown in Figure 13.21.

```
/*
   Purpose:
     This GUI-based program reads in a data set from a
     user-specified file and creates a histogram of the
     data.

   Record of revisions:
       Date         Programmer         Description of change
       ====         ==========         =====================
     10/14/98    S. J. Chapman         Original code
*/
import java.awt.*;
import java.awt.geom.*;
import java.awt.event.*;
import javax.swing.*;
import java.util.*;
import chapman.io.FileIn;
import chapman.graphics.JHist;
public class Histogram extends JPanel {

   // Instance variables
   private ActionListener hOpen, hExit;
                                    // Action listeners
   private JMenuBar bar;            // Menu bar
   private JMenu fileMenu;          // File Menu
   private JMenuItem open;          // Load "menu" item
   private JMenuItem exit;          // Exit "menu" item
   Vector data;                     // Input data
   double[] data1;                  // Data as an array
   String fileName;                 // File to open
   JHist hist;                      // Histogram

   //*********************************************
   //   init() method
   //*********************************************

   // Initialization method
   public void init() {

      // Set local system look and feel
      try {
         UIManager.setLookAndFeel(
            UIManager.getSystemLookAndFeelClassName());
      }
      catch (Exception e) {
         System.err.println("Couldn't use the "
                     + "look and feel: " + e);
      }

      // Set layout manager
      setLayout( new BorderLayout() );

       // Create event handlers
      hExit   = new ExitHandler();
      hOpen   = new OpenHandler(this);

      // Create and add histogram object
      hist = new JHist(21);
      hist.setTitle( "Histogram" );
```

Figure 13.21. *(cont.)*

```
        hist.setXLabel( "Distribution" );
        hist.setYLabel( "Count" );
        hist.setToolTipText("Displays Histogram");
        add( hist, BorderLayout.CENTER );

        // Create menu bar
        bar = new JMenuBar();

        // Create "File" menu
        fileMenu = new JMenu("File");
        fileMenu.setMnemonic('f');

        // Create and add "Open" menu item
        open = new JMenuItem( "Open" );
        open.addActionListener(hOpen);
        open.setMnemonic('o');
        fileMenu.add ( open );

        // Add separator
        fileMenu.addSeparator();

        // Create and add "Exit" menu item
        exit = new JMenuItem( "Exit" );
        exit.addActionListener(hExit);
        exit.setMnemonic('x');
        fileMenu.add ( exit );

        // Add the menu to the menu bar
        bar.add ( fileMenu );
    }

//*********************************************
//   Method to read data from a file
//*********************************************

public void openFile() {

    // Get name of file to open
    fileName = JOptionPane.showInputDialog(null,
             "Enter file to open", "Open Dialog",
             JOptionPane.PLAIN_MESSAGE);

    // Open file to read
    FileIn in = new FileIn(fileName);

    // Check for valid open
    if ( in.readStatus == in.FILE_NOT_FOUND ) {
        String s = "File " + fileName + " not found!";

         JOptionPane.showMessageDialog(null, s,
              "I/O Error", JOptionPane.ERROR_MESSAGE);
    }
    else {

        // Read numbers into a Vector
        data = new Vector();
        while ( in.readStatus != in.EOF ) {
            data.add(new Double(in.readDouble()));
        }
```

Figure 13.21. *(cont.)*

```
            // Convert to a double[] for use in processing
            data1 = new double[ data.size() ];
            for (int i = 0; i< data1.length; i++ ) {
               Object o = data.get(i);
               data1[i] = ((Double)o).doubleValue();
            }

             // Throw away the objects for recycling
            data = null;

            // Close file
            in.close();

            // Modify the title to reflect the number
            // of data values
            hist.setTitle("Histogram (N = " + data1.length + ")");

            // Set the new data into the histogram
            hist.setData( data1 );
            hist.repaint();
         }
      }

      //*********************************************
      //  main method
      //*********************************************

      // Main method to create frame
      public static void main(String s[]) {

         // Create a frame to hold the application
         JFrame fr = new JFrame("Histogram ...");
         fr.setSize(400,400);
         // Create a Window Listener to handle "close" events
         MyWindowListener l = new MyWindowListener();
         fr.addWindowListener(l);

         // Create and initialize a Histogram object
         Histogram tm = new Histogram();
         tm.init();

         // Add the menu bar to the frame
         fr.setJMenuBar( tm.bar );

         // Add the object to the center of the frame
         fr.getContentPane().add(tm, BorderLayout.CENTER);

         // Display the frame
         fr.setVisible( true );
      }
   }

   //*********************************************
   //  Event handlers
   //*********************************************

   class OpenHandler implements ActionListener {
      private Histogram h1;
```

Figure 13.21. *(cont.)*

```
   // Constructor
   public OpenHandler( Histogram h ) {h1 = h;}

   // Execute when an event occurs
   public void actionPerformed( ActionEvent e ) {
     h1.openFile();
   }
}

class ExitHandler implements ActionListener {

   // Execute when an event occurs
   public void actionPerformed( ActionEvent e ) {
      System.exit(0);
   }
}
```

Figure 13.21. GUI-based program to create a plot a histogram of a data set.

6. **Test the resulting Java program**. To test this program, we will execute it twice, once with a 2,000-value data set in file x.dat, and once with an invalid file name y.dat. When the program executes with the valid file name, the histogram shown in Figure 13.22a will be created. When the program executes with an invalid file name, the error message shown in Figure 13.22b will be displayed. Note that this program uses the Windows Look and Feel, since it executed on a PC.

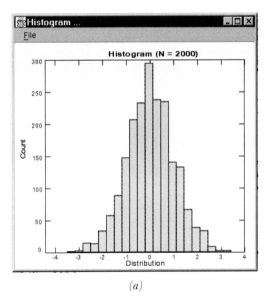

(a)

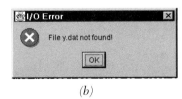

(b)

Figure 13.22. (a) Histogram of the data in file x.dat. (b) Results of attempting to open a nonexistent file.

13.7 INTRODUCTION TO APPLETS

An **applet** is a special type of Java program that is designed to work within a World Wide Web browser, such as Netscape Communicator, Microsoft Internet Explorer, or Sun's HotJava. Applets are usually quite small and are designed to be downloaded, executed, and discarded whenever the browser points to a site containing the Java applet.

Applets are quite restricted compared to Java applications. For security reasons, applets are not allowed access to the computer on which they are executing, so an applet cannot read or write disk files, for example. These restrictions make them less useful than applications for many data analysis purposes.

Applets are most commonly used for creating eye-catching graphics and animations on Web pages.

13.7.1 The `JApplet` Class

An *applet* is any class that extends class `javax.swing.JApplet`. Class `java.applet.Applet` is a container into which components can be placed. (See Figure 13-23.) It is very similar to `JFrame` in that the components must be added to a content pane retrieved by the `getContentPane()` method. In addition, class `JApplet` implements a set of methods that form the interface between the applet and the Web browser. These methods are summarized in Table 13-13.

Every applet has five key methods: `init`, `start`, `stop`, `destroy`, and `paintComponent`. Method `init()` is called by the browser when the applet is first loaded in memory. This method should allocate resources and create the GUI required for the applet. Method `start()` is called when the applet should start running. This call can be used to start animations, etc. when the applet becomes visible. Method `stop()` is called when the applet should stop running, for example, when its window is covered or when

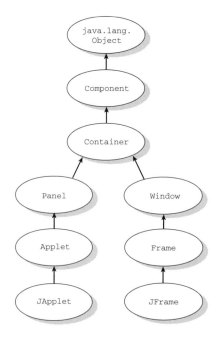

Figure 13.23. Partial class hierarchy of `Container` classes. Note that `JApplet` is a subclass of `Container`, so it can be used as a container for components.

TABLE 13-13 Selected `JApplet` Methods

METHOD	DESCRIPTION
`public boolean isActive();`	Determines if an applet is active.
`public void init();`	Method called by the browser to inform an applet that it has been loaded into the system.
`public void start();`	Method called by the browser to inform this applet that it should start execution. This call will always follow a call to `init()`.
`public void stop();`	Method called by the browser to inform an applet that it should stop execution.
`public void destroy();`	Method called by the browser to inform an applet that it is being destroyed, and it should deallocate an resources that it holds. This call will always follow a call to `stop()`.
`public String getAppletInfo();`	Returns information about an applet. This can be a version number, copyright, etc.
`public String getParameter(String name);`	Returns the value of the named parameter in the HTML tag.
`public String[][] getParameterInfo();`	Returns information about the parameters that are understood by an applet.
`public void paintComponent(Graphics g);`	Method to paint an applet.
`public void repaint();`	Repaints an applet.
`public void showStatus(String msg);`	Displays the argument string in the applet's "status window".

it is iconized. This call is also make just before an applet is destroyed. Method `destroy()` is the final call to the applet before it is destroyed. The applet should release all resources at the time of this call. Finally, method `paintComponent` is called whenever the applet must be drawn or redrawn.

Class `JApplet` implements all five of these methods as simple calls that do nothing. A practical applet will override as many of these methods as it needs to perform its function. Simple applets that only respond to user events will only need to override the `init()` and possibly the `paintComponent` methods.

13.7.2 Creating and Displaying an Applet

The basic steps required to create and run a Java applet are:

1. Create a container class to hold the GUI components. This class will always be a subclass of `JApplet`.
2. Select a layout manager for the container if the default layout manager (`FlowLayout`) is not acceptable.
3. Create components and add them to *the content pane* of the JApplet container.
4. Create listener objects to detect and respond to the events expected by each GUI component, and assign the listeners to appropriate components.
5. Create an HTML text file to specify to the browser which Java applet should be loaded and executed.

These steps are very similar to the one required to create a Java application, except that we use `JApplet` instead of `JPanel` as the container class, and we create an HTML file instead of a `JFrame` to execute the program. Note that all components must be added to the `JApplet`'s content pane, just as with `JFrame`.

Figure 13.24 shows an applet that creates a simple GUI with a single button and a single label field. The label field contains the number of times that the button has been pressed since the program started. This applet is identical to the `FirstGUI` application in Figure 12-4, except that it has been converted to run as an applet. Note that class `FirstApplet` extends `JApplet` and that this class serves as the container for our GUI components (step 1 above).

```java
1   // A first Applet.  This class creates a label and
2   // a button.  The count in the label is incremented
3   // each time that the button is pressed.
4   import java.awt.*;
5   import java.awt.event.*;
6   import javax.swing.*;
7   public class FirstApplet extends JApplet {
8
9      // Instance variables
10     private int count = 0;        // Number of pushes
11     private JButton pushButton;  // Push button
12     private JLabel label;         // Label
13
14     // Initialization method
15     public void init() {
16
17        // Set the layout manager
18        getContentPane().setLayout( new BorderLayout() );
19
20        // Create a label to hold push count
21        label = new JLabel("Push Count: 0");
22        getContentPane().add( label, BorderLayout.NORTH );
23        label.setHorizontalAlignment( label.CENTER );
24
25        // Create a button
26        pushButton = new JButton("Test Button");
27        pushButton.addActionListener( new ButtonHandler(this) );
28        getContentPane().add( pushButton, BorderLayout.SOUTH );
29     }
30
31     // Method to update push count
32     public void updateLabel() {
33        label.setText( "Push Count: " + (++count) );
34     }
35  }
36
37  class ButtonHandler implements ActionListener {
38     private FirstApplet fa;
37
40     // Constructor
41     public ButtonHandler ( FirstApplet fa1 ) {
42        fa = fa1;
43     }
44
45     // Execute when an event occurs
46     public void actionPerformed( ActionEvent e ) {
47        fa.updateLabel();
48     }
49  }
```

Figure 13.24. An applet that creates a container, sets a layout manager for the container, and adds components and listeners for the components. This is the basic core structure required to create Java applets.

This applet contains two classes: class `FirstApplet` to create and display the GUI, and class `ButtonHandler` to respond to mouse clicks on the button.

Class `FirstApplet` contains two methods: `init()` and `updateLabel()`. Method `init()` overrides the `init()` in class `JApplet`, and it initializes the GUI. It will be called by the browser when the applet is just starting. This class specifies which layout manager to use with the container (line 18), creates the `JLabel` and `JButton` components (lines 21 and 26), and adds them to the container (lines 22 and 28). In addition, it creates a listener object of class `ButtonHandler` to listen for and handle events generated by mouse clicks and assigns that object to monitor mouse clicks on the button (line 27).

Method `updateLabel()` (lines 32–34) is the method that should be called by the event handler every time that a button click occurs. It updates the label with the number of button clicks that have occurred. Class `ButtonHandler` is a listener class identical to those we discussed in Chapter 12. Its `actionPerformed` method calls method `updateLabel()` whenever a click occurs on the button.

To execute this applet in a Web browser, we must also create a Hypertext Markup Language (HTML) document to tell the browser to load and execute the applet. A sample HTML document is shown in Figure 13-25. An HTML document consists of a series of **tags** marking the beginning and ending of various items. For example, the beginning of an HTML document is marked by the `<html>` tag, and the end of the document is marked by the `</html>` tag. Similarly, the beginning of an applet description is marked by the `<applet>` tag, and the end of the applet description is marked by the `</applet>` tag. The series of values after the applet tag are known as *attributes*. The three required attributes specify the name of the class file to execute and the size of the applet in units of pixels.

```
1    <html>
2    <applet code="FirstApplet.class" width=200 height=100>
3    </applet>
4    </html>
```

Figure 13.25. HTML file required to execute the `FirstApplet` applet.

The applet is executed by loading the corresponding HTML document into a Java-enabled Web browser, such as Netscape Navigator, Microsoft Internet Explorer, or Sun's HotJava. In addition, an applet can be tested with a special program called `appletviewer`, which is supplied in the JDK. The applet can be executed with the following command, and the results are as shown in Figure 13.26:

```
D:book\java\chap13>appletviewer FirstApplet.html
```

Note that the GUI produced by this applet is identical to the GUI produced by the `FirstGUI` application, except that the applet includes a status line at the bottom of the window. (The status line says "Applet started.")

Figure 13.26. The display produced by applet `FirstApplet`.

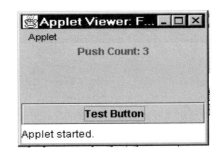

13.7.3 Displaying Status Information

The Applet Viewer and all browsers that support Java include a **status line** at the bottom of the display, where an applet can display useful information. For example, the status line in Figure 13.26 displays the message "Applet started". This field may be used to display information with the showStatus message.

The status line is very useful for programmers in the process of debugging an applet, but you should not count on it to supply information to the ultimate user. Many different messages are written to a browser's status line, and they replace any previous messages on the line. As a result, the messages that you send to the status line might only be visible for a fraction of a second before they are replaced by another message.

The applet shown in Figure 13.27 creates a GUI containing two buttons. When a button is pushed, it displays the number of times that button has been pushed on the status line of the applet.

```java
// This program sends messages to the status line
import java.awt.*;
import java.awt.event.*;
import javax.swing.*;
public class TestStatusLine extends JApplet
                    implements ActionListener {

    // Instance variables
    private int c1 = 0, c2 = 0;     // Counters
    private JButton b1, b2;         // Buttons

    // Initialization method
    public void init() {

        // Set the layout manager
        getContentPane().setLayout( new FlowLayout() );

        // Create buttons
        b1 = new JButton("Button 1");
        b1.addActionListener( this );
        getContentPane().add( b1 );
        b2 = new JButton("Button 2");
        b2.addActionListener( this );
        getContentPane().add( b2 );
    }

    // Method to handle button pushes
    public void actionPerformed(ActionEvent e) {
        String button = e.getActionCommand();
        if (button.equals("Button 1"))
            showStatus("Button 1 pressed: count = " + (++c1));
        else if (button.equals("Button 2"))
            showStatus("Button 2 pressed: count = " + (++c2));
    }
}
```

Figure 13.27. An applet that displays information on the status line whenever a user clicks a button.

To execute this applet, we must also create an HTML file to load the applet into the browser. The required file will be identical to the one shown in Figure 13.25, except

Figure 13.28. The display produced by applet
`TestStatusLine`.

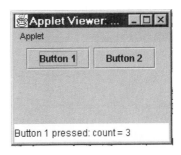

Figure 13.29. (*a*) The classes required by an applet that *are not* included in a package must appear in the same directory as the HTML file. (*b*) The classes required by an applet that *are* included in a package must appear in an appropriate subdirectory of the directory containing the HTML file. Class `chapman.io.Fmt` is shown in this figure.

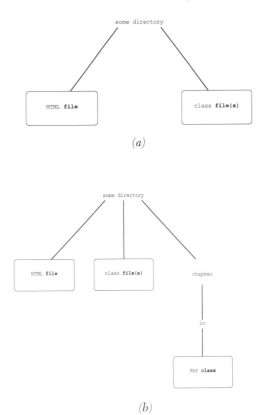

the class name to load is `TestStatusLine.class`. When this applet is executed with the Applet Viewer, the results are as shown in Figure 13.28.

13.7.4 Using Packages Within Applets

Because applets are designed to be transferred through the internet from a server to a browser, there must be a special convention to tell the applet where to find the classes that the applet needs to execute. This convention is illustrated in Figure 13-29.

If an applet uses a class that is *not* built into a package, then that class must be present in the *same directory* as the HTML file used to start the applet (see Figure 13.29*a*). This directory could be a local directory on your computer or a directory on a server on the other side of the world—it doesn't matter as long as the class files and the HTML file are in the same directory. When the HTML file is loaded into the browser, all of the required classes will be transferred over the network to the browser, so that they can be executed on the local computer. Note that applets should be small because they are transferred over the network each time that they are used.

If an applet uses a class that appears in a package that is *not* a part of standard Java, then *the package must appear in the appropriate subdirectory* of the directory containing the HTML file. For example, suppose that an applet uses the class Fmt from package chapman.io. When a browser executes this applet, it will look for the Fmt class in subdirectory chapman\io under the directory containing the HTML file (see Figure 13.29*b*). This structure is always the same whether the directory containing the HTML file is local to your computer or located on a remote server across the network. Unlike Java applications, applets ignore the CLASSPATH environment variable. They only look in subdirectories of the directory containing the HTML file to locate the classes in packages.

13.7.5 Creating an Applet That is Also an Application

It is possible to design a single Java program to run as either an applet or an application. We can create such a dual-purpose program by first creating a working applet, and then adding a main method to the applet. The main method will be designed to create a JFrame, place the applet into the frame, and execute the applet's init() and start() methods. The window listener associated with the frame will be designed to execute the applet's stop() and destroy() methods when the program is closed down.

A typical dual-purpose application/applet is shown in Figure 13.30. This is a version of the temperature conversion application from Chapter 12. When this program is executed as an applet, the main method is ignored and it runs as a conventional applet. When the program is executed as an application, the main method creates a JFrame, places the applet into the frame, and runs the applet's init() and start() methods. Note that the AppletWindowHandler executes the applet's stop() and destroy() methods when the frame is closed.

Figure 13.31 shows the GUI created by this program when it is executed as an application and as an applet. Note that the program behaves identically in either case.

Finally, note that this program uses the Fmt class from package chapman.io. In order for this program to work successfully as an applet, the file Fmt.class must be found in the subdirectory chapman\io below directory containing the file TempConversionApplet.html.

```
/*
   Purpose:
     This GUI-based program converts temperature in
     degrees Fahrenheit to degrees Celsius, and vice versa.

   Record of revisions:
      Date          Programmer            Description of change
      ====          ==========            =====================
      10/14/98      S. J. Chapman         Original code
   1. 12/22/98      S. J. Chapman         Modified for for applet
```

Figure 13.30. (*cont.*)

```
*/
import java.awt.*;
import java.awt.event.*;
import javax.swing.*;
import chapman.io.*;
public class TempConversionApplet extends JApplet {

   // Instance variables
   private JLabel l1, l2;          // Labels
   private JTextField t1, t2;      // Text Fields
   private DegCHandler cHnd;        // ActionEvent handler
   private DegFHandler fHnd;        // ActionEvent handler

   // Initialization method
   public void init() {

      // Set the layout manager
      getContentPane().setLayout( new FlowLayout() );

      // Create ActionEvent handlers
      cHnd = new DegCHandler( this );
      fHnd = new DegFHandler( this );

      // Create degrees Celsius field
      l1 = new JLabel("deg C:", JLabel.RIGHT);
      getContentPane().add( l1 );
      t1 = new JTextField("0.0",15);
      t1.addActionListener( cHnd );
      getContentPane().add( t1 );

      // Create degrees Celsius field
      l2 = new JLabel("deg F:", JLabel.RIGHT);
      getContentPane().add( l2 );
      t2 = new JTextField("32.0",15);
      t2.addActionListener( fHnd );
      getContentPane().add( t2 );
   }

   // Method to convert deg F to deg C
   // and display result
   public void toC( double degF ) {
      double degC = (5. / 9.) * (degF - 32);
      t1.setText( Fmt.sprintf("%5.1f",degC) );
      t2.setText( Fmt.sprintf("%5.1f",degF) );
   }

   // Method to convert deg C to deg F
   // and display result
   public void toF( double degC ) {
      double degF = (9. / 5.) * degC + 32;
      t1.setText( Fmt.sprintf("%5.1f",degC) );
      t2.setText( Fmt.sprintf("%5.1f",degF) );
   }

   // Main method to create frame
   public static void main(String s[]) {

      // Create a frame to hold the application
      JFrame fr = new JFrame("TempConversionApplet ...");
      fr.setSize(250,100);
```

Figure 13.30. *(cont.)*

```
                         // Create and initialize a TempConversionApplet object
                         TempConversionApplet tc = new TempConversionApplet();
                         tc.init();
                         tc.start();

                         // Create a Window Listener to handle "close" events
                         AppletWindowHandler l = new AppletWindowHandler(tc);
                         fr.addWindowListener(l);

                         // Add the object to the center of the frame
                         fr.getContentPane().add(tf, BorderLayout.CENTER);

                         // Display the frame
                         fr.setVisible( true );
                 }
        }

        class DegCHandler implements ActionListener {
            private TempConversionApplet tc;

            // Constructor
            public DegCHandler( TempConversionApplet t ) { tc = t; }

            // Execute when an event occurs
            public void actionPerformed( ActionEvent e ) {
                String input = e.getActionCommand();
                double degC = new Double(input).doubleValue();
                tc.toF( degC );
            }
        }

        class DegFHandler implements ActionListener {
            private TempConversionApplet tc;

            // Constructor
            public DegFHandler( TempConversionApplet t ) { tc = t; }

            // Execute when an event occurs
            public void actionPerformed( ActionEvent e ) {
                String input = e.getActionCommand();
                double degF = new Double(input).doubleValue();
                tc.toC( degF );
            }
        }

        public class AppletWindowHandler extends WindowAdapter {
            JApplet ap;

            // Constructor
            public AppletWindowHandler ( JApplet a ) { ap = a; }

            // This method implements a listener that detects
            // the "window closing event", shuts down the applet,
            // and stops the program.
            public void windowClosing(WindowEvent e) {
                ap.stop();
                ap.destroy();
                System.exit(0);
            };
        }
```

Figure 13.30. A dual-purpose application/applet version of the temperature conversion application from Chapter 12.

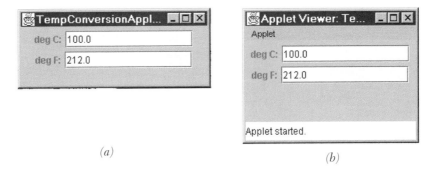

Figure 13.31. (a) The GUI produced when `TempConversionApplet` is run as an application. (b) The GUI produced when `TempConversionApplet` is run as an applet.

GOOD PROGRAMMING PRACTICE

Whenever possible, design your programs to be dual purpose applications/applets.

PRACTICE!

This quiz provides a quick check to see if you have understood the concepts introduced in Sections 13.1 through 13.7. If you have trouble with the quiz, reread the section, ask your instructor, or discuss the material with a fellow student. The answers to this quiz are found in the back of the book.

1. What is a `JList`? What type of events are generated by a `JList`?
2. Why should a `JList` be placed inside a `JScrollPane`?
3. What is necessary to add menus to an application or applet? What types of containers support menus?
4. What are dialog boxes? Write the statements required to create a dialog box asking a user whether or not to replace a file.
5. List the listener interfaces introduced in this chapter and in Chapter 12. What does each one do, and which components produce events handled by each interface?
6. What are adapter classes? Why are they useful?
7. How does a popup menu differ from an ordinary one?
8. How can you set up a Java application so that it looks the same across all types of computers? How can you set up a Java application so that it looks like a native application on each type of computer that it executes on?
9. What is an applet? How does it differ from an application?
10. What are the five key methods in an applet? What do they do?
11. How can you write a single program that can run as either an applet or an application?

SUMMARY

- The JList class creates a GUI component that implements single- or multiple-selection lists. JLists function in three modes: single selection mode, single interval selection mode, or multiple interval selection mode.
- A JList can be made scrollable by placing it inside a JScrollPane.
- JLists generate ListSelectionEvents, which are handled by classes implementing the ListSelectionListener interface.
- The JTable class creates a GUI component that displays a table of objects.
- Pull-down menus can be added to containers of type JFrame, JApplet, JDialog, JRootPane, or JInternalFrame.
- Popup menus can be added to any Java component.
- Menus are composed of five basic components: JMenuBar, JMenu, JMenuItems, JCheckBoxMenuItem, and JRadioButtonMenuItem.
- A menu bar is the bar across the top of the frame to which the menus are attached.
- A menu is an individual list of items that is pulled down from the menu bar when the user clicks on the menu name.
- A menu item is a string inside a menu that when selected causes an action to be performed.
- All types of menu items generate ActionEvents, which are handled by ActionListeners.
- A dialog box is a special type of container that is used to get information from a user or to provide error or warning messages. They may be modal or non-modal, but all examples in this text are modal. The standard types of dialog boxes are showMessageDialog, showConfirmDialog, showInputDialog, and showOptionDialog.
- The Look and Feel of a Java program can be set to be the same across all platforms, or the program can be made to match the Look and Feel of the computer on which it is executing. The Look and Feel of a program is controlled by class UIManager.
- An applet is a special type of Java program that is designed to work within a World Wide Web browser.
- Applets are usually quite small, and are designed to be downloaded, executed, and discarded whenever the browser points to a site containing the Java applet.
- For security reasons, applets are not allowed access to the computer on which they are executing.
- An applet is created by extending class javax.swing.JApplet.
- An applet is executed within a browser by loading an HTML page containing an <applet> tag referring to the applet.
- Information may be displayed on the browser's status line using the applet's showStatus method.
- If an applet uses a class that appears in a non-standard package, then the package must appear in a subdirectory of the directory containing the HTML file.
- We can create such a dual-purpose application/applet by first creating a working applet, and then adding a main method to the applet.

APPLICATIONS: GOOD PROGRAMMING PRACTICES

The following guidelines introduced in this chapter will help you to develop good programs:

1. Use class JList to create lists of objects for display and selection in a GUI.
2. Always use scrollable JLists in all of your programs to ensure that a user can see all of the values in the list.
3. Use JTables to display tabular data.
4. Use menus to display less frequently used options such as opening and saving files. This keeps infrequently used options from using up space in the GUI.
5. Use dialog boxes to display error and warning messages to the user, to confirm irrevocable actions such as overwriting files, and to get input values from a user.
6. Extend adapter classes to create event handling classes. If you extend existing adapter classes, you will not have to add empty methods to your event handlers.
7. Whenever possible, design your programs to be dual purpose applications / applets.

KEY TERMS

Adapter classes	JMenu class	Look and Feel
applet	JMenuBar class	menu
<applet> tag	JMenuItem class	menu bar
check box menu item	JRadioButtonMenuItem	menu item
destroy() method	class	modal dialog box
dialog box	JOptionPane class	showStatus() method
init() method	JScrollPane class	start() method
JApplet class	JTable class	stop() method
JCheckBoxMenuItem	ListSelectionEvent class	valueChanged method
class	ListSelectionListener	sub-menu
JList class	interface	

Problems

13.1. Add a set of menus to the spectral analysis program of Example 12-4. There should be two menus: "File" and "Options". The "File" menus should include "Load", "Save" and "Exit" menu items, with the "Load" and "Save" menu items loading and saving the program parameters from run to run. The "Options" menu should allow the user to select line color, line style, etc. for the two graphs.

13.2. Create a program that tests the showInputDialog methods described in Section 13.3.3.

13.3. Create a program with a blank canvas. The program should monitor mouse clicks and draw 30-pixel wide circle with a 2-pixel-wide solid border around the center of each mouse click. Note that you will need a MouseListener to determine the location of the clicks. Include menu on the program. The menu should allow the user to erase the canvas and start over, and should also allow the user to change the color of the circles.

13.4. Modify the program of Exercise 13.3 to include a popup menu. The popup menu should allow the user to erase the canvas.

13.5. Write a program that determines which Looks and Feels are installed on your computer. Uses the UIManager method getInstalledLookAndFeels to get the list, and use method `getSystemLookAndFeelClassName()` to determine the default Look and Feel for your system.

13.6.   Modify the spectrum analysis program of Example 12-4 by adding a menu that allows the user to select the Look and Feel of the program while it is running.

13.7.   Convert the spectrum analysis program of Example 12-4 so that it can run as either an application or an applet. Demonstrate its operation in both modes.

13.8.   Class `chapman.math.Statistics` includes many methods to calculate statistical measures of a data set. Modify the `Histogram` program of Example 13-2 to show the mean, median, standard deviation, and skewness of the displayed data set in non-editable text fields below the plot of the histogram. Use methods in class `Statistics` to calculate the values to display. Include appropriate labels for each text field. Note that you will need cascaded layout managers to create an appropriate GUI for this program.

13.9.   Modify the least squares fit program of Exercise 12.13 to include a "File" menu with "Open" and "Exit" menu items. Add a file open dialog box, and include appropriate error messages. Also, add a scrollable `JTable` to display the actual (x,y) points being plotted.

14

Input and Output

The Java input/output (I/O) system is very complex, both because of the wide variety of things it tries to do and because there are actually *two* different I/O systems created at different times. Java contains both the original I/O system released with the Java Development Kit version 1.0 and a newer system overlaid on top of it in JDK 1.1. The two systems intertwine in weird and wonderful ways, which doesn't make life any easier.

In other languages, such as Fortran and C, there are simple integrated statements for reading and writing data to files. For example, in Fortran the statement

```
WRITE (10,*) a, b, c
```

would write character representations of the values of a, b, and c to the file associated with unit 10. In these languages, any number of variables can be included in an input or output statement, and they may be of different types.

The Java I/O system does not do anything simply. Instead, it consists of many classes containing *components* of an I/O system, and it is the programmer's responsibility to string the components together in the proper order to accomplish whatever type of I/O operation is desired. The result is so messy that programmers almost always build **convenience classes** for each type of I/O operation that

SECTIONS

- 14.1 The Structure of the Java I/O System
- 14.2 Sequential Data Input
- 14.3 Sequential Data Output
- 14.4 Formatted Input and Output
- 14.5 Unformatted Input and Output
- 14.6 Random Access Files
- 14.7 Getting Information About Files: The File class
- Summary
- Key Terms

OBJECTIVES

After reading this chapter, you should be able to:

- Understand the structure of the Java I/O system
- Read Strings from a formatted sequential file or the standard input stream
- Read numeric data from a formatted sequential file or the standard input stream
- Write to a formatted sequential file
- Perform unformatted input and output to sequential files
- Perform unformatted input and output to random access files
- Get information about a file or directory using the File class

they wish to perform and use those convenience classes instead. Each convenience class contains all of the lower level Java I/O classes arranged in the proper order for one specific type of I/O operation. The classes `StdIn`, `FileIn`, and `FileOut` that we have used in this book are examples of such convenience classes.

There are several reasons for the Java I/O system's complexity, including

1. **Many different types of sources and sinks**. A **source** is a device that data can be read from, and a **sink** is a device that data can be written to. Java can read data from and write data to files, arrays of bytes, `Strings`, pipes (connections between two programs or threads), and other sources, such as Internet connections.

2. **Two different types of file access**. For historical reasons going back to the earliest computers, the data in most files are read sequentially from the beginning of the file to the end of the file. This **sequential access** was the standard, because many early I/O devices, such as tapes and card readers, could only be read sequentially. However, today's disks are **random access** devices; the data on a disk can be read in any arbitrary order. Random access is very useful for databases and other applications where any particular piece of information could be requested at any time. Java supports both sequential access and random access to files.

3. **Two different types of storage formats**. Java supports two different types of data storage formats, **formatted** and **unformatted**. A **formatted file** contains information written out as character strings, so that it is easy for a human to see and understand. For example, the statement

```
System.out.println("pi = " + Math.PI);
```

produces formatted output. It prints out a visible character string to the standard output stream, which is usually connected to our computer screen.

In contrast, an **unformatted file** contains data stored as raw bit patterns. Java can read and write these bit patterns in a platform-independent way, but they mean nothing to a human examining the file. Unformatted files typically pack data into less space than formatted files. Java supports both formatted and unformatted data storage, using different classes for each.

4. **Two different I/O systems**. The original Java Development Kit 1.0 contained an I/O system that was based on transferring *bytes* of data to and from sources and sinks. Unfortunately, all of Java's characters and strings are based on Unicode, which uses 16 bits to represent a character of data. Transferring characters is the most common operation in the I/O system, and it was awkward under JDK 1.0. To alleviate this problem, JDK 1.1 introduced a new parallel I/O system for formatted I/O based on transferring characters instead of bytes.

Unfortunately, the new character-based I/O system is *not* a complete replacement for the older byte-based I/O system. Many parts of Java were not converted to work with the character-based classes, including the standard input, output, and error streams, the data compression classes (zip file creators and users), and the direct access I/O classes. In addition, unformatted I/O is only supported though the older byte-based I/O system. As a result, we now have the original byte-based family of classes, the new character-based family of classes, and a set of bridges between them.

It is not possible for a programmer to only work with the old classes, because parts of them have been declared **deprecated**, meaning that they are candidates for deletion in future versions of the language. It is not possible for a programmer to only work with the new classes, because the new classes are not complete by themselves. Instead, the programmer must work will a complex mishmash of 50 or so classes and try to pick his or her own way through the mess.

5. **A variety of filter or modifier classes**. In addition to the basic I/O functions, Java includes a series of classes that filter or modify the input and output data streams. These classes improve the efficiency of I/O operations or provide other services, such as counting line numbers, dividing data into tokens, etc. Naturally, many of these classes come in pairs, one to work with the old I/O system and one to work with the new I/O system.

This chapter will only introduce the basics of the Java I/O system. We will learn how to do only the most important types of I/O operations, and we will ignore the rest.

14.1 THE STRUCTURE OF THE JAVA I/O SYSTEM

The Java I/O system can be divided into a series of categories based on the method of access, the direction of data transfer (input or output), the types of devices used, whether the data are transferred as bytes or characters, and whether the data are formatted or unformatted.

The first division in the Java I/O System is based on the method of access: sequential or random. (See Figure 14.1.)[1] Random access is supported for files and unformatted I/O only, by class `RandomAccessFile`. This class supports both reading and writing random access files. All other I/O classes support sequential access.

Sequential access may be subdivided by the *direction of data flow:* input or output. Except for random access files, Java I/O classes support data input only or data output

Figure 14.1. The Java I/O System may be divided by access method into random access and sequential access. Random access is implemented for files only using class `RandomAccess-File`. All other classes implement sequential access.

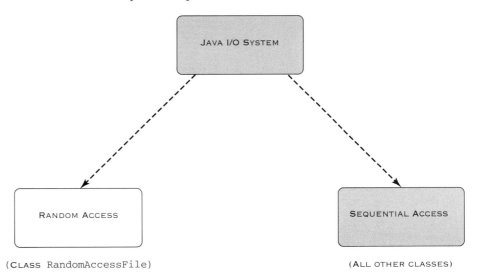

[1] Note that the dashed arrows in these figures indicate a logical relationship and that the solid arrows indicate data flow. Neither type of arrow has anything to do with inheritance or the class hierarchy of Java classes. Shaded boxes indicate logical categories within the I/O system, while white boxes indicate actual Java classes.

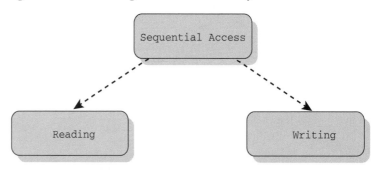

Figure 14.2.   Sequential I/O is subdivided into classes for reading and classes for writing. There is no such thing as read/write access in Java.

GOOD PROGRAMMING PRACTICE

Use class `RandomAccessFile` to read and write data in random access files.

Sequential access may be subdivided by the *direction of data flow:* input or output. Except for random access files, Java I/O classes support data input only or data output only. Unlike many other languages, it is not possible to open a sequential Java file for both read and write access. Instead, the file must be written completely, closed, and then opened separately for reading. Figure 14.2 shows this dichotomy between reading and writing.

14.2 SEQUENTIAL DATA INPUT

There are two ways to read sequential data streams: as a byte stream and as a character stream. The byte stream approach goes back to JDK 1.0, and classes that implement this approach usually have the words "`InputStream`" in their names. The character stream approach was introduced in JDK 1.1, and classes that implement this approach usually have the word "`Reader`" in their names. (See Figure 14.3.) Each of these approaches can be further subdivided by the type of the data source being read from: `byte` or `char` arrays, `Strings`, files, or pipes.

There is also a bridge class `InputStreamReader` that converts a byte-based `InputStream` into a character-based `Reader`. This class is necessary because certain parts of Java only work with byte streams. For example, the standard input device is implemented as a byte stream, and the classes that read zip files are implemented as byte streams. This bridge class allows byte data to be converted to character data for use with the `Reader` classes.

We mentioned before that Java supports formatted and unformatted data storage formats. The *unformatted* data storage format consists of data stored as raw bit patterns. Java reads these bit patterns in a platform-independent way through class `DataInput Stream`, which can be connected to any of the "`InputStream`" sources. This class provides methods such as `readInt()`, `readDouble()`, etc., to read unformatted data

Figure 14.3.   Sequential input streams are divided into two types, byte-based InputStreams and character-based Readers. Both InputStreams and Readers can read from arrays, Strings, files, or pipes. This picture illustrates the possible data flows from an input file for both unformatted and formatted data. The dotted
lines on this picture indicate logical relationships, and the solid black lines on the picture indicate the possible
directions of data flows.

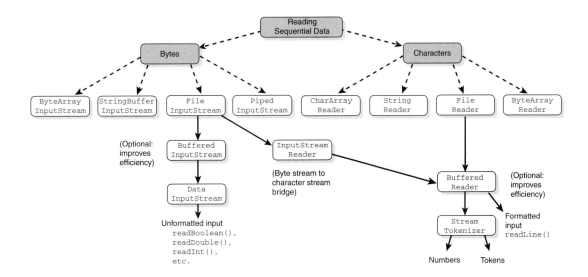

from an InputStream and convert it into the appropriate data type. The *formatted* data
storage format consists of data stored as sequences of human-readable characters. Java
converts these sequences of characters into Strings through class BufferedReader,
which can be connected to any of the Reader sources. This class provides methods such
as readLine() to read an entire line of characters and place them into a String.

There are also two **buffering classes**, one to support InputStreams and
one to support Readers. These classes greatly improve system performance when
reading from files. The normal input classes request data from the disk *a few bytes at
a time*, so they cause many delays while the computer reads from the disk. The buffering classes speed up operations by reading a large amount of data from the disk and
holding it in memory, and parceling it out a few bytes at a time as they are needed.
You should *always* use the BufferedInputStream class when reading from a
FileInputStream and the BufferedReader class when reading from a
FileReader or from an InputStreamReader whose original data source was a
FileInputStream.

Finally, there is a class StreamTokenizer that will accept a line of character
data from a Reader and break it up into individual tokens. Numeric tokens are automatically translated into double numbers, and character tokens are automatically
translated into Strings.

Figure 14.3 shows the overall sequential input data architecture. From it, we can
see that:

1. *Unformatted data* is read through any of the InputStream sources and is
    converted into usable data values by methods in class DataInputStream.
    If the source is a FileInputStream, then the data should be routed
    through a BufferedInputStream to improve performance.

2. *Formatted data* is read through any of the Reader sources and is converted into usable data values by methods in classes BufferedReader and / or StreamTokenizer. If the source is a FileReader or an Input-StreamReader whose original data source was a FileInputStream, then the data should be routed through a BufferedReader to improve performance.

GOOD PROGRAMMING PRACTICE

Read unformatted data using the InputStream sources, and convert the data to a useful form using the DataInput-Stream class.

GOOD PROGRAMMING PRACTICE

Read formatted data using the Reader sources, and convert the data to a useful form using the BufferedReader class. If you are reading from the standard input stream, convert the data into a Reader using the InputStreamReader class before sending it to the BufferedReader class.

GOOD PROGRAMMING PRACTICE

Always use the BufferedInputStream or BufferedReader classes to improve efficiency when reading data from a file.

14.3 SEQUENTIAL DATA OUTPUT

There are two ways to write sequential data streams: as a byte stream and as a character stream. The byte stream approach goes back to JDK 1.0, and classes that implement this approach usually have the words "OutputStream" in their names. The character stream approach was introduced in JDK 1.1, and classes that implement this approach usually have the word "Writer" in their names. (See Figure 14.4.) Each of these approaches can be further subdivided by the type of the data sink being written to: byte arrays, files, or pipes for the OutputStream classes and char arrays, Strings, files or pipes for the Writer classes.

There is also a bridge class OutputStreamWriter that converts a character based Writer into a byte-based OutputStream. This class is necessary because certain parts of Java only work with byte streams. For example, the standard output device is implemented as a byte stream, and the classes that write zip files are implemented as byte streams. This bridge class allows character data to be converted to byte data for use with the OutputStream classes.

Java can write both formatted and unformatted data storage formats. The *unformatted* data storage format consists of data stored as raw bit patterns. Java writes these bit patterns in a platform-independent way through class DataOutputStream, which can be connected to any of the OutputStream sinks. This class provides methods such as writeInt(), writeDouble(), etc., to write unformatted data to an OutputStream. The *formatted* data storage format consists of data stored as sequences of human-readable characters. Java writes formatted data through classes PrintStream and PrintWriter. These two classes each provide methods print() and println() to output formatted data to OutputStreams or Writers. Note that PrintWriter is the preferred class of the two, except for debugging purposes or for formatted data written to the standard output or standard error devices.

There are also two **buffering classes**, one to support OutputStreams and one to support Writers. These classes greatly improve system performance when writing to files. The normal output classes write data to the disk *a few bytes at a time,* so they cause many delays while the computer writes to the disk. The buffer classes speed up operations by saving up a large amount of data in memory and then writing it all at once to the disk. You should *always* use the BufferedOuputStream class when writing to a FileOutputStream and the BufferedWriter class when writing to a File- Writer or to an OutputStreamWriter whose final destination is a FileOutput- Stream.

Figure 14.4 shows the overall sequential output data architecture. From it, we can see that:

1. *Unformatted data* are created by methods in DataOutputStream and are written through any of the OutputStream sinks. If the destination is a FileOutputStream, then the data should be routed through a Buffered OutputStream to improve performance.

2. *Formatted data* are created by methods in PrintStream or in Print-Writer. The PrintStream data are written through any of

Figure 14.4.   Sequential output streams are divided into two types, byte-based Output- Streams and character-based Writers. OutputStreams can write to byte arrays, files, or pipes, and Writers can write to character arrays, Strings, files, or pipes. This picture illustrates the possible data flows to an output file for both unformatted and formatted data. The dotted lines on this picture indicate logical relationships, and the solid black lines on the picture indicate the possible directions of data flows.

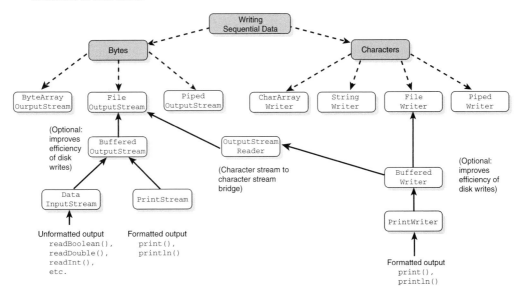

the Output Stream sinks. The PrintWriter data are written through any of the Writer sinks. The PrintWriter methods are preferred over the PrintStream methods, except when working with the standard output and standard error devices. If the destination is a FileOutputStream or a FileWriter, then the data should be routed through a Buffered OutputStream or a BufferedWriter to improve performance.

GOOD PROGRAMMING PRACTICE

Create unformatted output data with methods in the DataOutputStream class, and write it out using the Output-Stream sinks.

GOOD PROGRAMMING PRACTICE

Create formatted output data using the print() and println() methods found in the PrintStream and Print-Writer classes, and write it out using the OutputStream and OutputWriter sinks respectively. Use the Print-Writer methods, except when working with the standard output or standard error devices.

GOOD PROGRAMMING PRACTICE

Always use the BufferedOutputStream or BufferedWriter classes to improve efficiency when writing data to a file.

14.4 FORMATTED INPUT AND OUTPUT

As we saw in the previous sections, the preferred way to read character data is with the readLine() method of BufferedReader, and the preferred way to write character data is with the print() and println() methods of PrintWriter. We will now show how to read and write data files using these methods.

14.4.1 Reading Strings from a Formatted Sequential File

The class that allows us to open and read formatted character data from a file is FileReader. This class has three different forms of constructors, which contain different ways to specify the file to open and read data from:

```
FileReader(String fileName);
FileReader(File file);
FileReader(FileDescriptor fd);
```

The first constructor is the most common form. It specifies the file to open by its file name. The second form of the constructor specifies the file by an object of the File class, and the third form of the constructor specifies the object by a predefined file descriptor.

When a `FileReader` object is created, the corresponding file is automatically opened and prepared for reading. If the file cannot be opened, `FileReader` will throw a `FileNotFoundException`.

For efficiency reasons, the output of a `FileReader` should always be sent to a `BufferedReader`, as shown in Figure 14.3. (In Java terms, we say that the `FileReader` is *wrapped* in a `BufferedReader`, because the file data goes through the `BufferedReader` before it is used.) This is typically accomplished as follows:

```
BufferedReader br = new BufferedReader(
                    new FileReader( fileName ));
```

Once a `BufferedReader` has been created, each line of data in the file can be read with the `readLine()` method. When there are no more data available in the file, the `readline()` method will return a `null` reference.

After the data have been read from a file, the file should be explicitly closed with a call to the `close()` method. This should be done as soon as possible to release the file resources for possible reuse by this program or other programs. Note that once a file is closed, any attempt to read data from it will produce an `IOException`.

GOOD PROGRAMMING PRACTICE

Always close any files you use as soon as you are finished with them. This action releases the file resources for possible use elsewhere within the computer.

EXAMPLE 14-1: READING LINES OF DATA AS Strings FROM A FORMATTED SEQUENTIAL INPUT FILE

Write a program that reads and displays `Strings` a line at a time from a user-specified input file.

SOLUTION
A sample program that reads lines from a user-specified file and displays them is shown in Figure 14.5. The name of the file to read is passed as a command-line argument to the program. This program creates a new `FileReader` object and wraps it in a `BufferedReader` object for efficiency. It uses the `readLine()` method of the `BufferedReader` object to read the file one line at a time, and display the results on the standard output device. Note that the `BufferedReader` is created within a try/catch structure to trap `FileNotFound` and `IOExceptions`, if they occur.

```
// Read a formatted file
import java.io.*;
public class ReadFormattedFile {

    public static void main(String[] args) {

        // Define variables
        String s;           // String reference
```

Figure 14.5. *(cont.)*

```
                        // Trap exceptions if they occur
                        try {

                           // Create BufferedReader
                           BufferedReader in =
                              new BufferedReader(
                                 new FileReader(args[0]));

                           // Read file and display data
                           while( (s = in.readLine()) != null) {
                              System.out.println(s);
                           }

                           // Close file
                           in.close();
                        }

                        // Catch FileNotFoundException
                        catch (FileNotFoundException e) {
                           System.out.println("File not found: " + args[0]);
                        }

                        // Catch other IOExceptions
                        catch (IOException e) {
                           System.out.println("IOException: the stack trace is:");
                           e.printStackTrace();
                        }
                     }
                  }
```

Figure 14.5. A sample program that reads a formatted file and returns the data a line at a time as a String.

To test this program, we will execute it twice. The first time we will pass the program the name of an existing file, and the second time we will pass the program the name of a nonexistent file. When this program is executed with an existing file input.txt, the results are:

```
D:\book\java\chap14>java ReadFormattedFile input.txt
This is line 1 of the test file.
This is line 2 of the test file.
This is the last line of the test file.
```

When this program is executed with a nonexistent file input2.txt, the results are:

```
D:\book\java\chap14>java ReadFormattedFile input2.txt
File not found: input2.txt
```

The program appears to be working correctly in both cases.

GOOD PROGRAMMING PRACTICE

To read Strings from a formatted sequential input file, create a FileReader (wrapped in a BufferedReader for efficiency), and use the readLine() method of the BufferedReader to read the data a line at a time.

14.4.2 Reading Numeric Data from a Formatted Sequential File

If the output from a `BufferedReader` is sent to an object of the `StreamTokenizer` class, the data in a formatted sequential file can be separated into discrete tokens,[2] and the tokens that represent numbers can be automatically translated into `double` values by this class.

The `StreamTokenizer` class includes three `public` instance variables and a number of constants, which are summarized in Table 14-1.

TABLE 14-1   `StreamTokenizer` Instance Variables

INSTANCE VARIABLE	DESCRIPTION
double **nval**	If the current token is a number, this variable contains the value of the number.
String **sval**	If the current token is a word token (if it has alphabetic characters in it), this variable contains the characters in the token.
int **ttype**	After a call to the `nextToken()` method, this field contains the type of the token just read. For a quoted string token, its value is the quote character (34). Otherwise, its value is TT_WORD if the token is a word, TT_NUMBER if the token is a number, and TT_EOF if we are at the end of the file.
int **TT_EOF**	A constant indicating that the the end of the input file has been reached.
int **TT_NUMBER**	A constant indicating that the current token is a number.
int **TT_WORD**	A constant indicating that the current token is a word.

The class includes many methods, of which the most important is `next-Token()`. Each time that `nextToken()` is called, the method gets the next token from the `Reader`. Then, it decides whether the token is a word, a quoted string, or a number. If it is a word, the method sets `ttype` to `TT_WORD` and returns the word in `sval`. If it is a quoted string, the method sets `ttype` to the quote character and returns the string in `sval`. If it is a number, the method sets `ttype` to `TT_NUMBER` and returns the value in `nval`. If the token is a single character, then its value is returned directly in `ttype`.

This class is very flexible, with the ability to recognize quoted strings and escape characters such as \t and \n. However, it has one very important limitation. It does not recognize the exponent letter e in expressions such as 6.02e23, so such tokens will not be translated correctly.

EXAMPLE 14-2: READING TOKENS FROM A FORMATTED SEQUENTIAL INPUT FILE

Write a program that reads individual tokens from a formatted sequential input file and converts the tokens representing numbers into `double` values.

SOLUTION
This program must create a `FileReader` wrapped in a `BufferedReader` wrapped in a `StreamTokenizer`, so that the output of the `FileReader` goes to the `Buffered-`

---

[2] Remember from Chapter 10 that *tokens* are sequences of characters separated from other sequences of characters by whitespace.

Reader and the output of the buffered reader goes to the StreamTokenizer. Then, the method nextToken() can be used to recover and translate successive tokens from the file.

A sample program that using StreamTokenizer is shown in Figure 14.6.

```java
// Test the operation of StreamTokenizer
import java.io.*;
public class TestStreamTokenizer {

    public static void main(String[] args) {

        // Define variables
        String s;          // String reference

        // Trap exceptions if they occur
        try {

            // Create StreamTokenizer
            BufferedReader in =
                new BufferedReader(
                    new FileReader(args[0]));
            StreamTokenizer st = new StreamTokenizer(in);

            // Get and display tokens
            st.nextToken();
            while( st.ttype != st.TT_EOF ) {
                if ( st.ttype == st.TT_NUMBER )
                    System.out.println("Number: value = " + st.nval);
                else if ( st.ttype == st.TT_WORD )
                    System.out.println("String: value = " + st.sval);
                else if ( st.ttype == 34 )
                    System.out.println("Quote:  value = " + st.sval);
                else
                    System.out.println("Character: value = " + st.ttype);
                st.nextToken();
            }

            // Close file
            in.close();
        }

        // Catch FileNotFoundException
        catch (FileNotFoundException e) {
            System.out.println("File not found: " + args[0]);
        }
        // Catch other IOExceptions
        catch (IOException e) {
            System.out.println("IOException: the stack trace is:");
            e.printStackTrace();
        }
    }
}
```

Figure 14.6.   Program to test StreamTokenizer.

To test this program, we will create a file `tokens.txt` containing the following lines:

```
This is a test.
"This is a test."
123.45
4.2e6 +6
```

When this program is executed, the results are:

```
D:\book\java\chap14>java TestStreamTokenizer tokens.txt
String: value = This
String: value = is
String: value = a
String: value = test.
Quote: value = This is a test.
Number: value = 123.45
Number: value = 4.2
String: value = e6
Character: value = 43
Number: value = 6.0
```

For the most part, this program interpreted the data correctly. It made two errors in that it failed to recognize `4.2e6` as a number and it failed to recognize the + sign as a part of the number `+6`. With these limitations in mind, `StreamTokenizer` can be used to read `Strings` and numbers from a `Reader`.

Note that the convenience class chapman.io.FileIn uses a `FileReader`, `BufferedReader`, and `StreamTokenizer` to read numeric data. It does not use a `StreamTokenizer` because of the problems described in this section.

14.4.3 Reading Formatted Data from the Standard Input Stream

The standard input device on a computer is automatically opened and connected to object `System.in` whenever a Java program starts running. Unfortunately, `System.ini` is an `InputStream` instead of a `Reader`. To read formatted data, we need to send the data from `System.in` to an `InputStreamReader`, so that it can be translated into character data. For efficiency reasons, the `InputStreamReader` should always be wrapped in a `BufferedReader`, as shown in Figure 14.3. This is typically accomplished as follows:

```
BufferedReader br = new BufferedReader(
                    new InputStreamReader(System.in));
```

Once a `BufferedReader` has been created, a program can read lines of data from the standard input stream with the `readLine()` method. When there are no more data available, the `readline()` method will return a `null` reference.

If individual tokens are desired, then the `BufferedReader` can be wrapped in a `StreamTokenizer`, as we saw in Section 14.4.2, and the data from the standard input stream can be converted directly into tokens and numeric values.

EXAMPLE 14-3: READING LINES OF DATA AS STRINGs FROM THE STANDARD INPUT STREAM

Write a program that reads and displays `Strings` a line at a time from the standard input stream.

SOLUTION

This program must create an `InputStreamReader` wrapped in a `Buffered-Reader`, so that the `readLine()` method of the `BufferedReader` can be used to read lines of data from the standard input stream.

The program shown in Figure 14.7 reads lines from the standard input stream and displays them. This program reads lines of data from the standard input stream until there are either no more data to read or until there is an "x" in the first character of a line.

The program has two terminating conditions because of the nature of the standard input stream. If the standard input stream is redirected to come from a file, `read-Line()` will return `null` when there are no more data in the file, and the program will terminate. However, if the standard input stream comes from the keyboard, it will never be empty, and `readLine()` will never return `null`. The separate test to terminate the loop when an "x" is the first character in a line handles this case.

```java
// Read formatted data from the standard input stream
import java.io.*;
public class ReadFormattedStdin {

    public static void main(String[] args) {

        // Define variables
        String s;          // String reference
        String s1;         // First character in s

        // Trap exceptions if they occur
        try {

            // Create BufferedReader
            BufferedReader in =
                new BufferedReader(
                    new InputStreamReader(System.in));

            // Read file and display data.  Allow the
            // process to terminate if either the
            // input stream runs out of data or if an
            // "x" appears as the first character in
            // a line.
            s = in.readLine();
            while( s != null ) {
                s1 = s.substring(0,1);
                if ( s1.compareTo("x") == 0 ) break;
                 System.out.println("Line = " + s);
                s = in.readLine();
            }
        }

        // Catch IOExceptions
        catch (IOException e) {
            System.out.println("IOException: the stack trace is:");
            e.printStackTrace();
        }
    }
}
```

Figure 14.7. A sample program that reads a formatted data from the standard input stream and returns the data a line at a time as a `String`.

To test this program, we will execute it twice. The first time we will redirect the standard input stream to come from file `input.txt`. The second time we will enter data directly from the keyboard. When this program is executed with the standard input stream redirected to come from file `input.txt`, the results are:

```
D:\book\java\chap14>java ReadFormattedStdin < input.txt
Line = This is line 1 of the test file.
Line = This is line 2 of the test file.
Line = This is the last line of the test file.
```

When this program is executed with data read directly from the keyboard, the results are:

```
D:\book\java\chap14>java ReadFormattedStdin
Line 1
Line = Line 1
Line 2
Line = Line 2
x
```

The program appears to work correctly in both cases.

14.4.4 Formatted Output to a Sequential File

The class that allows us to open and write formatted character data to a file is `File-Writer`. This class has four different forms of constructors, which are four different ways to specify the file to open and write data to:

```
FileWriter(String fileName);
FileWriter(String fileName, boolean append);
FileWriter(File file);
FileWriter(FileDescriptor fd);
```

The first, third, and fourth constructors specify the file to open by file name, `File` object, and file descriptor respectively. When the file is opened with one of these constructors, any previously existing file is automatically deleted. The second constructor includes a `boolean` parameter `append`. If `append` is `true`, any previously existing file is opened and the new data is appended to the file. If `append` is `false`, any previously existing file is deleted.

When a `FileWriter` object is created, the corresponding file is automatically opened and prepared for writing. If the file cannot be opened, `FileWriter` will throw an `IOException`.

For efficiency reasons, a `FileWriter` should always be wrapped in a `Buffered Writer`, which should be wrapped in a `PrintWriter`, as shown in Figure 14.4. This is typically accomplished as follows:

```
PrintWriter out =
   new PrintWriter(
      new BufferedWriter(
         new FileWriter( fileName )));
```

Once a `PrintWriter` has been created, data can be written to the file with the `print()` and `println()` methods.

After the data has been written to a file, the file should be explicitly closed with a call to the `close()` method. This should be done as soon as possible to release the file resources for possible reuse by this program or other programs. Note that once a file is closed, any attempt to write data from it will produce an `IOException`.

EXAMPLE 14-4: WRITING DATA TO A FORMATTED SEQUENTIAL FILE

Create a program that writes output data to a formatted sequential output file.

SOLUTION

A sample program that writes lines to a user-specified file is shown in Figure 14.8. The name of the file to write and an append flag are passed as a command-line arguments to the program. This program creates a new PrintWriter object, with the data being transferred from a PrintWriter to a BufferedWriter to a FileWriter, as shown in Figure 14.4. If the append flag is false or absent, it deletes any previously existing file. If the append flag is true, it opens any previously existing file and adds the new data to the end of it.

The program uses the PrintWriter object to write data one line at a time to the file. Note that the PrintWriter is created within a try/catch structure to trap IOExceptions, if they occur.

```java
// Write a formatted file
import java.io.*;
import chapman.io.Fmt;
public class WriteFormattedFile {

    public static void main(String[] args) {

        // Define variables
        boolean append;  // Append flag
        String s;        // String reference

        // Trap exceptions if they occur
        try {

            // Get the append flag, if present
            append = false;
            if ( args.length >= 2 ) {
                if ( args[1].equalsIgnoreCase("true") )
                    append = true;
            }

            // Create PrintWriter
            PrintWriter out =
                new PrintWriter(
                    new BufferedWriter(
                        new FileWriter(args[0],append)));

            // Write data to file
            out.println("This is line 1.");
            out.println("This is line 2.");
            out.println("This is line 3.");
            out.println( Fmt.sprintf("pi = %.6f",Math.PI) );

            // Close file
            out.close();
        }
        // Catch IOExceptions
        catch (IOException e) {
            System.out.println("IOException: the stack trace is:");
            e.printStackTrace();
        }
    }
}
```

Figure 14.8. A sample program that writes data to a formatted file.

To test this program, we will execute it twice. The first time we will pass the program a file name without the append flag, and the second time we will pass the program the same file name with an append flag. When this program is executed with the file name output.txt, the results are:

```
D:\book\java\chap14>java WriteFormattedFile output.txt

D:\book\java\chap14>type output.txt

This is line 1.
This is line 2.
This is line 3.
pi = 3.141593
```

The contents of the file are the four lines that we expected. When this program is executed with the file name output.txt and the append flag, the results are:

```
D:\book\java\chap14>java WriteFormattedFile output.txt true

D:\book\java\chap14>type output.txt

This is line 1.
This is line 2.
This is line 3.
pi = 3.141593
This is line 1.
This is line 2.
This is line 3.
pi = 3.141593
```

This time the output data was appended to the previously-existing file. The program appears to work correctly in both cases.

This example also shows that we can use the formatting capabilities of class chapman.io.Fmt with output files. Method sprintf produces a String, and that String can be send to the output file with the println method just like any other String.

14.5 UNFORMATTED INPUT AND OUTPUT

As we saw in the Section 14.2, the preferred way to read unformatted data is with the readInt(), readDouble(), etc., methods of DataInputStream, and the preferred way to write unformatted data is with the writeInt(), writeDouble(), etc., methods of DataOutputStream. We will now show how to read and write data files using these methods.

14.5.1 Unformatted Input from a Sequential File

The class that allows us to read unformatted data from a sequential file in a machine-independent way is DataInputStream. As shown in Figure 14.3, unformatted input data flows from a FileInputStream object to a BufferedInputStream object, and from there to the DataInputStream object. The constructor of the Data InputStream class is

```
DataInputStream(InputStream in);
```

This constructor creates an object that reads data from in and translates it into the appropriate int, double, etc.

TABLE 14-2 Selected `DataInput` Methods

METHOD	DESCRIPTION
`boolean readBoolean()`	Reads one input byte and returns `true` if that byte is nonzero, and `false` if that byte is zero.
`byte readByte()`	Reads and returns one byte.
`char readChar()`	Reads and returns one `char` value.
`double readDouble()`	Reads and returns one `double` value.
`float readFloat()`	Reads and returns one `float` value.
`int readInt()`	Reads and returns one `int` value.
`Short readShort()`	Reads and returns one `short` value.
`String readUTF()`	Reads and returns a string coded in UTF format.

For efficiency reasons, a `FileInputStream` should always be wrapped in a `BufferedInputStream` before it is wrapped in a `DataInputStream`, as shown in Figure 14.3. This is typically accomplished as follows:

```
DataInputStream in = new DataInputStream(
                    new BufferedInputStream(
                        new FileInputStream( fileName )));
```

Once a `DataInputStream` has been created, each value can be read with the `readInt()`, `readDouble()`, etc., methods. When there are no more data available in the file, the read methods will throw an `EOFException`.

The methods in class `DataInputStream` are part of the `DataInput` interface, which is implemented by `DataInputStream`. Some of these methods are summarized in Table 14-2. All of them are listed in the JDK documentation.

After the data have been read from a file, the file should be explicitly closed with a call to the `close()` method. This should be done as soon as possible to release the file resources for possible reuse by this program or other programs. Note that once a file is closed, any attempt to read data from it will produce an `IOException`.

14.5.2 Unformatted Output to a Sequential File

The class that allows us to write unformatted data to a sequential file in a machine-independent way is `DataOutputStream`. As shown in Figure 14.4, unformatted output data flows from a `DataOutputStream` object to a `BufferedOutputStream` object, and from there to the `FileOutputStream` object. The constructor of the `DataOutputStream` class is

```
DataOutputStream(OutputStream out);
```

This constructor creates an object that writes unformatted `int`s, `double`s, etc., in a device-independent way to the output file.

For efficiency reasons, a `FileOutputStream` should always be wrapped in a `BufferedOutputStream` before it is wrapped in a `DataOutputStream`, as shown in Figure 14.4. This is typically accomplished as follows:

```
DataOutputStream out = new DataOutputStream(
                     new BufferedOutputStream(
                         new FileOutputStream( fileName )));
```

Once a `DataOutputStream` has been created, each value can be written to the file with calls to methods `writeInt()`, `writeDouble()`, etc.

TABLE 14-3 Selected `DataOutput` Methods

METHOD	DESCRIPTION
`void writeBoolean(boolean v)`	Writes a `boolean` value to the output stream.
`void writeByte(int v)`	Writes the eight low-order bits of the argument `v` to the output stream.
`void writeChar(int v)`	Writes a `char` value, which is comprised of two bytes, to the output stream.
`void writeDouble(double v)`	Writes a `double` value, which is comprised of eight bytes, to the output stream.
`void writeFloat(float v)`	Writes a `float` value, which is comprised of four bytes, to the output stream.
`void writeInt(int v)`	Writes an `int` value, which is comprised of four bytes, to the output stream.
`void writeLong(long v)`	Writes a `long` value, which is comprised of eight bytes, to the output stream.
`void writeShort(short v)`	Writes a `short` value, which is comprised of two bytes, to the output stream.
`void writeUTF(String s)`	Writes a string coded in UTF format.

After the data has been written to a file, the file should be explicitly closed with a call to the `close()` method. This should be done as soon as possible to release the file resources for possible reuse by this program or other programs. Note that once a file is closed, any attempt to write data from it will produce an `IOException`.

The methods in class `DataOutputStream` are part of the `DataOutput` interface, which is implemented by `DataOutputStream`. Some of these methods are summarized in Table 14-3. All of them are listed in the JDK documentation.

EXAMPLE 14-5: WRITING AND READING DATA WITH UNFORMATTED SEQUENTIAL FILES

Create a program that writes unformatted output data to a sequential output file and closes the file. The program should then open the file an read the data back in to confirm that it was written correctly.

SOLUTION
The example program shown in Figure 14.9 opens a file for output, writes unformatted data to it, and closes the file. Then it opens the file for reading, reads the same data back out, and closes the file again. This program illustrates the proper way to perform unformatted input and output to sequential files.

```
// Unformatted I/O
import java.io.*;
import chapman.io.Fmt;
public class TestUnformattedIO {

    public static void main(String[] args) {

        // Define variables
        double a1[] = {5., 10., 15., 20.};
        double a2[] = new double[4];
        int i1[] = {1, -10};
        int i2[] = new int[2];
```

Figure 14.9. *(cont.)*

```
                // Trap exceptions if they occur
                try {

                    // Create DataOutputStream
                    DataOutputStream out = new DataOutputStream(
                                        new BufferedOutputStream(
                                            new FileOutputStream("unf.dat")));

                    // Write data to file
                    for ( int i = 0; i < a1.length; i++ )
                        out.writeDouble( a1[i] );
                    for ( int i = 0; i < i1.length; i++ )
                        out.writeInt( i1[i] );

                    // Close file
                    out.close();

                    // Create DataInputStream
                    DataInputStream in = new DataInputStream(
                                        new BufferedInputStream(
                                            new FileInputStream("unf.dat")));

                    // Read data from file
                    for ( int i = 0; i < a2.length; i++ )
                        a2[i] = in.readDouble();
                    for ( int i = 0; i < i2.length; i++ )
                        i2[i] = in.readInt();

                     // Close file
                    in.close();

                    // Compare the data written to the data read back
                    System.out.println("Printing old and new values:");
                    for ( int i = 0; i < a1.length; i++ ) {
                        Fmt.printf("%8.4f   ",a1[i]);
                        Fmt.printf("%8.4f\n",a2[i]);
                    }
                    for ( int i = 0; i < i1.length; i++ ) {
                        Fmt.printf("%8d    ",i1[i]);
                        Fmt.printf("%8d\n",i2[i]);
                    }
                }

                // Catch IOExceptions
                catch (IOException e) {
                    System.out.println("IOException: the stack trace is:");
                    e.printStackTrace();
                }
            }
```

Figure 14.9. A sample program illustrating unformatted input and output.

When this program is executed, the results are:

```
C:\book\java\chap14>java TestUnformattedIO
Printing old and new values:
  5.0000      5.0000
 10.0000     10.0000
 15.0000     15.0000
 20.0000     20.0000
       1            1
     -10          -10
```

The contents of the data read from the file are identical to the contents of the data written to the file.

EXAMPLE 14-6:
COMPARING
FORMATTED
AND
UNFORMATTED
SEQUENTIAL
FILES

To compare the operation of formatted and unformatted sequential access files, we will create two files containing 20,000 `double` values. One file should be formatted and the other one should be unformatted. Compare the time that it takes to write the two files, and the sizes to the two files. Then read the two files into arrays, and compare the time that it takes to read the two files. How do formatted and unformatted files compare in terms of speed and size?

Use method `System.random()` to generate the 20,000 double values to be written out in each file, and user the `Timer` class to measure the elapsed time of file reads and writes.

SOLUTION
A program to write the two files and then to read them is shown in Figure 14.10. Note that this program calculates the elapsed time for both writes and reads.

```
/*
   Purpose:
     To compare the time required to read and write
     formatted and unformatted files, and the sizes
     of those files.

   Record of revisions:
      Date        Programmer         Description of change
      ====        ==========         =====================
      5/10/98    S. J. Chapman       Original code
*/
import java.io.*;
public class CompareFormat {

   public static void main(String[] args) throws IOException {

      // Define variables
      double a1[] = new double[20000]; // Original array
      double a2[] = new double[20000]; // Array from unformatted file
      double a3[] = new double[20000]; // Array from formatted file
      int i;                           // Loop index
      double readTimeFmt;              // Write time for fmt file
      double readTimeUnf;              // Write time for unf file
      Timer t = new Timer();           // Timer object
      double writeTimeFmt;             // Write time for fmt file
      double writeTimeUnf;             // Write time for unf file

      //*******************************************************
      // Create a data set to save
      //*******************************************************
      for ( i = 0; i < a1.length; i++ )
         a1[i] = Math.random();

      //*******************************************************
      // Write unformatted file
      //*******************************************************
      t.resetTimer();
```

Figure 14.10 *(cont.)*

```
// Create unformatted file
DataOutputStream out1 = new DataOutputStream(
                          new BufferedOutputStream(
                             new FileOutputStream(
                                "unformat.dat")));
// Write data
for ( i = 0; i < a1.length; i++ )
   out1.writeDouble( a1[i] );

// Close file
out1.close();

// Get elapsed time
writeTimeUnf = t.elapsedTime();

//*******************************************************
// Write formatted file
//*******************************************************
// Start timer
t.resetTimer();

// Create formatted file
PrintWriter out2 =
   new PrintWriter(
      new BufferedWriter(
         new FileWriter("format.dat")));

// Write data
for ( i = 0; i < a1.length; i++ )
   out2.println( a1[i] );

// Close file
out2.close();

// Get elapsed time
writeTimeFmt = t.elapsedTime();

//*******************************************************
// Read unformatted file
//*******************************************************
t.resetTimer();

// Open unformatted file
DataInputStream in1 = new DataInputStream(
                         new BufferedInputStream(
                            new FileInputStream(
                               "unformat.dat")));

// Read data
for ( i = 0; i < a1.length; i++ )
   a2[i] = in1.readDouble();

// Close file
in1.close();

// Get elapsed time
readTimeUnf = t.elapsedTime();
```

Figure 14.10 *(cont.)*

```
//*****************************************************
// Read formatted file
//*****************************************************
t.resetTimer();

  // Open formatted file
  BufferedReader in2 =
    new BufferedReader(
      new FileReader("format.dat"));
    StreamTokenizer st = new StreamTokenizer(in2);

// Read data
for ( i = 0; i < a1.length; i++ ) {
  st.nextToken();
  while( st.ttype != st.TT_NUMBER )
    st.nextToken();
  a3[i] = st.nval;
}

// Close file
in2.close();

// Get elapsed time
readTimeFmt = t.elapsedTime();

//*****************************************************
// Display results
//*****************************************************
System.out.println("Unformatted write time = " + writeTimeUnf);
System.out.println("Formatted write time   = " + writeTimeFmt);
System.out.println("Unformatted read time  = " + readTimeUnf);
System.out.println("Formatted read time    = " + readTimeFmt);
System.out.println("a1[19999] = " + a1[19999]);
System.out.println("a2[19999] = " + a2[19999]);
System.out.println("a3[19999] = " + a3[19999]);
  }
}
```

Figure 14.10. Program to compare the execution times and file sizes for formatted and unformatted sequential access files.

When the program is executed, the results are:

```
D:\book\java\chap14>java CompareFormat
Unformatted write time = 0.701
Formatted write time   = 8.983
Unformatted read time  = 0.862
Formatted read time    = 3.965
a1[19999] = 0.605629588261877
a2[19999] = 0.605629588261877
a3[19999] = 0.605629588261877
```

The formatted writes and reads took *much* longer than the unformatted writes and reads. If we compare the sizes of the resulting files, we see that the formatted file is also much larger than the unformatted file.

```
D:\book\java\chap14>dir *.dat
 Volume in drive D is DRIVE D
 Volume Serial Number is 1091-0CC3

 Directory of D:\book\java\chap14
05/11/98  05:42p                405,426 format.dat
05/11/98  05:42p                160,000 unformat.dat
                2 File(s)        565,426 bytes
                             251,916,800 bytes free
```

Unformatted sequential access files are both smaller and faster than formatted files, so they are the preferred way to store information when it will be read back in by a Java program. However, unformatted files cannot be examined by people, and they cannot be easily read in by programs written in other computer languages. If you need to manually type input that will be read by a Java program, if you need to examine the results of a program, or if you need to exchange data with non-Java programs, then you should use formatted I/O. Otherwise, you should use unformatted I/O.

GOOD PROGRAMMING PRACTICE

Unformatted sequential access files are both smaller and faster than formatted files, so they are the preferred way to store information when it will be read back in by a Java program. Use unformatted files to store and exchange data, unless a human needs to examine the data or it is to be exchanged with non-Java programs.

14.6 RANDOM ACCESS FILES

Random access files differ from sequential access files in that the records in a random access file can be accessed in *any* order. Random access files are implemented by class `RandomAccessFile`, and the `seek()` method of that class can be used to move around among the records of the file.

Interestingly, the records in a random access file do not have to be of any specific length; we just have to be able to determine how big a record is and where it is placed in the file.

Class `RandomAccessFile` handles both input and output to random access files. It implements the `DataInput` and `DataOutput` interfaces, so the methods in Tables 14-2 and 14-3 can be used to read or write data in these files. `RandomAccessFile` also supports the additional methods shown in Table 14-4

TABLE 14-4 Additional Methods in `class RandomAccessFile`

METHOD	DESCRIPTION
`void close()`	Close this random access file.
`long getFilePointer()`	Returns the current offset into this file, in bytes.
`long length()`	Returns the length of this file, in bytes.
`void seek(long pos)`	Sets the file-pointer offset in bytes, measured from the beginning of this file, at which the next read or write occurs. The offset may be set beyond the end of the file. Setting the offset beyond the end of the file does not change the file length. The file length will change only by writing after the offset has been set beyond the end of the file.
`void setLength(long len)`	Sets a new length in bytes for the file. If `len` is shorter than the current file length, the file is truncated and the file pointer points to the end of the file. If `len` is longer than the current file length, the file is extended, but the contents of the extended part of the file are undefined.

The constructors for this class take the following forms:

```
RandomAccessFile(String fileName, String mode)
RandomAccessFile(File file, String mode)
```

The first constructor is the most common form. It specifies the file to open by its file name. The second form of the constructor specifies the file by an object of the `File` class. In either case, the constructor takes a `mode` string to specify whether the file is to be opened for reading only or for reading and writing. The possible forms of this string are `"r"` and `"rw"`.

Once a file is opened, it is possible to move around freely within the file using `seek()`, and to read or write data at the specified location. However, any attempt to read data beyond the end of a file will produce an `EOFException`.

EXAMPLE 14-7: WRITING AND READING DATA WITH UNFORMATTED RANDOM ACCESS FILES

Create a program that writes 10 `double` values in sequence to a random access file, and then directly modifies the value in record 4. Then, show that the program can read back the data either sequentially or in random order.

SOLUTION

The example program shown in Figure 14.11 illustrates the use of random file access. It opens a random access file for reading and writing, writes 10 double values to it, and then closes the file. Then it illustrates random writing by reopening the file for reading and writing, going directly to record 4, and modifying the data in that record. (The program knows where record 4 is because each record is 8 bytes long, and the first record starts at byte 0.) Finally, it opens the file for reading only, reads the 10 records in order, and then jumps back and re-reads record 6.

```
/*
    Purpose:
      To test reading and writing to random access files.

    Record of revisions:
        Date          Programmer             Description of change
        ====          ==========             =====================
        5/10/98       S. J. Chapman          Original code
*/
import java.io.*;
public class TestRandomAccess {

    public static void main(String[] args)
                    throws IOException {
       // Define variables
       int i;                          // Loop index
       RandomAccessFile r;             // File reference

       //*******************************************************
       // Save data in a RandomAccessFile and close the file
       //*******************************************************
       r = new RandomAccessFile("random.dat","rw");
       for ( i = 0; i < 10; i++ )
          r.writeDouble( i * Math.PI );
       r.close();

       //*******************************************************
       // Re-open the file and change the fourth record.  Note
       // that each double is 8 bytes long.
       //*******************************************************
       r = new RandomAccessFile("random.dat","rw");
       r.seek ( 3*8 );
       r.writeDouble( 1.0 );
       r.close();
```

Figure 14.11.   *(cont.)*

```
//************************************************************
// Open and read data from the file in sequential order
//************************************************************
r = new RandomAccessFile("random.dat","r");
System.out.println("The data in the file is:");
for ( i = 0; i < 10; i++ )
    System.out.println(r.readDouble());

//************************************************************
// Recover the data from the sixth record
//************************************************************
r.seek( 5*8 );
System.out.println("Record 6 = " + r.readDouble());
r.close();
    }
}
```

Figure 14.11.   Program to test random access files.

When this program is executed, the results are:

```
D:\book\java\chap14>java TestRandomAccess
The data in the file is:
0.0
3.141592653589793
6.283185307179586
1.0
12.566370614359172
15.707963267948966
18.84955592153876
21.991148575128552
25.132741228718345
28.274333882308138
Record 6 = 15.707963267948966
```

This program correctly modified the fourth record, and correctly re-read the sixth record, so method seek() is working correctly.

14.7 GETTING INFORMATION ABOUT FILES: THE FILE CLASS

The File class can be used to recover information about files and directories. This class includes methods to get directory listings, to make directories, to create temporary files, to delete files, to determine if a specified file exists, and to perform similar utility functions. Note that a File object can be created to represent *either a file or a directory.*

A File constructor takes one of the following forms:

```
File (String path);
File (String path, String name);
File (File dir, String name);
```

where path is the path to a particular directory (without the terminating separator), name is a filename, and dir is a file object representing a parent directory. Some of the methods in class File are listed in Table 14-5. Descriptions of all of the methods in File may be found in the Java API documentation.

Figure 14.12 contains an example that uses the File class to recover a list of the files in a specific directory. Note the double backslashes used in the path name. Since a single backslash (\) is a escape character, a backslash must be represented by (\\).

TABLE 14-5   Selected Methods in `File`

METHOD	DESCRIPTION
`boolean canRead()`	Tests if an application can read a particular file.
`boolean canWrite()`	Tests if an application can write to particular file.
`File createTempFile(String p)`	Creates a temporary file in the system temporary directory, using string p as the base of the file name.
`boolean delete()`	Delete the file specified by this object.
`boolean exists()`	Tests if the file specified by this object exists.
`String getCanonicalPath()`	Returns the path to this file object.
`String getName()`	Get the name of this file object.
`boolean isDirectory()`	Tests if this object is a directory.
`boolean isFile()`	Tests if this object is a file.
`long lastModified()`	Returns date of last modification.
`long length()`	Returns length of file in bytes.
`String list()`	Returns the list of files in the current directory.
`boolean mkdir()`	Make the directory specified by this object.
`boolean mkdirs()`	Make the directory specified by this object, including any required parent directories.
`boolean renameTo(File n)`	Rename the file to the name specified in n.

```
// Get a directory listing
import java.io.*;
public class GetDirList {

    public static void main(String[] args) {
        // Define variables
        String path = "d:\\book\\java\\chap14";
        String s[];

        // Create a new File object representing a directory
        File f = new File(path);

        // Get a directory listing
        s = f.list();

        // Tell user.
        System.out.println("Directory " + path + " contains:");
        for (int i = 0; i < s.length; i++ )
            System.out.println(s[i]);
    }
}
```

Figure 14.12.   Program to get a directory listing using a `File` object.

When this program is executed, the results are:

```
D:\book\java\chap14>java GetDirList
Directory d:\book\java\chap14 contains:
capt14.doc
chap14.doc
CompareFormat.class
CompareFormat.java
fig14-1.drw
fig14-2.drw
```

```
fig14-3.drw
fig14-4.drw
format.dat
GetDirList.class
GetDirList.java
input.txt
output.txt
random.dat
ReadFormattedFile.class
ReadFormattedFile.java
ReadFormattedStdin.class
ReadFormattedStdin.java
test
test1
TestRandomAccess.class
TestRandomAccess.java
TestStreamTokenizer.class
TestStreamTokenizer.java
TestUnformattedIO.class
TestUnformattedIO.java
Timer.class
Timer.java
tokens.txt
unf.dat
unformat.dat
WriteFormattedFile.class
WriteFormattedFile.java
```

PRACTICE!

This quiz provides a quick check to see if you have understood the concepts introduced in Sections 14.1 through 14.7. If you have trouble with the quiz, reread the section, ask your instructor, or discuss the material with a fellow student. The answers to this quiz are found in the back of the book.

1. What is the difference between an `OutputStream` and `Writer`? What is the difference between an `InputStream` and a `Reader`?

2. What is the difference between sequential access and random access? How do you implement random access in Java?

3. What classes would you use to read character data from a formatted sequential file?

4. What classes would you use to read numeric data from a formatted sequential file?

5. What classes would you use to write data to a formatted sequential file?

6. What classes would you use to read unformatted data from a sequential file?

7. What classes would you use to write unformatted data to a sequential file?

8. What classes would you use to read and write data to a random access file?

SUMMARY

- The Java I/O system consists of many different classes, each performing a small part of the job. It is the responsibility of the programmer to string these classes together in useful ways to solve a particular problem.

- There are actually two Java I/O systems. Java version 1.0 had a byte-based I/O system, and Java version 1.1 introduced an additional character-based I/O system to better handle Unicode characters.

- In general, all unformatted and direct-access I/O should be done using the original byte-based I/O system. These classes implement the `DataInput` and `DataOutput` interfaces.
- Formatted I/O to files should be done using the character-based `Reader` and `Writer` classes.
- Formatted input from the standard input streams should use the bridge class `InputStreamReader` to convert it into character-based data.
- The `StreamTokenizer` class may be used to break formatted input streams up into discrete tokens, and to convert numeric tokens into their corresponding `double` values.
- Class `File` can be used to perform general-purpose file manipulations such as getting directory listings, getting information about files, creating temporary files, and so forth.

APPLICATIONS: SUMMARY OF GOOD PROGRAMMING PRACTICES

The following guidelines introduced in this chapter will help you to develop good programs:

1. Use class `RandomAccessFile` to read and write data in random access files.
2. Read unformatted data using the "`InputStream`" sources, and convert the data to a useful form using the `DataInputStream` class.
3. Read formatted data using the "`Reader`" sources, and convert the data to a useful form using the `BufferedReader` class. If you are reading from the standard input stream, convert the data into a `Reader` using the `InputStreamReader` class before sending it to the `BufferedReader` class.
4. Always use the `BufferedInputStream` or `BufferedReader` classes to improve efficiency when reading data from a file.
5. Create unformatted output data with methods in the `DataOutputStream` class, and write it out using the "`OutputStream`" sinks.
6. Create formatted output data using the `print()` and `println()` methods found in the `PrintStream` and `PrintWriter` classes, and write it out using the `Output Stream` and `OutputWriter` sinks respectively. Use the `PrintWriter` methods, except when working with the standard output or standard error devices.
7. Always use the `BufferedOutputStream` or `BufferedWriter` classes to improve efficiency when writing data to a file.
8. Always close any files you use just as soon as you are finished with them. This action releases the file resources for possible use elsewhere within the computer.

Unformatted sequential access files are both smaller and faster than formatted files, so they are the preferred way to store information when it will be read back in by a Java program. Use unformatted files to store and exchange data, unless a human needs to examine it, or it is to be exchanged with non-Java programs.

KEY TERMS

buffering class	formatted file	sink
convenience class	random access	source
deprecated	sequential access	unformatted file
filter class		

Problems

14.1.   Write a program to read a series of Strings from a formatted sequential input file, sort them into ascending order, and write them to a formatted sequential output file. You may assume that each string appears on a separate line in the input file. Pass the input and output file names to your program as command line arguments.

14.2.   Write a GUI program to read a series of Strings from a formatted sequential input file and display them in a List. The GUI should include a TextField for the input file name and a "Read File" button. You may assume that each string appears on a separate line in the input file.

14.3.   Create a GUI-based program that (1) reads a series of Strings from a formatted sequential input file, (2) displays them in a List, (3) allows the user to modify the order of the Strings, and (4) writes them to an output file. The program should include JTextFields for the input and output file names, as well as "Read File" and "Write File" Buttons. The program should allow the user to modify the order of the Strings by highlighting a particular item and moving it up or down in the list by clicking on "Up" or "Down" buttons. (You may assume that each string appears on a separate line in the input file.)

14.4.   Write a program to read a series of double values from a formatted sequential input file, sort them into ascending order, and write them to a formatted sequential output file. Pass the input and output file names to your program as command line arguments.

14.5.   Modify the program in Exercise 14.4 to read from the standard input stream instead of an input file.

14.6.   We mentioned in this chapter that the SteamTokenizer class has limitations, in that it fails to properly translate numbers in exponential format. Can you suggest a way to create an input class that will properly handle all forms of numeric inputs? (*Hint:* Consider using the StringTokenizer class and the Double type wrapper class.) Write such a class and test it using the following input data (this data can be found in file input1.txt):

| 10.0 | -12.1 | +14.4 |
| 32.e6 | -1.6e-19 | +6.02e23 |

14.7.   **File Copy while Trimming Trailing Blanks** Write a program that reads an input file name and an output file name from the command line, and then copies the input file to the output file, trimming trailing blanks off of the end of each line before writing it out. If no file names are present on the command line, the program should prompt the user for the input file name and the output file name. After the copy process is completed, the program should ask the user whether or not to delete the original file. If requested, the program should delete the input file using the delete() method in class File.

14.8.   Modify the program of Exercise 14.7 so that it checks for the existence of the specified output file, and prompts the user before overwriting the existing file if it already exists.

14.9.   Modify the program of Exercise 14.7 so that it supports an optional "-a" flag to cause the output data to be appended to the output file, if it already exists.

14.10. **Word Count** Write a program that reads a formatted sequential data set from an input file specified on the command line, and counts the number of words in the data set. Write the number of words to the standard output device. For these purposes, a word is defined as a set of characters separated by whitespace. (*Hint:* Use class StringTokenizer.)

14.11. **Histogram Program** Modify the histogram program of Example 13-2 so that the input dialog box offers the user a choice of all the files in the current directory ending with the extent ".dat". Use the File class to create this list, and use the proper form of input dialog box to display the list.

Appendix A:
ASCII Character Set

The ASCII character set is a subset of the Unicode character set. It contains the first 127 characters of the Unicode character set, which are the ones most commonly used in Java programs. The full details of the Unicode character set can be found by consulting the World Wide Web site http://unicode.org.

    The table shown below includes the first 127 characters, with the first two digits of the character number defined by the row, and the third digit defined by the column. For example, the letter 'R' is on row 8 and column 2, so it is character 82 in the ASCII (and Unicode) character set.

	0	1	2	3	4	5	6	7	8	9
0	nul	soh	stx	etx	eot	enq	ack	bel	bs	ht
1	nl	vt	ff	cr	so	si	dle	dc1	dc2	dc3
2	dc4	nak	syn	etb	can	em	sub	esc	fs	gs
3	rs	us	sp	!	"	#	$	%	&	'
4	(	)	*	+	,	-	.	/	0	1
5	2	3	4	5	6	7	8	9	:	;
6	<	=	>	?	@	A	B	C	D	E
7	F	G	H	I	J	K	L	M	N	O
8	P	Q	R	S	T	U	V	W	X	Y
9	Z	[	\	]	^	_	`	a	b	c
10	d	e	f	g	h	I	j	k	l	m
11	n	o	p	q	r	s	t	u	v	w
12	x	y	z	{	|	}	~	del		

Appendix B:
Operator Precedence Chart

The Java operators are shown in decreasing order of precedence from top to bottom, with the operators in each section having equal precedence.

OPERATOR	TYPE	ASSOCIATIVITY
( )	parentheses	left to right
[ ]	array subscript	
.	member selection	
++	unary preincrement	right to left
++	unary postincrement	
--	unary predecrement	
--	unary postdecrement	
+	unary plus	
-	unary minus	
!	unary logical negation	
~	unary bitwise complement	
(type)	unary cast	
*	multiplication	left to right
/	division	
%	modulus	
+	addition	left to right
-	subtraction	
<<	bitwise left shift	left to right
>>	bitwise right shift with sign extension	
>>>	bitwise right shift with zero extension	
<	relational less than	left to right
<=	relational less than or equal to	
>	relational greater than	
>=	relational greater than or equal to	
instanceOf	type comparison	
==	relational is equal to	left to right
!=	relational is not equal to	
&	bitwise AND	left to right
^	bitwise exclusive OR boolean logical exclusive OR	left to right
|	bitwise inclusive OR boolean logical inclusive OR	left to right
&&	logical AND	left to right

`||`		logical OR	left to right
`? :`		ternary conditional	right to left
`=`		assignment	right to left
`+=`		addition assignment	
`-=`		subtraction assignment	
`*=`		multiplication assignment	
`/=`		division assignment	
`%=`		modulus assignment	
`&=`		bitwise AND assignment	
`^=`		bitwise exclusive OR assignment	
`|=`		bitwise inclusive OR assignment	
`<<=`		bitwise left shift assignment	
`>>=`		bitwise right shift with sign extension assignment	
`>>>=`		bitwise right shift with zero extension assignment	

Appendix C:
Answers to Practice Boxes

CHAPTER 2

Practice Box, page 23

1. Valid `double` constant
2. Invalid—commas not allowed
3. Valid `double` constant
4. Valid `char` constant
5. Invalid—to create a `char` constant containing a single quote, use the backslash escape character: `'\''`
6. Valid `double` constant
7. Valid `String` constant
8. Valid `boolean` constant
9. Same value
10. Same value
11. Different value
12. Valid name—would be a variable or a method name
13. Valid name—would be a class name
14. Invalid—name may not begin with a number
15. Valid name—would be a constant (or `final` variable)
16. Valid
17. Invalid—`MAX_COUNT` is a `short`, and 100000 is an `int`. An explicit cast is required to convert `int` to `short`. In addition, 100000 is too large a number to be represented in a `short`.
18. Invalid—can't assign a `String` to a `char`.
19. These statements are illegal. They try to assign a new value to the constant (final variable) k.

Practice Box, page 31

1. The order of evaluation is:
    a. Expressions in parentheses, working from the innermost parentheses out
    b. Multiplications, divisions, and mod, working from left to right
    c. Additions and subtractions, working from left to right

2. *(a)* Legal—result is 12 *(b)* Legal—result is 42 *(c)* Legal—result is 2 *(d)* Legal—result is 2.25 *(e)* Legal—result is 2.3333333 *(f)* Legal—result is 1
3. *(a)* 7 *(b)* -21 *(c)* 7 *(d)* 9
4. These statements are legal: x = 16; y = 3; result = 17.5.
5. These statements are illegal. The expression evaluates to a double 17.5, but the variable result is an int. This assignment is a narrowing conversion, which is illegal unless an explicit cast is used.

Practice Box, pages 41-42

1. `rEq = r1 + r2 + r3 + r4;`
2. `rEq = 1 / (1/r1 + 1/r2 + 1/r3 + 1/r4);`
3. `t = 2 * Math.PI * Math.sqrt( 1 / g );`
4. `v = vm * Math.exp( -alpha*t ) * Math.cos( omega*t );`

5. $d = \frac{1}{2}at^2 + v_0 t + d_0$

6. $f = \dfrac{1}{2\pi\sqrt{LC}}$

7. $E = \frac{1}{2}Li^2$

8. *(a)* Illegal—mismatched parentheses. *(b)* Illegal—explicit cast needed to convert double to int. *(c)* Illegal—explicit cast needed to convert double to int. [*Note:* This one is tricky. Because the cast operator (int) is evaluated before division, a is converted to an int. Since a / b is an int divided by a double, the result is a double, and it illegal to assign the double value to k.] *(d)* Legal—b = 3.666667 *(e)* This is legal, but the calculation includes a floating-point division by zero; the result is infinite.
9. The results are: a = 2.0, b = 3.0, c = 4.666666666666667, i = 5, j = 0, k = 2.

CHAPTER 3

Practice Box, page 85

1. *(a)* `false` *(b)* Illegal—can't use the not (!) operator with a double value *(c)* `true` *(d)* `true` *(e)* `true` *(f)* `false`
2.
```
if ( x >= 0 ) {
    sqrtX = Math.sqrt(x);
}
else {
    System.out.println("Error: x < 0");
    sqrtX = 0;
}
```

3.
```
if ( Math.abs(denominator) < 1.0E-30 )
    System.out.println("Divide by 0 error.");
else {
    fun = numerator / denominator;
    System.out.println("fun = " + fun;
}
```

4.
```
if ( distance <= 100. )
    cost = 0.50 * distance;
else if ( distance <= 300. )
    cost = 50. + 0.30 * (distance - 100);
else
    cost = 110. + 0.20 * (distance - 300);
```

5. These statements will compile correctly, but they will not do what the programmer intended. Since there is no "else" in front of the second `if` statement, the second `if` statement will be executed regardless of the result of the first `if` statement. Thus if `volts` = 130, both `"WARNING: High voltage on line."` and `"Line voltage is within tolerances."` will be printed out.

6. Since i < j, the expression `j / i` will be executed, and the result will be k = 1.66666666666666667.

7. These statements are incorrect—a colon is required after the keyword `default`.

8. These statement will compile correctly, but they will not do what the programmer intended. If the `temperature` is 150, these statements will print out `"Human body temperature exceeded."` instead of `"Boiling point of water exceeded."`, because the `if` structure executes the first `true` condition and skips the rest. To get proper behavior, the order of these tests should be reversed.

CHAPTER 4

Practice Box, page 113

1. 4 times
2. This is an infinite loop. The values of j are 7, 6, 5, 4, 3, 2, 1, 0, -1, …. Since the loop terminates when j > 10, the loop will *never* terminate.
3. 1 time
4. 9 times
5. 7 times
6. 9 times
7. infinite loop
8. `ires` = 10, and the loop executes 10 times
9. `ires` = 55, and the loop executes 10 times
10. `ires` = 15, and the loop executes 5 times
11. `ires` = 15, and the loop executes 5 times

12. `ires` = 15, and the loop executes 5 times

13. `ires` = 18, and the loop executes 6 times

14. `ires` = 3, and the loop executes 3 times

15. `ires` = 25; the outer loop executes 5 times and the inner loop executes 25 times

16. `ires` = 15; the outer loop executes 5 times and the inner loop executes 15 times

17. `ires` = 2; the outer loop executes 1 time and the inner loop executes 3 times

18. `ires` = 10; the outer loop executes 5 times and the inner loop executes 15 times

19. Invalid. Variable `i` is used to control both loops.

20. Invalid. These statements will compile and execute, but they will produce an infinite loop. The semicolon after the `while` statement terminates the `while` loop without changing the value of x, so x will never be less than or equal to 0.

21. Invalid. The `i--` modifies the value of the loop variable, producing an infinite loop.

CHAPTER 5

Practice Box, pages 144-145

1. An array is a special object containing *(1)* a group of contiguous memory locations that all have the same name and same type, and *(2)* a separate instance variable containing an integer constant equal to the number of elements in the array. An element of an array is addressed by the array name followed by an integer subscript in square brackets (`[]`). The components of the array are the elements of the array plus the constant containing the length of the array.

2. A reference is a "handle" or "pointer" to an object that permits Java to locate the object in memory when it is needed.

3. An array object is created with the `new` operator. For example:

```
double[] x = new double[5];
```

creates a new five-element `double` array.

4. An array may be initialized by assignment statements, or by the use of an initializer when the array is created. For example,

```
int a[] = {1, 2, 3, 4, 5};
```

creates a new five-element `int` array, and initializes the values of the array elements to 1, 2, 3, 4, and 5.

5. A 100-element array would be addressed with the subscripts 0 to 99. Any other subscripts would produce an `ArrayIndexOutOfBoundsException`.

6. Valid. These statements create a new 10-element `double` array.

7. Invalid. A `double` reference cannot refer to an `int` array.

8. Invalid. An initializer can only be used in an array declaration, not in an assignment statement.

9. Valid. These statements will print out the second through fifth elements in the array. They will *not* print the first element, since the subscript for the first element is 0, and the loop begins at 1.

10. Valid. These statements will print out the first through fifth elements in the array *in reverse order*.

Practice Box, page 169

1. This array contains 35 elements, addressed by the subscripts `[0][0]` to `[4][6]`.

2. This array contains 9 elements, addressed by the subscripts `[0][0]`, `[0][1]`, `[1][0]`, `[1][1]`, `[1][2]`, `[1][3]`, `[2][0]`, `[2][1]`, and `[3][2]`.

3. Valid.

4. Invalid—an `int` array reference cannot refer to a `double` array.

5. Invalid—a one-dimensional reference cannot refer to a two-dimensional array.

CHAPTER 6

Practice Box, page 186

1. Incorrect. The `int` array is the first parameter in `method1`, but the second parameter in the call to `method1`.

2. Incorrect—`method2` is declared void but returns a value.

3. Correct. The `main` method calls `method3` with array x, and `method3` sums the values in the elements of array x, and divides that result by the number of elements in the array. The `main` method then prints out this result, which will be -0.5.

Practice Box, page 205

1. The duration of a variable is the time during which it exists. The types of duration in Java are automatic duration and static duration.

2. The scope of a variable is the portion of the program from which the variable can be addressed. The types of scope are class scope and block scope. Variables with block scope can be defined for any block size, such as a method body, a `for` loop, etc.

3. Variables defined within a Java method have automatic duration and block scope. The block in which they are visible is the method body, which is delineated by the open and closing braces `{}`.

4. A recursive method is a method that either directly or indirectly calls itself.

5. Method overloading is the process of defining several methods with the same name but different sets of parameters (based on the number, types, and order of the parameters). When an overloaded method is called, the Java compiler

selects the proper method by examining the number, type, and order of the calling arguments.

6. This program is incorrect. Variable i is redefined within the `while` loop, which will cause the loop to behave improperly.

7. This program is incorrect. The two overloaded methods m1 have the same signature, and so cannot be distinguished from each other.

CHAPTER 7

Practice Box, page 233

1. The major components of a class are fields, constructors, methods, and finalizers. Fields define the instance variables that will be created when an object is instantiated from a class. Constructors are special methods that specify how to initialize the instance variables in an object when it is created. Methods implement the behaviors of a class. A finalizer is a special method that is called just before an object is destroyed to release any resources allocated to the object.

2. The types of member access modifiers are `public`, `private`, `protected`, and `package`. Private access is normally used for instance variables, and public access is normally used for methods.

3. A variable with class scope is visible anywhere within the class in which it is defined, while a variable with block scope is only visible within the block in which it is defined.

4. If a method contains a local variable with the same name as an instance variable in the method's class, the instance variable will be "hidden", and so will not be directly accessible from the method. However, the method can still access the instance variable using the `this` reference.

5. To use classes in packages other than `java.lang`, you must include an `import` statement for each package at the beginning of the source file. Note that the `import` statements must appear *before* the class definition.

6. To create a user-defined package, include a `package` statement in the source file of each class to go into the package, and compile each class with the "`-d`" option to specify the location of the package directory structure. Include an `import` statement in each class using the package, and be sure to set the `CLASSPATH` environment variable so that the package can be found by the Java compiler.

7. The `CLASSPATH` environment variable tells the Java compiler and the Java runtime system where to look for packages being imported.

8. A variable or method declared with `public` access may be accessed from any class anywhere within a program. A variable or method declared with `private` access may only be accessed from within the class in which it is defined. A variable or method declared with package access may be accessed from within the class in which it is defined, or from any class within the same package. A variable or method declared with `protected` access may be accessed from within the class in which it is defined, from any class within the same package, or from any subclass of the class in which it is defined.

Practice Box, page 242

1. The garbage collector is a low-priority thread that searches for and destroys objects that are no longer needed. It runs automatically in the background while a Java program is executing. A Java object is eligible for garbage collection when no reference to the object exists, because the object can no longer be used once there are no longer any references to it.

2. Static variables are variables that are *shared* by all objects created from the class in which the variables are defined. These variables are automatically created as soon as a class is loaded into memory, and they remain in existence until the progam stops executing. Static variables are useful for keeping track of global information such as the number of objects instantiated from a class, or the number of those objects still surviving at any given time. They are also useful for defining single copies of final variables that will be shared among all objects of the class.

3. Static methods are commonly used to perform calculations that are independent of any instance data that might be defined in a class. The methods in class `java.lang.Math` (`sin`, `cos`, `sqrt`, etc.) are good examples of static methods.

CHAPTER 8

Practice Box, page 267

1. An exception is an event that interrupts the normal processing flow of a program. This event is usually an error of some sort.

2. Runtime exceptions are those exceptions that occur within the Java runtime system, including arithmetic exceptions, pointer exceptions, and indexing exceptions. These sorts of exceptions can occur *anywhere* in a program, so Java does not force a programmer to list every possible runtime exception that can occur in every method. All other exceptions in a Java program are known as checked exceptions, because the compiler checks that these exceptions are either caught or explicitly ignored by any method in which the exception could possibly occur.

3. The Java compiler checks to see that all checked exceptions are either caught or explicitly ignored by any method in which the exception could possibly occur. If an exception is to be ignored by a method, the method must explicitly "throw" the exception in it's method declaration, so that a method higher up the calling tree can have a chance to "catch" it. This is known as the "catch or specify" requirement.

CHAPTER 9

Practice Box, page 307

1. Inheritance is the process by which the non-private instance variables and methods of a class are automatically defined in all subclasses of that class unless they are explicitly overridden in the subclass. Once a behavior

(method) is defined in a superclass, that behavior is automatically inherited by all subclasses unless it is explicitly overridden with a modified method. Thus behaviors only need to be coded *once*, and they can be used by all subclasses. A subclass need only provide methods to implement the *differences* between itself and its parent.

2. Polymorphism is the ability to automatically select the proper version of a method to apply to objects of different subclasses when the objects are addressed using superclass references. In order for polymorphism to work, the method must be defined in the superclass, and that definition must be overridden with the appropriate methods in each subclass.

3. Abstract methods are method declarations that do not have code bodies attached to them. Abstract methods may be used in a parent class to declare a method that will be overridden in all of the subclasses of the class. If the method is going to be overridden in all subclasses, why bother to write code for it at all? Abstract classes are classes containing one or more abstract methods.

4. The principal advantage of declaring a class to be `final` is that the Java compiler can optimize the class for faster execution. Also, since the class cannot be overridden, its behavior will be the same on every Java virtual machine executing the class. The principal disadvantage of a `final` class is that it cannot serve as a superclass for further subclasses.

5. An interface is a special kind of block containing method signatures (and possibly constants) only. Interfaces define the signatures of a set of methods, without the method bodies that would implement their functionality. Interfaces have no direct inherited relationship with any particular class—they are defined independently. Therefore, methods that are designed to work with a particular interface can be re-used with any class that implements that interface. For example, a `sort` method that works with the `Comparable` interface can sort objects of any class implementing the interface—only one `sort` method is required to sort many different types of objects.

CHAPTER 10

Practice Box, page 342

1. The fundamental difference between `Strings` and `StringBuffers` is that the `String` class consists of strings that *never change* once they are created, while the `StringBuffer` class consists of modifiable strings. The `String-Buffers` should be used whenever you are working with strings that must be modified (for example, where you wish to insert or delete characters).

2. Invalid. These statements will compile successfully, but the will produce an `StringIndexOutOfBoundsException` at runtime, since `s1` is not eight characters long.

3. Valid. The statement "`s3 = s1.substring(1,3);`" selects the characters at indices 1 and 2 of `s1`, which is the string `"bc"`. The following statement concatenates the characters `"123"` to it, so the final result is `"bc123"`.

4. Invalid. You can't use the `substring` and `concat` methods with object of class `StringBuffer`, only with objects of class `String`.

5. Valid. The equals test will be false, because the two Strings are not identical. However, the equalsIgnoreCase test will be true.

6. Valid. The result is false, since the two references point to physically different objects, even though the contents of the objects are identical.

7. There are many ways to do this. One possible class is shown below, but it is *not* the only correct answer.

```
1   public class Finds {
2
3      public static void main(String[] args) {
4
5          String s1 = new String("Sassafras");
6          System.out.println("Locations of 's':");
7
8          int loc = 0;
9          while ( true ) {
10             loc = s1.indexOf("s",loc);
11             if ( loc >= 0 )
12                 System.out.println("s at position " + loc++);
13             if ( loc >= s1.length() )
14                 break;
15         }
16      }
17  }
```

When this program is executed, the results are:

```
C:\book\java\app_d>java Finds
Locations of 's':
s at position 2
s at position 3
s at position 8
```

To convert this program to find both uppercase and lowercase letters, add the line "s1 = s1.toLowerCase()" after line 5 above.

8. The length of a StringBuffer is the number of characters *actually stored* in the StringBuffer, while the capacity is the number of characters that *can be* stored without allocating additional memory.

9. Command line arguments are the arguments typed on the command line after the name of a Java program. The are passed to the main method in String array args.

CHAPTER 11

Practice Box, pag 396

1. A Container is a graphical object that can hold Components or other Containers. The type of container used in this chapter is a JFrame.

2. A Component is a visual object containing text or graphics, which can respond to keyboard or mouse inputs. The type of component used in this chapter is a JCanvas.

3. The basic steps required to display graphics in Java are:
    a. Create the component or components to display.
    b. Create a frame to hold the component(s), and place the component(s) into the frame(s).
    c. Create a "listener" object to detect and respond to mouse clicks, and assign the listener to the frame.

4. Java employs a coordinate system whose origin (0,0) is in the upper left hand corner of the screen, with positive x values to the right and positive y values down. The units of the coordinate system are pixels, with 72 pixels to an inch.

5. Method `getSize()` belongs to class `java.awt.Component`. Since this class is a superclass of any component or container, all components and containers include this method. The method is used to return the width and height of a particular component or container in pixels. This information can be used by the component to re-scale itself whenever the size of the window in which it is drawn changes.

6. The style of lines and borders is controlled by class `BasicStroke`.

7. Text is displayed on a graphics device using the `Graphics2D` method `drawString`. The font in which the text is displayed is specified by creating a new `Font` object, and using the `Graphics2D` method `setFont` to specify the use of that font. Information about a font can be recovered with the `FontMetrics` class.

8. An affine transform is a user-specified combination of translations, scalings, rotations, and shears that is automatically applied to any `Graphics2D` object whenever it is rendered on a graphics device. The term *affine transform* refers to a transformation that converts an input shape into an output shape while preserving parallel lines. It is used by creating a new `AffineTransform`, specifying the desired translations, rotations, etc., and using the `Graphics2D` method `setAffineTransform` to specify the use of that transform.

CHAPTER 12

Practice Box, page 444

1. A `Container` is a graphical object that can hold `Component`s or other `Containers`. We are using `JPanel`s and `JFrame`s in this chapter.

2. A `Component` is a visual object containing text or graphics, which can respond to keyboard or mouse inputs. The types of components used in this chapter are: `JButton`, `JCheckbox`, `JComboBox`, `JComponent`, `JLabel`, `JPasswordField`, `JRadioButton`, and `JTextField`.

3. A layout manager controls the location at which components will be placed within a container.

4. Cascaded layout managers permit a program to construct layouts that are more complex than can be accomplished with a single layout manager.

5. An event handler is a special method within a listener class that is called whenever a specific type of event occurs in a GUI component. The listener must first be registered with the GUI component.

6. The listener interface introduced in this chapter is the `ActionListener` interface. The `ActionListener` interface handles action events, which can be produced by all the components that we studied in this chapter, except for `JLabels`.

CHAPTER 13

Practice Box, page 513

1. A `JList` is a list of objects. Depending on the options selected, a user may select one item, one continuous interval of items, or many different intervals of items. A list can be made scrollable by placing it inside a `JScrollPane`. Lists generate `ListSelectionEvents` when an item is selected or deselected.

2. A `JList` should be placed inside a `JScrollPane` to allow the list to scroll so that all parts of the list will be visible. Even small lists should be placed in scroll panes, because the number of items in the list might grow.

3. Menus may be added to an application or an applet by creating a `JMenuBar` and adding it to the top-level container of the application or applet. `JMenus` can then be added to the `JMenuBar`, and `JMenuItems` can be added to the `JMenus`. Menus can be added to objects of classes `JFrame`, `JApplet`, `JDialog`, `JRootPane`, or `JInternalFrame`.

4. Dialog boxes are special windows that pop up with a warning or a question. They are usually modal, meaning that no other part of the application can be accessed until the dialog box is dismissed. A dialog asking a user whether or not to replace an existing file can be created by the statement:

```
res = JOptionPane.showConfirmDialog(null,
        "Replace the existing file?",
        "Warning",
        JOptionPane.YES_NO_OPTION,
        JOptionPane.WARNING_MESSAGE);
```

5. The listener interface introduced in Chapter 12 is the `ActionListener` interface. The `ActionListener` interface handles action events, which can be produced by classes `JButton`, `JCheckbox`, `JComboBox`, `JComponent`, `JPasswordField`, `JRadioButton`, and `JTextField`. The listener interfaces introduced in this chapter are the `ListSelectionListener`, `MouseListener`, `MouseMotionListener`, and `WindowListener` interfaces. The `ListSelectionListener` interface is produced by class `JList`. The `WindowListener` interface handles window events, such as opening, closing, iconifying, etc., which can be produced by class `JFrame`. The mouse interfaces are low-level interfaces whose events are normally converted into higher-level events before we use them. However, the `MouseListener` is used directly to detect popup events.

6. An adapter class is a class that implements all of the methods in an interface, *with each method doing nothing*. A programmer can write a new class that extends an adapter class, overriding only the methods that he or she wishes to

implement, and the adapter class will take care of all the "useless" interface method declarations.

7. Popup menus differ from ordinary menus in that they can be attached to any type of component, while ordinary menus can only be attached to `JFrame`, `JApplet`, `JDialog`, `JRootPane`, or `JInternalFrame`. Also, popup menus are triggered by a right-click on the mouse, while ordinary menus are triggered by a regular mouse click on the menu bar.

8. You can make an application appear the same across all type of computers by specifying that the application use the Java Look and Feel, which is guaranteed to be present in all implementations of Java. You can make a program look like a native application on each type of computer by detecting the standard look and feel for a particular computer and setting the application to use that. The code to do this automatic detection is

```
try {
    UIManager.setLookAndFeel(
        UIManager.getSystemLookAndFeelClassName());
}
catch (Exception e) {
    System.err.println("Couldn't use the "
                        + "look and feel: " + e);
}
```

9. An applet is a special type of Java program that is designed to work within a World Wide Web browser. Applets are usually quite small, and are designed to be downloaded, executed, and discarded whenever the browser points to a site containing the Java applet. They are restricted compared to applications, since they are usually not allowed access to the computer's resources (files, etc.) for security reasons.

10. Every applet has five key methods: `init`, `start`, `stop`, `destroy`, and `paintComponent`. Method `init()` is called by the browser when the applet is first loaded in memory. This method should allocate resources and create the GUI required for the applet. Method `start()` is called when the applet should start running. This call can be used to start animations, etc. when the applet becomes visible. Method `stop()` is called when the applet should stop running, for example when its window is covered or when it is iconized. This call is also make just before an applet is destroyed. Method `destroy()` is the final call to the applet before it is destroyed. The applet should release all resources at the time of this call. Finally, method `paintComponent` is called whenever the applet must be drawn or re-drawn.

11. This can be done by making the base class of the program extend `JApplet`, and then calling `init()` and `start()` in the program's `main` method. Methods `stop()` and `destroy()` should be called when the program is shutting down, for example when a window close event is detected.

Practice Box, page 544

1. `OutputStreams` output data a byte at a time, while `Writers` output data a character at a time. Similarly, `InputStreams` read data a byte at a time, while `Readers` read data a character at a time.

2. Sequential access involves reading the data in a file in order from the beginning of the file to the end of the file. Random access allows any part of the data in a file to be read in any order. Random access is implement with class `RandomAccessFile`.

3. To read character data from a formatted sequential file, use a `FileReader` wrapped by a `BufferedReader`. The `readLine()` method of the `BufferedReader` reads the data a line at a time.

4. To read numeric data from a formatted sequential file, use a `FileReader` wrapped by a `BufferedReader` wrapped by a `StreamTokenizer`. The character strings produced by the `BufferedReader` are converted into tokens by the `StreamTokenizer`, and then translated into numeric values.

5. To read numeric data from an unformatted sequential file, use a `FileInputStream` wrapped by a `BufferedInputStream` wrapped by a `DataInputStream`. The `DataInputStream` contains methods to read the unformatted data.

6. To write numeric data to an unformatted sequential file, use a `FileOutputStream` wrapped by a `BufferedOutputStream` wrapped by a `DataOutputStream`. The `DataOutputStream` contains methods to write the unformatted data.

7. All random access I/O is performed with class `RandomAccessFile`.

Index

A

Abstract classes, 288–290
    examples, 292–301
        good programming practice, 290
        programming pitfalls, 290
Abstract methods, 288
Abstract Windowing Toolkit (AWT), 10t, 158, 400
ActionEvent class, 410
    good programming practice, 414
    methods, 411t
ActionListener Interface, 410
    good programming practice, 414
    methods, 411t
ActionPerformed method, 406, 410
    good programming practice, 414
Adapter classes, 488–492
Affine transform, 388–393
    example, 390–393
AffineTransform class
    example, 390–393
    methods, 389t
Algorithm, 61
    selection sort
    good programming practice, 150
Alpha release, 62
Anonymous String objects, 319
Antialiasing, 363
Append method, 335–336
Appends data, 148
Applets, 504–513
    application creations, 509–513
    vs. applications, 10
    creating and displaying, 505–507
    packages, 509
Applet Viewer, 508
Applications
    vs. applets, 10
Arc2D, 372
Arcs, 372–375

Argument list, 180–181
Arithmetic calculations, 23–30
Array, 200
    and computer memory, 135f
    declaring, 136
    examples, 149–158
    good programming practice, 138, 200
    Java programming, 134–177
    multidimensional, 169
    one dimensional, 134–160, 161, 162
    programming pitfalls, 135
    two dimensional, 161–169
    use, 136–138
        examples, 141–145
Array declarations
    and named constants, 140–141
Array elements, 134, 138
ArrayIndexOutOfBoundsException, 139
Array initializers
    and declaration statements, 138
Array methods
    purpose, 203–204
Array object, 135f
    vs. array reference, 136
Array reference
    vs. array object, 136
Array size
    good programming practice, 141
Array subscripts, 139–140
Array values
    initializing, 138–139
Ascending order, 149
Assignment conversion, 29–30
Assignment operators, 24, 31, 32t
    programming pitfalls, 65
Assignment statements, 23–30

Associativity, 26
Automatic duration, 189
Automatic variables, 189–190
    good programming practice, 190

B

Back up, 51
BasicStroke
    parameters, 361t
Behavior, 4
Beta release, 62
Binary logical operators
    truth table, 66t
Binary operators, 24
    and numeric promotion, 28
Blank components, 431–435
Block, 190
Block scope, 190, 219
    programming pitfalls, 191
Body, 12
boolean
    primitive data type, 16–17, 17t
Boolean constants, 20
Boolean expression, 69
Boolean operands, 66
Boolean values, 58
Boolean variables, 20
BorderLayout, 402t, 436–437
Bounds checking, 139
Box, 402t
BoxLayout, 402t, 438–440
    control spacing methods, 439t
Braces, 12, 80
    method body, 181
    nested if structures
        good programming practice, 81
        programming pitfalls, 124–125

Brackets, 134
Branches
    Java programming, 58–89
Branching, 58
break statements, 82–84, 109–110, 111
    programming pitfalls, 84
Buffering classes, 521
    sequential data output, 523
Bugs, 50–51
ButtonGroup, 427
    methods, 428t
byte
    integer data type, 17, 17t
Bytecode, 2
Bytecode verifier, 13

C

Calculational methods, 201
Callback method, 406
Called method, 178
Calling interface methods, 305–306
Calling method, 182
Canvas, 355, 431–435
    creating and displaying, 355–357
    displaying graphics, 357–359
Capacity
    StringBuffer
        method, 332–335
Capitalization
    Java names, 16
        good programming practice, 16
    named constants, 22
CardLayout, 402t
Carriage return character, 20
Cascaded if/else structures, 72
Cascaded if structures, 73f
Casting conversion, 29–30
Cast operator, 30
    good programming practice, 30
catch block, 259
Catch exceptions, 250–251
Catch requirements, 252
chapman.graphics
    package, 158
chapman.io package, 115
    and arrays, 145
chapman.math, 200

methods, 202t
chapman.math.Array class, 203–204
chapman.math.Complex, 267–272
    example, 269–272
    instance methods, 268t
    static methods, 268t–269t
chapman.math.Math1
    class, 202t
chapman.math.SigProc
    class, 272
    static methods, 272t
Character constants, 20
Characters
    primitive data type, 16–17, 17t
Character variables, 20
Check boxes, 424–427
Check box menu items, 476
Checked exceptions, 251
Class, 6–7, 180, 213–249
    examples, 6f, 222–226, 236–241
    structure, 215
ClassCastException, 284
    programming pitfalls, 284
Class chapman.math.SigProc, 272
    static methods, 272t
Class chapman.io.FileIn
    methods, 146t
    reading files, 145–147
    readStatus values, 146t
Class chapman.io.FileOut
    methods, 147t
    writeStatus values, 147t
    writing files, 147–149
Class hierarchy, 8–9, 9f, 214, 276
Class inheritance, 8f, 9
Class java.util.arrays, 200
    methods, 201t
Class loader, 13
Class java.lang.Math, 34
Class java.lang.Math1, 200
Class member
    good programming practice, 219
Class methods, 8, 236
Class name
    programming pitfalls, 12
CLASSPATH, 231
    setting, 39–41
Class's data display

good programming practice, 221
Class chapman.io.StdIn
    method, 41t
Class variables, 7, 234–236
    example, 7f
Code block, 82
Coercion of arguments, 35
Collection interfaces, 307–314
Combo boxes, 421–424
Command-line arguments, 340–342
Command-line redirection, 145
Comments
compareTo, 324–325
Comparison operation, 65
Compile-time error, 50
Complex numbers
    Java programming, 267–275
Component classes
    inheritance hierarchy, 403f
Components, 354–360, 401
Compound statement, 72
Concatenates, 38
Concatenating strings, 320–323
concat method, 320–323
Concrete classes, 288
Conditional operator, 81–82
Confirm dialog boxes, 485–488
Constants, 16–22
    and consistency, 21–22
        good programming practice, 22
    defining
        using interfaces, 306–307
    named, 21–22
        good programming practice, 22
Constructors
    class structure, 215
Container, 354–360, 401
Container classes
    inheritance hierarchy, 403f
Content pane, 404
Continue statement, 109, 112
Control statements
Convenience class, 37, 39, 517–518
    chapman.io.FileIn and chapman.io.FileOut, 145

Cost
    program maintenance
        and modification, 63

D
Dangling-else problem, 80
Data, 214
    Java
        types, 16–17
        sort, example, 149–153
Data dictionary, 18
`DataInput` class
    methods, 534t
`DataOutput` class
    methods, 535t
Data streams, 37
`Date` class
    example, 222–226
Debugger
    with Java Software
        Development Kit, 51
Debugging
    exception, 50
    Java programs, 50–51, 124–128
Declaration statements, 18, 181
    and array initializers, 138
Decomposition, 61, 180
Decrement operators, 32–33, 33t
    good programming practice, 33
Default case, 82
Default constructor, 280
Degrees
    programming pitfalls, 35
Delimiters, 339
Depreciated classes, 518–519
Descending order, 149
Device-and platform-independent
    graphics, 158
Dialog boxes, 483–488
Displaying text, 383–385
Dot operator, 215
Double
    real data type, 17, 17t
`do`/`while` loops, 90, 97–98
    and debugging, 126
    good programming practice, 98
Downcast, 284
Drawing lines, 360–368
    controlling color, width,
        and style, 360–363
Drawing shapes, 369–382

`drawString`, 383–385
Duration, 189
    `static` variables, 235

E
Elapsed time calculator, 215
Ellipses, 371–372
Encapsulation, 4
    good programming practice, 5
Equality operator
    programming pitfalls, 324
Equality testing
    `if` structures, 79
`equals`, 324
`equalsIgnoreCase`, 324
Equivalence relational operators
    programming pitfalls, 65
Errors
    types, 50
Escape sequences, 20, 21t, 117
    descriptors, 117t
Event handler, 401, 406
Event handling, 406–407
Event interfaces
    inheritance hierarchy, 489f
Events, 401, 406–407
Exception handlers, 259
Exception handling, 250
Exceptions
    and arrays, 139
    creation, 252–253
    invalid results, 265–267
    Java programming, 250–267
    types, 251
Exceptions hierarchy, 261–262
Exceptions inheritance, 261–262
Exponent, 18, 19f

F
Fields, 6, 214
    class structure, 215
    numbers, 19f
File access, 518
`FileIn`, 145
File name
    programming pitfalls, 12, 13
`FileOut`, 145
Filter classes, 519
final
    keyword, 16t, 21–22

Final classes, 291
    type-wrapper class, 291
Finalizers, 233–234
    class structure, 215
    example, 236–239
    good programming practice, 281
final methods, 291
final variables, 21–22
    and array declarations, 140–141
float, 17, 17t
Floating-point arithmetic, 25
    and debugging, 126
Floating-point numbers, 18
Floating-point value, 117
FlowLayout, 402t, 437–438
`Fmt.printf` method, 116
    good programming practice,
        119
`Fmt.sprintf` method, 116
`Font.BOLD`, 384
`Font.ITALIC`, 384
`FontMetrics` class, 386
    methods, 386t
Font names, 384t
`Font.PLAIN`, 384
Fonts
    selecting and controlling,
        384–385
`for` loops, 90, 98–114
    and debugging, 126
    details of operation, 106–108
    examples, 100–106
    good programming practice, 106,
        107, 138
    structure, 99f
Format descriptors, 117, 117t
    components, 116f, 116t
Format string, 116–117
Formatted, 518
Formatted data, 522
    sequential data output, 524
Formatted file, 518
Formatted input, 524–531
Formatted output
    sequential file, 531
Formatted sequential file
    reading numeric data,
        527–529
    reading strings, 524–526
Formatting output data, 115–119
    examples, 118–124

`for` structure
    programming pitfalls, 108
Frames, 158, 355
    creating and displaying,
      355–357
Function
    vs. method, 213

G

Garbage collection, 233–234
`GeneralPath` methods, 375t
General paths, 375–378
Generate exceptions, 250
`getActionCommand`
    good programming practice, 414
Get methods, 220–221
Graphical User Interface (GUI),
    10t, 400–464
    components, 407–435
    creating and displaying,
      404–406
    elements, 402t
    examples, 444–462
Graphics class inheritance
    hierarchy, 355f
Graphics coordinate system,
    359–360
`GridBagLayout`, 402t
`GridLayout`, 402t, 438
GUI. *See* Graphical User Interface
    (GUI)

H

Handling exceptions, 250, 258–260
Hierarchy, 8–9, 9f
Hierarchy of operations, 26, 68, 68t
    Java rules governing, 26

I

`if/else` structures, 71–72
`if` structures, 69–70
    and debugging, 125–126
    equality testing, 79
    examples, 73–79
    and `if/else`, 72
    multiple statements, 72–73
    nested, 80–81
Immediate superclass, 214, 276
Implementing interfaces, 302–304

`import` statement, 229
Increment operators, 32–33, 33t
    good programming practice, 33
Independent testing
    sub-tasks, 180
`indexOf` method, 328–329
Infinite loop
    programming pitfalls, 92
Information hiding, 4, 181, 213, 214
Inheritance, 8f, 9, 214, 276–277
Inheritance hierarchy, 277f
Initializer, 138
Input, 517–539
Input dialog boxes, 488
Input/output, 37
Input stream
    reading formatted data,
      529–531
Inquiry methods, 201
`insert` method, 335–336
Instance methods, 4
    `chapman.math.Complex`, 268t
Instance variables, 4, 214, 218
    class scope, 219
    example, 7f
    good programming practice, 5,
      218
    `StreamTokenizer`, 527t
Instantiated, 136
    object, 6
`int`
    primitive data type, 16–17, 17t
Integer arithmetic, 24–25
    programming pitfalls, 25
Integer constants, 18
Integer variables, 18
    good programming practice,
      107
Interfaces, 302–307, 488–492
    defining constants, 306–307
    implementation, 302–304
    significance, 307
Invalid results
    not exceptions, 265–267
Invoked method, 178
Iterator interfaces, 307–314

J

`JApplet` class, 504–505
    methods, 505t

Java
    advantages, 1–2
    basic elements, 15–57
    vs. C and Fortran, 158
    vs. C language, 2
    elements, 2–3
    vs. Fortran, 2
    philosophy, 1
    rules governing
      hierarchy of operations, 26
    web site address, 2
Java API
    components, 3
    limitation, 115
Java API packages, 9, 10t, 228t–229t
`java.swing.Japplet`, 10t, 228t
`java.awt`, 10t, 228t
`java.awt.BasicStroke`, 360
`java.awt.datatransfer`, 228t
`java.awt.event`, 228t, 401
`java.awt.Font`, 384
    methods, 385t
`java.awt.FontMetrics`, 385
`java.awt.geom.AffineTrans-`
    `form`, 389
`java.awt.geom.Ellipse2D`,
    371
`java.awt.geom.GeneralPath`,
    375
`java.awt.geom.Line2D`, 360
`java.awt.geom.Rectangle2D`,
    369
`java.awt.geom.RoundRect-`
    `angle`
    2D, 370
`java.awt.image`, 228t
`java.awt.peer`, 228t
`java.beans`, 10t, 228t
Java colors
    predefined, 360t
Java data types, 16–17
Java Development Kit, 2
    web site address, 229
Java events and interfaces
    methods, 489t
Java graphics, 353–399
Java graphics package, 354t
Java GUI package, 354t
Java input/output (I/O), 517–539
    structure, 519–522
`java.io`, 10t, 228t

Java keywords, 16t
java.lang package, 10t, 228t
  math class, 34
Java mathematical method, 34
Java names, 15–16
java.net, 10t, 228t
Java programming
  arrays, file access, and plotting, 134–177
  branches and program design, 58–89
  classes and object-oriented programming, 213–249
  compiling and executing, 12
  complex numbers, 267–275
  creation, 3f
  debugging, 50–51, 124–128
  examples, 42–49
  exceptions, 250–267
  methods, 178–212
  repetition structures, 90–133
  required steps, 10–11
  suggestions and tips, 127
  types, 10
Java Software Development Kit
  debugger, 51
java.util.Arrays
  methods, 201t
java.util package, 9f, 10t, 229t
java.util.zip, 229t
Java Virtual Machine (Java VM), 2
javax.swing, 10t
JButton, 402t, 410
  methods, 411t
JCanvas (chapman.graphics), 431
JCheckBox, 402t, 424
  methods, 425t
JCheckBoxMenu, 402t
JComboBox, 402t
  methods, 421t
JComponent, 431
  methods, 432t
JDialog, 402t
JFrame, 401, 402t
JLabel, 402t, 408
  methods, 408t
JList, 402t, 466
  methods, 467t
JMenu, 402t
  methods, 477t

JMenuBar, 402t
  methods, 477t
JMenuItem, 402t
JPanel, 401, 402t
JPasswordField, 402t
JPlot2D, 158–161
JPopUpMenu, 402t
  methods, 492t
JRadioButton, 402t, 427
  methods, 425t
JTable, 402t, 474
  methods, 475t
JTextField, 402t

K
Keyboard shortcuts, 410
Keywords, 12, 16
  Java reserved list, 16t

L
Labeled break statement, 111–112
  good programming practice, 113
Labeled continue statement, 112–113
  good programming practice, 113
Labels, 111, 408–409
lastIndexOf method, 328–329
Layout managers, 401, 436–444
  combinations, 440–442
    example, 442–444
  elements, 436t
Left brace, 12
Length
  stringBuffer method, 332–335
Lexicographic sequence, 324
Line feed character, 20
Lines, 360–368
  eliminating jagged edges, 363
Linked lists, 308–309
  examples, 309–314
Listener classes, 401
Listener interfaces, 401
List interface methods, 310t
ListIterator, 307
ListIterator interface methods, 311t
Lists
  collection interfaces, 307
  GUI component, 466–473

  example, 468–473
ListSelectionEvent
  Methods, 468t
ListSelectionListener interface
  method, 468t
Local variables, 182, 189
Logical error, 50
Logical methods, 203
Logical operators, 64, 66–69
long
  integer data type, 17, 17t
Look and feel, 495–503
  class and description, 496t
Loop parameters
  and debugging, 126
Loops, 90
Lowercase letters
  Java names, 16

M
main method, 12
Maintenance
  program, 181
Mantissa, 18, 19f
Map
  collection interfaces, 307
Math.abs(x), 36t
Math.acos(x), 36t
Math.asin(x), 36t
Math.atan(x), 36t
Math.atan2(y,x), 36t
Math.ceil(x), 36t
Math class
  java.lang package, 34
Math.cos(x), 36t
Mathematical methods, 33–35, 36t
Math.exp(x), 36t
Math.floor (x), 36t
Math.log(x), 36t
Math.max(x,y), 36t
Math.min(x,y), 36t
Math.pow(x,y), 36t
Math.random(), 36t
Math.rint(x), 36t
Math.round(x), 36t
Math.sin(x), 36t
Math.sqrt(x), 36t
Math.tan(x), 36t
Member, 6
Member access modifiers, 218,

231–233
Member access operator, 215
Menu bar, 476
Menu components, 476–478
    associated events, 478–483
Menu item, 476
Menus, 476
    GUI component, 475–483
Message dialog boxes,
    484–485
Messages, 5–6
    components, 5
Method body, 181
Method call, 182
Method definition
    good programming practice, 218
Method invocation, 182
Method-name, 181
Method overloading, 193–199
    examples, 195–199
    programming pitfalls, 195
Methods, 4, 6, 178–212
    class structure, 215
    definitions, 181–183
    examples, 186–189
    purpose, 180–181
    types, 220–221
Mixed-mode arithmetic, 28
Mixed-mode expressions, 28
    programming pitfalls, 29
Mixed-mode operators
    good programming practice,
    30
Modal, 483
Modifier classes, 519
Modularity, 4, 214
Modulus operation, 24
MouseEvent
    methods, 493t
Multidimensional arrays, 169
Mythical Man-Month, 63

N
Named constants, 21–22
    and array declarations, 140–141
Names
    good programming practice, 17
    in Java, 15–16
Naming
    class and files

programming pitfalls, 12, 13
Narrowing conversion, 30
Near equality
    testing, 79
        good programming practice,
        80
Nested array initializers
    two dimensional arrays, 164
Nested if structures, 80–81
    braces
        good programming practice,
        81
Nested loops, 110
Nested loop structure, 111
Nested try/catch structures,
    262–263
Newline character, 117
New operator
    arrays, 136
    two dimensional arrays, 163
Non-modal, 483
NOT operator
    truth table, 66t
Null
    array, 136
Null statement, 92
Numeric promotion
    of operands, 28–29
    rules, 28

O
Object, 1, 4
    instantiated or created, 6
    Java language, 9
Object oriented, 1
Object-oriented language, 213
Object-oriented programming, 3–9,
    213–249
    examples, 222–226, 236–241
One dimensional arrays, 134–160,
    161, 162
Operands
    numeric promotion, 28–29
Operations
    hierarchy of, 68, 68t
        Java rules governing, 26
Out of bounds, 139
Out-of-bounds array subscripts,
    139–140

Output, 517–539
Output data
    formatting, 115–119
        examples, 118–124
Overloaded methods, 35
Override, 8, 221

P
Package access, 232
    danger *vs.* efficient, 233
Packages, 9, 10t, 227
    creation, 229–231
    good programming practice, 230
    member access modifier,
    231–233
package statement, 230
paintComponent, 355, 357
Parameter list, 181
Parameters, 34, 178
    trigonometric functions
        programming pitfalls, 35
Parentheses, 27
    good programming practice, 27
Pass-by-value scheme, 183–186
    good programming practice,
    184
Password fields, 415–421
    example, 418–421
    methods, 415t
Pixels, 359
Platform independent, 1
Plotting, 158–161
Plugable Look and Feel, 495–503
Polymorphism, 284–285, 303
    examples, 285–287, 292–301
Pop-up menus, 492–494
Postdecrement operator, 32
Postincrement operator, 32
Precision
    real number quantities, 19
Predecrement operator, 32
Predicate methods, 221
Preincrement operator, 32
Primitive data types, 16–17, 17t
    type-wrapper class, 291
print method, 37
println method., 37
    and debugging, 51
private
    keyword, 218

member access modifier, 231–233
Program design
  Java programming, 58–89
Program maintenance, 181
Programmer-defined types, 214
Programming language
  learning process, 49
protected
  member access modifier, 231–233
Protected access, 277
Prototype, 86
Pseudocode, 59, 61
  use of, 63–64
public, 5, 12, 218, 231–233
Push buttons, 410–414

R
Radians
  programming pitfalls, 35
Radio button menu items, 476
Radio buttons, 427–431
Random access, 518
Random number methods, 203
Range
  real number quantities, 19
Rapid prototyping, 86
readBoolean(), 41t
readByte(), 41t
readDouble(), 41t
readFloat(), 41t
Reading data from files, 145–149
  Class FileIn, 145–147
readInt(), 41t
readLong(), 41t
readShort(), 41t
readString(), 41t
Real constants, 18–20
Real numbers, 18
Real variables, 18–20
Rectangles, 369–370
  rounded, 370–371
Recursive methods, 191–193
Redirect, 145
Reference
  array, 136
regionMatch, 325–326
Relational methods, 203
Relational operators, 64–65, 64t

Repetition, 58
Repetition structures
  Java programming, 90–133
Replace method, 329
  example, 330
Reserved keywords, 16, 16t
Return statement, 181
Reusability, 214
Reusable code, 180
Reusable software, 180
Reverse method, 336
Right brace, 12
Rotations, 388
Rounded rectangles, 370–371
Round-off error, 19
Run-time error, 50
Run-time exceptions, 139, 251

S
Scalings, 388
Scope, 189, 190–191
Selection, 58
Selection sort, 149
  good programming practice, 150
Selection structures, 58, 69–86
  good programming practice, 70
Semicolon, 12
  programming pitfalls, 92, 108
Sequential access, 518
Sequential data output, 522–524
Sequential file
  comparing formatted and un-
    formatted, 537–539
Sequential input streams, 521f
Sequential output streams, 523f
Sequential programs, 58
Set
  collection interfaces, 307
setColor, 360
setFont, 384
setLayout, 436
Set methods, 220–221
Shapes
  drawing, 369–382
Shears, 388
Short
  integer data type, 17, 17t
ShowDialogs
  parameters, 484t
Signature

method overloading, 194
  programming pitfalls, 195
Sink, 518
Sort data example, 149–153
sortString example, 342–348
Source, 518
Specify requirement, 252
Square brackets, 134
Standard error stream, 37, 39
Standard font names, 384t
Standard input, 37–42
Standard input stream, 37, 39–42
Standard Java packages, 227–229
Standard method definition
  good programming practice, 303
Standard output, 37–42
Standard output stream, 37–39
Stars
  creating, 378–382
Statement, 12
static, 12, 234
Static class members, 234–242
Static duration, 190
Static methods, 236
  chapman.math.Complex, 268t–269t
  class chapman.math.SigProc, 272t
  example, 236–239
Static variables, 190, 234–236
Status line, 508
Stepwise refinement, 61
Storage formats, 518
StreamTokenizer
  instance variables, 527t
String, 21, 318–352
  comparison, 324–328
  concatenated, 320–323
  creating and initializing, 319
  locating character and substring, 328–329
  types, 319
StringBuffer class
  creating and initializing, 331–332
  methods, 332–339, 333t
  length and capacity, 332–335
StringBuffers
  comparing, 336–339
String constants, 319
String literals, 319

String methods, 320–331, 321t–322t
String object, 319
StringTokenizer method, 339–340
Strongly typed language, 17
Structured programs, 64
Structures, 64, 69–86
    good programming practice, 70
Subclass, 8, 214, 276
    definition, 277
    good programming practice, 280, 281
    superclass
        programming pitfalls, 284
        relationship between, 282–284
Submenu, 476
Subscripts, 134
    array, 139–140
Substrings, 320
Sub-tasks, 180
    independent testing, 180
Superclass, 8, 214, 276
    definition, 277
    good programming practice, 280, 281
    subclass
        programming pitfalls, 284
        relationship between, 282–284
Swing GUI, 400
Swing menu components
    inheritance hierarchy, 476f
switch structure, 82–84
    good programming practice, 84
    programming pitfalls, 84
Symbolic debuggers, 51, 125
Syntax errors, 50
System.currentTimeMillis(), 216
System.err, 37, 39
System.in, 37
System.out, 37
System.out.println method, 12

T
Tables
    GUI component, 474–475
Ternary operator, 81–82
Test driver, 182
Testing

if structures, 79
Testing process
    programs, 62f
Text
    displaying, 383–385
Text fields, 415–421
    example, 418–421
    methods, 415t
this, 219
Throw exceptions, 139, 250–251, 253–257
Throw point, 253
throw statement, 253
Timer class
    implementation, 215–219
Tokens, 339
toLowerCase () method, 329
    example, 330
Tool tips, 410
Top-down design, 180
    steps involved, 60–61
    techniques, 59–63
toString() method, 221
toUpperCase() method, 329
    example, 330
Translations, 388
Trigonometric functions
    parameters
        programming pitfalls, 35
Trim method, 329
    example, 330
try/catch structures, 258–260
    examples using, 263–265
    good programming practice, 260
    nested, 262–263
Two dimensional arrays, 161–169
    declaring, 162–163
    elements, 161–162
    examples, 165–169
    initializing, 164
        from file, 164–165
Type-wrapper classes, 291–292
Typographical errors, 50

U
UIManager
    methods, 495t
Unary operators, 24
Unformatted, 518

Unformatted data, 521
    sequential data output, 523
Unformatted file, 518
Unformatted input
    sequential file, 533–534
Unformatted output
    sequential file, 534–537
Unicode characters, 17
Unicode character set, 20
Unintended side effects, 180, 185
Units
    good programming practice, 43
Unit testing, 62, 180
Unsubscripted arrays
    programming pitfalls, 138
Upcast, 284
URL
    of Java, 2
Utility classes, 10t
Utility methods, 219
    good programming practice, 236

V
valueOf() method, 330–331
Variable passing, 183–186
Variables, 16–22
    automatic, 189–190
        good programming practice, 190
    boolean, 20
    character, 20
    class, 7, 234–236
        example, 7f
    final, 21–22
        and array declarations, 140–141
    instance variables, 4, 214, 218
        class scope, 219
        example, 7f
        good programming practice, 5
        StreamTokenizer, 527t
    integer, 18
    local, 182, 189
    static, 190, 234–236
        duration, 235
Vector, 308–309
    examples, 309–314
void, 12, 181

W

Web site
  Java, 2
  Java Development Kit (JDK)
    documentation, 229
while loops, 90–97
  and debugging, 126

examples, 92–97
good programming practice, 98
structure, 91f
Whitespace characters, 70
Widening conversion, 29
Writing data to files, 145–149
Writing files

Class FileOut, 147–149

X

XOR mode, 394–395